THE

PUBLICATIONS

OF THE

Lincoln Record Society

FOUNDED IN THE YEAR

1910

VOLUME 103

ISSN 0267–2634

LINCOLNSHIRE PARISH CLERGY, *c.*1214–1968

A BIOGRAPHICAL REGISTER

PART I:
THE DEANERIES OF ASLACOE AND AVELAND

NICHOLAS BENNETT

The Lincoln Record Society

The Boydell Press

First published 2013

A Lincoln Record Society Publication
published by The Boydell Press
an imprint of Boydell & Brewer Ltd
PO Box 9, Woodbridge, Suffolk IP12 3DF, UK
and of Boydell & Brewer Inc.
668 Mt Hope Avenue, Rochester, NY 14620–2731, USA
website: www.boydellandbrewer.com

ISBN 978 0 901503 96 1

A CIP catalogue record for this book is available
from the British Library

Details of other Lincoln Record Society volumes are available
from Boydell & Brewer Ltd

The publisher has no responsibility for the continued existence or accuracy of URLs for
external or third-party internet websites referred to in this book, and does not guarantee
that any content on such websites is, or will remain, accurate or appropriate.

Papers used by Boydell & Brewer Ltd are natural, recyclable products
made from wood grown in sustainable forests

MIX
Paper from
responsible sources
FSC
www.fsc.org   FSC® C013056

Printed and bound in Great Britain by
TJ International Ltd, Padstow, Cornwall

CONTENTS

ILLUSTRATIONS

ACKNOWLEDGEMENTS

The compilation of this volume has been made possible through the help of a great many people. I would like to express my thanks to the successive Bishops of Lincoln, Robert Hardy, John Saxbee and Christopher Lowson, who have encouraged my research into the records of the diocese. Caroline Mockford, the Diocesan Registrar, and the staff of the Registry have been unfailingly helpful in providing access to the records, allowing the temporary deposit of a register in Lincoln Cathedral Library for my use. Derek Wellman, the former Registrar, has given me a great deal of insight (and entertainment) from his experience of diocesan matters. The staff at Lincolnshire Archives, where I always receive a friendly welcome, have produced large numbers of episcopal registers, visitation records, wills, parish records and other, sometimes remarkably obscure, sources to enable me to pursue my researches. Professor Gerald Bray generously provided me with a copy of his valuable *Ely Clergy Lists*. I owe especial thanks to two scholars, Dr Philippa Hoskin and Dr Alison McHardy, for allowing me to see their unpublished work on the records of Bishops Robert Grosseteste and John Buckingham.

Over the years, a large number of Cathedral Library volunteers have worked on indexing projects relating to diocesan clergy; the fruits of their labours have made my task considerably easier. They include Rachel Walkinton, the late John Wells-Cole, Anne Senior and Katie Lord (now Flanagan). A large number of friends and colleagues have provided information and help, among them Rod Ambler, Richard Olney, Marianne Wilson and Rob Wheeler. The undertaking of this project would have been immeasurably more difficult without the foundations laid by Canon Charles Wilmer Foster, not only in his published work in the volumes of the Associated Architectural Societies and the Lincoln Record Society but also in the extensive collection of record transcripts, many of which were undertaken with a project such as this in mind.

My greatest debt, as always, is to my wife Carol, who has borne with great patience and good humour the constant presence of the Lincolnshire clergy in our lives.

Nicholas Bennett
Lincoln
Feast of the Conversion of St Paul, 2013

ABBREVIATIONS

County Abbreviations

Bd	Bedfordshire	Le	Leicestershire
Bk	Buckinghamshire	Li	Lincolnshire
Brec	Breconshire	Monm	Monmouthshire
Brk	Berkshire	Mont	Montgomeryshire
Ca	Cambridgeshire	Mx	Middlesex
Card	Cardiganshire	Nb	Northumberland
Chs	Cheshire	Nf	Norfolk
CI	Channel Islands	Np	Northamptonshire
Co	Cornwall	Nt	Nottinghamshire
Cu	Cumberland	Ox	Oxfordshire
Db	Derbyshire	Pemb	Pembrokeshire
Denb	Denbighshire	Radn	Radnorshire
Dev	Devonshire	Ru	Rutland
Do	Dorset	Sa	Shropshire
Du	Durham	Sf	Suffolk
Ess	Essex	So	Somerset
Flints	Flintshire	Sr	Surrey
Gl	Gloucestershire	St	Staffordshire
Glam	Glamorgan	Sx	Sussex
Ha	Hampshire	Wa	Warwickshire
He	Herefordshire	We	Westmorland
Hrt	Hertfordshire	Wlt	Wiltshire
Hu	Huntingdonshire	Wo	Worcestershire
IoM	Isle of Man	YER	Yorkshire East Riding
IoW	Isle of Wight	YNR	Yorkshire North Riding
K	Kent	YWR	Yorkshire West Riding
La	Lancashire		

Other Abbreviations

AKC	Associate of King's College, London
BA	Bachelor of Arts
BCL	Bachelor of Civil Law
BCnL	Bachelor of Canon Law

BD	Bachelor of Divinity
Borthwick	Borthwick Institute for Archives, York
br.	brother
Bt	Baronet
C.	Curate
CCED	Clergy of the Church of England Database
CETS	Church of England Temperance Society
CF	Chaplain to the Forces
C-in-C	curate-in-charge
CYS	Canterbury and York Society
DCL	Doctor of Civil Law
DCnL	Doctor of Canon Law
DD	Doctor of Divinity or Theology
Essex RO	Essex Record Office, Chelmsford
fo.	folio
GRO	General Register Office
GS	Grammar School
IGI	International Genealogical Index
Inc.	Incumbent
kt	knight
LAO	Lincolnshire Archives
LCL	Lincoln Cathedral Library
LD	letters dimissory
Liverpool RO	Liverpool Record Office
LMA	London Metropolitan Archives
LPL	Lambeth Palace Library
LRS	Lincoln Record Society
LTh	Licentiate in Theology
M.	Master
MA	Master of Arts
MI	Monumental inscription
MRST	Member of Royal Society of Teachers
OHS	Oxford Historical Society
ORO	Oxfordshire Record Office
par.	parish of
PC	Perpetual Curate
P-in-C	priest-in-charge
PRO	National Archives, Public Record Office
R.	Rector
RD	Rural Dean
SCL	Student in Civil Law
SLHA	Society for Lincolnshire History and Archaeology
TCF	Temporary Chaplain to the Forces
ThL	Licentiate in Theology

V.   Vicar
Warwicks RO Warwickshire Record Office
WYAS   West Yorkshire Archive Service

Bibliographical Sources
(with Abbreviated References)

Manuscripts

Chelmsford, Essex Record Office:
  D/DU 918/1
Dorchester, Dorset History Centre
  Bristol Consistory Court wills
  parish registers
Leeds, West Yorkshire Archives Service
  parish registers
Lincoln, Lincoln Cathedral Library
  Lincoln Theological College archives
Lincoln, Lincolnshire Archives
  Ancaster archives (ANC)
  Brownlow archives (BNLW)
  Dean and Chapter archives:
    chapter act books
    'Taxatio ecclesiastica Nicholai IV' (A/1/11)
  Diocesan records:
    bishop's correspondence (COR/B)
    bishop's transcripts (BTs)
    curates' licences (CR)
    episcopal registers (REG)
    faculty papers (FAC)
    induction registers (IND)
    libri cleri (LC)
    letters testimonial and dimissory (LTD)
    letters testimonial and licences (LIC)
    mortgages under Gilbert Acts (MGA)
    non-residence licences (NRL)
    Orders in Council (OC)
    ordination registers (OR)
    presentation deeds (PD)
    probate inventories (INV)
    resignations (RES)
    subscription books (SUB)
    visitation records (Vj)

Foster Library transcripts (FL)
Lincoln Consistory Court wills
Monson archives (MON)
parish registers
Stow wills
Tennyson d'Eyncourt archives (TDE)
Liverpool, Liverpool Record Office
parish registers
London, Lambeth Palace Library
Commonwealth Records
Sancroft Reg. 2
W3/32/1/3
London, London Metropolitan Archives
parish registers
London, National Archives, Kew (Public Record Office)
Common Pleas Records (Feet of Fines): CP 25/1
Exchequer Records: E134; E334
General Register Office Records (Census Returns)
Probate (Prerogative Court of Canterbury): PROB 11
War Office: WO 100
Oxford, Oxfordshire Record Office
MS Oxf. Dioc. Papers b.21
MS Oxf. Dioc. Papers c.266
MS Oxf. Dioc. Papers d.106
parish registers
Warwick, Warwickshire Record Office
parish registers
York, Borthwick Institute for Archives
Bishop Neile's Subscription Book (Sub. Bk. 2)

Printed Books and Articles

AASRP: *Associated Architectural Societies Reports and Papers*.
Acta of Hugh of Wells: D. M. Smith (ed.), *The Acta of Hugh of Wells, Bishop of Lincoln 1209–1235*, LRS 88 (2000).
Ambler, 'Return': R. W. Ambler, 'Religious life in Kesteven: a return of the number of places of worship not of the Church of England, 1829', *LHA* 20 (1985), 59–64.
Archbishop Drummond's Visitation Returns: Cressida Annesley and Philippa Hoskin, *Archbishop Drummond's Visitation Returns 1764*, Borthwick Texts and Calendars 21, 23, 26 (1997–2001).
Archivists' Report: Lincolnshire Archives Committee, *Archivists' Reports* (Lincoln, 1948–75).
Atkin, 'Frances Brooke': Wendy J. Atkin, ' "A most ingenious Authress":

Frances Brooke (1724–1789) and her Lincolnshire connections', *LHA* 32 (1997), 12–20.

Baker, *Nettleham*: Florence L. Baker, *The History of Nettleham* (Gainsborough, 1957).

Balliofergus: Henry Savage, *Balliofergus: or, a Commentary upon the Foundation, Founders and Affaires of Balliol Colledge* (Oxford, 1668).

Banstead Register: F. A. H. Lambert (ed.), *The Registers of Banstead in the County of Surrey 1547–1789*, Parish Register Society 1 (1896).

Berry, *Sussex Pedigrees*: William Berry, *Pedigrees of the Families in the County of Sussex* (London, 1830).

Bertie, *Scottish Episcopal Clergy*: David M. Bertie, *Scottish Episcopal Clergy 1689–2000* (Edinburgh, 2000).

Binnall, *Hemswell*: Peter B. G. Binnall, *Hemswell 1086–1901* (Lincoln, 1985).

Binney Genealogy: C. J. F. Binney, *Genealogy of the Binney Family in the United States* (Albany NY, 1886).

Binns, *Intellectual Culture*: J. W. Binns, *Intellectual Culture in Elizabethan and Jacobean England: The Latin Writings of the Age* (Leeds, 1990).

Birch, *Royal Charters*: W. de Gray Birch, *The Royal Charters of the City of Lincoln* (Cambridge, 1911).

Bishop Cooper: C. W. Foster (ed.), *Lincoln Episcopal Records in the time of Thomas Cooper STP, Bishop of Lincoln AD 1571 to AD 1584*, LRS 2 (1912).

Blomefield: Francis Blomefield, *An Essay towards a Topographical History of the County of Norfolk* (2nd ed., 11 vols, London, 1805–10).

Bloxam: J. R. Bloxam, *A Register of the Presidents, Fellows, Demies ... and other Members of Saint Mary Magdalen College in the University of Oxford* (8 vols, Oxford, 1853–85).

Blundell's Register: Arthur Fisher (ed.), *The Register of Blundell's School* (Exeter, 1904).

Bonney's Church Notes: N. S. Harding (ed.), *Bonney's Church Notes: Being Notes on the Churches in the Archdeaconry of Lincoln 1845–1848 by The Venerable H. K. Bonney* (Lincoln, 1937).

Book of Fees: *Liber Feodorum: The Book of Fees* (2 vols in 3, London, 1920–31).

Brasenose Register: *Brasenose College Register 1509–1909*, OHS 55 (1909).

Bray, *Ely Lists*: Gerald Bray (comp.), *Ely Clergy Lists* (London, 2009).

Brayley, *History of Surrey*: E. W. Brayley, *A Topographical History of Surrey* (5 vols, London, 1841–8).

Browne Willis: Browne Willis, *A Survey of the Cathedrals* (2 vols in 3, London, 1727–30).

Buckingham Writs: A. K. McHardy (ed.), *Royal Writs addressed to John Buckingham, Bishop of Lincoln 1363–1398*, LRS 86 (1997).

Burke, *Landed Gentry* (1837): John Burke, *A Genealogical and Heraldic History of the Landed Gentry* (4 vols, London, 1837).

Burke, *Landed Gentry* (1863): Sir Bernard Burke, *A Genealogical and Heraldic Dictionary of the Landed Gentry* (4th ed., London, 1863).

Burke, *Landed Gentry* (1894): Sir Bernard Burke, *A Genealogical and Heraldic History of the Landed Gentry* (8th ed., London, 1894).

Burke, *Landed Gentry* (1900): Ashworth P. Burke (ed.), *A Genealogical and Heraldic History of the Landed Gentry of Great Britain* (10th ed., London, 1900).

Burke, *Landed Gentry* (1921): A. W. Thorpe (ed.), *A Genealogical and Heraldic History of the Landed Gentry of Great Britain, by Sir Bernard Burke* (13th ed., London, 1921).

Burke, *Landed Gentry* (1937): H. Pirie-Gordon (ed.), *Burke's Genealogical and Heraldic History of the Landed Gentry* (15th ed., London, 1937).

Burke, *Landed Gentry* (18th ed.): Peter Townend (ed.), *Burke's Genealogical and Heraldic History of the Landed Gentry* (18th ed., 3 vols, London, 1965–72).

Burke, *Landed Gentry of Ireland* (1899): Sir Bernard Burke, *A Genealogical and Heraldic History of the Landed Gentry of Ireland* (9th ed., London, 1899).

Burke, *Peerage* (1906): Sir Bernard Burke, *Peerage, Baronetage and Knightage* (68th ed., London, 1906).

Burke, *Peerage* (1938): *Burke's Genealogical and Heraldic History of the Peerage, Baronetage and Knightage* (96th ed., London, 1938).

Burke, *Peerage* (1959): L. G. Pine (ed.), *Burke's Genealogical and Heraldic History of the Peerage, Baronetage and Knightage* (102nd ed., London, 1959).

Burke, *Peerage* (1999): Charles Mosley (ed.), *Burke's Peerage and Baronetage* (106th ed., London, 1999).

Burke, *Peerage* (2003): Charles Mosley (ed.), *Burke's Peerage, Baronetage and Knightage* (107th ed., 3 vols, Stokesley, 2003).

Bury Grammar School List: [S. H. A. Hervey], *Biographical List of Boys Educated at King Edward VI Free Grammar School, Bury St Edmunds from 1550 to 1900*, Suffolk Green Books 13 (1908).

Calamy Revised: A. G. Matthews, *Calamy Revised, Being a Revision of Edmund Calamy's Account of the Ministers and Others Ejected and Silenced, 1660–2* (Oxford, 1943).

Canterbury Act Books: E. H. W. Dunkin, Claude Jenkins and E. A. Fry (eds), *Index to the Act Books of the Archbishops of Canterbury 1663–1859*, British Record Society 55, 63 (1929–38).

CBS Quarterly: *Confraternity of the Blessed Sacrament Quarterly*.

CCC: M. A. Everett Green (ed.), *Calendar of the Proceedings of the Committee for Compounding 1643–1660* (1 vol in 5, London, 1889–92).

Change and Continuity: P. L. Everson, C. C. Taylor and C. J. Dunn, *Change and Continuity*: *Rural Settlement in North-West Lincolnshire* (London, 1991).

Chapter Acts of Lincoln: R. E. G. Cole (ed.), *Chapter Acts of the Cathedral Church of St Mary of Lincoln AD 1520–1559*, LRS 12–13, 15 (1915–20).

Charterhouse Register 1769–1872: R. L. Arrowsmith (ed), *Charterhouse Register June 1769–May 1872* (Godalming, 1964).

Charterhouse Register 1872–1910: F. K. W. Girdlestone, E. T. Hardman and A. H. Tod (eds), *Charterhouse Register 1872–1910* (2 vols, London, 1911).

Chester of Chicheley: R. E. C. Waters, *Genealogical Memoirs of the Extinct Family of Chester of Chicheley* (2 vols, London, 1878).

CIPM: *Calendar of Inquisitions Post Mortem* (HMSO, London, 1904–).

Clergy List: *The Clergy List* (London, 1841–1917).

Clerical Poll-Taxes: A. K. McHardy (ed.), *Clerical Poll-Taxes of the Diocese of Lincoln 1377–1381*, LRS 81 (1992).

Clifton College Register: F. Borwick (ed.), *Clifton College Annals and Register 1862–1925* (Bristol, 1925).

Colvin, *White Canons*: H. M. Colvin, *The White Canons in England* (Oxford, 1951).

Complete Baronetage: G. E. Cockayne, *Complete Baronetage* (5 vols, Exeter, 1900–6).

CPL: *Calendar of Papal Letters* (HMSO, London, 1893–).

CPR: *Calendar of Patent Rolls* (HMSO, London, 1891–).

Crisp, *Fragmenta Genealogica*: F. A. Crisp, *Fragmenta Genealogica* (13 vols, London, 1889–1909).

Crisp, *Visitation*: J. J. Howard and F. A. Crisp, *Visitation of England and Wales* (35 vols, London, 1893–1921).

Crockford: *Crockford's Clerical Directory* (1858–).

Crook, 'Jordan Castle': David Crook, 'Jordan Castle and the Foliot family of Grimston', *Transactions of the Thoroton Society* 112 (2008), 143–58.

Cross, *York Clergy Wills*: Claire Cross (ed.), *York Clergy Wills 1520–1600*, Borthwick Texts and Calendars 10, 15 (1984–9).

CSPD: *Calendar of State Papers Domestic*.

Curia Regis Rolls: *Curia Regis Rolls Preserved in the Public Record Office* (HMSO, London, 1922–).

Cussans, *Hertfordshire*: John Edwin Cussans, *History of Hertfordshire* (3 vols, London, 1870–81).

Custodians of Continuity: Paul Everson and David Stocker, *Custodians of Continuity? The Premonstratensian Abbey at Barlings and the Landscape of Ritual* (Sleaford, 2011).

Danelaw Charters: F. M. Stenton (ed.), *Documents Illustrative of the Social and Economic History of the Danelaw*, British Academy Records of the Social and Economic History of England and Wales 5 (1920).

Dickinson, *Austin Canons*: J. C. Dickinson, *The Origins of the Austin Canons and their Introduction into England* (London, 1950).

Dictionary of Canadian Biography: Ramsay Cook (ed.), *Dictionary of Canadian Biography* (Toronto, 2005).

Diocesan Visitations: A. Hamilton Thompson (ed.), *Visitations in the Diocese of Lincoln 1517–1531* I–III, LRS 33, 35, 37 (1940–7).

Durham School Register: T. H. Burbidge (ed.), *Durham School Register,* 3rd ed. (Cambridge, 1940).

Early Lincoln Wills: Alfred Gibbons, *Early Lincoln Wills: An Abstract of all the Wills and Administrations recorded in the Episcopal Registers of the old Diocese of Lincoln ... 1280–1547* (Lincoln, 1888).

Early Motor Vehicle Registration in Wiltshire: Ian Hicks (ed.), *Early Motor Vehicle Registration in Wiltshire 1903–1914*, Wiltshire Record Society 58 (2006).

Ecclesiastical Register of Ireland (1827): John C. Erck (ed.), *The Ecclesiastical Register containing the Names of the Dignitaries and Parochial Clergy of Ireland* (Dublin, 1827).

EEA: *English Episcopal Acta* (London, 1980–).

Emden, *BRUC*: A. B. Emden, *A Biographical Register of the University of Cambridge to 1500* (Cambridge, 1963).

Emden, *BRUO*: A. B. Emden, *A Biographical Register of the University of Oxford to 1500* (3 vols, Oxford, 1957–9).

Emden, *BRUO 1501–1540*: A. B. Emden, *A Biographical Register of the University of Oxford 1501 to 1540* (Oxford, 1974).

ESTC: English Short Title Catalogue.

Eton College Register 1753–1790: R. A. Austen-Leigh (ed.), *The Eton College Register 1753–1790* (Eton, 1921).

Eton School Lists: H. E. C. Stapylton, *The Eton School Lists from 1791 to 1877* (Eton, 1885).

Eton School Register: *The Eton Register 1841–1909* (7 vols, Eton, 1903–22).

Exeter College Register: A. B. How, *Register of Exeter College Oxford 1891–1921* (Oxford, 1928).

Ex-Religious: G. A. J. Hodgett (ed.), *The State of the Ex-Religious and Former Chantry Priests in the Diocese of Lincoln 1547–1574*, LRS 53 (1959).

EYC: William Farrer and C. T. Clay (eds), *Early Yorkshire Charters*, Yorkshire Archaeological Society Record Series, Extra Series 1–12 (1914–65).

Fasti Parochiales: A. Hamilton Thompson, C. T. Clay, N. A. H. Lawrance and N. K. M. Gurney (eds), *Fasti Parochiales* I–V, Yorkshire Archaeological Society Record Series 85, 107, 129, 133, 143 (1933–85).

Fasti Wyndesorienses: S. L. Ollard, *Fasti Wyndesorienses: The Deans and Canons of Windsor* (Windsor, 1950).

Feudal Aids: *Inquisitions and Assessments relating to Feudal Aids* (6 vols, London, 1899–1920).

Final Concords, I: W. O. Massingberd (ed.), *Lincolnshire Records*: *Abstracts of Final Concords temp. Richard I, John and Henry III* (London, 1896).

Final Concords, II: C. W. Foster (ed.), *Final Concords of the County of Lincoln ... AD 1244–1272*, LRS 17 (1920).

Flinders: Martyn Beardsley and Nicholas Bennett (eds), *Gratefull to Providence*: *The Diary and Accounts of Matthew Flinders, Surgeon, Apothecary and Man-Midwife, 1775–1802*, LRS, 95, 97 (2007–9).

Foster, *Aisthorpe*: C. W. Foster, *A History of the Villages of Aisthorpe and Thorpe in the Fallows* (Lincoln, 1927).

Foster, *Alumni*: J. Foster, *Alumni Oxonienses 1500–1886* (2 parts in 8 vols, Oxford, 1887–92).

Foster, *Burrell of Dowsby*: C. W. Foster, *Burrell of Dowsby, co. Lincoln, and of Ryhall, co. Rutland* (Rotherham, 1885).

Foster, *Oxford Men*: J. Foster, *Oxford Men 1880–1892* (Oxford, 1893).

Foster, *Plundered Ministers*: W. E. Foster, *The Plundered Ministers of Lincolnshire*: *Being Extracts from the Minutes of the Committee of Plundered Ministers* (Guildford, 1900).

Foster, *Visitation of Yorkshire*: J. Foster (ed.), *The Visitation of Yorkshire Made in the Years 1584/5* (London, 1875).

Franklin, 'The Bishop, the Abbot and Warmington Rectory': M. J. Franklin, 'The Bishop, the Abbot and Warmington Rectory: a mediaeval church appropriation struggle', *Northamptonshire Past and Present* 6 (1980–1), 197–206.

Garton, 'Lincoln School': Charles Garton, 'Lincoln School: A Draft History' (1980–8). Typescript in Lincoln Cathedral Library.

GEC: G. E. Cokayne, *Complete Peerage of England, Scotland, Ireland, Great Britain and United Kingdom, extant, extinct, or dormant*, new ed., revised and much enlarged, by V. Gibbs, H. A. Doubleday, D. Warrand, Lord Howard de Walden, G. H. White and P. W. Hammond (13 vols in 14, London, 1910–98).

Georgian Lincoln: Sir Francis Hill, *Georgian Lincoln* (Cambridge, 1966).

GM: *The Gentleman's Magazine* (1731–1907).

Gibbons, *Visitation*: Alfred Gibbons, *Notes on the Visitation of Lincolnshire 1634* (Lincoln, 1898).

Godfrey, *Notts Churches*: *Bingham*: J. T. Godfrey, *Notes on the Churches of Nottinghamshire*: *Hundred of Bingham* (London, 1907).

Godfrey, *Notts Churches*: *Rushcliffe*: J. T. Godfrey, *Notes on the Churches of Nottinghamshire*: *Hundred of Rushcliffe* (London, 1887).

Golding, *Gilbertine Order*: Brian Golding, *Gilbert of Sempringham and the Gilbertine Order c.1130–c.1300* (Oxford, 1995).

Gorman, *Converts to Rome*: W. Gordon Gorman, *Converts to Rome*: *A Biographical List of the More Notable Converts to the Catholic Church in the United Kingdom during the last Sixty Years* (London, 1910).

Goulding, *Louth Records*: R. W. Goulding, *Louth Old Corporation Records* (Louth, 1891).

Goulding, Miscellany: A collection of miscellaneous articles by R. W. Goulding, mainly relating to Louth (Lincoln Cathedral Library).

Greenhill, *Incised Slabs*: F. A. Greenhill, *Monumental Incised Slabs in the County of Lincoln* (Newport Pagnell, 1986).

Greenway, *Mowbray Charters*: D. E. Greenway (ed), *Charters of the Honour of Mowbray 1107–1191*, British Academy Records of Social and Economic History, New Series 1 (1972).

Gribbin, *Premonstratensian Order*: J. A. Gribbin, *The Premonstratensian Order in Late Medieval England* (Woodbridge, 2001).

Grimaldi, *Miscellaneous Writings*: A. B. Grimaldi (ed.), *Miscellaneous Writings: Prose and Poetry from Printed and Manuscript Sources* (London, 1874–81).

Haileybury Register: Norman C. King (ed.), *Haileybury Register 1862–1946* (7th ed., Hertford, 1947).

Hamilton Thompson, 'Bardney Abbey': A. Hamilton Thompson, 'Notes on the history of the Abbey of St Peter, St Paul and St Oswald, Bardney', *AASRP* 32 (1913–14), 35–96, 351–402.

Hamilton Thompson, *Leicester Abbey*: A. Hamilton Thompson, *The Abbey of St Mary of the Meadows, Leicester* (Leicester, 1949).

Hamilton Thompson, *Welbeck Abbey*: A. Hamilton Thompson, *The Premonstratensian Abbey of Welbeck* (London, 1938).

Harrow Register 1571–1800: W. T. J. Gun (ed.), *The Harrow School Register, 1571–1800* (London, 1934).

Harrow Register 1800–1911: M. G. Dauglish and P. K. Stephenson (eds), *The Harrow School Register, 1800–1911* (3rd ed., London, 1911).

Hasted, *History of Kent*: Edward Hasted, *The History and Topographical Survey of the County of Kent* (2nd ed., 12 vols, Canterbury, 1797–1801).

Heads: D. Knowles, C. N. L. Brooke, V. C. M. London and David M. Smith (eds), *The Heads of Religious Houses: England & Wales*, I–III (Cambridge, 1972–2008).

Hebgin-Barnes: Penny Hebgin-Barnes, *The Medieval Stained Glass of the County of Lincolnshire* (Oxford, 1996).

Hennessy: George Hennessy, *Novum Repertorium Ecclesiasticum Parochiale Londinense* (London, 1898).

Hicks Diaries: G. Neville (ed.), *The Diaries of Edward Lee Hicks Bishop of Lincoln 1910–1919*, LRS 82 (1993).

History of Hemingbrough: James Raine (ed.), *The History and Antiquities of the Parish of Hemingbrough* by Thomas Burton (York, 1888).

History of Parliament: House of Commons 1386–1421: J. S. Roskell (ed.), *The House of Commons 1386–1421* (4 vols, History of Parliament Trust, 1992).

HMC, Lincoln Corporation: Historical Manuscripts Commission, *The Manu-*

scripts of the Corporation of Bury St Edmunds, Lincoln, Great Grimsby etc. (London, 1895).

Holles Church Notes: R. E. G. Cole (ed.), *Lincolnshire Church Notes made by Gervase Holles AD 1634 to AD 1642*, LRS 1 (1911).

Honors and Knights' Fees: William Farrer, *Honors and Knights' Fees* (3 vols, London, 1923–5).

Hoskin: Philippa M. Hoskin, *The Rolls of Bishop Robert Grosseteste*, LRS (forthcoming).

Hutton of Gate Burton: A. W. Hutton, *Some Account of the Family of Hutton of Gate Burton, Lincolnshire* (Devizes, 1898).

Jones, *Balliol*: John Jones, *Balliol College: A History 1263–1939* (Oxford, 1988).

Kaye Parish Correspondence: R. W. Ambler (ed.), *Lincolnshire Parish Correspondence of John Kaye, Bishop of Lincoln 1827–53*, LRS 94 (2006).

Keble Register: Basil St G. Drennan, *The Keble College Centenary Register 1870–1970* (Oxford, 1970).

Kelly, *Essex* (1902): *Kelly's Directory of Essex* (London, 1902).

Kelly, *Essex* (1917): *Kelly's Directory of Essex* (London, 1917).

Kelly, *Lincolnshire* (1900): *Kelly's Directory of Lincolnshire* (London, 1900).

Kelly, *Lincolnshire* (1913): *Kelly's Directory of Lincolnshire* (London, 1913).

Kelly, *Lincolnshire* (1919): *Kelly's Directory of Lincolnshire* (London, 1919).

Kelly, *Lincolnshire* (1926): *Kelly's Directory of Lincolnshire* (London, 1926).

King's School Canterbury Register: *King's School Canterbury Register 1859 to 1931* (Canterbury, 1932).

Lambeth Institutions: A. Hamilton Thompson, 'Lambeth Institutions to Benefices', *AASRP* 40 (1930), 33–110.

Lancing Register: E. B. Gordon (ed.), *The Lancing Register: The Third Edition revised and continued to 1932* (Cambridge, 1933).

Law, *Oundle's Story*: W. S. Law, *Oundle's Story: A History of Town and School* (London, 1922).

LDC: *Lincoln Diocesan Church Calendar, Clergy List and General Almanack* (Lincoln, 1866–1965).

LDM: *Lincoln Diocesan Magazine* (Lincoln, 1885–1976).

Leeds GS Admission Books: Edmund Wilson (ed.), *Leeds Grammar School Admission Books from 1820 to 1900*, Thoresby Society 14 (1906).

Le Neve Fasti 1300–1541: H. P. F. King, J. M. Horn and B. Jones (eds), *John Le Neve, Fasti Ecclesiae Anglicanae 1300–1541,* 12 vols (London, 1962–7).

Le Neve Fasti 1541–1857: J. M. Horn, D. M. Smith, D. S. Bailey, P. Mussett and W. H. Campbell (eds), *John Le Neve, Fasti Ecclesiae Anglicanae 1541–1857*, 12 vols (London, 1969–2007).

Le Neve-Hardy: John Le Neve and T. Duffus Hardy, *Fasti Ecclesiae Anglicanae*, 3 vols (Oxford, 1854).

LHA: *Lincolnshire History and Archaeology*.

Lincoln Wills: C. W. Foster and David Hickman (eds), *Lincoln Wills*, LRS 5, 10, 24, 89 (1914–2001).

Lincolnshire Domesday: C. W. Foster and T. Longley (eds), *The Lincolnshire Domesday and the Lindsey Survey*, LRS 19 (1924).

Lincolnshire Feet of Fines: Margaret S. Walker (ed.), *Feet of Fines for the County of Lincoln for the Reign of King John 1199–1216*, Pipe Roll Society, New Series 29 (1954).

Lincolnshire Pedigrees: A. R. Maddison (ed.), *Lincolnshire Pedigrees*, Harleian Society 50–52, 55 (1902–6).

Lipscomb: George Lipscomb, *The History and Antiquities of the County of Buckingham* (4 vols, London, 1831–47).

LNQ: *Lincolnshire Notes and Queries*: *A Quarterly Journal* (24 vols, Horncastle, 1889–1938).

Lodge, *Peerage*: Edmund Lodge, *The Peerage and Baronetage of the British Empire* (36th ed., London, 1867).

Longden: H. I. Longden, *Northamptonshire and Rutland Clergy from 1500*, 16 vols (Northampton, 1938–52).

Lunt, *Financial Relations*: W. E. Lunt, *Financial Relations of the Papacy with England to 1327* (Cambridge MA 1939).

Macdonald, *Holbeach*: G. W. Macdonald, *Historical Notices of the Parish of Holbeach ... with Memorials of its Clergy from AD 1225 to the Present Time* (King's Lynn, 1890).

Maddison, 'Lincoln Cathedral Choir 1640–1700': A. R. Maddison, 'Lincoln Cathedral Choir AD 1640 to 1700', *AASRP* 20 (1889–90), 41–55.

Maddison, 'Lincoln Cathedral Choir 1700–1750': A. R. Maddison, 'Lincoln Cathedral Choir AD 1700 to 1750', *AASRP* 20 (1889–90), 213–26.

Maddison, 'Lincoln Cathedral Choir 1750–1875': A. R. Maddison, 'Lincoln Cathedral Choir AD 1750 to 1875', *AASRP* 21 (1891–2), 208–26.

Maddison, 'Tournay family': A. R. Maddison, 'The Tournays of Caenby', *AASRP* 29 (1907–8), 1–42.

Major, *Blyborough Charters*: Kathleen Major, 'Blyborough Charters', in Patricia M. Barnes and C. F. Slade (eds), *A Medieval Miscellany for Doris Mary Stenton,* Pipe Roll Society, New Series 36 (1962), 203–19.

Manchester School Register: Jeremiah Finch Smith, *The Admission Register of the Manchester School*, Chetham Society, Old Series 69, 73, 93–94 (1866–74).

Marcombe, *Leper Knights*: David Marcombe, *Leper Knights*: *The Order of St Lazarus of Jerusalem in England c.1150–1544* (Woodbridge, 2003).

Marlborough College Register: L. W. James (ed.), *Marlborough College Register 1843–1952* (9th ed., Marlborough, 1952).

Medieval Lincoln: J. W. F. Hill, *Medieval Lincoln* (Cambridge, 1948).

Memorials of Canterbury: C. E. Woodruff and W. Danks, *Memorials of the Cathedral and Priory of Christ in Canterbury* (London, 1912).

Mentmore Registers: Mrs C. H. Parez (ed.), *The Register of the Parish of Mentmore 1685–1829* (Buckinghamshire Parish Register Society, 1909).

Merchant Taylors' Register: Charles J. Robinson (ed.), *A Register of the Scholars Admitted into Merchant Taylors' School from AD 1562 to 1874* (2 vols, Lewes, 1882–3).

Monasticon: W. Dugdale, *Monasticon Anglicanum*, ed. J. Caley, H. Ellis and B. Bandinel (6 vols in 8, London, 1817–30).

Monson: John, Lord Monson (ed.), *Lincolnshire Church Notes made by William John Monson FSA, 1828–1840*, LRS 31 (1936).

Musgrave: Sir G. J. Armytage (ed.), *Obituary Prior to 1800 ... Compiled by Sir William Musgrave*, Harleian Society 44–49 (1899–1901).

Muss-Arnolt, *BCP Among the Nations*: William Muss-Arnolt, *The Book of Common Prayer among the Nations of the World* (London, 1914).

Newcourt: Richard Newcourt, *Repertorium Ecclesiasticum Parochiale Londiniense: An Ecclesiastical Parochial History of the Diocese of London* (2 vols, London, 1708–10).

Nicholas, *County Families of Wales*: Thomas Nicholas, *Annals and Antiquities of the Counties and County Families of Wales* (London, 1872).

Nichols, *Leicestershire*: John Nichols, *The History and Antiquities of the County of Leicester* (8 parts in 4 vols, London, 1795–1811).

Norfolk Benefices: Dawson Turner, *List of Norfolk Benefices* (Norwich, 1847).

Notes on the Foster Family: W. E. Foster, *Notes on the Foster Family of Dowsby and Moulton, co. Lincoln* (London, 1907).

'Notes for a History of Nocton': K. Norgate and M. H. Footman, 'Some notes for a history of Nocton', *AASRP* 24 (1897), 347–81.

ODNB: *Oxford Dictionary of National Biography*.

Oggins, *The Kings and their Hawks*: Robin S. Oggins, *The Kings and their Hawks: Falconry in Medieval England* (London, 2004).

Oliver, *Caribbeana*: V. L. Oliver (ed.), *Caribbeana: Being Miscellaneous Papers relating to the History, Genealogy, Topography and Antiquities of the British West Indies*, 6 vols (London, 1909–19).

Owen, 'Medieval Chapels': D. M. Owen, 'Medieval chapels in Lincolnshire', *LHA* 10 (1975), 15–22.

Peacock, *Church Furniture*: Edward Peacock (ed.), *English Church Furniture, Ornaments and Decorations at the Period of the Reformation* (London, 1866).

Peck, *Antiquities of Stamford*: Francis Peck, *The Antiquities of Stamford and St Martin's* (2 vols, London, 1785).

Peile: John Peile, *Biographical Register of Christ's College 1505–1905*, 2 vols (Cambridge, 1910–13).

Perkin: Michael Perkin (ed.), *A Directory of the Parochial Libraries of the Church of England and the Church in Wales* (revised ed., London, 2004).

Phillips, *Wiltoniae*: Sir Thomas Phillipps, *Institutiones Clericorum in Comitatu Wiltoniae* (2 vols, Salisbury, 1821–5).

Pickford, *Bedfordshire Churches*: Chris Pickford (ed.), *Bedfordshire Churches in the Nineteenth Century*, Bedfordshire Historical Record Society 73, 77, 79–80 (1994–2001).

Porter, *The London Charterhouse*: Stephen Porter, *The London Charter-house*: *A History of Thomas Sutton's Charity* (Stroud, 2009).

Poulson, *Holderness*: George Poulson, *The History and Antiquities of the Seigniory of Holderness*, 2 vols (Hull, 1840–1).

PR Bourne: C. W. Foster (ed.), *The Parish Registers of Bourne ... 1562–1650*, LRS Parish Register Section 7 (1921).

Probate Calendar: Principal Probate Registry, *Calendar of Grants of Probate and Letters of Administration* (1858–).

Record of Old Westminsters: G. F. Russell Barker and A. H. Stenning, *The Record of Old Westminsters*: *A Biographical List of all those who are known to have been educated at Westminster School from the earliest times to 1927* (2 vols, London, 1928).

Records of the Templars: Beatrice A. Lees (ed.), *Records of the Templars in England*, British Academy Records of the Social and Economic History of England and Wales 9 (1935).

Reg. Ant: C. W. Foster and K. Major (eds), *The Registrum Antiquissimum of the Cathedral Church of Lincoln*, LRS 27–29, 32, 34, 41–42, 46, 51, 62, 67–68 (1931–73).

Reg. Burghersh: Nicholas Bennett (ed.), *The Registers of Henry Burghersh 1320–1342* I–III, LRS 87, 90, 101 (1999–2011).

Reg. Catterick: R. N. Swanson (ed.), *The Register of John Catterick, Bishop of Coventry and Lichfield 1415–1419*, CYS 77 (1990).

Reg. Chichele: E. F. Jacob (ed.), *The Register of Henry Chichele, Archbishop of Canterbury 1414–1443*, CYS 42, 45–47 (1937–47).

Reg. Edington: S. F. Hockey (ed.), *The Register of William Edington, Bishop of Winchester 1346–1366* I–II, Hampshire Record Series 7–8 (1986–7).

Regesta: H. W. C. Davis, C. Johnson, H. A. Cronne and R. H. C. Davis (eds), *Regesta Regum Anglo-Normannorum 1066–1154* (4 vols, Oxford, 1913–69).

Reg. Fleming: Nicholas Bennett (ed.), *The Register of Richard Fleming, Bishop of Lincoln 1420–31* I–II, CYS 73, 99 (1984–2009).

Reg. Greenfield: A. Hamilton Thompson (ed.), *The Register of William Greenfield, Lord Archbishop of York, 1306–1315* I–V, Surtees Society 145, 149, 151–153 (1931–40).

Registrum Collegii Exoniensis: C. W. Boase (ed.), *Registrum Collegii Exoniensis*: *Register of the Rectors, Fellows and other Members on the Foundation of Exeter College, Oxford*, OHS 27 (1894).

Reg. Langley: R. L. Storey (ed.), *The Register of Thomas Langley, Bishop of Durham 1406–1437* I–VI, Surtees Society 164, 166, 169–170, 177, 182 (1956–70).

Reg. Melton: R. M. T. Hill, D. Robinson, R. Brocklesby and T. C. B. Timmins (eds), *The Register of William Melton* I–VI, CYS 70–71, 76, 85, 93, 101 (1977–2011).

Reg. Pal. Dunelm: Sir Thomas Duffus Hardy (ed), *Registrum Palatinum Dunelmense. The Register of Richard de Kellawe, Lord Palatine and Bishop of Durham, 1314–1316*, 4 vols, Rolls Series (1873–8).

Reg. Repingdon: Margaret Archer (ed.), *The Register of Bishop Philip Repingdon 1405–1419*, LRS 57–58, 74 (1963–82).

Reg. Scrope: R. N. Swanson (ed.), *A Calendar of the Register of Richard Scrope, Archbishop of York 1398–1405*, Borthwick Texts and Calendars 8, 11 (1981–5).

Reg. Sudbury: R. C. Fowler (ed.), *Registrum Simonis de Sudbiria Diocesis Londoniensis AD 1362–1375*, CYS 34, 38 (1927–38).

Reg. Sutton: R. M. T. Hill (ed.), *The Rolls and Register of Bishop Oliver Sutton* I–VIII, LRS 39, 43, 48, 52, 60, 64, 69, 76 (1948–86).

Reg. Waltham: T. C. B. Timmins (ed.), *The Register of John Waltham, Bishop of Salisbury 1388–1395*, CYS 80 (1994).

Repton Register: G. S. Messiter (ed.), *Repton School Register 1557–1905* (Repton, 1905).

'Rolls of Hugh of Wells': D. M. Smith, 'The rolls of Hugh of Wells, Bishop of Lincoln 1209–35', *Bulletin of the Institute of Historical Research* 45 (1972), 155–95.

Rossall Register: L. R. Furneaux (ed.), *Rossall School Register 1844–1923* (6th ed., Godalming, 1923).

Rot. Gravesend: F. N. Davis (ed.), *Rotuli Ricardi Gravesend episcopi Lincolniensis*, LRS 20 (1925).

Rot. Welles: W. P. W. Phillimore, F. N. Davis and H. E. Salter (eds), *Rotuli Hugonis de Welles episcopi Lincolniensis* I–III, LRS 3, 6, 9 (1912–14).

Rugby Register: A. T. Michell (ed.), *Rugby School Register* (2 vols, Rugby, 1901–2).

St Bees College Calendar: *The Saint Bees College Calendar* (London, 1853–68).

St John's Admissions: R. F. Scott (ed.), *Admissions to the College of St John the Evangelist in the University of Cambridge*, 4 parts in 3 vols (Cambridge, 1893–1931).

St John's College Register: V. Sillery, *St John's College Biographical Register 1919–1975* (2nd ed., Oxford, 1994).

St John's Register: A. Hegarty (ed.), *A Biographical Register of St John's College Oxford 1555–1660*, OHS, New Series 43 (2011).

St Paul's School Register: R. B. Gardiner (ed.), *The Admission Registers of St Paul's School from 1748 to 1905* (2 vols, London, 1884–1906).

Sanders, *English Baronies*: I. J. Sanders, *English Baronies: A Study of their Origin and Descent* (London, 1960).

Sedbergh Register: [Bernard Wilson (ed.)], *The Sedbergh School Register 1546 to 1895* (Leeds, 1895).

Shrewsbury Register: J. E. Auden and H. N. Dawson, *Shrewsbury School Register* (2 vols, Oswestry and Shrewsbury, 1898, 1964).

Snape, *Army Chaplains*: M. F. Snape, *The Royal Army Chaplains' Department 1796–1953: Clergy Under Fire* (Woodbridge, 2008).

Somerset Incumbents: F. W. Weaver (ed.), *Somerset Incumbents* (Bristol, 1889).

Southwell Monuments: *Southwell Minster: Schedule of Gravestones, Ledger Stones, Monuments, Dedications*, Nottinghamshire Family History Society Records Series 118 (1998).

Speculum: R. E. G. Cole (ed.), *Speculum Dioeceseos Lincolniensis*, LRS 4 (1913).

State of the Church: C. W. Foster (ed.), *The State of the Church in the Reigns of Elizabeth and James I*, LRS 23 (1926).

Stenton: *Facsimiles of Early Charters*: F. M. Stenton (ed.), *Facsimiles of Early Charters from Northamptonshire Collections*, Northamptonshire Record Society 4 (1930).

Stenton, *Rolls of the Justices in Eyre*: D. M. Stenton (ed.), *Rolls of the Justices in Eyre, being the Rolls of Pleas and Assizes for Lincolnshire 1218–9 and Worcestershire 1221*, Selden Society 53 (1934).

Stonor Letters and Papers: Christine Carpenter (ed.), *Kingsford's Stonor Letters and Papers 1290–1483* (Cambridge, 1996).

Stow Admons: Lincolnshire Archives, Stow Administrations.

Stow Church Restored: Mark Spurrell (ed.), *Stow Church Restored 1846–1866*, LRS 75 (1984).

Stow Visitation: N. S. Harding (ed.), *A Stow Visitation, Being Notes on the Churches in the Archdeaconry of Stow 1845 by The Venerable W. B. Stonehouse* (Lincoln, 1940).

Subsidy: H. Salter (ed.), *A Subsidy Collected in the Diocese of Lincoln in 1526*, OHS 63 (1909).

Summoning St Michael: David Stocker and Paul Everson, *Summoning St Michael: Early Romanesque Towers in Lincolnshire* (Oxford, 2006).

Swaby: J. E. Swaby, 'Lincolnshire Parish Clergy in the Seventeenth Century' (1983). Typescript list in Lincoln Cathedral Library.

Thompson, *Boston*: Pishey Thompson, *The History and Antiquities of Boston* (Boston, 1856).

Todd, *Life of Walton*: H. J. Todd, *Memoirs of the Life and Writings of the Right Rev. Brian Walton, Lord Bishop of Chester* (2 vols, London, 1821).

Train, *Central Notts Clergy*: K. S. S. Train (ed.), *Lists of the Clergy of Central Nottinghamshire* I–III, Thoroton Society Record Series 15 (1953–5).

Train, *North Notts Clergy*: K. S. S. Train (ed.), *Lists of the Clergy of North Nottinghamshire*, Thoroton Society Record Series 20 (1961).

Trollope, *Sleaford*: E. Trollope, *Sleaford and the Wapentakes of Flaxwell and Aswardhurn* (London, 1872).

Tyerman, *Harrow School*: Christopher Tyerman, *A History of Harrow School 1324–1991* (Oxford, 2000).

Valor: J. Caley (ed.), *Valor Ecclesiasticus* (6 vols, London, 1810–34).

VCH Cambridge: L. F. Salzman *et al.* (eds), *The Victoria History of the County of Cambridgeshire and the Isle of Ely* (10 vols, Oxford, 1938–2002).

VCH Essex: William Page *et al.* (eds), *The Victoria History of the County of Essex* (11 vols, London, 1903–), in progress.

VCH Hertford: William Page (ed.), *The Victoria History of the County of Hertford* (5 vols, London, 1902–23).

VCH Lincoln: William Page (ed.), *The Victoria History of the County of Lincoln, II* (London, 1906).

Venn, *Alumni*: John and J. A. Venn, *Alumni Cantabrigienses: A Biographical List of all known Students, Graduates and Holders of Office at the University of Cambridge from the Earliest Times to 1900* (2 parts in 10 vols, Cambridge, 1922–54).

Visitation of London: J. J. Howard and G. J. Armytage (eds), *The Visitation of London in the Year 1568 Taken by Robert Cooke, Clarenceux King of Arms*, Harleian Society 1 (1869).

Visitations of Southwell: A. F. Leach (ed.), *Visitations and Memorials of Southwell Minster*, Camden Society, New Series 48 (1891).

Wadham Registers: R. B. Gardiner (ed.), *The Registers of Wadham College Oxford from 1613 to 1719 (1719 to 1871)* (2 vols, London, 1889–95).

Walker Revised: A. G. Matthews, *Walker Revised, Being a Revision of John Walker's Sufferings of the Clergy during the Grand Rebellion 1642–60* (Oxford, 1948).

Westbury-on-Trym: Nicholas Orme and Jon Cannon, *Westbury-on-Trym: Monastery, Minster, College*, Bristol Record Society 62 (2010).

Wheater, *Sherburn and Cawood*: William Wheater, *The History of the Parishes of Sherburn and Cawood: with incidental accounts of the village and prebendal church of Wistow* (Selby, 1865).

Whichcot Letters: C. M. Lloyd (ed.), *Letters from John Wallace to Madam Whichcot*, LRS 66 (1973).

White, *Lincolnshire* (1842): William White, *History, Gazetteer and Directory of Lincolnshire* (Sheffield, 1842).

White, *Lincolnshire* (1856): William White, *History, Gazetteer and Directory of Lincolnshire* (Sheffield, 1856).

White, *Lincolnshire* (1872): *White's History, Gazetteer and Directory of Lincolnshire* (Sheffield, 1872).

White, *Lincolnshire* (1892): *White's History, Gazetteer and Directory of Lincolnshire* (Sheffield, 1892).

Who Was Who 1929–1940: *Who Was Who 1929–1940: A Companion to Who's Who Containing the Biographies of Those who Died during the Period 1929–1940* (London, 1947).

Winchester College 1836–1906: J. B. Wainewright (ed.), *Winchester College 1836–1906: A Register* (Winchester, 1907).

Winchester Ordinations: A. J. Willis, *Winchester Ordinations 1660–1829* (2 vols, Folkestone, 1964–5).

Wisden (1913): Sydney H. Pardon (ed.), *John Wisden's Cricketer's Almanack for 1913* (50th ed., London, 1913).

Wood, *Athenae*: Philip Bliss (ed.), *Athenae Oxonienses, an Exact History of Writers and Bishops who have had their Education in the University of Oxford* [by Anthony à Wood] (new ed., 4 vols, London, 1813–20).

Woodforde at Oxford: W. N. Hargreaves-Mawdsley (ed.), *Woodforde at Oxford 1759–1776*, OHS, New Series 21 (1969).

York Ordinations 1500–1509: Claire Cross (comp.), *York Clergy Ordinations 1500–1509*, Borthwick List and Index 30 (2001).

York Ordinations 1520–1559: Claire Cross (comp.), *York Clergy Ordinations 1520–1559*, Borthwick List and Index 32 (2002).

York Ordinations 1561–1642: Claire Cross (comp.), *York Clergy Ordinations 1561–1642*, Borthwick List and Index 24 (2000).

York Ordinations 1662–1699: Anna B. Bisset (comp.), *York Clergy Ordinations 1662–1699*, Borthwick List and Index 20 (1998).

York Ordinations 1700–1749: Anna B. Bisset (comp.), *York Clergy Ordinations 1700–1749*, Borthwick List and Index 25 (2000).

York Ordinations 1750–1799: Debbie Usher (comp.), *York Clergy Ordinations 1750–1799*, Borthwick List and Index 33 (2002).

York Ordinations 1800–1849: Sara Slinn (comp.), *York Clergy Ordinations 1800–1849*, Borthwick List and Index 28 (2001).

York Sede Vacante Register 1423–26: Joan Kirby (ed), *The York Sede Vacante Register 1423–26: a Calendar*, Borthwick Texts and Studies 38 (2009).

INTRODUCTION

The Lincolnshire landscape is thickly populated with parish churches, their towers and spires rising from the villages and towns of the county. In 1914, on the eve of the First World War, there were some 700 Anglican parish churches and parochial chapels in the diocese.[1] During the past hundred years, some of these have been declared 'redundant', or even destroyed, but the great majority remain as witnesses to the central role of the Christian faith in the history of Lincolnshire communities. The fabric of these buildings, nave and chancel, font, pulpit and reading desk, stained glass and monuments, all tell of the long history of their parishes. But what of the clergy who served them? Go inside one of these churches, savour the familiar smell of hassocks and hymn books, and you will often see beside the door a framed list of past incumbents. Some of these lists are the work of local historians; a surprising number were compiled by Canon C. W. Foster, Vicar of Timberland and founder of the Lincoln Record Society. They serve to remind us that in order to understand the history of the towns and villages in which these churches stand, we must go beyond the buildings themselves and explore the lives of those who used them. In a parish church, we must begin with the parson.

The infrastructure of historical enquiry lies, as Sir Isaiah Berlin used to say, in asking such basic questions as 'Who did what, and when?' A list of parochial clergy can supply an essential part of such a foundation. My own first venture in 1984 into the publication of medieval episcopal registers, an edition of the first part of the register of Richard Fleming (Bishop of Lincoln, 1420–31), was met with incredulity by a Northamptonshire reviewer who asked why it was necessary to print such records of institutions, when all the enquirer needed to do was to look in the pages of the county history. It is indeed true that some parts of the ancient diocese of Lincoln are well-favoured in this respect. Northamptonshire and Leicestershire, Buckinghamshire and Hertfordshire can all boast extensive histories, compiled by eighteenth- and nineteenth-century antiquaries such as Bridges, Nichols and Cussans, giving for each parish details of the descent of the manor and the succession of incumbents.[2] Other counties however (and Lincolnshire is one of them) have

---

[1] *LDC* (1914).
[2] See C. R. J. Currie and C. P. Lewis (eds), *English County Histories: A Guide* (Stroud, 1994).

never enjoyed the luxury of these handsome leather-bound folios. A guide to the rectors and vicars of the parishes of Lincolnshire is long overdue.

The present volume is planned as the first of a series which, when complete, will make up a biographical register of Lincolnshire parish clergy. Taking the rural deaneries of the county in alphabetical order, it will list the succession of incumbents, parish by parish, with dates of institution and names of patrons. Where possible, a brief biographical sketch of the incumbent is attached. Little can be done in this regard for the great majority of medieval incumbents, but from the sixteenth century, when more sources become available, it has been the aim to provide basic information about birth, parentage, education, ordination, clerical career and date of death. An attempt has been made where possible to ascertain the extent to which the incumbent was resident. It must be stressed, however, that these biographies are simply an outline, a starting-point from which further work can be done by others.

Dates and Sources

The diocese of Lincoln has the distinction of having produced the earliest system of episcopal registration known to exist. The rolls of Bishop Hugh of Wells, dating from *c*.1214, provide the starting date of this biographical register, for although the names of earlier incumbents can occasionally be found in legal records or in the witness lists of charters, it is the systematic recording of institutions by the bishop's chancery that makes the present undertaking possible. It has been less easy to determine when to draw the lists to a close. The most appropriate date would seem to be that of the Pastoral Measure 1968 which in many ways marked the end of an era by giving the diocesan bishop a much more active role in managing parochial resources, enabling the establishment of groups and team ministries, the suspension of patronage and the redundancy of churches, and diluting the historic links between patron, incumbent and benefice. Outside the major town parishes, the concept of a 'parish priest' has become a rarity, as rural congregations find themselves sharing their incumbent with ever-expanding groups of churches.

The principal source for this project is the majestic series of episcopal registers of the bishops of Lincoln, beginning with Hugh of Wells in the early thirteenth century and continuing right down to the present day as the staff of the Diocesan Registry add current entries to the register of Bishop Christopher Lowson. The registers thus cover a span of eight hundred years, with only one serious gap extending from the death of Bishop John Longland in 1547 until the Restoration of Church and King in 1660. Some registers survive from this period, among them those of Bishops Thomas Cooper and William Chaderton, but much has been lost. Other sources from the diocesan records can be used to fill these gaps: presentation deeds, subscription registers, records of inductions and the lists of clergy exhibiting at visitations. Many such sources for the sixteenth century were printed by Canon Foster.[3]

Records of episcopal and archidiaconal visitation can also be used to determine the extent to which a particular incumbent was resident in his parish. The visitation book used in 1768 and 1778 is particularly fruitful in this regard, and comments such as 'Absent, lives in Yorkshire' or 'Lives in Norwich' can provide valuable clues. One incumbent of Spridlington defeated all enquiries, however, and it could only be recorded 'No account where he lives'.[4] Enquiries as to residence can be pursued further in parish registers, bishop's transcripts, wills and probate inventories and non-residence licences. Parish registers have also been used to establish dates of baptism and burial. Details of education have been supplied by the registers of alumni, notably the majestic registers compiled by A. B. Emden for medieval graduates of Oxford and Cambridge, those of Foster (Oxford) and Venn (Cambridge) for their post-medieval graduates, and numerous registers of historic schools, of which there is an extensive collection in Lincoln Cathedral Library. Dates of ordination may be found in the episcopal registers, in visitation records and, for the nineteenth century, a separate series of ordination registers. For clerical careers during the period from 1540 to 1835, the Clergy of the Church of England Database, based at King's College, London, is a valuable guide; after this period, the successive editions of *Crockford's Clerical Directory* and the *Lincoln Diocesan Calendar* are essential reading.

The Making of an Incumbent

The process whereby a clerk in holy orders gained possession of a parochial benefice changed very little during the 750 years covered by this project.[5] When a vacancy occurred, the choice of a new incumbent fell upon the patron of the living, the possessor of the advowson. Having made his choice, the patron would cause a presentation deed to be drawn up, addressed to the diocesan bishop, naming the candidate and humbly requesting that he be instituted. On receiving the presentation deed, the bishop would order an inquiry to be held, usually by the archdeacon's official or the rural dean, to ascertain the facts of the case: whether the living was in fact vacant, when and how the vacancy began, whether the patron truly had the right of presentation and who had presented at the last vacancy, and finally, concerning

---

[3]   See D. M. Smith, *Guide to Bishops' Registers of England and Wales* (London, 1981); Kathleen Major, *A Handlist of the Records of the Bishop of Lincoln and of the Archdeacons of Lincoln and Stow* (Oxford, 1953).

[4]   LC 31, *passim*.

[5]   For a survey of the procedure in the early fourteenth century, see *Reg. Burghersh* i. xix–xxvii.

the candidate who had been presented, whether he were of honest life and conversation, duly ordained and in possession of any other benefice. The inquiry would be held before clergy from neighbouring parishes and laity from the parish itself. Occasionally its conclusions were incorporated in the registration of the subsequent institution, as at Rippingale in 1497 when the alternate turns of patronage shared by the Grey family and Shelford Priory, a regular cause of friction, were set down in writing.

Once the inquiry had been held, its findings were communicated to the bishop, and the institution of the candidate could take place. An exception to this pattern of presentation and inquiry may be found in those parishes where the patronage was in the hands of the bishop himself. The church of Kirkby Underwood was in the bishop's gift from 1337 onwards, and those of Horbling and Morton-by-Bourne came into his possession at the Reformation. In such cases there was no need for a presentation deed, and it would appear that the formal inquiry was usually omitted. Admission to these benefices was by collation rather than institution, the bishop in his joint capacity as patron and diocesan conferring the living on the clerk. The final stage in all admissions to benefices was induction, traditionally carried out by the archdeacon, where the new incumbent was given possession of the temporal, as opposed to the spiritual, rights of the benefice.

Deaneries and Parishes

The medieval diocese of Lincoln comprised eight archdeaconries, whose extent was normally based on county boundaries. The archdeaconries of Leicester, Oxford, Buckingham and Bedford corresponded to their respective counties. That of Northampton included Rutland as well as Northamptonshire. The archdeaconry of Huntingdon comprised the county of that name together with a large part of Hertfordshire. Lincolnshire was divided unequally into two archdeaconries. Much the greater part fell within the archdeaconry of Lincoln but a small area in the north-west of the county, based on the West Riding of Lindsey, made up the small archdeaconry of Stow. The archdeaconries were themselves subdivided into rural deaneries. There were twenty-two deaneries in Lincoln Archdeaconry and a further four in Stow, ranging in size from Ness in the extreme south of the county, with fourteen parishes, to Louthesk and Ludborough with fifty.

The two deaneries covered in this volume (the first two in alphabetical sequence) are Aslacoe and Aveland. As with most of the Lincolnshire deaneries, both corresponded closely to the boundaries of the civil wapentakes of those names. The name Aslacoe is said to mean 'Aslak's mound or hill', no doubt with reference to the site where the wapentake met (the site has not been identified). In the middle ages, the deanery included twenty parishes grouped around a north–south spine along the Roman Ermine Street, a pattern sometimes referred to as the 'ladder' parishes. On the west side of the road, the deanery stretched from Blyborough in the north to Cammeringham in the south; on the east side it extended from Waddingham in the north to Hackthorn and Cold Hanworth in the south. Like Aslacoe, the deanery of Aveland was based on the wapentake of that name. Aveland ('Afi's grove') was also the meeting-place of the wapentake, identified as a moated enclosure known as *The Aveland*, one mile west of Aslackby. The deanery comprised twenty-three parishes, extending from Dembleby, Osbournby and Swaton in the north to Bourne in the south.[6]

As was the case elsewhere, the pattern of church foundations reflected that of land tenure. A single or dominant holding usually resulted in one parish church, whereas multiple holdings might result in two churches being built in one village (as at Spridlington, Hemswell and Waddingham) or in two patrons each presenting to a different mediety of the church (as at Hackthorn and Kirkby Underwood). The church of Rippingale was divided into three parts, of which two were united during the thirteenth century to form one benefice, the third remaining a separate living until 1725. Nearly three-quarters of the parish churches in these two deaneries were in ecclesiastical patronage during the medieval period, many being in the gift of religious houses. Local monasteries were predominant among these patrons, among them Bourne Abbey (Bourne itself, Dunsby and Morton-by-Bourne), Barlings Abbey (Caenby and Swaton), Bullington Priory (Ingham, Spridlington St Albin and a mediety of Hackthorn) and Sempringham Priory (Billingborough, Horbling, Laughton-by-Folkingham, Sempringham, Stow-by-Threckingham, Walcot and a mediety of Kirkby Underwood). Some were in the gift of houses further afield: Blyborough (Durham Priory), Newton-by-Folkingham (St Andrew's Priory, Northampton). Two churches belonged to monasteries in France; these were Cammeringham (Blanchland Abbey) and Fillingham (Lessay Abbey, until the advowson was purchased in 1343 by Balliol College, Oxford); in addition, the Abbey of St Nicholas in Angers held an alternate share in the patronage of Willoughton.

With so many advowsons in the hands of abbeys, priories and cathedral chapters, it is not surprising to find that nearly half of the churches in these two deaneries were appropriated at some stage during the medieval period, allowing the religious corporation to take the revenues of the rectory, leaving a smaller share for a vicar who would undertake the cure of souls in the parish. On occasion, the ordination of a vicarage in an appropriated church was omitted, as at Walcot-by-Folkingham, where the spiritual care of the parishioners fell to a stipendiary curate, employed by the appropriator but with no security of tenure. Appropriation naturally affected the income that the incumbent derived from a living. Assessments for clerical taxation give

---

[6]   Kenneth Cameron, *A Dictionary of Lincolnshire Place-Names* (Nottingham, 1998), 5, 7–8.

us an occasional indication of the values of benefices and although (as with all such assessments) they are unlikely to give an accurate picture they do afford some comparison between one church and another. In the assessment for the Taxation of Pope Nicholas IV of 1291, the mean value of an incumbent's income in Aslacoe deanery was £5; in the deanery of Aveland it was slightly higher, at £7 3s 4d. Despite this, there were more of the richest benefices (those assessed at £20 or more) in Aslacoe (Blyborough, Fillingham, Hemswell All Saints, each valued at £20) than in Aveland, where only Rippingale (£36 8s 4d, shared unequally between the two portions) and Swaton (£51 6s 8d) fell into this category. It is unsurprising to find that not long afterwards Swaton was appropriated by Barlings Abbey.[7]

Clergy

The clergy who served these forty-five parishes over this long period of some 750 years provide a cross-section of the clerical population of the county across the centuries. They include some whose illustrious careers passed far beyond the confines of a Lincolnshire rectory. Two medieval incumbents, Henry de Beningworth (Folkingham 1284) and Hugh de Houcton (Rippingale 1247/8), were preferred to the Subdeanery of Lincoln, the latter having previously held office as Chancellor of Cambridge University. Another who held (briefly) the post of Subdean at Lincoln was Brian Higdon (Kirkby Underwood 1511) whose later promotion to the Deanery of York was due to the patronage of Cardinal Wolsey.

The celebrated hymn to the goddess of Learning

> Make me, O sphere-descended Queen,
> A Bishop – or, at least, a Dean …

was a refrain sung by not a few eighteenth-century pluralists.[8] Rowney Noel (Bourne 1756) had to settle for a deanery (Salisbury 1780) but there were others from our two deaneries who travelled all the way to the episcopal bench. Thomas Earle Welby (Newton-by-Folkingham 1847) had indeed a long journey to reach in 1861 the bishopric of St Helena but others attained sees closer at hand. John Hacket (Kirkby Underwood 1621) not only wrote a celebrated life of a prelate (John Williams) but became one himself in 1661, as Bishop of Coventry and Lichfield. The rectory of Fillingham, more or less reserved for Fellows of Balliol College, produced no fewer than three future bishops: George Cotes (Chester 1554), Robert Abbot, whose brother was himself an Archbishop (Salisbury 1615) and John Piers who rose almost to the top of the hierarchy as Archbishop of York (1589).

---

[7] D&C A/1/11 (Taxatio Ecclesiastica Nicholai IV).
[8] *Blackwood's Edinburgh Magazine* 2 (1818), 82.

Among the many scholars whose names grace these pages, one whose influence stands far beyond all others is John Wycliffe (Fillingham 1361). With its Oxford connection, Fillingham inevitably produced more than its share of learned incumbents, although it should be noted that wisdom is not always accompanied by practical ability. The election of George Cotes as Master was opposed by Bishop Longland ('if [he] shulde obtaine itt, I reckon the colledge undone'), while the Mastership of Henry Savage (Fillingham 1662) nearly brought the Foundation to an untimely end. When his successor examined the financial situation, he commented that 'had Dr Savage livd but a year longer the colledge gates has been shut up'. Another college head was Gabriel Silvestre (Folkingham 1502), Master of Clare from 1496 until 1506.

Complaints about the lack of learning among the parish clergy can be found during the episcopate of Hugh of Wells at the beginning of the thirteenth century. Hugh de Scalleby (Cold Hanworth 1218/19) was ordered to attend the schools because he was lacking in learning. By the sixteenth century, such comments were endemic. The note on John Jackson (Billingborough 1546) made at Bishop Cooper's visitation in 1576 ('knows but little Latin; but little versed in sacred learning') was repeated many times. Thomas Gamon (Hacconby 1577) was admonished in 1611, when he had already been incumbent for more than thirty years, 'to appeare at Buckden before his Lordship touching his insufficiency in learninge'. An indication that standards were improving comes not only from the growing number of graduates presented to livings during the course of the seventeenth century but also from the appearance of books among the items listed in the probate inventories of the clergy of this period. Some collections were meagre; the books of John Wilson (Dembleby 1515) may have been valued at a mere ten shillings and those of Richard Potter, who held the same living a century later, at only three shillings and sixpence. On the other hand, John Wetherall (Spridlington 1626), whose energetic participation in the disputes of the period bore fruit in his tract *A Discovery and Confutation of the Opinions and Practises of Some False Brethren Betwixt Bridge and Lincoln* (1652), had a collection of books worthy to be described in the inventory of his goods as 'his Librarie', valued at £30. The 'librarie of Bookes' belonging to Thomas Grainger (Horbling 1621) were appraised at £11; significantly, they were listed among the contents of 'his studdie'. By the time of Abraham Page (Folkingham 1657) it was possible for the appraisers to record a well-equipped room: 'In the Library: All the Bookes there, £16 … one Table, one Deske, and the shelves there, 5s.'

Presentation to a living depended ultimately on the patron knowing something about the candidate. It has already been noted that the great majority of rectors of Fillingham were graduates of Balliol College. Indeed it is something of an irony that Theophilus Leigh, whose Mastership of the College endured for almost sixty years, was unable to secure for himself this valuable living because, during the protracted dispute caused by his election in

1726, the presentation to Fillingham lapsed to the Bishop of Lincoln, who conferred it on one of his own sons, thereby keeping Leigh out of the rectory for forty years. The link between Balliol and Fillingham can be traced elsewhere. A number of the medieval rectors of Blyborough can be found to have a connection with the Bishop or Priory of Durham. A lay patron might well present a member of his family. This can be seen from the thirteenth century, as with Peter de Paris (Owmby 1231/2), Henry de Haneword (Cold Hanworth 1251/2) and Henry son of Henry de Hauvill, presented by his father to Hacconby in 1244/5. John Bourryau Spooner (Blyborough 1795) was presented by the Crown but his candidacy would not have been adversely affected by his kinship to the Luard family, owners of the Blyborough estate. Similarly, Hugh Nanney (Caenby 1848) was a kinsman of the patron, Sir Charles Monck, and John Cracroft (Hackthorn 1821) was presented by his father. Edwin George Jarvis (Hackthorn with Cold Hanworth 1844) was also linked to the Cracroft family through his marriage with the daughter of his patron. The pattern of the family living can be seen at Newton-by-Folkingham, held between 1802 and 1858 by three successive members of the Welby family in whose gift it was. Nineteenth-century Spridlington furnishes a good example of the activities of a 'squarson'. Henry Frederick Hutton, who inherited the manor and advowson from his cousin, presented himself to the living in 1841 and went on to build a new parsonage (1842), enlarge the church (1865) and erect a school (1870). After his death in 1873 the church was once more rebuilt in his memory.

There were many clergy who were not so fortunately situated, and there was at times a considerable underclass of stipendiary chaplains (in the medieval period) or assistant curates (in post-Reformation times) who struggled to obtain the security of a living. Victorian editions of *Crockford's Clerical Directory* furnish numerous examples of clergy who served a succession of curacies. Henry Simpson Blink (Owmby 1887) was ordained in 1857 and spent thirty years as a curate in nine different parishes, moving from Staffordshire to south-east England, then to Wales and finally to Lincolnshire. James Johnson (Glentham 1844) had waited twenty-seven years for a benefice, including twenty-four years as curate of Crowle. Johnson had not had a university education, having been ordained as a literate, but a university degree did not necessarily help in finding a living. William Norton Howe (Caenby 1914) had graduated from Exeter College, Oxford, but it was twenty years before he received the offer of Caenby Rectory from Bishop Hicks.

Some clergy sought ordination later in life. Charles Ethelbert Milton (Owmby 1899) was in his forties when he was ordained deacon, having previously worked in commerce as a clerk and accountant. David Cuthbert Rosser (Spridlington 1938) embarked on higher education at the age of thirty, his entry into the ordained ministry having been postponed by the First World War and service in the Royal Naval Volunteer Reserve. Leonard Garnier Pilkington (Sempringham 1937) was over fifty when he was ordained; his earlier career included a post as Warden of a Boys Club run by J. S. Fry and Sons, the Bristol chocolate manufacturers. Some incumbents had seen military service before ordination. Charles Ramsay Flint (Glentworth 1852) had been with the East India Company in Madras. Edward Revell Eardley-Wilmot (Waddingham 1872) had been in the Bengal Artillery. Francis George Frost (Caenby 1936) had served during the First World War with the Canadian Infantry Battalion, being awarded the DCM at Courcelette in 1916. John Cracroft (Hackthorn 1821) was an Army Chaplain, serving in the Peninsular War in 1812–14.

The most usual alternative career among the clergy, either before or after ordination, was that of schoolmaster. James Adamson (Rippingale 1615) and Robert Kelham (Billingborough 1702) were also schoolmasters in those villages. Benjamin Peacocke, a baker's son from Tillingham in Essex, became a pupil teacher at the age of fourteen and spent nearly fifty years as a schoolmaster before being ordained by Bishop Swayne in 1929. William Sadler (Dembleby 1877) had previously been Classics Master at St Paul's School in Darjeeling. More locally, the curacy of Hemswell, in the gift of the City of Lincoln, was used to supplement the income of William White (1749) and Richard Thomas (1823), both Ushers of Lincoln School. Samuel Rolt (Bishop Norton c.1745) and John Hewthwaite (Morton-by-Bourne 1766) each served as Headmaster of Lincoln School. Other local schools were served by incumbents in these two deaneries. John Banks (Cammeringham 1813) was Headmaster of Boston School from 1790 until 1825. Arthur Madge (Kirkby Underwood 1907) was Headmaster of Horncastle Grammar School from 1891 to 1907. Further afield, William Bolton (Dunsby-by-Bourne 1686) was successively an Assistant Master at Charterhouse and Headmaster at Harrow School, while John Jones (Kirkby Underwood 1722) had previously served as Headmaster at Oundle where his enthusiastic flogging of the boys gave him the reputation of 'a very Orbilius'.

When not teaching classical languages to the boys at Harrow, William Bolton spent some of his leisure moments in the writing of verse. His *Poem upon a Laurel Leaf*, published in 1680, offers a touching account of the cure of his rheumatism. Other poets to be found among the clergy of these parishes are William Gurden Moore (Aslackby 1840), author of *A Dream of Life, or, Augustine and Geraldine* (1837) and Edwin Wrenford (Sempringham 1887) whose works included *First-fruits of Sacred Song* (1876); *Carmina Regia and other Songs of the Heart* (1878); *'The Kiss of Death' and 'In Memoriam'*: *Alice Maud Mary, Princess of England* (1878). Other incumbents employed their spare time at the easel. The painting *The Poultry Seller* by Richard Heighway (Fillingham 1782) is in the collection of the Victoria and Albert Museum. William Norton Howe (Caenby 1914) was an enthusiastic amateur artist and the author of *Animal Life in Italian Painting* (1912).

The theological disputes that have from time to time beset the Church in England are reflected in the careers of the clergy from these two deaneries.

John Wycliffe (Fillingham 1361) is of course pre-eminent in the line of English reformers (his non-residence at Fillingham can be seen to sit not altogether comfortably with his reforming views). In the controversies that engaged the Elizabethan and early Stuart Church, John Jackson (Bourne 1585), Robert Atkinson (Glentworth 1600) and Simon Bradstreet (Horbling 1596) were among those who refused to wear the surplice or to engage in ceremonies such as signing with the cross in baptism. Their treatment by the episcopal authorities seems surprisingly lenient and few such men were removed from office. The situation of the next generation of clergy was very different. Robert Haslewood (Kirkby Underwood 1622) and Adam Cranwell (Rippingale 1619) were among the many Royalist clergy sequestered during the Civil War period. George Beck, who was intruded in Cranwell's place in 1646, was himself one of the nonconformist clergy ejected from their livings in 1662, along with Michael Drake (Pickworth 1647). Jeremy Dunn (Waddingham 1686) and Richard Brocklesby (Folkingham 1673) were both deprived as non-jurors in the years after 1689. At the end of the nineteenth century, David Lloyd Thomas (Cammeringham 1884) was received into the Roman Catholic Church following the publication of the Bull *Apostolicae Curae*, denying the validity of Anglican Orders.

The parish churches of these two deaneries bear ample testimony in furnishings, stained glass and memorials to their incumbents of past generations. There are monuments to Robert Conyng (Blyborough 1424) and William Beauchaump (Harpswell 1349) in their respective churches. Robert Kelham (Billingborough 1702), George Bassett (Glentworth 1765) and John Shinglar (Walcot 1798) are among the many others commemorated. There is a charming acrostic verse memorial to John Audley (Hacconby 1631); in the same church is a remarkable monument to Samuel Hopkinson (Morton with Hacconby 1795), designed by A. W. N. Pugin.

This survey of Lincolnshire clergy will, it is hoped, serve as a starting-point for further investigation, helping to understand the role they have played in the history of the Church in this county.

DEANERY OF ASLACOE

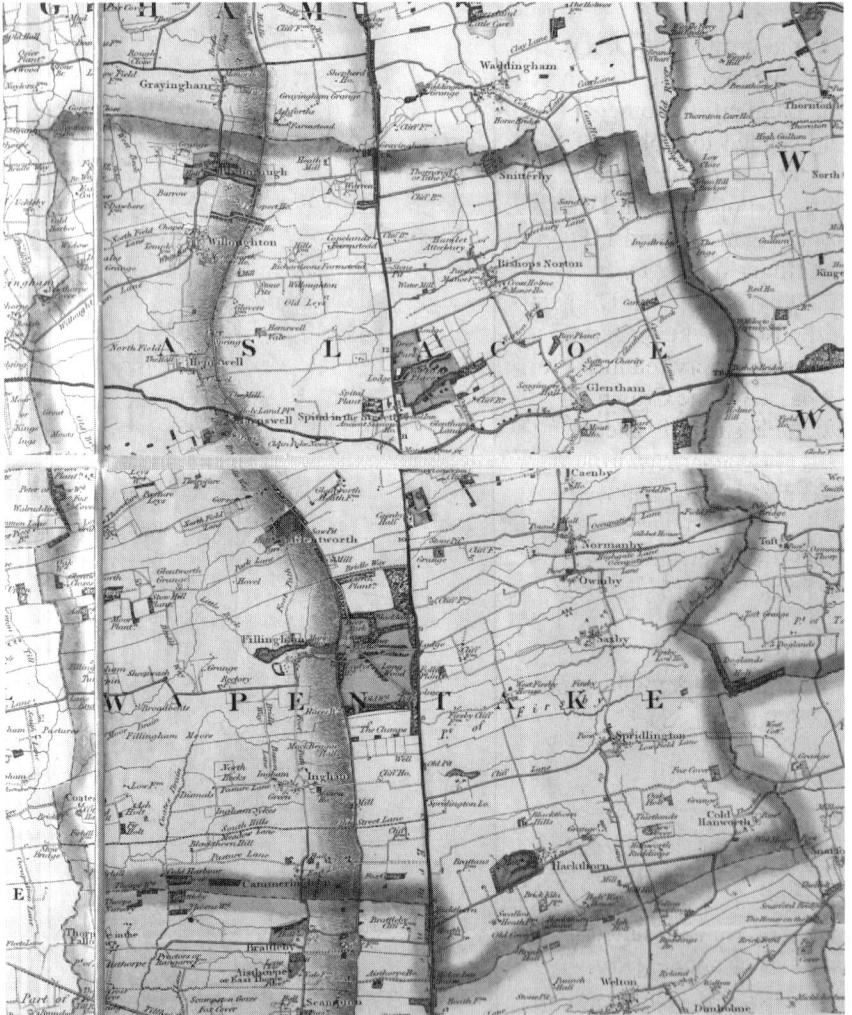

1. Deanery and Wapentake of Aslacoe. The parish of Waddingham St Peter
was formerly in Aslacoe Deanery, while that of Waddingham St Mary
or Stainton was in that of Manlake.
Detail from A. Bryant, *Map of the County of Lincoln*
(London, 1828) (Lincoln Cathedral Library)

BLYBOROUGH

At the time of the Domesday Survey, the church of Blyborough was divided into two medieties, one belonging to the Bishop of Durham with Gocelin son of Lambert, the other to the estate of Geoffrey de Wirce. The latter portion descended to Robert of St Martin who gave it to Durham Priory when he became a monk there in 1148; his gift was confirmed in 1166 by his son Roger. Pope Adrian IV in 1157 confirmed the whole church of Blyborough to Durham. Around 1180 the monks conferred the church on Robert, nephew of Roger of St Martin. It seems that Robert was still alive in 1206 but had died by 1213 when Durham's right to the advowson was disputed by Roger, grandson of the Robert of St Martin who had made the original gift in 1148. Durham Priory retained the right of presentation until the Reformation, when it passed to the Crown. In 1958 the patronage was transferred from the Crown to the Bishop of Lincoln by Order in Council; the Bishop remained patron in 1965. [Major, *Blyborough Charters*; Greenway, *Mowbray Charters*, 68; Reg. 44, p.253; *LDC* (1965), 112–13.]

Hugh de Pateshull
Occurs 1218. [*Blyborough Charters*, 213–14.]

Walter
Instituted before 8 June 1275. [*Rot. Gravesend*, 94.]

Grant (28 December 1312) by Richard, Bishop of Durham, of indulgence of 40 days to those who visit church of St Alkmund, Blyborough, and pray for the soul of Walter, late Rector of the same, who is buried there. [*Reg. Pal. Dunelm*. i. 264–5.]

William de Bibisworth (Byblesworth) subdeacon
Instituted 8 June 1275 to church of Blyborough, on death of Walter. Patron: Prior and Convent of Durham. Reinstituted 16 November 1284 on re-presentation (having failed to be ordained priest within a year of his institution); patron: as above. [*Rot. Gravesend*, 94; *Reg. Sutton* viii. 6.]

Commission to hear accounts of executors of his will, 29 December 1320. [*Reg. Burghersh* iii. no.1623.]

M. Henry de Lusceby chaplain
Instituted 17 November 1312 to church of Blyborough, on death of William de Bybelisword, having first resigned the church of Wooler. Patron: Prior and Convent of Durham. [Reg. 2, fo.96; Durham Cathedral Muniments, Register II, fo.3v.]

Subdeacon: before 19 January 1305/6; LD for diaconate and priesthood, 1306; priest: before 8 January 1322 when he was licensed to study in England or abroad for 3 years. Clerk of Bishop of Durham. Also: R. of Wooler (Nb), occ. 1308, 1311, resigned 1312; R. of Wold Newton, 1306–18. Papal dispensations for plurality, 1307, 1311. Proctor of Bishop Dalderby at Roman Curia, 1317. Involved in lawsuit against M. William de Gotham, R. of Althorpe, 1320. [Reg. 2, fo.16v; Reg. 3, fo.97v; *Reg. Burghersh* iii. no.229; *Reg. Pal. Dunelm.* i. 105, 274, 306, 480; ii. 1167, 1190, 1194, 1212; Reg. 2, fo.96; *CPL* ii. 34, 91, 174; Reg. 3, fo.362v; Reg. 5, fo.263v.]

M. Peter de Fissheburn clerk
Instituted 6 March 1323 to church of Blyborough, on death of M. Henry de Lusceby. Patron: Prior and Convent of Durham. [*Reg. Burghersh* i. no.728.]

Deacon: before 29 February 1311/12. Formerly: V. of Northallerton, 1312–23 (to receive money collected for rebuilding the church there after it was burned by the Scots, 1319). [*Reg. Greenfield* v. 149; *Reg. Melton* i. 120–1; Durham Cathedral Muniments, Register II, fo.84v.]

M. John de Bekingham priest
Instituted 22 September 1331 to church of Blyborough, on death of M. Peter de Fisseburn. Patron: William, Prior, and Convent of Durham. [*Reg. Burghersh* i. no.766.]

Licensed to be absent for 1 year, 16 October 1331. Bishop's auditor of causes, 1334; bishop's commissary, 7 February 1334/5 and 26 March 1335. Licence to choose a confessor, 3 November 1334. Afterwards: Archdeacon of Stow, 1335–9. Died by 17 February 1338/9. [*Reg. Burghersh* i. no. 465; ii. nos 2604–5; iii. no.1034; Reg. 5, fos 222, 485v; *Le Neve Fasti: Lincoln 1300–1541*, 18.]

Thomas de Repplyngham priest
Instituted 9 April 1335 to church of Blyborough, on resignation of M. John de Bekyngham (by exchange with the archdeaconry of Stow). Patron: Prior (William) and Convent of Durham (26 March 1335). [*Reg. Burghersh* i. no.793; Durham Cathedral Muniments, Register II, fo.106.]

Formerly: R. of Moor Monkton (YWR), 1317–22; R. of Winceby, 1322; R. of Lowthorpe (YER), 1333–5; Archdeacon of Stow, March–April 1335. Afterwards: R. of Ryther (YWR), 1336; R. of Brompton (YNR), 1338; R. of Huggate (YER), 1338–9; R. of Stokesley (YNR), April–November 1339; R. of Clayworth (Nt), 1339–43; R. of Wistow (Le), 1343–5; R. of Chalton (Ha), 1345; R. of Fishlake (YWR), 1345–6; R. of Witley (Sr), to 1351; R. of Boothby Graffoe, 1351–2; R. of Kirkby Thore (We), 1352. [*Reg. Greenfield* v. 256–7; *Fasti Parochiales* iii. 56; *Le Neve Fasti: Lincoln 1300–1541*, 18; *Reg. Melton* ii. 183–4, 189; Train, *North Notts Clergy*, 41–2; Reg. 6, fos 33v, 42v; *Fasti Parochiales* i. 118–19; *Reg. Edington* i. 123.]

John de Killum
Instituted 30 March 1336 to church of Blyborough, on resignation of Thomas de Repplingham (by exchange with church of Ryther, dioc. York). Patron: Prior and Convent of Durham. [*Reg. Burghersh* i. no.801.]

Formerly: R. of Ryther (YWR), to 1336. Licence to study in England for 1 year, 21 May 1340; to be absent from his church for 1 year, 7 January 1342/3; for 1 year, 15 January 1343/4; for 1 year, 28 August 1345; for 1 year, 28 September 1346; for half-year, 6 December 1347. [Reg. 5, fo.200v; Reg. 7, fos 132v, 134v, 137, 138v; Reg 9C, fo.6v.]

John de Wynstowe acolyte
Instituted 7 May 1364 to church of Blyborough, on death of John Killum. Patron: Prior (John) and Convent of Durham (22 April 1364). [Reg. 10, fo.127; Durham Cathedral Muniments, Register II, fo.179.]

Afterwards: R. of North Scarle, 1404. Royal writs issued against JW as R. of Blyborough in 1369–70, concerning tithes alleged to be payable to the alien priory of Willoughton while it was in the king's hands during the French war. Assessed for poll tax, 1377. Died before 23 January 1404/5. [*Buckingham Writs*, nos 88, 97, 105, 120; *Clerical Poll-Taxes*, no.816; Reg. 13, fo.174.]

Thomas atte Hall priest
Instituted 25 November 1404 to church of Blyborough, on resignation of John Wystowe (by exchange with church of North Scarle). Patron: Prior and Convent of Durham. [Reg. 13, fo.184.]

Priest: before 30 November 1403. Formerly: R. of North Scarle, 1403–4. [Reg. 13, fo.163.]

Thomas de Ryhale acolyte
Instituted 1 March 1411/12 to church of Blyborough, on resignation of Thomas atte Hall who had accepted another benefice. Patron: Prior and Convent of Durham (31 January 1411/12). [Reg. 14, fo.120v; Durham Cathedral Muniments, Register III, fo.36.]

Roger de Saxton priest
Instituted 8 December 1412 to church of Blyborough, on resignation of Thomas de Ryhale. Patron: Prior and Convent of Durham. [Reg. 14, fo.122v.]

Afterwards: V. of Preston in Holderness (YER), 1415–19; V. of Great Limber, 1419–20; R. of St Mary Magdalene, Bermondsey, 1420. [Poulson, *Holderness* ii. 185; *Reg. Fleming* i. no.72.]

M. John (Bron de) Tetford
Instituted 28 November 1415 to church of Blyborough, on resignation of Roger de Saxton (by exchange with vicarage of Preston in Holderness, dioc. York). Patron: Prior (John) and Convent of Durham (19 November 1415). [Reg. 14, fo.127v; Durham Cathedral Muniments, Register III, fo.43.]

Of Norwich diocese. Educated: Cambridge University (BCL by 1390). Priest: by 1390. Formerly: V. of Preston in Holderness, 1398–1415. Afterwards: V. of Sutton on Trent (Nt), 1418–23; R. of Great Bradley (Sf), resigned 1438; R. of Croxton (Ca), 1438–54. [Emden, *BRUC*, 97; Poulson, *Holderness* ii. 185; Bray, *Ely Lists*.]

Adam de Louth
Instituted 16 September 1418 to church of Blyborough, on resignation of M. John Tetford (by exchange with vicarage of Sutton on Trent, dioc. York). Patron: Prior (John) and Convent of Durham (12 September 1418). [Reg. 14, fo.133v; Durham Cathedral Muniments, Register III, fo.62.]

Formerly: V. of Sutton on Trent (Nt). Afterwards: R. of Ordsall (Nt), 1424–8. Died before
25 November 1428. [Train, *North Notts Clergy*, 147.]

Robert Conynge

Instituted 26 July 1424 to church of Blyborough, on resignation of Adam
Louth (by exchange with church of Ordsall, Notts). Patron: Prior (John) and
Chapter of Durham (2 June 1424). [*Lambeth Institutions*, 48; Durham Cathe-
dral Muniments, Register III, fo.105.]

Formerly: R. of a mediety of Grayingham (to 1418); R. of Ordsall (Nt), 1418–24. Died 3
May 1434; monument in Blyborough Church. [Train, *North Notts Clergy*, 147; *Monson*,
44.]

M. Robert Burton DD priest

Instituted 14 June 1434 to church of Blyborough, on death of Robert
Conynges. Patron: Prior (John) and Convent of Durham (15 May 1434).
Vacated by resignation before 22 October 1441. [Reg. 17, fo.17; Durham
Cathedral Muniments, Register III, fos 158v, 272v.]

Of Durham diocese. Educated: Merton College (portionist *c*.1393–5) and University
College, Oxford (fellow 1406–20; master 1420–6); MA; BD by 1418; DD by 1421. LD
for all orders, 9 August 1406 (Durham); subdeacon: 18 December 1406 (Worcester).
Formerly: R. of First Portion of Waddesdon, 1420; R. of Drayton Parslow (Bk), 1421–2;
R. of Stepney (Mx), 1422–7; R. of Burmarsh (K), 1424–7; Precentor of Lincoln, 1427, still
in 1440; Archdeacon of Northumberland, 1427, still in 1435. Also: Canon of Lanchester
and Prebendary of Grenecroft by 1435. Afterwards: R. of Wheathampstead (Hrt), 1440–9.
Died by May 1449. [Emden, *BRUO*, 319–20; *Reg. Langley*, nos 13, 673; *Le Neve Fasti:
Lincoln 1300–1541*, 20; *Le Neve Fasti: Northern Province 1300–1541*, 115.]

John Leeke

Presented to church of Blyborough, on resignation of M. Robert Burton (by
exchange with church of Broxholme). Patron: Prior and Chapter of Durham
(3 April 1440). [Durham Cathedral Muniments, Register III, fo.252v.]

Presentation presumably ineffective (see below).

John Bewmarys

Instituted to church of Blyborough, on resignation of M. Robert Burton.
Patron: Prior (John) and Chapter of Durham (22 October 1441). [Durham
Cathedral Muniments, Register III, fo.272v.]

M. Thomas Portyngton MA acolyte

Instituted 4 October 1453 to church of Blyborough, on death of John Beau-
marys. Patron: Prior (William) and Chapter of Durham (28 September 1453).
[Reg. 20, fo.157; Durham Cathedral Muniments, Register IV, fo.94v.]

Son of John Portington of Portington (YER) kt. Educated: Cambridge. Deacon: 15 June
1454; priest: 21 December 1454 (York). Also: Prebendary of Osmotherley (YNR), 1443;
Prebendary of Third Prebend of Hemingbrough (YER), 1447–58; Warden of St Nicholas's Chapel, Sheering (Ess). Papal dispensations to receive an additional benefice, 1456,

1479. Afterwards: Provost of Hemingbrough, 1458–71; Canon of York and Prebendary of Apesthorpe, 1470–6; Canon of Lincoln and Prebendary of Nassington, 1471–85; Treasurer of York, 1477–85; R. of Shillington (Bd), before 20 April 1479. Died 11 June/13 July 1485; buried at Shillington (monumental brass). [*History of Hemingbrough*, 71–2; *CPL* xi. 27; *CPL* xiii. 695; *Le Neve Fasti: Northern Province 1300–1541*, 14, 30; *Le Neve Fasti: Lincoln 1300–1541*, 96.]

M. Thomas Candell

Instituted 3 March 1457/8 to church of Blyborough, on resignation of M. Thomas Portyngton (by exchange with provostship of collegiate church of Hemingbrough, dioc. York). Patron: Prior and Chapter of Durham (17 February 1457/8). Vacated by resignation ('in John Abbay's house, Wakefield'), 5 June 1460. [Reg. 20, fo.159r–v; Durham Cathedral Muniments, Register IV, fo.108v, 121v.]

Education: BCL by 1436; BCn&CL by 1440. Acolyte: 3 March 1435/6; subdeacon: 24 March 1435/6; deacon: 7 April 1436; priest: 2 June 1436 (York). Formerly: Canon and Prebendary of Royal Free Chapel of Wolverhampton, 1436; Provost of Hemingbrough (YER), 1440–58. Also: Warden of St Nicholas's Chapel, Sheering (Ess), 1458; Prebendary of Osmotherley (YNR), 1458. [Emden, *BRUO*, 345.]

William Joys chaplain

Instituted to church of Blyborough, on resignation of M. Thomas Candell. Patron: Prior and Chapter of Durham (10 June 1460). [Durham Cathedral Muniments, Register IV, fo.122.]

Richard Hyndmerse BA

Instituted 6 August 1484 to church of Blyborough, on death of William Jones. Patron: Subprior (William) and Chapter of Durham (2 July 1484). [Reg. 22, fo.163v; Durham Cathedral Muniments, Register IV, fo.224.]

Of Durham diocese. Educated: University College, Oxford (MA); Fellow, *c*.1468–96. [Emden, *BRUO*, 995.]

Richard Grauntte chaplain

Instituted 21 June 1510 to church of Blyborough, on death of M. Richard Hyndmars. Patron: Prior and Convent of Durham. [Reg. 23, fo.140v.]

Non-resident (1519); resided at Beverley where he had a chantry. Assessed for subsidy (£14) in 1526. Died before 12 March 1533/4 when the church was granted *in commendam* to M. Robert Hole. [*Diocesan Visitations* i. 94; *Subsidy*, 36; Reg. 27, fo.96.]

M. Robert Hole BD

Instituted 2 July 1534 to church of Blyborough, on death of Richard Graunte. Patron: Prior (Hugh) and Convent of Durham (21 February 1533/4). [Reg. 27, fo.96; PD 1534/2.]

Of Lincoln diocese. Educated: Corpus Christi College, Oxford (Foundation Fellow 1517; MA 1521; BD 1533). Formerly: R. of Nettleton, 1523–38. Dispensed to hold additional benefice, 29 June 1534. [Emden, *BRUO 1501–1540*, 293–4.]

John Farmery

Instituted 23 June 1538 to church of Blyborough, on death of M. Robert Hole. Patron: Prior (Hugh) and Chapter of Durham (26 April 1538). [Reg. 27, fo.97; PD 1538/42.]

Born c.1506. Priest: 1538 (Philadelphia for Lincoln). Occurs as rector in 1551 and 1576. Resident at Blyborough (1576). Also: R. of Grayingham. Died December 1582. Will dated 9 December 1582; proved 24 December 1582. [Vj 13, fo.58; *Bishop Cooper*, 168; Stow Wills 1582–6/73.]

Anthony Hill BA

Instituted 13 December 1582 to rectory of Blyborough. Patron: Henry Aiscoghe esquire (10 December 1582), by reason of a grant from King Henry VIII. [*Bishop Cooper*, 79; PD 1582/40.]

Afterwards: V. of Billingborough, 1592–1621 (*q.v.*).

Simon Robson BD

Instituted 2 August 1593 to rectory of Blyborough. Patron: Queen Elizabeth I (10 July 1593). [BC; PD 1593/68.]

Henry Aiscoughe BA

Instituted 26 September 1594 to rectory of Blyborough, on resignation of last incumbent. Patron: Queen Elizabeth I (2 July 1594). [BC; PD 1594/33.]

Probably son of Sir Henry A., of Blyborough. Education: 'no graduate … able to catechise'. Resident: signed BTs 1600–9. [*Lincs. Pedigrees*, 57; *State of the Church*, 329, 356; BTs Blyborough.]

Henry Hoddesdon MA

Instituted 15 June 1610 to rectory of Blyborough, on resignation of last incumbent. Patron: King James I (14 June 1610). [BC; PD 1610/3.]

Born at Edgware (Mx); son of Nicholas H. (and nephew of Sir Christopher H., merchant). Educated: Corpus Christi College, Cambridge (matric. 1583; BA 1586–7; MA 1590). Deacon: 12 April 1597; priest: 13 April 1597 (London). Formerly: C. of Stanford-le-Hope (Ess). Non-resident at Blyborough. Will dated 1 April 1617 ('of Islington'); proved 12 April 1617. Bequeathed to the parish of Blyborough 'all my houshould stuffe remayning in the Parsonage House' for the use of the poor of the parish. [Venn, *Alumni*; *Visitation of London*, 36; LC 4, fo.10; PROB 11/129.]

Laurence Carliell

Instituted 18 December 1618 to rectory of Blyborough. Patron: King James I. [BC.]

Educated: Westminster School, Trinity College, Cambridge (matric. 1602; BA ?1607–8), and University of Basle (MA). Non-resident (but signed BT for 1620). Also: V. of Bishop Norton, 1614; Canon of Lincoln and Prebendary of Sexaginta Solidorum, 1617–24. Resigned Blyborough 21 January 1624/5. R. of Healing, 1637–43. [Venn, *Alumni*; BTs Blyborough; RES 1625/2; *Le Neve Fasti: Lincoln, 1541–1857*, 110; *Walker Revised*, 248.]

John Peachell MA

Instituted 12 February 1624/5 to rectory of Blyborough. Patron: King James I (9 February 1624/5). [BC; PD 1625/49.]

Educated: Jesus College, Cambridge (matric. 1615; BA 1618–19; MA 1622; BD 1630). Deacon: 11 October 1622; priest: 6 March 1624/5 (Peterborough). Also: R. of Normanton, 1625; Canon of Lincoln and Prebendary of Decem Librarum, 1636–48. Buried at Carlton Scroop, 24 June 1648. Will. [Venn, *Alumni*; Longden x. 211; *Le Neve Fasti: Lincoln, 1541–1857*, 62; LCC Wills 1647–8/959.]

William Branston

Instituted *c*.1647–8. [Swaby, 13.]

Deacon: 16 June 1644; priest: 9 August 1646 (Lincoln). Resident (1662): signed BTs 1646 (as Curate), 1663–71. Buried at Blyborough, 28 February 1671/2. Will dated 18 February 1671/2; proved at Lincoln, 22 March 1671/2. [LC 5, fo.74; BTs Blyborough; Stow Wills 1669–71/643.]

Robert Wild MA

Instituted 4 April 1672 to rectory of Blyborough, on death of last incumbent. Patron: King Charles II. [Reg. 33, fo.148.]

Born *c*.1645; son of Robert W. of Tatenhill (St), DD. Educated: Brasenose College, Oxford (matric. 1661, aged 16; BA 1664/5) and King's College, Cambridge (MA 1668). Priest: 10 June 1667 (Exeter). Non-resident at Blyborough: BTs signed by curate William Brumby (1673–4). Afterwards: R. of Toppesfield (Ess), 1674–91. Died 25 February 1690/1; MI at Toppesfield. Will. [Foster, *Alumni*; Venn, *Alumni*; Reg. 33, fo.148; PCC Wills.]

John Hill BA

Instituted 25 September 1675 to rectory of Blyborough, on cession of Robert Wild. Patron: King Charles II (29 May 1675). [Reg. 34, fo.2v; PD 1675/19.]

Priest: 19 September 1675 (Oxford). Resident: signed BTs 1676–81. Died 1682. Will dated 20 April 1682; proved 23 July 1682. Legatee and executor: 'my brother Robert Hill, haberdasher in the City of York'. Goods appraised for inventory, 6 May 1682. [Reg. 34, fo.2v; SUB Va, fo.74; BTs Blyborough; Stow Wills 1681–3/193; INV 183/336.]

Abraham Crowther BA

Instituted 24 June 1682 to rectory of Blyborough, on [death] of John Hill. Patron: King Charles II. [Reg. 34, fo.67v.]

Educated: Trinity College, Cambridge (matric. 1664; BA 1668–9; MA 1672); incorporated at Oxford, 1675. Priest: 20 February 1675/6 (London). Resident: signed BTs 1683–91. Also R. of Messingham, 1683–91. Died 1691. Administration granted 1691; probate inventory dated 18 January 1691/2. [Venn, *Alumni*; Reg. 34, fo.67v; Stow Admons Axix/138; INV 190/103.]

Richard Hill MA

Instituted 26 January 1691/2 to rectory of Blyborough, on death of Abraham Crowther. Patron: King William III and Queen Mary II (11 January 1691/2). [Reg. 35, fo.1v; PD 1692/15.]

Of Kent. Educated: Westminster School and Trinity College, Cambridge (matric. 1657; BA 1657–8; MA 1661); Fellow, 1659. Deacon: 20 September 1662; priest: 21 December 1662 (Ely). Formerly: V. of St Michael, Cambridge, 1663–7. Perhaps Canon of York and Prebendary of Apesthorpe, 1671–1704. Resident at Blyborough: signed BTs 1693–1703. Buried at Blyborough, 1 December 1704. [Venn, *Alumni*; Bray, *Ely Lists*; Reg. 35, fo.1v; LC 14, p.229; *Le Neve Fasti: York, 1541–1857*, 22; BTs Blyborough.]

Miles Hodgson MA
Instituted 22 October 1705 to rectory of Blyborough, on death of last incumbent. Patron: Queen Anne (5 September 1705). [Reg. 36, p.1; PD 1705/18.]

Born *c.*1664 at Dent; son of Rowland H., husbandman. Educated: Sedbergh School and St John's College, Cambridge (matric. 1682; BA 1685–6; MA 1693). Priest: 21 February 1691/2 (Lincoln). Formerly: C. of Ropsley, 1691/2; V. of Caistor, 1692–3. Non-resident at Blyborough, which was served by curates including Laurence Robinson (signed BTs 1710–17). Also: Master of Louth GS, *c.*1700–20 (where he resided); C. of Cawkwell; C. of Farforth cum Maidenwell; C. of Scamblesby. Buried at Louth, 18 December 1719. [Venn, *Alumni*; Reg. 35, fo.2v; BTs Blyborough; Goulding, *Louth Records*, 117; *Speculum*, 28, 46, 84, 104, 152; PR Louth.]

Godfrey Inman
Instituted 2 April 1720 to rectory of Blyborough, on death of Miles Hodgson. Patron: King George I (3 March 1719/20). [Reg. 37, p.98; PD 1720/10.]

Of Yorkshire. Educated: Jesus College, Cambridge (matric. 1686; BA 1689–90). Deacon: 22 May 1692 (York); priest: 20 December 1719 (Lincoln). Formerly: C. of Northorpe, 1719. [Venn, *Alumni*; *York Ordinations 1662–1699*, 35; Reg. 37, p.91.]

George Herbert BA
Instituted 27 January 1720/1 to rectory of Blyborough, on death of Godfrey Inman. Patron: King George I (7 January 1720/1). [Reg. 37, p.111; PD 1721/38.]

Baptised 5 March 1687/8; third son of John H. of Dolforgan and Upper Cwmyddalfa (Mont), gent. Educated: Balliol College, Oxford (matric. 1705; BA 1709). Also: Schoolmaster at Blyborough, 1721. Signed BTs between 1721 and 1731 but thereafter lived at Upper Cwmyddalfa, Blyborough being served by curates including Michael Fawell (1733–42) and Richard Willis (1743–79). Buried at Kerry, 27 December 1768. [Burke, *Landed Gentry* (1937), 1098; SUB V/6, fo.99; J. B. Willans, 'Houses and some families connected with Kerry', *Collections Historical & Archaeological relating to Montgomeryshire* 47 (1942), 148–63; Foster, *Alumni*; BTs Blyborough; LC 31, fo.197r.]

Thomas Holme
Instituted 6 May 1769 to rectory of Blyborough, on death of last incumbent. Patron: King George III (6 April 1769). [Reg. 39, p.113; PD 1769/5.]

Baptised 29 July 1732 at Kirkby Ireleth (La); son of Thomas H., Master of Wellingborough School and V. of Kirkby Ireleth. Educated: Wellingborough School and St John's College, Cambridge (matric. 1749; BA 1752). Formerly: PC of Upholland (La), 1758–67. Afterwards: R. of Covenham St Mary, 1769–97. Non-resident at Blyborough; lived at Upholland House. Succeeded in 1800 to the estate of his cousin William Bankes at

Winstanley, where he died 17 August 1803. [Venn, *Alumni*; Burke, *Landed Gentry* (1863), 51; LC 31, fo.129; *Manchester School Register* ii. 109–10.]

William Welfitt

Instituted 5 February 1770 to rectory of Blyborough, on cession of last incumbent. Patron: King George III (8 January 1770). [Reg. 39, p.132; PD 1770/1.]

Baptised 4 April 1745 at Holy Trinity, Hull; son of William W., gent. Educated: University College, Oxford (matric. 1764; BA 1768; MA 1772; DD 1785). Priest: 21 May 1769 (York). Formerly: C. of Welton (YER), 1769. Non-resident at Blyborough ('lives at Welton near Hull', 1778). Also: R. of Rand with Fulnetby, 1773–80; V. of Welton (YER), 1779–95; Canon of 3rd Prebend, Canterbury, 1785–1833 (where he was said to reside nine months each year, attending service twice daily). Afterwards: R. of Hastingleigh and V. of Elmstead (K), and V. of Ticehurst (Sx), 1795–1833. Died 3 February 1833; buried at Canterbury Cathedral (MI). [*York Ordinations 1750–1799*, 108; Foster, *Alumni*; LC 31, fo.189v; *Le Neve Fasti: Canterbury, Rochester and Winchester, 1541–1857*, 22; *Memorials of Canterbury*, 355.]

John Bourryau Spooner

Instituted 29 May 1795 to rectory of Blyborough, on cession of last incumbent. Patron: King George III (20 May 1795). [Reg. 39, p.605; PD 1795/4.]

Born *c*.1761; younger son of Hungerford Spooner of St Christopher's, West Indies. His elder brother Hungerford married Harriet, dau. of Peter Robert Luard (1727–1802) who inherited the Blyborough estate through his wife Jane, dau. and co-heiress of Zachariah Bourryau. Educated: Trinity College, Cambridge (matric. 1780; BA 1783). Deacon: 26 September 1784; priest: 25 September 1785 (Lincoln). Formerly: C. of Blyborough, 1784–95. Resident: signed BTs and registers, 1784–1825. On account of the unfitness of the Rectory House he was permitted to reside in the adjoining parish of Pilham (1804). A new Rectory House was built in 1811. Assisted by Octavius Luard as curate, 1827–46. Buried at Blyborough, 10 June 1846 (aged 84). [V. L. Oliver (ed.), *Caribbeana* (1910) i. 2; Venn, *Alumni* (where his later career is confused with that of another); Reg. 39, pp. 417–18, 433; BTs Blyborough; NRL 1804/8; MGA 62; Census Returns 1841; White, *Lincolnshire* (1842), 478; PR Blyborough.]

William Paley Graham

Instituted 18 July 1846 to rectory of Blyborough, on death of John Bourryau Spooner. Patron: Queen Victoria (30 June 1846). [Reg. 40, p.512; PD/Crown/42.]

Born 12 April 1817; son of Fergus G., Rector of Arthuret (Cu), by his second wife Jane, eldest dau. of William Paley DD. Educated: Shrewsbury School and Queen's College, Oxford (matric. 1835, aged 18; BA 1839; MA 1843). Deacon: 14 June 1840 (Oxford); priest: 19 September 1841 (Carlisle). Resident at Blyborough to 1867; licensed for non-residence (1867), on account of ill-health. Died 29 April 1870; buried at Blyborough, 4 May 1870. [Crisp, *Visitation* vi. 76; *Shrewsbury Register,* 49; Foster, *Alumni*; *Oxford Journal*, 20 June 1840; *Carlisle Journal*, 25 September 1841; White, *Lincolnshire* (1856), 210; Census Returns 1851, 1861; NRL 31/10; PR Blyborough.]

Francis Thomas Clark Margetts MA

Instituted 30 July 1870 to rectory of Blyborough, on death of William

Paley Graham. Patron: Queen Victoria (14 July 1870). [Reg. 41, p.319; PD/ Crown/148.]

Born August 1821; son of Thomas M. of Hemingford Grey (Hu), clerk. Educated: Uppingham School and Clare College, Cambridge (matric. 1839, BA 1843, MA 1846). Deacon: 1844; priest: 1845 (Ely). Formerly: C. of Fenstanton (Hu), 1851–3; V. of Duxford (Ca), 1853–63; V. of Aldbrough (YER), 1863–70. Resident at Blyborough; his household in 1871 included his wife, son, five daughters, a nephew and two nieces, a French governess, two nurses, a cook, housemaid, laundress and under-housemaid. Resigned 26 January (accepted 29 January) 1883. Afterwards: V. of Wendron (Co), 1883–93. Resided latterly at Elland Lodge, Cleveland Road, Torquay. Died 11 April 1897. [Venn, *Alumni*; Census Returns 1871; RES 248/3; *Probate Calendar* 1897.]

Thomas Binfield Ludlow MA

Instituted 15 February 1883 to rectory of Blyborough, on resignation of Francis Thomas Clark Margetts. Patron: Queen Victoria. [Reg. 42, p.181.]

Baptised 13 January 1822; son of Stephen L. of Cowley (Ox), dealer. Educated: Christ Church, Oxford (matric. 1841, aged 19; BA 1845, MA 1848). Deacon: 1845; priest: 1846 (Oxford). Formerly: Chaplain of Christ Church, 1845–53; R. of Slapton (Bk), 1853–74; V. of Wendron (Co), 1874–83. Resident at Blyborough. Resignation accepted 8 November 1894. Afterwards: R. of Wolverton cum Ewhurst (Ha), 1894. Died 15 May 1899 at Wolverton Rectory (aged 77). [ORO, PR Cowley; Foster, *Alumni*; *Crockford* (1895); Census Returns 1891; Reg. 42, p.368; *The Guardian*, 24 May 1899.]

Robert Haynes Cave MA

Instituted 10 December 1894 to rectory of Blyborough, on resignation of Thomas Binfield Ludlow. Patron: Queen Victoria. [Reg. 42, p.369.]

Born 1830 in Barbados; son of Nathaniel C., esquire. Educated: Exeter College, Oxford (matric. 1849, aged 18; BA 1853; MA 1862). Deacon: 1853; priest: 1855 (Lichfield). Formerly: R. of Lidgate (Sf), 1858–71; C. of St Thomas Stamford Hill, Upper Clapton, 1871–3; R. of Covenham St Bartholomew, 1873–80; R. of Wolverton cum Ewhurst (Ha), 1880–94. Author: *Sermons* (1861, 1872); *In The Days of Good Queen Bess* (1897), an historical novel. Died 28 September 1899 at Blyborough, aged 69. [Foster, *Alumni*; *LDC* (1900), 71.]

John Thomas Halland BA

Instituted 10 April 1900, on death of Robert Haynes Cave. Patron: Queen Victoria. [Reg. 42, p.473.]

Born 22 February 1857 in Westminster; son of James H., of 2 Milnes Terrace, Upper Chelsea, SW. Educated: King's College School, London, and Corpus Christi College, Cambridge (matric. 1877; Organ Scholar; BA 1881; MA 1912). Deacon: 1881; priest: 1882 (St Albans). Formerly: C. of Witham (Ess), 1881–5; V. of Witham on the Hill, 1885–9. Resided at Blyborough; licensed for non-residence (illness of wife and daughter), 26 March 1904. Discovered and restored the medieval rood figure in Blyborough Church. 'An accomplished chess player'. Resigned with effect 11 September 1939. Retired to 'Bronygarth', Ryland Road, Welton by Lincoln, where he died 22 May 1941. Buried 26 May 1941 at Blyborough. [Venn, *Alumni*; NRL 68/4; *Hicks Diaries*, no.422; RES 1939/17; *Probate Calendar* 1941; *LDM* (1941), 109, 171.]

Bryant Burgess Tucker BSc

Instituted 22 April 1940 to rectory of Blyborough, on resignation of John Thomas Halland. Patron: King George VI. [Reg. 43, p.650.]

Born 16 October 1895. Fought in World War I (East Surrey Regiment, gazetted Second Lieutenant, 24 July 1915). Educated: McGill University, Montreal (BSc 1923); Trinity College, Cambridge (1926); Ridley Hall, Cambridge (1929). Deacon: 1931; priest: 1932 (Birmingham). Formerly: C. of St George, Birmingham, 1931–3; C. of All Saints, Highgate, 1938–40. Resigned 23 October (accepted 27 October) 1941. Afterwards: Chaplain to the Forces (Emergency Commission), 1941–9; Chaplain to the Forces, 1941–55. Died at Plymouth, December 1982. [*Crockford* (1961–2); *London Gazette*, 23 July 1915; RES 1941/12; GRO, Death Index.]

Hugh Frank Riches MA MLitt

Instituted 6 June 1942 by Official *sede vacante* to rectory of Blyborough, on resignation of Bryant Burgess Tucker. Patron: King George VI. Note that on 14 May 1942, the Archbishop of Canterbury granted a dispensation enabling the said HFR to hold together the Rectory of Blyborough and the Vicarage of Willoughton. [Reg. 43, pp.674–5.]

Also: V. of Willoughton, 1942–52 (*q.v.*).

Jonathan Ernest Draper LTh

Instituted 5 December 1952 to rectory of Blyborough, on cession of Hugh Frank Riches. Patron: Queen Elizabeth II. Note that on 16 May 1952, the Archbishop of Canterbury granted a dispensation enabling the said JED to hold together the rectory of Blyborough and the vicarage of Willoughton. [Reg. 44, p.168.]

Also: V. of Willoughton, 1952–60 (*q.v.*).

Benjamin Owen Whitfield BA

Instituted 23 September 1960 to rectory of Blyborough, on cession of Jonathan Ernest Draper. Patron: Bishop of Lincoln. Note that on 13 September 1960, the Archbishop of Canterbury granted a dispensation enabling the said BOW to hold together the rectory of Blyborough and the vicarage of Willoughton. [Reg. 44, p.302.]

Also: V. of Willoughton, 1960–2 (*q.v.*).

Edward Denzil Chetwood Wright MA

Instituted 20 December 1962 to rectory of Blyborough, on cession of Benjamin Owen Whitfield. Patron: Bishop of Lincoln. Note that on 22 November 1962, the Archbishop of Canterbury granted a dispensation enabling the said EDCW to hold together the rectory of Blyborough and the vicarage of Willoughton. Vacated by resignation, 31 May 1972. [Reg. 44, pp. 340–1, 468.]

Also: V. of Willoughton, 1962–72 (*q.v.*).

CAENBY

The manor and advowson of Caenby descended in the twelfth century from Alice de Condet via her son Roger to Roger's daughter Agnes who married Walter Clifford the elder. Their son, Walter Clifford the younger, presented to the rectory twice during the episcopate of Robert Grosseteste. Maud de Clifford, the daughter of the younger Walter, together with her husband William de Longespée, gave the manor and advowson of Caenby to Barlings Abbey some time before 1271. Barlings continued to present to the living until the Dissolution. By the late seventeenth century, the advowson had come into the possession of the Tournay family, whence it passed by marriage to Lawrence Monck. In 1799 Sir Charles Middleton of Belsay Castle changed his surname to Monck on inheriting the Caenby property. The advowson was transferred from Sir Arthur Edward Middleton Bt in 1914 to the See of Lincoln. The Bishop of Lincoln was patron in 1965. The church of St Nicholas,Caenby, was declared redundant in 1975. [*Reg. Ant.* i. 283–4; Maddison, 'Tournay family'; Reg. 43, p.62; *LDC* (1965), 108–9.]

Robert de Stowa Sancti Edwardi chaplain
Instituted in the first pontifical year of Bishop Robert Grosseteste (17 June 1235/16 June 1236) to church of Caenby. Patron: Walter de Clifford. [Hoskin, no.1225.]

Thomas de Weng subdeacon
Instituted in the tenth pontifical year of Bishop Robert Grosseteste (17 June 1244/16 June 1245) to church of Caenby, on resignation of Robert. Patron: W. de Clyfford. [Hoskin, no.1264.]

William de Caneford chaplain
Instituted 5 October 1271 to church of Caenby, on death of Thomas. Patron: Abbot and Convent of Barlings. [*Rot. Gravesend*, 93.]

William de Braundon priest
Instituted 25 July 1275 to church of Caenby, on resignation of William. Patron: Abbot and Convent of Barlings. [*Rot. Gravesend*, 94.]

Robert de Clisseby deacon
Instituted in the twenty-first pontifical year of Bishop Richard Gravesend (3 November 1278/2 November 1279) to church of Caenby, on death of William. Patron: Abbot and Convent of Barlings. [*Rot. Gravesend*, 97.]

M. William de Clisseby priest
Instituted 3 May 1286 to church of Caenby, on institution of Robert de Clisseby to church of Great Carlton. Patron: Abbot and Convent of Barlings. [*Reg. Sutton* viii. 8.]

Involved in dispute over tithes with Richard, Vicar of Glentham, 1292. [*Reg. Sutton* iv. 21.]

John de Burwell chaplain
Instituted 18 September 1294 to church of Caenby, on death of M. William de Clisseby. Patron: Abbot and Convent of Barlings. [*Reg. Sutton* viii. 24–5.]

Geoffrey de Langwath chaplain
Instituted 3 April 1299 to church of Caenby, on death of John de Burwell. Patron: Abbot and Convent of Barlings. [*Reg. Sutton* viii. 30.]

Geoffrey de Undel
Instituted before 6 February 1300/1. [Reg. 2, fo.83v.]

Elias de Wheteley clerk
Instituted 6 February 1300/1 to church of Caenby, on death of Geoffrey de Undel. Patron: Abbot and Convent of Barlings. [Reg. 2, fo.83v.]

Afterwards: R. of Stoke, dioc. Norwich; R. of Maltby, dioc. York; R. of Sudbrooke, 1312–14; R. of Sibsey, 1314–20; R. of Great Hale, 1320–31; Canon of Lincoln and Prebendary of Liddington, 1317–31. Appointed proctor to contract a loan of £100 secured on the bishop's possessions, 6 November 1320. Appointed to provide all things necessary for solemn enthronement of Bishop Burghersh; rendered account for same, 4 January 1320/1. Died before 21 June 1331. Brother of Hugh de Wheteley, R. of Stainton by Langworth, who founded a chantry in church of Great Hale for the souls of Elias and others, 1337. [*CPL* ii. 98–9; *Le Neve Fasti: Lincoln 1300–1541*, 85; Reg. 5, fos 268, 271; *Reg. Burghersh* i. nos 300, 532.]

Robert de Askeby chaplain
Instituted 5 January 1304/5 to church of Caenby, on resignation of Elias de Weteley. Patron: Abbot and Convent of Barlings. [Reg. 2, fo.87v.]

John de Hole
Instituted before 30 September 1330. [*Reg. Burghersh* i. no.763.]

Henry son of John de Bayus clerk
Instituted 30 September 1330 to church of Caenby, on death of John de Hole. Patron: Abbot and Convent of Barlings. [*Reg. Burghersh* i. no.763.]

Acolyte: before 28 February 1331; subdeacon: before 16 July 1331; priest: before 21 May 1335. Dispensation to study for 1 year, 28 February 1330/1; in England for 1 year, 16 July 1331; for 1 year, 25 October 1333. Licence to study at University of Oxford and to farm his church, 21 May 1335; to farm his church for 2 years, 28 September 1336. [*Reg. Burghersh* iii. nos 562, 573, 630; Reg. 5, fos 195, 197.]

John de Brex clerk
Instituted 27 September 1349 to church of St Nicholas, Caenby, on death of Henry. Patron: Abbot and Convent of Barlings. [Reg. 9, fo.159.]

William de Claxby
Instituted before 19 September 1380. [Reg. 10, fo.146.]

Perhaps to be indentified with William, R. of Caenby, assessed for poll-tax in 1377. [*Clerical Poll-Taxes*, no.818.]

Robert Carter de Lymbergh priest
Instituted 19 September 1380 to church of Caenby, on death of William de Claxby. Patron: Abbot and Convent of Barlings. [Reg. 10, fo.146.]

John Couper de Stoke iuxta Newerk priest
Instituted 7 June 1392 to church of Caenby (cause of vacancy not stated). Patron: Abbot and Convent of Barlings. [Reg. 11, fo.108.]

Afterwards: R. of Miningsby, 1399–1400; R. of Caenby (again), 1400.

Thomas (Dunham de) Ely chaplain
Instituted 27 June 1399 to church of Caenby, on resignation of John Stokes (by exchange with church of Miningsby). Patron: Abbot and Convent of Barlings. [Reg. 13, fos 122v, 178.]

Priest: before 4 August 1382. Formerly: R. of Brauncewell, by 1377; R. of St Peter at Arches, Lincoln, *c*.1377–82; R. of Miningsby, 1382–99. [Reg. 10, fos 88, 120.]

Hugh de Hemyngby priest
Instituted 1 August 1399 to church of Caenby, on death of Thomas Ely. Patron: Abbot and Convent of Barlings. [Reg. 13, fo.178v.]

Alan Hakeney
Instituted before 25 January 1399/1400. [Reg. 13, fos 126v, 179.]

Also: V. of Glentham, 1378–1413 (*q.v.*).

John de Stokes chaplain
Instituted 25 January 1399/1400 to church of Caenby, on resignation of Alan Hakeney (by exchange with church of Miningsby). Patron: Abbot and Convent of Barlings. [Reg. 13, fos 126v, 179.]

Formerly: R. of Caenby (see above), 1392–9; R. of Miningsby, 1399–1400.

John Albertoft
Instituted before 6 July 1456. [Reg. 20, fo.158.]

John Herve chaplain
Instituted 6 July 1456 to church of Caenby, on death of John Albertoft. Patron: Abbot and Convent of Barlings. [Reg. 20, fo.158.]

Hugh Ingoldesby
Instituted 24 February 1486/7 to church of Caenby, on resignation of John Hervy. Patron: Abbot and Convent of Barlings. [Reg. 22, fo.164v.]

Walter Munk
Instituted before 30 March 1510. [Reg. 23, fo.159v.]

Christopher Raner
Instituted 30 March 1510 to church of St Nicholas, Caenby, on resignation of Walter Munk. Patron: Abbot and Convent of Barlings. [Reg. 23, fo.159v.]

Guy Carington chaplain
Instituted 18 March 1518/19 to church of Caenby, on death of Christopher Rayner. Patron: Abbot and Convent of Barlings. [Reg. 25, fo.26v.]

Assessed for subsidy (£4 13s 4d) in 1526. [*Subsidy*, 37.]

Richard Whelpdale chaplain
Instituted 8 October 1539 to church of Caenby, on death of Guy Carington. Patron: Matthew Sayntpal of Snarford, esquire, and Richard Nayler yeoman, by grant of advowson to them for this turn by the late Abbot and Convent of Barlings. [Reg. 27, fo.97v.]

Witnessed wills in Caenby and Normanby, 1550–9. [Stow Wills 1530–52/485; LCC Wills 1551–3/265; Stow Wills 1553–67/297; Stow Wills 1559–62/22v.]

Humphrey Wallen
Instituted 1564 to church of Caenby, on death of last incumbent. Patron: Adrian Stokes of Beaumanor (Leics), esquire. [Reg. 28, fo.38.]

Richard Laminge
Instituted 11 May 1566 to church of Caenby, on resignation of last incumbent. Patron: Adrian Stokes esquire. [Reg. 28, fo.114v.]

Born *c*.1538. Education: 'understands Latin; but little versed in sacred learning'. Priest: 19 September 1563 (Lincoln). Resident: signed BTs 1600–21. Also: V. of Glentham, 1564–80. Buried at Caenby, 2 September 1621. [*Bishop Cooper*, 167; BTs Caenby.]

Theodore Hayward MA
Instituted 8 December 1621 to rectory of Caenby. Patron: Anne, Lady Beauchamp, widow of Edward, Lord Beauchamp (14 November 1621). [BC; PD 1621/10.]

Of Essex. Educated: Queens' College (matric. 1602) and St Catharine's College, Cambridge (BA 1605–6). Signed BT 1635. Died by 1650. Will dated 16 November 1649; proved at Lincoln, 11 March 1649/50. [Venn, *Alumni*; BTs Caenby; Stow Wills 1640–50/420.]

John Bulcock
Instituted 11 March 1660/1 to rectory of Caenby, on [death] of Theodore Heward. Patron: King Charles II (29 September 1660). [Reg. 32, fo.7.]

Baptised March 1635/6; son of Hamond B. of Harpswell, clerk (*q.v.*). Educated: Lincoln School and Magdalene College, Cambridge (matric. 1653; BA 1656–7). Deacon: 22

September 1660 (Chichester); priest: 23 September 1660 (Bath and Wells). Resident (1662): signed BTs 1663–83. Also: C. of Hemswell, 1670–83. Buried at Caenby, 3 February 1683/4. Will dated 28 January 1683/4; proved at Lincoln, 13 February 1683/4. [Harpswell PR; Venn, *Alumni*; LC 5, fo.74v; BTs Caenby; Stow Wills 1681–3/330; INV 184/71.]

Dennis Pepper MA

Instituted 18 April 1684 to rectory of Caenby, on death of John Bullcock. Patron: Edward Tourney esquire (24 March 1683/4). [Reg. 34, fo.78; PD 1684/47.]

Also: V. of Glentham (*q.v.*).

William Brearcliffe BA

Instituted 12 August 1696 to rectory of Caenby, on death of Denis Pepper. Patron: Edward Tournay esquire (29 May 1696). [Reg. 35, fo.34; PD 1696/46.]

Baptised 13 February 1666/7 at Brantingham (YER); son of Stephen B., Rector of Brantingham. Educated: Elloughton and Howden Schools and Sidney Sussex College, Cambridge (matric. 1683; BA 1686–7). Deacon: 21 September 1689; priest: 3 June 1694 (York). Letters testimonial issued for WB, 5 August 1696. Resident at Caenby: signed BTs 1697–1712. Buried at Caenby, 9 October 1712. [IGI; Venn, *Alumni*; *York Ordinations 1662–1699*, 9; LTD 1696/16; LC 14, p.230; BTs Caenby.]

John Dunn MA

Instituted 26 January 1712/13 to rectory of Caenby, on death of William Bearecliffe. Patron: Edward Tournay esquire (24 December 1712). [Reg. 36, p.190; PD 1712/14.]

Educated: Edinburgh University (MA). Priest: 4 June 1710 (Lincoln). Formerly: C. of Owersby, 1710. Resident: signed BTs 1713–48; carried out repairs to rectory house. Also: sequestrator of Normanby; C. of Glentham. Buried at Caenby, 7 October 1748. [Reg. 36, pp.133–4; BTs Caenby; *Speculum*, 155; LC 18b, p.306.]

Abraham Walker

Instituted 21 February 1748/9 to rectory of Caenby, on death of John Dunn. Patron: Lawrence Monck of Caenby, esquire. [Reg. 38, p.486.]

Of East Retford (Nt). Educated: Jesus College, Cambridge (matric. 1735; BA 1737–8). Deacon: 26 February 1737/8; priest: 20 September 1741 (Lincoln). Formerly: C. of Lea, 1738; C. of Worlaby, 1741. Resident at Caenby: signed BTs 1749–63. Also: R. of Newton by Toft, 1763–77. Afterwards: V. of Alford, 1764–77. Died 27 August 1777; buried at Alford, 29 August 1777. [Venn, *Alumni*; Reg. 38, pp. 342, 404; BTs Caenby; *Monson*, 3; PR Alford.]

Jeremiah Dixon

Instituted 8 June 1764 to rectory of Caenby, on death [*recte* cession] of Abraham Walker. Patron: Lawrence Monck esquire. [Reg. 39, p.32.]

Education: literate. Deacon: 29 May 1743 (Chester); priest: 17 June 1753 (York). Also: Master of Worsborough GS (YWR), 1753–74. Non-resident at Caenby ('Absent: lives in Yorkshire at Worsbrough near Barnsley'). Caenby served by curates, including Anthony

Furness (1768–9). Died 'at his house at Worsbrough', November 1773. [*Archbishop Drummond's Visitation Returns* iii. 140; *York Ordinations 1750–99*, 31; LC 31, fo.197; BTs Caenby; *Leeds Intelligencer 1769–1776*, 107.]

Lawrence Gibbs BA
Instituted 1 March 1774 to rectory of Caenby, on death of Jeremiah Dixon. Patron: Lawrence Monck of Caenby, esquire. [Reg. 39, p.224.]

Baptised 30 January 1741/2 at Pulham St Mary (Nf); son of Samuel G., farmer. Educated: Bury St Edmunds GS (1753–60) and Sidney Sussex College, Cambridge (matric. 1760; BA 1764). Deacon: 13 May 1764 (Lincoln from Norwich); priest: 8 June 1766 (Norwich). Formerly: C. of Thorpe Abbots (Nf), 1764. Also: R. of Brockdish (Nf), 1766–1825. Non-resident at Caenby ('Absent: lives in Norwich', 1778; 'house unfit', 1815; 'age and ill-health', 1818); the living served by curates, including Samuel Proctor (1770–80), Thomas Dawson (1771–99) and William Wilkinson (1811–27). Died 28 April 1825, aged 84. [IGI; *Bury Grammar School List*, 154; Venn, *Alumni*; Reg. 39, p.32; LC 31, fo.197; NRL 1815/46, 1818/63; MI (St Peter Mancroft, Norwich).]

John Johnson MA
Instituted 22 July 1825 to rectory of Caenby, on death of Lawrence Gibbs. Patron: Sir Charles Miles Lambert Monck Bt. [Reg. 40, p.341b.]

Born 1779; son of John J., of Bengal. Educated: Durham School and Trinity College, Cambridge (matric. 1799; BA 1803; MA 1806). Deacon: 16 March 1806; priest: 22 March 1807 (Peterborough). Formerly: C. of Charwelton (Np), 1806; C. of East Haddon, 1807. Also: V. of Little Houghton with Brafield (Np), 1817–38; R. of Outwell (Nf), 1838–48. Non-resident at Caenby, which was served by curates, including William Wilkinson, William Worsley and Richard Thomas. Died at Leamington (Wa), 8 October 1848 (aged 66). [*Durham School Register*, 76; Venn, *Alumni*; Longden viii. 27; CR 1, pp. 56, 398; CR 3, fo.51v; PR Caenby; White, *Lincolnshire* (1842), 479; *GM* 184 (1848), 551.]

Hugh Nanney
Instituted 7 December 1848 to rectory of Caenby, on death of John Johnson. Patron: Sir Charles Miles Lambert Monck Bt. [Reg. 40, p.520.]

Born 20 June (baptised 18 July) 1810 at Haltwhistle (Nb); son of Lewis N., gent. (through whose mother Barbara he was descended from Sir John Middleton, 2nd Bt) and grandson of Hugh N., Vicar of Haltwhistle. Educated: St Bees College (adm. 1831) and Queens' College, Cambridge (adm. 1845 as a 'ten year man'). Deacon: 3 August 1834; priest: 2 August 1835 (York). Formerly: C. of Whitley (Nb), 1834; PC of Jarrow (Du), 1836–48. Resident at Caenby where he built a new rectory house (1849–50). Also: V. of Saxby with Firsby, 1852–63. Licensed for non-residence (1860) on account of incapacity of body; Caenby served by George Carter Cardale as curate. Lived latterly at High Street, Swinton (YWR). Died at York, 5 January 1863 (aged 52). [*York Ordinations 1800–1849*, 136; Burke, *Peerage* (1938), 1731; *St Bees College Calendar 1858*, 43; Venn, *Alumni*; MGA 331; Census Returns 1851; White, *Lincolnshire* (1856), 210; NRL 24/18; CR 4, fo.90v; Census Returns 1861; *Probate Calendar*, 1863.]

Thomas Middleton Nanney
Instituted 27 February 1863 to rectory of Caenby, on death of Hugh Nanney. Patron: Sir Charles Miles Lambert Monck of Belsay (Nb), Bt. [Reg. 41, p.97.]

Baptised 17 June 1824 at Haltwhistle (Nb); son of Lewis N (and brother of Hugh N., above). Educated: St Bees College (adm. 1847). Deacon: 26 May 1850; priest: 15 June 1851 (Chester). Formerly: C. of Rippingale, 1861–2. Also: V. of Saxby with Firsby, 1863–7. Died at Caenby, 10 October 1867. [IGI; *St Bees College Calendar 1858*, 65; *Ecclesiastical Gazette* (9 July 1850 and 12 August 1851); PR Rippingale; *Probate Calendar*, 1867.]

George Banastre Pix MA

Instituted 17 January 1868 to rectory of Caenby, on death of Thomas Middleton Nanney. Patron: Sir Arthur Edward Monck of Belsay (Nb), Bt. [Reg. 41, p.255.]

Born 10 July 1825; son of Samuel P., of Rolvenden (K). Educated: Christ's Hospital School and Lincoln College, Oxford (matric. 1843; BA 1846; MA 1849). Deacon: 1849; priest: 1851 (Worcester). Formerly: Vice-Principal of York Training College; Headmaster of Trinidad GS, 1853–6; PC of Acaster Selby (YWR), 1859–68. Resided at Caenby Rectory. Also: V. of Saxby, 1868–74. Restored Caenby Church, 1869. Latterly becoming insane, he was taken to London; escaped from his keeper while out for a walk and was later found hanging from a tree in Gravel Pit Wood, Highgate. Died 6 November 1874. [*Christ's Hospital Exhibitioners*, 65; Foster, *Alumni*; White, *Lincolnshire* (1872), 156; Fac. Papers 1869/5; *Oxford Journal*, 21 November 1874; *Probate Calendar* 1875.]

Robert Boyce Spoor (Courtenay)

Instituted 11 March 1875 to rectory of Caenby, on death of George Banastre Pix. Patron: Sir Edward Arthur Monck of Belsay (Nb), Bt. [Reg. 41, p.493.]

Born 27 February 1837 at Bishop Wearmouth (Du); son of John S., woollen draper. Educated: St Bees College (adm. 1858). Deacon: 1860; priest: 1861 (Hereford). Formerly: C. of Chirbury (Sa), 1860–3; C. of Ulgham (Nb), 1863–8; Domestic Chaplain to Earl of Scarbrough, 1868–75 (resident at Sandbeck). Also: V. of Saxby with Firsby, 1875–1909. Changed name to Courtenay, 1875. Resided at Caenby Rectory. Member of Diocesan Conference and Lincoln Board of Guardians; Chairman of Glentham and Caenby School Board. Author: *Sermons Preached in Sandbeck Chapel* (1871). Died at Caenby Rectory, 12 February 1909. [IGI; Census Returns 1851; *St Bees College Calendar 1866*, 88; *Crockford* (1907); Census Returns 1871; *Probate Calendar* 1909; *LDM* 23 (1909), 47.]

John Booth MA

Instituted 19 July 1909 to rectory of Caenby, on death of Robert Boyce Courtenay. Patron: Sir Arthur Edward Middleton of Belsay Castle (Nb), Bt. Note that on 24 June 1909, the Archbishop of Canterbury granted a dispensation enabling the said JB to hold together the rectory of Caenby and the vicarage of Saxby with the rectory of Firsby annexed. [Reg. 42, p.613.]

Born 23 June 1872; son of Thomas Christopher Booth of Warlaby, Northallerton (YNR). Educated: Durham School (1886–91), Exeter College, Oxford (matric. 1891; BA 1895; MA 1898) and Wycliffe Hall, Oxford (1895–6). Deacon: 1896; priest: 1897 (Southwell). Formerly: C. of New Radford (Nt), 1896–8; of Beverley Minster, 1898–9; of Fishtoft, 1899–1901; of St Mark, Victoria Park, 1901–2; Vice-Principal, CMS College, Kottayam (South India), 1902–8; C. of Sandal Magna (YWR), 1908–9. Also: V. of Saxby with Firsby, 1909–14. Resided at Caenby Rectory, 1909–14. Afterwards: V. of Reepham, 1914–36; V. of Colston Bassett (Nt), 1936–42. Latterly of Moorside, Hilton, Appleby (We), where he died 8 May 1958. [*Durham School Register*, 344; Foster, *Oxford Men; Crockford* (1957–8); Census Returns 1911; *Probate Calendar* 1958.]

William Norton Howe MA

Instituted 13 June 1914 to rectory of Caenby, on cession of John Booth. Patron: Sir Arthur Edward Middleton of Belsay Castle (Nb), Bt. Note that on 22 May 1914, the Archbishop of Canterbury granted a dispensation enabling the said WNH to hold together the Rectory of Caenby and the Vicarage of Saxby with the Rectory of Firsby annexed. [Reg. 43, p.70.]

Born 5 October 1870 at Castleton (La); son of Alfred Howe, cotton manufacturer. Educated: Exeter College, Oxford (matric. 1889; BA 1893; MA 1896) and St Stephen's House, Oxford (1893). Deacon: 1894; priest: 1895 (Peterborough). Formerly: C. of St George, Leicester, 1894–8; of St Bridget with St Martin, Chester, 1898–1902; of All Saints Margaret Street, London, 1902–4; of All Saints Odd Rode with St Luke Mow Cop (Chs), 1904–9; Lecturer at Boston, 1909–11. Bishop Hicks noted (21 March 1914): 'Offered Caenby to Norton Howe.' Resided at Caenby Rectory. Also: V. of Saxby with Firsby, 1914–26; RD of Aslacoe, 1918–26. Afterwards: V. of New Sleaford, 1926–38; RD of South Lafford, 1929–38; Canon of Lincoln and Prebendary of Aylesbury, 1936–45; R. of Withern, 1938–45. Author: *Animal Life in Italian Painting* (1912); *The Eye of Erasmus* (1925). Died 11 August 1945. [Foster, *Oxford Men*; *Crockford* (1920, 1941); *Hicks Diaries*, no.465; *Probate Calendar* 1945.]

The vicarage of Glentham was united to the rectory of Caenby by Order in Council dated 25 October 1922 to form the united benefice of Caenby with Glentham. [Reg. 43, pp. 285–9.]

Frederick Anthony Williams

Instituted 26 March 1926 to united benefice of Caenby with Glentham, on cession of rectory of Caenby by William Norton Howe. [Reg. 43, p.393.]

Baptised 23 June 1854 at Sherborne (Do); son of Thomas Williams (Curate of Sherborne). Educated: Durham School (1869–71). Deacon: 18 December 1881; priest: 17 December 1882 (Lincoln). Formerly: Asst Master, Lincoln GS, 1881–94; C. of St Mark, Lincoln, 1888–91; V. of Cherry Willingham and of Greetwell, 1891–4. Also: V. of Glentham, 1894–1926. Resided at Glentham Vicarage to 1926; thereafter at Caenby Rectory. Bishop Hicks noted: 'Old bachelor, v. tidy: a scholar: but oh! how deliberate of speech and shy. Has been v. long in this remote spot.' Died 24 March 1931. [Dorset History Centre, PR Sherborne; *Durham School Register*, 244; Census Returns 1871; OR 2, pp. 47, 53; *LDC* (1915), 93; *Crockford* (1923, 1927); *Hicks Diaries*, no.579; *Probate Calendar* 1931.]

George Jordan LTh

Instituted 16 September 1931 to united benefice of Caenby with Glentham, on death of Frederick Anthony Williams. Patron: Dean (Robert Andrew Mitchell MA) and Chapter of Lincoln, for this alternate turn. [Reg. 43, p.490.]

Educated: University of Durham (LTh 1902). Deacon: 1902; priest: 1904 (Newcastle). Formerly: C. of Bywell St Andrew (Nb), 1902–5; of St Ives, 1905–13; R. of Brandiston-with-Haveringland (Nf), 1913–15; V. of St Michael, Louth, 1915–29; RD of Louthesk West, 1928–9; R. of Rothwell with Cuxwold, 1929–31. Resided at Caenby Rectory. Also:

Canon of Lincoln and Prebendary of Kilsby, 1928–36. Died 30 March 1936 at Caerleon Nursing Home, Grimsby. [*Crockford* (1935); *Probate Calendar* 1936.]

Francis George Frost MA

Instituted 22 June 1936 by collation to united benefice of Caenby with Glentham, on death of George Jordan. Patron: Bishop of Lincoln, for this alternate turn. Vacated by resignation, 1 December 1953. [Reg. 43, p.581; Reg. 44, p.186.]

Born 13 August 1886; son of John Hale F. of Leytonstone. Educated: Bancroft School, Woodford; Emmanuel College, Saskatchewan (Th.Test. 1913); University of Saskatchewan (BA 1915); Exeter College, Oxford (BA 1921; MA 1925). Deacon: 1913; priest 1914 (Saskatchewan). Formerly: C. of St George, Asquith, 1914–15; 28th Canadian Infantry Battalion, 1914–16: wounded in action, DCM 1916 (Courcelette); Chaplain to the Forces, 1917–19; Asst Master and Chaplain, Sherborne School, 1921–2; C. of St Mary, Longfleet, Poole, 1922–3; of Holy Trinity, Selhurst (Sr), 1923–4; of Faversham (K), 1924–8; V. of Leysdown with Harty (K), 1928–30; C. of St Peter, Paddington, 1930–2; V. of North Rauceby, 1932–6. Resided at Caenby Rectory. Author: *The Message of F. W. Robertson* (1926). Resigned 1 December 1953. Retired to 4 The Drive, Buckhurst Hill (Ess). Later V. of Castle Bytham, 1956–7. Died 19 January 1957 at The Isolation Hospital, Bourne. [*Exeter College Register 1891–1921*, 191; *Crockford* (1955–6); *Probate Calendar* 1957; *LDM* 73 (1957), 47.]

Thomas Hugh Roberts BA

Instituted 2 September 1954 to united benefice of Caenby with Glentham, on resignation of Francis George Frost. Patron: Dean (David Colin Dunlop) and Chapter of Lincoln, for this alternate turn. [Reg. 44, p.198.]

Educated: University of Wales (BA 1929); Ripon Hall, Oxford (1929). Deacon: 1930; priest: 1931 (St Asaph). Formerly: C. of Denbigh, 1930–2; of St Agnes, Moseley (Wo), 1932–4; of Acock's Green (Wa), 1934–6; V. of Boulton (Db), 1936–42; R. of Eyam, 1942–6; PC of King Sterndale, 1946–50; V. of Chelmorton, 1946–50; of Milford, 1950–4. Resided at Caenby Rectory. Afterwards: V. of Elsham, 1958–62; of Worlaby, 1958–62; of New Bolingbroke with Carrington, 1962–7. Retired to 87 Cliffe Road, Grantham. Disappears from *Crockford* after 1975–6. [*Crockford* (1971–2, 1975–6); *LDC* (1957), 54.]

Oliver Alfred Ernest Comely

Instituted 11 May 1959 by collation to united benefice of Caenby with Glentham, on cession of Thomas Hugh Roberts. Patron: Bishop of Lincoln, for this alternate turn. [Reg. 44, p.271.]

Born January 1905 at Osmington (Do); son of William John C., seaman (Royal Navy). Educated: Knutsford Test School (1931); Bishop Wilson Theological College (IoM) (1933); Clifton Theological College (1935). Deacon: 1936; priest: 1937 (Sheffield). Formerly: C. of Brinsworth (YWR), 1936–8; of Rawmarsh (YWR), 1938–9; of Ashtead (Sr), 1939–43; of St Michael, Aldershot, 1943–7; Minister of St George, Badshot Lea (Sr), 1947–51; R. of Somerby with Searby and Owmby, 1951–4; V. of Grasby, 1951–4; V. of Longham with Wendling and Bittering Parva (Nf), 1954–6; of Kenninghall (Nf), 1956–9. Resided at Caenby Rectory. Afterwards: V. of Barrow on Humber with New Holland, 1962–70. Died 28 April 1970. [GRO, Death Index; Census Returns 1911; *Crockford* (1969–70); *LDC* (1971), 65.]

John Forbes Thomson MA
Instituted 3 October 1963 to united benefice of Caenby with Glentham, on cession of Oliver Alfred Ernest Comely. Note that on 29 May 1963, an Order for Plurality was made under Section 5 of the Pastoral Reorganisation Measure 1949, authorising the said JFT to hold the benefices of Caenby with Glentham and Owmby with Normanby in plurality. [Reg. 44, pp. 352.]
Also: V. of Owmby, 1963–70 (*q.v.*).

CAMMERINGHAM

The church and manor of Cammeringham were given before 1126 by Robert de Haia to the abbey of Lessay in Normandy. Robert's son, Richard, was the founder of the Norman Premonstratensian abbey of Blanchland to which he in turn granted Cammeringham. The resulting dispute between the two houses was eventually settled in 1192, in favour of Blanchland, which established an alien priory at Cammeringham, appropriating the church. A vicarage was ordained, consisting of the altarage of the church, a toft and three bovates of land, and tithes of eight bovates of land in Cammeringham. The Abbots of Blanchland presented to the vicarage until 1326, shortly after which Cammeringham was taken into the possession of the King as an alien priory. Towards the end of the fourteenth century, the alien priory was suppressed and its assets sold to the Cistercian house of Hulton in Staffordshire. After the Dissolution, the right of presentation passed into the hands of the Cammeringham branch of the Tyrwhitt family. By the early nineteenth century it had come into the possession of Lord Monson. [Colvin, *White Canons*, 71–2; *Acta of Hugh of Wells*, no.104; Gribbin, *Premonstratensian Order*, 6.]

Gilbert de Wivelingehame chaplain
Instituted in the tenth pontifical year of Bishop Hugh of Wells (20 December 1218/19 December 1219) to vicarage of Cammeringham. Patron: Robert, Prior of Cammeringham. [*Rot. Welles* i. 133; *Acta of Hugh of Wells*, no.104.]

William de Evesham chaplain
Instituted in the twenty-third pontifical year of Bishop Hugh of Wells (20 December 1231/19 December 1232) to vicarage of Cammeringham. Patron: Br. Peter, proctor-general in England of Abbot and Convent of Blanchland (*Alba Landa*). [*Rot. Welles* i. 231–2.]

Ralph
Instituted before 1 June 1282. [*Reg. Sutton* viii. 3.]

William of Halton chaplain
Instituted 1 June 1282 to vicarage of Cammeringham, on death of Ralph.
Patron: Abbot and Convent of Blanchland. [*Reg. Sutton* viii. 3.]

Commission to hear confessions of clergy in deanery of Aslacoe, 1292. [*Reg. Sutton* iv. 46.]

Ralph of Bottesford chaplain
Instituted 13 April 1293 to vicarage of Cammeringham, on death of William.
Patron: Abbot and Convent of Blanchland. [*Reg. Sutton* viii. 23.]

John de Ringeden chaplain
Instituted 9 May 1298 to vicarage of Cammeringham, on death of Ralph.
Patron: Abbot and Convent of Blanchland. [*Reg. Sutton* viii. 29.]

Geoffrey de la Haye priest
Instituted 1 April 1318 to vicarage of Cammeringham, on death of John.
Patron: Br. Nicholas Fouet, proctor-general in England of Abbot and Convent
of St Nicholas, Blanchland. [Reg. 2, fo.99v.]

William de Baggenderby priest
Instituted 4 December 1326 to vicarage of Cammeringham, on death of Geoffrey. Patron: Abbot and Convent of Blanchland. [*Reg. Burghersh* i. no.742.]

William de Wadyngham
Instituted 14 July 1349 to vicarage of Cammeringham, on death of William.
Patron: King Edward III (24 June 1349), the temporalities of the alien Priory
of Cammeringham being in his hands. [Reg. 9, fo.155v; *CPR Edward III
1348–1350*, 332.]

John de Barow de Ingham priest
Instituted 11 November 1349 to vicarage of Cammeringham, on resignation of William. Patron: King Edward III (8 October 1349), the Priory of Cammeringham being in his hands. [Reg. 9, fo.159v; *CPR Edward III 1348–1350*, 401.]

Afterwards: V. of Wootton, 1357–68. Died before 10 September 1368 ('John de Cameryngham'). [Reg. 10, fo.26.]

Alan son of Simon de Barowe priest
Instituted 25 May 1357 to vicarage of Cammeringham, on resignation of John de Barowe (son of Peter de Alkebarowe) (by exchange with vicarage of Wootton). Patron: King Edward III (27 August 1356), the Priory of Cammeringham being in his hands on account of the war with France. [Reg. 9, fos 127, 168v; *CPR Edward III 1354–1358*, 432.]

Priest: before 22 August 1349. Formerly: V. of Wootton, 1349–57. [Reg. 9, fo.64.]

John Martyn priest
Instituted 16 June 1373 to vicarage of Cammeringham, on death of Alan de Barowe. Patron: King Edward III (19 May 1373), the temporalities of the Priory of Cammeringham being in his hands on account of the war with France. [Reg. 10, fo.138v; *CPR Edward III 1370–1374*, 286.]

John de Denton
Instituted before 17 August 1375. [Reg. 10, fo.142.]

John son of John de Botesford (de Grantham) priest
Instituted 17 August 1375 to vicarage of Cammeringham, on resignation of John de Denton. Patron: King Edward III (24 June 1375), the alien Priory of Cammeringham being in his hands on account of the war with France. [Reg. 10, fo.142; *CPR Edward III 1374–1377*, 114.]
Afterwards: V. of Digby, 1379–83 (assessed for poll-tax, 1381); V. of Billinghay, 1383. [Reg. 10, fo.126v; *Clerical Poll-Taxes*, no.1304.]

Robert de Rampton priest
Instituted 24 September 1379 to vicarage of Cammeringham, on resignation of John de Grantham (by exchange with vicarage of Digby). Patron: King Richard II (20 July 1379), the temporalities of the alien Priory of Cammeringham being in his hands on account of the war with France. [Reg. 10, fos 98, 145v; *CPR Richard II 1377–1381*, 374.]
Formerly: R. of St Paul in the Bail, Lincoln, to 1372; V. of a mediety of Leasingham, 1372–3/4; V. of Digby, 1373/4–9. Assessed for poll-tax, 1381. Afterwards: R. of Maidwell St Peter (Np), 1382–90. Died before 16 September 1390. [Reg. 10, fos 50v, 61v; *Clerical Poll-Taxes*, no.2162; Reg. 11, fo.156.]

Thomas de Kelsterne priest
Instituted 16 October 1382 to vicarage of Cammeringham, on resignation of Robert de Rampton [MS *Brampton*] (by exchange with church of St Peter, Maidwell). Patron: King Richard II (16 October 1382), the alien Priory of Cammeringham being in his hands on account of the war with France. [Reg. 10, fos 148, 228v; *CPR Richard II 1381–1385*, 172.]
Priest: before 28 September 1379. Formerly: R. of Maidwell St Peter (Np), 1379–82. Afterwards: V. of Eagle, 1384–5; Chaplain of Chantry of John Barton in Lincoln Cathedral, 1385. [Reg. 10, fo.214v; Reg. 11, fos 3v, 19.]

John Send priest
Instituted 17 March 1383/4 to vicarage of Cammeringham, on resignation of Thomas de Kelsterne (by exchange with vicarage of Eagle). Patron: King Richard II (24 February 1383/4), the alien Priory of Cammeringham being in his hands on account of the war with France. [Reg. 10, fo.151v; *CPR Richard II 1377–1381*, 379–80.]

Formerly: V. of Rainham (Ess), to 1383; of Eagle, 1383–4. Afterwards: Chaplain of St Mary Chantry in Church of West Rasen, 1385–7. [Newcourt ii. 481; Reg. 10, fo.126; Reg. 11, fo.31v.]

William Kelhode (de Spaldyng) priest

Instituted 23 November 1385 to vicarage of Cammeringham, on resignation of John de Sende (by exchange with chantry at altar of St Mary in church of West Rasen). Patron: King Richard II, the alien Priory of Cammeringham being in his hands on account of the war with France. [Reg. 11, fo.98.]

Priest: before 18 October 1381. Formerly: Chaplain of St Mary Chantry in Church of West Rasen, 1381–5. [Reg. 10, fo.117.]

Simon de Sproxton chaplain

Instituted 12 August 1388 to vicarage of Cammeringham, on death of William Kelhood de Spaldyng. Patron: King Richard II. [Reg. 11, fo.101v.]

John de Sneed priest

Instituted 15 October 1395 to church of Cammeringham. Patron: Abbot and Convent of St Mary, Hulton. Note that Elizabeth, widow of Nicholas de Audeley kt had paid £100 for a royal licence permitting the Abbot and Convent of Blanchland in Normandy to grant to the Abbot (Richard) and Convent of St Mary, Hulton (Staffs) the manor or priory of Cammeringham together with the advowson and appropriation of the church. [Reg. 11, fo.116.]

Institution apparently ineffective (see below).

Robert Theleby priest

Instituted 13 April 1441 to vicarage of Cammeringham, on death of Simon Sproxton. Patron: Abbot and Convent of Hulton. [Reg. 18, fos 86, 113.]

Robert Coleby

Instituted before 1 February 1478/9. [Reg. 21, fo.33.]

William Hustewat priest

Instituted 1 February 1478/9 to vicarage of Cammeringham, on death of Robert Coleby. Patron: Abbot and Convent of Hulton. [Reg. 21, fo.33.]

Charles Rome priest

Instituted 27 March 1497 to vicarage of Cammeringham, on resignation of William Hustwhaite. Patron: Abbot and Convent of Hulton. [Reg. 23, fo.148.]

Robert Northerby chaplain

Instituted 20 September 1505 to vicarage of Cammeringham, on death of Charles Rome. Patron: Abbot and Convent of Hulton. [Reg. 23, fo.156v.]

Assessed for subsidy (£5 18s 4d) in 1526. Still Vicar in 1535. [*Subsidy*, 36; *Valor* iv. 133.]

John Hanley

Instituted *c*.1552 (compounded for first-fruits, 24 January 1552). [FL.h.12, 308.]

Subdeacon: 31 March 1537; deacon: 22 September 1537; priest: 20 April 1538. Formerly: Chaplain of Chantry in Church of Burton-by-Lincoln, 1542–8; granted pension of £3 3s, September 1548. Died *c*.1557. Will dated 19 September 1557 (LCC). [*Chapter Acts* ii. 4, 8, 14, 65; *Ex-Religious*, 80; LCC Wills 1557/ii/111.]

Thomas Tompson

Instituted before 23 June 1563. [Reg. 28, fo.119.]

Died 1563. Will (Stow), dated 18 April 1563; proved at Lincoln 21 April 1563. [Stow Wills 1563/39.]

Peter Toller

Instituted 23 June 1563 to vicarage of Cammeringham, on death of Thomas Tompson. Patron: Robert Tyrwhite esquire. [Reg. 28, fo.119.]

Simon Arrowsmithe

Instituted in the tenth year of Queen Elizabeth I (17 November 1567 x 16 November 1568) to vicarage of Cammeringham, on death of Peter Toller. Patron: John Aistroppe. [Reg. 28, fo.39.]

Born *c*.1543. Education: 'ignorant of Latin; moderately versed in sacred learning'. Priest: 8 April 1562 (Lincoln). Resident at Cammeringham (signed BTs 1604–7). Died June 1607. Will dated 2 June 1607; proved at Lincoln, 19 June 1607. [*Bishop Cooper*, 167; BTs Cammeringham; Stow Wills 1607/22.]

William Davenporte

Instituted 19 August 1607 to vicarage of Cammeringham, on death of Simon Arrowsmith. Patron: Robert Tirwhitt of Cammeringham, esquire (14 August 1607). [Reg. 30, fo.311; PD 1607/18.]

Born *c*.1574 at Fillingham. Literate. Deacon: 9 June 1602; priest: 1 December 1602 (York). Died 1611. Will dated 19 February 1610/11; proved at Lincoln, 10 January 1611/12. [*York Ordinations 1561–1642*, 18; PD 1607/18; Stow Wills 1611/56.]

William May

Instituted 20 May 1611 to vicarage of Cammeringham, on death of William Davenport. Patron: Robert Tirwhitte esquire (24 April 1611). [BC; PD 1611/10.]

Deacon and priest: 31 March 1602 (York). Resident at Cammeringham: signed BTs 1612–25. Died June 1629. Will dated 8 June 1629; proved at Lincoln, 30 June 1629. [*York Ordinations 1561–1642*, 44; LC 4, fo.10; BTs Cammeringham; Stow Wills 1627–9/229.]

Nathaniel Smyth

Instituted 26 August 1629 to vicarage of Cammeringham, on death of William May. Patron: Anne Tirwhitt widow and Marmaduke Tirwhitt esquire, her son (29 July 1629). [BC; PD 1629/5.]

Of Lincolnshire. Educated: Trinity College (matric. 1618) and Sidney Sussex College, Cambridge (BA 1621–2). Deacon: 31 October 1624; priest: 9 March 1627/8 (Peterborough). [Venn, *Alumni*; Longden xii. 225.]

John Leigh

Instituted 25 September 1643 to vicarage of Cammeringham (cause of vacancy not stated). Patron: Ann Tirwhit widow. [Reg. 31, p.40.]

Perhaps to be identified with JL of Magdalene College, Cambridge (matric. 1637; BA 1639–40; MA 1643). Deacon: 24 September 1643; priest: 17 March 1643/4 (Lincoln). Married (22 April 1650) Elizabeth Tyrwhitt of Harmston. Preached funeral sermon of Anne, widow of Robert Tyrwhitt of Cammeringham (1652), printed as *The saints' rest and reward in heaven* (1654). R. of Silk Willoughby, 1661. Buried there, 30 January 1681/2. [Venn, *Alumni*; Reg. 31, fos 103v, 107; LC 5, fo.56v; PR Harmston; ESTC; PR Silk Willoughby; LCC Wills 1681/ii/649.]

Richard Gibson BA

Instituted 5 November 1661 to vicarage of Cammeringham, on cession of John Leigh. Patron: Cecil Tirwhit esquire (13 September 1661). [Reg. 32, fo.13v; PD 1661/37.]

Of Yorkshire. Educated: Trinity College, Cambridge (matric. 1656; BA 1661–2; MA 1665). Deacon: 2 November 1661; priest: 4 November 1661 (Lincoln). Resident (1662): signed BTs 1663–7. Also: C. of Ingham, 1662. Afterwards: R. of Kelham (Nt), 1667–89; Canon of Southwell and Prebendary of Norwell Tertia Pars, 1688–90. [Venn, *Alumni*; Reg. 32, fo.13; LC 5, fos 74, 82v; BTs Cammeringham; Le Neve-Hardy iii. 445.]

Arthur Noell BA

Instituted 5 September 1668 to vicarage of Cammeringham, on cession of last incumbent. Patron: Cecil Tyrwhitt esquire. [Reg. 33, fo.109.]

Baptised 7 November 1640 at Brompton by Sawdon (YNR); son of Arthur N., gent. Educated: Pocklington School and St John's College, Cambridge (matric. 1661; BA 1664–5; MA 1673). Deacon: 21 May 1665; priest: 11 March 1665/6 (York). Signed BTs at Cammeringham 1668. Afterwards: V. of Seaham (Du), 1668–91. Died 22 November 1691; buried at Seaham. [IGI; *St John's Admissions* i. 152; Venn, *Alumni*; *York Ordinations 1662–1699*, 49; BTs Cammeringham.]

Anthony Todd BA

Instituted 22 June 1669 to vicarage of Cammeringham, on cession of last incumbent. Patron: Cecil Tyrwhit esquire. [Reg. 33, fo.120.]

Baptised 6 January 1645/6 at St James, Grimsby; son of Thomas T., Alderman. Educated: Alford School and Magdalene College, Cambridge (matric. 1664; BA 1667–8). Deacon: 6 June 1669 (Lincoln); priest: 29 May 1670 (Peterborough). Signed BTs at Cammeringham 1670–6. Buried at Cammeringham, 18 September 1676. Will dated 9 September 1676; proved at Lincoln, 14 October 1676. [PR Grimsby St James; Venn, *Alumni*; Reg. 33, fo.119v; Longden xiii. 237; BTs Cammeringham; Stow Wills 1675–8/88.]

Samuel Lownes BA

Instituted 13 February 1676/7 to vicarage of Cammeringham, on death of

Anthony Todd. Patron: Cecil Tyrwhitt esquire (15 January 1676/7). [Reg. 34, fo.17v; PD 1677/19.]

Priest: 30 May 1675 (Gloucester). Also: V. of Ingham, 1675–95. Signed BTs at Cammeringham 1677–94. Died 3 April 1695; buried at Cammeringham, 4 April 1695. Probate inventory dated 13 April 1695: Library £3. [Reg. 34, fo.3; PR Cammeringham; Stow Admons Axix/181; INV 191/297.]

William Gibson MA

Instituted 31 May 1695 to vicarage of Cammeringham, on death of Samuel Lownes. Patron: Robert Tyrwhitt esquire (29 May 1695). [Reg. 35, fo.25; PD 1695/20.]

Baptised at Laughton, 7 May 1660; son of Robert Gibson, clerk. Educated: Kelham School (Nt) and Christ's College, Cambridge (matric. 1678; BA 1681–2; MA 1685). Deacon: 11 June 1682 (York); priest: 30 May 1686 (Lincoln). Formerly: C. of Kilvington (Nt), 1683–94; C. of Redmile (Le), 1686; V. of Norwell, 1689–90. Signed BTs at Cammeringham 1696–1704. Also: C. of Ingham, 1695–1705. Buried at Cammeringham, 1 February 1704/5. Will dated 26 November 1702; executrix sworn, 15 March 1704/5. [PR Laughton; Venn, *Alumni*; Peile ii. 66; *York Ordinations 1662–1699*, 26; Reg. 34, fo.92; LC 14, p.231; PR Cammeringham; Stow Wills 1700–4/67.]

John Johnson

Instituted 1705. [*Speculum*, 155.]

Of Nottinghamshire. Educated: Jesus College, Cambridge (matric. 1698; BA 1701–2; MA 1705). Deacon: 12 March 1704 (Lincoln); priest: 4 March 1704/5 (Peterborough). Resident: signed BTs 1705–30. Also: C. of Ingham, 1705–30. Buried at Cammeringham, 22 August 1730. Will dated 21 April 1730; executor sworn, 9 October 1730. [Venn, *Alumni*; Longden viii. 27; SUB VI; *Speculum*, 155; BTs Cammeringham; Stow Wills 1728–31/121.]

Francis Howson MA

Instituted 5 September 1730 to vicarage of Cammeringham, on death of John Johnson. Patron: Francis, Earl Godolphin, and Henrietta, Duchess of Marlborough. Reinstituted 29 June 1733, on resignation of last incumbent. [Reg. 38, pp. 230, 277.]

Baptised 29 July 1704 at Ulceby by Grimsby; son of Francis H. of Ulceby, gent. Educated: Lincoln College, Oxford (matric. 1724; BA 1727–8; MA 1731). Deacon: 21 December 1729; priest: 25 December 1729 (Lincoln). Formerly: C. of Fillingham, 1729–30. Also: V. of Great Carlton, 1742–73. Signed BTs at Cammeringham, 1730–70. Lived latterly in Lincoln. Buried at Ulceby by Grimsby, 27 March 1773 ('from Lincoln'). [PR Ulceby by Grimsby; *Lincolnshire Pedigrees*, 516; Foster, *Alumni*; Reg. 38, p.216; BTs Cammeringham.]

Tillotson Laycock BA

Instituted 17 June 1773 to vicarage of Cammeringham, on death of Francis Howson. Patron: Lord Robert Spencer. [Reg. 39, p.200.]

Baptised 8 July 1741 at Wrawby; son of Tillotson Laycock. Educated: Clare College, Cambridge (matric. 1758; BA 1762). Deacon: 25 September 1763; priest: 6 October 1765

(Lincoln). Formerly: C. of Wrawby, 1763; V. of Owersby, 1767–73. Also: V. of Hackthorn, 1773–1813; V. of Ingham, 1773–1813. Resided in Lincoln (on account of unfitness of Vicarage House and the infirmity of his wife) but served the church (signed BTs at Cammeringham, 1772–1810). Latterly of St Pancras (Mx). Died by July 1813. Will dated 15 March 1813; proved 30 July 1813 (PCC). [PR Wrawby; Venn, *Alumni*; Reg. 39, pp. 23, 47; LC 31, fo.197r; NRL 1803/29, 1806/18, 1812/39, 1814/11; BTs Cammeringham; *GM* 83 (1813), 94; PROB 11/1546.]

John Banks BD

Instituted 7 December 1813 to vicarage of Cammeringham, on death of Tillotson Laycock. Patron: Frederick John, Lord Monson (3 November 1813). [Reg. 40, p.193; PD 169/5.]

Born *c.*1765 at Keswick (Cu); son of John B. Educated: Keswick School and Christ's College, Cambridge (matric. 1798; BD 1800 as a 'ten year man'). FSA. Also: Master of Boston School, 1790–1825; R. of Bratoft, 1809–42; C. of Benington, 1816–20. Non-resident, on account of the house being small and unfit – a small, low thatched cottage. Cammeringham served by curates, including Thomas Francis Beckwith, Samuel Martin, Christopher Milnes, John Hull, William Henry Flowers and Joseph Green. Buried at Spilsby, 26 March 1842 (aged 78). Will. [Venn, *Alumni*; Peile ii. 327; Thompson, *Boston*, 285; CR 1, pp. 67, 90; PR Benington in Holland; NRL 1816/14; NRL 1823/27; NRL 1829/23; NRL 1835/1; NRL 1/59; NRL 6/117; CR 1, pp. 18, 153, 228, 394; CR 2, pp. 160, 208; PR Spilsby; LCC Wills 1842/27.]

Joseph Green MA

Instituted 15 July 1842 to vicarage of Cammeringham, on death of John Banks. Patron: Lord Monson. [Reg. 40, p.485.]

Also: R. of Owmby (*q.v.*).

David Lloyd Thomas MA

Instituted 8 February 1884 to vicarage of Cammeringham, on death of Joseph Green. Patron: William John, Lord Monson. [Reg. 42, p.197.]

Born *c.*1849 at Carmarthen; son of Benjamin David T., clerk. Educated: Shrewsbury School (1866–7) and Jesus College, Oxford (matric. 1868; BA 1872; MA 1881). Deacon: 1872; priest: 1873 (St Asaph). Formerly: various curacies, 1872–81; V. of Aslacton (Nf), 1881–2; R. of Lewcombe (Do), 1882–3. Afterwards: V. of Talland (Co), 1886–7; R. of Grainsby and V. of Waithe, 1887. For presentation, see MON 25/13/24. Received (with his wife and family) into the Roman Catholic Church following the publication of the Bull *Apostolicae Curae*, 1896. [*Shrewsbury Register 1798–1898*, 140; Foster, *Alumni*; Gorman, *Converts to Rome*, 220.]

William Wilton Smith MA

Instituted 10 April 1886 to vicarage of Cammeringham, on cession of David Lloyd Thomas. Patron: William John, Lord Monson. [Reg. 42, p.236.]

Also: R. of Fillingham, 1897–1913 (*q.v.*).

John Francis Edward Cudmore MA

Instituted 28 February 1914 to vicarage of Cammeringham, on death of

William Wilton Smith. Patron: Augustus Debonnaire John, Lord Monson, of Burton Hall. Note that on 28 January 1914, the Archbishop of Canterbury granted a dispensation enabling the said JFEC to hold together the Vicarage of Cammeringham and the Vicarage of Ingham. [Reg. 43, p.61.]

Also: V. of Ingham, 1894–1928 (*q.v.*).

The Vicarage of Cammeringham was united to the Vicarage of Ingham by Order in Council dated 12 October 1925 to form the United Benefice of Ingham with Cammeringham. [Reg. 43, pp. 379–80.]

COATES-BY-STOW

The church of Coates-by-Stow was granted to the Premonstratensian Abbey of Welbeck in Nottinghamshire by Peter of Cotes, and confirmed by Bishop Hugh of Avalon between 1189 and 1194. The church was appropriated and a vicarage (consisting of the altarage, 20 shillings from the great tithes, and a house) had been ordained by 1219–20. Welbeck took advantage of the privilege granted to the Premonstratensian Order to present their own canons to the churches in their gift, and the Abbey can be seen exercising this right, particularly in the first half of the fourteenth century and the second half of the fifteenth. After the Dissolution, the impropriate rectory passed into lay hands, the vicarage disappeared and the parish was served by a succession of curates until 1842 when the bishop's right to institute was re-established. The Bishop retained the patronage in 1965. [Hamilton Thompson, *Welbeck Abbey*, 51–2; *EEA* iv, no.208; Colvin, *White Canons*, 277–80; *LDC* (1965), 108–9.]

Adam chaplain
Instituted in the eleventh pontifical year of Bishop Hugh of Wells (20 December 1219/19 December 1220) to vicarage of Coates-by-Stow. Patron: Abbot and Convent of Welbeck. [*Rot. Welles* i. 214.]

Walter chaplain
Instituted in the fourth pontifical year of Bishop Robert Grosseteste (17 June 1238/16 June 1239) to vicarage of Coates-by-Stow. Patron: Abbot and Convent of Welbeck. [Hoskin, no.1244.]

Hugh de Stretton chaplain
Instituted in the thirteenth pontifical year of Bishop Robert Grosseteste (17 June 1247/16 June 1248) to vicarage of Coates-by-Stow, on resignation of Walter. Patron: Abbot and Convent of Welbeck. [Hoskin, no.1288.]

Henry
Instituted before 6 July 1292. [*Reg. Sutton* iv. 10.]

Commission to Archdeacon of Stow to provide Henry with a guardian, as he was said to be out of his mind (*mentis incompositionem ut dicitur patienti…*). [*Reg. Sutton* iv. 10.]

Br. William de Cestrefeld canon of Welbeck
Instituted 11 August 1296 to vicarage of Coates-by-Stow, on death of Henry. Patron: Abbot and Convent of Welbeck. [*Reg. Sutton* viii. 27.]

Br. John de Ettewell, canon of Welbeck
Instituted 5 June 1314 to vicarage of Coates-by-Stow, on death of br. William de Cestrefeld. Patron: Abbot and Convent of Welbeck. [Reg. 2, fo.97.]

Br. Robert de Lincoln, canon of Welbeck
Instituted 26 January 1320/1 to vicarage of Coates-by-Stow, on resignation of br. John de Etwell. Patron: Abbot and Convent of Welbeck. [*Reg. Burghersh* i. no.719.]

He was to have a fellow canon, in priest's orders, residing with him. [*Reg. Burghersh* i. no.719.]

Br. John de Hauteberg, canon of Welbeck
Instituted 30 June 1324 to vicarage of Coates-by-Stow, on resignation of br. Robert de Lincoln. Patron: Abbot and Convent of Welbeck. [*Reg. Burghersh* i. no.732.]

Perhaps to be identified with br. John de Alkebarwe, on whose behalf letters questuary were issued (12 March 1334/5) to the archdeaconry of Stow after his house, corn and other goods were destroyed by fire. [Reg. 5, fo.492r; Thompson, *Welbeck Abbey*, 77.]

Richard de Malberthorp priest
Instituted 14 January 1349/50 to vicarage of Coates-by-Stow, on death of br. John. Patron: Abbot and Convent of Welbeck. [Reg. 9, fo.160v.]

William de Scremby
Instituted before 5 December 1369. [Reg. 10, fo.132v.]

Afterwards: V. of Cuxwold, 1369–71. [Reg. 10, fos 37v, 44.]

John son of John de Botelesford (de Grantham) priest
Instituted 5 December 1369 to vicarage of Coates-by-Stow, on resignation of William de Scremby (by exchange with vicarage of Cuxwold). Patron: Abbot and Convent of Welbeck. [Reg. 10, fos 37v, 132v.]

Formerly: V. of Cuxwold, 1362–9. Afterwards: V. of Cammeringham, 1375 (*q.v.*) [Reg. 9, fo.153v.]

John Cotes
Instituted before 30 September 1375. [Reg. 10, fo.142v.]

John al Grene priest
Instituted 30 September 1375 to vicarage of Coates-by-Stow, on resignation of John Cotes. Patron: Abbot and Convent of Welbeck. [Reg. 10, fo.142v.]
Assessed for poll-tax, 1377 and 1381. [*Clerical Poll-Taxes*, nos 810, 2160.]

Br. John de Norton canon of Welbeck, priest
Instituted 12 March 1389/90 to vicarage of Coates-by-Stow (cause of vacancy not stated). Patron: Abbot and Convent of Welbeck. [Reg. 11, fo.104.]

John Stacy priest
Instituted 10 January 1394/5 to vicarage of Coates-by-Stow (cause of vacancy not stated). Patron: Abbot and Convent of Welbeck. [Reg. 11, fo.114v.]

Robert son of Richard Barbur de Langwath priest
Instituted 16 August 1397 to vicarage of Coates-by-Stow, on resignation of John Stacy. Patron: Abbot and Convent of Welbeck. [Reg. 11, fo.119.]

William de Laceby priest
Instituted 27 May 1407 to vicarage of Coates-by-Stow, on death of last incumbent. Patron: Abbot and Convent of Welbeck. [Reg. 14, fo.110.]
Afterwards: V. of Neatishead (Nf), 1412.

John Fogheler
Instituted 25 May 1412 to vicarage of Coates-by-Stow, on resignation of William de Laceby (by exchange with vicarage of Neatishead (*Netesherde*), dioc. Norwich). Patron: Abbot and Convent of Welbeck. [Reg. 14, fo.121v.]
Priest: before 5 December 1413. Previously: V. of Neatishead (Nf) to 1412. Afterwards: V. of Anwick, 1413–16; R. of Bradley (Db), 1416--17; Vicar of Sutton le Marsh, 1417; Vicar of Crowle, March–April 1422. [Reg. 14, fos 66v, 121v; *Reg. Catterick*, nos 78–80; *Reg. Fleming* i. nos 409–10.]

Hugh Nobyll priest
Instituted 5 December 1413 to vicarage of Coates-by-Stow, on resignation of John Fogheler (by exchange with vicarage of Anwick). Patron: Abbot and Convent of Welbeck. [Reg. 14, fos 66v, 123v.]
Priest: before 21 March 1412/3. Formerly: V. of Anwick, March–December 1413. [Reg. 14, fo.62.]

Thomas Caldewell priest
Instituted 19 August 1414 to vicarage of Coates-by-Stow, on resignation of Hugh Nobull. Patron: Abbot and Convent of Welbeck. [Reg. 14, fo.124v.]

Hugh Weryngton chaplain
Instituted 27 October 1417 to vicarage of Coates-by-Stow, on resignation

of Thomas Caldewell. Patron: Abbot and Convent of Welbeck. [Reg. 14, fo.132.]

John Ferrour priest
Instituted 15 October 1420 to vicarage of Coates-by-Stow, on death of Hugh Weryngton. Patron: Abbot and Convent of Welbeck. [*Reg. Fleming* i. no.397.]

William Carleton priest
Instituted 29 May 1423 to vicarage of Coates-by-Stow, on resignation of John Ferrour. Patron: Abbot and Convent of Welbeck. [*Reg. Fleming* i. no.424.]

John Feryby
Instituted 9 October 1451 by Official of Lincoln *sede vacante* to vicarage of Coates-by-Stow (cause of vacancy not stated). Patron: Official of Lincoln as above, by lapse. [Reg. 19, fos 65v, 79v.]

Br. John Rawnfeld, canon of Welbeck
Instituted 21 April 1452 by Official *sede vacante* to church [*sic*] of Coates-by-Stow, on resignation of John Feryby. Patron: Abbot and Convent of Welbeck. [Reg. 19, fo.71v.]

Richard Cambrigge
Instituted before 19 May 1485. [Reg. 22, fo.164.]

Br. John Hyrste
Instituted 19 May 1485 to vicarage of Coates-by-Stow, on resignation of Richard Cambrigge. Patron: Abbot and Convent of Welbeck. [Reg. 22, fo.164.]

Br. Edward Colinson, canon of Welbeck, priest
Instituted 13 March 1494/5 to vicarage of Coates-by-Stow, on death of John Hurst. Patron: Abbot and Convent of Welbeck. [Reg. 23, fo.7v.]

Br. Robert Sharpe, canon [of Welbeck], priest
Instituted 17 June 1498 to vicarage of Coates-by-Stow, on resignation of br. Edward Colynson. Patron: Abbot and Convent of Welbeck. [Reg. 23, fo.149.]

Br. William Crosse, canon of Welbeck, priest
Instituted 31 July 1504 to vicarage of Coates-by-Stow, on resignation of br. Robert Sharpe. Patron: Abbot and Convent of Welbeck. [Reg. 23, fo.155r–v.]

John Grene
Instituted 10 April 1510 to vicarage of Coates-by-Stow, on resignation of William Crosse. Patron: Abbot and Convent of Welbeck. [Reg. 23, fo.140.]

The cure was served by Percival Ellys as stipendiary chaplain in 1526. JG was still Vicar in 1535. [*Subsidy*, 36; *Valor* iv. 133.]

After the Dissolution, Coates-by-Stow was served by curates including John Thorpe (1551), Richard Glosse (1662), William Blyth (1697), Robert Broughton, William Whitlam, Thomas Clarke, John Bassett. [Vj 13, fo.58v; LC 5, fo.74; LC 14, p.231; LC 31, fo.197; PR Coates-by-Stow.]

George Atkinson

Instituted 15 July 1842 to vicarage of Coates-by-Stow, on death of last incumbent. Patron: Queen Victoria, by lapse. [Reg. 40, p.485.]

Born 29 December 1801 at Rochdale (La); son of Francis A., cotton manufacturer. Educated: Queens' College, Cambridge (matric. 1820; BA 1824; MA 1827). Deacon: 25 September 1825; priest: 24 September 1826 (Lincoln). Formerly: C. of Heapham and Springthorpe, 1826–36; of Corringham, 1831–6. Also: PC of Stow-in-Lindsey, 1836–65. Resided at Stow. 'Worked strenuously to carry out the restoration of [Stow] Church.' Died 23 May 1865 at Stow Rectory. [*Stow Church Restored*, xi; Venn, *Alumni*; OR 1, pp. 21, 25; PR Heapham; CR 2, p.14; *Probate Calendar* 1865.]

Edward Henry Julius Hawke MA

Instituted 22 December 1865 by collation to vicarage of Coates-by-Stow, on death of George Atkinson. Patron: Bishop of Lincoln, by lapse. [Reg. 41, p.147.]

Born 24 December 1815 at Brussels; son of Hon. Martin Edward Bladen Hawke. Educated: St Catharine's Hall, Cambridge (matric. 1835; BA 1839; MA 1843). Deacon: 22 December 1839; priest: 20 December 1840 (York). Formerly: C. of Helmsley (YNR), 1839; C. of Stonegrave, 1853. Also: R. of Willingham-by-Stow, 1854–75. Resignation of Coates accepted 9 April 1875. Succeeded his cousin as 6th Baron Hawke, 1870. Father of Martin Bladen Hawke (7th Baron Hawke), the Yorkshire and England cricketer. Died 5 December 1887, suddenly at Midland Hotel, St Pancras (Middx). [*GEC* vi. 415; Venn, *Alumni*; *York Ordinations 1800–1849*, 87; Reg. 41, p.494.]

William Reynard

Instituted 30 July 1875 to vicarage of Coates-by-Stow, on resignation of Rt Hon. Henry Edward Julius, Baron Hawke. Patron: Sir John William Ramsden of Byram (Yorks), Bt. Note that the Archbishop of Canterbury granted a dispensation enabling the said WR to hold together the Vicarage of Coates and the Rectory of Willingham-by-Stow. [Reg. 41, p.501.]

Born 17 August 1840 at Hob Green, par. Markington (YWR); son of Charles R. Educated: University of Durham. Deacon: 1868; priest: 1869 (Ripon). Formerly: C. of Middleham (YNR), 1868–72; V. of Lockington-with-Hemington (Db), 1872–3; C. of Sutton Bonington St Anne with Kingston-on-Soar (Nt), 1873–4. Also: R. of Willingham-by-Stow, 1875–8. Resided at Willingham Rectory. Died 1 August 1878 at Willingham; buried there, 5 August 1878 (aged 37). Will. [Crisp, *Visitation* iii. 165; Burke, *Landed Gentry* (1937), 1909; *Crockford* (1878); *Probate Calendar* 1878; PR Willingham by Stow; Wills 1878/ii/580.]

Charles Nevile MA

Instituted 21 March 1879 to vicarage of Coates-by-Stow, on death of William Reynard. Patron: Bishop of Lincoln, for this turn (by lapse). Note that on 15 March 1879, the Archbishop of Canterbury granted a dispensation enabling the said CN to hold together the Vicarage of Coates and the Rectory of Stow in Lindsey. [Reg. 42, p.80.]

Born 10 December 1816; 3rd son of Christopher N. of Scaftworth, Everton (Nt), esquire. Educated: Trinity College, Oxford (matric. 1835; BA 1839; MA 1842). Deacon: 22 December 1839; priest: 20 December 1840 (Lincoln). Formerly: C. of Thorney (Nt), 1839–44; of Wickenby, 1845–53; R. of Fledborough (Nt), 1853–77. Also: Canon of Lincoln and Prebendary of South Scarle, 1868–1902; R. of Stow in Lindsey, 1877–87. Resided at Stow Rectory. Married (31 January 1860) at St Marylebone (Mx), Maria, daughter of Revd William Hammond, R. of Whitchurch (Ox). Retired 1887; lived at 6 Lindum Terrace, Lincoln. Died 26 April 1902 at Lincoln. [Burke, *Landed Gentry* (1894), 1469; Foster, *Alumni*; OR 1, pp. 78, 82; Reg. 40, p.539; *Crockford* (1878); LMA, PR St Marylebone; Census Returns 1901; *Probate Calendar* 1902; *LDM* (1902), 80.]

Octavius Appleby Garwood MA

Instituted 16 October 1885 to vicarage of Coates-by-Stow, on resignation of Charles Nevile. Patron: Sir John William Ramsden of Byram (YWR), Bt. Note that on 1 October 1885, the Archbishop of Canterbury granted a dispensation enabling the said OAG to hold together the Vicarage of Coates and the Rectory of Willingham-by-Stow. [Reg. 42, p.229.]

Baptised 4 April 1843 at St Mary Castlegate, York; son of William G. of Castlegate, York, gent. Educated: Worcester College, Oxford (matric. 1861; BA 1865; MA 1870). Deacon: 1866 (Lincoln); priest: 1870 (Oxford). Formerly: C. of Willingham-by-Stow, 1866–9; of Christ Church, Reading, 1870–4; of Upton with Chalvey (Bk), 1874–6; of St Martin, Brighton, 1876–8; of Betchworth (Sr), 1878–81; of Crickhowell, 1881–2. Also: R. of Willingham-by-Stow, 1882–1908. Resided at Willingham Rectory. Died 10 October 1908. [PR York St Mary Castlegate; Foster, *Alumni*; *Crockford* (1907); Census Returns 1901; *Probate Calendar* 1908.]

James Ernest Christie

Instituted 12 February 1909 to vicarage of Coates-by-Stow, on death of Octavius Appleby Garwood. Patron: Sir John William Ramsden of Byram (YWR), Bt. Note that on 4 February 1909, the Archbishop of Canterbury granted a dispensation enabling the said JEC to hold together the vicarage of Coates and the rectory of Stow in Lindsey. [Reg. 42, p.607.]

Born *c.*1862 at Hull; son of James C., merchant. Educated: King's College, London (AKC 1892). Deacon: 1893; priest: 1894 (St Albans). Formerly: C. of St Mary, Plaistow (Ess), 1893–4; of Addlestone (Sr), 1894–6; R. of Ingoldmells, 1896–1901. Also: R. of Stow in Lindsey, 1901–16. Resided at Stow Rectory. Afterwards: R. of Thornton-le-Moor, 1916–31. Died at Thornton-le-Moor Rectory, 16 February 1931. [*Crockford* (1931); *Probate Calendar* 1931.]

John Barber MA

Instituted 2 September 1916 to vicarage of Coates-by-Stow, on cession of

James Ernest Christie. Patron: Sir John Frecheville Ramsden of Byram (Yorks), Bt. Note that on 10 August 1916, the Archbishop of Canterbury granted a dispensation enabling the said JB to hold together the rectory of Stow in Lindsey and the vicarage of Coates. [Reg. 43, p.135.]

Born 30 June 1881 at Stanton (St); son of Lewis Pasteur B. of Burton on Trent. Educated: Repton School and Trinity College, Cambridge (matric. 1900; BA 1903; MA 1908). Deacon: 1904; priest: 1905 (Liverpool). Formerly: C. of All SS Prince's Park, Liverpool, 1904–6; of Holy Trinity Toxteth Park, Liverpool, 1906–8; of Grimsby, 1908–10; UMCA Missioner, Northern Rhodesia, 1910–12; C. of Grimsby, 1912–13; of Bishop's Hatfield (Hrt), 1913–16. Also: R. of Stow in Lindsey, 1916–27; RD of Lawres, 1920–7. Resided at Stow Rectory. Afterwards: R. of Great Coates, 1927–54; RD of North Grimsby, 1940–8; Canon of Lincoln and Prebendary of Bedford Major, 1943–54. Retired 1954. Latterly of 12 Dudley Street, Grimsby. Died 7 January 1957 at The General Hospital, Grimsby. [*Repton Register*, 362; Venn, *Alumni*; *Crockford* (1916, 1923, 1955–6); *Probate Calendar* 1957.]

Norman Kershaw Leach MA

Instituted 31 October 1927 to vicarage of Coates-by-Stow, on cession of John Barber. Patron: Sir John Frecheville Ramsden of Turweston Manor, Brackley (Northants), Bt. Note that on 28 September 1927, the Archbishop of Canterbury granted a dispensation enabling the said NKL to hold together the rectory of Stow in Lindsey and the vicarage of Coates. [Reg. 43, p.424.]

Born 26 June 1881; son of Abraham L. of Oldham, medical practioner. Educated: Giggleswick School and Christ's College, Cambridge (matric. 1900; BA 1903; MA 1907); Ridley Hall, Cambridge. Deacon: 1904; priest: 1905 (Manchester). Formerly: C. of St Silas, Blackburn, 1904–6; of Sandal Magna (YWR), 1906–7; V. of Wainfleet St Mary, 1907–27. Resided at Stow Rectory. Afterwards: C. of Riseholme, 1937–49. Died 31 January 1949 at Riseholme Rectory. [Venn, *Alumni*; *Crockford* (1948); *Probate Calendar* 1949.]

Henry Cecil Orr MA

Instituted 1 July 1935 to vicarage of Coates-by-Stow, on resignation of Norman Kershaw Leach. Patron: Sir John Frecheville Ramsden of Turweston Manor, Brackley (Northants), Bt. Note that on 13 June 1935, the Archbishop of Canterbury granted a dispensation enabling the said HCO to hold together the rectory of Stow in Lindsey and the vicarage of Coates. [Reg. 43, pp. 560–1.]

Born 26 January 1888; son of John Orr, V. of Ashted, Birmingham. Educated: King Edward School, Birmingham, and Keble College, Oxford (matric. 1907; BA 1910; MA 1914); Scholae Cancellarii, Lincoln (1910). Deacon: 11 June 1911; priest: 2 June 1912 (Lincoln). Formerly: C. of St Andrew, Grimsby, 1911–15; TCF 1915–19; C. of St James, Louth, 1919–20; V. of All SS, Grimsby, 1920–35; Chaplain of Grimsby Union, 1921–5. Also: RD of West Lawres, 1944–9; Canon of Lincoln and Prebendary of Bedford Minor, 1945–55. Resided at Stow Rectory. Afterwards: V. of Harmston, 1949–55. Retired 1955. Latterly of Ellesborough Manor, Aylesbury. Died 19 July 1981. [GRO, Death Index; Census Returns 1891; *Keble Register*, 356–7; *LDC* (1911, 1912); *Crockford* (1955–6, 1977–9).]

Philip Ellard Ellard-Handley MA

Instituted 29 November 1949 to vicarage of Coates-by-Stow, on cession of Henry Cecil Orr. Patron: Sir John Frecheville Ramsden of Ardverikie, Kingussie, co. Inverness, Bart. Note that on 14 November 1949, the Archbishop of Canterbury granted a dispensation enabling the said PEE-H to hold together the rectory of Stow in Lindsey and the vicarage of Coates. [Reg. 44, p.117.]

Born 18 January 1911. Educated: St Catharine's College, Cambridge (BA 1932; MA 1936); Lichfield Theological College (1933). Deacon: 1934; priest: 1935 (Bradford). Formerly: C. of Holy Trinity, Queensbury (YWR), 1934–7; Chaplain of Orleton School and C. of St Martin, Scarborough, 1937–8; Chaplain, Dinapore (India), 1938–42; Chaplain, RAFVR, 1942–4; Head Master of Prebendal School, Priest Vicar and Succentor, Chichester, 1945–6; R. of North Scarle, 1946–9. Also: R. of Willingham-by-Stow, 1951–6. Resided at Stow Rectory. Afterwards: V. of Sark (CI), 1956–77. Retired 1977. Latterly of Terry's Cross, Woodmancote, Henfield (Sx). Died February 1990. [GRO, Death Index; *Crockford* (1955–6, 1961–2, 1989–90).]

Walter Nicholson

Instituted 26 September 1957 to vicarage of Coates-by-Stow, on cession of Philip Ellard Ellard-Handley. Patron: Bishop of Lincoln, for this turn by virtue of an Order made on 6 November 1951. Note that on 14 June 1957, a Renewal Order was made under Section 5 of the Pastoral Reorganisation Measure 1949, authorising the said WN to hold the benefices of Stow in Lindsey, Coates and Willingham-by-Stow in plurality. [Reg. 44, pp. 246–7.]

Born *c*.1899. Educated: Westcott House, Cambridge (1951). Deacon: 1952; priest: 1953 (Manchester). Formerly: C. of St Luke with All SS Weaste, Salford, 1952–4; R. of St Clement, Ordsall, Salford, 1954–6. Also: R. of Stow in Lindsey, 1956–61; R. of Willingham-by-Stow, 1956–61. Resided at Stow Rectory. Afterwards: V. of Nicholforest (Cu), 1962–6. Retired 1966. Latterly of Fairview, Saxilby Road, Sturton-by-Stow. Died 18 November 1968. [GRO, Death Index; *Crockford* (1967–8); *LDC* (1969), 57.]

John William Parker AKC

Instituted 29 May 1963 to vicarage of Coates-by-Stow, on cession of Walter Nicholson. Patron: Bishop of Lincoln. Note that on 5 February 1963, a Renewal Order was made under Section 5 of the Pastoral Reorganisation Measure 1949, authorising the said JWP to hold the benefices of Stow in Lindsey, Coates and Willingham by Stow in plurality. [Reg. 44, p.346.]

Born 22 December 1906. Educated: King's College, London (AKC 1934) and Sarum Theological College (1934). Deacon: 16 June 1935; priest: 7 June 1936 (Lincoln). Formerly: C. of St Aidan, New Cleethorpes, 1935–7; of St Martin, Lincoln, 1937–41; V. of Gosberton Clough, 1941–6; R. of St John Baptist with St Clement, Stamford, 1946–62; Domestic Chaplain to Marquis of Exeter, 1948–58; Confrater of Browne's Hospital, Stamford, 1958–62. Also: R. of Stow, 1962–75; R. of Willingham-by-Stow, 1962–75; Canon of Lincoln and Prebendary of Marston St Lawrence, 1974. Resided at Stow Rectory. Retired 1975; lived at 6 Minster Yard, Lincoln. Died 18 August 1996. [GRO, Death Index; *Crockford* (1980–2); *LDM* (1935, 1936); Lincoln Cathedral Obit Book.]

1. Willoughton: Church of St Andrew.
(Nicholas Bennett)

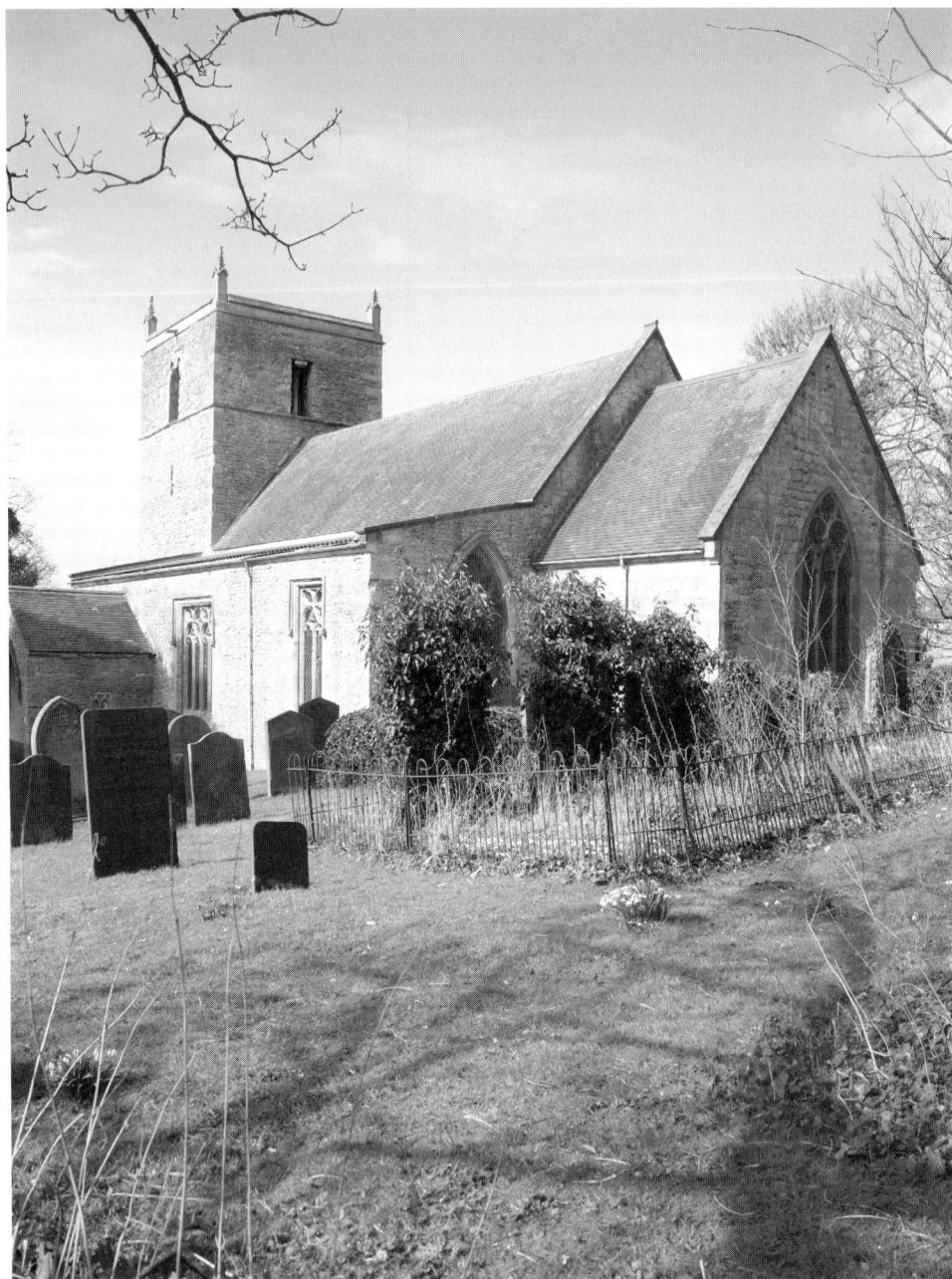

2. Harpswell: Church of St Chad.
(Nicholas Bennett)

3(a). Fillingham: Church of St Andrew.
(Lincoln Cathedral Library)

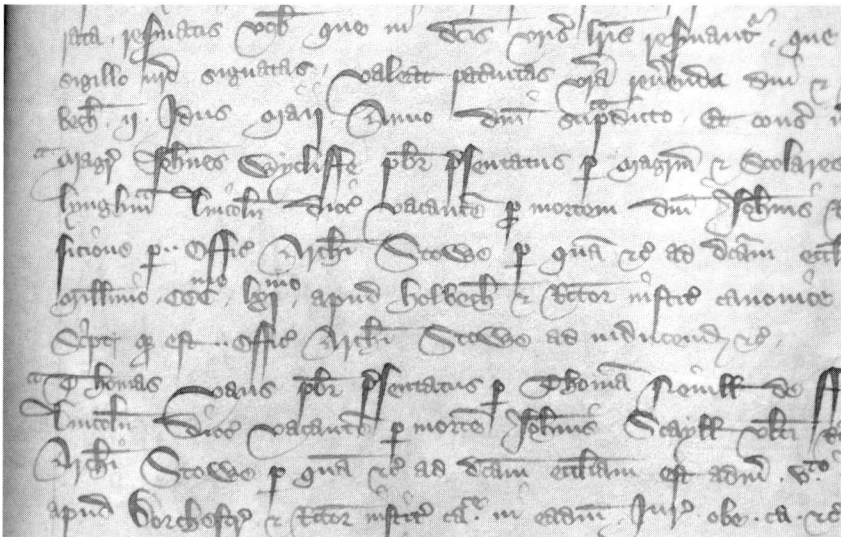

3(b). Institution of John Wycliffe to Fillingham, 1361.
(Detail from Lincolnshire Archives, Bishop's Register 9, fo.172.
With the permission of Lincolnshire Archives.)

4. Waddingham: Rectory House, south elevation
(James Fowler of Louth for William Windsor Berry, 1858–9).
(Detail from Lincolnshire Archives, MGA 406. With the
permission of Lincolnshire Archives.)

5. Harpswell, Church of St Chad:
effigy of William de Harington, Rector (d.1349).
(Nicholas Bennett)

6. Snitterby: Church of St Nicholas (interior).
(Nicholas Bennett)

In the name of god amen: I Theodor Haward of Caenby in the County of Lincolne Clarke being perfect in minde but weake in bodie thanks be unto god doe ordaine this my last will and testament, As Followeth

First I bequeath my soule into the hands of almighty god my creator and redeemer: and my body to be buried in the body of the Chancell of the Quire of Caenby aforesaid/

It give unto all my Godchildren one Shillinge a peece to be payed unto them within a yeare after my decease

It give unto my Servant Sarah Woode two poundes whereof one half to be payed unto her in money and the rest in goods which shalbe payed unto her att the day of her marriage or att the age of One and twenty yeares

It give unto Judie Pirkinge and unto all her children ^ a peece
It to Mary Woode and to all her Children except Sarah j^ a peece
It to Jonie Flitchett and to her childe j^ a peere

I desire that my debtes may be payed as Followeth/
To the poore of Caenby Five poundes eight Shillinges
To Mr Hotch of Marquett Rason Draper three poundes
To Mr Berk of Lincolne Draper thirteene Shillings sixpence
To Honorie Bitton of Briggs seaventeene Shillings tenpence

These debtes and Legaries being payed, I give unto my wife all my goods and chattells both within dores and without for her maintenance dureinge her life; and that in the time of her life shee imbrace none of them away: but what is neffessarie for her maintenance and after her decease I bequeath them all to my Cosen Mary Bright now servant to Mr Edw: Journey of Caenby and doe make her sole executrix/ In witness whereof I have sett to my hand & seale of this my last will and Testament/

Signum
Will. [...] Todd   Theodore Hayward   Daydard [...]

7. Will of Theodore Hayward, Rector of Caenby (1649).
(Detail from Lincolnshire Archives, Stow Wills 1640–50/420.
With the permission of Lincolnshire Archives.)

CHRISTIAN
HOSPITALITIE

Handled Common-place-wise in the
Chappel of Trinity Colledge in
CAMBRIDGE:

Whereunto is added, *A short but honourable*
Narration of the life and death of Mr
HARRISON, *the late hospital Vice-*
master of that Royal and Ma-
gnificent Societie:

By
CALEB DALECHAMP Minister
of Gods Word, and Master of
Arts in the said Colledge.

GREG. NAZIAN. Orat. 16.
Καλὸν ἡ φιλοξενία, δι᾽ ἣν Ῥαὰβ ἐπαγγεθεῖσα τε
ἠ σωθεῖσα.

PET. MART. in Judic.19.18.
Vt vitium est gravissimum hospites contemnere,
ità excellentissima Virtus est Hospitalitas.

¶ Printed by TH. BUCK, printer to the
Universitie of *Cambridge.* 1632.

8. Caleb Dalechamp (Vicar of Ingham), *Christian Hospitalitie*
(Cambridge, 1632).
(Lincoln Cathedral Library)

FILLINGHAM

The church of Fillingham, together with that of Brattleby, was given in 1123 to Lessay Abbey in Normandy by Robert de Haia and this gift was confirmed three years later by King Henry I. Some time before 1232, Bishop Hugh of Wells issued an ordination setting out that Lessay should receive an annual pension of twenty marks from Fillingham church and that, when a vacancy occurred, they were to present a suitable clerk to the bishop for institution. In practice, such presentations were often made by the abbey's proctor-general in England. In 1343 the advowson was purchased by Balliol College, Oxford, using money left for that purpose by Thomas Cave. The first Balliol presentee was John Wycliffe, at that time Master of Balliol; he became the first of many Balliol incumbents who preferred to reside in Oxford, leaving Fillingham to be served by a curate. The College still held the advowson in 1965. [*Honors and Knight's Fees* iii. 56; *Acta of Hugh of Wells*, no.420; Jones, *Balliol*, 15, 26; *LDC* (1965), 108–9.]

Thomas de Sancto Martino deacon
Instituted in the first pontifical year of Bishop Robert Grosseteste (17 June 1235/16 June 1236) to church of Fillingham. Patron: Abbot and Convent of Lessay. Letters of institution issued 16 November 1240. [Hoskin, nos 1226, 1319.]

Robert de Wytten subdeacon
Instituted in the thirteenth pontifical year of Bishop Robert Grosseteste (17 June 1247/16 June 1248) to church of Fillingham. Patron: Abbot and Convent of Lessay. [Hoskin, no.1293.]

Pagan de Liskered
Instituted before 20 December 1287. [*Reg. Sutton* viii. 11–12, 19.]

M. Thomas le Fleming
Instituted 20 December 1287 to church of Fillingham, on resignation of Pagan de Liskered. Patron: M. John le Fleming, canon of Lincoln and proctor-general in England of Abbot and Convent of Lessay. Reinstituted 25 May 1289, because he had not been ordained priest within a year of institution; patron, as above. [*Reg. Sutton* viii. 11–12, 19.]
Subdeacon: 20 December 1287 (Lincoln). [*Reg. Sutton* viii. 12.]

Thomas de Foxele chaplain
Instituted 22 December 1293 to church of Fillingham, on lapse of grant *in commendam* to M. Thomas le Fleming who had now been instituted to Burton Latimer. Patron: M. John le Fleming, canon of Lincoln and proctor of Abbot and Convent of Lessay. [*Reg. Sutton* viii. 23.]

Richard de Bodekesham chaplain
Instituted 11 October 1296 to church of Fillingham, on resignation of Thomas
de Foxele. Patron: M. John le Fleming, proctor-general in England of Abbot
and Convent of Lessay. [*Reg. Sutton* viii. 28.]

Formerly: R. of Gravenhurst (Bd), 1294–6. [*Reg. Sutton* viii. 113, 117.]

William de Broklesby priest
Instituted 13 September 1330 to church of Fillingham, on death of Richard de
Bodekesham. Patron: Adam de Lymbergh, canon of Chichester and proctor
of Abbot and Convent of Lessay. [*Reg. Burghersh* i. no.762.]

John de Rasne priest
Instituted 19 October 1331 to church of Fillingham, on dimission of William
de Broklesby. Patron: William de Broklesby clerk, proctor of Abbot and
Convent of Holy Trinity, Lessay. [*Reg. Burghersh* i. no.768.]

John Reyner priest
Instituted 31 May 1335 to church of Fillingham, on death of John de Rasyn.
Patron: William de Broklesby clerk, proctor of Abbot and Convent of Holy
Trinity, Lessay. [*Reg. Burghersh* i. no.796.]

M. John Wycliffe priest
Instituted 14 May 1361 to church of Fillingham, on death of John Reyner.
Patron: Master and Scholars of Balliol Hall, Oxford. [Reg. 9, fo.172.]

Perhaps to be identified with a JW who was ordained subdeacon 12 March 1350/1; deacon
18 April 1351; priest 24 September 1351 (York). Educated: Merton College, Oxford (BA
by 1356); Master of Balliol College, by summer 1360. Also: Warden of Canterbury
College, Oxford, 1365–7; Canon of Westbury-on-Trym and prebendary of Aust (Gl),
1366–84. Licence for non-residence at Fillingham, 29 August 1363 (1 year) and April
1368 (2 years). Residing at Queen's College, Oxford, by 1363–4. Afterwards: R. of Ludgershall (Bk), 1368–74; R. of Lutterworth (Le), 1374–84; Canon of Lincoln and Prebendary of Caistor, *c*.1376. Author: works on logic, theology, dominion and law; inspired
the translation of the Bible into English. The celebrated theologian and reformer. Died
31 December 1384 at Lutterworth. [Anne Hudson and Anthony Kenny, 'Wyclif, John'
in *ODNB*; Emden, *BRUO*, 2103–6; Jones, *Balliol*, 26–9; *Westbury-on-Trym*, 48–9, 214.]

John de Wythornewyk priest
Instituted 12 November 1368 to church of Fillingham, on resignation of M.
John de Wyclif (by exchange with church of Ludgershall). Patron: Master
and Scholars of Balliol Hall in the University of Oxford. [Reg. 10, fos 130v,
419.]

Priest: before November 1366. Formerly: R. of Silverton (Dev), 1366–8; Canon of Salisbury and Prebendary of Preston, 1367; R. of Ludgershall (Bk), February–November 1368.
Royal writs issued against JW as R. of Fillingham in 1369–70, concerning tithes alleged
to be payable to the alien priory of Willoughton while it was in the king's hands during
the French war. Assessed for poll-tax in 1377 and 1381. Afterwards: R. of Riseholme,

1395–1402. [*Reg. Sudbury* ii. 153; *Le Neve Fasti: Salisbury 1300–1541*, 77; Reg. 10, fo.415; *Buckingham Writs*, nos 88, 97, 120; *Clerical Poll-Taxes*, nos 811, 2164, 2171; Reg. 13, fo.181v.]

M. Thomas Tyrwhit priest
Instituted 31 July 1395 to church of Fillingham, on resignation of John Wythornwyk (by exchange with church of Riseholme). Patron: Master and Scholars of Balliol Hall, Oxford. [Reg. 11, fo.115v.]

Educated: Balliol Hall Oxford (MA by 1371; BTh by 1386). Formerly: R. of Riseholme, 1381–95. Died by January 1399. [Emden, *BRUO*, 1925.]

Thomas Barry priest
Instituted 22 January 1398/9 to church of Fillingham, on death of Thomas Tyrwhite. Patron: Master and Scholars of Balliol Hall, Oxford. [Reg. 13, fo.177v.]

Of York diocese. Educated: Balliol Hall Oxford (MA by 1390). Deacon: 26 February 1390 (London); priest: by 22 January 1398/9. A benefactor of his college. [Emden, *BRUO*, 120.]

Thomas Lovecok DD priest
Instituted 8 November 1431 to church of Fillingham, on death of M. Thomas Barre. Patron: Master and Scholars of Balliol Hall, Oxford. [Reg. 17, fo.16.]

Educated: Balliol Hall Oxford (MA by 1417; DD by 1431); Fellow by 1417. Deacon: 19 February 1418 (London); priest: 12 March 1418 (Salisbury). [Emden, *BRUO*, 1165–6.]

M. William Lambton
Instituted before 16 May 1448. [*CPL* x. 24.]

Educated: Balliol Hall Oxford (BA by 1443; MA by 1448). Formerly: Principal of Staple Hall Oxford, 1443. Fellow of Balliol by 1446. Papal dispensation to hold another benefice with Fillingham, 16 May 1448. Subdeacon: before 11 June 1448; priest: 21 March 1450 (Lincoln). Also: R. of Pyworthy (Dev), 1449–69; Master of Hospital of SS James and John, Aynho (Np), 1455–69. Afterwards: R. of Aynho, 1458–69; Master of Balliol College, 1458–69. [Emden, *BRUO*, 1088; *CPL* x. 38.]

M. Thomas Jakeson MA
Instituted 26 October 1458 to church of Fillingham, on resignation of M. William Lambton. Patron: Master and Fellows of Balliol College, Oxford. [Reg. 20, fo.160.]

Educated: Oxford University (MA by 1452): Principal of Staple Hall, 1453–8; Fellow of Balliol, by 1456. Deacon: 13 March 1456; priest: 27 March 1456 (Salisbury). Papal dispensation to hold another benefice with Fillingham, 15 September 1463. Also: V. of Abbotsley (Hu), 1463–5; R. of Friesthorpe, 1467. Died by June 1480. [Emden, *BRUO*, 1011–12.]

M. Thomas Brereton MA priest
Instituted 21 June 1480 to church of Fillingham, on death of M. Thomas Jakson. Patron: Master and Fellows of Balliol Hall or College, Oxford. [Reg. 21, fo.35v.]

M. John Smyth
Instituted before April 1490. [Reg. 22, fo.165v.]

Educated: Balliol College, Oxford (MA); Fellow in 1485. Borrowed copy of Robert Holcote, *Super Sapientiam*, from Merton College Library. [Emden, *BRUO*, 1717.]

M. William Lambton MA
Instituted 29 April 1490 to church of Fillingham, on death of M. John Smyth. Patron: Master and Fellows of Balliol College, Oxford (24 April 1490). [Reg. 22, fo.165v; PD 1490/21.]

Of Lincoln diocese. Educated: Balliol College, Oxford (MA); Fellow in 1486, still in 1490. Junior Proctor of University, 1492–3. Subdeacon: 6 March 1489/90; deacon: 27 March 1490 (Lincoln). [Emden, *BRUO*, 1087.]

M. Thomas Scisson BD
Instituted 29 July 1516 to church of Fillingham, on death of M. William Lambton. Patron: Master and Fellows of Balliol College, Oxford. [Reg. 25, fo.26.]

Educated: Balliol College, Oxford (MA; BD by 1512); Fellow, probably by May 1495, still in 1503; Bursar in 1501 and 1503; Master, 1511–18. Formerly: R. of Brattleby, 1514–15. Also: V. of St Margaret, Leicester, by 1526. Assessed at Fillingham for subsidy (£15 13s 4d) in 1526; for *Valor*, 1535. Owned copy of Augustine, *Expositio Psalterii* (*c*.1485), now in Bodleian Library. Died before 26 March 1543. [Emden, *BRUO*, 1703; Jones, *Balliol*, 286; *Subsidy*, 35; *Valor* iv. 133.]

M. George Cotes DD
Instituted 26 March 1543 to church of Fillingham, on death of last incumbent. Patron: Richard Salven clerk and John Cotes yeoman, by grant made to them for this turn by Master and Fellows of Balliol College, Oxford. [Reg. 27, fo.101.]

Of Leeds. Educated: Balliol College, Oxford (BA 1522; MA 1526; BD 1534; DD 1536); Fellow, 1523–7; Master, 1539–45; and Magdalen College, Oxford: Fellow 1527–39; Dean of Divinity, 1535, 1537–8. His appointment as Master of Balliol was opposed by Bishop Longland ('if [he] shulde obtaine itt, I reckon the colledge undone … the man is so wilful, headye parcyall and factyous …'). Acolyte: 23 December 1525 (York). Also: R. of Belton (Sf), 1535; of Ashmore (Do), 1539–48; V. of Godshill (IoW), 1540–55; Canon of Chester and Prebendary of 5th Prebend, 1544–54; R. of mediety of Cotgrave (Nt), 1544–55; R. of Tackley (Ox), 1549–55. Afterwards: Bishop of Chester, 1554–5. Died December 1555. [Emden, *BRUO 1501–1540*, 140; *York Clergy Ordinations 1520–1559*, 50; Jones, *Balliol*, 52–3, 286; *Le Neve Fasti: Chester 1541–1857*.]

M. William Wright
Instituted 1 February 1555/6 to church of Fillingham, on death of George, Bishop of Chester. Patron: Senior Fellow (M. John Smithe) and the other Fellows of Balliol College, Oxford. [Reg. 28, fo.156v.]

Of London diocese. Educated: Balliol College, Oxford (BA 1523; MA 1528; BD 1537; DD 1556); Fellow, 1527; Master, 1545–7 and 1555–9. Subdeacon: 23 December 1531;

deacon: 24 February 1531/2; priest: 16 March 1531/2 (London). Formerly: R. of Rise-holme, 1532–40; Canon of Lincoln and Prebendary of Crackpole St Mary, 1539–43; R. of Conington (Hu), 1539; V. of High Wycombe (Bk), 1540–56; Canon of Lincoln and Prebendary of Decem Librarum, 1543–52 and 1554–5. Chaplain to Bishop Longland, by 1544. [Emden, *BRUO 1501–1540*, 642; *Le Neve Fasti: Lincoln 1541–1857*, 58, 61.]

John Piers DD

Instituted 30 May 1570 to church of Fillingham, on deprivation of William Wrighte. Patron: Master and Fellows of Balliol College, Oxford. [Reg. 28, fo.37.]

Born *c*.1522/3 at South Hinksey (Brk). Educated: Magdalen College School and Magdalen College, Oxford (demy 1542; BA 1545; MA 1549; BD 1558; DD 1566); Fellow, 1545–59. Formerly: R. of Quainton (Bk), 1558–67. Also: Dean of Chester, 1567–72; Master of Balliol, 1570–1; Dean of Christ Church, Oxford, 1571–6. Afterwards: Dean of Salisbury, 1572–7; Bishop of Rochester, 1576–7; of Salisbury, 1577–89; Archbishop of York, 1589–94. Died 28 September 1594 at Bishopthorpe; buried in York Minster. [Claire Cross, 'Piers, John' in *ODNB*; Foster, *Alumni*; *Le Neve Fasti: Chester 1541–1857; Oxford 1541–1857; Salisbury 1541–1857*, 1, 6.]

Adam Squier MA

Instituted 24 April 1572 to church of Fillingham, on resignation of John Piers DD. Patron: Master (Adam Squier) and Fellows of Balliol College, Oxford (20 April 1572). [*Bishop Cooper*, 74.]

Educated: Balliol College, Oxford (BA 1560; MA 1564; BD 1575; DD 1576); Fellow, 1560; Master, 1571–80. Non-resident at Fillingham: 'dwells in the university of Oxford'. Also: V. of Cumnor (Brk), 1568; R. of Wollaton (Nt), 1571–6; of Winterbourne Earls (Wlt), 1571; of Drayton (Ox), 1576–7; Canon of St Paul's and Prebendary of Totenhall, 1577–88; Archdeacon of Middlesex, 1577–88; R. of Longworth (Brk), 1578; Canon of Lichfield and Prebendary of Colwich, 1587–8. Died by 26 October 1588. [Foster, *Alumni*; *Bishop Cooper*, 168; Train, *Central Notts Clergy* iii. 51; *Le Neve Fasti: St Paul's 1541–1857*, 11, 58; *Lichfield 1541–1857*, 27.]

M. Edmund Lilye DD

Instituted 18 August 1580 to church of Fillingham, on resignation of M. Adam Squier. Patron: Vice-Master (Robert Crane) and Scholars of Balliol College, Oxford. Reinstituted 7 August 1601; patron: Queen Elizabeth I (7 May 1601), by lapse. [*Bishop Cooper*, 78; Reg. 30, fo.160v; PD 1601/53.]

Born *c*.1544 at Saxilby. Educated: Magdalen College, Oxford (BA 1564, MA 1570, BD 1578, DD 1580): Fellow of Magdalen, 1563; Master of Balliol, 1580–1610. Priest: (Lichfield). Also: Archdeacon of Wiltshire, 1590–1610; V. of Highworth (Wlt), 1589–1610. Chaplain to Queen Elizabeth I but failed to secure further preferment because 'his long-winded Sermon displeased her'. Died 7 February 1609/10; buried (12 February 1609/10) in church of St Mary, Oxford. [Foster, *Alumni*; Jones, *Balliol*, 286; PD 1601/53; *Le Neve Fasti: Salisbury, 1541–1857*, 18; H. Savage, *Balliofergus* (1668), 115.]

Robert Abbot DD

Instituted 20 April 1610 to rectory of Fillingham, on death of Edmund Lillye.

Patron: Master (Robert Abbot) and Fellows of Balliol College, Oxford. [PD 1610/14.]

Born 1559/60 at Guildford; son of Maurice A., clothworker; brother of George A., later Archbishop of Canterbury. Educated: King Edward VI School, Guildford, and Balliol College, Oxford (matric. 1577; BA 1579; MA 1583; BD 1594; DD 1597); Fellow, 1581; Master, 1610–16. Formerly: R. of All Saints, Worcester, 1589–98. Also: R. of Bingham (Nt), 1598–1615; Chaplain to James I; Canon of Southwell and Prebendary of Normanton, 1610–15. Bishop of Salisbury, 1615–18. Died 2 March 1617/18 at Salisbury; buried in the Cathedral. [Julian Lock, 'Abbot, Robert' in *ODNB*; Foster, *Alumni*; Godfrey, *Notts Churches: Bingham*, 16–17; Jones, *Balliol*, 286, 289.]

James Forsyth
Instituted 16 January 1615/16. [Borthwick, Sub. Bk. 2, fo.40.]

Ralph Hollingworth BD
Instituted 21 January 1629/30 to rectory of Fillingham. Patron: King Charles I (19 January 1629/30), by lapse. [BC; PD 1630/55.]

Son of Ralph H. of Whetstone (Le). Educated: Merton College (BA 1614), Lincoln College (MA 1617) and Magdalen Hall, Oxford (BD 1635). Also: Canon of Lincoln and Prebendary of Gretton, 1660–1. Buried at Fillingham, 10 October 1661. [Nichols, *Leicestershire* iv. 166; Foster, *Alumni*; *Le Neve Fasti: Lincoln 1541–1857*, 69; BT Fillingham.]

Henry Savage DD
Instituted 28 February 1661/2 to rectory of Fillingham, on death of Ralph Hollingworth. Patron: Master and Scholars of Balliol College, Oxford. [Reg. 32, fo.16; PD 1661/99.]

Born *c*.1605; son of Francis S. of Eldersfield (Worcs), gent. Educated: Balliol College, Oxford (matric. 1625; BA 1625; MA 1630; BD 1637; DD 1651); Fellow, 1635; Master, 1651–72. Deacon: 19 February 1631/2 (Oxford); priest: 1 June 1634 (St David's). Under his Mastership the financial position of the College suffered; his successor wrote in 1676, 'had Dr Savage livd but a year longer the colledge gates has been shut up'. Non-resident at Fillingham, by dispensation; lived mostly in Oxford, apart from travels in France in the 1640s. Also: R. of Sherborne St John (Ha), 1647–72; R. of Riseholme, 1662–72; R. of Bladon (Ox), 1662–72; Canon of Gloucester, 1665–72; R. of Crowmarsh Gifford (Ox), 1670–2. Dispensed to hold Bladon with Fillingham (1662). Author: works on infant baptism; *The dew of Hermon which fell upon the hill of Sion* (1663); *Balliofergus* (1668), a history of his College. Died 2 June 1672 (aged 68); buried in Balliol College Chapel, 'next below the steps leading to the altar'. [Foster, *Alumni*; Wood, *Athenae* iii. 957; LC 5, fo.74v; John Jones, 'Savage, Henry' in *ODNB*; *CSPD Charles II 1661–1662*, 275.]

John Good DD
Instituted 9 November 1672 to rectory of Fillingham, on death of Henry Savage. Patron: Master, Fellows and Scholars of Balliol College, Oxford. [Reg. 33, fo.157v.]

Born *c*.1623; son of William G. of Oxford, gent. Educated: Balliol College, Oxford (matric. 1638; BA 1642; MA 1648–9; BD 1661); Fellow, 1645. Remained in residence at Balliol until his death; known as a 'scholastical retired and melancholy man'. Deacon and priest: 2 August 1660 (Oxford). Non-resident at Fillingham. Died 26 February 1675/6; buried in the College Chapel. [Foster, *Alumni*; Jones, *Balliol*, 107–8, 290; ORO, MS. Oxf. Dioc. Papers d.106, fo.1; Reg. 33, fo.157v.]

William Goode MA

Instituted 26 July 1676 to rectory of Fillingham, on death of John Goode. Patron: Master and Fellows of Balliol College, Oxford. [Reg. 34, fo.10v.]

Born *c*.1648; son of Richard G. of Oxford. Educated: Balliol College, Oxford (matric. 1661/2; BA 1665; MA 1667/8); Fellow, 1666. Priest: 13 October 1672 (Oxford). Also: R. of Brattleby, 1680–1. [Foster, *Alumni*; Jones, *Balliol*, 290; Reg. 34, fo.10v.]

John Venn MA

Instituted 26 January 1680/1 to rectory of Fillingham, on death of William Goode. Patron: Benjamin Cooper gent., for this turn (18 December 1680). [Reg. 34, fo.56v; PD 1680/26.]

Born *c*.1647; son of Simon V. of Lydeard St Lawrence (So). Educated: Balliol College, Oxford (matric. 1662; BA 1666; MA 1669; BD and DD 1685); Fellow, 1668; Master, 1678–87. Priest: 10 July 1670 (Oxford). Formerly: R. of Riseholme, 1672–80; V. of Yarnton (Ox), 1678–81. Also: R. of Brattleby, 1681–7. Died 8 October 1687 at Lydeard St Lawrence; buried there. [Foster, *Alumni*; Jones, *Balliol*, 129, 286, 290; ORO, MS. Oxf. Dioc. Papers d.106, fo.33v; Reg. 34, fo.56v.]

Thomas Norwood MA

Instituted 22 February 1687/8 to rectory of Fillingham, on death of John Venne. Patron: Master and Fellows of Balliol College, Oxford (3 January 1687/8). [Reg. 34, fo.103; PD 1688/13.]

Born *c*.1654; son of Francis N. of Leckhampton (Gl). Educated: Balliol College, Oxford (matric. 1669/70; BA 1673; MA 1676); Fellow, 1676. Deacon and priest: 29 January 1675/6 (Canterbury). Also: R. of Brattleby, 1688–97. Resigned Fillingham and Brattleby 30 January 1696/7. Afterwards: R. of Leckhampton (Gl), 1707–34. Died 15 August 1734. [Foster, *Alumni*; Jones, *Balliol*, 290; Reg. 34, fo.103; RES 1697/1.]

Adam Lugg MA

Instituted 16 February 1696/7 to rectory of Fillingham, on resignation of Thomas Norwood. Patron: Master and Fellows of Balliol College, Oxford. [Reg. 35, fo.38v.]

Born *c*.1664; son of James L. of Tiverton (Dev). Educated: Balliol College, Oxford (matric. 1680; BA 1684; MA 1687); Fellow, 1686. Deacon: 18 December 1687 (Sodor & Man); priest: 29 December 1689 (Bristol). Resident: signed BTs 1700–20. Also: R. of Brattleby, 1697–1722. Buried at Fillingham, 20 September 1722. [Foster, *Alumni*; Jones, *Balliol*, 290; CCED; LC 14, p.231; *Speculum*, 157; BTs Fillingham.]

Joseph Hunt DD

Instituted 1 January 1722/3 to rectory of Fillingham, on death of Adam Lugg. Patron: Master and Scholars of Balliol College, Oxford. [Reg. 37, p.184.]

Born c.1681; son of Stephen H. of Kingsclere (Ha), gent. Educated: Balliol College, Oxford (matric. 1696/7; BA 1700; MA 1703; BD 1718; DD 1721); Fellow, 1700; Master, 1722–6. Deacon: 11 June 1704; priest: 4 March 1704/5 (Oxford). Formerly: V. of Nether Stowey (So), 1716–22. Died May 1726; buried at King's Sutton (Np). Will dated 16 May 1726 (PCC). [Foster, *Alumni*; Jones, *Balliol*, 287, 290; ORO, MS. Oxf. Dioc. Papers c.266, fos 7v, 8v; *Somerset Incumbents*, 449; PROB 11/609/110.]

Charles Reynolds MA

Instituted 16 September 1726 by collation to rectory of Fillingham, on death of [Joseph] Hunt. Patron: Bishop of Lincoln, by lapse. [Reg. 38, p.139.]

Baptised 27 May 1702 in Peterborough Cathedral; son of Richard R., Dean of Peterborough. Educated: Trinity Hall (matric. 1720; BA 1723–4) and Jesus College, Cambridge (MA 1727; DD 1740); Fellow of Jesus, 1723–7. Deacon: 17 October 1725; priest: 5 June 1726 (Lincoln). Also: Chancellor of Lincoln, 1728–66; Canon of Lincoln and Prebendary of Liddington (1727–8) and of Gretton (1737–66); R. of Spridlington, 1737–66; V. of Gretton (Np), 1737–42. Died 5 October 1766. [Venn, *Alumni*; Reg. 38, pp. 60, 128; *Le Neve Fasti: Lincoln, 1541–1857*, 27, 70, 88, 141.]

Theophilus Leigh DD

Instituted 28 October 1766 to rectory of Fillingham, on death of Dr Charles Reynolds. Patron: Master and Fellows of Balliol College, Oxford. [Reg. 39, p.59.]

Born c.1694; son of Theophilus L. of Adlestrop (Gl), esquire. Educated: Trinity College (matric. 1709), Corpus Christi College (BA 1713; MA 1716) and Balliol College, Oxford (BD 1727; DD 1727). Master of Balliol, 1726–85. Deacon: 23 December 1716 (Oxford); priest: 29 December 1717 (Rochester). Formerly: R. of Broadwell (Gl), 1718. Resigned Fillingham 15 May (accepted 16 May) 1767. Afterwards: R. of Huntspill (So), 1767–78. Died in College, 3 January 1785; buried at Adlestrop, 10 January 1785. Will (PCC). [Foster, *Alumni*; ORO, MS. Oxf. Dioc. Papers c.266, fo.35v; CCED; PR Fillingham; RES 238/119; Jones, *Balliol*, 155–73, 287.]

John Darch BD

Instituted 21 May 1767 to rectory of Fillingham, on resignation of Dr Theophilus Leigh. Patron: Master and Scholars of Balliol College, Oxford. [Reg. 39, p.75.]

Born c.1724; son of Thomas D. of Luxborough (So). Educated: Balliol College, Oxford (matric. 1741; BA 1745; MA 1748; BD 1756); Fellow, 1745. Deacon: 25 September 1748; priest: 24 September 1749 (Oxford). Formerly: V. of Abbotsley (Hu), 1752–5; V. of Long Benton (Nb), 1754–67. Resided at Fillingham. Died 17 November 1768. Will dated 12 September 1763 (codicil 3 November 1764); proved 8 December 1768. [Foster, *Alumni*; Jones, *Balliol*, 291; ORO, MS. Oxf. Dioc. Papers b.21, fos 29, 31; Reg. 38, pp. 514, 534; LC 31, fo.197v; Musgrave ii. 141; *GM* 38 (1768), 543; Stow Wills 1766–71/99.]

John Coxe MA

Instituted 8 March 1769 to rectory of Fillingham, on death of John Darch. Patron: Master and Scholars of Balliol College, Oxford. [Reg. 39, p.111.]

Born c.1729; son of Charles C. of Cirencester (Gl). Educated: Balliol College, Oxford (matric. 1747; BA 1751; MA 1754); Fellow, 1752. Deacon: 23 February 1754; priest: 14

March 1756 (Oxford). [Foster, *Alumni*; Jones, *Balliol*, 291; ORO, MS. Oxf. Dioc. Papers b.21, fos 42, 43v.]

John Davey MA

Instituted 11 December 1770 to rectory of Fillingham, on death of John Coxe. Patron: Master and Scholars of Balliol College, Oxford (28 November 1770). [Reg. 39, p.144; PD 1770/6.]

Born *c*.1732; son of John D., of Tiverton (Dev), gent. Educated: Balliol College, Oxford (matric. 1749; BA 1753; MA 1757; BD 1784; DD 1785); Fellow, 1752. Deacon: 23 February 1754; priest: 14 March 1756 (Oxford). Also: R. of Brattleby, 1766–85. Afterwards: Master of Balliol, 1785–98 ('a painstaking, efficient administrator'); V. of Bledlow (Bk), 1775–98. Died 5 October 1798; buried at Bledlow. Will (PCC). [Foster, *Alumni*; Jones, *Balliol*, 176–7, 287, 291; Reg. 39, p.59; ORO, MS. Oxf. Dioc. Papers b.21, fos 42, 43v.]

Roger Watkins MA

Instituted 7 March 1772 to rectory of Fillingham, on resignation of John Davey. Patron: Master and Scholars of Balliol College, Oxford. [Reg. 39, p.172.]

Born *c*.1717; son of Roger W. of Kentchurch (He). Educated: Balliol College (matric. 1734/5), All Souls' College (BA 1738) and St Mary Hall, Oxford (MA 1741); Fellow of Balliol, 1754. Formerly: V. of Abbotsley (Hu), 1760–72. Resided at Fillingham: signed BTs 1774–80. Buried at Fillingham, 23 September 1781. [Foster, *Alumni*; Reg. 38, p.579; Jones, *Balliol*, 291; LC 31, fo.197v; BTs Fillingham.]

Richard Heighway MA

Instituted 10 January 1782 to rectory of Fillingham, on death of Roger Watkins. Patron: Master and Scholars of Balliol College, Oxford. [Reg. 39, p.373.]

Born *c*.1752; son of Richard H. of Ludlow (Sa), gent. Educated: Balliol College, Oxford (matric. 1766; BA 1770; MA 1773; BD 1796); Fellow, 1770; Nominal Proctor at Encaenia, July 1774 ('Mr Woodhouse a Gentleman Commoner of University College was very drunk at the Theatre and cascaded in the middle of the Theatre. Mr Highway one of the nominal Proctors for this Week desired him to withdraw very civilly'). Deacon: 29 May 1774; priest: 21 September 1776 (Hereford). Non-resident at Fillingham: ill-health (licensed 1804, 1806, 1810, 1812). Also: R. of North Thoresby, 1796–1802; C. of Myddle (Sa). Artist: *The Poultry Seller* (Victoria and Albert Museum) is attributed to him. Died 2 May 1817. Will (PCC). [Foster, *Alumni*; Jones, *Balliol*, 291; *Woodforde at Oxford*, 236; CCED; NRL 1804/27, 1806/77, 1810/43, 1812/43; PR Fillingham; PROB 11/1598/159.]

Matthew Hodge MA

Instituted 21 October 1817 to rectory of Fillingham, on death of Richard Heighway. Patron: Master and Scholars of Balliol College, Oxford. Reinstituted 27 January 1824, on his own cession; patron: as above. [Reg. 40, pp. 259, 336.]

Born *c*.1777; son of Matthew H., of North Petherton (So), clerk; nephew of Revd Dr Davey, Master of Balliol. Educated: Rugby School (1790) and Balliol College, Oxford (matric. 1795; BA 1799; MA 1804); Fellow, 1798–1818. Deacon: 21 September 1799 (Bath and Wells); priest: 20 December 1801 (Oxford). Resided at Fillingham Rectory. Licensed for non-residence (1838–46) on account of ill-health of himself and his wife, advanced years, death of his wife. Fillingham served by curates, including James Pearson and John Peacock. Also: V. of Ingham, 1823–52 (*q.v.*). Died 15 January 1852; buried at Fillingham. [*Rugby Register* i. 108; Foster, *Alumni*; CCED; ORO, MS. Oxf. Dioc. Papers b.21, fo.168v; Census Returns (1851); NRL 2/45; NRL 4/68; NRL 8/24; NRL 10/23; CR 2, p.194; CR 3, fo.65v; White, *Lincolnshire* (1842), 480; PR Fillingham.]

William James Jenkins MA

Instituted 14 April 1852 to rectory of Fillingham, on death of Matthew Hodge. Patron: Master and Scholars of Balliol College, Oxford. [Reg. 40, p.534.]

Born *c*.1821; son of John J. of Meerut, East Indies. Educated: Blundell's School (1831–7) and Balliol College, Oxford (matric. 1837; BA 1841; MA 1846). Fellow of Balliol, 1840–52. Formerly: C. of Ramsgate, 1846–52. Resided at Fillingham where he built a new Rectory House in 1853 (Thomas Calvert of Branston, builder). Also: Chaplain to Earl of Cardigan. Found guilty at Lindsey Petty Sessions of assault against one of his servants (1884). Charges of indecency heard before Bishop of Lincoln and sentence of suspension passed, May 1884. Subjected to 'rantanning' by villagers of Fillingham; an effigy, adorned with ritualistic vestments, was burned in a field adjoining the Rectory. Latterly of 1 Grove Villas, Muswell Hill (Mx). Died 9 July 1897. [Foster, *Alumni*; *Blundell's Register*; Foster, *Oxford Men*; MGA 354; White, *Lincolnshire* (1856), 212; Census Returns 1861; Ron Drury, 'A Fillingham centenary', *SLHA Newsletter* 43 (1985), 8–10; NRL 48/15; *Probate Calendar* 1897.]

William Wilton Smith MA

Instituted 25 November 1897 to rectory of Fillingham, on death of William James Jenkins. Patron: Master and Scholars of Balliol College, Oxford. [Reg. 42, p.423.]

Born 1835 at Bleasdale nr Garstang (La). Educated: Sedbergh School (1852–5) and Emmanuel College, Cambridge (matric. 1855; BA 1859; MA 1864). Deacon: 3 June 1860; priest: 26 May 1861 (Lincoln). Formerly: C. of Biscathorpe, 1860–2; C. of Kelstern, 1862–8; C. of Greatford, 1868–9; C. of Lavington, 1869–84; C. of Fillingham, 1884–97; R. of Fillingham, 1897–1914. Resided at Fillingham Rectory. Also: V. of Cammeringham, 1886–1914. Married (23 August 1866) at Biscathorpe, Louisa Jane, daughter of Revd Dionysius Prittie O'Connor (R. of Gayton-le-Wold with Biscathorpe). Latterly became senile. Died 17 September 1913; buried at Fillingham. [Venn, *Alumni*; *Sedbergh Register*; OR 1, pp. 150, 152a; *Louth and North Lincolnshire Advertiser*, 1 September 1866; *Hicks Diaries*, no.262; PR Fillingham; *Probate Calendar* 1913.]

Philip Druitt MA

Instituted 24 January 1914 to rectory of Fillingham, on death of William Wilton Smith. Patron: Master and Scholars of Balliol College, Oxford. [Reg. 43, pp. 61, 254.]

Born 4 October 1865 at Christchurch (Ha); son of James D., esquire. Educated: Westminster School (1878–84) and St Mary Hall (matric. 1884) and University College, Oxford (BA 1888; MA 1896); Leeds Clergy School (1891). Deacon: 1891; priest: 1892 (Ripon). Formerly: C. of Armley (YWR), 1891–1914. Resided at Fillingham Rectory. Resigned 21 January (accepted 26 January) 1922. Latterly of Wick Cottage, Carr Hill Lane, Sleights

(YNR); died there, 16 March 1928. [*Record of Old Westminsters* i. 286; Foster, *Oxford Men*, 175; *LDC* (1921), 52; *Crockford* (1927); RES 248g/12; *Probate Calendar* 1928.]

David Marshall Lang MA

Instituted 27 March 1922 to rectory of Fillingham, on resignation of Philip Druitt. Patron: Master and Scholars of Balliol College, Oxford. [Reg. 43, p.258.]

Born 9 July 1862 at 61 St Vincent Crescent, Glasgow; son of David L. Educated: Highgate School and Corpus Christi College, Cambridge (matric. 1881; BA 1884; MA 1888). Deacon: 1885 (Worcester); priest: 1886 (Rochester). Formerly: C. of St Matthias, Birmingham, 1885–6; of Kidbrooke (K), 1886–9; of St Mark, Reigate, 1889–90; Missioner (CMS) in Japan: at Kumamoto, 1890–2; at Osaka, 1892–4; at Hakodate, 1894–1920; Chaplain to Bishop of Hokkaido, 1910–20. Resided at Fillingham Rectory. Died 1 January 1946; buried at Fillingham (MI). [Venn, *Alumni*; *Crockford* (1932); Census Returns 1881.]

Leonard Walter Hicks Withers-Lancashire

Instituted 25 July 1946 to rectory of Fillingham, on death of David Marshall Lang. Patron: Master and Scholars of Balliol College, Oxford. [Reg. 44, p.56.]

Also: V. of Ingham with Cammeringham, 1948–54 (*q.v.*).

Ronald Palin Woods

Instituted 13 July 1954 to rectory of Fillingham, on cession of Leonard Walter Hicks Withers-Lancashire. Patron: Master and Scholars of Balliol College, Oxford. Note that on 5 July 1954, the Archbishop of Canterbury granted a dispensation enabling the said RPW to hold together the united benefice of Ingham with Cammeringham and the rectory of Fillingham. [Reg. 44, p.195.]

Also: V. of Ingham with Cammeringham, 1954–9 (*q.v.*).

Alun John Morris Virgin MA

Instituted 27 July 1960 to rectory of Fillingham, on resignation of Ronald Palin Woods. Patron: Master and Scholars of Balliol College, Oxford. Note that on 20 April 1960, the Archbishop of Canterbury granted a dispensation enabling the said AJMV to hold together the united benefice of Ingham with Cammeringham and the rectory of Fillingham. [Reg. 44, pp. 298–9.]

Also: V. of Ingham with Cammeringham, 1960–71 (*q.v.*).

FIRSBY

The church of Firsby was in the possession of the Foliot family before 1185, when a grant made to the Knights Templar by Jordan Foliot was recorded. This grant does not appear to have been effective, and by a final concord of 1214 the Master of the Templars remitted the advowson to Jordan Foliot in return for four shillings of rent. Members of the Foliot family continued to present to the living until 1349, after which Firsby was acquired by William de la Pole, whose son Michael, the future Earl of Suffolk, presented in 1367 and 1369. After Suffolk's attainder, the estate came into the hands successively of William Tynton and Robert Tyrwhitt. The church was vacant on account of its poverty for a long period in the fifteenth century. In 1447 William Tyrwhitt petitioned Bishop Alnwick for its union with Buslingthorpe, but this was not effected. The last institution took place in 1470, and by 1526 Firsby was described as a parochial chapel annexed to the vicarage of Ingham. [*Records of the Templars*, clx, 80; *Curia Regis Rolls* vii. 14; 'Foliot' in *GEC* v. 538–42; Crook, 'Jordan Castle'; *Change and Continuity*, 211; *Subsidy*, 36.]

John de Stangrave subdeacon
Instituted in the sixteenth pontifical year of Bishop Robert Grosseteste (17 June 1250/16 June 1251) to church of East Firsby. Patron: R[ichard] Foliot kt. [Hoskin, no.1305.]

Nicholas de Hedon subdeacon
Instituted 18 June 1272 to church of East Firsby, vacant because John de Staynegrave had become a knight and was married (*miles est et uxoratus*). Patron: Richard Folyot kt. [*Rot. Gravesend*, 93.]

Died before 20 March 1307/8 when the living was granted *in commendam* to Hugh de Normanton priest; patron Richard Foliot, lord of Firsby. [Reg. 2, fo.332v.]

Walter de Ingelby acolyte
Instituted 4 February 1308/9 to church of Firsby, on death of Nicholas de Hedon and lapse of commend to Hugh de Normanton. Patron: Richard Foliot. [Reg. 2, fo.92.]

Subdeacon by 18 April 1309. Dispensation for absence to study in England for 5 years, 18 April 1309. [Reg. 2, fo.315v.]

M. Walter de Atherby clerk
Instituted 7 August 1332 to church of Firsby, on death of Walter. Patron: Robert Foliot of Firsby. [*Reg. Burghersh* i. no.769.]

Walter de Kernetby priest

Instituted 29 April 1335 to church of Firsby, on death of M. Walter de
Adtherby. Patron: Robert Foliot. [*Reg. Burghersh* i. no.794.]

Licence to study at University of Oxford for 1 year, 4 June 1335; to study in England for
1 year, 30 October 1337. [Reg. 5, fos 195, 198.]

Robert Mawe de Hacthorn priest

Instituted 5 August 1349 to church of Firsby, on death of Walter. Patron:
Robert Foliot of Firsby. [Reg. 9, fo.158.]

[NB the Register gives the name of the church as Hackthorn (*Hacthorp' iuxta
Frisby*) but the entry clearly refers to Firsby. See also Hackthorn below.]

Afterwards: R. of Owmby, 1374–83 (*q.v.*).

William de Bourgh

Instituted 10 June 1367 to church of Firsby, on resignation of Robert Mawe
(by exchange with church of Saundby, dioc. York). Patron: Michael de la
Pole kt. [Reg. 10, fo.129v.]

Son of Eustace de Burgh iuxta Waynflete. Formerly: R. of Saundby (Nt), 1361–7 (licence
for non-residence for 1 year, April 1367). [Train, *North Notts Clergy*, 162.]

Nicholas de Sapirton priest

Instituted 16 April 1369 to church of Firsby, on resignation of William de
Burgh. Patron: Michael de la Pole kt. [Reg. 10, fo.131.]

Afterwards: Chaplain of William de Burton Chantry in Church of Burton-by-Lincoln,
1404.

Robert Kelsaye

Instituted 27 March 1404 to church of Firsby, on resignation of Nicholas de
Saperton (by exchange with chantry of M. William de Burton in church of
Burton-by-Lincoln). Patron: William Tynton *domicellus*, lord of Firsby. [Reg.
13, fo.164v.]

Formerly: Chaplain of William de Burton Chantry in Church of Burton-by-Lincoln, to
1404. Afterwards: Chaplain of Chantry of St Mary's Gild in Church of Newark (Nt),
1404. [*Reg. Scrope* i. 98.]

William Chester

Instituted 30 December 1404 to church of Firsby, on resignation of Robert
de Kelsay (by exchange with chaplaincy of chantry of Gild of St Mary in
church of Newark, dioc. York). Patron: William Tynton, lord of Firsby. [Reg.
13, fo.183v.]

Formerly: Chaplain of Chantry of St Mary's Gild in Church of Newark (Nt), to 1404.
[*Reg. Scrope* i. 98.]

John Bryce priest
Instituted 1 March 1404/5 to church of Firsby, on resignation of William
Chestre. Patron: William Tynton, as above. [Reg. 13, fo.184.]

Afterwards: Chaplain of St Giles Chantry in Church of Great Stretton (Le), 1413.

Robert Chaumberlayn (de Aslokby) priest
Instituted 27 February 1412/13 to church of Firsby, on resignation of John
Bryce (by exchange with chantry of St Giles, Great Stretton). Patron: William
Tynton of Firsby. [Reg. 14, fos 122v, 172.]

Priest: before 18 August 1408. Formerly: V. of Preston Deanery (Np), 1408–9; Chaplain
of St Giles Chantry in Church of Great Stretton, 1409–13. [Reg. 14, fos 158, 233.]

Thomas Jonson Almotson de Keleby
Instituted before 26 April 1417. [Reg. 14, fo.131.]

John Est chaplain
Instituted 26 April 1417 to church of Firsby, on resignation of Thomas Jonson
Almotson de Keleby. Patron: Robert Tirwhit. [Reg. 14, fo.131.]

Laurence Bertlot clerk
Instituted 1461 (day and month left blank) by collation to church of Firsby.
Patron: Bishop of Lincoln, by lapse. [Reg. 20, fo.160v.]

John Sharp priest
Instituted 2 December 1470 to church of Firsby, on death of Laurence
Bertlot. Patron: John Meidley and John Broughton, for this turn as feoffees
of William Tyrwhitt in the advowson of Firsby. [Reg. 20, fo.162.]

GLENTHAM

In the twelfth century the church of Glentham was divided into two medieties, one belonging to Sixhills Priory, the other being granted to Lincoln
Cathedral in the time of St Hugh by Gilbert son of Alfred of Glentham. The
Sixhills mediety was acquired before 1268 by the Chapter of Lincoln and
it was then appropriated to them and a vicarage ordained. The Dean and
Chapter still held the patronage in 1965. [*Reg. Ant*. iii. 361–3; iv. 11; *EEA* iv.
no.100; *Rot. Gravesend*, 93; LDC (1965), 108–9.]

Church

Geoffrey
Instituted before *c*.1190. [*Reg. Ant*. iv. 11–14.]

M. Richard de Radeclive
Instituted before 1235–6. [Hoskin, nos 540, 1222, 1312.]

William de Stok chaplain
Instituted in the first pontifical year of Bishop Robert Grosseteste (17 June 1235/16 June 1236) to a mediety of church of Glentham, formerly held by M. Richard de Radeclive. Patron: Master of the Order of Sempringham and Prior and Convent of Sixhills. Letters of institution issued 27 November 1236. [Hoskin, nos 540, 1222, 1312.]

Vicarage

Richard de Staunford chaplain
Instituted 25 December 1273 to vicarage of Glentham, newly ordained. Patron: Dean and Chapter of Lincoln. [*Rot. Gravesend*, 93.]
Involved in dispute over tithes with M. William, Rector of Caenby, 1292. [*Reg. Sutton* iv. 21.]

Bartholomew de Dunham chaplain
Instituted 1 November 1296 to vicarage of Glentham, on resignation of Richard de Staunford. Patron: Dean and Chapter of Lincoln. [*Reg. Sutton* viii. 28.]

John de Somerdeby priest
Instituted *c*.1328 (date not given) to vicarage of Glentham, on death of Bartholomew. Patron: Dean and Chapter of Lincoln. [*Reg. Burghersh* i. no.751.]
Appointed penitentiary in Glentham, 28 January 1338/9. [*Reg. Burghersh* iii. no.4752.]

Richard de Brunneby
Instituted 11 February 1339/40 to vicarage of Glentham (cause of vacancy not stated). Patron: Chapter of Lincoln. [*Reg. Burghersh* i. no.819.]

John atte Bek de Hospitali super Stratam priest
Instituted 1 July 1349 to vicarage of Glentham, on death of Richard. Patron: Chapter of Lincoln (Dean being absent). [Reg. 9, fo.155.]

John de Brantyngham priest
Instituted 30 July 1349 to vicarage of Glentham, on death of John. Patron: Chapter of Lincoln. [Reg. 9, fo.158.]

Simon de Ketilby priest
Instituted 1 December 1361 to vicarage of Glentham, on death of John [son

of] Sir John de Brantyngham. Patron: Subdean and Chapter of Lincoln (Dean being absent). [Reg. 9, fo.173.]

Afterwards: V. of Kirkby cum Osgodby, 1378–97. Died before 10 November 1397. [Reg. 11, fo.90v.]

Alan (Hakenaye) de Welton (iuxta Orby)

Instituted 1 April 1378 to vicarage of Glentham, on resignation of Simon Clerk de Ketilby (by exchange with vicarage of Kirkby cum Osgodby). Patron: Subdean and Chapter of Lincoln (the Dean being absent). [Reg. 10, fo.88v.]

Priest: before 15 April 1374. Formerly: R. of Dalderby, 1374–5; V. of Kirkby cum Osgodby, 1375–8. Also: R. of Caenby, to 1400 (*q.v.*); R. of Miningsby, 1400–2; R. of Hatton, 1402–13. [Reg. 10, fo.69v; Reg. 13, fo.144v; Reg. 14, fo.65v.]

John Duffeld priest

Instituted 16 June 1413 to vicarage of Glentham, on death of Alan Hakeney. Patron: Subdean and Chapter of Lincoln (the Dean being absent). [Reg. 14, fo.122v.]

John Pyrt chaplain

Instituted 7 August 1418 to vicarage of Glentham, on resignation of John Duffeld. Patron: President and Chapter of Lincoln (the Dean and Subdean being absent). [Reg. 14, fo.133.]

John Edirston

Instituted before 28 November 1418. [Reg. 14, fo.134.]

Thomas Igett of North Kelsey chaplain

Instituted 28 November 1418 to vicarage of Glentham, on resignation of John Edirston. Patron: President and Chapter of Lincoln (the Dean and Subdean being absent). [Reg. 14, fo.134.]

Will dated 8 February 1455/6. To be buried in churchyard of Glentham. [D & C A/2/35, fo.50.]

Richard Halton priest

Instituted 4 February 1455/6 to vicarage of Glentham, on resignation of Thomas Igett. Patron: President and Chapter of Lincoln (the Dean and Subdean being absent). [Reg. 20, fo.158.]

Thomas Barowgby priest

Instituted 26 May 1481 to vicarage of Glentham, on resignation of Richard Halton. Patron: Dean and Chapter of Lincoln. [Reg. 22, fo.162v.]

Thomas Clerk

Instituted 18 October 1486 to vicarage of Glentham, on resignation of Thomas Barowby. Patron: Dean and Chapter of Lincoln. [Reg. 22, fo.164v.]

Died before 14 April 1494 when administration of his goods was granted to Thomas Megott, V. of Bishop Norton, and William Tubbyng of Glentham. [D & C A/3/1, fo.93v.]

Robert Lownde priest

Instituted 24 April 1494 to vicarage of Glentham, on death of Thomas Clerke. Patron: Subdean and Chapter of Lincoln. [Reg. 22, fo.168.]

John Craven priest

Instituted 3 October 1503 to vicarage of Glentham, on resignation of Robert Lond. Patron: Dean and Chapter of Lincoln. Note that an annual pension of 10 shillings was reserved to the said Robert Lond for life from the fruits of the church. [Reg. 23, fo.80.]

Probate of his will granted 3 January 1507/8. [D & C A/3/3, fo.4v.]

William Lees chaplain

Instituted 27 October 1507 to vicarage of Glentham, on death of John Crawen. Patron: President and Chapter of Lincoln (the Dean and Subdean being absent). [Reg. 23, fo.158.]

Thomas Hawe chaplain

Instituted 11 May 1508 to vicarage of Glentham, on resignation of William Lees. Patron: Dean and Chapter of Lincoln (6 May 1508). [Reg. 23, fo.131; PD 1508/3.]

Assessed for subsidy (£5) in 1526. [*Subsidy*, 35.]

John Clarke chaplain

Instituted 28 February 1533/4 to vicarage of Glentham, on death of Thomas Hawe. Patron: Dean and Chapter of Lincoln (21 February 1533/4). [Reg. 27, fo.96; Cole, *Chapter Acts of Lincoln* i. 172.]

Robert Whelpdale

Instituted before 9 January 1561/2.

Witnessed wills, 1562–3. [D&C Wills 3/28; 3/30; 3/35.]

Richard Lamynge

Instituted 6 June 1564 to vicarage of Glentham. Patron: Dean and Chapter of Lincoln. Inducted the same day. [SUB 1, fo.21; D & C A/3/7, fo.36.]

Born *c*.1538. Education: 'understands Latin; but little versed in sacred learning'. Married. Also: R. of Caenby. Accused of non-residence (for which he claimed to need no dispensation, as Glentham was valued at only £7) during his dispute with Henry Cooke, fishmonger, over rights of common at Burton Stather, in the course of which blows were exchanged and Cooke was alleged to have called Lamynge 'a foole, a doltish fool & a knave, a doty-pole preest and a knave preest'. Witnessed wills 1566–7. [*Bishop Cooper*, 116, 167; D&C Wills 3/40; 3/53.]

Matthew Walker

Instituted 7 March 1579/80 to vicarage of Glentham, on resignation of last incumbent. Patron: Dean (William Wyckham) and Chapter of Lincoln. [*Bishop Cooper*, 78.]

Thomas Wye MA

Instituted 7 March 1628/9 to vicarage of Glentham, on death of Matthew Walker. Patron: Dean and Chapter of Lincoln (24 January 1628/9). [BC; PD 1629/56.]

Henry Wilce

Instituted by 1662. [LC 5, fo.80v.]

Deacon: 26 May 1616 (Lincoln); priest: 15 June 1617 (Peterborough). Signed BTs at Glentham 1663–76. [LC 5, fo.80v; BTs Glentham.]

Thomas Elford BA

Instituted 15 August 1677 to vicarage of Glentham, on death of Henry Wilce. Patron: Dean and Chapter of Lincoln (30 July 1677). [Reg. 34, fo.22; PD 1677/41.]

Born *c*.1647; son of Thomas E. of Acton (Mx), minister. Educated: Christ Church, Oxford (matric. 1667; BA 1671). Signed BTs at Glentham 1678–81. Also: Priest Vicar of Lincoln Cathedral, 1673–94; Canon of Lincoln and Prebendary of Decem Librarum, 1673–94. Afterwards: R. of Sudbrooke, 1681–94; V. of Thorpe-on-the-Hill, 1691. Died 1694. Will (D&C). [Foster, *Alumni*; BTs Glentham; Maddison, 'Lincoln Cathedral Choir 1640–1700', 45–6; *Le Neve Fasti: Lincoln 1541–1857*, 62; D&C Wills 26/28.]

Nathaniel Gibson MA

Instituted 12 August 1681 to vicarage of Glentham, on cession of Thomas Elford. Patron: Dean and Chapter of Lincoln (30 July 1681). [Reg. 34, fo.62; PD 1681/78.]

Educated: King's College, Cambridge (matric. 1672; BA 1675–6; MA 1679). Deacon: 23 July 1677; priest: 23 September 1677 (Peterborough). Non-resident at Glentham, which was served by Bryan Smith as curate. Also: Priest Vicar of Lincoln Cathedral, 1681–5; R. of Denton (Hu), 1682–9; Canon of Lincoln and Prebendary of Sanctae Crucis, 1683–1706; V. of Reepham, 1684. Afterwards: R. of Sawtry St Andrew (Hu), 1689–1706; buried there, 20 September 1706. [Venn, *Alumni*; Longden v. 219; Reg. 34, fo.62; BTs Glentham; Maddison, 'Lincoln Cathedral Choir 1640–1700', 49; *Le Neve Fasti: Lincoln 1541–1857*, 106.]

Dennis Pepper MA

Instituted 4 June 1688 to vicarage of Glentham (cause of vacancy not stated). Patron: King James II (31 May 1688), by lapse. [Reg. 34, fo.104v; PD 1688/30.]

Baptised 28 July 1652 at Barton-upon-Humber; son of Gilbert P. of Barton, clerk. Educated: York (private school) and Magdalene College, Cambridge (matric. 1667; BA 1670–1; MA 1674). Deacon: 25 September 1670 (York); priest: 8 May 1671 (Lincoln). Formerly: R. of Rothwell, 1671–84. Also: R. of Caenby, 1684–96; signed BTs there 1684–94. Resided at Glentham. Buried at Glentham, 9 April 1696; goods appraised for probate inventory, 17 April 1696. Will. [PR Barton-upon-Humber St Peter; Venn, *Alumni*; *York Ordinations 1662–1699*, 51; Reg. 34, fo.78; BTs Caenby; PR Glentham; INV 192/316; D&C Wills 16/21.]

Richard Cantrell BA

Instituted 6 June 1696 to vicarage of Glentham, on death of Dennis Pepper. Patron: Dean (Samuel Fuller DD) and Chapter of Lincoln (13 May 1696). [Reg. 35, fo.30v; PD 1696/34.]

Born October 1670; son of Thomas C. of London, gent. Educated: Merchant Taylors School and St John's College, Oxford (matric. 1688; BA 1692). Priest: 4 November 1694 (Lincoln). Also: Priest Vicar of Lincoln Cathedral, 1694–1712; R. of Sudbrooke, 1694–1712; Canon of Lincoln and Prebendary of Decem Librarum, 1694–1712. Afterwards: R. of Thorpe on the Hill, 1700–12. Died 23 March 1711/12; buried in Lincoln Cathedral, 25 March 1712. [Foster, *Alumni*; LC 14, p.235; Maddison, 'Lincoln Cathedral Choir 1700–1750', 218; *Le Neve Fasti; Lincoln 1541–1857*, 62; PR Lincoln St Margaret.]

Christopher Coulson BA

Instituted 7 August 1700 to vicarage of Glentham, on cession of Richard Cantrell. Patron: Dean and Chapter of Lincoln (5 August 1700). [Reg. 35, fo.68; PD 1700/32.]

Born c.1663 at Waddington; son of Edward C. Educated: Lincoln School and Magdalene College, Cambridge (matric. 1682; BA 1685–6). Deacon: 19 December 1686; priest: 22 May 1687 (Lincoln). Formerly: C. of Waddington, 1686; C. of South Hykeham, 1692–1701. Non-resident at Glentham, which was served by Thomas Cunington as curate. Died 26 February 1700/1. [Venn, *Alumni*; Reg. 34, fos 94v, 98; CCED; PR Glentham; PR South Hykeham.]

Thomas Cunington BA

Instituted 1 June 1702 to vicarage of Glentham, on death of Christopher Colson. Patron: Dean and Chapter of Lincoln (25 May 1702). [Reg. 35, fo.86v; PD 1702/23.]

Born c.1678 at Ely; son of Thomas C., blacksmith. Educated: Ely School; St John's College (matric. 1695) and King's College, Cambridge (BA 1698–9; MA 1702). Lay Clerk at King's, 1695. Deacon: 4 August 1700; priest: 30 May 1702 (Lincoln). Signed BTs 1705–34: 'Performs Divine Service on Sundays, at other times serves the Cathedral as Vicar Choral.' Also: Priest Vicar of Lincoln Cathedral (where he resided), 1700–34; Canon of Lincoln and Prebendary of Welton Westhall, 1714–34. Married (14 November 1705) at Welton-by-Lincoln, Jane Tournay. Took part in 1727 in defence of Minster Yard against Lincoln rioters enraged by chapter proposal to remove western spires of Cathedral; it was said that the mob formed a circle and forced him to dance to chants of 'High church or low, jump again, Cunington'. Buried at Glentham, 20 May 1734. [Venn, *Alumni*; Reg. 35, fos 67v, 86; BTs Glentham; *Speculum*, 160; Maddison, 'Lincoln Cathedral Choir 1700–1750', 214–21; *Le Neve Fasti; Lincoln 1541–1857*, 132; PR Welton-by-Lincoln; *Georgian Lincoln*, 39–41; *Lincolnshire Pedigrees*, 1004.]

Samuel Drake BA

Instituted 28 September 1734 to vicarage of Glentham, on death of Thomas Cunington. Patron: Dean and Chapter of Lincoln. [Reg. 38, p.292.]

Baptised 13 March 1696/7 at St Peter, Nottingham; son of Nathan D., Vicar of St Peter, Nottingham (1695–1705). Educated: All Souls' College (matric. 1714); Magdalen College (Chorister, 1714–19) and Magdalen Hall, Oxford (BA 1718). Deacon: 24 May 1719 (York); priest: 6 November 1725 (Lincoln). Signed BTs 1735–45. Also: Priest Vicar of Lincoln Cathedral (where he resided), 1725–46. Buried at St Margaret, Lincoln, 14 April 1746. [IGI; Foster, *Alumni*; Train, *Central Notts Clergy* ii. 45; *York Ordinations 1700–1749*, 20; Reg. 38, p.110; BTs Glentham; Maddison, 'Lincoln Cathedral Choir 1700–1750', 220–3; PR Lincoln St Margaret.]

Thomas Newcomen

Instituted 26 May 1746 to vicarage of Glentham, on death of Samuel Drake. Patron: Dean and Chapter of Lincoln (17 May 1746). [Reg. 38, p.466; PD 110/16.]

Born *c*.1721; son of Theophilus N. of the Close of Lincoln, gent. Educated: Lincoln School (Dr Goodall) and Trinity College, Cambridge (matric. 1738). Deacon: 20 September 1741; priest: 25 May 1746 (Lincoln). Formerly: C. of Fillingham, 1741. Non-resident at Glentham, which was served by John Dunn, Curate. Also: Senior Vicar of Lincoln Cathedral, 1746–9. Died 8 February 1748/9; buried in Lincoln Cathedral (MI). [*Lincolnshire Pedigrees*, 720; Venn, *Alumni*; Reg. 38, pp. 404, 465; Maddison, 'Lincoln Cathedral Choir 1700–1750', 221–2.]

John Austin MA

Instituted 18 May 1749 to vicarage of Glentham, on death of [Thomas] Newcomen. Patron: Dean and Chapter of Lincoln (26 April 1749). Reinstituted 30 August 1751; patron, as above. [Reg. 38, pp. 487, 503; PD 1749/9.]

Baptised 20 May 1712 at St Mary Magdalene, Lincoln; son of William A. Educated: Balliol College, Oxford (matric. 1732; BA 1736; MA 1739). Priest: 5 June 1737 (Oxford). Also: V. of Normanby, 1749; V. of Gosberton, 1751–8. Afterwards: R. of Thorpe on the Hill, 1757–8; Canon of Lincoln and Prebendary of Bedford Minor, 1757–8. Buried at St Mary Magdalene, Lincoln, 24 December 1758. [PR Lincoln St Mary Magdalene; Foster, *Alumni*; ORO, MS. Oxf. Dioc. Papers b.21, fo.1; *Le Neve Fasti: Lincoln, 1541–1857*, 39; CCED.]

Thomas Sympson BA

Instituted 13 April 1758 to vicarage of Glentham, on cession of John Austin. Patron: Dean and Chapter of Lincoln. Reinstituted 21 January 1766, on his own cession; patron, as above. [Reg. 38, p. 558; Reg. 39, p.51.]

Baptised 21 December 1726 at Lincoln St Michael on the Mount; son of Thomas S. of Lincoln. Educated: Lincoln School and Trinity College, Cambridge (matric. 1744; BA 1748–9). Deacon: 19 February 1748/9 (Ely); priest: 23 December 1750 (Lincoln). Formerly: C. of Papworth Everard (Ca), 1749. Resided in Lincoln; signed BTs at Glentham 1762–6. Also: Priest Vicar of Lincoln Cathedral, 1749–86; Canon of Lincoln and Prebendary of Bedford Minor, 1759–86; V. of Lincoln St Mary-le-Wigford, 1765–86; V. of Messingham with Bottesford, 1773–84; R. of Sudbrooke, 1784–6. Buried at Lincoln St

Peter in Eastgate, 22 March 1786. [PR Lincoln St Michael on the Mount; Venn, *Alumni*; BTs Glentham; *Le Neve Fasti: Lincoln, 1541–1857*, 39; PR Lincoln St Peter in Eastgate.]

Peter Moon

Instituted 11 November 1773 to vicarage of Glentham, on cession of Thomas Sympson. Patron: Dean and Chapter of Lincoln. Reinstituted 16 August 1781, on his own cession; patron, as above. [Reg. 39, pp. 215, 367.]

Literate. Deacon: 23 December 1764; priest: 20 September 1767 (Lincoln). Formerly: C. of Ramsey and Upwood (Hu), 1764; V. of Orston (Nt), 1772–3. Also: V. of Kirton Lindsey, 1769–88; Priest Vicar of Lincoln Cathedral, 1771–88; Canon of Lincoln and Prebendary of Crackpole St Mary, 1780–8; V. of Welton by Lincoln, 1781–8. Buried in the cloister of Lincoln Cathedral, 18 June 1788. [Reg. 39, pp. 38, 82; *Notts Churches: Bingham*, 328; *Le Neve Fasti: Lincoln, 1541–1857*, 59; PR Lincoln St Margaret in the Close.]

George Jepson

Instituted 11 November 1788 to vicarage of Glentham, on death of Peter Moon. Patron: Dean and Chapter of Lincoln. Reinstituted 2 June 1795, on his own cession; patron, as above. Reinstituted a second time 19 June 1806, on his own cession; patron, as above. [Reg. 39, pp. 486, 606; Reg. 40, p.106.]

Baptised 14 February 1753 at St Mary Magdalene, Lincoln; son of William J. Educated: Emmanuel College, Cambridge (matric. 1773; BA 1777; MA 1780). Deacon: 2 June 1776; priest: 24 February 1777 (Lincoln). Formerly: C. of Thorpe on the Hill, 1776; V. of Saxilby, 1778–88. Also: Priest Vicar of Lincoln Cathedral; Canon of Lincoln and Prebendary of St Botolph, 1781–1837; V. of Hainton, 1795–1831; V. of Ashby Puerorum, 1806–37. Died 21 April 1837 (aged 84). [PR Lincoln St Mary Magdalene; Venn, *Alumni*; Reg. 39, pp. 270, 286; *Le Neve Fasti: Lincoln 1541–1857*, 104; *GM* 161 (1837), 553.]

William Wilkinson

Instituted 27 December 1837 to vicarage of Glentham, on death of George Jepson. Patron: Dean and Chapter of Lincoln. [Reg. 40, p.455.]

Born *c*.1783. Formerly: C. of Glentham and Normanby, 1809–37; Schoolmaster at Glentham, by 1814; C. of Spridlington, 1814; C. of Caenby, 1815. Resided at Glentham; married there (9 December 1818) Caroline Robinson (she was buried at Glentham 26 July 1890, aged 91). Buried at Glentham 2 January 1842, aged 59. [Reg. 40, p.144; CR 1, pp. 13, 56, 356; Census Returns 1841; White, *Lincolnshire* (1842), 481; PR Glentham.]

Edward Sunderland

Instituted 24 January 1842 to vicarage of Glentham, on death of William Wilkinson. Patron: Dean and Chapter of Lincoln. [Reg. 40, p.482.]

Born 5 June 1792; son of John S., Curate of Kirkheaton (YWR). Literate. Deacon: 22 December 1816; priest: 3 August 1817 (York). Formerly: C. of Greasbrough (YWR), 1816; of Gainsborough, 1820; of Waddingham, 1823; of Luddington, 1825; of Messingham with Bottesford, 1831–40. Married at Leeds (25 January 1817), Diana Brook. Resident in Kirton Lindsey, 1841. Buried 2 June 1844 at Glentham. [*York Ordinations 1800–1849*, 177; CR 1, pp. 114, 217, 275; CR 2, p.20; WYAS, PR Leeds St Peter; Census Returns, 1841; PR Glentham.]

James Johnson

Instituted 29 July 1844 to vicarage of Glentham, on death of Edward Sunderland. Patron: Dean and Chapter of Lincoln. [Reg. 40, p.498.]

Baptised 12 April 1789 at Kirklinton (Cu); son of Anthony J. Deacon: 3 August 1817; priest: 21 June 1818 (York). Formerly: C. of Thorganby (YER), 1817; of Crowle, 1820–44. Also: V. of Normanby, 1844–58. Resided at Glentham (1851), subsequently at Normanby (1856). Buried 3 August 1858 at Glentham, aged 69. [*York Ordinations 1800–1849*, 108; CR 1, p. 113; Census Returns 1841, 1851; White, *Lincolnshire* (1842), 546; White, *Lincolnshire* (1856), 218; PR Glentham.]

John Fardell Bassett BA

Instituted 26 November 1858 to vicarage of Glentham, on death of James Johnson. Patron: Dean and Chapter of Lincoln. [Reg. 40, p.597.]

Born 24 March 1827; son of Henry B., Vicar of Glentworth (*q.v.*). Brother of Richard B., R. of North Thoresby (1852–92). Educated: Louth GS (1835–46) and Caius College, Cambridge (matric. 1846; BA 1850). Deacon: 22 December 1850; priest: 21 December 1851 (Lincoln). Formerly: C. of Willoughton, 1850–8. Also: V. of Normanby, 1858–94; RD of Aslacoe, 1883–94. Built new vicarage house at Glentham (architect: Michael Drury of Lincoln), 1861. Married (29 July 1862) at Aberystwyth, Anne Palmer, daughter of Revd C. Moffat of Minster Yard, Lincoln. Died 5 March 1894. [*Lincolnshire Pedigrees*, 107; Census Returns 1851; Goulding, *Miscellany*, 345; Venn, *Alumni*; OR 1, pp. 121, 125; MGA 422; *Lincolnshire Chronicle*, 1 August 1862; *LDC* (1895), 119; *Probate Calendar* 1894.]

Frederick Anthony Williams

Instituted 28 April 1894 to vicarage of Glentham, on death of John Fardell Bassett. Patron: Dean and Chapter of Lincoln. [Reg. 42, p.361.]

Also: R. of Caenby (*q.v.*).

The Vicarage of Glentham was united to the Rectory of Caenby by Order in Council dated 25 October 1922 to form the United Benefice of Caenby with Glentham. [Reg. 43, pp. 285–9.]

GLENTWORTH

The church of St Michael in Glentworth was granted to Newhouse Abbey by King Stephen in 1153–4. It was subsequently appropriated to the Abbey and a vicarage was ordained, consisting of the whole altarage and a vicarage house. Newhouse Abbey held the advowson until the Dissolution, after which it came into the hands of the Wray family of Glentworth, from whom it descended through the Saunderson family (Earls of Castleton) to the Earls of Scarbrough. The patronage was still in the hands of the Earl in 1965. [*Regesta* iii. no.606; *EEA* i. nos 178–9; *Rot. Welles* i. 200; *LDC* (1965), 108–9.]

Richard
Instituted in the first pontifical year of Bishop Robert Grosseteste (17 June 1235/16 June 1236) to vicarage of Glentworth. Patron: Abbot and Convent of Newhouse. [Hoskin, no.1219.]

William de Thirneby chaplain
Instituted in the thirteenth pontifical year of Bishop Robert Grosseteste (17 June 1247/16 June 1248) to vicarage of Glentworth. Patron: Abbot and Convent of Newhouse. [Hoskin, no.1289.]

Peter de Huntingdon chaplain
Instituted 5 December 1283 to vicarage of Glentworth, on death of William. Patron: Abbot and Convent of Newhouse. [*Reg. Sutton* viii. 5.]

Robert de Cava chaplain
Instituted 29 January 1309/10 to vicarage of Glentworth, on death of Peter de Huntingdon. Patron: Abbot and Convent of Newhouse. [Reg. 2, fo.92v.]

Robert de Kyngeston deacon
Instituted 14 November 1324 to vicarage of Glentworth, on death of Robert de Cave. Patron: Abbot and Convent of Newhouse. [*Reg. Burghersh* i. nos 114, 733.]

Robert de Wyk
Instituted before 5 July 1348. [Reg. 9, fo.154.]

Richard son of Gilbert Wright de Haltone super Humbre
Admitted 5 July 1348 to vicarage of Glentworth by collation following papal provision, on death of Robert de Wyk. [Reg. 9, fo.154.]

Thomas Peronell
Instituted before 8 August 1357. [Reg. 9, fo.169.]
Afterwards: R. of a mediety of Hackthorn, 1357–70 (*q.v.*).

Thomas de Houton priest
Instituted 8 August 1357 to vicarage of Glentworth, on resignation of Thomas Peronell (by exchange with a mediety of church of Hackthorn). Patron: Abbot and Convent of Newhouse. [Reg. 9, fo.169.]
Formerly: R. of a mediety of Hackthorn, 1349–57 (*q.v.*).

Thomas Rider
Instituted before 16 September 1369. [Reg. 10, fo.132.]
Afterwards: Vicar Choral of York Minster, 1369.

John de Oustewyk
Instituted 16 September 1369 to vicarage of Glentworth, on resignation of Thomas Rider (by exchange with vicar-choralship in York Minster). [Reg. 10, fo.132.]
Formerly: Vicar Choral of York Minster, to 1369. Assessed for poll-tax, 1381. [*Clerical Poll-Taxes*, no.2165.]

John Forman
Instituted before 22 December 1384. [Reg. 10, fo.152v.]

Adam de Media Rasyn priest
Instituted 22 December 1384 to vicarage of Glentworth, on death of John Forman. Patron: Abbot and Convent of Newhouse. [Reg. 10, fo.152v.]

Robert Cowper
Instituted before 10 December 1473. [Reg. 21, fo.32v.]

Edmund Moseley priest
Instituted 10 December 1473 to vicarage of Glentworth, on death of Robert Cowper. Patron: Abbot and Convent of Newhouse. [Reg. 21, fo.32v.]

Richard Grene priest
Instituted 20 October 1475 to vicarage of Glentworth (cause of vacancy not stated). Patron: Abbot and Convent of Newhouse. [Reg. 21, fo.33v.]

Roger Smyth
Instituted before 17 May 1485. [Reg. 22, fo.164.]
Afterwards: R. of Aisthorpe, 1485. [Foster, *Aisthorpe*, 121.]

Richard Tone
Instituted 17 May 1485 to vicarage of Glentworth, on resignation of Roger Smyth (by exchange with church of Aisthorpe). Patron: Abbot and Convent of Newhouse. [Reg. 22, fo.164.]
Formerly: R. of Aisthorpe, 1476–85. [Foster, *Aisthorpe*, 121.]

John Dyghton deacon
Instituted 5 June 1512 to vicarage of Glentworth (cause of vacancy not stated). Patron: Robert Trowyth, by grant of advowson made to him by Abbot and Convent of Newhouse. [Reg. 23, fo.144.]

Thomas Bowland chaplain
Instituted 16 June 1514 to vicarage of Glentworth, on death of John Dighton. Patron: Abbot and Convent of Newhouse. [Reg. 25, fo.1.]

Thomas Hawe chaplain
Instituted 3 April 1518 to vicarage of Glentworth, on death of Thomas
Bowland. Patron: Abbot and Convent of Newhouse. [Reg. 25, fo.26v.]

Also: V. of Glentham, 1508–34 (*q.v.*). Assessed for subsidy (£4 18s 4d) in 1526. [*Subsidy*, 35.]

Richard Tathewell chaplain
Instituted 28 February 1533/4 to vicarage of Glentworth, on death of Thomas
Hawe. Patron: Robert Brokelsbe yeoman, by grant made to him for this turn
by Abbot and Convent of Newhouse. [Reg. 27, fo.95v.]

Thomas Hopkynson chaplain
Instituted 13 July 1542 to vicarage of Glentworth, on death of Richard
Tathewell. Patron: Robert Dighton gent., by grant made to him for this turn
by the late Abbot and Convent of the dissolved monastery of St Martial,
Newhouse. [Reg. 27, fo.101.]

Witnessed wills, 1545, 1553. Exhibited at visitation, 1551. [Stow Wills 1530–52/267;
1553–67/147v; Vj 13, fo.58. For the dedication of Newhouse Abbey to St Martial of
Limoges, see Colvin, *White Canons*, 51.]

Robert Chapman
Instituted before 26 March 1554.

Witnessed wills, 1554–7. [LCC Wills 1557/ii/46, 52, 61–2, 122.]

The vicarage of Glentworth was said to be vacant in 1576. [*Bishop Cooper*, 168.]

Robert Catline
Instituted 10 September 1594 to vicarage of Glentworth. Patron: William
Wraye esquire. [BC; IND/S 1.]

Robert Atkinson
Instituted 11 November 1600 to vicarage of Glentworth, on resignation of
Robert Catlin. Patron: Sir William Wraye kt (27 October 1600). [PD 1600/19;
LC 4, fo.10.]

Deacon and priest: 20 March 1585/6 (Peterborough). Signed BTs, 1601–22, 1625. Nonconformist: objected to wearing the surplice and using the sign of the cross in baptism.
Resigned 1626. [LC 4, fo.10; *State of the Church*, civ; PD 1626/26.]

William Stevenson MA
Instituted 10 September 1626 to vicarage of Glentworth, on resignation of
Robert Atkinson. Patron: Sir John Wray of Glentworth, Bt (9 September
1626). [BC; PD 1626/26.]

Buried at Glentworth, 11 April 1636 (his daughter Frances was baptised the same day). [PR Glentworth.]

John Ashburne MA
Instituted 11 September 1636 to vicarage of Glentworth, on death of William Stephenson. Patron: Sir John Wray of Glentworth, Bt. (8 July 1636). [PD 1636/28.]

His sons John (19 October 1637) and Samuel (3 March 1639/40) and his daughter Deborah (12 January 1641/2) were baptised at Glentworth; Deborah was buried there 10 October 1642. Afterwards: R. of Norton by Woolpit (Sf), 1646. [PR Glentworth; Swaby, 14.]

--- Aires
Instituted before 29 October 1663. Ejected. [*Calamy Revised,* 4.]

Oswald Rumney
Instituted 29 October 1663 to vicarage of Glentworth, on death of last incumbent. Patron: Sir John Wray Bt (2 September 1663). [Reg. 33, fo.19v; PD 1663/81.]

Deacon and priest (Carlisle). Also: C. of Hemswell, 1660–5. Buried at Glentworth, 24 February 1664/5. [LC 5, fos 82, 94v; BTs Hemswell; PR Glentworth.]

Robert Janney
Instituted 31 August 1665 to vicarage of Glentworth, on death of Oswald Rumney. Patron: Anthony Thorold and John Cooper (28 August 1665). [Reg. 33, fo.48; PD 1665/43.]

Born *c.*1638 at Timperley in Bowdon (Chs); son of Robert J., Vicar of Bowdon. Educated: Dronfield School (Db) and St John's College, Cambridge (matric. 1656). Deacon: 10 March 1660/1; priest: 13 March 1660/1 (Lincoln). Also: V. of Honington, 1662. Signed BTs at Glentworth 1666–83. Afterwards: PC of Shotwick (Chs), 1697–1701; V. of Woodchurch, 1704–5; PC of Overchurch, 1705–16. Died 10 October 1719. [*St John's Admissions* i. 128; Venn, *Alumni*; Reg. 32, fo.7; BTs Glentworth.]

Anthony Smith BA
Instituted 14 August 1686 to vicarage of Glentworth, on resignation of Robert Janny. Patron: Nicholas Saunderson esquire. [LPL, Sancroft Reg. 2, fo.294.]

Born 10 April (baptised 18 April) 1657; son of Anthony S. of Theddlethorpe (Lincs), gent. Educated: Charterhouse School; St John's (matric. 1673) and St Catharine's College, Cambridge (BA 1676–7; MA 1692). Deacon: 16 March 1678/9; priest: 7 March 1679/80 (Lincoln). Formerly: C. of Fulletby, 1679; C. of Glentworth, 1684–6. Also: R. of Laceby, 1681–96. Signed BTs at Glentworth 1687–95. Afterwards: V. of Gainsborough, 1696–1719; Canon of Lincoln and Prebendary of Corringham, 1696–1719. Buried at Gainsborough, 22 April 1719. [PR Theddlethorpe All Saints; *St John's Admissions* ii. 46; Venn, *Alumni*; Reg. 34, fos 33v, 46v; BTs Glentworth; *Le Neve Fasti: Lincoln, 1541–1857,* 57; PR Gainsborough All Saints.]

William Bassett BA
Instituted 7 May 1696 to vicarage of Glentworth, on cession of Anthony

Smith. Patron: Elizabeth Saunderson widow (27 April 1696). [Reg. 35, fo.29v; PD 1696/28.]

Of Yorkshire. Educated: Jesus College, Cambridge (matric. 1682; BA 1685–6). Priest: 21 December 1689 (York). Formerly: C. of Arksey (YWR), 1689. Also: PC of Harpswell, 1696; R. of Toft-by-Newton, 1719–29. Signed BTs at Glentworth 1697–1728. Died 10 May 1729 (aged 66); buried at Glentworth same day. [Venn, *Alumni*; *York Ordinations 1662–1699*, 4; LC 14, p.231b; *Lincolnshire Pedigrees*, 106; BTs Glentworth.]

William Bassett

Instituted 22 September 1729 to vicarage of Glentworth, on death of William Bassett. Patron: Sir Thomas Saunderson of Glentworth, kt. [Reg. 38, p.212.]

Born 7 June, baptised 11 June 1703 at Glentworth; son of William B., above. Brother of Ralph B., Vicar of Corringham (1724–40). Father of George B. and John B., Vicars of Glentworth (below). Educated: Magdalene College, Cambridge (matric. 1723; BA 1726–7). Deacon: 5 June 1726; priest: 21 September 1729 (Lincoln). Formerly: C. of Toft-by-Newton (of which his father was Rector), 1726. Signed BTs at Glentworth 1730–63. Also: Archdeacon of Stow, 1751–65; R. of Waddingham, 1754–65. Married (19 February 1729/30) Elizabeth, daughter of George Whichcote of Harpswell. Buried at Glentworth, 13 July 1765. [*Lincolnshire Pedigrees*, 107; PR Glentworth; Venn, *Alumni*; Reg. 38, pp. 127, 212; *Le Neve Fasti: Lincoln 1541–1857*, 23; BTs Glentworth.]

George Bassett

Instituted 21 September 1765 to vicarage of Glentworth, on death of William Bassett. Patron: Richard, Earl of Scarbrough. [Reg. 39, p.46.]

Born 27 September 1740; son of William B., Vicar of Glentworth, above. Brother of John B., Vicar of Glentworth (1788–93) and uncle of Henry B., Vicar of Glentworth (1802–52). Educated: Beverley School and Peterhouse, Cambridge (matric. 1761; LLB 1766). Deacon: 27 February 1763; priest: 1 November 1764 (Lincoln). Formerly: C. of Willoughton, 1763. Resided at Glentworth (1768, 1778); signed BTs 1767–77. Also: V. of Owersby, 1764–7; C. of Kirkby with Osgodby, 1765; R. of Toft-by-Newton, 1767–79; V. of Willoughton, 1768–93 (*q.v.*); V. of Gainsborough, 1779–91; Canon of Lincoln and Prebendary of Corringham, 1779–91; V. of Stainton-by-Langworth, 1788–97; V. of Wigtoft with Quadring, 1791–7. Reinstituted to Glentworth, 1793 (see below). Died 16 December 1796 at Bath (MI Glentworth). Will (PCC). [*Lincolnshire Pedigrees*, 107; Venn, *Alumni*; Reg. 39, pp. 15, 36; BTs Glentworth; *Le Neve Fasti: Lincoln 1541–1857*, 57; LC 31, fo.197v; *Monson*, 142; PROB 11/1284/17.]

John Bassett

Instituted 9 July 1788 to vicarage of Glentworth, on cession of George Bassett. Patron: George Augusta, Earl of Scarbrough. [Reg. 39, p.481.]

Also: V. of Willoughton (*q.v.*).

George Bassett LLB

Instituted again 17 April 1793 to vicarage of Glentworth, on resignation of John Bassett. Patron: George Augusta Lumley Sanderson, Earl of Scarbrough. [Reg. 39, p.574.]

John Hartley

Instituted 18 May 1797 to vicarage of Glentworth, on death of George Bassett. Patron: George Augusta, Earl of Scarbrough. [Reg. 39, p.633.]

Baptised 6 February 1763; son of William and Elizabeth H. of Dent, par. Sedbergh. Literate. Deacon: 20 December 1789 (St Asaph for York); priest: 10 October 1790 (York). Formerly: C. of Gamston (Nt), 1789. Also: C. of Corringham, 1793–1815; of Willoughton, 1792–1827. Afterwards: C. of Glentworth, 1814; of Stow in Lindsey, 1815–27; V. of Corringham, 1815–27. Resided at Gainsborough where he was school-master; buried there, 29 May 1827 (aged 64). [*York Ordinations 1750–1799*, 49; CCED; PR Corringham; PR Willoughton; CR 1, pp. 21, 42; PD 171/46; PR Gainsborough All Saints; Stow Admons/1821–29/75.]

Henry Bassett BA

Instituted 13 June 1802 to vicarage of Glentworth, on resignation of John Hartley. Patron: George Augusta, Earl of Scarbrough (12 June 1802). [Reg. 40, p.40; PD 158/28.]

Born 12 April 1778 at Glentworth; son of Richard B. Educated: Balliol College, Oxford (matric. 1797; BA 1801). Deacon: 31 May 1801; priest: 13 June 1802 (Lincoln). Formerly: C. of Saxby, 1801. Also: R. of North Thoresby, 1802–52; V. of Saxby, 1805–52. Resided at Glentworth; Archdeacon Stonehouse noted (1845) 'There is a good vicarage house'. Married at St Margaret, Lincoln (1 October 1811), Catherine, daughter of John Fardell, Deputy Registrar of Lincoln Diocese. Died 1 May, buried at Glentworth 6 May 1852. Will (PCC). [*Lincolnshire Pedigrees*, 107; Foster, *Alumni*; Reg. 40, pp. 24, 39; Census Returns 1841, 1851; White, *Lincolnshire* (1842), 482; *Stow Visitation*, 79; PR Glentworth; PROB 11/2154/87.]

Charles Ramsay Flint BCL

Instituted 13 May 1852 to vicarage of Glentworth, on death of Henry Bassett. Patron: John Savile Lumley Savile, Earl of Scarbrough. [Reg. 40, p.534.]

Born 13 September, baptised 30 November 1805 at St George, Hanover Square (Mx); son of Charles William F. Educated: Westminster School (adm. 1812); Addiscombe College (1821). Cadet, East India Company (Madras), 1821; Cornet, 4th Light Cavalry, 1823; Lieutenant, 1825; retired 1828. Peterhouse, Cambridge (matric. 1828; First Class in Civil Law, 1830–1). Deacon: 31 July 1831; priest: 4 August 1833 (York). Formerly: C. of Loversall (YWR), 1831; R. of Bilsthorpe (Nt), 1839–47 and PC of Wellow (Nt), 1841–7 (Patron of both: Earl of Scarbrough); V. of Scothern, 1850–2. Married (24 May 1842) Frances, daughter of Robert Hodgson Fowler, Minor Canon of Southwell and Vicar of Rolleston (Nt). Resident at Glentworth. Licence for temporary non-residence (1859–60), on account of ill-health; Glentworth served by John Park and Samuel Webb Thomas as curates. Died 13 October 1876 at Bath. [LMA, PR St George Hanover Square; *Record of Old Westminsters* i. 337; Venn, *Alumni*; *York Ordinations 1800–1849*, 69; Reg. 40, pp. 466, 469, 516; Train, *North Notts Clergy*, 11–12; White, *Lincolnshire* (1856), 214; NRL 23/6; CR 4, fos 76, 85; *Probate Calendar* 1877.]

John Sanderson MA

Instituted 24 November 1876 to vicarage of Glentworth, on death of Charles Ramsay Flint. Patron: Richard George Lumley, Earl of Scarbrough, of Sand-beck Park (Yorks). [Reg. 41, p.544.]

Born *c*.1842 at Sheffield; son of Charles S., steel manufacturer's clerk. Educated: Shrewsbury School (1858) and Jesus College, Cambridge (matric. 1861; BA 1865; MA 1871). Deacon: 1872; priest: 1873 (Winchester). Formerly: C. of Little Walsingham (Nf), 1872–3; V. of Hartley Wintney (Ha), 1873–6. Also: V. of Ingham, 1887–8. Resided at Glentworth Vicarage. Afterwards: R. of Winchfield (Ha), 1890–1907. Married (11 April 1871) Maria, daughter of Francis Beaufort Edgeworth of Edgeworthstown, co. Longford (Ireland), half-niece of Maria Edgeworth. Retired to Westbay, Bridport (Do). Died 12 October 1914 at Mornish, Summerlease Crescent, Bude (Co). [*Shrewsbury Register*, 122; Venn, *Alumni*; Census Returns 1851, 1881; *Crockford* (1911); Burke, *Landed Gentry of Ireland* (1899), 130; *Probate Calendar* 1914.]

John Edmund Bettison

Instituted 17 December 1890 to vicarage of Glentworth, on cession of John Sanderson. Patron: Aldred Frederick George Beresford, Earl of Scarbrough. [Reg. 42, p.324.]

Born *c*.1846 at Bridge (K); son of William George Bettison, fundholder. Educated: King's School Canterbury (1857); Chichester Theological College (1880). Deacon: 1880; priest: 1882 (Salisbury). Fomerly: C. of Berwick Bassett (Wlt), 1880–4; of St Michael, Beckton, 1884–5; Domestic Chaplain to Lord Lamington, 1885–90. Resided at Glentworth Vicarage. Resigned 10 November (accepted 11 November) 1908. Afterwards: R. of Jacobstow (Co). Died 27 April 1917 at Jacobstow Rectory near Bude (Co). [Census Returns 1851; *King's School Canterbury Register*; *Crockford* (1905, 1916); Bertie, *Scottish Episcopal Clergy*, 176; RES 248d/14; *Probate Calendar* 1918.]

Edward Wilcocks Raby MA

Instituted 4 January 1909 to vicarage of Glentworth, on resignation of John Edmund Bettison. Patron: Aldred Frederick George Beresford Lumley, Earl of Scarbrough, of Sandbeck Park, Rotherham. [Reg. 42, p.605.]

Baptised 22 February 1860 at St Stephen by Saltash (Co); son of Hugh Snell R., yeoman. Educated: St John's College, Cambridge (matric. 1880; BA 1884; MA 1895). Deacon: 1885; priest: 1887 (Ripon). Formerly: C. of St Matthew, Leeds, 1885–7; of St John, Chatham, 1887–90; of St Marylebone (Mx), 1890–1902; R. of Jacobstow (Co), 1902–9. Also: PC of Harpswell, 1912–30. Resided at Glentworth Vicarage. Latterly of 45 Balfour Road, Walmer (K). Died 18 June 1943 at Victoria Hospital, Deal. [Venn, *Alumni*; *Crockford* (1932); *LDC* (1914), 90; *Probate Calendar* 1943.]

Benjamin Peacocke

Instituted 27 June 1930 to vicarage of Glentworth, on resignation of Edward Wilcocks Raby. Patron: Aldred Frederick George Beresford, Earl of Scarbrough, of Sandbeck Hall, Rotherham (Yorks). [Reg. 43, p.468.]

Born *c*.1867 at Tillingham (Ess); son of Thomas P., bread and biscuit baker. Pupil teacher (1881); schoolmaster at Loves Green, par. Writtle (1891); Tollesbury (1901, 1902); Tillingham (1911); Heybridge (1917) (all Essex); Willoughby in the Marsh (1926). Deacon: 26 May 1929; priest: 15 June 1930 (Lincoln). Formerly: C. of Alkborough with Whitton, 1929–30. Resided at Glentworth Vicarage. Afterwards: V. of North Reston with South Reston and Castle Carlton, 1934–8; V. of Elsham, 1938–46. Latterly of Ravenstone, 40 George Street, Mablethorpe. Died 26 April 1948 at Holmecroft, Louth. [Census Returns 1871–1911; Kelly, *Essex* (1902, 1917); Kelly, *Lincolnshire* (1926); *LDM* (1929, 1930); *Crockford* (1932); *Probate Calendar* 1948.]

Percy Warwick Richardson
Instituted 8 May 1934 to vicarage of Glentworth, on cession of Benjamin Peacocke. Patron: Aldred Frederick George Beresford, Earl of Scarbrough, of Sandbeck Hall, Rotherham (Yorks). [Reg. 43, p.543.]

Baptised 21 April 1880 at Normanton (YWR); son of Richard Hepton R., railway agent. Educated: Emmanuel College, Saskatchewan. Deacon: 1910; priest: 1912 (Saskatchewan). Formerly: C. of Kitscoty, 1914–15; Inc. of King with Maple, 1915–17; of Tapleytown with Woodburn and Rymal, 1917–23; of Mount Forest, Riverton and Farewell, 1923–5; R. of Caledonia (Ontario), 1925–34; RD of Haldinand, 1929–34. Resided at Glentworth Vicarage. Also: PC of Hemswell with Harpswell, 1934–50 (*q.v.*). Resigned 27 September (accepted 30 September) 1950. Lived at 49 Skellingthorpe Road, Lincoln. Latterly of 3 Princess Royal Close, Lincoln. Died 6 February 1965. [WYAS, PR Normanton; *Crockford* (1951–2); RES 1950/14; *Probate Calendar* 1965.]

George Arthur Tyson
Instituted 8 February 1952 to vicarage of Glentworth, on resignation of Percy Warwick Richardson. Patron: Lawrence Roger, Earl of Scarbrough, of Sandbeck Park, Rotherham (YWR). Note that on 12 September 1951, the Archbishop of Canterbury granted a dispensation enabling the said GAT to hold together the vicarage of Glentworth and the united benefice of Hemswell with Harpswell. [Reg. 44, p.154.]

Born 13 March 1889. Educated: St Chad's College, Regina, Canada (1914). Deacon: 1917; priest: 1918 (Qu'Appelle). Formerly: C. of Pelly, 1917–18; Incumbent of Pelly, 1918–21; of Foam Lake, 1921–8; P-in-C of Brock, 1928–31; V. of Marton, 1931–8; R. of Hameringham with Scrafield and Winceby, 1938–43; V. of Deeping St Nicholas, 1943–6; R. of Mavis Enderby with Raithby, 1946–51. Also: V. of Hemswell with Harpswell, 1951–6. Afterwards: V. of Dunholme, 1956–9. Retired 1959. Lived at St Chad's, Great Coates Road, Healing; latterly at Manormead, Tilford Road, Hindhead (Sr). Died December 1982. [GRO, Death Index; *Crockford* (1971–2, 1980–2).]

Guy Colville Nicholson
Instituted 30 October 1956 to vicarage of Glentworth, on cession of George Arthur Tyson. Patron: Lawrence Roger, Earl of Scarbrough, as above. Note that on 21 September 1956, the Archbishop of Canterbury granted a dispensation enabling the said GCN to hold together the united benefice of Hemswell with Harpswell and the vicarage of Glentworth. [Reg. 44, p.232.]

Of New Zealand. Educated: University of New Zealand (BE 1945) and Oak Hill Theological College (1951). Deacon: 1953; priest: 1954 (Rochester). Formerly: C. of Christ Church, Beckenham, 1953–6. Also: V. of Hemswell with Harpswell, 1956–63; RD of Aslacoe, 1960–3. Resignation of Glentworth accepted 4 January 1963. Afterwards: V. of Ellerslie, 1963–71. Returned to New Zealand: licence to officiate, diocese of Auckland, 1971. [*Crockford* (1970–2); Reg. 44, p.342.]

Gordon Bottomley
Instituted 9 February 1963 to vicarage of Glentworth, on resignation of Guy Colville Nicholson. Patron: Lawrence Roger, Earl of Scarbrough, as above. Note that on 29 January 1963, the Archbishop of Canterbury granted

a dispensation enabling the said GB to hold together the united benefice of Hemswell with Harpswell and the vicarage of Glentworth. [Reg. 44, p.343.]

Born 1931. Educated: Oak Hill Theological College (1951). Deacon: 1955; priest: 1956 (Sarum). Formerly: C. of Kinson (Do), 1955–8; Northern Area Secretary, Bible Churchmen's Missionary Society, 1958–63. Resided at Glentworth Vicarage. Also: V. of Hemswell with Harpswell, 1963–72; Chaplain, RAF Hemswell, 1963–71. Afterwards: R. of Bucknall with Bagnall (St), 1972–82; P-in-C of Holy Trinity, Worthing, 1982–8; V. of Camelsdale (Sx), 1988–96. Retired 1996. Of Fareham (Ha). [*Crockford* (1969–70, 2010–11).]

HACKTHORN

One mediety of the church of Hackthorn was granted to Bullington Priory by William of Otringham in the reign of Henry II. This mediety was appropriated and a vicarage ordained. Bullington continued to present to this mediety until the late fourteenth century, although from 1277 they appear to have presented alternately with the rector of the other mediety. This second mediety was held by the Dene family. In 1313 William Dene conveyed it to Roger de Morwode who in turn conveyed it in 1321 to Simon de Herford. Shortly before 1390 the mediety was acquired by the Gilbertine Priory of St Katherine outside Lincoln, to whom it was appropriated in that year. Thereafter the two medieties were merged, the two priories presenting alternately. After the Dissolution the advowson remained with the Crown until it was acquired in the seventeenth century by the Saunderson family. Between 1660 and 1773 the living was under sequestration and no vicars were instituted. The Cracroft family, who rebuilt Hackthorn Hall adjacent to the church in 1792, became patrons of the living at that time. In 1965 the advowson was held by Sir Weston Cracroft-Amcotts. [*Danelaw Charters*, 21; *Rot. Welles* i. 200; FL, Feet of Fines, B.187, B.479; *Change and Continuity*, 106; *LDC* (1965), 108–9.]

Bullington Mediety

Alan parson of Hackthorn
Witnessed grants to Bullington Priory, late twelfth century. [*Danelaw Charters*, 24, 26–31.]

Robert son of Gilbert chaplain
Instituted in the twenty-second pontifical year of Bishop Hugh of Wells (20 December 1230/19 December 1231) to vicarage of mediety of Hackthorn. Patron: Prior and Convent of Bullington. [*Rot. Welles* i. 230.]

Henry
Instituted before 1232/3. [*Rot. Welles* i. 233–4.]

Robert de Wrageby chaplain
Instituted in the twenty-fourth pontifical year of Bishop Hugh of Wells (20 December 1232/19 December 1233) to vicarage of mediety of Hackthorn, formerly held by Henry. Patron: Prior and Convent of Bullington. Note that a mandate was issued to William, Archdeacon of Stow, to induct the said Robert, notwithstanding that the Bishop had granted the fruits of the said vicarage for a time (*ad tempus*) to Robert, parson of the other mediety. [*Rot. Welles* i. 233–4.]

Ralph de Salmonby chaplain
Instituted in the ninth pontifical year of Bishop Robert Grosseteste (17 June 1243–16 June 1244) to vicarage of [mediety of] Hackthorn. Patron: Prior and Convent of Bullington. [Hoskin, no.1263.]

Thomas
Instituted before 28 April 1277. [*Rot. Gravesend*, 96.]

John de Horkistowe priest
Instituted 28 April 1277 to vicarage of [mediety of] Hackthorn, on death of Thomas. Patron: Geoffrey, rector of a mediety of Hackthorn, for this turn. [*Rot. Gravesend*, 96.]

Richard de Houton subdeacon
Instituted 22 March 1298 to vicarage of [mediety of] Hackthorn, on death of John. Patron: Prior and Convent of Bullington. [*Reg. Sutton* viii. 29.]
Deacon: 22 March 1298; priest: 31 May 1298 (Lincoln). [*Reg. Sutton* vii. 105, 107.]

John
Instituted before 1 March 1337/8.
Licensed as penitentiary in deanery of Aslacoe, 1 March 1337/8. [*Reg. Burghersh* iii. no.4595.]

William Dupton priest
Instituted 29 October 1349 to vicarage of [mediety of] Hackthorn, on death of John. Patron: Prior and Convent of Bullington. [Reg. 9, fo.159v.]

William son of John de Lafford de Luda priest
Instituted 25 March 1352 to vicarage of [mediety of] Hackthorn, on resignation of William de Upton. Patron: Thomas son of Simon de Hawton de Filyngham. [Reg. 9, fo.163.]
[MS gives the year as 1351/2 in error.]

John de Hemyngby priest
Instituted 31 January 1354/5 to vicarage of [mediety of] Hackthorn, on resignation of William de Luda. Patron: Prior and Convent of Bullington. [Reg. 9, fo.167.]

John Ingram de Spridlyngton priest
Instituted 15 July 1361 to vicarage of [mediety of] Hackthorn, on resignation of John de Hemyngby. Patron: Thomas Peronell, rector of mediety of Hackthorn. [Reg. 9, fo.171v.]

Peter de Lyssyngton
Instituted by 1377. [*Clerical Poll-Taxes*, no.826.]
Afterwards: V. of Haugham, 1389–90; Chaplain of second chantry of Roger son of Benedict in church of St Peter in Eastgate, Lincoln, 1390. [Reg. 11, fo.45v.]

John South (de Beltesford) priest
Instituted 5 May 1389 to vicarage of Hackthorn, on resignation of Peter de Lyssyngton (by exchange with vicarage of Haugham). Patron: Alan, Rector of Hackthorn. [Reg. 11, fos 39, 102.]
Formerly: V. of Haugham, 1383–9.

Dene Mediety

M. Reginald de Bathon
Instituted in the seventeenth pontifical year of Bishop Hugh of Wells (20 December 1225/19 December 1226) to a mediety of church of Hackthorn, saving to Robert son of Gilbert a perpetual vicarage in the same). Patron: William son of Gilbert. [*Rot. Welles* i. 224.]
Educated: University of Oxford (MA); gave the University a tenement in parish of St Edward, which became the School of Canon Law. [Emden, *BRUO*, 131.]

Robert son of Gilbert chaplain
Instituted in the eighteenth pontifical year of Bishop Hugh of Wells (20 December 1226/19 December 1227) to vicarage of a mediety of Hackthorn. Patron: M. Reginald de Bathon, rector of the said mediety. [*Rot. Welles* i. 225.]

Robert de Hakethorn chaplain
Instituted in the twenty-third pontifical year of Bishop Hugh of Wells (20 December 1231/19 December 1232) to a mediety of church of Hackthorn. Patron: Gilbert de Hakethorn. [*Rot. Welles* i. 233.]

Geoffrey of Norton
Instituted before 28 April 1277. [*Rot. Gravesend*, 96.]

Philip of Norton clerk in minor orders
Instituted 22 March 1287 to a mediety of church of Hackthorn, on death of Geoffrey of Norton. Patron: John de Dene. Reinstituted 21 May 1288 because he had not been ordained priest within a year of his institution; patron: John de Dene and Alice his wife. [*Reg. Sutton* viii. 9, 17.]
Described as under age in March 1287. Subdeacon: 22 March 1287 (Lincoln); deacon by 21 May 1288. [*Reg. Sutton* viii. 9, 17.]

Simon de Dene clerk in minor orders
Instituted 22 September 1291 to a mediety of church of Hackthorn, on death of Philip de Norton. Patron: John son of William de Dene. [Reg. 1, fo.247.]
Subdeacon: 22 September 1291; deacon: 20 September 1292; priest: 19 September 1293 (Lincoln). [*Reg. Sutton* vii. 18, 33, 44.]

John de Herford in Westrasen clerk
Instituted 14 June 1322 to a mediety of church of Hackthorn, on death of Simon de Deen. Patron: Simon de Herford. [*Reg. Burghersh* i. no.725.]
Afterwards: R. of West Rasen, by 16 January 1330/1. [*CPR 1330–34*, 40.]

Edmund
Instituted before 14 July 1349. [Reg. 9, fo.155.]

Thomas de Houton de Filyngham priest
Instituted 14 July 1349 to a mediety of church of Hackthorn, on death of Edmund. Patron: Simon de Herford of Hackthorn. [Reg. 9, fo.155.]
Afterwards: V. of Glentworth, 1357 (*q.v.*).

Thomas Peronell priest
Instituted 8 August 1357 to a mediety of church of Hackthorn, on resignation of Thomas de Houton (by exchange with vicarage of Glentworth). Patron: James de Herford of Hackthorn. [Reg. 9, fo.168v.]
Formerly: V. of Glentworth, to 1357. Afterwards: R. of Salmonby, 1370 (still incumbent there in 1377 when he resided in the cathedral close at Lincoln). Royal writs issued against TP as R. of Hackthorn in 1369–70, concerning tithes alleged to be payable to the alien priory of Willoughton while it was in the king's hands during the French war. It was returned that TP could not be found in Lincoln diocese, as 'he remains in London diocese'. He came to Stow Park in November 1370 and promised to pay the sum owing. [*Clerical Poll-Taxes*, no.3; *Buckingham Writs*, nos 92, 106, 121.]

Alan Benselyn (de Askeby) priest
Instituted 26 November 1370 to a mediety of church of Hackthorn, on resig-

nation of Thomas Peronell (by exchange with church of Salmonby). Patron: Isolde, widow of James de Herford of Hackthorn. [Reg. 10, fos 43v, 136.]

Priest: before 28 May 1365. Formerly: R. of Salmonby, 1365–70. [Reg. 10, fo.11.]

John Knote de Skeftelyng priest
Instituted 13 June 1376 to a mediety of church of Hackthorn, on death of Alan. Patron: James de Hoton. [Reg. 10, fo.143v.]

Licence to be absent for 3 years and to farm his benefice, 5 April 1377. [Reg. 12, fo.168.]

Alan Cothon priest
Instituted 22 July 1387 to a mediety of church of Hackthorn, on resignation of John Skeftlynge. Patron: John Grymesby kt. [Reg. 11, fo.30v.]

A mediety of the church of Hackthorn was appropriated to the Prior and Convent of St Katherine outside Lincoln, 15 June 1390. [Reg. 12, fo.371.]

Vicarage of Whole Church

William Hawkeswell priest
Instituted 29 March 1432 to vicarage of Hackthorn (cause of vacancy not stated). Patron: Prior and Convent of Bullington. [Reg. 17, fo.16.]

Richard Waynflete Abbot of Kirkstead
Instituted 23 August 1462 to vicarage of Hackthorn (cause of vacancy not stated). Patron: Prior and Convent of Bullington. [Reg. 20, fo.161.]

Abbot of Kirkstead, c.1433/4–63. [*Heads* iii. 305.]

Br. John Staynfeld Canon of Priory of St Katherine outside Lincoln
Instituted 14 September 1465 to vicarage of Hackthorn, on renunciation and demission of br. Richard Waynflet. Patron: Prior and Convent of St Katherine outside Lincoln. [Reg. 20, fo.161v.]

John Mynting
Instituted before 26 April 1490. [Reg. 22, fo.165v.]

Richard Wytheryn
Instituted 26 April 1490 to vicarage of Hackthorn, on death of John Mynting. Patron: Prior and Convent of St Katherine outside Lincoln. [Reg. 22, fo.165v.]

Br. John Bradley Canon of Bullington Priory
Instituted 26 October 1500 to vicarage of Hackthorn, on resignation of Richard Wethern. Patron: Prior and Convent of Bullington. [Reg. 23, fo.151.]

Witnessed wills, 3 April 1507; 17 June 1523. Was said to keep a woman in his house (1519). [*Lincoln Wills* ii. 4–5, 11; *Diocesan Visitations* i. 94.]

John Gibson priest
Instituted 19 October 1524 to vicarage of Hackthorn, on death of John Bradley. Patron: Prior and Convent of St Katherine outside Lincoln. [Reg. 27, fo.99.]

Assessed for subsidy (£4) in 1526. Witnessed wills, 12 August 1528; 2 March 1530/1. [*Subsidy*, 36; *Lincoln Wills* ii. 95; iii. 110.]

Thomas Boys (or Byggs) clerk
Instituted 10 November 1541 to vicarage of Hackthorn, on death of last incumbent. Patron: John Broxolme and John Bucke, by reason of a grant made to them for this turn by the late Prior and Convent of Bullington. [Reg. 27, fo.100v.]

Formerly: Canon of Bullington Priory; allotted pension of £2 in 1539. Died *c*.1559. Will dated 20 April 1559. [*Ex-Religious*, 80; Stow Wills 1553–67/261.]

The vicarage of Hackthorn was vacant in 1576. [*Bishop Cooper*, 165.]

Henry Nelson
Instituted 27 March 1579 to vicarage of Hackthorn, on death of last incumbent. Patron: Queen Elizabeth I, on the petition and recommendation of Mr Seyntpole. [*Bishop Cooper*, 77.]

Education: 'bred in the schools'. Priest: 17 August 1575 (Peterborough). Licensed preacher. Still Vicar in 1590. [*State of the Church*, 97, 155.]

George Dale BA
Instituted 8 June 1592 to vicarage of Hackthorn, on death of last incumbent. Patron: Queen Elizabeth I (6 June 1592). [BC; PD 1592/65.]

Born *c*.1569; of Lincolnshire. Educated: St John's College, Oxford (matric. 1585; BA 1588/9). Resigned 10 October 1597. [Foster, *Alumni*; *St John's Register*, 247; RES 1597/11.]

Christopher Feilden
Instituted 29 October 1597 to vicarage of Hackthorn, on resignation of last incumbent. Patron: Queen Elizabeth I (24 October 1597). [Reg. 30, fo.77; PD 1597/38.]

William Lincoln BA
Instituted 10 August 1603 to vicarage of Hackthorn, on cession of last incumbent. Patron: King James I. [Reg. 30, fo.195; BC.]

Educated: Corpus Christi College (matric. *c*.1597; BA 1601–2; MA 1605) and Pembroke College, Cambridge (DD 1623). Deacon and priest: 28 October 1602 (Peterborough).

Signed BTs at Hackthorn 1604–8. Also: R. of mediety of Treswell (Nt), 1605–13. After-wards: R. of West Halton, 1613–39; R. of Scotter, 1613–39; Chaplain to the King; Canon of Lincoln and Prebendary of Centum Solidorum, 1631–9. Father of John Lincoln, V. of Hackthorn (1639), below. Died 1639; buried 24 October 1639 at St Giles in the Fields (Mx). Administration granted to Okley Lincoln of West Halton, his widow. [Venn, *Alumni*; BTs Hackthorn; Train, *North Notts Clergy*, 183; *Le Neve Fasti: Lincoln 1541–1857*, 52; LCC Admons 1639/221.]

Christopher Riddinge BA

Instituted 30 October 1610 to vicarage of Hackthorn, on resignation of last incumbent. Patron: King James I (29 October 1610). Reinstituted 28 April 1613, on resignation of William Lincoln; patron: Nicholas Saunderson Bt (15 March 1612/13), to whom the patronage had lately been adjudged by the King's justices at Westminster. [BC; PD 1610/19; PD 1613/39.]

Born *c.*1581. Educated: St John's College, Cambridge (matric. *c.*1594; BA 1598–9). Deacon: 1 July 1604 (Colchester); priest: 22 May 1608 (Peterborough). Signed BTs at Hackthorn 1610–22, 1628. Died 1631. Admon (LCC). [PD 1613/39; Venn, *Alumni*; LC 4, fo.11; BTs Hackthorn; LCC Admons 1632/216.]

Thomas Eland MA

Instituted 25 September 1631 to vicarage of Hackthorn, on death of Christo-pher Reddinge. Patron: Nicholas, Viscount Castleton (16 September 1631). [BC; PD 1631/39.]

Baptised 19 March 1606/7 at Tempsford (Bd); son of George E., Rector of Tempsford. Educated: Magdalen College, Oxford (matric. 1621/2; BA 1625/6; MA 1628). Afterwards: R. of Bigby, 1632–6. [PR Tempsford; Bloxam v. 108–9; Foster, *Alumni*.]

Edward Smyth MA

Instituted 11 March 1632/3 to vicarage of Hackthorn, on cession of Thomas Eland. Patron: Nicholas, Viscount Castleton (6 March 1632/3). [BC; PD 1633/5.]

Educated: Magdalene College, Cambridge (matric. 1622; BA 1625–6; MA 1629). Deacon and priest: 23 December 1632 (Lincoln). Afterwards: R. of Beelsby, 1648–71. Buried 18 April 1671 at Beelsby. [Venn, *Alumni*; LC 5, fo.43v; Swaby, 47; PR Beelsby.]

John Lincoln

Instituted 22 June 1639 to vicarage of Hackthorn. Patron: Nicholas Sanderson Bt, Lord Saunderson. [AC.]

Baptised 18 September 1614 at West Halton; son of William L., Rector of West Halton (and V. of Hackthorn, 1603–10, above). Educated: Magdalene College, Cambridge (matric. 1631; BA 1634; MA 1638). [BTs West Halton; Venn, *Alumni*.]

Between 1660 and 1773 the living of Hackthorn was under sequestration and served by curates, including George Langley (*c.*1663–73); Thomas Elford (*c*.1675–9); Robert Dixon (*c*.1682–8); Joseph Lister (*c*.1689–1715); John Eastland (*c*.1717–24); John Arnold (*c*.1725–53). [BTs Hackthorn; LC 14, p.231c.]

Tillotson Laycock BA
Instituted 17 June 1773 to vicarage of Hackthorn, on death of last incumbent. Patron: King George III (by lapse). [Reg. 39, p.200.]

Signed BTs at Hackthorn 1774–1810. Also: V. of Cammeringham, 1773–1813 (*q.v.*).

Thomas Brown MA
Instituted 27 December 1813 to vicarage of Hackthorn, on death of Tillotson Laycock. Patron: John Cracroft of Hackthorn, esquire (14 December 1813). [Reg. 40, p.193; PD 169/4.]

Baptised 14 February 1779 at Cammeringham; son of Hezekiah B., esquire. Educated: Oriel College, Oxford (matric. 1797; BA 1801; MA 1804). Deacon: 20 December 1801; priest: 12 June 1803 (Lincoln). Formerly: C. of South Hykeham, 1801–13. Resided in Lincoln. Also: C. of Burton-by-Lincoln, 1816; C. of Spridlington, 1820. Afterwards: R. of Leadenham, 1821–35. Buried at Leadenham, 21 December 1835. [PR Cammeringham; Foster, *Alumni*; Reg. 40, pp. 28, 70; PR South Hykeham; CR 1, pp. 67, 113; PR Leadenham.]

John Cracroft (the younger) MA
Instituted 16 August 1821 to vicarage of Hackthorn, on resignation of Thomas Brown. Patron: John Cracroft of Hackthorn, esquire. [Reg. 40, p.318.]

Born 4 October 1784 at Dawlish; son of John C. of Hackthorn. Educated: Eton College and Brasenose College, Oxford (matric. 1803; BA 1807; MA 1812). Deacon: 21 December 1807 (Salisbury); LD (13 April 1809) for priesthood (Exeter for London). Formerly: C. of Tisbury (Wlt), 1807; of Stratford-le-Bow, 1809. Also: Chaplain to the Forces, 1812–42; R. of West Keal, 1821–2; R. of Ripley (YWR), 1822–42. Married 1st (22 December 1807) Eliza (d.1811), daughter of James Lewis. Served in Napoleonic Wars: invalided home from the Peninsula (August 1814), being 'very ill of an intermittent fever'. Married 2nd (10 November 1814) at St Peter-in-Eastgate, Lincoln, Jane, daughter of Hezekiah Brown of the Close of Lincoln. On Army half-pay, 1819. Non-resident at Hackthorn: lived at Lincoln (1821), Spa (1823, 1828), Dieppe (1824). Died 21 September 1842 at Neuwied-on-the-Rhine; buried there. [Crisp, *Fragmenta Genealogica* (1901), 9; *Lincolnshire Pedigrees*, 281; *Brasenose Register*, 411; CCED; *GM* 82 (1812), 587; PRO, WO 100/2, p.128; Snape, *Army Chaplains*, 50; *Army List* (1841), 423.]

Hibbert Binney LLD
Instituted 6 July 1827 to vicarage of Hackthorn, on cession of John Cracroft. Patron: Robert Cracroft esquire. [Reg. 40, p.353.]

Born 22 April 1793 at Halifax, Nova Scotia; son of Hibbert Newton B. Educated: King's College, Nova Scotia (BA 1811; MA 1814; LLD 1827). Ordained 1816 (London). Formerly: R. of Cape Breton (NS), 1818. Non-resident at Hackthorn, which was served by curates: Richard Greaves Moore (1826–8), Robert Edward Blackwell (1828–35), William Henry Flowers (1836–8), Richard Stanley (1839–43) and Edwin George Jarvis (1843–4). Also: R. of Cold Hanworth, 1827–44; Chaplain of Holy Trinity, Knightsbridge, 1833–57; R. of Newbury (Brk), 1838–57. Married (25 September 1818) Henrietta Lavinia, daughter of Hon. Richard Stout of Sidney (NS). Father of Hibbert B., later Bishop of Nova Scotia (1851–87). Died 6 June 1857. [*Binney Genealogy*, 113; PR Hackthorn; CR 1, pp. 324, 404; CR 2, pp. 160, 226; CR 3, fo.40v; White, *Lincolnshire* (1842), 482–3; Census Returns 1851; *Dictionary of Canadian Biography*; *The Guardian*, 17 June 1857.]

The Rectory of Cold Hanworth was united to the Vicarage of Hackthorn by Order in Council dated 17 April 1844. [OC/27.]

Edwin George Jarvis MB
Instituted 7 May 1844 to vicarage of Hackthorn with rectory of Cold Hanworth annexed, on cession of Hibbert Binney. Patron: Robert Cracroft of Hackthorn, esquire. [Reg. 40, p.496.]

Born 16 February 1816 at Dover; son of George Ralph Payne J. of Doddington Hall. Educated: Winchester College and Trinity College, Cambridge (matric. 1834; MB 1840). Deacon: 11 June 1843; priest: 3 March 1844 (Lincoln). Formerly: C. of Doddington, 1843. Resided at Hackthorn. Built new vicarage house (architect, W. A. Nicholson of Lincoln), 1844. Married (1841) Frances Amcotts, daughter of Robert Cracroft of Hackthorn. Father of Francis Amcotts J., Rector of Kettlethorpe (1874–82) and of Burton Stather (1882–1921). Died 11 November 1876 at Hackthorn. [Venn, *Alumni*; OR 1, pp. 92, 95; CR 3, fo.39v; MGA 290; JARVIS 5/A/11/147; *Probate Calendar* 1877.]

Charles Henry Fairfax BA
Instituted 12 January 1877 to vicarage of Hackthorn with rectory of Cold Hanworth annexed, on death of Edwin George Jarvis. Patron: Weston Cracroft Amcotts of Hackthorn, esquire. [Reg. 41, p.546.]

Born 2 January 1849; son of Thomas F. of Newton Kyme (YNR), esquire. Educated: Eton College (1859) and St John's College, Oxford (matric. 1867; BA 1871; MA 1879). Deacon: 30 June 1872; priest: 29 June 1873 (Durham). Formerly: C. of Hurworth (Du), 1872–4; V. of Maltby (YWR), 1875–7. Married (1873) Emmeline Marian, daughter of James Sawrey Cookson of Neasham Hall (Du). Resided at Hackthorn. Afterwards: R. of Dumbleton (Gl), 1894–1904; R. of Brailsford (Db), 1904–19. Died 1 July 1919 at Brailsford Rectory. [Burke, *Landed Gentry* (1863), 450; *Eton School Register (1853–59)*, 87; Foster, *Alumni*; Durham UL, DDR/EA/CL; *Crockford* (1916); Census Returns 1881, 1891; *Probate Calendar* 1919.]

William Hathorn Mills MA
Instituted 5 April 1895, on cession of Charles Henry Fairfax. Patron: Edward Weston Cracroft of Hackthorn, esquire. [Reg. 42, p.379.]

Born 28 April 1848; son of Revd John M., Rector of Orton Waterville (Hu). Educated: Haileybury School (1863–6) and Pembroke College, Cambridge (matric. 1866; BA 1870; MA 1873). Deacon: 1873; priest: 1874 (Hereford). Formerly: Assistant Master, Hereford Cathedral School, 1872–5; C. of Pipe and Lyde (He), 1873–5; Head Master of Ruthin GS, 1875–81; Senior Assistant Master, Louth GS, 1881–95; C. of South Thoresby, 1882–92; V. of Kelstern, 1892–5; R. of Calcethorpe, 1894–5. Resided at Hackthorn Vicarage. Afterwards: R. of North Thoresby, 1902–8; R. of Rand with Fulnetby, 1908–9. Author: *Ballads of Hellas for School Use* (1878); *The Odes of Horace; The Antigone of Sophocles*. Retired 1909. Of 1 Lemsford Road, St Albans (1911); Birkland Villa, Worksop (1915, 1916). Latterly of San Bernardino, California (USA), where he died 29 September 1923.

[*The Guardian*, 10 May 1848; *Haileybury Register*; Venn, *Alumni*; Census Returns 1901; *Crockford* (1915); *Probate Calendar* 1925.]

Thomas William Hills

Instituted 8 December 1902, on cession of William Hathorn Mills. Patron: Edward Weston Cracroft of Hackthorn, esquire. [Reg. 42, p.503.]

Born *c*.1856 at Gravesend; son of William H., agricultural labourer. Educated: King's College, London (AKC 1891). Deacon: 1892; priest: 1893 (London). Formerly: C. of St Paul, Old Ford, 1892–3; of St Matthew, Ponders End, 1893–6; of St Paul, Stratford, 1896–1901; C-in-C of St Luke's Mission Church, Leyton, 1901–2. Resided at Hackthorn Vicarage. Died 1 July 1916 at 1 College Road, Eastbourne. [Census Returns 1861, 1911; *Crockford* (1908); *Probate Calendar* 1916.]

Benjamin James Boodle MA

Instituted 21 October 1916 to vicarage of Hackthorn with Cold Hanworth, on death of Thomas William Hills. Patron: Edward Weston Cracroft of Hackthorn, esquire. [Reg. 43, p.140.]

Born 9 March 1868 at Chilcompton (So); son of Robert Hockin B., general practitioner. Educated: St John's Wood School and St John's College, Oxford (matric. 1887; BA 1891; MA 1894); Wells Theological College (1892). Deacon: 1893; priest: 1894 (Winchester). Formerly: C. of Godalming, 1893–8; of Thames Ditton, 1898–1901; of Beaminster (Do), 1901–5; of Westbury (Wlt), 1905–6; of Hungerford (Brk), 1906–9; of Ringwood (Ha), 1909–16. Resided at Hackthorn Vicarage. Bishop Hicks noted (September 1918): 'a good Parish Priest, tho' not a very clever man. They run into Lincoln most weeks in a motor bike & side-car for shopping.' Resigned 7 July 1923. Afterwards: C. of Henfield (Sx), 1923–35; V. of Icklesham (Sx), 1935–41. Retired 1941. Lived at Gully Shute, Colyford (Dev). Died 24 April 1959 at Lusways Nursing Home, Salcombe Hill, Sidmouth. [*Oxford Men*, 61; Census Returns 1881, 1911; *Crockford* (1908, 1952); Kelly, *Lincolnshire* (1919); *Hicks Diaries*, no.1318; Reg. 43, p.313; *Probate Calendar* 1959.]

John Duncan Jowitt

Instituted 10 October 1923 to vicarage of Hackthorn with Cold Hanworth, on resignation of Benjamin James Boodle. Patron: Edward Weston Cracroft of Hackthorn, esquire. [Reg. 43, p.330.]

Born 1867 at Reading; son of Revd John Henry J., Vicar of Alford. Educated: Newark, Alford and Louth Schools; Christ's College (matric. 1886) and St Catharine's College, Cambridge; Lincoln Theological College (1892). Deacon: 1896; priest: 1898 (St Albans). Formerly: C. of St Giles, Colchester, 1896–8; of Eastville, 1898–1900; of West Fordington (Do), 1900–1; of Charminster, 1901–2; of Holy Trinity, Dorchester, 1902–4; of St John Baptist, Hoxton, 1904–7; of St Andrew, Fulham, 1909–12; R. of St James the Less, Springburn, Glasgow, 1913–23. Resided at Hackthorn Vicarage. Also: RD of Aslacoe, 1926. Resigned 26 March 1942. Lived at Wootton House, Wootton, Boars Hill, Oxford. Died there, 4 September 1943. [GRO, Birth Index; Venn, *Alumni*; *Crockford* (1932); Reg. 43, p.672; *Probate Calendar* 1943.]

Arthur James Westcott DD PhD

Instituted 6 October 1947 to vicarage of Hackthorn with Cold Hanworth, on resignation of John Duncan Jowitt. Patron: King George VI, for this turn, by lapse. [Reg. 44, p.77.]

Baptised at St Mary, Lambeth, 3 December 1876; son of James W., carpenter. Educated: New Windsor College, Maryland (USA) (PhD 1904; DD 1908). Deacon: 1901; priest: 1902 (Milwaukee). In Wisconsin and Nebraska. Formerly: Organising Secretary for SPG, 1909–22; C. of St Margaret, Burley, Leeds, 1910–16; V. of St Oswald, Abbeydale, Sheffield, 1918–23; V. of Walton, 1923–4; of Kirk Hammerton, 1924–5; Secretary of Church of England Children's Society, 1924–32; Chaplain of Bournabat, Izmir and Buca (Turkey), 1932–47. Resided at Hackthorn Vicarage. Resignation accepted 18 February 1952. Disappears from *Crockford* 1957–8. [LMA, PR Lambeth St Mary; Census Returns 1911; *Crockford* (1952, 1957–8); Reg. 44, p.154.]

Henry Bursey BA

Instituted 15 October 1954 to vicarage of Hackthorn with Cold Hanworth, on resignation of Arthur James Westcott. Note that on 3 July 1954, an Order was made under Section 5 of the Pastoral Reorganisation Measure 1949, authorising the said HB to hold the benefices of Spridlington with Saxby and Firsby, and of Hackthorn with Cold Hanworth, in plurality. [Reg. 44, p.200.]

Also: R. of Spridlington with Saxby and Firsby, 1953–8 (*q.v.*).

Richard Laurence Crampton LTh

Instituted 11 December 1959 to vicarage of Hackthorn with Cold Hanworth, on cession of Henry Bursey. Patron: Sir Weston Cracroft Amcotts of Hackthorn Hall, Lt Col. (retd), Lawrence Roger, Earl of Scarbrough, of Sandbeck Park, Rotherham (YWR), and Brigadier Walter Morland Hutton DSO MC, for this turn. Note that on 28 September 1959, a Renewal Order was made under Section 5 of the Pastoral Reorganisation Measure 1949, authorising the said RLC to hold the benefices of Spridlington with Saxby and Firsby, and of Hackthorn with Cold Hanworth, in plurality. Vacated by resignation (accepted 1 September 1962). [Reg. 44, pp. 286, 336.]

Also: R. of Spridlington with Saxby and Firsby, 1959–62 (*q.v.*).

Michael Roy Sinker MA

Instituted 28 August 1963 to vicarage of Hackthorn with Cold Hanworth, on resignation of Richard Laurence Crampton. Patron: Sir Weston Cracroft Amcotts of Hackthorn Hall, Lt Col. (retd). [Reg. 44, p.348.]

Born 28 September 1908; son of Revd F. Sinker of Kendal. Educated: Haileybury (1922–7) and Clare College, Cambridge (BA 1930; MA 1934); Cuddesdon College (1931). Deacon: 1932; priest: 1933 (Carlisle). Formerly: C. of Dalston, 1933–4; Missioner, South African Church Railway Mission, Alicedale, 1934–8; C. of Bishop's Hatfield, 1938–9; V. of Dalton-in-Furness, 1939–46; V. of Saffron Walden, 1946–63; Hon. Canon of Chelmsford, 1955–63. Resided at Hackthorn Vicarage. Also: Archdeacon of Stow, 1963–7; Canon of Lincoln and Prebendary of Leicester St Margaret, 1963–7. Afterwards: R. of St Matthew, Ipswich, 1967–77. Retired 1977. Lived at 8 White Horse Way, Westbury (Wlt) and latterly at 31 The Gowers, Amersham (Bk). Died 8 March 1994. [*Haileybury Register*; *Crockford* (1963–4, 1980–2, 1993–4); GRO, Death Index; Lincoln Cathedral Obit Book.]

Sidney Harvie Clark MA

Instituted 13 September 1967 to vicarage of Hackthorn with Cold Hanworth, on cession of Michael Roy Sinker. Patron: Sir Weston Cracroft Amcotts of Hackthorn Hall, Lt Col. (retd). Vacated by resignation, accepted 30 April 1975. [Reg. 44, pp. 406, 496.]

Born 26 July 1905 at Nunhead (Sr). Educated: Jesus College, Cambridge (BA 1927; MA 1931); Westcott House, Cambridge (1929). Deacon: 21 December 1930; priest: 20 December 1931 (Durham). Formerly: C. of St Mary, Gateshead, 1930–4; of St Mary, Portsea, 1934–6; R. of Jarrow, 1936–40; of St John, Edinburgh, 1940–7; Archdeacon of Birmingham and Hon. Canon of Birmingham, 1947–67; R. of Wishaw, 1947–8; V. of Harborne, 1948–67. Also: Archdeacon of Stow, 1967–75; Canon of Lincoln and Prebendary of Leicester St Margaret, 1967–77. Resided at Hackthorn Vicarage. Retired 1975. Latterly of Stow House, Skillington. Died 12 February 1991. [GRO, Death Index; Census Returns 1911; Durham UL, DDR/EA/CL; *Crockford* (1969–70, 1980–2); Lincoln Cathedral Obit Book.]

COLD HANWORTH

In the thirteenth century, the advowson of Cold Hanworth appears to have belonged to the holding of the Costentin family, which had passed by 1303 to William de Ouneby. William's son Thomas was killed at Warsop (Nt) in 1322; his heir was his brother Walter. By the later fourteenth century the village had come into the possession of the powerful Sutton family of Lincoln, whose descendants were still presenting to the rectory in the reign of Queen Elizabeth I. In the early eighteenth century the advowson was acquired by the Cracroft family of neighbouring Hackthorn. The patron in 1965 was Sir Weston Cracroft-Amcotts. [*Book of Fees*, 1073; *Feudal Aids* iii. 136; *CIPM* vi. no.355; *Change and Continuity*, 93; *LDC* (1965), 108–9.]

Hugh de Scalleby clerk

Instituted in the tenth pontifical year of Bishop Hugh of Wells (20 December 1218/19 December 1219) to church of Cold Hanworth. Patron: Nigel Costentin. Hugh had previously been given custody of the church, to give him time for study and the practice of singing. He was to proceed to the subdiaconate at the next ordination and, because of his insufficient learning, he was to attend the schools. [*Rot. Welles* i. 81, 147.]

Henry de Haneword subdeacon

Instituted in the seventeenth pontifical year of Bishop Robert Grosseteste (17 June 1251/16 June 1252) to church of Cold Hanworth. Patron: Alexander de Haneword. [Hoskin, no.1306.]

Richard de Ouneby acolyte

Instituted 24 May 1304 to church of Cold Hanworth, on death of M. Henry.

Patron: Henry de Lascy, Earl of Lincoln (by reason of minority of Thomas son and heir of William de Ouneby). [Reg. 2, fo.87.]

Subdeacon: by 21 August 1305. Dispensations for absence to study for 1 year, 12 March 1304/5; for 1 year, 21 August 1305. Letters of caption issued, 6 March 1330/1 and 25 April 1331. [Reg. 2, fo.309r–v; Reg. 5, fo.445.]

Walter Barow
Instituted before 1377. [*Clerical Poll-Taxes*, no.827.]

William son of John Smyth de Keleby priest
Instituted 15 December 1389, on death of Walter Barow. Patron: Robert de Sutton, Citizen of Lincoln. [Reg. 11, fo.103.]

Afterwards: V. of Kirkby cum Osgodby, 1398.

John Maysand (de Croxton) priest
Instituted 28 February 1397/8 to church of Cold Hanworth, on resignation of William Smyth de Keleby (by exchange with vicarage of Kirkby cum Osgodby). Patron: Robert de Sutton, Citizen of Lincoln. [Reg. 11, fos 92, 120.]

Formerly: V. of Kirkby cum Osgodby, 1397–8. [Reg. 11, fo.90v.]

John Sherman priest
Instituted 1 November 1403 to church of Cold Hanworth, on resignation of John Maysant. Patron: Robert Sutton, Citizen of Lincoln. [Reg. 13, fo.182v.]

John Thymulby priest
Instituted 4 June 1405 to church of Cold Hanworth, on death of John Sherman. Patron: Robert Sutton, Citizen of Lincoln. [Reg. 14, fo.105.]

John Chetour chaplain
Instituted 17 April 1409 to church of Cold Hanworth, on resignation of John Thymelby. Patron: Robert Sutton, Citizen of Lincoln. [Reg. 14, fo.113.]

Henry o'the Hill chaplain
Instituted 29 June 1411 to church of Cold Hanworth, on resignation of John Cheytoure. Patron: Robert Sutton, Citizen of Lincoln. [*Lambeth Institutions*, 49.]

John Seriaunt priest
Instituted 30 April 1451 to church of Cold Hanworth, on death of Henry de Hill. Patron: Hamon Sutton, Citizen of Lincoln. [Reg. 19, fos 61, 76v.]

Alan Braytoft chaplain
Instituted 20 February 1455/6 to church of Cold Hanworth, on dimission of John Sergiant. Patron: Hamon Sutton the elder, esquire. [Reg. 20, fo.158.]

Thomas Hodgeson priest
Instituted 17 July 1457 to church of Cold Hanworth, on resignation of Alan Braytofte. Patron: Hamon Sutton the elder, of Lincoln. [Reg. 20, fo.159.]

Hugh Barleby priest
Instituted 20 August 1464 to church of Cold Hanworth, on resignation of Thomas Hogeson. Patron: Hamon Sutton esquire, lord of Cold Hanworth. [Reg. 20, fo.161.]

Hugh Carlyll
Instituted before 13 January 1470/1. [Reg. 20, fo.162.]

Christopher Mersden priest
Instituted 13 January 1470/1 to church of Cold Hanworth, on resignation of Hugh Carlyll. Patron: Hugh Tapton clerk, Thomas Fitzwilliam the younger, William Rither and Thomas Dymmok, for this turn by feoffment of manor and advowson of Cold Hanworth made to them by Hamon Sutton the elder, esquire, decd. [Reg. 20, fo.162.]

John Colyn priest
Instituted 14 May 1493 to church of Cold Hanworth, on resignation of Christopher Marsden. Patron: Hamon Sutton esquire (8 May 1493). [Reg. 22, fo.153v; PD 1493/44.]

John Londesdale priest
Instituted 22 October 1500 to church of Cold Hanworth, on resignation of John Colyn. Patron: Hamon Sutton esquire. [Reg. 23, fo.56v.]

Robert Norton priest
Instituted 5 March 1505/6 to church of Cold Hanworth, on resignation of John Londisdale. Patron: Hamon Sutton, lord of Cold Hanworth. [Reg. 23, fo.157v.]

[Note: a collation of the church of Cold Hanworth made by the Bishop of Lincoln, by lapse, on 28 June 1507 to Arthur [blank] BA appears to have been ineffective.]

John Roper chaplain
Instituted 25 April 1508 to church of Cold Hanworth, on resignation of Robert Norton. Patron: Hamon Sutton of Norton Disney. [Reg. 23, fo.158v.]
Was said to keep his mother and his sister in his house (1519). Assessed for subsidy (£6) in 1526. [*Diocesan Visitations* i. 94; *Subsidy*, 36.]

Robert Tailor deacon
Instituted 8 August 1534, during metropolitical visitation of Archbishop

of Canterbury, to church of Cold Hanworth, on resignation of John Roper. Patron: Robert Taylor of Langworth, by grant made to him by Hamond Sutton esquire. [Reg. 27, fo.59.]

Robert Langtonne

Instituted 10 March 1558/9 to church of Cold Hanworth, on death of last incumbent. Patron: Hamond Sutton esquire. [Reg. 28, fo.126v.]

Witnessed wills, 1559–67. Died *c*.1568. Will (Stow), dated 18 December 1568; proved 22 April 1569. [Stow Wills 1559–62/113v; Stow Wills 1553–67/21, 33; Stow Wills 1569–74/15.]

John Stregit

Instituted before 9 October 1570. [Reg. 28, fo.37.]

John Pailie

Instituted 9 October 1570 to church of Cold Hanworth, on death of John Stregit. Patron: Elizabeth Sutton of Washingborough, gentlewoman. [Reg. 28, fo.37.]

Robert Oram

Instituted 10 February 1573/4 to church of Cold Hanworth. [*Bishop Cooper*, 75.]

Education: 'bred in the schools'. Deacon: 30 March 1572; priest: 24 July 1573 (York). Resident (1598, 1614): signed BTs 1600–13. Father of John Oram, V. of Canwick (1609). Died December–January 1613–14. Will dated 13 December 1613; proved at Lincoln, 27 January 1613/14. [*State of the Church*, 97, 329; *York Ordinations 1561–1642*, 50; LC 4, fo.10v; BTs Cold Hanworth; Stow Wills 1613/73.]

Thomas Langley

Instituted 31 January 1613/14 to rectory of Cold Hanworth. [AC; Add. Reg. 3, fo.66.]

Perhaps to be identified with TL of Queens' College, Cambridge (matric. 1587; BA 1591–2). Deacon: 9 December 1591; priest: 17 March 1591/2 (Lincoln). Also: R. of Irby on Humber (where he resided), 1591–1622. Perhaps father of George L. (Rector of Cold Hanworth, 1653–74 below). Non-resident at Cold Hanworth: BTs signed by a curate, 1615–17. Resignation accepted 22 November 1617. Died at Irby before 17 January 1621/2 (probate inventory). [Venn, *Alumni*; LC 4, fo.34; BTs Cold Hanworth; Add. Reg. 3, fo.66; LCC Wills 1622/i/93; INV 126/85.]

Robert Marland MA

Instituted 24 November 1617 by John Williams, Official *sede vacante*, to rectory of Cold Hanworth, on resignation of Thomas Langley. Patron: Robert Grantham of Whisby. [Add. Reg. 3, fo.66v.]

Born *c*.1583; son of James M. of Rochdale, yeoman. Educated: St John's College and Caius College, Cambridge (adm. 1600; BA 1603–4; MA 1609). Deacon: 26 May 1605 (Colchester); priest: 26 May 1616 (Lincoln). Formerly: Head Master of Rochdale GS,

1605–10; C. of Buslingthorpe, 1616; V. of Middle Rasen, 1617. Signed BTs at Cold Hanworth 1619–22, 1628. Died 1639. Will (Stow) dated 5 May 1639, proved at Lincoln 13 May 1639. [Venn, *Alumni*; LC 4, fo.11v; Borthwick, Sub. Bk. 2, fo.61; BTs Cold Hanworth; Stow Wills 1638–40/65.]

Thomas Daniell

Instituted 6 June 1639 to rectory of Cold Hanworth. Patron: Robert Cracroft esquire and Francis Cracroft gent. [AC.]

Born *c*.1603; of Kent. Educated: St John's College, Oxford (matric. 1618; BA 1621). Also: R. of Snarford. Perhaps plundered. [Foster, *Alumni*; *St John's Register*, 249; *Walker Revised*, 249.]

George Langley BA

Presented 1 June 1653 to rectory of Cold Hanworth by Robert and Francis Cracroft, esquires. Subscribed 14 August 1662. [LC 5, fo.82.]

Deacon and priest: 9 October 1645 (Lincoln). Signed BTs at Cold Hanworth 1663–73. Buried 12 April 1674 at Cold Hanworth; probate inventory praised 22 April 1674 ('His Library, £5'). Will. [LC 5, fo.82; BTs Cold Hanworth; INV 178/3; Stow Wills 1672–4/335.]

Samuel Welfit BA

Instituted 25 June 1674 to rectory of Cold Hanworth, on death of George Langley. Patron: John Lodington, esquire (9 May 1674). [SUB Va, fo.59; PD 1674/20.]

Born *c*.1650; son of Jeremy W., yeoman, of Idle, Bradford. Educated: Bridlington School and St John's College, Cambridge (matric. 1667; BA 1670–1; MA 1674). Deacon: 24 September 1671; priest: 25 May 1673 (Lincoln). Formerly: C. of Buslingthorpe, 1673. Signed BTs at Cold Hanworth, 1675–88. Also: R. of Faldingworth, 1682–1720; resided there. Buried at Faldingworth, 2 March 1719/20. Will (Stow). [Venn, *Alumni*; Reg. 33, fos 144v, 161v; *Speculum*, 157; PR Faldingworth; Stow Wills 1717–27/373.]

Joseph Lister BA

Instituted 5 June 1688 to rectory of Cold Hanworth, on cession of Samuel Welfitt. Patron: Francis Grantham and Ann his wife (21 May 1688). [Reg. 34, fo.104v; PD 1688/35.]

Born *c*.1652; son of Thomas L. of Barton (Y). Educated: 'Sheerburne' School and St John's College, Cambridge (matric. 1671; BA 1674–5). Deacon: 19 September 1675; priest: 21 May 1676 (York). Formerly: C. of Panton, 1678; of Goltho, 1681; of Appleby, 1681. Resident at Cold Hanworth: signed BTs 1690–1715. Died before 4 May 1716. [*St John's Admissions* ii. 34; Venn, *Alumni*; *York Ordinations 1662–1699*, 41 (*sub* 'Lister, James'); Reg. 34, fo.104v; CCED; *Speculum*, 161; BTs Cold Hanworth; PD 1716/10.]

John Eastland BA

Instituted 23 June 1716 to rectory of Cold Hanworth, on death of Joseph Lister. Patron: Thomas Dixon of Owmby, gent., and John Hoggard of Cold Hanworth, gent. (4 May 1716), for this turn. [Reg. 37, p.18; PD 1716/10.]

Baptised 29 February 1691/2 at Stow-in-Lindsey; son of John E. of Bransby, gent. Educated:

Pembroke College, Cambridge (matric. 1710/11; BA 1714–15). Deacon: 25 September 1715; priest: 27 May 1716 (Lincoln). Formerly: C. of Brattleby and of Fillingham, 1715. Also: Sequestrator of Hackthorn; resided there, and later at Spridlington. Signed BTs at Cold Hanworth 1717–24. Died before 13 March 1724/5. [PR Stow-in-Lindsey; Venn, *Alumni*; Reg. 36, fo.258v; Reg. 37, p.15; *Speculum*, 161; BTs Cold Hanworth.]

John Arnold BA

Instituted 13 March 1724/5 to rectory of Cold Hanworth, on death of John Eastland. Patron: Robert Craycroft, esquire. [Reg. 38, p.85.]

Baptised 9 June 1696 at St Martin, Lincoln; son of Alexander A. Educated: Lincoln School and Magdalene College, Cambridge (matric. 1715; BA 1718–19). Deacon: 24 May 1719; priest: 12 June 1720 (Lincoln). Formerly: C. of Nettleham and of Greetwell, 1719. Signed BTs at Cold Hanworth 1725–39 and intermittently thereafter. Also: R. of Burton-by-Lincoln, 1739–54; Sequestrator of Hackthorn, 1745; Canon of Lincoln and Prebendary of Welton Beckhall, 1746–54. Died 12 April 1754; buried at Burton-by-Lincoln (MI). [PR Lincoln St Martin; Venn, *Alumni*; Reg. 37, pp. 81, 101; BTs Cold Hanworth; LC 18B, p.306; *Le Neve Fasti: Lincoln 1541–1857*, 124; PR Burton-by-Lincoln.]

William Green MA

Instituted 3 June 1754 to rectory of Cold Hanworth, on death of John Arnold. Patron: Robert Cracroft, esquire. [Reg. 38, p.526.]

Born *c*.1714 at Newark (Nt). Educated: Clare College, Cambridge (matric. 1735; BA 1737–8; MA 1741); Fellow of Clare, 1738–59. Deacon: 24 September 1738 (Lincoln); priest: June 1740 (Norwich). Formerly: C. of Everton with Tetworth (Hu), 1738. Also: R. of Hardingham (Nf), 1759–94; R. of Barnham Broom (Nf), 1790–4. Non-resident at Cold Hanworth ('Absent – lives at Hardingham'); the cure was served by Tillotson Laycock as curate. A noted Hebraist: 'a dedicated scholar and insightful translator of the scriptures'. Author: *The Song of Deborah Reduced to Metre* (1753); *A New Translation of the Prayer of Habbakuk* (1755) and other works. Died 31 October 1794 at Hardingham. [*ODNB*; Venn, *Alumni*; Reg. 38, p.353; LC 31, p.198; CCED; *Norfolk Benefices*, 47, 49.]

Bernard Cracroft

Instituted 28 February 1777 to rectory of Cold Hanworth, on cession of William Green. Patron: Rebecca Cracroft, widow. [Reg. 39, p.286.]

Afterwards: R. of Rippingale, 1801–16 (*q.v.*).

Charles Robert Marshall BD

Instituted 7 May 1802 to rectory of Cold Hanworth, on cession of Bernard Cracroft. Patron: Rebecca Cracroft of The Close of Lincoln, widow (15 April 1802). [Reg. 40, p.38; PD 158/33.]

Baptised 2 September 1764 at Theddlethorpe St Helen; 4th son of William M., esquire, and Grace (daughter of Robert Cracroft of Hackthorn) his wife. Educated: Lincoln College, Oxford (matric. 1782; BA 1786; MA 1789; BD 1799). Deacon: 18 May 1788; priest: 7 June 1789 (Oxford). Also: V. of Exning (Sf), 1806–23. Died 19 April 1823 at Greenhithe (K); buried at Eversley (Ha). [*Lincolnshire Pedigrees*, 650; PR Theddlethorpe St Helen; Foster, *Alumni*; ORO, MS. Oxf. Dioc. Papers b.21, fos 127, 131.]

Henry John Ingilby MA
Instituted 16 October 1823 to rectory of Cold Hanworth, on death of Charles
Robert Marshall. Patron: Robert Cracroft of the City of York, esquire. [Reg.
40, p.335.]

Born 28 January 1790; son of Revd Henry I., of North Deighton (YWR). Educated:
University College, Oxford (matric. 1808; BA 1812; MA 1816). Priest: 12 June 1814
(Salisbury). Non-resident at Cold Hanworth, which was served by curates, including
William Williamson (1825). Also: R. of West Keal, 1822–55; resided there. Succeeded to
the estates of Sir William Amcotts Ingilby Bt (who d.s.p. 14 May 1854); resided there-
after at Ripley Castle. Was created a baronet, 26 July 1866. Died 4 July 1870 at Ripley
Castle. [Burke, *Peerage* (1906 edn), 883; Foster, *Alumni*; CCED; CR 1, p.262; White,
Lincolnshire (1842), 277; Census Returns 1851, 1861; *Probate Calendar* 1870.]

Hibbert Binney LLD
Instituted 6 July 1827 to rectory of Cold Hanworth, on cession of Henry John
Ingilby. Patron: Robert Cracroft, esquire. [Reg. 40, p.353.]

Also: V. of Hackthorn, 1827–44 (*q.v.*).

**The Rectory of Cold Hanworth was united to the Vicarage of Hackthorn
by Order in Council dated 17 April 1844. [OC/27.]**

HARPSWELL

The Domesday Survey of 1086 refers to half a church at Harpswell, and
while no evidence has been found to suggest that the church was divided
into two medieties, the right of presentation was disputed in 1306, 1335
and *c*.1370. In the early thirteenth century it belonged to the manor of the
Nevill family. In 1299 the manor and advowson were conveyed to William
Tuchet, whose attempt to present to the rectory in 1306 was challenged by
Roger de Nevill and the right lapsed to the bishop. After Tuchet's execution following the battle of Boroughbridge (1322) the advowson passed to
Robert son of Robert le Clerk and his wife Alice; they conveyed it in 1326
to Master John de Haryngton, who presented in 1333 and 1335. In 1327 the
manor and advowson were settled on Haryngton for life (he died in 1344),
with remainder to John de Beauchamp and Matilda his wife, and their heirs
male. Members of the Beauchamp family presented between 1349 and 1370.
By 1374 the advowson had been acquired for Michael de la Pole, the future
Earl of Suffolk. After Suffolk's attainder, the Crown presented in 1389 but
later in that year Michael de la Pole the younger received livery of the manor
of Harpswell. The patronage appears to have been granted to Louth Park
Abbey by 1438, and it seems possible that the church was appropriated to
that house without a vicarage being ordained. At any rate, no further institutions were made to Harpswell until the nineteenth century, the parish being

served by curates appointed by the Whichcote family who acquired the Harpswell estate in the sixteenth century. Sir George Whichcote nominated to the perpetual curacy in 1909 and 1912; in 1931 he transferred the advowson to Lincoln Diocesan Trust. In 1965 the right of presentation was held by the Diocesan Board of Patronage. [*Lincolnshire Domesday*, 132; *Summoning St Michael*, 182–4; FL Feet of Fines A.845, B.650, C.8; *Le Neve Fasti: Lincoln 1300–1541*, 100; *CPR 1388–92*, 58.]

Peter de Alencun subdeacon
Instituted in the eighteenth pontifical year of Bishop Hugh of Wells (20 December 1226/19 December 1227) to church of Harpswell. Patron: Richard de Alencun kt, by reason of the custody of the land and heir of Alexander de Nevill. [*Rot. Welles* i. 225.]

John Gere
Occurs *c*.1275.

Incised slab in church ('Iadys Person de Herpeswelle'), perhaps *c*.1275. [Greenhill, *Incised Slabs*, 54.]

Alexander de Hothum
Instituted before 8 March 1289/90. [*Reg. Sutton* viii. 19.]

M. Thomas de Perariis
Instituted 8 March 1289/90 to church of Harpswell, on death of Alexander de Hothum. Patron: M. Thomas de Luda. Reinstituted 17 March 1290/1 because he had not been ordained priest within a year of his institution; patron: M. Thomas de Luda. [*Reg. Sutton* viii. 19, 21.]

Educated: University of Oxford (MA by 1277). Deacon: 23 December 1290; priest: 17 March 1290/1 (Lincoln). Formerly: R. of Skegness, to 1290. Also: Canon of Lincoln and Prebendary of Dunham, *c*.1274–1305; R. of Panton, 1300. [Emden, *BRUO*, 1463; *Reg. Sutton* i. 139; vii. 10, 13; *Le Neve Fasti: Lincoln 1066–1300*, 67.]

M. John de Harington priest
Instituted 10 May 1306 by collation to church of Harpswell, on death of M. Thomas de Perariis. Patron: Bishop of Lincoln, by lapse (the advowson having been disputed between William Tuchet kt and Roger de Nevill for over six months). [Reg. 2, fo.90.]

Also: Canon of Lincoln and Prebendary of Sexaginta Solidorum, 1305; of Carlton cum Dalby, 1307–8; of All Saints in Hungate, 1311–17; of Sanctae Crucis, 1317–44. Afterwards: R. of Sibsey, 1333. [*Le Neve Fasti: Lincoln 1300–1541*, 27, 44, 100, 106; *Reg. Burghersh* i. no.366.]

John de Navenby (Severesby) priest
Instituted 15 February 1332/3 to church of Harpswell, on institution of M. John de Harington to church of Sibsey. Patron: M. John de Haryngton, clerk. [*Reg. Burghersh* i. no.776.]

M. William de Harington priest
Instituted 27 May 1335 to church of Harpswell, on death of John de Severesby. Patron: M. John de Harington (after advowson had been disputed unsuccessfully by Crown). [*Reg. Burghersh* i. no.795.]

Educated: Merton College, Oxford (Fellow by 1320/1; Subwarden 1334–5; MA; DD); Senior Proctor, November 1325. Priest: before 27 May 1335. Licence to study at University of Oxford for 1 year, 27 May 1335. Licence to reside in Lincoln Cathedral for 2 years and to lecture on holy writ to the canons there, 1 November 1338. Died 1349; effigy in Harpswell Church (see Plate 5). [Emden, *BRUO*, 874; *Reg Burghersh* i. no.795; Reg. 5, fo.195; *Reg. Burghersh* iii. no.1446.]

William Beauchaump
Instituted 9 August 1349 to church of Harpswell, on death of M. William de Haryngton. Patron: Peter Beauchaump. [Reg. 9, fo.158.]

Royal writs issued against WB as R. of Harpswell in 1369–70, concerning tithes alleged to be payable to the alien priory of Willoughton while it was in the king's hands during the French war. In January 1370 it was returned that WB was dead. Buried at Harpswell (MI). [*Buckingham Writs*, nos 88, 97, 105, 120; Greenhill, *Incised Slabs*, 54.]

William son of William Wasselyn clerk
Instituted to church of Harpswell after appeal to the Court of Canterbury. Patron: Elizabeth late wife of Peter de Beauchamp (*Bello Campo*) and Alice late wife of John son of the said Peter. No date (*c*.1370). [Reg. 10, fo.132.]

Afterwards: R. of Greetwell, 1370.

Stephen de Whitewell
Instituted 16 January 1369/70 to church of Harpswell, on resignation of M. William Wascelyn (by exchange with church of Greetwell). Patron: John de Beauchamp (*Bello Campo*). [Reg. 10, fo.132v.]

Formerly: R. of Greetwell, to 1370. Afterwards: R. of Peakirk (Np), 1374–94; V. of Oakham (Ru), 1394. [Reg. 11, fo.171v.]

Stephen of the Bothe priest
Instituted 20 March 1373/4 to church of Harpswell, on resignation of Stephen de Whittewell (by exchange with church of Peakirk). Patron: Katherine de la Pole, attorney of Michael de la Pole kt, her son. [Reg. 10, fos 139v, 196v.]

Formerly: R. of Peakirk (Np), to 1374. Licence to be in service of M. Richard Lyncheford, Canon of Lincoln, for 2 years, 20 June 1378. Still Rector in 1381. [Reg. 12, fo.171v; *Clerical Poll-Taxes*, no. 2166.]

W· iiam de Wrangell priest
Instituted 16 May 1386 to church of Harpswell (cause of vacancy not stated). Patron: Michael de la Pole, Earl of Suffolk and lord of Huntingfield. [Reg. 11, fo.99.]

Afterwards: Chaplain of Chantry in Ingleby Chapel, 1389.

John Elys
Instituted 8 March 1388/9 to church of Harpswell, on resignation of William de Wrangell (by exchange with chantry of Ingleby in parish of Saxilby). Patron: King Richard II, for this turn (13 February 1388/9). [Reg. 11, fo.101v; *CPR 1388–92*, 7.]
Formerly: Chaplain of Chantry in Ingleby Chapel, to 1389.

John Farthyngton priest
Instituted 28 February 1437/8 to vicarage of Harpswell (cause of vacancy not stated). Patron: Abbot and Convent of Louth Park. [Reg. 18, fo.80.]

No further institutions to Harpswell are recorded until the nineteenth century. In 1526 the cure was being served by Francis Tailbois as curate [*Subsidy*, 37]. After the Reformation, Harpswell became a donative curacy in the gift of the Whichcote family. It was served by curates, including:

Edward Hudson
Occurs 1586.
Formerly: Canon of Thornton Abbey; allotted pension of £6 at the Dissolution. Roger Norton (Vicar of Hemswell, 1532–59) bequeathed to him a copy of 'Denys upon the Evaungelists wiche he hayth in his hands already'. Buried at Harpswell, 3 April 1586. [*Ex-Religious*, 45, 148; PR Harpswell.]

Thomas Bulcock
Licensed 2 December 1594. [LC 4, fo.10.]
Deacon and priest: 16 December 1590 (Lincoln). Buried at Harpswell, 10 May 1633: 'Preacher of God's Word, having served the cure of Harpswell 38 years'. Will. [LC 4, fo.10; PR Harpswell; Stow Wills 1632–3/73.]

Hamond Bulcock
Occurs 1633–70. [PR Harpswell; BTs Harpswell.]
Baptised at Hemswell, 18 July 1602; son of Thomas B., above. Educated: Jesus College, Cambridge (matric. 1621; BA 1624–5; MA 1628). Deacon: 21 July 1625; priest: 22 July 1625 (Peterborough). V. of Saxby by Owmby, 1628–31 (*q.v.*). Resident at Harpswell (1662). Also: C. of Hemswell, 1667–70. Buried at Harpswell, 13 October 1670. [BTs Hemswell; Venn, *Alumni*; LC 5, fo.82; BTs Harpswell.]

Robert Janny
Occurs 1671–83. [BTs Harpswell.]

William Bassett
Licensed 7 May 1696. [Reg. 35, fo.29v.]
Signed BTs 1696–1728. [BTs Harpswell.]

Samuel Rolt
Occurs 1744–57.
Signed BTs 1744–57. [BTs Harpswell.]

Robert Wells
Appointed before 1768. [LC 31, fo.198r.]
Also: V. of Market Rasen, 1766.

Thomas Dawson
Occurs 1774–1804. [PR Harpswell.]
Signed registers 1774–1804. 'Late Vicar of North Kelsey and Perpetual Curate of Harpswell 30 years who died 25 March 1804 aged 58 years. Also Mary his wife who died 2 March 1822 aged 72 years. Likewise Edward their son who died 28 September 1823 aged 37 years and Elizabeth their daughter who died 12 February 1789 in the 3rd year of her age.' [MI Harpswell]

James Septimus Cox
Licensed 20 December 1829. [CR 1, p.454.]

Henry William Richter
Occurs 1835–43. [PR Harpswell.]
Born 22 May, baptised 13 June 1794 at St Pancras Church (Mx). Literate. Deacon: 16 December 1821; priest: 22 December 1822 (York). Formerly: C. of Leconfield (YER), 1821–3; C. of South Ferriby, 1823–5; C. of Winterton, 1824. Also: Chaplain of House of Correction, Kirton Lindsey, 1825–44. Later: R. of St Paul, Lincoln, 1844–73; Chaplain of Lincoln County Gaol, 1844–78. [*York Ordinations 1800–1849*; PR South Ferriby; White, *Lincolnshire* (1842), 483.]

George Dodds DD
Licensed 1844. [*Crockford* (1874).]
Educated: Pembroke College, Cambridge (BD 1833; DD 1839). Deacon: 1822; priest: 1823 (York). Formerly: C. of Skipwith, 1822–5; of Ledsham, 1825–7; of Rochdale, 1827; of Gainsborough, 1828. Also: V. of Corringham, 1831–79. Resided at Corringham Vicarage. Signed Harpswell registers. Died at Corringham, 5 October 1879. [PR Harpswell; White, *Lincolnshire* (1856), 215; *Probate Calendar* 1879.]

Timothy Gascoigne Lynde
Licensed 1880. [*Crockford* (1898).]
Signed registers 1880–99. Resigned 1908. Also: PC of Hemswell (*q.v.*), where he resided. [PR Harpswell.]

Ernest Wentworth Vaughan MA
Licensed 16 April 1909 to perpetual curacy of Harpswell, on resignation of Timothy Gascoigne Lynde. Nominated by Sir George Whichcote of Aswarby Park, Bt. Note that on 26 February 1909, the Archbishop of Canterbury

granted a dispensation enabling the said EWV to hold together the perpetual curacy of Hemswell and the perpetual curacy of Harpswell. [Reg. 42, p.608.]

Also: PC of Hemswell (*q.v.*).

Edward Wilcocks Raby MA

Licensed 10 May 1912 to perpetual curacy of Harpswell, on death of Ernest Wentworth Vaughan. Nominated by Sir George Whichcote of Aswarby Park, Bt. Note that on 16 April 1912, the Archbishop of Canterbury granted a dispensation enabling the said EWR to hold together the Vicarage of Glentworth and the Perpetual Curacy of Harpswell. [Reg. 43, p.26.]

Also: V. of Glentworth (*q.v.*).

The Perpetual Curacy of Harpswell was united to the Perpetual Curacy of Hemswell by Order in Council dated 10 August 1926 to form the United Benefice of Hemswell with Harpswell. [Reg. 43, pp. 400–2.]

HEMSWELL ALL SAINTS

The advowson of the church of All Saints appertained to the Soke of Kirton, held during the thirteenth century by the Earls of Cornwall, during much of the fourteenth by the Black Prince or his assignee, Sir John Chandos, and after 1437 by the Crown. In 1546 King Henry VIII sold the rectory and advowson to the City of Lincoln, which retained the revenues of the rectory, out of which it paid the stipend of a curate. The City nominated curates to Hemswell until 1823. By 1956 the right of presentation had been acquired by the Martyrs Memorial Trust which still held it in 1965. [*Archivists' Report* 9 (1957–8), 26; Birch, *Royal Charters*, xliii–xliv; *LDC* (1965), 108–9.]

Simon de Offeham chaplain

Instituted in the twenty-second pontifical year of Bishop Hugh of Wells (20 December 1230/19 December 1231) to church of [All Saints], Hemswell. Patron: Hubert de Burgh, Earl of Kent, Justiciar of England. [*Rot. Welles* i. 230.]

Michael of Northampton

Instituted before 17 June 1283. [*Reg. Sutton* viii. 4.]

John of Helpston subdeacon

Instituted 17 June 1283 to church of Hemswell, on death of Michael of Northampton. Patron: Edmund, Earl of Cornwall. [*Reg. Sutton* viii. 4.]

Roger de Merlawe chaplain
Instituted 5 September 1289 to church of All Saints, Hemswell, on death of John. Patron: Edmund, Earl of Cornwall. [*Reg. Sutton* viii. 19.]

William de Brueria chaplain
Instituted 30 May 1292 to church of All Saints, Hemswell, on institution of Roger de Merlawe to Harwell, dioc. Salisbury. Patron: Edmund, Earl of Cornwall. [*Reg. Sutton* viii. 22.]

John de Capella chaplain
Instituted 7 June 1311 to church of All Saints, Hemswell, on death of William. Patron: Margaret, Countess of Cornwall. [Reg. 2, fo.95v.]

John de London acolyte
Instituted 8 April 1318 to church of All Saints, Hemswell, on dimission of John de Capella *in forma constitutionis*. Patron: Hugh Daudele the younger. [Reg. 2, fo.99v.]
Afterwards: Prebendary of St Mary, Shrewsbury, 1319.

Richard de Berkhamstede acolyte
Instituted 1 January 1318/19 to church of All Saints, Hemswell, on resignation of John de London (by exchange with prebend in royal free chapel of St Mary, Shrewsbury). Patron: King Edward II (13 November 1318). [Reg. 2, fo.100; *CPR 1317–21*, 227.]
Subdeacon: by 28 May 1319. Formerly: Prebendary of St Mary, Shrewsbury, to 1319. Dispensations for absence to study in England for 2 years, 28 May 1319; for 4 years, 4 August 1321. [Reg. 2, fo.327; *Reg. Burghersh* iii. no.161.]

Thomas de Rasyn priest
Instituted 23 February 1359/60 to church of All Saints, Hemswell, on death of Richard de Berkamsted. Patron: John Chaundos kt, lord of Kirton Lindsey (by John de Buckyngham, Archdeacon of Northampton, his attorney-general). Note that Thomas was instituted in person of Thomas Vaus, Vicar of Messingham, his proctor. [Reg. 9, fo.170.]

Roger de Rasyn clerk
Instituted 17 February 1361/2 to church of All Saints, Hemswell, on resignation of Thomas de Rasyn. Patron: John Chaundos kt, lord of St Sauveur le Vicomte (*Seynt Savoriis le Viscounte*) (by Robert de Morton his attorney-general). [Reg. 9, fo.173.]
Dispensation to study at Oxford, 20 September 1363. Still Rector in 1377 and 1381. [Reg. 12, fo.18v; Emden, *BRUO*, 1548; *Clerical Poll-Taxes*, nos 814, 2167, 2171.]

Simon Melburne
Instituted 23 October 1400 to church of Hemswell (cause of vacancy not stated). Patron: Henry, Prince of Wales. [Reg. 13, fo.131v.]

Roger Hampton clerk
Instituted 11 February 1400/1 to church of Hemswell, on resignation of Simon Melbourne. Patron: Prince Henry. [Reg. 13, fo.179v.]

Afterwards: R. of Houghton (Ha), 1410.

Robert Trays
Instituted 12 June 1410 to church of All Saints, Hemswell, on resignation of Roger Hampton (by exchange with church of Houghton, dioc. Winchester). Patron: Henry, Prince of Wales. [Reg. 14, fo.116v.]

Formerly: R. of Wadenhoe (Np), to 1401; R. of Two Parts of Rippingale, 1401–6 (*q.v.*); R. of Houghton (Ha), to 1410. Also: Canon of Lincoln and Prebendary of Bedford Major, 1401–2, and of Buckden, 1402–26. Residentiary canon; was unable through infirmity to attend Bishop Fleming's arbitration in the dispute between Dean Mackworth and the Chapter, April 1421. Died 21 December 1426. [*Le Neve Fasti: Lincoln 1300–1541*, 33, 43; *CPR 1416–22*, 404; Browne Willis iii. 155.]

John Tevelby
Instituted before 3 June 1433. [Reg. 17, fo.16v.]

Thomas Patteshull priest
Instituted 3 June 1433 to church of All Saints, Hemswell, on death of John Tevelby. Patron: Queen Katherine, daughter of King Charles of France and mother of the King of England. [Reg. 17, fo.16v.]

William Estby priest
Instituted 12 January 1434/5 to church of All Saints, Hemswell, on resignation of Thomas Patteshull. Patron: Queen Katherine, as above. [Reg. 17, fo.17.]

John Cotes chaplain
Instituted to church of All Saints, Hemswell, on resignation of William Estby. Patron: King Henry VI (18 August 1437). [*CPR Henry VI 1436–1441*, 78.]

There is no record of the institution of John Cotes in the episcopal register.

Clement Argent priest
Instituted 18 January 1451/2 to church of Hemswell, on death of John Cotes. Patron: King Henry VI. [Reg. 19, fos 69v, 81v.]

M. John Topclyf
Instituted 28 February 1484/5 to church of Hemswell, on resignation of Clement Argent. Patron: King Richard III. [Reg. 22 fo.163v.]

Educated: University of Oxford (BA, BCn&CL). Formerly: V. of Crowle (Wo), 1454–5. Papal dispensation to hold additional benefice, 1483. Also: R. of All SS Pavement, York, 1466–89; R. of Kirkby Underdale (YER), 1489; V. of Briston (Nf), 1494–1505. Died 1505. Will (PCC): dated 15 August 1505, proved 9 December 1505. [Emden, *BRUO*, 1886.]

Roger Adamson chaplain
Instituted 1 November 1505 to church of Hemswell, on death of last incumbent. Patron: King Henry VII. [Reg. 23, fo.156v.]

John Maltby chaplain
Instituted 22 April 1513 to church of Hemswell, on death of last incumbent. Patron: King Henry VIII. [Reg. 23, fo.146.]

Assessed for subsidy (£19 13s 4d) in 1526. [*Subsidy*, 37.]

Roger Norton BA
Instituted 15 April 1532 to church of Hemswell, on resignation of M. John Maltby. Patron: King Henry VIII, by reason of his Duchy of Cornwall. Note that an annual pension of £10 was reserved to the said M. John Maltby for life from the fruits of the church. [Reg. 27, fo.94v.]

Poor Clerk of Lincoln Cathedral, 1522. Educated: Magdalen College, Oxford (BA 1529; MA 1533); Fellow. Subdeacon: 20 September 1532; deacon: 21 December 1532 (Lincoln). Also: R. of Winteringham, 1554. Died 1559, probably in the plague ('one masse boke a manuell and a prossessoner, gone in parson Norton dayes in the plage tyme frome the parsonage and no man knoweth howe'). Will (Stow) dated 22 September 1559, proved at Lincoln 17 November 1559. To be buried in the chancel on the north side of the high altar, 'wherein the saynt [se]pulcre howse was sett in tymes heretofore'; bequeathed to Edward Wymark, Vicar of Searby, five books of Rogers; to John Berridge, Vicar of Blyton, a book of church history; to Mr Robinson of Springthorpe, 'my booke concernyng the blyssyd Sacramente'; requested his executors to cause 'some lernyd man to wryte me an Ephytath in verses or prose'. [*Chapter Acts of Lincoln* i. 30; Emden, *BRUO 1501–1540*, 419; Peacock, *Church Furniture*, 103; Stow Wills 1553–67/238.]

After the Reformation, Hemswell became a donative curacy in the gift of the Mayor and Citizens of Lincoln. It was served by curates, including:

Henry Greene
Occurs 1562–3.

Witnessed wills, 1562–3. [Stow Wills 1563/11v, 21v; Stow Wills 1564/3v.]

Richard Byrkyt
Presented by the Mayor and Citizens of Lincoln, 9 June 1565. [*HMC, Lincoln Corporation*, 60.]

Priest: 7 April 1566 (Lincoln). Witnessed wills, 1565–71. Afterwards: V. of Bishop Norton, 1575–93 (*q.v.*). [*Bishop Cooper*, 168; Stow Wills 1553–67/43v, 55; 1565–6/69, 72; 1568–75/23; 1572–4/157.]

Christopher Kitchingman
Admitted 15 September 1580. [*State of the Church*, 97.]

Education: 'bred in the schools'. Priest: 23 September 1576 (Chester). Still at Hemswell, 1586–7. Afterwards: R. of Ingoldmells, 1590–4. [*Ibid.*, 11, 97.]

Thomas Bulcocke
Curate by 1594. [*State of the Church*, 394.]

Signed BTs at Hemswell 1600–6. Also: C. of Harpswell, *c*.1594–1633. [BTs Hemswell.]

Oliver Mather
Granted sequestration of vicarage, 15 July 1607. Presented by the Mayor and Citizens of Lincoln, 28 July 1607. [Reg. 30, fo.310v; *HMC, Lincoln Corporation*, 81.]

Signed BTs at Hemswell 1608–10. [BTs Hemswell.]

Nicholas Cartwright
Licensed 21 July 1610. [LC 4, fo.11.]

Signed BTs at Hemswell 1611–17. Also: V. of Willoughton, 1612 (*q.v.*). [BTs Hemswell.]

Peter Coates
Occurs as curate, 1618–22. [BTs Hemswell.]

Christopher Dennis
Occurs as curate, 1623. [BTs Hemswell.]

Also: V. of Saxby, *c*.1620–8 (*q.v.*).

William Parkinson
Occurs as curate, 1635. [BTs Hemswell.]

Signed Protestation Return as Minister, 1642. Also: V. of Willoughton, 1646. [Binnall, *Hemswell*, 24.]

Nathaniel Tuke
Granted £5 per annum, 25 July 1657, for preaching at Hemswell. [*HMC, Lincoln Corporation*, 103.]

Oswald Rumney
Presented by the Mayor and Citizens of Lincoln, 2 June 1660. [*HMC, Lincoln Corporation*, 103.]

Deacon and priest (Carlisle). Resident (1662); signed BTs 1663–4. Also: V. of Glentworth, 1663–5 (*q.v.*). [LC 5, fos 82, 95; BTs Hemswell.]

Hamond Bulcocke
Occurs as minister, 1666–7. [BTs Hemswell.]

John Bulcock
Occurs as curate, 1670–83. [BTs Hemswell.]

Also: R. of Caenby, 1661–83 (*q.v.*).

Robert Gibson
Admitted 2 February 1683/4. [PR Hemswell.]

Education: Literate. Deacon: 31 August 1662 (Lincoln); priest: 14 June 1663 (York). Signed BTs at Hemswell 1684–91. Also: C. of Northorpe, 1663–90; Master of Laughton School. Father of William G. (see under Cammeringham). Buried at Laughton, 17 March 1691/2. [Reg. 32, fo.19v; *York Ordinations 1662–1699*, 26; BTs Hemswell; PR Laughton.]

Christopher Hillyard
Presented by Mayor and Citizens of Lincoln, 2 April 1692, 'in room of Mr Gibson, deceased'. [*HMC, Lincoln Corporation*, 112.]

Born 8 November 1668; son of Christopher H., Rector of Routh (YER). Educated: Beverley School and Peterhouse, Cambridge (matric. 1688; BA 1689–90). Deacon: 15 June 1690 (York); priest: 22 May 1692 (Lincoln). Also: C. of West Rasen, 1692. Afterwards: R. of Claxby by Normanby, 1693–1734; R. of Winestead (YER), 1711–22; R. of Rowley (YER), 1715–34. Buried at Rowley, 24 September 1734. [Venn, *Alumni*; Reg. 35, fo.4.]

John Towne
Presented by Mayor and Citizens of Lincoln, 4 August 1693, Christopher Hillyard 'having left the same and had taken no care to serve it'. [*HMC, Lincoln Corporation*, 112.]

Son of John T. of Sudbrook, par. Ancaster. Educated: Newark GS and Christ's College, Cambridge (matric. 1688; BA 1691–2). Deacon: 22 May 1692; priest: 3 June 1694 (Lincoln). Signed BTs at Hemswell 1696, 1705–23. Listed as Curate, 1697. Also: C. of Grayingham, 1692; R. of Grayingham (where he resided), 1694–1724. Died 1724. [Venn, *Alumni*; Peile ii. 107; Reg. 35, fos 4, 20; BTs Hemswell; LC 14, p.231c.]

Abraham Bigos
Licensed as curate, 9 September 1698. [Reg. 35, fo.51.]

Literate. Deacon: 11 June 1693 (Coventry & Lichfield); priest: 19 May 1695 (Lincoln). Formerly: C. of Weston under Lizard, 1693; C. of Waddingham, 1695. Also: C. of Willoughton, 1698. Signed BTs at Hemswell 1701–2. Afterwards: V. of Saxilby, 1702–7. [CCED; Reg. 35, fos 24v–25; BTs Hemswell.]

John Towne
Licensed as curate, 23 June 1703. [Reg. 35, fo.96v.]

See above.

John Whitehead
Occurs as curate, 1724–49. [BTs Hemswell.]

Deacon: 19 February 1721/2; priest: 9 June 1734 (Lincoln). Also: C. of Blyton; R. of Pilham, 1735–50. [Reg. 37, p.150; Reg. 38, p.290; LC 18B, 279.]

William White

Presented by Mayor and Citizens of Lincoln, 26 September 1749. [*HMC, Lincoln Corporation*, 117.]

Signed BTs at Hemswell 1750. Also: V. of Blyton, 1748–58; Usher of Lincoln School. Resided in Lincoln. Died 1758. Will (LCC). [BTs Hemswell; LCC Wills 1758/176.]

Edward Threlfal

Licensed as curate, 4 July 1759. [Reg. 38, p.568.]

Literate. Priest: 24 December 1752 (Lincoln). Also: C. of Blyton (where he resided), 1752–69; served cure of Hemswell for William White (signed BTs 1752–9); R. of Covenham St Mary, 1768–9. Buried at Blyton, 29 May 1769. [Reg. 38, p.516; BTs Hemswell; PR Blyton.]

Robert Wells DD

Instituted 6 September 1774. Patron: Mayor and Citizens of Lincoln. [Reg. 39, p.232.]

Born *c*.1734; son of Thomas W., R. of Willingham by Stow. Educated: Lincoln College, Oxford (matric. 1752; BA 1756; MA 1774; BD and DD 1774). Deacon: 19 September 1756; priest: 21 May 1758 (Lincoln). Formerly: C. of Springthorpe, 1756; served cure of Hemswell, 1763–71. Non-resident thereafter, Hemswell being served by Thomas Dawson, 1774–1802. Also: V. of Market Rasen, 1766–81; R. of Springthorpe, 1775–1807; R. of Willingham by Stow, 1781–1807. Died 26 March 1807; buried at Willingham, 1 April 1807. [Venn, *Alumni*; Reg. 38, pp. 545, 559; BTs Hemswell; PR Willingham by Stow.]

William Jackson LLB

Licensed 8 July 1807 to perpetual curacy of Hemswell, on death of Robert Wells. Nominated by Mayor, Sheriffs, Citizens and Commonalty of Lincoln (27 June 1807). [Reg. 40, p.122; PD 163/26.]

Also: V. of Ingham (*q.v.*).

Richard Thomas

Licensed 20 September 1823 to perpetual curacy of Hemswell, on death of William Jackson. Nominated by Mayor, Sheriffs, Citizens and Commonalty of Lincoln. [Reg. 40, p.335.]

Non-resident at Hemswell (which was served by curates) until 1839 when a new Vicarage House was built. Also: Usher of Lincoln School (resided at Lincoln); C. of Skellingthorpe, 1824; C. of Thorpe on the Hill, 1824. Buried at Hemswell, 9 June 1848 (aged 60). [Binnall, *Hemswell*, 60; CR 1, p.242; White, *Lincolnshire* (1842), 483–5; PR Hemswell.]

William Frankland Hood BA

Licensed 24 September 1848 to perpetual curacy of Hemswell, on death of Richard Thomas. Nominated by Revd James Adcock of Lincoln, clerk. Vacated by resignation, 9 August 1853 (accepted 11 August 1853). [Reg. 40, p.519; RES 243/44.]

Born *c*.1825; son of John H. of Yafforth (YNR) and subsequently of Nettleham Hall, esquire. Educated: Exeter College, Oxford (matric. 1843; BA 1847; MA 1849). Deacon: 18 June 1848; priest: 24 September 1848 (Lincoln). Resided at Hemswell Vicarage. Resigned 1853. Later of Nettleham Hall. On account of his delicate health, spent winters abroad, particularly in Egypt where he carried out archaeological research. Died 21 September 1864. [Foster, *Alumni*; Burke, *Landed Gentry* (1894), 983; OR 1, pp. 112–13; Census Returns 1851; Baker, *Nettleham*, 60; *Probate Calendar* 1864.]

James Basnett Mills MA

Licensed 29 December 1853 to perpetual curacy of Hemswell, on resignation of William Frankland Hood. Nominated by James Adcock of Greetham, clerk. [Reg. 40, p.548.]

Born *c*.1804; son of Samuel M. of Portsmouth, gent. Educated: Queen's College, Oxford (matric. 1825; MA 1827). Deacon: 1836 (Gloucester); priest: 1849 (Hereford). Also: Chaplain of St Edmund's Chapel, Spital; Domestic Chaplain to Earl of Zetland. Resided at Hemswell Vicarage. Died 13 March 1874 (aged 70). Memorial window in Hemswell Church. [Foster, *Alumni*; *Crockford* (1870); Census Returns 1861; White, *Lincolnshire* (1872), 160; *LDC* (1875), 114; Binnall, *Hemswell*, 75.]

Henry Williams

Licensed 28 September 1874 to perpetual curacy of Hemswell, on death of James Basnett Mills. Nominated by the Bishop of Lincoln, for this turn (by lapse). [Reg. 41, p.478.]

Born *c*.1828; son of Henry W. of Llangyfelach (Glam), clerk. Educated: Jesus College, Oxford (matric. 1847; BA 1851; MA 1854). Deacon: 1852 (Lichfield); priest: 1854 (Worcester). Formerly: C. of Blockley (Wo), 1859–61; of Bishops Canning (Wlt), 1861–2; of Overton and Fyfield (Wlt), 1862–4; of Malmesbury, 1864–6; of South Collingham (Nt), 1866–8; of Sutton-in-Ashfield (Nt), 1868–9; of Flintham (Nt), 1870–1; of Timberland, 1871–3; of Silk Willoughby, 1873–4. Resided at Hemswell Vicarage. Afterwards: V. of Sutton in the Marsh, 1879–92. Author: *The Medea, Alcestis and Hippolytus of Euripides translated into blank verse* (1871). Died 22 February 1892. [Foster, *Alumni*; *Crockford* (1878); *LDC* (1893), 109.]

Timothy Gascoigne Lynde

Licensed 2 July 1879 to perpetual curacy of Hemswell, on cession of Henry Williams. Nominated by Alexander Dickson Mills of Brook House, Godalming (Surrey), esquire. [Reg. 42, p.88.]

Born *c*.1824 at Westminster; son of James Gascoigne L., Secretary to Chelsea Water Works. Educated: University College, Durham (LTh 1855). Deacon: 1855 (Ripon); priest: 25 January 1857 (Durham). Formerly: C. of Bywell (Nb), 1856–8; of St Thomas, Ryde (IoW), 1858–9; R. of Whitchurch (He), 1859–63; C. of Eynesbury (Hu), 1863–5; of St Columba, Haggerston, London, 1865–70 and 1873–4; of St Leonard, Shoreditch, 1874–6; of St Peter, Vauxhall, 1876–9. Resided at Hemswell Vicarage. Also: PC of Harpswell, 1880–1908. Author: *Some Sacred Thoughts in Verse* (1901). Resigned 30 January 1908 (accepted 1 February 1908). Died 28 July 1913 at 141 Carholme Road, Lincoln. [PR Paddington St Mary Magdalene (1877); Census Returns 1891; Durham UL, DDR/EA/CL; *Crockford* (1908); Binnall, *Hemswell*, 75–6; White, *Lincolnshire* (1892); RES 248d/5; *Probate Calendar* 1913.]

Ernest Wentworth Vaughan MA

Licensed 16 April 1909 to perpetual curacy of Hemswell, on resignation of Timothy Gascoigne Lynde. Nominated by Randall Thomas, Archbishop of Canterbury, for this turn, by lapse. Note that on 26 February 1909, the Archbishop of Canterbury granted a dispensation enabling the said EWV to hold together the perpetual curacy of Hemswell and the perpetual curacy of Harpswell. [Reg. 42, p.608.]

Baptised 15 February 1867 at St Mary, Lambeth; son of James Henry Vaughan of Upper Norwood, stockbroker. Educated: St Leonards School, Jesus College, Cambridge (matric. 1885; BA 1888; MA 1892) and Wells Theological College (1888). Deacon: 1 June 1890; priest: 28 May 1891 (Lincoln). Formerly: C. of Alford, 1890–2; of Clewer (Brk), 1892–5; R. of Maltby-le-Marsh, 1895–7; C. of Hemswell, 1897–1908; of Woodhall Spa, 1908–9. Died 7 February 1911 at Hemswell (aged 44). [PR Lambeth St Mary; Venn, *Alumni*; *Crockford* (1909); *LDC* (1912), 189.]

Robert Phippen Carroll MA

Licensed 4 November 1911 to perpetual curacy of Hemswell, on death of Ernest Wentworth Vaughan. Nominated by Thomas William Rodwell of The Gables, Hacheston near Wickham Market (Suffolk), gentleman. Vacated by resignation, 22 January 1915 (accepted 29 January 1915). [Reg. 43, p.20; RES 248e/40.]

Born *c*.1858 at Kingstown, Dublin, Ireland. Educated: Trinity College, Dublin (BA 1885; MA 1892). Clerk in Church Temporalities Commission (Ireland), 1879. Deacon: 1889; priest: 1890 (Sodor and Man). Formerly: C. of St George, Douglas (IoM), 1889–91; of Christ Church, Bridlington (YER), 1891–2; of St Thomas, Dublin, 1893–7; of Christ Church, Gladesville, Sydney (NSW), 1898–9; of St Cuthbert, West Hampstead, 1902–4; of St Helen, Stapleford (Nt), 1904–6; of St Peter, Islington, 1906–8; of Shirley, Southampton, 1909–11. Afterwards: V. of Weybread (Sf), 1919–23. Latterly of 52 Ceylon Place, Eastbourne. Died 26 October 1934. [Census Returns 1901; *London Gazette*, 1 April 1879; *Crockford* (1932); *Probate Calendar* 1934.]

John Herbert Chisam Smith

Licensed 7 May 1915 to perpetual curacy of Hemswell, on resignation of Robert Phippen Carroll. Nominated by Thomas William Rodwell, as above. [Reg. 43, p.98.]

Born *c*.1874 at Whitehaven (Cu). Educated: St Bees College. Deacon: 1901; priest: 1902 (Llandaff). Formerly: C. of Merthyr Tydfil, 1901–5; of St Giles, Newcastle-under-Lyme, 1905–6; of All SS, Southport, 1906–12; of St George, Tufnell Park, 1912–13; of St Matthias, Upper Tulse Hill, 1913–15. Afterwards: C. of St Thomas, Edinburgh, 1915–16; Incumbent of Montrose Qualified Chapel, 1916–18; C. of St James, Ealing, 1918–23. Permission to officiate at St Simon, Hammersmith, from 1923. Changed name to Chisam-Smith. At 48 Granville Gardens, Shepherds Bush (1934). Retired to Montrose. Disappears from *Crockford*, 1955–6. [Census Returns 1911; *Crockford* (1951–2, 1955–6); Bertie, *Scottish Episcopal Clergy*.]

Henry Edward Bennett BA

Licensed 27 November 1915 to perpetual curacy of Hemswell, on resignation of John Herbert Chisam Smith. Nominated by Thomas William Rodwell, as above. Vacated by resignation, 14 September (accepted 12 October) 1917. [Reg. 43, p.127; RES 248f/25.]

Born *c*.1852 at North Anston (YWR); son of Samuel Bennett, shoemaker. Educated: Rotherham Theological College (1872) and Royal University of Ireland (BA 1888). Congregational Minister: at Uppingham (1881). Deacon: 1908; priest: 1909 (London). Formerly: C. of Holy Trinity, Hounslow, 1908–11; of Terrington St Clement (Nf), 1911–12; of St George Martyr, Deal (K), 1912–13; of Holy Trinity, Worthing, 1913–15. Retired 1917. Latterly of 24 Avondale Road, Southport: died there, 14 May 1922. [Census Returns 1861, 1881; *Crockford* (1916); *Probate Calendar* 1922.]

Robert Foster Burrow LLD

Licensed 22 May 1918 to perpetual curacy of Hemswell, on resignation of Henry Edward Bennett. Nominated by Thomas William Rodwell, as above. [Reg. 43, p.163.]

Born *c*.1848 at Cullompton (Dev). Educated: Scholae Cancellarii, Lincoln (1874); Philadelphia (LLD 1874). Deacon: 23 March 1875; priest: 17 December 1876 (Lincoln). Formerly: C. of St Paul-in-the-Bail, Lincoln, 1875–6; of Glentworth, 1876–7; of Cockfield (Du), 1877; of St Cuthbert, Darlington, 1877–8; of St Paul, Bath, 1878–9; PC of Laura Chapel, Bath, 1879–80; C. of Fordwich (K), 1880; R. of St Andrew, Droitwich with St Mary, Witton, 1880–7; V. of St Andrew, Bordesley, Birmingham, 1887–1900; C. of Symondsbury (Do), 1909–14. Died 16 January 1922. [Census Returns 1901; LTC 1; *Crockford* (1916); OR 2, pp.24, 30; *Probate Calendar* 1922.]

Edward Dalzell MA

Licensed 11 September 1922 to perpetual curacy of Hemswell, on death of Robert Foster Burrow. Nominated by Thomas William Rodwell, as above. [Reg. 43, p.282.]

The Perpetual Curacy of Harpswell was united to the Perpetual Curacy of Hemswell by Order in Council dated 10 August 1926 to form the United Benefice of Hemswell with Harpswell. [Reg. 43, pp. 400–2.]

Edward Dalzell MA

Licensed 20 May 1930 to united benefice of perpetual curacy of Hemswell with perpetual curacy of Harpswell, the perpetual curacy of Harpswell being vacant by resignation of Edward Wilcocks Raby. [Reg. 43, p.465.]

Born 15 May 1870; son of John D. of Loughgall, Armagh, Ireland. Assistant Schoolmaster at Park Villa School, Condover (Sa), 1891. Educated: Trinity College Dublin (BA 1894; MA 1898). Deacon: 1896; priest: 1897 (Cork). Formerly: C. of Nohoval with Tracton (Cork), 1896–1904; Incumbent of Castle Ventry with Kilkerranmore, 1904–17; C. of Marlesford (Sf), 1917–18; of Cretingham (Sf), 1918–19; of St Michael, Ipswich, 1919–22. Resignation accepted 15 December 1945. Latterly of 75 Southbourne Road, Southbourne, Bournemouth. Died 23 June 1959 at Bournemouth. [Census Returns 1891; *Crockford* (1951–2); Reg. 44, p.42; *LDC* (1960), 179; *Probate Calendar* 1959.]

George Arthur Tyson

Instituted 8 February 1952 to united benefice of Hemswell with Harpswell, on resignation of Edward Dalzell. Patron: King George VI for this turn, by lapse. Note that on 12 September 1951, the Archbishop of Canterbury granted a dispensation enabling the said GAT to hold together the vicarage of Glentworth and the united benefice of Hemswell with Harpswell. [Reg. 44, p.154.]

Also: V. of Glentworth (*q.v.*).

Guy Colville Nicholson
Instituted 30 October 1956 to united benefice of Hemswell with Harpswell, on cession of George Arthur Tyson. Patron: The Martyrs Memorial and Church of England Trust. Note that on 21 September 1956, the Archbishop of Canterbury granted a dispensation enabling the said GCN to hold together the united benefice of Hemswell with Harpswell and the vicarage of Glentworth. [Reg. 44, p.232.]

Also: V. of Glentworth (*q.v.*).

Gordon Bottomley
Instituted 9 February 1963 to united benefice of Hemswell with Harpswell, on resignation of Guy Colville Nicholson. Patron: The Martyrs Memorial and Church of England Trust. Note that on 29 January 1963, the Archbishop of Canterbury granted a dispensation enabling the said GB to hold together the united benefice of Hemswell with Harpswell and the vicarage of Glentworth. [Reg. 44, p.343.]

Also: V. of Glentworth (*q.v.*).

HEMSWELL ST HELEN

The advowson of the church of St Helen was held with Martin's manor by Oliver de Wendovere. By 1333 it had passed to the Crosholm family of Bishop Norton. No institutions to the church are recorded after 1379. [Binnall, *Hemswell*, 3; *Feudal Aids* iii. 152.]

Hugh
Instituted before 20 December 1287. [*Reg. Sutton* viii. 11.]

William de Wendovere clerk
Instituted 20 December 1287 to church of St Helen, Hemswell, on death of Hugh. Patron: Oliver de Wendovere. [*Reg. Sutton* viii. 11.]

Subdeacon: 20 December 1287 (Lincoln). Commissions to audit his accounts as coadjutor to Robert de Nevill, R. of Scotton, 22 January 1320/1, 20 December 1321 and 5 January 1321/2. [*Reg. Sutton* viii. 11; Reg. 5, fos 274, 300v, 301v.]

Robert Jackes de Norton priest
Instituted 29 December 1333 to church of St Helen, Hemswell, on death of

William. Patron: Joan widow of John de Crosholm senior. [*Reg. Burghersh* i. no.781.]

William de Langrave priest
Instituted 1 September 1349 to church of St Helen, Hemswell, on death of Robert. Patron: John de Croxholm. [Reg. 9, fo.156.]

Afterwards: V. of Eagle, 1353–72. [Reg. 10, fo.50v.]

Robert Hert de Haversham priest
Instituted 3 January 1352/3 to church of St Helen, Hemswell, on resignation of William (by exchange with vicarage of Eagle). Patron: John de Crosholm. [Reg. 9, fos 103v, 165.]

Priest: before 21 July 1349. Formerly: V. of Eagle, 1349–53. [Reg. 9, fo.61v.]

Simon Bray
Instituted 26 June 1361 to church of St Helen, Hemswell (cause of vacancy not stated). Patron: John de Crosholm. [Reg. 9, fo.171v.]

John (son of Hugh) de Garwell clerk
Instituted 9 April 1378 to church of St Helen, Hemswell, on death of Simon Bray. Patron: Robert de Grenefeld. [Reg. 10, fo.145.]

Afterwards: R. of Thorpe-on-the-Hill, 1379–90; V. of Saxilby, 1390–1; V. of Hose (Le), 1391. [Reg. 11, fos 46v, 105v, 107v.]

Thomas Stubbes priest
Instituted 1 April 1379 to church of St Helen, Hemswell, on resignation of John de Garewell (by exchange with church of Thorpe-on-the-Hill). Patron: Robert Grenefeld. [Reg. 10, fos 94v, 145.]

Formerly: R. of Wickenby, to 1379; R. of Thorpe-on-the-Hill, 1379. Still Rector in 1381. [Reg. 10, fo.93; *Clerical Poll-Taxes*, no.2168.]

INGHAM

The church of Ingham was granted to the Gilbertine Priory of Bullington by Philip of Kyme early in the reign of King Henry II. In 1214 a case of darrein presentment was brought against the Prior by two tenants of the Kyme family. This lawsuit was eventually settled in favour of the Priory in 1219, and this may explain why in 1218 the church was conferred on Gilbert de Jone by the Bishop. Although a charter of Geoffrey Plantagenet had authorised the appropriation by Bullington of twelve churches, it was not until 1310 that Ingham was appropriated, a vicarage being ordained in the following year. Bullington continued to present to the vicarage until the Dissolution. The advowson subsequently passed to the Bertie and then the

Monson families. Between 1695 and 1730 the living was under sequestration and no vicars were instituted. In the eighteenth century the advowson was acquired by the Nevile family of Wellingore. In 1887 and 1888, when the head of the family was a Roman Catholic, the patronage passed to the University of Cambridge for those turns. In 1913 the advowson was transferred to the Bishop of Lincoln, who still held it in 1965. [*Danelaw Charters*, 38–9; Golding, *Gilbertine Order*, 331–2; *EEA* i. no.286; Reg. 2, fo.95; Patronage/115; *LDC* (1965), 108–9.]

Church

Gilbert de Jone' Dean of City of Lincoln
Instituted before 20 December 1218 by collation to church of Ingham. Patron: Bishop of Lincoln. [*Rot. Welles* i. 125.]

M. Stephen de Cantebrigia clerk
Instituted in the tenth pontifical year of Bishop Hugh of Wells (20 December 1218/19 December 1219) to church of Ingham. Patron: G[ilbert], Prior of the Order of Sempringham, and the Convent of Bullington. [*Rot. Welles* i. 171.]

M. Robert de Paxton subdeacon
Instituted in the twenty-second pontifical year of Bishop Hugh of Wells (20 December 1230/19 December 1231) to church of Ingham. Patron: Master of the Order of Sempringham and Prior and Convent of Bullington. [*Rot. Welles* i. 230.]
Educated: University of Oxford (MA by 1230). Also: R. of Fordington, 1230/1–1232/3. [Emden, *BRUO*, 1440.]

William de Esenden chaplain
Instituted in the fourth pontifical year of Bishop Robert Grosseteste (17 June 1238/16 June 1239) to church of Ingham, on resignation of M. Robert de Paxton. Patron: Master of the Order of Sempringham and Prior and Convent of Bullington. Letters of institution issued 14 November 1240. [Hoskin, nos 565, 1246.]

M. Thomas (Malherbe) de Luda
Instituted before 31 March 1283. [Lunt, *Financial Relations*, 646.]
Educated: MA (perhaps University of Oxford). Formerly: R. of Adstock (Bk), 1259/60. Also: R. of Grainsby, 1264–90; R. of Thimbleby, 1265–95; R. of Bottesford, 1290–5. [Emden, *BRUO*, 1165.]

M. (Hugh son of) Durand of Lincoln subdeacon
Instituted 21 January 1285/6 to church of Ingham, on resignation of

M. Thomas de Luda. Patron: Prior and Convent of Bullington. [*Reg. Sutton* viii. 7.]

M. William de Louther clerk
Instituted 19 December 1293 to church of Ingham, on death of Hugh Durand. Patron: Prior and Convent of Bullington. Reinstituted 24 April 1295, because he had not been ordained priest within a year of institution; patron, as above. [*Reg. Sutton* viii. 23, 25.]

Subdeacon: 19 December 1293; LD for diaconate and priesthood: 1 March 1293/4 (Lincoln). Made agreement with Bullington (1294) for the profits of the church to be given to the Priory for 18 months, in return for the sum of £40 to be paid to William or his proctors at Bullington, Paris, Bologna or the Papal Curia, depending where he was. [*Reg. Sutton* vii. 46, 49; Golding, *Gilbertine Order*, 391.]

Roger de Bullingbrok subdeacon
Instituted 22 July 1296 to church of Ingham, on death of M. William de Louther. Patron: Prior and Convent of Bullington. [*Reg. Sutton* viii. 27.]

Deacon: 22 December 1296; priest: 25 February 1296/7 (Lincoln). [*Reg. Sutton* vii. 88, 91.]

M. William de Burgo acolyte
Instituted 21 May 1310 to church of Ingham, on death of Roger de Bolyngbrok. Patron: Prior and Convent of Bullington. [Reg. 2, fo.93v.]

Vicarage

William de Burg chaplain
Instituted 2 February 1310/11 to vicarage of Ingham, newly ordained. Patron: Prior and Convent of Bullington. [Reg. 2, fo.94v.]

John son of William de Thedelthorp priest
Instituted 31 January 1316/17 to vicarage of Ingham, on death of William de Burgo. Patron: Prior and Convent of Bullington. [Reg. 2, fo.98v.]

Gilbert Wilek priest
Instituted 1 August 1365 to vicarage of All Saints, Ingham, on death of John Thetilthorp. Patron: Prior and Convent of Bullington. [Reg. 10, fo.128.]

John Payntour de Luda priest
Instituted 11 March 1369/70 to vicarage of Ingham, on resignation of Gilbert. Patron: Prior and Convent of Bullington. [Reg. 10, fo.134.]

Afterwards: V. of Stow-by-Threckingham, 1370 (*q.v.*).

Thomas de Salteby (alias Sproxton) priest
Instituted 9 December 1370 to vicarage of Ingham, on resignation of John de
Luda (by exchange with vicarage of Stow-by-Threckingham). Patron: Prior
and Convent of Bullington. [Reg. 10, fos 43v, 136v.]
Formerly: V. of Stow-by-Threckingham, 1357–70 (*q.v.*).

William son of John Fligher priest
Instituted 3 October 1395 to vicarage of Ingham, on resignation of Thomas
de Sproxton. Patron: Prior and Convent of Bullington. [Reg. 11, fo.115v.]
Afterwards: V. of Kingerby, 1398.

Thomas Burnet priest
Instituted 22 January 1397/8 to vicarage of Ingham, on resignation of William
Flygher (by exchange with vicarage of Kingerby). Patron: Prior and Convent
of Bullington. [Reg. 11, fos 92, 120.]
Priest: before 8 January 1390/1. Formerly: V. of Kingerby, 1391–8. Afterwards: V. of
Legsby, 1400–1. [Reg. 11, fo.48v; Reg. 13, fo.142v.]

William son of Roger in le Hole de Asterby chaplain
Instituted 10 January 1399/1400 to vicarage of Ingham, on resignation of
Thomas Burnet (by exchange with vicarage of Legsby). Patron: Prior and
Convent of Bullington. [Reg. 13, fos 125v, 179.]
Priest: before 5 December 1386. Formerly: V. of Waddingworth, 1386–90; V. of Legsby,
1390–1400. Afterwards: V. of Hallington, 1403–12; V. of Longdon (St), 1412; V. of
Ingham (again), 1414. [Reg. 11, fos 27, 47; Reg. 14, fo.58.]

Ralph de Halyngton chaplain
Instituted 22 April 1403 to vicarage of Ingham, on resignation of William son
of Roger in le Hole de Asterby (by exchange with vicarage of Hallington).
Patron: Prior and Convent of Bullington. [Reg. 13, fos 158v, 181v.]
Priest: before 15 December 1376. Formerly: V. of Hallington, 1376–1403. [Reg. 10,
fo.81v.]

William son of Roger in le Hole de Aysterby priest
Instituted 3 April 1414 to vicarage of Ingham, on death of Ralph de Halyn-
gton. Patron: Prior and Convent of Bullington. [Reg. 14, fo.124v.]
V. of Ingham (1400–3), above.

John Lofte chaplain
Instituted 9 May 1457 to vicarage of Ingham (cause of vacancy not stated).
Patron: Prior and Convent of Bullington. [Reg. 20, fo.159.]

John Bacheler priest
Instituted 6 April 1464 to vicarage of Ingham, on resignation of John Lofte.
Patron: Prior and Convent of Bullington. [Reg. 20, fo.161.]

Richard Dighton
Instituted 16 April 1485 to vicarage of Ingham, on resignation of John
Bacheler. Patron: Prior and Convent of Bullington. [Reg. 22, fo.164.]
Assessed for subsidy (£4 13s 4d) in 1526. [*Subsidy*, 36.]

John Grifeson
Instituted 16 January 1535/6 to vicarage of Ingham, on death of Richard
Dighton. Patron: Prior (Richard) and Convent of Bullington (31 August
1535). [Reg. 27, fo.96v; PD 1535/13.]
Witnessed wills, 20 April 1538; 23 October 1548. Died *c*.1553 (Will). [Stow Wills 1530–
52/24v, 465; 1531–56/46.]

Brian Fycheborn
Instituted *c*.1553 (compounded for first-fruits, 3 July 1553) to vicarage of
Ingham, on death of John Greveson. Patron: John Halle (14 June 1553) by
grant of next presentation made by dissolved Prior and Convent of Bullington
to John Draycotes and by John Draycotes to John Halle. [FL.h.13, 505; PD
1553/15.]

Peter Toller
Instituted before 17 May 1568. [Reg. 28, fo.39.]

Thomas Walker
Instituted 17 May 1568 to vicarage of Ingham, on death of Peter Toller.
Patron: Richard Bertie of Eresby, esquire. [Reg. 28, fo.39.]
Deacon: 17 May 1568; priest: 16 April 1569 (Lincoln). Resident: signed BTs 1600–22.
Buried at Ingham, 16 January 1625/6. Will. [LC 4, fo.10; BTs Ingham; PR Ingham; Stow
Wills 1624–5/263.]

Richard Clayton MA
Instituted 7 March 1625/6 to vicarage of Ingham, on death of last incumbent.
Patron: Sir Robert Mounson kt (4 March 1625/6). [PD 1626/39.]

Robert Coulton BA
Instituted 12 June 1629 to vicarage of Ingham, on resignation of Richard
Clayton. Patron: Sir Robert Mounson kt (2 June 1629). [BC; PD 1629/30.]
Educated: Magdalene College, Cambridge (matric. 1618). Deacon: 23 May 1624; priest:
24 May 1624 (Peterborough). Buried at Ingham, 14 January 1631/2. [Venn, *Alumni*; PR
Ingham.]

Caleb Dalechamp MA
Instituted 28 September 1632 to vicarage of Ingham. Patron: Bishop of
Lincoln (by lapse). [BC.]
Born Sedan; perhaps of Huguenot extraction. Educated: Trinity College, Cambridge (MA

1634; BD 1633). Resident at Ingham, 1637–45. Also: R. of South Ferriby, 1634. Author: *Christian Hospitalitie* (1632) and other works. Father of Robert D., baptised at Ingham 11 October 1638. [Binns, *Intellectual Culture* (1990), 150; Venn, *Alumni*; PR Ingham.]

Samuel Lownes BA

Instituted 15 October 1675 to vicarage of Ingham, on death of Caleb de la Champ. Patron: Brian Nevile esquire. [Reg. 34, fo.3.]

Signed BTs at Ingham 1676–94. Also: V. of Cammeringham, 1677–95 (*q.v.*).

Between 1695 and 1730 the Vicarage of Ingham was under sequestration and served by curates William Gibson (1695–1705) and John Johnson (1705–30). [PR Ingham; LC 14, p.231c; *Speculum*, 163.]

Francis Howson

Instituted 5 September 1730 to vicarage of Ingham, on death of [John] Johnson. Patron: Bishop of Lincoln (by lapse). [Reg. 38, p.230.]

Also: V. of Cammeringham, 1730–73 (*q.v.*).

Tillotson Laycock BA

Instituted 17 June 1773 to vicarage of Ingham, on death of Francis Howson. Patron: Christopher Nevile of Wellingore, esquire. [Reg. 39, p.200.]

Also: V. of Cammeringham, 1773–1813 (*q.v.*).

William Jackson LLB

Instituted 27 October 1813 to vicarage of Ingham, on death of Tillotson Laycock. Patron: Christopher Nevile of Wellingore, esquire (11 October 1813). [Reg. 40, p.191; PD 169/11.]

Educated: St Catharine's College, Cambridge (LLB 1795). Deacon: 24 February 1793; priest: 6 April 1794 (Lincoln). Formerly: C. of Willingham by Stow, 1793. Also: R. of Nettleton, 1801–23; C. of Fillingham (resident), 1802–18; PC of Hemswell, 1807–23 (*q.v.*); C. of Burton by Lincoln (resident), 1818–23. Licensed for non-residence at Hemswell, 'the House of Residence being a small Cottage unfit for the residence of a Clergyman'. Died 4 June 1823. [Venn, *Alumni* (his Cambridge career is difficult to disentangle from that of a contemporary); Reg. 39, pp. 571, 589; CR 1, pp. 21, 90; NRL 1811/14; 1813/25; PR Nettleton.]

Matthew Hodge MA

Instituted 10 September 1823 to vicarage of Ingham, on death of William Jackson. Patron: Christopher Nevile of Bath, esquire. [Reg. 40, p.334.]

Also: R. of Fillingham (*q.v.*).

Samuel King Webster MA

Instituted 17 November 1852 to vicarage of Ingham, on death of Matthew Hodge. Patron: Henry Nevile of Walcot Park near Stamford, esquire. [Reg. 40, p.538.]

Baptised 30 April 1819 at Oakington (Ca); son of Thomas W., Vicar of Oakington. Educated: St Paul's School (1826–38) and Emmanuel College, Cambridge (matric. 1838; BA 1842; MA 1845). Deacon: 1842; priest: 1843 (Peterborough). Formerly: C. of Barnack (Np), 1842–51. Married (12 July 1842) Maria, daughter of Revd Herbert Randolph, Rector of Letcombe Basset (Brk). Built new Vicarage House (1852), where he resided. Died there, 30 March 1887. The sale of his effects, held at the Vicarage on 3 May 1887, included two pianofortes, a mahogany telescope, a 'set lawn tennis', a gig, a pony cart and four hives of bees. [Venn, *Alumni*; *St Paul's School Register*; *Reading Mercury*, 16 July 1842; Census Returns 1851 (Barnack), 1861; White, *Lincolnshire* (1872); *Probate Calendar* 1887; *Lincolnshire Chronicle*, 29 April 1887.]

John Sanderson MA

Instituted 2 November 1887 to vicarage of Ingham, on death of Samuel King Webster. Patron: University of Cambridge (the patron being a Roman Catholic). [Reg. 42, p.259.]

Also: V. of Glentworth (*q.v.*).

Henry Christopher Ricketts Macpherson BA

Instituted 4 August 1888 to vicarage of Ingham, on resignation of John Sanderson. Patron: University of Cambridge, as above. [Reg. 42, p.282.]

Born 1847 at Bath; son of Alexander John M., Captain in HM Army. Educated: Hatfield College, Durham (BA 1872; MA 1897). Lt RMLI, 1865–70. Deacon: 21 September 1873 (Ripon); priest: 23 March 1875 (Lincoln). Formerly: C. of Penistone, 1873–4; of St John, Nottingham, 1874–5; of Thurgarton (Nt), 1876–9; of Thwing (Y), 1880–3; of St Thomas, Regent St (Mx), 1883–5; of Binbrook, 1886–7; of St John, Buenos Aires, 1887–8. Resided at Ingham Vicarage. Afterwards: V. of St James, Isle of Grayne (K), 1893–1916; R. of Copdock with Washbrook (Sf), 1916–23; Chaplain to Lord Walsingham, 1916–19. Founder and Head of Clergy Rating Federation, which procured Tithe Act of 1899. Latterly of 8 Norman Avenue, Henley-on-Thames; died there, 13 May 1936. [*Crockford* (1932); OR 2, p.24; Census Returns 1891; White, *Lincolnshire* (1892); *Probate Calendar* 1936.]

John Francis Edward Cudmore MA

Instituted 28 April 1894 to vicarage of Ingham, on cession of Henry Christopher Ricketts Macpherson. Patron: Thomas Henry Burroughes of Ketton, esquire. [Reg. 42, p.362.]

Born *c*.1858 in Ireland. Educated: Trinity College, Dublin (BA 1883; MA 1888). Deacon: 1885; priest: 1886 (London). Formerly: C. of Christ Church, Clapton (Mx), 1885–6; C. of St Stephen, Poplar, 1886–8; C. of St Peter, Bushey Heath, 1888–9; V. of Sutton St Nicholas, 1890–4. Resided at Ingham Vicarage. Also: V. of Cammeringham, 1914–28. Resigned 26 July (accepted 30 August) 1928. Retired to 'Andover', Lacey Green, Wilmslow. Died 17 March 1935. [*Crockford* (1932); *LDC* (1914), 83; RES 1928/11; *Probate Calendar* 1935.]

The Vicarage of Cammeringham was united to the Vicarage of Ingham by Order in Council dated 12 October 1925 to form the United Benefice of Ingham with Cammeringham. [Reg. 43, pp. 379–80.]

Arthur Cecil Northon
Instituted 5 November 1928 by collation to united benefice of Ingham with Cammeringham, on resignation of John Francis Edward Cudmore. Patron: Bishop of Lincoln. [Reg. 43, p.438.]

Worked as a farmer for most of his life. Deacon: 19 December 1926; priest: 18 December 1927 (Lincoln). Formerly: C. of Pinchbeck, 1926–8. Resigned 30 September 1947. Latterly of 'The Poplars', Fiskerton (Li). Died 12 December 1949 (aged 79). 'A faithful parish priest, of gentle disposition.' [*Crockford* (1947); *LDM* 1926–7; Reg. 44, p.77; *Probate Calendar* 1950; *LDM* 66 (1950), 54.]

Leonard Walter Hicks Withers-Lancashire
Instituted 14 April 1948 to united benefice of Ingham with Cammeringham, on resignation of Arthur Cecil Northon. Patron: Bishop of Lincoln. Note that on 19 March 1948, the Archbishop of Canterbury granted a dispensation enabling the said LWHW-L to hold together the rectory of Fillingham and the united benefice of Ingham with Cammeringham. [Reg. 44, p.85.]

Born 4 October 1908; son of Gerald W-L. Educated: Kelham Theological College (1927). Deacon: 1932; priest: 1933 (Canterbury). Formerly: C. of Westbere, 1932–4; of St Michael, Beckenham, 1934–8; of All SS, Brighton, 1938–40; Chaplain of All Hallows, Ditchingham, 1940–3; C. of St Edmund, Forest Gate, 1943–4; of St Andrew, Coulsdon, 1944–6. Also: R. of Fillingham, 1946–54 (*q.v.*). Resided at Fillingham Rectory, 1946–8; at Ingham Vicarage, 1948–54. Afterwards: V. of St John Divine, Gainsborough, 1954–9; C. of Stanwell, 1959; of West Wycombe, 1962–9; of Gedling and of Netherfield, 1969–76. Retired 1976. Lived at 19a Bridge Road, Worthing. Died there June 1983. [GRO, Death Index; *Crockford* (1980–2).]

Ronald Palin Woods
Instituted 13 July 1954 to united benefice of Ingham with Cammeringham, on cession of Leonard Walter Hicks Withers-Lancashire. Patron: Bishop of Lincoln. Note that on 5 July 1954, the Archbishop of Canterbury granted a dispensation enabling the said RPW to hold together the united benefice of Ingham with Cammeringham and the rectory of Fillingham. [Reg. 44, p.195.]

Born 24 December 1916. Educated: Bishops' College, Cheshunt (1948). Deacon: 12 June 1949; priest: 4 June 1950 (Lincoln). Formerly: C. of St Mary and St James, Grimsby, 1949–54. Also: R. of Fillingham, 1954–9. Resided at Ingham Vicarage. Resigned 21 September (accepted 30 September) 1959. Afterwards: in Matabeleland as C. of Shangani Reserve, 1959–61; P-in-C of Bembesi, 1961–3; and Asst P. of Que Que, 1963–4; R. of Diego Martin (Trinidad), 1965–70; V. of Balsall Heath (Wo), 1970–2; Missioner, Rhodesia Railway Mission, 1972–3; C. of St Cuthbert, Gwelo, 1973–5; V. of Wankie (both Matabeleland), 1975–6; C. of Spalding, 1977–8; V. of Wrangle, 1978–81; of All SS, Grimsby, 1981–5. Retired 1985. Latterly of St Paul's House, Clarence Place, Penzance. Died October 1987. [GRO, Death Index; *LDM* (1949, 1950); RES 1959/17; Reg. 44, p.283; *LDC* (1959), 56; *Crockford* (1980–2).]

Alun John Morris Virgin MA
Instituted 27 July 1960 to united benefice of Ingham with Cammeringham, on resignation of Ronald Palin Woods. Patron: Bishop of Lincoln. Note

that on 20 April 1960, the Archbishop of Canterbury granted a dispensation enabling the said AJMV to hold together the united benefice of Ingham with Cammeringham and the rectory of Fillingham. [Reg. 44, pp.298–9.]

Born 15 October 1927. Educated: Balliol College, Oxford (BA 1950; MA 1957) and Wycliffe Hall, Oxford (1951). Deacon: 1953 (Chelmsford); priest: 1954 (Birmingham). Formerly: C. of St Matthias, Canning Town (Ess), 1953–4; of Northfield, 1954–5; of Acock's Green (Wa), 1955–6; Chaplain of Wellesbourne School, 1956–60. Resided at Ingham Vicarage. Also: R. of Fillingham, 1960–71 (*q.v.*). Afterwards: R. of Huntspill (So), 1971–82. Died September 1982. [GRO, Death Index; *Crockford* (1969–70, 1980–2).]

NORMANBY-BY-SPITAL

The Domesday Survey recorded a priest and a church on the holding of Ivo Taillebois at Normanby. This manor passed to Ranulf Meschin by *c.*1115 and in 1189x1191 William de Roumare, who had inherited Meschin's estate, granted the church of Normanby to Peterborough Abbey. Peterborough continued to present to the rectory until 1312. In 1314, as part of the negotiations involved in the projected appropriation of the wealthy Northampton-shire church of Warmington, the Abbey granted the advowson of Normanby to Bishop Dalderby and the Chapter of Lincoln. The abbey also surrendered its right to an annual pension of 10 marks from the church, in order that it might be used to endow a chantry for Dalderby's soul. Normanby was appropriated to the Dean and Chapter in 1317, and in 1322 a vicarage was ordained, whereby the vicar was to receive an annual stipend of seven marks from the Chapter. The Dean and Chapter still held the advowson in 1965. [*Lincolnshire Domesday*, 81, 239; *Summoning St Michael*, 226–7; *EEA* iv. no.154; *White Book*, no.247; Franklin, 'The Bishop, the Abbot and Warmington Rectory', 202–5; Reg. 2, fo.99v; *Reg. Burghersh* i. no.41; *LDC* (1965), 108–9.]

Church

Roger de Ver
Instituted before 1223–4. [*Rot. Welles* i. 220.]

William de Burgo clerk
Instituted in the fifteenth pontifical year of Bishop Hugh of Wells (20 December 1223/19 December 1224) to church of Normanby-by-Spital, on resignation of Roger de Ver. Patron: Abbot and Convent of Peterborough. [*Rot. Welles* i. 220.]

John de Monte Pessolano subdeacon
Instituted in the sixteenth pontifical year of Bishop Hugh of Wells (20

December 1224/19 December 1225) to church of Normanby-by-Spital, on resignation of William de Burgo. Patron: Abbot and Convent of Peterborough. [*Rot. Welles* i. 223.]

John de Hothum
Instituted before 29 February 1275/6. [*Rot. Gravesend*, 94.]

William de Alwalton subdeacon
Instituted 29 February 1275/6 to church of Normanby-by-Spital, on death of John de Hothum. Patron: Abbot and Convent of Peterborough. [*Rot. Gravesend*, 94.]

Nicholas de Ludington subdeacon
Instituted 27 August 1277 to church of Normanby-by-Spital, on death of William. Patron: Abbot and Convent of Peterborough. [*Rot. Gravesend*, 96.]

Afterwards: R. of Paston (Np), 1283–94. Died before 24 September 1294. [*Reg. Sutton* ii. 27, 117.]

Robert de Ferrariis of Fotheringhay subdeacon
Instituted 17 June 1283 to church of Normanby-by-Spital, on institution of Nicholas de Lodington to church of Paston. Patron: Abbot and Convent of Peterborough. [*Reg. Sutton* viii. 4.]

M. John de Aylington acolyte
Instituted 24 August 1312 to church of Normanby-by-Spital, on death of Robert. Patron: Abbot and Convent of Peterborough. [Reg. 2, fo.96.]

John de Ulseby
Instituted before 15 February 1316/17. [Reg. 2, fo.337.]

M. Thomas de Luda priest
Granted church of Normanby-by-Spital *in commendam* 15 February 1317, on resignation of John de Ulseby. Patron: Dean and Chapter of Lincoln. [Reg. 2, fo.337.]

Resigned commend 21 February 1316/17, on appropriation of church to Dean and Chapter.

Vicarage

Robert de Drayton priest
Instituted 10 March 1321/2 to vicarage of Normanby-by-Spital, newly ordained. Patron: Dean and Chapter of Lincoln. [*Reg. Burghersh* i. no.41.]

Hugh de Burton iuxta Beverlacum priest
Instituted 7 August 1332 to vicarage of Normanby-by-Spital, on resignation

of Robert. Patron: Subdean and Chapter of Lincoln (the Dean being absent). [*Reg. Burghersh* i. no.770.]

John de Osgodby priest
Instituted 5 July 1349 to vicarage of Normanby-by-Spital, on death of Hugh. Patron: Chapter of Lincoln. [Reg. 9, fo.155.]

William de Malteby priest
Instituted 15 August 1349 to vicarage of Normanby-by-Spital, on death of John de Osgodby. Patron: Chapter of Lincoln. [Reg. 9, fo.156.]

Walter de Risceby priest
Instituted 5 April 1353 to vicarage of Normanby-by-Spital, on resignation of William son of Robert de Malteby. Patron: Subdean and Chapter of Lincoln (the Dean being absent). [Reg. 9, fo.166.]

Walter de Welwyk
Instituted before 14 June 1374. [Reg. 10, fo.140.]

Robert son of William de Malberthorp priest
Instituted 14 June 1374 to vicarage of Normanby-by-Spital, on death of Walter de Welwyk. Patron: Subdean and Chapter of Lincoln (the Dean being *in remotis*). [Reg. 10, fo.140.]

Robert Marschall de Twyford priest
Instituted 26 September 1390 to vicarage of Normanby-by-Spital, on death of Robert. Patron: Dean and Chapter of Lincoln. [Reg. 11, fo.105v.]

Thomas Burnett chaplain
Instituted 20 December 1401 to vicarage of Normanby-by-Spital, on resignation of Robert Twyford. Patron: Subdean and Chapter of Lincoln. [Reg. 13, fo.180v.]

John de Osgodby chaplain
Instituted 25 April 1403 to vicarage of Normanby-by-Spital, on death of Thomas Burnet. Patron: Subdean and Chapter of Lincoln (the Dean being absent). [Reg. 13, fo.182.]

John Kyrkeby
Instituted before 10 November 1412. [Reg. 14, fo.122v.]
Afterwards: R. of St Paul, Lincoln, 1412.

David de Worthyn priest
Instituted 10 November 1412 to vicarage of Normanby-by-Spital, on resigna-

tion of John Kyrkeby (by exchange with church of St Paul, Lincoln). Patron: Dean and Chapter of Lincoln. [Reg. 14, fos 58v, 122v.]

Formerly: R. of mediety of Llandinam (Mont), to 1411; R. of St Paul, Lincoln, 1411–12. Afterwards: Chaplain of St Mary Chantry in Church of Heckington, 1413–14. [Reg. 14, fos 50v, 68.]

William Otryngham de Wotton priest

Instituted 31 October 1413 to vicarage of Normanby-by-Spital, on resignation of David Worthin (by exchange with chantry of St Mary in parish church of Heckington). Patron: Subdean and Chapter of Lincoln (the Dean being absent). [Reg. 14, fo.123.]

Formerly: Chaplain of St Mary Chantry in Church of Heckington, to 1413. Afterwards: V. of Cherry Willingham, 1418–22; V. of Martin-by-Horncastle, 1422. [Reg. Fleming i. nos 157, 412.]

James [Burgh]

Instituted 27 October 1418 to vicarage of Normanby-by-Spital, on resignation of William Otryngham (by exchange with vicarage of Cherry Willingham). Patron: President and Chapter of Lincoln (the Dean and Subdean being absent). [Reg. 14, fo.134.]

Priest: before 13 January 1411/12. Formerly: V. of Cherry Willingham, 1412–18. [Reg. 14, fo.120.]

Hugh Mawnus priest

Instituted 19 August 1420 to vicarage of Normanby-by-Spital, on resignation of James Burgh. Patron: Dean and Chapter of Lincoln. [Reg. Fleming i. no.402.]

Afterwards: Chaplain of Chantry in Church of West Rasen, 1423.

William Halton

Instituted 29 July 1423 to vicarage of Normanby-by-Spital, on resignation of Hugh Mawnus (by exchange with chantry in church of West Rasen). Patron: Subdean and Chapter of Lincoln (the Dean being absent). [Reg. Fleming i. nos 206, 426.]

Priest: before 25 September 1416. Formerly: Chaplain of Chantry in Church of West Rasen, 1416–23. [Reg. 14, fo.83.]

Thomas Medley priest

Instituted 19 April 1457 to vicarage of Normanby-by-Spital (cause of vacancy not stated). Patron: President and Chapter of Lincoln (the Dean and Subdean being absent). [Reg. 20, fo.159.]

Afterwards: Chaplain of Burghersh Chantry in Lincoln Cathedral, 1465.

William Grey alias Elryk priest

Instituted 15 September 1465 to vicarage of Normanby-by-Spital, on resignation of Thomas Medley (by exchange with chaplaincy of Burghersh chantry in Lincoln Cathedral). Patron: Dean and Chapter of Lincoln. [Reg. 20, fo.161.]

Formerly: Chaplain of Burghersh Chantry in Lincoln Cathedral, to 1465.

Thomas Oldham priest
Instituted 8 May 1476 to vicarage of Normanby-by-Spital, on death of William Gray. Patron: Dean and Chapter of Lincoln. [Reg. 21, fo.33v.]

William Walker priest
Instituted 11 February 1498/9 to vicarage of Normanby-by-Spital, on resignation of Thomas Oldham. Patron: Dean and Chapter of Lincoln. [Reg. 23, fo.150v.]

Richard Chylde priest
Instituted 22 January 1506/7 to vicarage of Normanby-by-Spital, on resignation of William Wakar. Patron: Dean and Chapter of Lincoln. [Reg. 23, fo.119.]

John Clerc
Instituted 1522 to vicarage of Normanby-by-Spital. Patron: Dean and Chapter of Lincoln, on nomination of the Dean (1 April 1522). [*Chapter Acts of Lincoln* i. 26.]

Assessed for subsidy (£7 13s 4d) in 1526. [*Subsidy*, 36.]

Robert Larke chaplain
Instituted 7 July 1529 to vicarage of Normanby-by-Spital, on death of John Clarke. Patron: Subdean and Chapter of Lincoln (3 July 1529). [Reg. 27, fo.99v; *Chapter Acts of Lincoln* i. 122.]

Thomas Barnes
Instituted 14 April 1536 to vicarage of Normanby-by-Spital, on resignation of Robert Larke. Patron: Dean and Chapter of Lincoln, on nomination of Subdean (25 March 1535). [Reg. 27, fo.62; *Chapter Acts of Lincoln* i. 190.]

Oliver Clayton priest
Instituted 1 February 1542/3 to vicarage of Normanby-by-Spital, on death of Thomas Barnes. Patron: Dean and Chapter of Lincoln, on nomination of George Heneage, Archdeacon of Lincoln (16 January 1542/3). [Reg. 27, fo.101; *Chapter Acts of Lincoln* ii. 72.]

Witnessed will, 11 October 1548; 20 May 1552. [Stow Wills 1530–52/456v; 1531–56/48.]

Robert Freman priest
Instituted 1556 to vicarage of Normanby-by-Spital, on dimission of Oliver

Clayton. Patron: Subdean and Chapter of Lincoln, on nomination of the Subdean (14 April 1556). [*Chapter Acts of Lincoln* iii. 126.]

George Johnson
Occurs as Vicar 12 May 1559 as witness to will. [Stow Wills 1553–67/243v.]

Richard Wright
Occurs as Vicar 11 September 1561 as witness to will. [Stow Wills 1569–71/41v.]

The vicarage of Normanby-by-Spital was said to be vacant in 1576 and was served by Philip Wright as curate in 1594. [*Bishop Cooper*, 168; *State of the Church*, 394.]

Thomas Wade
Instituted 28 June 1594 to vicarage of Normanby-by-Spital (cause of vacancy not stated). Patron: Queen Elizabeth I (26 June 1594), by lapse. [BC; PD 1594/35.]

Education: 'no graduate; no preacher'. Resident. Held no other benefice. [*State of the Church*, 330.]

Richard Cater
Instituted 28 September 1601 to vicarage of Normanby-by-Spital, on death of last incumbent. Patron: Dean (Laurence Stanton) and Chapter of Lincoln (26 September 1601). [BC; PD 1601/34.]

Baptised 9 July 1575 at Boston; son of Thomas C. Educated: Trinity College, Cambridge; no graduate. At Butterwick, 1595–1600. Deacon: 16 March 1599/1600; priest: 27 September 1601 (Lincoln). Resident (1611); signed BTs at Normanby between 1602 and 1628. Died 1637. [PR Boston; PD 1601/34; Venn, *Alumni*; LC 3, fo.99v; LC 4, fo.10v; BTs Normanby-by-Spital; Stow Admons 1636–8/271.]

Christopher Bagshawe MA
Instituted 10 November 1637 to vicarage of Normanby-by-Spital, on death of Master Cater. Patron: Dean and Chapter of Lincoln (19 September 1637). [AC; D & C A/3/9, fo.197.]

Perhaps to be identified with CB, son of George B., Vicar of Haselbech (Np). Educated: St John's College, Oxford (BA). Deacon: 28 August 1629; priest: 29 August 1629 (Peterborough). Was serving Haselbech in 1650. [Longden i. 137; *Walker Revised*, 238.]

Between 1660 and 1749 the vicarage of Normanby-by-Spital was under sequestration and the living was served by curates, including William Nunwick (1660–78); Joseph Dawber (1678–88); Brian Smyth (1688–1704); Thomas Reith (1707–18); and John Dunn (1718–48). [BTs Normanby-by-Spital; LC 14, p.232; *Speculum*, 166.]

John Austin MA
Instituted 18 May 1749 to vicarage of Normanby-by-Spital (cause of vacancy
not stated). Patron: Dean and Chapter of Lincoln. [Reg. 38, p.487.]

Also: V. of Glentham (*q.v.*).

Between 1758 and 1843 the vicarage of Normanby-by-Spital was under
sequestration and the living was served by curates, including Wyvell Blen-
nerhassett (1764–6); Samuel Proctor (1770–80); William Pearson (1797–9);
Thomas Wilson (1800–8); William Wilkinson (1809–41). [PR Normanby-by-
Spital; LC 31, p.199.]

Oswald Joseph Cresswell
Instituted 1843 to vicarage of Normanby-by-Spital, on death of last incumbent. Patron: Queen Victoria (2 January 1843). [PD/Crown/76.]

Born *c.*1803; 5th son of Francis C. (formerly Easterby) of Charlton (K), gent., and Frances
Dorothea Cresswell of Cresswell (Nb), his wife. Educated: Corpus Christi College, Oxford
(matric. 1820; BA 1824; MA 1827). Deacon: 1826; priest: 10 June 1827 (Ely for Durham).
Formerly: C. of Mitford. Also: V. of Seaham (Du), 1827. Married (10 January 1837) Anna
Maria, daughter of Canon Strong, R. of Sedgefield (Du). Resigned 21 June (accepted 24
June) 1844. Afterwards: R. of Hanworth (Mx), 1846–71. Died at Hanworth Rectory, 7
June 1871. [Burke, *Landed Gentry* (1900), 343; *Oxford Journal*, 23 June 1827; Census
Returns 1851; RES 242/45; *Probate Calendar* 1871.]

James Johnson
Instituted 21 September 1844 to vicarage of Normanby-by-Spital, on resig-
nation of Oswald Joseph Cresswell. Patron: Dean and Chapter of Lincoln.
[Reg. 40, p.499.]

Also: V. of Glentham (*q.v.*).

John Fardell Bassett BA
Instituted 26 November 1858 to vicarage of Normanby-by-Spital, on death
of James Johnson. Patron: Dean and Chapter of Lincoln. [Reg. 40, p.597.]

Also: V. of Glentham (*q.v.*).

Henry Simpson Blink
Instituted 28 April 1894 to vicarage of Normanby-by-Spital, on death of John
Fardell Bassett. Patron: Dean and Chapter of Lincoln. [Reg. 42, p.360.]

Also: R. of Owmby (*q.v.*).

**The Vicarage of Normanby-by-Spital was united to the Rectory of
Owmby by Order in Council dated 26 October 1899. [Reg. 42, pp. 451–5.]**

BISHOP NORTON

The church of Bishop Norton formed part of the episcopal manor of Stow before 1066. It had become the endowment of a prebend in Lincoln Cathedral by 1254. A vicarage was ordained in 1323. The vicar was to have one third part of a messuage on the north side of the church, in which the prebendary as rector was to build a hall, a chamber with solar, a kitchen, barn and stable. The vicar was to receive tithes of hay in Atterby and all other tithes, oblations and mortuaries, except tithes of grain and wool, and tithes of hay from other lands. Successive prebendaries continued to present to the vicarage until the death of Frederick Borradaile in 1876, when the prebendal estate passed to the Ecclesiastical Commissioners and the advowson was transferred to the Bishop of Lincoln. The Bishop was patron in 1965. [*Le Neve Fasti: Lincoln 1066–1300*, 91; *Reg. Burghersh* i. no.119; *LDC* (1965), 108–9.]

Vicarage

Philip de Burgo sancti Petri chaplain
Instituted 1323 to vicarage of Bishop Norton, newly ordained. Patron: M. Robert de Pyncebek, Prebendary of Norton Episcopi. [*Reg. Burghersh* i. no.119.]

Adam de Halum
Instituted before 30 May 1349. [Reg. 9, fo.154v.]

John de Alkebarowe priest
Instituted 30 May 1349 to vicarage of Bishop Norton, on death of Adam de Halum. Patron: Thomas de Northwode, Prebendary of Norton Episcopi. [Reg. 9, fo.154v.]

Henry de Berughby priest
Instituted 28 October 1361 to vicarage of Bishop Norton, on death of John. Patron: Br. Hugh, Prior of Lewes, vicar-general of Audoyin, Cardinal Priest of St John and St Paul, Prebendary of Norton Episcopi. [Reg. 9, fo.172v.]
Still Vicar in 1377. [*Clerical Poll-Taxes*, no. 819.]

John de Glentham priest
Instituted 4 April 1380 to vicarage of Bishop Norton (cause of vacancy not stated). Patron: Richard de Chestrefeld, Prebendary of Norton Episcopi. [Reg. 10, fo.102v.]

John Norton
Instituted before 27 October 1411. [Reg. 14, fo.120.]

Afterwards: V. of Saxilby, 1411–47. [Reg. 18, fo.101.]

John son of William Smyth de Derlyngton
Instituted 27 October 1411 to vicarage of Bishop Norton, on resignation of John Norton (by exchange with vicarage of Saxilby). Patron: John Brymmesgrove, Canon of Lincoln and Prebendary of Norton Episcopi. [Reg. 14, fo.120.]

Formerly: V. of Croydon (Ca), March–December 1389; V. of Hose (Le), 1389–91; V. of Saxilby, 1391–1411. Afterwards: V. of St James, Grimsby, 1413–17. [Bray, *Ely Lists*; Reg. 11, fos 107v, 213v, 219v; Reg. 14, fo.90v.]

Simon Gunny (de Waynflete) priest
Instituted 16 September 1413 to vicarage of Bishop Norton, on resignation of John son of William Smyth de Dalyngton (by exchange with vicarage of church of St James, Grimsby). Patron: John Brymmesgrove, Canon of Lincoln and Prebendary of Norton Episcopi. [Reg. 14, fo.123.]

Priest: before 10 December 1408. Formerly: V. of St James, Grimsby, 1408–13. Afterwards: V. of Killingholme, 1415–22. [Reg. 14, fo.30; *Reg. Fleming* i. no.155.]

John Almot chaplain
Instituted 10 May 1415 to vicarage of Bishop Norton, on resignation of Simon Gunny (by exchange with vicarage of Killingholme). Patron: John Wodham, Canon of Lincoln and Prebendary of Norton Episcopi. [Reg. 14, fo.127.]

Formerly: Chaplain of Chantry in Church of Wigston (Le), to 1412; V. of Killingholme, 1412–15. [Reg. 14, fo.59v.]

Richard Ford priest
Instituted 5 December 1416 to vicarage of Bishop Norton, on resignation of John Almot. Patron: Thomas Grenewod, Canon of Lincoln and Prebendary of Norton Episcopi. [Reg. 14, fo.130v.]

William Walson of Malton priest
Instituted 15 November 1423 to vicarage of Bishop Norton, on resignation of Richard de Forth. Patron: Thomas de Wykeresley, Canon of Lincoln and Prebendary of Norton Episcopi. [*Reg. Fleming* i. no.430.]

Thomas Meygott
Instituted before 14 April 1494. [D&C A/3/1, fo.93v.]

On 14 April 1494 the Chapter of Lincoln granted administration of the goods of Thomas Clerk, Vicar of Glentham, to Thomas Megott, Vicar of Bishop Norton, and William Tubbyng of Glentham. [D & C A/3/1, fo.93v.]

John Waynwright chaplain

Instituted 1 April 1527 to vicarage of Bishop Norton, on death of Thomas Meygott. Patron: John Elton *alias* Baker, Canon of Lincoln and Prebendary of Norton Episcopi. [Reg. 27, fo.42; *Chapter Acts of Lincoln* i. 76.]

Assessed for subsidy (£6 13s 4d) in 1526. [*Subsidy*, 36.]

Richard Tyson

Inducted 4 November 1540 to vicarage of Bishop Norton, on death of John Waynwright. [*Chapter Acts of Lincoln* ii. 39.]

Formerly: Canon of St Katherine's Priory outside Lincoln; allotted pension of £5 6s 8d in 1538. 'He is not married nor ever was (1554).' Will dated 13 December 1558; proved 8 October 1559 (PCC). To be buried on the north side of the choir before St Peter and beneath the lowest step ('grice') of the altar; bequeathed wax 'for ij tapers the one to be before the Trynitie and the other before our ladye and durynge the tyme that the sepulcre is in the quere at Easter I will that the same ij Tapers shalbe burnynge before the sepulcre … yff the lawes of this Realme do suffre it'. [*Ex-Religious*, 80; PROB 11/42B/709.]

Gervase Fishborne chaplain

Inducted 28 April 1559 to vicarage of Bishop Norton, on death of last incumbent. [*Chapter Acts of Lincoln* iii. 166.]

George Cave

Instituted 11 July 1560 to vicarage of Bishop Norton, on resignation of John [*sic*] Fishburne. Patron: Thomas Lark, Canon of Lincoln and Prebendary of Norton Episcopi. [Reg. 19, fo.101.]

Admon., 1574. [D&C Wills 3/85.]

Richard Byrkitt

Instituted 25 March 1575 to vicarage of Bishop Norton, on death of last incumbent. Patron: Henry Ince, Canon of Lincoln and Prebendary of Norton Episcopi. [*Bishop Cooper*, 75.]

Education: 'ignorant of Latin; but little versed in sacred learning'. Priest: 7 April 1566 (Lincoln). Married. Resident; signed BTs 1579–92. Buried at Bishop Norton, 19 March 1592/3. [*Bishop Cooper*, 168; BTs Bishop Norton.]

John Herde BA

Instituted 6 July 1593 to vicarage of Bishop Norton, on death of Richard Burkett. Patron: Thomas Fryar, Canon of Lincoln and Prebendary of Norton Episcopi (23 June 1593). [BC; PD 1593/40.]

Buried at Bishop Norton, 29 August 1614. [PR Bishop Norton.]

Laurence Carliell

Instituted 16 October 1614 to vicarage of Bishop Norton. Inducted 2 June 1615. [BC; D & C A/3/9, fo.107v.]

Also: R. of Blyborough (*q.v.*). Signed BTs at Bishop Norton, 1635. Still Vicar in 1651. [*LNQ* 19 (1927), Appendix, 133.]

Simon Deanes

Perhaps presented in 1655.

'Simon Deanes which was supposed to have beene our Vicar was buried October 21th 1655.' [PR Bishop Norton.]

William Stapylton

Instituted 1656. Patron: under Great Seal. [Swaby, 13.]

Perhaps curate at Bishop Norton from 1645. Occurs in BTs 1645–57; signed BTs 1663.

Brian Smyth

Instituted 17 February 1663/4 to vicarage of Bishop Norton (cause of vacancy not stated). Patron: Anthony Scattergood, Prebendary of Norton Episcopi (16 November 1663). [Reg. 33, fo.24v; PD 1663/55.]

Baptised 28 April 1639 at Hibaldstow; son of Brian S. Educated: Lincoln School and Magdalene College, Cambridge (matric. 1655; BA 1658–9). Deacon: 2 December 1660 (Lincoln); priest: 14 June 1663 (Oxford). Formerly: V. of Hibaldstow, 1660–1. Signed BTs at Bishop Norton 1694–1704. Also: C. of Normanby, 1688–1704. [PR Hibaldstow; Venn, *Alumni*; LC 14, p.229; BTs Bishop Norton.]

Thomas Reith BA

Instituted 15 December 1704 to vicarage of Bishop Norton, on death of Brian Smith. Patron: William Needham BD, Prebendary of Norton Episcopi (1 December 1704). [SUB VI, p.167; D&C Dj/34/2/48; PD 1704/17.]

Priest: 19 September 1703 (Winchester). Also: C. of Normanby, 1707–18; V. of Willoughton, 1718. Resided at Bishop Norton. Witnessed will of Helen Child of Bishop Norton, 31 March 1742. [*Winchester Ordinations* ii. 18; *Speculum*, 166–7; 174; TDE/A/Middle Rasen/2/3.]

Samuel Rolt

Instituted before 1745. [LC 18B, 307.]

Born *c.*1698; son of Oliver R. of Alderton (Np), gent. Educated: Wadham College, Oxford (matric. 1716; BA 1719; MA 1722). Deacon: 29 October 1721; priest: 24 December 1721 (Lincoln). Formerly: V. of Caistor, 1722–43; Head Master of Caistor GS, 1724–42. Also: R. of Croxton, 1727–57; Head Master of Lincoln School, 1742–58. Died 19 July 1758 (aged 61); buried at Bishop Norton, 23 July 1758. [*Wadham Registers* i. 461; Foster, *Alumni*; Reg. 37, pp. 127, 145; LC 18B, 307; Garton, 'Lincoln School', 1462–3; PR Bishop Norton.]

George Jolland

Instituted 8 November 1758 to vicarage of Bishop Norton, on death of [Samuel] Rolt. Patron: Thomas Balgay, Prebendary of Norton Episcopi. [Reg. 38, p.562.]

Baptised 4 May 1705 at Wrawby; son of George J. Educated: Bury St Edmunds and

Colchester Schools and St John's College, Cambridge (matric. 1727). Married (17 October 1729) at South Wingfield (Db), Bridget Hurt of Wirksworth. Non-resident at Bishop Norton, which was served by curates including John Hewthwaite (1760), Christopher Metcalfe (1764–6); Anthony Furness (1768–9) and Samuel Proctor (1769–79). Lived at Stafford, where he died in 1779. Will (PCC) dated 28 April 1779; proved 1 July 1780. [PR Wrawby; *Bury Grammar School List*, 213; Venn, *Alumni*; IGI; LC 31, fo.198v; PR Bishop Norton; PROB 11/1067.]

Robert Cane MA

Instituted 29 September 1779 to vicarage of Bishop Norton, on death of William [*sic*] Jolland. Patron: Thomas Balguy, Prebendary of Norton Episcopi. Reinstituted 16 September 1788, on his own cession; patron: as above. Reinstituted a second time 15 March 1798, on his own cession; patron: John Applebee BD, Prebendary of Norton Episcopi (10 March 1798). [Reg. 39, pp. 341, 484, 648; PD 154/62.]

Baptised 2 March 1755 at Welby; son of Robert C., Rector of Welby (1750–71). Educated: Winchester and St John's College, Cambridge (matric. 1772; BA 1776; MA 1779; Fellow of St John's, 1777–85). Deacon: 28 September 1777 (Oxford); priest: 27 June 1779 (Peterborough). Non-resident at Bishop Norton, which was served by Thomas Dawson as curate (1781–1802). Also: Vicar-Choral of Southwell, 1784–1802; R. of Brigsley, 1788–98; V. of Barnby-in-the-Willows (Nt), 1798–1802. Resided at Southwell; died there, 6 January 1802, aged 42 (MI). Will (PCC), dated 17 April 1801. [PR Welby; Venn, *Alumni*; PR Bishop Norton; *Southwell Monuments*, 97; PROB 11/1371/107.]

Thomas Calthorpe Blofeld BA

Inducted 19 March 1802 to vicarage of Bishop Norton, on death of Robert Cane. Patron: John Applebee BD, Prebendary of Norton Episcopi (8 March 1802). Reinstituted after 16 December 1803, on his own cession; patron: as above. Reinstituted a second time 24 November 1819, on his own cession; patron: as above. [D&C Dj/35/1/75; PD 158/46; Dj/35/1/79; Reg. 40, p.299.]

Born 16 August 1777 at Dyers Buildings, Holborn; son of Thomas B., barrister. Educated: Merchant Taylors' School (1789); St John's College (matric. 1795) and Pembroke College, Cambridge (BA 1801; MA 1805). Deacon: 20 December 1801; priest: 14 March 1802 (Norwich). Married (7 May 1802) at Walton (Nf), Mary Caroline, third daughter of Francis Grose FSA. Also: V. of Felmingham (Nf), 1803–19; of Hoveton St Peter and St John (Nf), 1819–51; RD of Waxham, 1842–51. Non-resident at Bishop Norton, which was served by curates, including William Bowerbank (1807–16) and Joseph Stockdale (1818–51). Resided from 1819 at Hoveton. Afterwards: R. of Drayton with Hellesdon, 1851–5. Died 24 February 1855 at Hoveton House. [LMA, PR Holborn St Andrew; Crisp, *Visitation* xx. 193; *Merchant Taylors' Register* ii. 159; *St John's College Admissions* iv. 141–2; Venn, *Alumni*; *Norfolk Benefices*, 63–4; CR 1, pp. 25, 381.]

Rose Fuller Whistler BA

Instituted 10 December 1851 to vicarage of Bishop Norton cum Atterby, on cession of Thomas Calthorpe Blofield. Patron: Frederick Borradaile, Prebendary of Norton Episcopi. [Reg. 40, p.532.]

Born 9 December 1825; son of Edward Webster W. of Grange Buildings, West Hackney, gent. Educated: Sutton Valence GS and Emmanuel College, Cambridge (matric. 1845;

BA 1849; MA 1853). Deacon: 1849; priest: 1850 (Chichester). Formerly: C. of Battle, 1849–51. Resided at Bishop Norton. Resigned, 29 September 1853. Afterwards: R. of Hollington (Sx), 1854–67; of Ilketshall St John with St Lawrence (Sf), 1867–79; R. of Penshurst and V. of Ashburnham (Sx), 1879–88; R. of Elton (Hu), 1888–94. Author: *History of Elton* (1892). Died 16 June 1894 at Elton Rectory. [LMA, PR Hackney; Venn, *Alumni*; PR Bishop Norton; RES 243/45; *Probate Calendar* 1894.]

Frederick Borradaile MA (the younger)

Instituted 3 November 1853 to vicarage of Bishop Norton cum Atterby, on resignation of Rose Fuller Whistler. Patron: Frederick Borradaile (the elder) of Upper Tooting (Sr), Prebendary of Norton Episcopi. [Reg. 40, p.543.]

Resided at Bishop's Norton Vicarage. Afterwards: R. of Spridlington, 1876–98 (*q.v.*).

William Alfred Plumptre MA

Instituted 26 May 1876 by collation to vicarage of Bishop Norton cum Atterby, on cession of Frederick Borradaile. Patron: Bishop of Lincoln. [Reg. 41, p.529.]

Baptised 22 December 1830 at St George-the-Martyr, Bloomsbury; 4th son of Edward Hallows P. of East Street, solicitor. Educated: University College, Oxford (matric. 1849; BA 1853; MA 1858). Deacon: 1853; priest: 1854 (Lichfield). Formerly: SPG Missionary (Incumbent of St John, Egmore, Madras), 1858–62 (invalided home); Chaplain to Duke of Marlborough, 1867; C. of Woodstock, 1867–70; V. of Whatton (Nt), 1871–6. Died 3 September 1879 at 3 St Giles Road East, Oxford. [LMA, PR St George-the-Martyr; Foster, *Alumni*; Frank Perry, *The Church in Madras* (1904); *Crockford* (1874); *Probate Calendar* 1879.]

Christopher Harrison BA

Instituted 25 March 1879 by collation to vicarage of Bishop Norton, on resignation of William Alfred Plumptre. Patron: Bishop of Lincoln. [Reg. 42, p.81.]

Born *c*.1848 at Brandesburton (YER). Educated: Shrewsbury School and Clare College, Cambridge (matric. 1866; BA 1870). Deacon: 24 December 1871; priest: 22 December 1872 (Lincoln). Formerly: C. of Carlton-in-Lindrick (Nt), 1871–4; of Langar, 1874–6; of Hickling (Nt), 1876–8; of Edwinstowe, 1878–9. Also: Chaplain of St Edmund's Chapel, Spital, 1881. Resided at Bishop Norton Vicarage. Died 23 February 1932; buried at Bishop Norton (MI). [Venn, *Alumni*; OR 2, pp. 11, 14; *Crockford* (1898); White, *Lincolnshire* (1892); *Probate Calendar* 1932.]

Frank Brian Lys

Instituted 21 July 1932 by collation to vicarage of Bishop Norton cum Atterby, on death of Christopher Harrison. Patron: Bishop of Lincoln. [Reg. 43, p.509.]

Born 21 June 1865 in Madras, India. Educated: Lancing College (1881–3) and St John's College, Manitoba (BA). Deacon: 1903 (Qu'Appelle for Rupert's Land); priest: 1904 (Coadjutor Bishop of Rupert's Land). Formerly: Missioner at Woodlands (Rupert's Land), 1903–6; Incumbent of Holland (Brandon), 1908–14; of Rapid City, 1914–15; R. of Souris, 1915–18; of St John, Sedgewick (Edmonton), 1921–8; C. of Scunthorpe, 1928–32.

Resided at Bishop Norton Vicarage. Resigned 4 December (accepted 9 December) 1946. Died 5 June 1949 at The White House, Bishop Norton. [*Lancing Register*, 130; Census Returns 1871 (Leamington), 1881 (Lancing); *Crockford* (1932); RES 1946/28; *Probate Calendar* 1949.]

Johnston Redmond ThL
Instituted 6 March 1948 to vicarage of Bishop Norton cum Atterby, on resignation of Frank Bryan Lys. Patron: King George VI for this turn, by reason of the late vacancy of the see of Lincoln. [Reg. 44, p.84.]

Afterwards: R. of Owmby with Normanby (*q.v.*).

Eric Marcus Vanston
Instituted 14 February 1953 by collation to vicarage of Bishop Norton cum Atterby, on cession of Johnston Redmond. Patron: Bishop of Lincoln. [Reg. 44, p.173.]

Born 1903; son of George Thomas Barrett Vanston of Dublin. Educated: Trinity College, Dublin (1920); London College of Divinity (1922). Deacon: 1926; priest: 1927 (London). Formerly: C. of All SS, Harlesden (Mx), 1926–7; of St Luke, West Holloway, 1927–9; Missioner, Queens' College Mission, Rotherhithe, 1929–32; C. of St Barnabas, Mitcham, 1932–7; of Warlingham with Chelsham (Sr), 1937–42; V. of Ditton Priors, 1942–6; R. of Bratoft with Irby, 1946–51; of Kilgobbin Union, Kerry (Ireland), 1951–3. Resided at Bishop Norton Vicarage. Afterwards: V. of Strubby with Woodthorpe and Maltby, 1958–60. Retired 1960. Lived at The White House, Timberland. Died there, 4 March 1965. [Census Returns (Ireland) 1911; *Crockford* (1961–2); *LDC* (1957), 56; *Probate Calendar* 1965.]

Albert Edward Swain
Instituted 11 April 1959 by collation to vicarage of Bishop Norton cum Atterby, on cession of Eric Marcus Vanston. Patron: Bishop of Lincoln. [Reg. 44, p.269.]

Born *c*.1898; son of James Thomas S. of St Helen's (La), glass cutter. Deacon: 1926; priest: 1927 (Liverpool). Formerly: C. of St Paul, Widnes, 1926–8; C-in-C of Holy Trinity, Cowgate, Newcastle, 1928–34; R. of Elton (Nt), 1934–8; PC of Mapperley (Nt), 1938–45; V. of St Mary, Widnes, 1945–53; of Mold Green (YWR), 1953–9. Resided at Bishop Norton Vicarage. Died 15 January 1967 (memorial on credence table in Bishop Norton Church). [Census Returns 1911 (St Helens); *Crockford* (1961–2).]

William Harrison
Instituted 3 November 1967 by collation to vicarage of Bishop Norton cum Atterby, on death of Albert Edward Swain. Patron: Bishop of Lincoln. [Reg. 44, p.406.]

Born 17 November 1903. Educated: Bishops' College, Cheshunt (1945). Deacon: 1948; priest: 1949 (Lincoln). Formerly: C. of Old Brumby, 1948–52; V. of Stainton-by-Langworth with Newball, 1952–7; of Torksey, 1957–67; of Marton, 1958–67; R. of Gate Burton, 1958–67. Resided at Bishop Norton Vicarage. Retired 1971. Lived at 27 Mill Crescent, Scotter. Died March 1975. [GRO, Death Index; *Crockford* (1969–70, 1971–2).]

OWMBY-BY-SPITAL

The church of Owmby may have been held by the Arsic family as early as *c*.1115, when Manaset Arsic was recorded as holding 2 bovates there in the Lindsey Survey. Osbert Arsic kt presented in 1227–8; shortly afterwards the advowson was conveyed to Peter of Paris, to whom it was confirmed by Ralph Arsic, brother of Osbert, in February 1231/2. Members of the Paris family (most of whom were active in the civic affairs of Lincoln) presented to the rectory during the remainder of the thirteenth century but by 1304 the advowson had passed to Hugh Bardolf kt. The Bardolf family continued to present to the living (apart from two occasions in 1367–8 when Queen Philippa did so during the minority of William Bardolf) until the attainder and subsequent death of Thomas Bardolf in 1406–8. The right of presentation was then exercised by William Clifford and Reginald Cobham as successive husbands of Anne daughter and co-heir of Thomas Bardolf. After Anne's death in 1453 the advowson passed to John, Viscount Beaumont, as husband of her niece Elizabeth; he presented in 1455. Since 1467 the advowson has been in the possession of the Crown. [*Lincolnshire Domesday*, 240; *Final Concords* i. 249; *Summoning St Michael*, 235; *Medieval Lincoln*, 391–2; *GEC* i. 417–21; *LDC* (1965), 108–9.]

John son of Ralph son of Reginald subdeacon
Instituted in the nineteenth pontifical year of Bishop Hugh of Wells (20 December 1227/19 December 1228) to church of Owmby-by-Spital. Patron: Osbert Arsich kt (the advowson having been unsuccessfully disputed by Jordan le Rat and Michael de Stocton, and Peter de Paris having renounced his claim). [*Rot. Welles* i. 226.]

Peter de Paris chaplain
Instituted in the twenty-third pontifical year of Bishop Hugh of Wells (20 December 1231/19 December 1232) to church of Owmby-by-Spital. Patron: Peter de Paris, citizen of Lincoln (the advowson having been unsuccessfully disputed by Ralph Arsic). [*Rot. Welles* i. 231.]

Alexander de Hothun subdeacon
Instituted in the eighth pontifical year of Bishop Robert Grosseteste (17 June 1242/16 June 1243) to church of Owmby-by-Spital. Patron: William and John de Paris (brothers), by reason of their wardship of the lands and heirs of the late P. de Paris. [Hoskin, no.1261.]

Peter de Ingoldemeles subdeacon
Instituted in the fourth pontifical year of Bishop Richard Gravesend (3 November 1261/2 November 1262) to church of Owmby-by-Spital, on

resignation of Alexander. Patron: John son of Peter de Paris. [*Rot. Gravesend,* 89.]

Also: R. of Northorpe, to 1304. Died 26 April 1304. [Reg. 2, fo. 87; D&C A/1/14.]

Stephen de Whitelwode chaplain
Instituted 13 May 1304 to church of Owmby-by-Spital, on death of Peter de Ingoldemeles. Patron: Hugh Bardolf kt. [Reg. 2, fo.87.]

Walter Power acolyte
Instituted 28 January 1334 to church of Owmby-by-Spital, on death of Stephen. Patron: King Edward III, by custody of land and heir of Thomas Bardolf decd. [*Reg. Burghersh* i. no.782.]

Richard de Therlesthorp clerk
Instituted 2 August 1338 to church of Owmby-by-Spital, on resignation of Walter Power. Patron: John Bardolf kt. [*Reg. Burghersh* i. no.804.]

John de Chestre
Instituted 28 May 1367 to church of Owmby-by-Spital, on death of Richard. Patron: Queen Philippa. [Reg. 10, fo.18.]

Afterwards: R. of Teigh (Ru), 1368–77; R. of Thurlaston (Le), 1377–83; R. of Strixton (Np), 1383–7. Died before 4 October 1387. [Reg. 10, fos 172v, 207v; Reg. 11, fos 124v, 145.]

Henry Drury priest
Instituted 3 August 1368 to church of Owmby-by-Spital, on resignation of John de Chestre (by exchange with church of Teigh). Patron: Queen Philippa. [Reg. 10, fos 25, 129, 131v.]

Afterwards: R. of Dunsby-by-Bourne, 1376 and again 1394 (*q.v.*).

Robert Mawe
Instituted 13 September 1374 to church of Owmby-by-Spital, on resignation of Henry Drewry (by exchange with church of Saundby, dioc. York). Patron: William Bardolf, lord of Wormegay. [Reg. 10, fo.140.]

Formerly: R. of Firsby, 1349–67 (*q.v.*); R. of Saundby (Nt), 1367–74. Afterwards: R. of a mediety of Sedgebrook, 1383–7; R. of a mediety of Grimoldby, 1387–94. [Train, *North Notts Clergy*, 162; Reg. 11, fos 30v, 70v.]

Robert de Pothowe priest
Instituted 11 August 1383 to church of Owmby-by-Spital, on resignation of Robert Mawe (by exchange with a mediety of church of Sedgebrook). Patron: William Bardolf kt. [Reg. 10, fos 126v, 149.]

Formerly: V. of Lastingham (YNR), to 1380; R. of a mediety of Sedgebrook, 1380–3. Afterwards: R. of Broughton-in-Craven (YWR), 1393. [Reg. 10, fo.104v; *Fasti Parochiales* iv. 27.]

Thomas de Toynton
Instituted 19 June 1393 to church of Owmby-by-Spital, on resignation of
Robert de Pothowe (by exchange with church of Broughton-in-Craven, dioc.
York). Patron: Thomas Bardolf. [Reg. 11, fo.110.]

Formerly: R. of a mediety of Treswell (Nt), to 1391; R. of Broughton-in-Craven (YWR),
1391–3. Afterwards: V. of Preston in Holderness (YER), 1396–8. [Train, *North Notts
Clergy*, 184; *Fasti Parochiales* iv. 27; Poulson, *Holderness* ii. 185.]

Thomas de Neuton priest
Instituted 28 August 1396 to church of Owmby-by-Spital, on resignation of
Thomas Tynton (by exchange with vicarage of prebendal church of Preston,
dioc. York). Patron: Thomas Bardolf, lord of Wormegay. [Reg. 11, fo.118.]

Formerly: V. of Preston in Holderness (YER), 1382–96. [Poulson, *Holderness* ii. 185.]

Thomas Rasyn
Instituted before 13 October 1401. [Reg. 13, fo.180.]

Afterwards: V. of Dunham (Nt), 1401.

William Morepath
Instituted 13 October 1401 to church of Owmby-by-Spital, on resignation of
Thomas Rasyn (by exchange with vicarage of Dunham on Trent, dioc. York
and in the jurisdiction of chapter of Southwell). Patron: Thomas Bardolf kt,
lord of Wormegay. [Reg. 13, fo.180.]

Formerly: V. of Dunham (Nt), until 1401. Afterwards: R. of Gate Burton, June–October
1402; R. of Newton-by-Toft, 1402. [Reg. 13, fos 148v, 181v.]

Richard de Wartyr
Instituted 7 June 1402 to church of Owmby-by-Spital, on resignation of
William Morpath (by exchange with church of Gate Burton). Patron: Thomas
Bardolf kt, lord of Wormegay. [Reg. 13, fo.180v.]

Formerly: R. of Gate Burton, 1384–1402. Afterwards: Master of Hospital of St John
Baptist, King's Lynn, 1410. [Reg. 11, fo.97.]

M. John Warde
Instituted 17 April 1410 to church of Owmby-by-Spital, on resignation of
Richard Wartyr (by exchange with office of Master of Hospital of St John
Baptist, King's Lynn, dioc. Norwich). Patron: William Clyfford kt, lord of
Caythorpe. [Reg. 14, fo.116v.]

Formerly: Master of Hospital of St John Baptist, King's Lynn, 1410. Afterwards: Chaplain
of Chantry in St Mary Magdalene Chapel, Bawtry (YWR), 1416.

John son of Simon de Saltfletby chaplain
Instituted 25 May 1416 to church of Owmby-by-Spital, on resignation of

John Ward (by exchange with chantry in chapel of St Mary Magdalene by Bawtry, dioc. York). Patron: William Clifford kt, lord of Caythorpe. [Reg. 14, fo.128.]

Formerly: Chaplain of Chantry in St Mary Magdalene Chapel, Bawtry (YWR), to 1416. Afterwards: V. of Market Rasen, 1422.

Robert Grene de Quarnedon

Instituted 31 December 1422 to church of Owmby-by-Spital, on resignation of John Symkynson *alias* son of Simon de Salfletby (by exchange with vicarage of Market Rasen). Patron: Reginald Cobham, lord of Sterborough and Caythorpe, in right of his wife Ann, a daughter and heiress of Thomas, Lord Bardolf, decd. [*Reg. Fleming* i. nos 176, 420.]

Afterwards: V. of Swaton, 1429–31 (*q.v.*).

Henry Bilbourgh

Instituted 10 July 1424 to church of Owmby-by-Spital, on resignation of Robert Grene de Quaryndon (by exchange with church of Coppingford. Patron: Reginald Cobbeham of Sterborough, kt. [*Lambeth Institutions*, 18.]

Formerly: Chaplain of Buckingham Chantry in Lincoln Cathedral, to 1423; R. of Coppingford (Hu), 1423–4. [*Reg. Fleming* ii. no.176.]

James Rudde chaplain

Instituted 19 November 1455 to church of Owmby-by-Spital, on resignation of Henry Bylburgh. Patron: John Beaumont, Viscount Beaumont. [Reg. 20, fo.157v.]

Thomas Sheffeld priest

Instituted 22 July 1467 to church of Owmby-by-Spital (cause of vacancy not stated). Patron: King Edward IV. [Reg. 20, fos 146, 161v.]

John Malteby clerk

Instituted 22 December 1505 to church of Owmby-by-Spital, on death of last incumbent. Patron: King Henry VII. [Reg. 23, fo.157.]

William Hugate chaplain

Instituted 28 April 1511 to church of Owmby-by-Spital, on resignation of John Maltby. Patron: King Henry VII, in right of his duchy of Lancaster. [Reg. 23, fo.160.]

Assessed for subsidy (£8) in 1526. Witnessed will, 15 July 1553. [*Subsidy*, 36; Stow Wills 1553–67/123.]

Anthony Holmes

Instituted *c*.1554 (compounded for first-fruits 12 July 1554) to church of Owmby-by-Spital. Patron: Queen Mary I. [FL.h.13, 626.]

Born *c*.1508. Educated: University of Cambridge (BA 1530–1; MA 1534). Priest: 1536 (suffragan for Lincoln). Also: R. of Normanby-le-Wold, 1558–83; resided there (1576). Witnessed Owmby wills, 1557–64. Died before 23 April 1583. Will (LCC). [Venn, *Alumni*; *Bishop Cooper*, 32, 173; LCC Wills 1557/ii/74v; Stow Wills 1559–62/98v; Stow Wills 1563–6/26; LCC Wills 1583/ii/176.]

James Nayler

Instituted 13 January 1580/1 to church of Owmby-by-Spital. Patron: Queen Elizabeth I. [*Bishop Cooper*, 78.]

[James Nayler was inducted to Owmby on the day after his institution, 14 January 1580/1; he compounded for first-fruits on 26 January 1580/1. It would appear, however, from the institution of John Wrighte below that Nayler was unsuccessful in securing possession of the living. See IND/S 1; FL.h.13, 626.]

John Wrighte

Instituted 18 May 1581 to church of Owmby-by-Spital, on resignation of Anthony Holmes. Patron: Queen Elizabeth I. [*Bishop Cooper*, 78.]

Educated (MA); perhaps of Clare College, Cambridge (matric. 1572; BA 1575–6; MA 1579). Priest: 9 March 1581/2 (Lincoln). Died before 23 March 1591/2. [Venn, *Alumni*; *State of the Church*, 97.]

Philip Wright BA

Instituted 23 March 1591/2 to rectory of Owmby-by-Spital, on death of John Wright. Patron: Queen Elizabeth I (18 March 1591/2), in right of her duchy of Lancaster. [PD 1592/7.]

Educated: Clare College, Cambridge (matric. 1582; BA 1585–6). Deacon and priest: 1 July 1590 (Lincoln). Resident (1614): signed BTs 1600–22. Died *c*.1627. Will dated 21 November 1625; proved at Lincoln, 10 August 1627. [Venn, *Alumni*; LC 4, fo.10v; BTs Owmby-by-Spital; Stow Wills 1627–9/98.]

Thomas Bancks MA

Instituted 19 September 1627 to rectory of Owmby-by-Spital, on death of last incumbent. Patron: King Charles I (9 July 1627), in right of his duchy of Lancaster. [PD 1627/22.]

William Nunwicke MA

Instituted 27 October 1630 to rectory of Owmby-by-Spital, on cession of Thomas Banckes. Patron: King Charles I (20 October 1630), in right of his duchy of Lancaster. [PD 1630/39.]

Educated: Clare Hall, Cambridge (matric. 1614; BA 1616–17; MA 1620). Deacon: 8 April 1621; priest: 9 April 1621 (Peterborough). Resident (1662): signed BTs 1660–77. Also: C. of Normanby-by-Spital, 1660–78; buried there, 20 December 1678. [Venn, *Alumni*; LC 5, fo.82v; BTs Owmby-by-Spital; BTs Normanby-by-Spital.]

Joseph Dawbor

Instituted 17 April 1677 to rectory of Owmby-by-Spital, on resignation of William Nunwick. Patron: King Charles II. [Reg. 34, fo.19v.]

Born *c*.1653; son of William D. of Kirton Lindsey. Educated: Kirton School and Magdalene College, Cambridge (matric. 1670; BA 1673–4). Deacon: 20 September 1674 (Lincoln). Formerly: V. of Redbourne, 1675–7. Died *c*.1688. [Venn, *Alumni*; CCED; Stow Wills 1687–90, 73.]

John Lord MA

Instituted 25 February 1688/9 to rectory of Owmby-by-Spital, on death of last incumbent. Patron: King James II. [Reg. 34, fo.107v.]

Robert Dixon MA

Instituted 27 January 1692/3 to rectory of Owmby-by-Spital, on resignation of John Lord. Patron: King William III and Queen Mary II. [Reg. 35, fo.13.]

Son of Christopher D. of Owmby. Educated: Lincoln College, Oxford (matric. 1675; BA 1679). Deacon: 7 March 1679/80; priest: 26 June 1681 (Lincoln). Formerly: C. of Newton-by-Toft, 1679/80. Also: V. of Saxby, 1681–1729; R. of Newton-by-Toft, 1682–96. Resided at Owmby; signed BTs there, 1693–1729. Buried at Owmby, 11 October 1729. [Foster, *Alumni*; Reg. 34, fo.46v; *Speculum*, 167; BTs Owmby-by-Spital; PR Owmby-by-Spital.]

William Jepson BA

Instituted 18 October 1729 to rectory of Owmby-by-Spital, on death of Robert Dixon. Patron: King George II (by reason of his Duchy of Lancaster). [Reg. 38, p.213.]

Baptised 18 October 1694 at Welney (Nf); son of Thomas J., Rector of Melton St Mary. Educated: Oundle School and St John's College, Cambridge (matric. 1712; BA 1716–17). Deacon: 15 June 1717 (Peterborough); priest: 12 June 1720 (Lincoln). Formerly: C. of St Martin, Stamford, 1717; C. of Langtoft, 1720; Schoolmaster in Stamford, 1720. Non-resident at Owmby, which was served by John Barr as Curate. Afterwards: V. of Holbeach, 1731–41. Died 6 March 1740/1; buried at Holbeach, 8 March 1740/1. [*St John's Admissions* ii. pp. lxxxv, 203; Venn, *Alumni*; Longden viii. 15–17; Reg. 37, p.101; *Speculum*, 77, 114; Reg. 38, p.237; PR Holbeach; Macdonald, *Holbeach*, 176.]

Charles Reynolds

Licensed curate, 30 April 1731. Instituted before 17 July 1736. [SUB VII, p.254; Reg. 38, p.319.]

Also: R. of Fillingham (*q.v.*).

John Barr

Instituted 17 July 1736 to rectory of Owmby-by-Spital, on cession of Charles Reynolds. Patron: King George II. Reinstituted 16 December 1747, benefice being legally void; patron, as above. [Reg. 38, pp. 319, 477.]

Baptised 19 January 1709/10 at Normanby-by-Spital; son of John B, farmer. Educated: Kirton Lindsey School and Sidney Sussex College, Cambridge (matric. 1727; BA 1730–1). Deacon: 19 December 1731; priest: 10 March 1733/4 (Lincoln). Formerly: C. of Blyton, 1731; C. of Owmby-by-Spital, 1732 (signed BTs as Curate, 1732–6). Resided at Owmby; signed BTs and registers 1738–76. Also: V. of Saxby, 1747–78 (*q.v.*); Canon of Lincoln and Prebendary of Welton Beckhall, 1755–78. Died 16 July 1778; buried at Owmby, 18 July 1778 (MI). [PR Normanby-by-Spital; Venn, *Alumni*; Reg. 38, pp. 254,

286; *Le Neve Fasti: Lincoln 1541–1857*, 124; LC 31, fo.197v; BTs Owmby-by-Spital; PR Owmby-by-Spital.]

Thomas Kipling MA

Instituted 30 July 1778 to rectory of Owmby-by-Spital, on death of John Barr. Patron: King George III, in right of his Duchy of Lancaster. [Reg. 39, p.313.]

Baptised 20 October 1745 at Bowes (YNR); son of William K. of Richmond (YNR), cattle salesman. Educated: Scorton and Sedbergh Schools and St John's College, Cambridge (matric. 1764; BA (Senior Wrangler) 1768; MA 1771; BD 1779; DD 1784); Fellow of St John's, 1771. Deputy Regius Professor of Divinity, 1787–1802. Deacon: 29 May 1768 (London); priest: 9 June 1770 (Peterborough). Chaplain to the King at Whitehall, 1778. Non-resident at Owmby. Also: V. of Holme-on-Spalding-Moor (YER), 1784–1822. Master of the Temple, 1797. Afterwards: R. of Fiskerton, 1798–1822; Dean of Peterborough, 1798–1822. His edition of *Codex Bezae* (1792) was distinguished by its outstanding typography, but the Latin of the preface was so full of errors that at Cambridge a 'Kiplingism' came to denote a grammatical blunder. Died 28 January 1822 at Holme-on-Spalding-Moor Vicarage. [Robert Hole, 'Kipling, Thomas' in *ODNB*; *Sedbergh School Register*, 149; Venn, *Alumni*; Longden viii. 107; LC 31, fo. 198v; *Le Neve Fasti: Peterborough 1541–1857*, 121.]

William Short MA

Instituted 5 April 1799 to rectory of Owmby-by-Spital, on cession of Thomas Kipling. Patron: King George III, in right of his Duchy of Lancaster. [Reg. 39, p.665.]

Baptised 29 February 1760; son of John S. of Bickham (Dev), esquire. Educated: Eton College (1772–7) and Christ Church, Oxford (matric. 1778; BA 1782; MA 1785; BD & DD 1811). Formerly: Chaplain of East and West Teignmouth (Dev), 1792. Afterwards: R. of King's Worthy (Ha), 1805–26; Canon of Exeter, 1805; Archdeacon of Cornwall, 1807–26; Sub-Preceptor and Chaplain to Princess Charlotte, 1810; Canon of Westminster, 1816–26. Married (22 August 1787) at West Teignmouth (Dev), Elizabeth, daughter of Tilleman Hodgkinson, R. of Sarsden (Ox). Father of Thomas Vowler S. (1790–1872), successively Bishop of Sodor and Man and of St Asaph. Died 18 May 1826 'deeply lamented', at King's Worthy Rectory. [*Eton College Register 1753–1790*, 473; Foster, *Alumni*; *Le Neve Fasti: Westminster 1541–1857*, 96; *Record of Old Westminsters* ii. 847; *GM* 96 pt 1 (1826), 645–6.]

John Nedham MA

Instituted 3 December 1802 to rectory of Owmby-by-Spital, on resignation of William Short. Patron: King George III, in right of his Duchy of Lancaster. [Reg. 40, p.46.]

Born 7 January 1774; son of William Dandy N. of Hanover Square, London (Speaker of House of Assembly, Jamaica, 1766). Educated: Westminster School (1781); Oriel College, Oxford (matric. 1793; BA 1797) and Peterhouse, Cambridge (MA 1803). Formerly: R. of Mundesley (Nf), 1798–1802. Resided at Owmby. Also: C. of Saxby, 1814; C. of Newton by Toft, 1814. Died 31 December 1822 at Newark-on-Trent. [*Record of Old Westminsters* ii. 685; Venn, *Alumni*; CR 1, pp. 26, 44.]

George Moore BA

Instituted 4 February 1823 to rectory of Owmby-by-Spital, on death of John Nedham. Patron: King George IV, in right of his Duchy of Lancaster. [Reg. 40, p.330.]

Born *c*.1792; son of George M. of Lincoln, esq. Educated: Heighington School (Li); St John's College (matric. 1808) and Pembroke College, Cambridge (BA 1813). Deacon: 13 March 1814; priest: 9 June 1816 (Lincoln). Formerly: C. of Coleby, 1814–22 (resided in Lincoln). Also: PC of St Peter in Eastgate with St Margaret, Lincoln, 1819–41. Non-resident at Owmby, which was served by curates, including Thomas Townsend (1828–34), John Mandell (1834–8) and Joseph Green (1839–41), all of whom resided in Owmby Rectory. Living at 19 Eastgate, Lincoln (1841). Died at Lincoln, 19 October 1841 (aged 49). [Venn, *Alumni*; Reg. 40, pp. 195, 241; CR 1, pp. 24, 71, 381; CR 2, pp. 89, 220; PR Coleby; PR Owmby-by-Spital; Census Returns 1841; *GM* 170 (1841), 661.]

Joseph Green MA

Instituted 16 December 1841 to rectory of Owmby-by-Spital, on death of George Moore. Patron: Queen Victoria, in right of her Duchy of Lancaster. [Reg. 40, p.481.]

Born 26 March 1807 at Amsterdam. Educated: Corpus Christi College, Cambridge (matric. 1826; BA 1830; MA 1836). Deacon: 27 February 1831; priest: 17 June 1832 (Lincoln). Formerly: C. of Saxby, 1831; C. of Cammeringham, 1839; C. of Owmby-by-Spital, 1839. Also: V. of Cammeringham, 1842–83. Did duty at Cammeringham and Owmby until 1871. Built new Rectory House at Owmby (architect: Charles Vickers of Pontefract), 1844; resided there. Died 28 September 1883 at Owmby; buried at Owmby (MI). Churchyard cross at Owmby dedicated to his memory. [Venn, *Alumni*; OR 1, pp. 43, 48; CR 2, pp. 4, 208, 220; PR Cammeringham; PR Owmby-by-Spital; MGA 292; Census Returns 1861; *Probate Calendar* 1884; PR Owmby-by-Spital.]

Thomas Stamford Raffles MA

Instituted 14 December 1883 to rectory of Owmby-by-Spital, on death of Joseph Green. Patron: Queen Victoria, in right of her Duchy of Lancaster. [Reg. 42, p.195.]

Born 11 July 1853; son of Sir Thomas Stamford R. of Liverpool, barrister. Educated: Rugby School and Clare College, Cambridge (matric. 1877; BA 1880; MA 1883). Deacon: 1880 (Oxford for St Albans); priest: 1881 (St Albans). Formerly: C. of Hawarden, 1880; of Whittington (Sa), 1880–2; of Ashton-on-Mersey (Ch), 1882–3. Resided at Owmby Rectory. Afterwards: R. of Langham (Ess), 1887–1914; of Lexden, 1914–26. Married (6 November 1884) Cecil Helen, daughter of Col. Thomas Lovett of Henlle (Sa). Died 1 March 1926 at 29 Wimpole Street (Mx). [Burke, *Landed Gentry* (1894), 1677; Venn, *Alumni*; *Crockford* (1886); *Probate Calendar* 1926.]

Henry Simpson Blink

Instituted 15 July 1887 to rectory of Owmby-by-Spital, on cession of Thomas Stamford Raffles. Patron: Queen Victoria, in right of her Duchy of Lancaster. [Reg. 42, p.255.]

Baptised 14 August 1831 at St James, Clerkenwell; son of George B., gent. Educated: King's College, London (AKC 1855). Deacon: 1856; priest: 1857 (Lichfield). Formerly:

C. of Audley (St), 1856–8; of Reigate (Sr), 1858–61; of Battle (Sx), 1861–2; of Sitting-bourne (K), 1862–4; of Little Munden (Hrt), 1864–6; of Watlington (Ox), 1866–8; of St Mary with St Michael, Pembroke, 1868–77; of Panteg (Monm), 1877–9; of Revesby, 1879–87. Resided at Owmby Rectory. Also: V. of Normanby-by-Spital, 1894–9 (*q.v.*). An advocate of Rackham's Liver Pills ('I have distributed them amongst my parishioners with marked effect'). Died 16 February 1899; buried at Owmby, 20 February 1899. [LMA, PR Clerkenwell St James; *Crockford* (1891); Census Returns 1891; MI, Owmby by Spital; *Whitstable Times and Herne Bay Herald*, 11 April 1891; *Probate Calendar* 1899; PR Owmby-by-Spital.]

The Vicarage of Normanby-by-Spital was united to the Rectory of Owmby-by-Spital by Order in Council dated 26 October 1899. [Reg. 42, pp. 451–5.]

Charles Ethelbert Milton
Instituted 18 November 1899 to rectory of Owmby-by-Spital with vicarage of Normanby annexed, on death of Henry Simpson Blink. Patron: Queen Victoria (in right of her Duchy of Lancaster) and Dean (Edward Charles Wickham DD) and Chapter of Lincoln. [Reg. 42, p.456.]

Born 20 May 1849, baptised 15 July 1849 at St Mary, Islington; son of John M. of Doctors Commons, gent. Worked as a banker's clerk (1871); hide factor's clerk (1881); accountant (1883). Married (10 October 1883) at St Paul, Canonbury, Helen Sophia, daughter of Robert Simons. Educated: King's College, London (AKC 1894). Deacon: 1894; priest: 1895 (Rochester). Formerly: C. of St Laurence, Catford, 1894–9. Resigned 31 December 1920. Latterly of 70 Burford Gardens, Palmers Green (Mx). Died 27 April 1921 at Prince of Wales Hospital, Tottenham. [LMA, PR Islington St Mary, PR Canonbury St Paul; Census Returns 1871, 1881, 1911. *Crockford* (1920); RES A/94; *Probate Calendar* 1921.]

Arthur Evelyn Nelson
Instituted 13 May 1921 to rectory of Owmby-by-Spital with vicarage of Normanby, on resignation of Charles Ethelbert Milton. Patron: King George V (in right of his Duchy of Lancaster), for this turn. [Reg. 43, p.228.]

Born March 1895; son of William Joseph N., C. of Churston Ferrers (Dev). Educated: Bishop Wilson Theological College (1916). Deacon: 1916; priest: 1919 (Sodor and Man). Formerly: Asst Chaplain to Bishop of Sodor and Man, 1916–18; Chaplain of St John, Cronk-y-Voddy (IoM), 1918–21. Resignation accepted 30 November 1925. Died 12 December 1925 at The County Hospital, Lincoln. [GRO, Birth Index; Census Returns 1911; *Crockford* (1923); Reg. 43, p.383; *Probate Calendar*, 1926.]

Austin Locke Richards
Instituted 27 May 1926 to rectory of Owmby-by-Spital with vicarage of Normanby, on resignation of Arthur Evelyn Nelson. Patron: Dean (Thomas Charles Fry DD) and Chapter of Lincoln, for this turn. [Reg. 43, p.396.]

Born *c*.1884 at Horsham (Sx); son of William Joseph Richards, clerk in holy orders. Educated: St Augustine's College, Canterbury (1903). Deacon: 1906 (Dover for Canter-bury for Colonies); priest: 1908 (Bombay). Formerly: SPG Missionary at Dapoli, 1906–8; at Miri, 1908–10; residing with his father at Dowsby Rectory (*q.v.*), 1911; C. of St Peter-in-Eastgate, Lincoln, 1911–13; of Pinchbeck, 1913–15; of Stoke Rochford with Easton, 1915–18; V. of Gosberton Clough, 1918–21; of Tallington, 1921–6. Resided at Owmby Rectory. Also: RD of Aslacoe, 1927–30. Afterwards: V. of Heckington with Howell, 1930–7; PC of Tattershall, 1937–9; V. of North Kelsey, 1939–43; of Netley Marsh (Ha), 1943–8. Retired 1948. Lived at 21a High Street, Christchurch (Ha). Died 1965. [Census Returns 1911 (Dowsby); *Crockford* (1959–60); GRO, Death Index.]

Cyril Alexander Sheehan-Dare MA

Instituted 10 February 1931 to rectory of Owmby-by-Spital with vicarage of Normanby, on cession of Austin Locke Richards. Patron: King George V (27 October 1930), in right of his Duchy of Lancaster, for this turn. [Reg. 43, p.478; PD/Duchy of Lancaster/44.]

Born 16 October 1888 at Hatfield; son of John Raymond S-D, schoolmaster. Educated: Worcester College, Oxford (BA 1913; MA 1928) and Cuddesdon College (1913). Deacon: 1914; priest: 1915 (Exeter). Formerly: C. of Littleham with Exmouth, 1914–17; TCF 1917–19; C. of St Paul, Middlesbrough, 1919–23; of Banstead, 1923–6; of Christ Church, Radlett, 1926–8. Resided at Owmby Rectory. Resigned 12 March (accepted 26 March) 1940. Lived afterwards at 15 Malvern Drive, Acklam, Middlesbrough. Died 1971. [GRO, Death Index; Census Returns 1911; *Crockford* (1931–2, 1961–2); RES 1940/4.]

Thomas Aubrey Sankey MA

Instituted 17 September 1940 to rectory of Owmby-by-Spital with vicarage of Normanby, on resignation of Cyril Alexander Sheehan-Dare. Patron: King George VI (in right of his Duchy of Lancaster), for this turn. [Reg. 43, p.655.]

Born 1881 at Thame (Ox); son of Thomas S. schoolmaster. Educated: University of Durham (BA 1907; MA 1911). Deacon: 1907; priest: 1908 (Manchester). Formerly: C. of Christ Church, Glodwick, 1907–8; of Christ Church, Pendlebury, 1908–14; of Whalley, 1914–16; of Holme-in-Cliviger, 1916–17; of Padiham, 1917–19; V. of St Michael, Cornholme, 1919–28; C. of Darrington (in charge of Wentbridge), 1928. Resided at Owmby Rectory. Died 26 March 1950; buried at Owmby, 29 March 1950. [GRO, Birth Index; Census Returns 1891; *Crockford* (1932); *Probate Calendar* 1950; PR Owmby-by-Spital.]

Ronald Metcalfe

Instituted 24 August 1950 to rectory of Owmby-by-Spital with vicarage of Normanby, on death of Thomas Aubrey Sankey. Patron: Dean (David Colin Dunlop) and Chapter of Lincoln, for this turn. [Reg. 44, p.128.]

Deacon: 1923; priest: 1924 (Ripon). Formerly: C. of St Augustine, Wrangthorn, 1923–6; of Stranton, 1926–8; of Ockbrook with Borrowash, 1928–9; V. of Bassingthorpe with Westby and Bitchfield, 1929–40; R. of Burton Coggles, 1940–50; V. of Swayfield, 1947–50. Resided at Owmby Rectory. Afterwards: V. of Thornton with Bagworth (Le), 1952–5. Retired 1955. Lived at 42d Station Road, Whitstable. [*Crockford* (1961–2).]

Johnston Redmond

Instituted 18 November 1952 to rectory of Owmby-by-Spital with vicarage of Normanby, on cession of Ronald Metcalfe. Patron: Queen Elizabeth II (in right of her Duchy of Lancaster), for this turn. [Reg. 44, p.167.]

Educated: St Aidan's Theological College, Ballarat (ThL 1905). Deacon: 1905; priest: 1908 (Ballarat). Formerly: D-in-C of Apsley, 1906; C. of Camperdown, 1907–9; of Ararat,

1909; of Coleraine, 1910; P-in-C of Heywood, 1910–11; C-in-C of Murtoa, 1911–17; Acting Sub-Warden of St Aidan's, Ballarat, 1915–16; TCF 1916–18; V. of Warrnambool, 1917–23; of Furlough, 1923–4; Minister of Mount Dandenong, 1924–6; P-in-C of Millicent, 1926–31; R. of St Aidan, Payneham, 1931–5; V. of Carlton-on-Trent (Nt), 1937–40; PC of St Andrew, East Kirkby, 1940–8; V. of Bishop Norton, 1948–52 (*q.v.*). Resided at Owmby Rectory. Resigned 14 September (accepted 30 September) 1956. Latterly of 32 Hollin Lane, Middleton, Manchester. Died 13 July 1964. [*Crockford* (1955–6, 1961–2); RES 1956/12; *Probate Calendar* 1965.]

Alexander Charles Edward Bennett

Instituted 4 March 1957 to rectory of Owmby-by-Spital with vicarage of Normanby, on resignation of Johnston Redmond. Patron: Queen Elizabeth II (in right of her Duchy of Lancaster), for this turn. [Reg. 44, p.237.]

Born 21 September 1884. Educated: St Aidan's College, Birkenhead (1931). Deacon: 1932; priest: 1933 (Worcester). Formerly: C. of Cradley (Wo), 1932–4; C-in-C of Dunscroft (YWR), 1934–7; V. of St Hilda, Thurnscoe (YWR), 1937–43; of Thorpe Hesley (YWR), 1943–53; R. of Toft with Newton, 1953–7; R. of Faldingworth with Buslingthorpe, 1955–7. Resided at Owmby Rectory. Resignation accepted 31 October 1962. Died 1971. [GRO, Death Index; *Crockford* (1961–2); Reg. 44, p.338.]

John Forbes Thomson MA

Instituted 16 January 1963 to rectory of Owmby-by-Spital with vicarage of Normanby, on resignation of Alexander Charles Edward Bennett. Patron: Dean (David Colin Dunlop) and Chapter of Lincoln, for this turn. [Reg. 44, p.342.]

Born 21 March 1912. Educated: University of St Andrews (MA 1935); St Stephen's House, Oxford (1935). Deacon: 1936; priest: 1937 (London). Formerly: C. of St Mary Magdalene, Paddington, 1936–9; of St Frideswide, Poplar, 1939–40; of Tong with St John, Tong Street, 1940–5; V. of St Margaret, Burnley, 1945–60; of St Peter, Blackburn, 1960–3. Resided at Owmby Rectory. Resignation accepted 6 April 1970. Latterly of The Pantiles, Middle Street, Rippingale. Died March 1982. [GRO, Death Index; *Crockford* (1965–6, 1980–2); Reg. 44, p.437.]

SAXBY

The church of Saxby was given by William Foliot to the Gilbertine Priory of St Katherine outside Lincoln at some time during the episcopate of Robert Chesney (1148 x 1166). In 1236 Jordan Foliot, nephew of William, acknowledged by a final concord that the advowson was the right of the Prior and Convent. The church was appropriated to the Priory on 16 July 1306 and a vicarage was ordained. St Katherine's Priory continued to present to the vicarage until the Dissolution, after which the advowson passed into the possession of the Saunderson family (later Earls of Castleton) and from them, like Glentworth, to the Lumleys (Earls of Scarbrough). The Earl was patron in 1965. [*Reg. Sutton* v. 87–8; *EEA* iv. (App I), no.xiii; *Final Concords* i. 293; Reg. 2, fos 90v, 92; *LDC* (1965), 110–11.]

M. John de Kaifas chaplain
Instituted in the first pontifical year of Bishop Robert Grosseteste (17 June 1235/16 June 1236) to church of Saxby (wrongly identified as 'Saxilby' in MS). Patron: Prior and Convent of St Katherine outside Lincoln. [Hoskin, no.1221.]

M. Paul
Instituted before 23 June 1276. [*Rot. Gravesend*, 95.]

M. William de Bolington subdeacon
Instituted 23 June 1276 to church of Saxby, on death of M. Paul. Patron: Prior and Convent of St Katherine outside Lincoln. [*Rot. Gravesend*, 95.]

Thomas of Bradwell
Instituted before 19 December 1282. [*Reg. Sutton* viii. 4.]

John de Lathebiry clerk
Instituted 19 December 1282 to church of Saxby, on death of Thomas of Bradwell. Patron: Prior and Convent of St Katherine outside Lincoln. [*Reg. Sutton* viii. 4.]
Subdeacon: 12 December 1282 (Lincoln). [*Ibid.*]

Richard of Burton chaplain
Instituted 30 January 1293/4 to church of Saxby, on death of John. Patron: Prior and Convent of St Katherine outside Lincoln. [*Reg. Sutton* viii. 24.]

Vicarage

John de Marton chaplain
Instituted 7 September 1309 to vicarage of Saxby, newly ordained. Patron: Prior and Convent of St Katherine outside Lincoln. [Reg. 2, fo.92v.]

Walter
Instituted before 15 March 1352/3. [Reg. 9, fo.165v.]

William son of Robert de Malteby priest
Instituted 15 March 1352/3 to vicarage of Saxby, on resignation of Walter. Patron: Prior and Convent of St Katherine outside Lincoln. [Reg. 9, fo.165v.]

Richard de Malberthorp
Instituted before 26 August 1384. [Reg. 10, fo.151v.]

Robert son of William de Stok iuxta Newerk priest
Instituted 26 August 1384 to vicarage of Saxby, on death of Richard de

Malberthorp. Patron: Prior and Convent of St Katherine outside Lincoln. [Reg. 10, fo.151v.]

William de Wrangill priest
Instituted 5 August 1391 to vicarage of Saxby, on resignation of Robert de Stoke. Patron: Prior and Convent of St Katherine outside Lincoln. [Reg. 11, fo.107.]

[Roger son of] Thomas Tayllour de Helmeswell priest
Instituted 11 March 1395/6 to vicarage of Saxby, on death of William de Wranghill. Patron: Prior and Convent of St Katherine outside Lincoln. [Reg. 11, fo.117.]

Afterwards: R. of Southorpe, 1396.

William Fynche priest
Instituted 3 October 1396 to vicarage of Saxby, on resignation of Roger son of Thomas Tayllour de Helmeswell (by exchange with church of Southorpe). Patron: Prior and Convent of St Katherine outside Lincoln. [Reg. 11, fo.118v.]

Priest: before 13 March 1380/1. Formerly: R. of Southorpe, 1381–96. [Reg. 10, fo.147.]

Robert de Kellesey priest
Instituted 17 November 1397 to vicarage of Saxby, on resignation of William Fynche. Patron: Prior and Convent of St Katherine outside Lincoln. [Reg. 11, fo.119v.]

Thomas Staunton
Instituted before 9 December 1404. [Reg. 13, fo.183.]

John Wrote chaplain
Instituted 9 December 1404 to vicarage of Saxby, on resignation of Thomas Staunton. Patron: Prior and Convent of St Katherine outside Lincoln. [Reg. 13, fo.183.]

Br. John Grave Canon of Bridlington
Instituted 10 October 1466 to vicarage of Saxby (cause of vacancy not stated). Patron: not specified. [Reg. 20, fo.161v.]

Robert Ossyt priest
Instituted 14 April 1474 to vicarage of Saxby, on deprivation of br. John Gray, Augustinian canon of York diocese. Patron: Prior and Convent of St Katherine outside Lincoln. [Reg. 21, fo.32v.]

Afterwards: R. of St Hilary, Spridlington, 1479–1501 (q.v.).

Richard Gybson priest
Instituted 4 October 1479 to vicarage of Saxby, on resignation of Robert
Ossitt (by exchange with church of Spridlington). Patron: Prior and Convent
of St Katherine outside Lincoln. [Reg. 21, fo.34v.]
Formerly: R. of St Hilary, Spridlington, 1473–9 (*q.v.*).

William Wynter
Instituted before 30 March 1499. [Reg. 23, fo.150v.]

Oliver Horner priest
Instituted 30 March 1499 to vicarage of Saxby, on death of William Wynter.
Patron: Prior and Convent of St Katherine outside Lincoln. [Reg. 23, fo.150v.]

Richard Redyshe priest
Instituted 20 April 1499 to vicarage of Saxby, on resignation of Oliver
Horner. Patron: Prior and Convent of St Katherine outside Lincoln. [Reg.
23, fo.152v.]

Thomas Waleys
Instituted 1 August 1514 to vicarage of Saxby, on death of last incumbent.
Patron: Prior and Convent of St Katherine outside Lincoln. [Reg. 25, fo.1.]
Assessed for subsidy (£9) in 1526. [*Subsidy*, 36.]

Thomas Sheffeld
Instituted 28 April 1529 to vicarage of Saxby, on death of last incumbent.
Patron: Prior and Convent of St Katherine outside Lincoln. [Reg. 27, fo.100.]
Witnessed wills as Vicar, 1540–56. [Stow Wills 1530–52/103; Stow Wills 1553–67/86,
161; LCC Wills 1557/ii/53v.]

William Clerke
Instituted 24 February 1582/3 to vicarage of Saxby (cause of vacancy not
stated). Patron: Nicholas Saunderson of Fillingham, esquire. [*Bishop Cooper*,
79.]
Education: 'bred in the schools'. Priest: 25 March 1566 (Lincoln). [*State of the Church*,
97.]

Thomas Watson
Instituted 17 July 1586 to vicarage of Saxby, on death of William Clerke.
Patron: Nicholas Saunderson of Fillingham, esquire (16 July 1586). [BC;
PD 1586/35.]
Education: 'no graduate; no preacher'. Non-resident; 'his behaviour not knowen for that
he lyeuthe not in the countie' (1598). Living served by Richard Laminge (1594) and
Robert Shawe (1603), curates. TW still vicar in 1607. [*State of the Church*, 330, 339,
394, 428.]

Andrew Harrington MA
Instituted 20 June 1610 to vicarage of Saxby. [BC.]

Educated: King's College (matric. *c*.1595; BA 1598–9) and Sidney Sussex College, Cambridge (MA 1602). Deacon: 25 March 1601 (Norwich); priest: 23 September 1604 (Peterborough). Non-resident (1611): 'Hee is Curate at Fillingham, and monished to leave either that cure or this vicaredge.' Signed BTs 1611–12. Afterwards: V. of Stainton-by-Langworth, 1612–24. Died before 26 January 1623/4. [Venn, *Alumni*; LC 4, fo.15; LC 3, fo.100; BTs Saxby; PD 1624/59.]

Sebastian Walker
Instituted 17 October 1612 to vicarage of Saxby, on cession of Andrew Harrington. Patron: Sir Nicholas Sanderson Bt (18 September 1612). [BC; PD 1612/57.]

Born *c*.1582. Deacon: 12 January 1603/4; priest: 24 May 1605 (York). Married. [PD 1612/57; *York Ordinations 1561–1642*, 71.]

The vicarage of Saxby was under sequestration in 1614. [LC 4, fo.10v.]

Christopher Denn[is BA]
Instituted before 3 April 1628. [PD 1628/42.]

Son of Edward D., citizen of Lincoln. Educated: Christ's College, Cambridge (BA 1603). Deacon: 23 May 1619; priest: 12 March 1619/20 (Peterborough). Signed BTs at Saxby as curate or minister, 1620–8. Also: C. of Hemswell, *c*.1623–4. Afterwards: R. of Little Warley (Ess), 1627–32; R. of Beelsby, 1632–48. Buried at Beelsby, 26 November 1648. [Binnall, *Hemswell*, 24; Venn, *Alumni*; Longden iv. 61; BTs Saxby; PR Beelsby.]

Hamond Bulcocke MA
Instituted 3 April 1628 to vicarage of Saxby, on cession of Christopher Denn[is]. Patron: Nicholas Sanderson, Viscount Castleton (24 March 1627/8). [BC; PD 1628/42.]

Also: C. of Harpswell, *c*.1633–70 (*q.v.*).

Robert Mattins BA
Instituted 8 December 1631 to vicarage of Saxby, on cession of Hamond Bulcock. Patron: Nicholas Saunderson, Viscount Castleton (11 October 1631). [BC; PD 1631/24.]

Educated: Trinity College, Cambridge (matric. 1623; BA 1626–7). Deacon and priest: 20 May 1628 (Lincoln). Resident (1662); signed BTs at Saxby 1661–4. Buried at Saxby, 15 September 1665. [Venn, *Alumni*; LC 5, fo.96; BTs Saxby.]

John Smith MA
Instituted 12 May 1666 to vicarage of Saxby, on death of Robert Mattens. Patron: George Saunderson, Viscount Castleton (16 February 1665/6). [Reg. 33, fo.58v; PD 1666/7.]

Born *c*.1609; son of John S. of Gainsborough. Educated: New Inn Hall (matric. 1624/5) and St Alban Hall, Oxford (BA 1628; MA 1631). Deacon and priest: 23 September 1632 (Lincoln). Formerly: R. of Heapham, 1638–69. Signed BTs at Saxby 1667–76. Afterwards: R. of Mareham-le-Fen, 1675–81. Buried at Mareham-le-Fen, 5 March 1680/1. Will (LCC). [Foster, *Alumni*; LC 5, fo.76; BTs Saxby; PR Mareham-le-Fen; LCC Wills 1680/ii/446.]

John Curtois MA

Instituted 11 July 1676 to vicarage of Saxby, on cession of John Smith. Patron: George Saunderson, Viscount Castleton (7 March 1675/6). [Reg. 34, fo.10; SUB Va, fo.84; PD 1676/14.]

Born *c*.1651; son of Robert C. of the City of Lincoln. Educated: Lincoln College (matric. 1667) and Magdalen College, Oxford (BA 1670; MA 1674); Fellow of Magdalen, 1671–4. Priest: 11 July 1676 (Lincoln). Signed BTs at Saxby 1677–80. Afterwards: R. of Branston, 1680–1719; Canon of Lincoln and Prebendary of Welton Beckhall, 1700–19. Buried at Branston, 10 April 1719. [Foster, *Alumni*; Reg. 34, fo.20; *Speculum*, 21; *Le Neve Fasti: Lincoln 1541–1857*, 124; PR Branston.]

Robert Dixon BA

Instituted 27 June 1681 to vicarage of Saxby, on cession of John Curtois. Patron: George, Viscount Castleton. [Reg. 34, fo.61v.]

Also: R. of Owmby-by-Spital, 1693–1729 (*q.v.*).

John Whichcot BA

Instituted 3 January 1729/30 to vicarage of Saxby, on death of Robert Dixon. Patron: Sir Thomas Saunderson of Glentworth, kt. [Reg. 38, p.217.]

Born 1 June 1702, baptised 6 June 1702 at Harpswell; son of George W., esquire. Educated: Brigg GS and Magdalene College, Cambridge (matric. 1723; LLB 1727). His bills at Cambridge a recurring theme in family letters: 'He complains … very much of Poverty and … says I must leave him a Guinea, which I durst not but submitt to, Concidering the Horse-course and the Assemblys at Stamford.' Deacon: 2 March 1728/9; priest: 21 December 1729 (Lincoln). Also: V. of Blyton, 1729–31. Afterwards: R. of Scotton, 1731–50; R. of Althorpe, 1741–50. Died 29 September 1750; buried at St Margaret, Lincoln, 2 October 1750. [PR Harpswell; *Lincolnshire Pedigrees*, 1073; Venn, *Alumni*; *Whichcot Letters*, 23; Reg. 38, pp. 200, 216; PR Lincoln St Margaret.]

Richard Bursey

Instituted 26 August 1730 to vicarage of Saxby, on cession of John Whichcote. Patron: Sir Thomas Saunderson of Sandbeck, kt (29 July 1730). [Reg. 38, p.230; PD 1730/1.]

Also: R. of Skegness, 1719–47. Buried at Croft, 17 September 1747. [PR Croft.]

John Barr BA

Instituted 10 December 1747 to vicarage of Saxby, on death of Richard Bursey. Patron: Thomas, Earl of Scarbrough. [Reg. 38, p.477.]

Signed BTs at Saxby 1747–78. Also: R. of Owmby-by-Spital, 1736–78 (*q.v.*).

John Bassett
Instituted 8 January 1779 to vicarage of Saxby, on death of John Barr. Patron: Richard, Earl of Scarbrough. [Reg. 39, p.325.]

Also: V. of Willoughton, 1793–1805 (*q.v.*).

Henry Bassett BA
Instituted 21 June 1805 to vicarage of Saxby, on death of John Bassett. Patron: George Augustus, Earl of Scarbrough. [Reg. 40, p.96.]

Also: V. of Glentworth, 1802–52 (*q.v.*).

Hugh Nanney BA
Instituted 24 September 1852 to vicarage of Saxby with rectory of Firsby annexed, on death of Henry Bassett. Patron: John Savile Lumley Savile, Earl of Scarbrough. [Reg. 40, p.537.]

Also: R. of Caenby, 1848–63 (*q.v.*).

Thomas Middleton Nanney
Instituted 19 June 1863 to vicarage of Saxby with rectory of Firsby annexed, on death of Hugh Nanney. Patron: Richard George Lumley, Earl of Scarbrough, of Sandbeck Park, Rotherham. Note that on 9 June 1863, the Archbishop of Canterbury granted a dispensation enabling the said TMN to hold together the rectory of Caenby and the vicarage of Saxby with the rectory of Firsby annexed. [Reg. 41, p.100.]

Also: R. of Caenby, 1863–7 (*q.v.*).

George Banastre Pix MA
Instituted 17 January 1868 to vicarage of Saxby with rectory of Firsby annexed, on death of Thomas Middleton Nanney. Patron: Richard Lumley, Earl of Scarbrough, of Sandbeck Park, Rotherham. [Reg. 41, p.256.]

Also: R. of Caenby, 1868–74 (*q.v.*).

Robert Boyce Spoor (Courtenay)
Instituted 11 March 1875 to vicarage of Saxby with rectory of Firsby annexed, on death of George Banastre Pix. Patron: Richard George Lumley, Earl of Scarbrough, of Sandbeck Park. [Reg. 41, p.493.]

Also: R. of Caenby, 1875–1909 (*q.v.*).

John Booth MA
Instituted 19 July 1909 to vicarage of Saxby with rectory of Firsby annexed, on death of Robert Boyce Courtenay. Patron: Aldred Frederick George Beresford Lumley, Earl of Scarbrough, of Sandbeck Park, Rotherham. Note that on 24 June 1909, the Archbishop of Canterbury granted a dispensation enabling the said JB to hold together the rectory of Caenby and the vicarage of Saxby with the rectory of Firsby annexed. [Reg. 42, p.613.]

Also: R. of Caenby, 1909–14 (*q.v.*).

William Norton Howe MA

Instituted 13 June 1914 to vicarage of Saxby with rectory of Firsby annexed, on cession of John Booth. Patron: Aldred Frederick George Beresford Lumley, Earl of Scarbrough, of Sandbeck Park, Rotherham. Note that on 22 May 1914, the Archbishop of Canterbury granted a dispensation enabling the said WNH to hold together the rectory of Caenby and the vicarage of Saxby with the rectory of Firsby annexed. [Reg. 43, p.70.]

Also: R. of Caenby, 1914–26 (*q.v.*).

The Benefice of Saxby with Firsby was united to the Rectory of Spridlington by Order in Council dated 10 August 1922 to form the United Benefice of Spridlington with Saxby and Firsby. [Reg. 43, pp. 277–81.]

SNITTERBY

Snitterby was a chapelry in the parish of Waddingham by 1277, when Bishop Gravesend ratified an agreement relating to the endowment of the chapel and the provision of sacraments (except burial) there. By Order in Council dated 20 March 1857, it was constituted a separate perpetual curacy. The advowson was vested in the Crown, which remained the patron in 1965. [Reg. 3, fo.56; Owen, 'Medieval Chapels', 21; *Subsidy*, 35; Reg. 40, pp. 588–90; *LDC* (1965), 132–3.]

Richard Morey BA

Licensed 26 February 1858 to perpetual curacy of Snitterby, on death of William Cooper. Nominated by Queen Victoria (17 February 1858). [Reg. 40, p.593; PD/Crown/100.]

Born *c*.1807 at North Marden (Sx); son of Richard Marden M. Educated: Sherborne School and Trinity College, Cambridge (matric. 1827; BA 1831). Deacon: 23 December 1832; priest: 22 December 1833 (Chichester). Formerly: C. of Messingham with Bottesford, 1836–40; of Waddingham, 1841–58. First Incumbent of Snitterby; resided in Rectory House. Died 13 November 1861; buried at Snitterby, 16 November 1861. [Census Returns 1861; Venn, *Alumni*; *Hampshire Telegraph*, 31 December 1832; *Hampshire Advertiser*, 4 January 1834; CR 2, p.155; CR 3, fo.15v; PR Waddingham; *Probate Calendar* 1862; PR Snitterby.]

Richard Edward Warner MA

Licensed 21 February 1862 to perpetual curacy of Snitterby, on death of Richard Morey. Nominated by Queen Victoria (7 February 1862). [Reg. 41, p.80; PD/Crown/118.]

Born c.1837; son of Richard W. of Lifton (Dev), esquire. Educated: Exeter College, Oxford (matric. 1855; BA 1858; MA 1861). Deacon: 1859; priest: 1860 (Peterborough). Formerly: C. of Finedon (Np), 1859–61. Resided at Snitterby Rectory. Also: Canon of Lincoln and Prebendary of Dunholme, 1887–9. Afterwards: V. of Gainsborough, 1889–94; Canon of Lincoln and Prebendary of Corringham, 1889–94; RD of Corringham, 1889–94; R. of Stoke Rochford, 1894–1910; Canon of Lincoln and Prebendary of Bedford Major, 1895–1910. Father of Constance Weigall (1865–1951), the authoress of *An Angel Unawares* (1899), *A Counsel of Uprightness* (1905) and other works. Died 3 May 1910; buried 6 May 1910 at Stoke Rochford. [Foster, *Alumni*; *Crockford* (1908); Census Returns 1881; *Probate Calendar* 1910; PR Stoke Rochford.]

Henry Usher

Instituted 31 August 1889 to rectory of Snitterby, on cession of Richard Edward Warner. Patron: Queen Victoria. [Reg. 42, p.303.]

Baptised 28 December 1816 at St Swithin, Lincoln; son of Richard U. of Broadgate, sawyer. Educated: St Bees College (1845). Deacon: 1846; priest: 1847 (Worcester). Formerly: C. of St James, Birmingham, 1846–8; of Oddington (Gl), 1848–56; of Broadwell (Gl), 1856–63; of Barrowby, 1863–7; R. of Saltfleetby St Clement, 1867–89. Resided at Snitterby Rectory. Died 7 December 1896. [PR Lincoln St Swithin; Census Returns 1891; *St Bees College Calendar* (1854), 42; *Crockford* (1895); *Probate Calendar* 1897.]

Clifford Coleridge Chamberlain MA

Instituted 24 April 1897 to rectory of Snitterby, on death of Henry Usher. Patron: Queen Victoria. [Reg. 42, p.413.]

Born 1843; son of Henry Edwin C., Curate of Chelwood (So). Educated: Worcester College, Oxford (matric. 1861; BA 1865; MA 1872). Deacon: 1869; priest: 1873 (London). Formerly: Second Master of Swansea GS, 1865–7; Asst Classics Master, Eagle House School, Wimbledon, 1868–74; C. of Wimbledon, 1874–97. Resided at Snitterby Rectory. Resigned 25 September (accepted 9 October) 1906. Lived abroad: at Grand Hotel, Pallanza, Lake Maggiore, Italy (1909); at Hôtel Schweizerhof, Lucerne, Switzerland (1911); latterly of Redhill (Sr). Died 10 August 1913 at the house of Edward Eustace Chamberlain, Chaplain of County Asylum at Rainhill (La). [GRO, Birth Index; *Clergy List* (1841); Foster, *Alumni; Crockford* (1905, 1909); RES 248c/14; *Probate Calendar* 1913.]

John Swalwell BA

Instituted 19 June 1906 to rectory of Snitterby, on resignation of Clifford Coleridge Chamberlain. Patron: King Edward VII. [Reg. 42, p.548.]

Born c.1864 at Scarborough; son of Revd John S., Headmaster of Scarborough GS. Brother of Marmaduke Frederick Thomas S., Vicar of Linwood 1906–32, and of Sidney Rupert S., Vicar of Willoughton 1901–14 (*q.v.*). Educated: St Catharine's College, Cambridge (matric. 1884; BA 1888). Deacon: 1890 (York); priest: 1891 (Beverley). Formerly: C. of North Otterington, 1890–2; of Emmanuel Church, Sheffield, 1893; of Danby (Y), 1894–6; of St Luke, Nottingham, 1896–1901; of St Jude, Sheffield, 1901–5; of St Stephen, Sheffield, 1905–6. Resided at Snitterby Rectory. In October 1908 an Order of Affiliation was made against JS for the maintenance of the bastard daughter of Mary Wright of Blyborough, formerly a servant at Snitterby Rectory; he denied the charge and appealed against the Order, unsuccessfully. The living was declared vacant on 25 January 1909. Afterwards: R. of Swift Current, Saskatchewan (Canada), 1912–17; of Estevan, Saskatchewan,

1917–19. Retired 1919. Died *c*.1920. [Venn, *Alumni*; *Crockford* (1907, 1920); Census Returns 1901; COR/B/7A/1/Snitterby; *Sheffield Daily Telegraph*, 28–30 October 1908; *Manchester Courier*, 25 January 1909.]

Robert John Anderson BA

Instituted 6 April 1909 to rectory of Snitterby, on ejection of John Swalwell under Clergy Discipline Act 1892. Patron: King Edward VII. [Reg. 42, p.608.]

Born *c*.1871 at Dublin. Educated: University of Dublin (BA 1900; Divinity Testimonium 1902). Deacon: 1900 (Southwell); priest: 1902 (Lincoln). Formerly: C. of Eckington, 1900–2; of St Peter-in-Eastgate, Lincoln, 1902–9. Resided at Snitterby Rectory. Bishop Hicks noted (February 1914): 'a good man. Nice little wife, v. pretty, & the good m[other] of 2 sweet babes.' Afterwards: R. of Little Ponton, 1921–32. Died 19 December 1932 at St Clement's Nursing Home, Barrowby Road, Grantham. [Census Returns 1911; *Crockford* (1932); *Hicks Diaries*, no.444; *Probate Calendar* 1933.]

Graeme Maurice Elliott

Instituted 21 March 1921 to rectory of Snitterby, on cession of Robert John Anderson. Patron: King George V. [Reg. 43, p.212.]

Born 1883, baptised 10 February 1884 at Christ Church, Hampstead; son of Alfred Harraden E. of Hampstead, merchant. Educated: University of London, Hackney College (1905). Deacon: 1915; priest: 1917 (Winchester). Formerly: C. of Havant, 1915–17; of Christchurch, 1917–20; R. of Honiley, 1920. Resided at Snitterby Rectory. Afterwards: V. of Sutton St Nicholas alias Lutton, 1927–30; R. of Over Wallop, 1930–4; of St Peter, Cricklewood, 1934–6; C. of Glynde, 1950–2; R. of Birdham with West Itchenor, 1952–4. Author: *Angels Seen To-day* (1919); *The Challenge of Spiritualism* (1920); *A Modern Miracle: being the story of how a little girl was saved by an angel* (1922). Retired to 39 West Heath Drive, London NW11. Latterly of 31a Chapel Road, Worthing. Died there, 1959. [GRO, Birth Index; LMA, PR Hampstead Christ Church; *Crockford* (1923, 1957–8); GRO, Death Index.]

The Rectory of Snitterby was united to the Rectory of Waddingham by Order in Council dated 6 February 1928. [Reg. 43, p.428.]

SPRIDLINGTON ST ALBIN

The church of St Albin, Spridlington, was given by Philip of Kyme to the Gilbertine Priory of Bullington during the reign of Henry II. It was appropriated to the Priory by Geoffrey Plantagenet and a vicarage was ordained. Bullington continued to present to the vicarage until its union with the church of St Hilary, Spridlington, in 1417. [*Danelaw Charters*, 3–4; *EEA* i. no.286.]

Thomas de Burgo chaplain

Instituted in the ninth pontifical year of Bishop Hugh of Wells (20 December 1217/19 December 1218) to vicarage of [church of St Albin], Spridlington.

Patron: G[ilbert], Prior of Order of Sempringham, Prior (G.) and Nuns of Bullington. [*Rot. Welles* i. 103–4; 'Rolls of Hugh of Wells', 166.]

Simon de Bamburg chaplain
Instituted in the fifteenth pontifical year of Bishop Robert Grosseteste (17 June 1249/16 June 1250) to vicarage of church of St Albinus, Spridlington, on resignation of Thomas. Patron: Prior and Convent of Bullington. [Hoskin, no.1300.]

William de Ingham priest
Instituted 24 February 1265/6 to vicarage of church of St Albin, Spridlington, on death of Simon. Patron: Prior and Convent of Bullington. [*Rot. Gravesend*, 91, 291.]

Richard de Witton chaplain
Instituted 18 March 1267/8 to vicarage of church of St Albin, Spridlington, on resignation of William de Ingham. Patron: Prior and Convent of Bullington. [*Rot. Gravesend*, 92.]

Robert of Chafford chaplain
Instituted 25 June 1288 to vicarage of church of St Albin, Spridlington, on death of Richard. Patron: Prior and Convent of Bullington. [*Reg. Sutton* viii. 17–18.]

Commission to hear confessions of clergy in deanery of Aslacoe, 1292. Licence to grant absolution to Nicholas de Crevecuer, Eleanor his wife and their household (except in reserved cases), 8 January 1321/2. [*Reg. Sutton* iv. 46; Reg. 5, fo.302v.]

John
Instituted before 23 September 1349. [Reg. 9, fo.159.]

John Ingram de Spridlyngton priest
Instituted 23 September 1349 to vicarage of church of St Albin the Confessor, Spridlington, on death of John. Patron: Prior and Convent of Bullington. [Reg. 9, fo.159.]

John de Bradefeld
Instituted before 21 August 1358. [Reg. 9, fo.169v.]

William de Croxton priest
Instituted 21 August 1358 to vicarage of church of St Albin, Spridlington, on resignation of John de Bradefeld. Patron: Prior and Convent of Bullington. [Reg. 9, fo.169v.]

Afterwards: V. of Risby, 1359–65; V. of Willoughton, 1365 (*q.v.*). [Reg. 9, fo.169v; Reg. 10, fo.127v.]

Roger de Chirchewawer priest
Instituted 11 April 1359 to vicarage of church of St Albin, Spridlington, on institution of William de Croxton to vicarage of Risby. Patron: Prior and Convent of Bullington. [Reg. 9, fo.169v.]

William de Malteby priest
Instituted by collation 26 February 1361/2 to vicarage of church of St Albin, Spridlington (cause of vacancy not stated). Patron: Bishop of Lincoln, by lapse. [Reg. 9, fo.173.]

William de Stoke
Instituted before 1 July 1381. [Reg. 10, fo.147.]

John Othebrigge priest
Instituted 1 July 1381 to vicarage of church of [St Albin], Spridlington, on death of William de Stoke. Patron: Prior and Convent of Bullington. [Reg. 10, fo.147.]

Afterwards: V. of Bishopthorpe (YWR), 1390–1401. [*Reg. Scrope* i. 31.]

John de Thornton
Instituted 25 July 1390 to vicarage of church of St Albin, Spridlington, on resignation of John de Brigg (by exchange with vicarage of Bishopthorpe (*Thorp' iuxta Ebor'*), dioc. York). Patron: Prior and Convent of Bullington. [Reg. 11, fo.105.]

Formerly: V. of Bishopthorpe, to 1390.

John de Hawardeby priest
Instituted 13 October 1390 to vicarage of church of St Albin, Spridlington, on resignation of John de Thornton. Patron: Prior and Convent of Bullington. [Reg. 11, fo.105v.]

John de Schalby priest
Instituted 14 November 1391 to vicarage of church of St Albin, Spridlington, on resignation of John de Hawardeby. Patron: Prior (Robert) and Convent of Bullington. [Reg. 11, fo.107v.]

John Chetur priest
Instituted 12 October 1395 to vicarage of church of St Albin, Spridlington, on resignation of John de Scalby. Patron: Prior and Convent of Bullington. [Reg. 11, fo.115v.]

Thomas Couper priest
Instituted 31 May 1408 to vicarage of church of St Albin, Spridlington, on resignation of John Chetour. Patron: Prior and Convent of Bullington. [Reg. 14, fo.26v.]

Thomas Kynyardeby
Instituted before 20 March 1408/9. [Reg. 14, fo.113.]

John Coke de Wythern priest
Instituted 20 March 1408/9 to vicarage of church of St Albin, Spridlington, on resignation of Thomas Kynyardeby. Patron: Prior and Convent of Bullington. [Reg. 14, fo.113.]

Thomas de Neuton priest
Instituted 5 September 1414 to vicarage of church of St Albin, Spridlington, on resignation of John Coke. Patron: Prior and Convent of Bullington. [Reg. 14, fo.124v.]

John Prest de Threkyngham chaplain
Instituted 26 February 1414/15 to vicarage of church of St Albin, Spridlington, on resignation of Thomas Newton. Patron: Prior and Convent of Bullington. [Reg. 14, fo.125v.]
Resigned 2 January 1416/17. [*Reg. Repingdon* iii. no.303.]

The vicarage of the church of St Albin, Spridlington, was united to the church of St Hilary, Spridlington, following an inquiry held by the bishop's commissary, 14 January 1416/17. [*Reg. Repingdon* iii. no.303.]

SPRIDLINGTON ST HILARY

The church of St Hilary, Spridlington, was given by Geoffrey son of Ruallan to Bardney Abbey during the episcopate of Robert Chesney. Around 1200, the Abbot of Bardney quitclaimed the advowson to Ralph de la Mare, in consideration of an annual pension of twenty shillings on the Feast of St Oswald. Ralph de la Mare was succeeded by his son William, whose daughter Mabel married Geoffrey de Neville. Geoffrey presented in 1248–9. On his death in 1249, Geoffrey's son Hugh acquired the advowson but it had passed from the Neville family by 1280 when the Spridlington fee was held by Walter de Stokes. The Stokes family continued to present until the early fifteenth century, after which the advowson passed to Gerard Sothill of Redbourne, who presented in 1453 and 1460. Gerard's daughter Jane married Gilbert

Lacy of Brearley near Halifax, who presented in 1479. The Lacy family retained the advowson until the middle of the sixteenth century. By 1671 it was in the hands of Richard Sherbrooke, from whom it passed to Mary Mead (née Sherbrooke) of St Sepulchre, London, the mother-in-law of John Wilkes the politician. It was afterwards held by Frederick Gildart, who presented himself to the living in 1822 and who bequeathed it to his cousin, Henry Frederick Hutton of Gate Burton. The Hutton family still held the patronage in 1965. [Hamilton Thompson, 'Bardney Abbey', 74–5; *Danelaw Charters*, lxxv; *EYC* v. 290–1; *Lincolnshire Pedigrees*, 914–15; Foster, *Visitation of Yorkshire* (1875), 330–1; *Archivists' Report* 13 (1961–2), 18–19; *Hutton of Gate Burton* (1898), 39; *LDC* (1965), 110–11.]

Richard of Beckingham
Instituted before *c*.1200. [Hamilton Thompson, 'Bardney Abbey', 74.]

Theobald son of Roger de Stikeswald
Instituted *c*.1200 to church of St Hilary, Spridlington, on resignation of Richard of Beckingham. Patron: Ralph de la Mare. [Hamilton Thompson, 'Bardney Abbey', 74.]

Francis chaplain
Instituted in the fourteenth pontifical year of Bishop Robert Grosseteste (17 June 1248/16 June 1249) to church of [St Hilary], Spridlington, on resignation of Theobald de Stikeswaud. Patron: Geoffrey de Novavill kt. [Hoskin, no.1299.]

William son of John Clerk de Caden' chaplain
Instituted in the second pontifical year of Bishop Richard Gravesend (3 November 1259/2 November 1260) to church of St Hilary, Spridlington. Patron: Hugh de Nevill kt. Thomas Haunsard and Roger de Claxton, clerks, who had been presented earlier, renounced their claims. [*Rot. Gravesend*, 88, 290.]

William de Axeby subdeacon
Instituted 13 March 1276/7 to church of [St Hilary], Spridlington, on resignation of William. Patron: Abbot and Convent of Bardney. [*Rot. Gravesend*, 95, 292.]

William de Spridelington chaplain
Instituted 30 October 1305 to church of St Hilary, Spridlington, on death of William de Haxeby. Patron: Robert de Stokes. [Reg. 2, fo.88v.]

A William, Rector of Spridlington, was appointed a commissary to audit executors' accounts of will of John Colbyng de Ouneby, 28 November 1323. [*Reg. Burghersh* iii. no.1815.]

William Cadenay
Instituted before 4 February 1342/3. [Reg. 6, fo.29.]

Nicholas Stokes priest
Instituted 4 February 1342/3 to church of St Hilary, Spridlington, on death
of William Cadenay. Patron: Robert Stokes de Spridlington. [Reg. 6, fo.29.]
Afterwards: R. of a mediety of Weldon (Np), 1343–4; R. of St Hilary, Spridlington
(again), 1344–85 (see below).

Thomas Besevill de Lufwyk priest
Instituted 15 October 1343 to church of St Hilary, Spridlington, on resignation
of Nicholas de Stokes (by exchange with a mediety of church of Weldon).
Patron: Robert de Stokes, lord of Spridlington. [Reg. 6, fo.29.]
Formerly: R. of a mediety of Weldon, 1327–43. [*Reg. Burghersh* ii. no.1310.]

William son of Thomas de Spridlyngton clerk
Instituted 28 October 1343 to church of St Hilary, Spridlington, on resignation of Thomas Besevill de Lufwyk. Patron: Robert de Stokes, lord of Spridlington. [Reg. 6, fo.29.]
Afterwards: R. of a mediety of Weldon (Np), 1344–58; R. of Sileby (Le), 1358. [Reg. 9,
fo.216.]

Nicholas de Stokes priest
Instituted 15 April 1344 to church of St Hilary, Spridlington, on resigna-
tion of William de Spridelyngton (by exchange with a mediety of church
of Weldon). Patron: Robert de Stokes, lord of Spridlington. [Reg. 6, fo.29.]
Formerly: R. of St Hilary, Spridlington, 1343; R. of a mediety of Weldon (Np), 1343–4.
Assessed for poll tax, 1377. [*Clerical Poll-Taxes*, no.825.]

John de Wadingham priest
Instituted 7 March 1384/5 to church of St Hilary, Spridlington, on death of
Nicholas Stokes. Patron: Richard de Stokes. [Reg. 11, fo.97.]

William de Patryngton
Instituted before 22 November 1398. [Reg. 13, fo.177.]
Afterwards: V. of Clarborough (Nt), 1398–1404; Chaplain of Melton Chantry in York
Minster, 1404; Chaplain of Thorpe Chantry in York Minster, until 1407; V. of Laneham
(Nt), 1407–15; R. of Saxby All Saints, 1415–18; R. of Linby (Nt), 1418. [Train, *North
Notts Clergy*, 36, 108; Reg. 14, fos.76v, 95v.]

Thomas Coke (de Cressingham)
Instituted 22 November 1398 to church of Spridlington, on resignation of
William de Patryngton (by exchange with vicarage of Clarborough, dioc.
York). Patron: Walter Stokes of Spridlington. [Reg. 13, fo.177.]
Formerly: R. of All SS Peaseholme Green, York, to 1392; V. of Clarborough (Nt), 1392–8.
Afterwards: V. of Billinghay, 1399–1401. [Train, *North Notts Clergy*, 36; Reg. 13, fo.143.]

John Katyrton chaplain

Instituted 18 September 1399 to church of St Hilary, Spridlington, on resignation of Thomas Cook (by exchange with vicarage of Billinghay). Patron: Walter Stokes *domicellus*. [Reg. 13, fo.178v.]

Formerly: Chaplain of St Mary Chantry in Church of St Martin Cony Street, York, to 1391; V. of Redbourne, 1391–4; V. of Billinghay, 1394–9. Afterwards: V. of Scothern, 1404–6; V. of Misterton (Nt), 1406–11; V. of Lavington, 1411–14. [Reg. 11, fos 69, 106v; Reg. 14, fos 70v, 108v; Train, *North Notts Clergy*, 138.]

Robert in the Blomes

Instituted 9 March 1403/4 to church of St Hilary, Spridlington, on resignation of John Caterton (by exchange with vicarage of Scothern). Patron: Walter Stokes of Spridlington. [Reg. 13, fo.182v.]

Formerly: Chaplain of Lexington Chantry in Lincoln Cathedral, to 1397; V. of Wootton, 1397–8; V. of Scothern, 1398–1404. Afterwards: V. of Middle Rasen Drax, 1407–9; Chaplain of Chantry in Church of Burton-by-Lincoln, 1409. [Reg. 11, fos 85, 120; Reg. 14, fo.36v.]

John Weldon priest

Instituted 23 May 1407 to church of St Hilary, Spridlington, on resignation of Robert in the Blomes (by exchange with vicarage of Middle Rasen Drax). Patron: Walter Stokes, lord of Spridlington. [Reg. 14, fos 19, 110.]

Formerly: V. of Middle Rasen Drax, to 1407. Afterwards: V. of Everton (Nt), 1409–13; of Mattersey (Nt), 1413–16. [Train, *North Notts Clergy*, 65, 130.]

John Shafton

Instituted 10 September 1409 to church of St Hilary, Spridlington, on resignation of John Weldon (by exchange with vicarage of Everton, dioc. York). Patron: Walter Stokes, lord of Spridlington. [Reg. 14, fo.114v.]

Formerly: V. of Everton (Nt), 1406–9. [Train, *North Notts Clergy*, 65.]

William Malkynson chaplain

Instituted 15 September 1409 to church of St Hilary, Spridlington (cause of vacancy not stated). Patron: Walter Stokes of Spridlington. [Reg. 14, fo.115.]

William Greyngham

Instituted before 10 September 1416. [Reg. 14, fo.129.]

John Cristyanson de Sutton chaplain

Instituted 10 September 1416 to church of St Hilary, Spridlington, on death of William Greyngham. Patron: Sir Thomas Hawley kt, Thomas Enderby, William Blesby and Ralph de Gouxhill chaplain. [Reg. 14, fo.129.]

William Grene

Instituted before 24 October 1419. [Reg. 14, fo.137.]

Afterwards: V. of St Martin, Stamford, 1419–22; V. of Mundon (Ess), 1422. [*Reg. Fleming* i. no.219.]

Thomas son of Richard Smyth de Stykeney priest

Instituted 24 October 1419 to church of St Hilary, Spridlington, on resignation of William Grene (by exchange with vicarage of St Martin, Stamford). Patron: Thomas Enderby, William Bleseby and Ralph Gouxhill chaplain. [Reg. 14, fos 102, 137.]

Formerly: V. of St Martin, Stamford, to 1419. Afterwards: R. of Croxby, 1428.

John Sparwe

Instituted 19 August 1428 to church of St Hilary, Spridlington, on resignation of Thomas son of Richard Smyth de Stykeney (by exchange with church of Croxby). [*Reg. Fleming* i. no.290.]

Formerly: R. of Croxby, to 1428.

John Miskyn

Instituted before 19 April 1443. [Reg. 18, fo.113.]

William Burden priest

Instituted 19 April 1443 to church of Spridlington, on resignation of John Miskyn. Patron: Gerard Sothill. [Reg. 18, fo.113.]

Simon Waryn

Instituted before 23 September 1453. [Reg. 20, fo.157.]

John Feryby chaplain

Instituted 23 September 1453 to church of Spridlington, on resignation of Simon Waryn. Patron: Gerard Sothyll esquire. [Reg. 20, fo.157.]

William Husthwayte chaplain

Instituted 3 November 1456 to church of Spridlington, on death of John Feriby. Patron: Gerard Sothill. [Reg. 20, fo.158.]

William Grewe priest

Instituted 4 June 1460 to church of Spridlington, on resignation of William Hustwayte. Patron: Gerard Sothyll of Redbourne. [Reg. 20, fo.160v.]

William Sleight

Instituted before 1 April 1473. [Reg. 21, fo.4.]

Richard Gibson priest

Instituted 1 April 1473 to church of St Hilary, Spridlington, on resignation of William Sleight. Patron: William Gibson of Halifax. [Reg. 21, fos 4, 31v.]

Afterwards: V. of Saxby, 1479 (*q.v.*).

Robert Ossyt priest

Instituted 4 October 1479 to church of Spridlington, on resignation of Richard Gybson (by exchange with vicarage of Saxby). Patron: Gilbert Lacy esquire. [Reg. 21, fo.34v.]

Formerly: V. of Saxby, 1474–9 (*q.v.*).

Arthur Lacy MA priest

Instituted 21 May 1501 to church of Spridlington, on death of Robert Ossett. Patron: Gerard Lacy esquire. [Reg. 23, fo.153.]

Educated: University of Oxford (BA by 1495; MA by 1501). Also: V. of Braithwell (YWR), to 1511. [Emden, *BRUO*, 1081.]

Thomas Peck chaplain

Instituted 18 August 1511 to church of Spridlington, on death of Arthur Lacy. Patron: John Savile, John Russhworth, Thomas Savile and John Waterhouse, for this turn by reason of a feoffment made to them by Edward Grisakar, Hugh Boswell and Pertinella Amyas to the use of Hugh son and heir of Gerard Lacy decd, to whom the right of presentation belonged while he lived. [Reg. 23, fo.160.]

Edward Lacy

Instituted before 1526.

Assessed for subsidy (£12 10s) in 1526. [*Subsidy*, 36.]

Alexander Lacye

Instituted 31 May 1536 to church of Spridlington, on death of Edward Lacye. Patron: Hugh Lacye esquire. [Reg. 27, fo.96v.]

William Foxcrofte chaplain

Instituted 27 August 1539 to church of Spridlington, on death of Alexander Lacye. Patron: Hugh Lacye of Brearley (YWR), esquire. [Reg. 27, fo.70.]

Born *c*.1515. Education: 'competently skilled in Latin; well versed in sacred learning'. Priest: 20 March 1539/40 (London). Witnessed Spridlington will, 4 January 1541. Appears to have been deprived, *c*.1554; restored after 1558 (see below). Also: R. of Althorpe, 1564–82, where he resided (1576). Will dated 10 December 1581, proved 7 May 1582. [*Bishop Cooper*, 169; Stow Wills 1530–52/118v; Stow Wills 1582–6, 17.]

William Constable

Instituted 1554 (compounded for first-fruits, 4 June 1554). [FL.h.13, 733.]

Jasper Hanson

Instituted 1554 (compounded for first-fruits, 21 October 1554). [FL.h.13, 733.]

Witnessed Spridlington will, 9 March 1555. [Stow Wills 1553–67/183v.]

William Foxcrofte chaplain
Restored after 1558.

Non-resident after 1564 (see above); Spridlington served by curates, including Simon Arrowsmith (1565). [Stow Wills 1563–6/61v.]

Robert Shawe
Instituted 4 July 1582 (compounded for first-fruits, 17 November 1582). [*Bishop Cooper*, 79; LC 4, fo.10v.]

Education: 'bred in the schools'. Deacon: 18 June 1570 (Coventry); priest: 26 June (or July) 1573 (Chester). Signed BTs 1600–22. Buried at Spridlington, 20 December 1626. [*State of the Church*, 97; LC 4, fo.10v; BTs Spridlington; PR Spridlington.]

John Wetherall MA
Instituted 29 December 1626 to rectory of Spridlington, on death of Robert Shawe. Patron: Edward Blawe, alderman of Lincoln (26 December 1626), for this turn by reason of an assignment made to him (26 November 1626) by John Wetherall of Market Rasen, clerk, of a grant of next presentation made to him (1 September 1626) by George Lowe of London, esquire. [BC; PD 1626/55–7.]

Educated: Magdalene College, Cambridge (matric. 1617; BA 1620–1; MA 1624). Deacon and priest: 19 September 1624 (Llandaff). Resident (1662); signed BTs 1663–70. Married (1627) Anne, daughter of Sir James Bogg kt. Author: *A Discovery and Confutation of the Opinions and Practises of Some False Brethren Betwixt Bridge and Lincoln* (1652). Buried at Spridlington, 7 March 1670/1. Probate inventory praised, 11 March 1670/1 ('his Librarie, £30'). [Venn, *Alumni*; LC 5, fo.82v; BTs Spridlington; *Lincolnshire Pedigrees*, 148; ESTC; PR Spridlington; INV 171/12.]

Thomas Croe BA
Instituted 1 July 1671 to rectory of Spridlington, on death of Master Waterall. Patron: Richard Sherbrooke, gent. [Reg. 33, fo.142.]

Educated: Trinity Hall, Cambridge (BA 1670). Priest: 18 June 1671 (Ely). Resided at Spridlington; signed BTs 1672–1717. Also: R. of Aisthorpe, 1674–1723. Buried at Spridlington, 16 November 1723. [Venn, *Alumni*; LC 14, p.233; *Speculum*, 172; Foster, *Aisthorpe*, 129; BTs Spridlington; PR Spridlington.]

William Mason BA
Instituted 2 December 1723 to rectory of Spridlington, on death of Mr Croe. Patron: Mary Mead, widow (30 November 1723). [Reg. 38, p.15; PD 103/14.]

Licensed for non-residence, 21 May 1724. Perhaps to be identified with WM who was baptised 27 October 1682; son of John M., Rector of Water Stratford (Bk) and hymn writer. Educated: King's College, Cambridge (matric. 1701; BA 1704–5). Deacon: 22 September 1706; priest: 9 December 1706 (Lincoln). Also: V. of Mentmore (Bk), 1706–44. Afterwards: R. of Bonsall (Db), 1736–44. Died at Mentmore, 29 March 1744; buried there, 2 April 1744 (MI). [Reg. 38, p.47; Venn, *Alumni*; Reg. 36, pp. 31, 37; SUB VII, p.33; Lipscomb iii. 423; *Mentmore Registers*.]

Charles Reynolds

Instituted 1 March 1736/7 to rectory of Spridlington, on cession of William Masson. Patron: Mary Mead of St Sepulchre, London, widow. [Reg. 38, p.327.]

Also: R. of Fillingham (*q.v.*).

Henry Taylor

Instituted 24 November 1766 to rectory of Spridlington, on death of Dr Charles Reynolds. Patron: Mary Mead of St Sepulchre, London, widow. [Reg. 39, p.60.]

Baptised 4 July 1742 at Wheatfield (Ox); son of Henry T., Rector of Wheatfield. Educated: Queens' College, Cambridge (matric. 1761; LLB 1767). Deacon: 2 June 1765; priest: 23 November 1766 (Winchester). Formerly: C. of Crawley (Ha), 1765. Non-resident at Spridlington: 'No account where he lives' (1768). Licensed for non-residence, 31 December 1803 'on account of the smallness of the Parsonage House and your infirmity of deafness'. Acted as trustee for property devised by Mary Wilkes (granddaughter of Mary Mead above and daughter of John Wilkes, the politician). Resided latterly at Banstead (Sr) where he died, 27 February 1822 (MI). [*Winchester Ordinations* i. 45 (for his father, see *ODNB*); Venn, *Alumni*; LC 31, fo.198v; NRL 1803/4; Peter D. G. Thomas, 'Wilkes, John' in *ODNB*; 1 Fane 2/1/4/20; *Banstead Register*, 120.]

Frederick Gildart

Instituted 1822 [day and month not given] to rectory of Spridlington, on death of Henry Taylor. Patron: Frederick Gildart himself. [Reg. 40, p.325.]

Baptised 8 April 1769 at St Botolph Bishopsgate, London; son of Richard G. of London, esquire (and grandson of Richard G., MP for Liverpool). Educated: Queen's College, Oxford (matric. 1787; BCL 1797). Deacon: 11 March 1792; priest: 31 May 1795 (Lincoln). Inherited estate of Norton Hall (St). Married Anne, daughter of Edward Hussey of Scotney Castle (K), esquire. Resided principally at West Wickham (K); died there, 23 April 1841. Will (PCC). [LMA, PR St Botolph Bishopsgate; Foster, *Alumni*; Reg. 39, pp. 555, 605; Berry, *Sussex Pedigrees*, 126; *Clergy List* (1841); *GM* ns 16 (1841), 213; PROB 11/1948/321.]

Henry Frederick Hutton BA

Instituted 17 September 1841 to rectory of Spridlington, on death of Frederick Gildart. Patron: Henry Frederick Hutton himself. [Reg. 40, p.479.]

Born 10 August 1810; son of William H. of Gate Burton. Educated: Rugby School and Trinity College, Oxford (matric. 1828; BA 1832; MA 1855). Deacon: 22 December 1833; priest: 21 September 1834 (Lincoln). Formerly: C. of Gate Burton, 1833–4; R. of Gate Burton, 1834–41. Married (25 September 1834) at Byfield (Np), Louisa, daughter of Revd Henry John Wollaston, R. of Scotter. Inherited manor and advowson of Spridlington from his cousin, Frederick Gildart (see above). Father of Henry Wollaston H., Priest-Vicar and Canon of Lincoln; Vernon Wollaston H., Rector of Sneinton (Nt) and Canon of Lincoln; Arthur Wollaston H. (see below). Enlarged Spridlington Church and built new Rectory House ('affording every necessary accommodation'), where he resided. The new church (1874–5) was built in his memory. Died 16 July 1873 at Spridlington. [*Hutton of Gate Burton*, 39–43; Foster, *Alumni*; OR 1, pp. 54, 57; *Crockford* (1868); CR 2, p.77; *Stow Visitation*, 81; *Probate Calendar* 1873.]

Arthur Wollaston Hutton MA
Instituted 3 October 1873 to rectory of Spridlington, on death of Henry Frederick Hutton. Patron: Revd Henry Wollaston Hutton of Lincoln, clerk. [Reg. 41, p.418.]

Born 5 September 1848; 7th son of Henry Frederick H., above. Educated: Bury St Edmunds GS (1859–61); Cheltenham College; Exeter College, Oxford (matric. 1867; BA 1871; MA 1873). Deacon: 1871; priest: 1872 (Oxford). Formerly: C. of St Barnabas, Oxford, 1871–3. Joined Church of Rome 1876; with Newman at Birmingham Oratory, 1876–83. Librarian of National Liberal Club, 1887–99. Returned to Church of England, 1899. R. of Easthope (Sa), 1899–1901; C. of St Luke, Richmond, 1901–3; R. of St Mary-le-Bow with St Pancras Soper Lane, All Hallows Bread Street, All Hallows Honey Lane and St John Evangelist, London, 1903–12. Author: *Our Position as Catholics in the Church of England* (1872); *Cardinal Manning* (1892). Latterly of 16 The Grove, Greenwich. Died 25 March 1912. [*Hutton of Gate Burton*, 43, 48–50; *Bury Grammar School List*, 203; Foster, *Alumni*; *Crockford* (1911); *Probate Calendar* 1912.]

Frederick Borradaile MA
Instituted 21 April 1876 to rectory of Spridlington, on resignation of Arthur Wollaston Hutton. Patron: Revd Henry Wollaston Hutton of Lincoln, clerk. [Reg. 41, p.529.]

Born 16 April, baptised 26 May 1827 at Clapham (Sr); son of Frederick B. of Battersea, clerk. Educated: Trinity College, Cambridge (matric. 1846; BA 1850; MA 1853). Deacon: 1851; priest: 1852 (Chichester). Formerly: C. of Worth (Sx), 1851–3; V. of Bishop Norton, 1853–76. Also: RD of Aslacoe, 1875–83. Resigned 6 January 1898. Resided latterly at Lincoln. Died 23 April 1907 at St Hilary, Greetwell Road, Lincoln; buried 26 April 1907 at Spridlington. [LMA, PR Clapham; Venn, *Alumni*; Census Returns 1871; *Crockford* (1874); Reg. 42, p.426; *Probate Calendar* 1907; PR Spridlington.]

Edward Page MA
Instituted 22 January 1898 to rectory of Spridlington, on resignation of Frederick Borradaile. Patron: Revd Henry Wollaston Hutton of Lincoln. [Reg. 42, p.426.]

Born *c*.1861 at Arundel (Sx); son of John P. Educated: Jesus College, Cambridge (matric. 1880; BA 1885; MA 1889). Deacon: 1886; priest: 1887 (Rochester). Formerly: C. of St John, Battersea, 1886–9; R. of Whitchurch (He), 1890–7. Resided at Spridlington Rectory. Resignation accepted 20 August 1910. Resided latterly at The Birks, Branksome Wood Road, Bournemouth. Died 1 March 1912 at Hartington, Poole Road, Bournemouth. [Venn, *Alumni*; *Crockford* (1911); Kelly, *Lincolnshire* (1900); Reg. 43, p.5; *Probate Calendar* 1912.]

Arthur Samuel Wright MA
Instituted 11 October 1910 to rectory of Spridlington, on resignation of Edward Page. Patron: Revd Henry Wollaston Hutton of Lincoln. [Reg. 43, p.7.]

Born 16 November 1867 at Brattleby Hall; son of Samuel W., esquire. Educated: Charterhouse (1881–5) and New College, Oxford (matric. 1886; BA 1890; MA 1898). Deacon: 24 September 1893; priest: 9 June 1895 (Durham). Formerly: C. of Chester-le-Street

(Du), 1893–4; of Holy Trinity, Stockton-on-Tees, 1895–8; of St Peter, Norbiton (Sr), 1899–1901; of Kingswood (Sr), 1901–4; V. of Bonby, 1908–10. Resided at Spridlington Rectory. Dined with Bishop Hicks (February 1914) to meet Warde Fowler the ornithologist. Resigned 29 September (accepted 30 November) 1914. Afterwards: Missioner of St Andrew's Mission (SPG), dioc. South Tokyo, 1914–20; R. of Snelland, 1924–9; of Brattleby, 1929–37. Retired 1937. Died 25 January 1938 at Sarratt Hill (Hrt). [*Charterhouse Register 1872–1910*, 242; Foster, *Oxford Men*; Durham UL, DDR/EA/CL; *Crockford* (1911, 1932); *Hicks Diaries*, no.441; RES 248e/32; *Probate Calendar* 1938.]

George Henry Round-Turner

Instituted 30 January 1915 to rectory of Spridlington, on resignation of Arthur Samuel Wright. Patron: Revd Henry Wollaston Hutton of Lincoln. [Reg. 43, p.84.]

Born 11 February, baptised 9 March 1877 at Holy Trinity, Chelsea; son of Henry Lewes R-T. of Grundisburgh (Sf), Captain RN. Educated: St John's College, Oxford (1896); Lincoln Theological College (1905). Deacon: 1906 (Ipswich for Norwich); priest: 1907 (Norwich). Formerly: C. of St Bartholomew, Heigham (Nf), 1906–9; of St Mark, Lakenham, 1909–14. Resided at Spridlington Rectory. Resignation accepted 9 October 1919. Afterwards: V. of Scothern with Sudbrooke, 1919–29; of Gainsborough, 1929–36; Canon of Lincoln and Prebendary of Lafford, 1927–9, and Prebendary of Corringham, 1929–36; RD of Corringham, 1929–36. Afterwards: R. of Great with Little Bealings (Sf), 1936–45. Married (17 April 1901) at Alverstoke (Ha), Irene, daughter of Col. George Hobart. Latterly of Ransome, Aldeburgh (Sf). Died 10 January 1951. [LMA, PR Chelsea Holy Trinity; Crisp, *Visitation* xii. 5; xvi. (Appendix), xli; *Crockford* (1916, 1949–50); Reg. 43, p.185; *Probate Calendar* 1951.]

Henry Falkner Allison MA

Instituted 17 February 1920 to rectory of Spridlington, on resignation of George Henry Round-Turner. Patron: Francis Henry Hutton of Greyland, Lee Road, Lincoln, esquire. [Reg. 43, p.191.]

The Benefice of Saxby with Firsby was united to the Rectory of Spridlington by Order in Council dated 10 August 1922 to form the United Benefice of Spridlington with Saxby and Firsby. [Reg. 43, pp. 277–81.]

Henry Falkner Allison MA

Instituted 26 March 1926 to united benefice of rectory of Spridlington with vicarage of Saxby with rectory of Firsby annexed, the vicarage of Saxby with rectory of Firsby annexed being vacant by cession of William Norton Howe. [Reg. 43, p.391.]

Born 9 September 1859; son of Thomas Falkner A. of Louth, solicitor. Educated: Clare College, Cambridge (matric. 1878; BA 1882; MA 1885). Deacon: 1883 (Lincoln); priest: 1884 (Nottingham for Lincoln). Formerly: C. of Beckingham, 1883–91; of Foston, 1891–6; R. of Sudbrooke, 1896–1919; V. of Scothern, 1904–19. Resided at Spridlington Rectory. Also: RD of Aslacoe, 1930–2. Resignation accepted 1 March 1938. Latterly of Lynford, Nettleham. Died 4 November 1940. [*Lincolnshire Pedigrees*, 1135; Venn, *Alumni*; *Crockford* (1938); Reg. 43, p.612; *Probate Calendar* 1941.]

David Cuthbert Rosser MA

Instituted 6 April 1938 to united benefice of rectory of Spridlington with vicarage of Saxby with rectory of Firsby annexed, on resignation of Henry Falkner Allison. Patron: Francis Henry Hutton of Greyland Place, Lee Road, City of Lincoln, esquire, for this turn. [Reg. 43, p.614.]

Born 1888 at Bridgend. Served in RNVR, 1914–19. Registered owner (at The Rectory, Aberkenfig, Bridgend) of a four-cylinder FN (Fabrique Nationale) motorcycle (1915). Educated: Jesus College, Oxford (BA 1918; MA 1922); Lincoln Theological College (1921). Deacon: 1921 (St Asaph); priest: 1922 (Bangor for St Asaph). Formerly: C. of Colwyn Bay, 1921–4; Clergy Secretary, Church of England Children's Society, 1925–6; R. of Woodeaton, 1926–9; of West Keal, 1929–38. Resided at Spridlington Rectory. Also: RD of Aslacoe, 1946–53. Afterwards: R. of Little Ponton with Stroxton, 1952–4. Latterly at Ellesborough Manor, Aylesbury. Died 26 April 1964. [GRO, Birth Index; *Navy List*; *Early Motor Vehicle Registration in Wiltshire* (2006), 27; (*Crockford* (1963–4); *Probate Calendar* 1964.]

Henry Bursey BA

Instituted 7 January 1953 to united benefice of rectory of Spridlington with vicarage of Saxby with rectory of Firsby annexed, on cession of David Cuthbert Rosser. Patron: Major Walter Morland Hutton DSO MC of 2 Stevenson Crescent, Parkstone (Do), for this turn. [Reg. 44, p.171.]

Born *c*.1909. Educated: St David's College, Lampeter (BA 1932). Deacon: 1932; priest: 1933 (St Asaph). Formerly: C. of Chirk, 1932–6; Chaplain, Toc H, 1936–42; C-in-C of Norton, 1942–6; V. of Elloughton, 1946–52. Resided at Spridlington Rectory. Also: V. of Hackthorn with Cold Hanworth, 1954–8. Afterwards: R. of Skegness, 1958–63. Died 7 September 1963 at The Royal Infirmary, Sheffield. [*Crockford* (1961–2); *Probate Calendar* 1963.]

Richard Laurence Crampton LTh

Instituted 7 March 1959 to united benefice of rectory of Spridlington with vicarage of Saxby with rectory of Firsby annexed, on cession of Henry Bursey. Patron: Brigadier Walter Morland Hutton DSO MC, for this turn. [Reg. 44, p.267.]

Born 13 April 1908. Educated: University of Durham (LTh 1936). Deacon: 1934; priest: 1935 (Rochester). Formerly: C. of Crayford, 1934–7; in Polynesia: V. of Levuka, 1937–8; Superintendent of Indian Mission, Labasa, 1938–45; V. of Vanua Levu, 1938–45; C. of Weybridge, 1945–7; Minister of St Augustine, Aldershot, 1947–50; V. of Reepham, 1950–5; R. of Great Gonerby, 1955–9. Resided at Spridlington Rectory. Afterwards: R. of Beaufort West and of Victoria West (South Africa), 1962–6; V. of Nocton, 1967–73; V. of Dunston, 1967–73. Latterly of 3 Tor-o-Moor Gardens, Woodhall Spa. Died June 1984. [GRO, Death Index; *Crockford* (1961–2, 1980–2).]

Harold Alfred Standbrook

Instituted 14 October 1963 to united benefice of Spridlington with Saxby and Firsby, on resignation of Richard Laurence Crampton. Patron: Bishop of Lincoln for this turn, by lapse. (Note that the lapse was of the fourth turn of presentation, belonging to the Earl of Scarbrough.) [Reg. 44, p.353.]

Born: 29 September 1912. Educated: St Paul's Theological College, Grahamstown, South Africa (1946). Deacon: 1947; priest: 1948 (Cape Town). Formerly: C. of Good Shepherd, Kensington, Cape Town, 1947–9; of St Philip, Cape Town, 1949–50; Chaplain, St Ninian's Cathedral, Perth, 1950–2; CF 1952–5; R. of St Aidan, Clarkston, 1955–9; Precentor, St Paul's Cathedral, Dundee, 1959–61; P-in-C of All SS, Muizenberg, Cape Town, 1961–3. Resided at Spridlington Rectory. Afterwards: R. of Fochabers and Aberlour, 1972–4; C. of East Preston with Kingston (Sx), 1974–5; of St Mary, Dover, 1975–7. Latterly at 6 Bramwell Lodge, Woodmancote, Henfield (Sx). Died January 1989. [GRO, Death Index; *Crockford* (1980–2); *LDC* (1967–8); Bertie, *Scottish Episcopal Clergy*, 447.]

WADDINGHAM ST PETER

The advowson of the church of St Peter, Waddingham, belonged to Thornholm Priory by the early thirteenth century; in the absence of either foundation deeds or a cartulary of this house, it is impossible to ascertain precisely when the gift was made. The church was never appropriated and the Prior and Convent continued to present to the rectory until the Dissolution, after which the patronage passed to the Crown. In 1687 the church of St Peter was united with the neighbouring church of St Mary Stainton, otherwise known as Waddingham St Mary, which had been in the deanery of Manlake. The united benefice was in the gift of the Crown, which still held the advowson in 1965. [*Monasticon* vi. 356; *VCH Lincoln* ii. 166–8; *Lincolnshire Domesday*, lxvi; *LDC* (1965), 132–3.]

M. William de Osolveston subdeacon
Instituted in the thirteenth pontifical year of Bishop Robert Grosseteste (17 June 1247/16 June 1248) to church of St Peter, Waddingham. Patron: Prior and Convent of Thornholme. [Hoskin, no.1287.]

William de Beverlaco subdeacon
Instituted 19 October 1284 to church of St Peter, Waddingham, on death of William de Osolveston. Patron: Prior and Convent of Thornholme. [*Reg. Sutton* viii. 6.]

Afterwards: R. of a mediety of Gedling (Nt), 1286.

Richard de Saham clerk
Instituted 9 June 1286 to church of St Peter, Waddingham, on institution of William de Beverlaco to mediety of church of Gedling, dioc. York. Patron: Prior and Convent of Thornholme. [*Reg. Sutton* viii. 8.]

Subdeacon: 8 June 1286 (Lincoln). [*Reg. Sutton* viii. 8.]

William de Nevill acolyte
Instituted 1 November 1305 to church of St Peter, Waddingham, on death of Richard de Saham. Patron: Prior and Convent of Thornholme. [Reg. 2, fo.88v.]

John de Bekeby
Instituted before 22 September 1349. [Reg. 9, fo.69v.]

John Wodcok de Feriby acolyte
Instituted 22 September 1349 to church of [St Peter], Waddingham, on death
of John de Bekeby. Patron: Prior and Convent of Thornholme. [Reg. 9,
fo.69v.]

Subdeacon: 20 February 1349/50 (Lincoln); deacon: before 27 August 1350. Afterwards:
V. of Messingham, August–September 1350. [Reg. 9, fos 160v, 162; Reg. 9D, fo.21v.]

Thomas de Thetelthorp priest
Instituted 27 August 1350 to church of St Peter, Waddingham, on resignation
of John Wodecok de Feriby (by exchange with vicarage of Messingham).
Patron: Prior and Convent of Thornholme. [Reg. 9, fo.160v.]

Formerly: V. of Messingham, to 1350.

Robert de Lyndewode de Messyngham priest
Instituted 30 January 1352/3 to church of St Peter, Waddingham, on death of
Thomas de Thedilthorp. By reason of a papal grace made to him of a benefice
in the gift of Prior and Convent of Thornholme. [Reg. 9, fo.165v.]

Licensed to celebrate one anniversary on account of the poverty of his church, 25
November 1363. Afterwards: V. of altar of St Andrew in St John, Beverley, 1373. [Reg.
12, fo.18v.]

Robert de Wragby
Instituted 3 August 1373 to church of St Peter, Waddingham, on resignation of Robert de Lyndewode (by exchange with vicarage of the altar of St
Andrew in collegiate church of St John, Beverley). Patron: Prior and Convent
of Thornholme. [Reg. 10, fo.139.]

Formerly: V. of altar of St Andrew in St John, Beverley, to 1373. Assessed for poll-tax,
1377 (as 'John de Wragby'). [*Clerical Poll-Taxes*, no.817.]

John Coke de South Feryby priest
Instituted 7 November 1393 to church of St Peter, Waddingham, on death
of Robert de Wragby. Patron: Prior and Convent of Thornholme. [Reg. 11,
fo.111.]

Afterwards: R. of Nettleham, 1418.

Walter Gunny chaplain
Instituted 5 April 1418 to church of St Peter, Waddingham, on resignation of
John Coke de Southferiby (by exchange with church of Nettleham). Patron:
Prior and Convent of Thornholme. [Reg. 14, fo.132v.]

Formerly: V. of South Elkington, to 1402; R. of Stewton, 1402–8; V. of Bottesford, 1408–
10; R. of Nettleham, 1410–18. Afterwards: V. of Wadsworth (YWR), 1419–24; Chaplain

of St Mary Chantry in Church of Misson (Nt), 1424. [Reg. 13, fo.152v; Reg. 14, fos 112, 118; *York Sede Vacante Register 1423–26*, nos 39–40, 235.]

John Ward
Instituted 23 June 1419 to church of St Peter, Waddingham, on resignation of Walter Gunny (by exchange with vicarage of Wadsworth, dioc. York). Patron: Prior and Convent of Thornholme. [Reg. 14, fo.135.]

Formerly: V. of Wadsworth (YWR), to 1419.

William Andrewe priest
Instituted 1 March 1422 to church of St Peter, Waddingham, on death of last incumbent. Patron: Prior and Convent of Thornholme. [*Reg. Fleming* i. no.404.]

Afterwards: Chaplain of St Laurence Chantry in Church of Leake, 1422–36. [Reg. 17, fo.14v.]

Thomas Enderby priest
Instituted 7 December 1422 to church of St Peter, Waddingham, on resignation of William Andrewe (by exchange with chantry at altar of St Laurence in church of Leake). Patron: Prior and Convent of Thornholme. [*Reg. Fleming* i. no.418.]

Formerly: Chaplain of St Laurence Chantry in Church of Leake, to 1422.

William Mason
Instituted before 13 August 1435. [Reg. 17, fo.17v.]

Afterwards: V. of Wistow (YWR), 1435–9. [Wheater, *Sherburn and Cawood*, 137.]

M. William Waryn
Instituted 13 August 1435 to church of St Peter, Waddingham, on resignation of William Mason (by exchange with vicarage of prebendal church of Wistow, dioc. York). Patron: Prior and Convent of St Mary, Thornholme. [Reg. 17, fo.17v.]

Formerly: V. of Wistow (YWR), 1422–35. [Wheater, *Sherburn and Cawood*, 137.]

Hugh Noon priest
Instituted 11 December 1440 to church of St Peter, Waddingham, on resignation of M. William Waryne. Patron: Prior and Convent of Thornholme. [Reg. 18, fos. 86, 113.]

Thomas Brigham priest
Instituted 26 April 1474 to church of St Peter, Waddingham, on death of Hugh Nonne. Patron: Prior and Convent of Thornholme. [Reg. 21, fo.32v.]

John Jeffrason priest
Instituted 4 October 1479 to church of St Peter, Waddingham, on resignation

of Thomas Bynkham. Patron: Prior and Convent of Thornholme. [Reg. 21, fo.34v.]

William Robynson priest
Instituted 9 September 1480 to church of St Peter, Waddingham, on resignation of John Jeffrayson. Patron: Prior and Convent of Thornholme. [Reg. 22, fo.162.]

Thomas Kendall priest
Instituted 2 October 1499 to church of St Peter, Waddingham, on death of William Robynson. Patron: Prior and Convent of Thornholme. [Reg. 23, fo.153v.]

Reported (1519) to have an old woman in his house with two young kinswomen; all however were of good repute. Assessed for subsidy (£4 9s 10d) in 1526. [*Diocesan Visitations* i. 95; *Subsidy*, 35.]

Thomas Clayton acolyte
Instituted 14 November 1530 to church of St Peter, Waddingham, on death of Thomas Kendall. Patron: Prior and Convent of Thornholme. Reinstituted 26 June 1534, on his own resignation; patron, as above. [Reg. 27, fos 58v, 100.]

Subdeacon: 17 December 1530; deacon: 8 April 1531; priest: 3 June 1531 ('Reonensis' for Lincoln). Witnessed Waddingham will as 'late parson of Saynt Peters', 4 March 1554/5. [Reg. 26, fos 27, 27v, 28v; Stow Wills 1553–67/126.]

Thomas Patrick
Instituted 21 October 1554 to church of St Peter, Waddingham, on deprivation of Thomas Clayton. Patron: William Anderson, for this turn. [Reg. 28, fo.109v.]

Robert Towne
Instituted 2 March 1560/1 to church of St Peter, Waddingham, on death of last incumbent. Patron: Queen Elizabeth I (12 December 1560). [Reg. 19, fo.115; FL.h.19, p.16.]

David Vaughan
Instituted *c*.1566 to rectory of St Peter, Waddingham. Patron: Queen Elizabeth I (8 July 1566). [FL.h.19, p.26.]

Resigned, 16 February 1567. [RES 1567/3.]

William Smith
Instituted 1566–7 to church of St Peter, Waddingham, on resignation of last incumbent. Patron: Queen Elizabeth I (13 March 1566/7). [Reg. 28, fo.38v; FL.h.19, p.27.]

Non-resident (1576). [*Bishop Cooper*, 168.]

Christopher Banyster

Instituted 1 February 1577/8 to rectory of St Peter, Waddingham (cause of vacancy not stated). Patron: Queen Elizabeth I. [*Bishop Cooper*, 76–7.]

Educated: St John's College, Cambridge (matric. 1569; 'Bred in the schools'). Priest: 18 September 1572 (Peterborough). Assessed for subsidy of armour, 1590. [Venn, *Alumni*; Longden i. 175; *State of the Church*, 97.]

Richard Turswell BD

Instituted 1592 to rectory of St Peter, Waddingham, on death of last incumbent. Patron: Queen Elizabeth I (20 September 1592). [FL.h.19, p.93.]

Of Lincolnshire. Educated: Queens' College, Cambridge (matric. 1569; BA 1571–2; MA 1575; BD 1582); Fellow, 1572–82. Deacon and priest: 11 July 1573 (Peterborough). Listed as Rector in *Liber Cleri* of 1594. Also: R. of St Mary, Waddingham, 1577–1610; R. of Manton, 1588–1610; Canon of Lincoln and Prebendary of Luda, 1582–1610 (residentiary 1602–10). Will (PCC). [Venn, *Alumni*; Longden xiv. 53; *State of the Church*, 394; *Bishop Cooper*, 76; *Le Neve Fasti: Lincoln 1541–1857*, 89, 137; PROB 11/119/626.]

William Crowther

Instituted before 16 August 1596 (mandate to induct) to rectory of St Peter, Waddingham. Patron: Queen Elizabeth I (2 July 1596). [IND/S/1; FL.h.19, p.101.]

Returned as Rector in election of proctors, 27 September 1597. [*State of the Church*, 185.]

Francis Rawlinson MA

Instituted 27 April 1597 to rectory of St Peter, Waddingham, on cession of last incumbent. Patron: Queen Elizabeth I (14 April 1597). Presentation revoked, 26 April 1597; did not receive induction. [BC; PD 1597/35; FL.h.19, p.104; Reg. 30, fo.88.]

Born *c.*1565 at Market Rasen. Also: V. of Middle Rasen Drax (where he resided), 1589–1603; R. of St Nicholas, South Kelsey, 1603–30. [PD 1597/35.]

Robert Prichard MA

Instituted 3 August 1597 to rectory of St Peter, Waddingham, on resignation of last incumbent. Patron: Queen Elizabeth I (15 July 1597). Inducted 17 June 1598 by M. Richard Turswell, R. of St Mary, Waddingham. [BC; PD 1597/36; IND/S/1.]

Non-resident in 1598. Signed BTs at Waddingham 1603, 1605–9. [*State of the Church*, 330; BTs Waddingham.]

John Lewis MA

Instituted 5 September 1609 to rectory of St Peter, Waddingham, on cession of last incumbent. Patron: King James I (18 August 1609). [BC; PD 1609/45.]

Non-resident; held no other benefice (1611). Signed BTs 1610–15. [LC 3, fo.100v; BTs Waddingham.]

Stephen Bunting

Instituted 3 June 1615 to rectory of St Peter, Waddingham. [BC.]

Educated: Jesus College, Cambridge (matric. 1605; BA 1608–9; MA 1612). Deacon: 20 December 1612; priest: 22 December 1612 (Lincoln). Formerly: R. of West Deeping, 1612–15. Signed BTs at Waddingham, 1616–28. Married (11 May 1620) at Ramsey, Elizabeth Cervington. Died 1634. Will dated 31 August 1631; proved 6 February 1633/4 (PCC). The portions of his two eldest sons, John and Stephen, to be paid to 'my welbe-loved Friend' Paul le Marchant, Rector of Kirkby on Bain, as trustee; meanwhile his wife was to maintain them at Kirton School in board, apparel and other necessaries. [Venn, *Alumni*; PROB 11/165/192.]

Henry Smith MA

Instituted 13 January 1634 to rectory of St Peter, Waddingham. Patron: King Charles I. [BC.]

Educated: Magdalene College, Cambridge (matric. 1618; BA 1621–2; MA 1625). Deacon: 7 June 1623; priest: 8 June 1623 (Peterborough). Resident (1662): signed BTs at Waddingham 1635, 1645, 1663–75. Buried 6 November 1675 at Waddingham. [Venn, *Alumni*; Longden xii. 215; LC 5, fo.83; BTs Waddingham.]

George Huddlestone MA

Instituted 14 December 1675 to rectory of St Peter, Waddingham, on death of last incumbent. Patron: King Charles II (7 December 1675). [Reg. 34, fo.5; PD 1675/11.]

Son of Robert H. of Lincoln. Educated: Magdalene College, Cambridge (matric. 1631; BA 1634–5; MA 1638); Fellow. Priest: 10 March 1638/9 (Peterborough). Also: R. of Waddingham St Mary, 1673–86; Canon of Lincoln and Prebendary of Carlton Kyme, 1675–86. Signed BTs at Waddingham, 1676–85. Buried 11 January 1685/6 at Waddingham. [*Lincolnshire Pedigrees*, 518–19; Venn, *Alumni*; Longden vii. 137; BTs Waddingham; *Le Neve Fasti: Lincoln 1541–1857*, 48.]

Jerman Dunn MA

Instituted 9 March 1685/6 to rectory of St Peter, Waddingham, on death of George Hudleston. Patron: King James II (26 January 1685/6). [Reg. 34, fo.90v; PD 1686/11.]

Baptised 28 March 1655 at St Giles Cripplegate, London; son of Isaac D., skinner. Educated: St Catharine's College, Cambridge (admitted 1670; matric. 1673; BA 1673–4; MA 1677). Priest: 19 December 1680 (London). Formerly: R. of Orlestone (K), 1685–6. Also: R. of Waddingham St Mary, 1686–91. Deprived 1691 as non-juror. [LMA, PR St Giles Cripplegate; Venn, *Alumni*; Hasted, *History of Kent* viii. 360–5.]

The Rectory of Waddingham St Mary was united to the Rectory of Waddingham St Peter by act of Bishop Barlow dated 30 July 1687. [Reg. 34, fo.99v.]

Thomas Harvey

Instituted 30 June 1691 to rectory of Waddingham St Mary and St Peter with Snitterby, on deprivation of last incumbent under the Act for Abrogating the Oaths of Allegiance and Supremacy. Patron: King William III and Queen Mary II. [Reg. 34, fo.123.]

Of Derbyshire. Educated: Queens' College, Cambridge (adm. 1681; BA 1684–5). Signed BTs 1692–1703. Patron of Magdalen Laver (Ess.) Died 1708. Will (London) dated 18 May 1708; proved 30 September 1708. [Venn, *Alumni*; BTs Waddingham; *VCH Essex* iv. 107–8; Essex RO, D/DU 918/1.]

Brian Sixesmith MA

Instituted 3 February 1707/8 to rectory of Waddingham St Mary and St Peter with Snitterby, on resignation of Thomas Harvey. Patron: Queen Anne. [Reg. 36, p.59.]

Of Lancashire. Educated: Jesus College, Cambridge (matric. 1695; BA 1697–8; MA 1701). Deacon: 23 September 1699 (Ely); priest: 21 September 1700 (London). Formerly: C. of Waddingham, 1703–5; R. of Magdalen Laver (Ess), 1703–8. Resident: signed BTs at Waddingham, 1704–5, 1708–14. Buried 7 July 1714 at Waddingham. Administration (Stow), 1715. [Venn, *Alumni*; CCED; *Speculum*, 172; Reg. 35, fo.94; BTs Waddingham; Stow Admons/1700–20/295A.]

Edward Parker MA

Instituted 28 October 1714 to rectory of Waddingham St Mary and St Peter with chapel of Snitterby, on death of Brian Sixesmith. Patron: King George I. [Reg. 36, p.242.]

Of Derbyshire. Educated: Emmanuel College, Cambridge (matric. 1698; BA 1700–1; MA 1704). Deacon: 20 September 1702; priest: 28 October 1714 (Lincoln). Formerly: C. of Nether Seal (Le). Signed BTs at Waddingham 1716–50. Also: Canon of Southwell and Prebendary of Halloughton, 1724–54. Buried 21 January 1754 at Waddingham. [Venn, *Alumni*; Reg. 35, fo.88; Reg. 36, p.242; BTs Waddingham; Le Neve-Hardy iii. 425; PR Waddingham.]

William Basset BA

Instituted 13 April 1754 to rectory of Waddingham St Mary and St Peter with chapel of Snitterby, on death of Edward Parker. Patron: King George II (28 March 1754). [Reg. 38, p.525; PD 1754/8.]

Also: V. of Glentworth, 1729–65 (*q.v.*).

Robert Carter (Thelwall) MA

Instituted 20 November 1765 to rectory of Waddingham St Mary and St Peter, on death of William Bassett. Patron: King George III (30 July 1765). [Reg. 39, p.48; PD 1765/14.]

Born 1721; son of William C. of Kinmel (Denb), esquire. Educated: Oriel College, Oxford (matric. 1739; BA 1742–3; MA 1747). Deacon: 20 December 1747 (Lincoln). Formerly: C. of Waddingham, 1747; R. of South Hykeham, 1749–66; of Silk Willoughby, 1753–60. Inherited Redbourne and Pickworth estates on death of his brother Thomas. Married (1 January 1767) at Redbourne, Charlotte, daughter of Sir Henry Nelthorpe Bt. Took the additional name of Thelwall, c.1780. Non-resident: resided at Redbourne Hall. Waddingham served by Christopher Metcalfe as curate (1755–93). Also: R. of Broughton, 1760–87; Canon of Lincoln and Prebendary of Caistor, 1775–87. Died 18 October 1767 (MI Redbourne). [Foster, *Alumni*; Reg. 38, p.478; 'Redbourne Hall', *LAR* 8 (1956–7), 46–51; *Lincolnshire Pedigrees*, 705; PR Redbourne; LC 31, pp. 170, 173; *Le Neve Fasti: Lincoln 1541–1857*, 47; *Monson*, 300.]

John Barker DD

Instituted 22 November 1787 to rectory of Waddingham St Mary and St Peter with chapel of Snitterby, on death of Robert Carter Thelwall. Patron: King George III (15 November 1787). [Reg. 39, p.468; PD 1787/7.]

Baptised 10 October 1727 at Earsdon (Nb); son of George B. of Seghill (Nb) and Mary (daughter of John Lawson of Longhirst, esquire). Educated: Newcastle School and Christ's College, Cambridge (matric. 1745; BA 1748–9; MA 1752; DD 1781); Fellow 1749; Master 1780–1808. Deacon: 24 May 1752; priest: 25 December 1752 (Ely). Formerly: C. of Fen Drayton, 1761–3; V. of Bourn (Ca), 1763–72; V. of Caldecote (Ca), 1772–86. Non-resident: Waddingham served by curates. Married (13 December 1787) at St John, Newcastle-upon-Tyne, Hannah, daughter of Robert Ellison esquire, widow of Thomas Dockwray DD. Died 18 February 1808; buried in Ante-Chapel at Christ's College. [IGI; Burke, *Landed Gentry* (1837 edn) ii. 106; Venn, *Alumni*; Bray, *Ely Lists*.]

William Cooper BD

Instituted 15 July 1808 to rectory of Waddingham St Mary and St Peter, on death of John Barker. Patron: King George III (26 March 1808). [Reg. 40, p.134; PD 1808/5.]

Born c.1770 at Wistow (Hu); son of Samuel C., Curate of Upwood and Ramsey. Educated: Oakham School and St John's College, Cambridge (matric. 1788; BA 1792; MA 1795; BD 1802); Fellow 1794–1810. Deacon: 1 July 1792 (Lincoln); priest: 31 May 1795 (Ely). Formerly: C. of Wistow, 1792; Chaplain of Horningsea (Ca), 1802–9. Also: R. of West Rasen, 1802–56 (where he succeeded his father). Non-resident at Waddingham, which was served by curates, including William Bowerbank (1794–1819). Resided at West Rasen Rectory. Married (2 December 1822) at Swinhope, Anne, daughter of Revd Marmaduke Alington of Swinhope. Author: *An Examination of the Case of the Penitent on the Cross* (1812). Died 24 August 1856; buried at West Rasen. [Venn, *Alumni*; Reg. 39, p.563; Bray, *Ely Lists*; White, *Lincolnshire* (1842), 416; Census Returns 1851 (West Rasen); PR Swinhope; Burke, *Landed Gentry* (18th edn) iii. 12; PR West Rasen.]

William Windsor Berry MA

Instituted 26 February 1858 to rectory of Waddingham, on death of William Cooper. Patron: Queen Victoria. [Reg. 40, p.593.]

Baptised 25 November 1801 at St Mary, Lambeth; son of William B. of Lambeth, gent. Educated: Exeter College, Oxford (matric. 1818; BA 1824; MA 1826). Deacon: 1832; priest: 1833 (Canterbury). Formerly: C. of Putney, 1832–4; British Chaplain at Leghorn, 1834–9; V. of Stanwell (Mx), 1839–58; RD of Staines, 1841–58. Built new Rectory House

1859 (architect: James Fowler of Louth), where he resided. Married (17 June 1840) at Cheltenham, Arethusa Georgiana St Vincent Sarah, daughter of Admiral Sir Charles Brisbane KCB. Also: Canon of St Paul's and Prebendary of Mapesbury, 1853–67. Died 12 December 1867; buried at Waddingham. [LMA, PR Lambeth St Mary; Foster, *Alumni*; *Crockford* (1865); Hennessy, 37, 408; MGA 406; *Nautical Magazine* (1840), 535; Census Returns 1861; *Le Neve Fasti: St Paul's London 1541–1857*, 43; *Probate Calendar* 1867; PR Waddingham.]

Lewis Welsh Owen MA

Instituted 12 June 1868 to rectory of Waddingham, on death of William Windsor Berry. Patron: Queen Victoria. [Reg. 41, p.261.]

Born *c*.1813; son of George Welsh O. of Tiverton (Dev), esquire. Educated: Tiverton School and Balliol College, Oxford (matric. 1830; BA 1834; MA 1838); Fellow 1836–9. Deacon: 1837; priest: 1838 (Oxford). Formerly: R. of Holy Trinity, Colchester and V. of Marks Tey (Ess), 1839–68; RD of Colchester. Also: Canon of Lincoln and Prebendary of Brampton, 1869–76. Afterwards: R. of Wonston (Ha), 1870–84. Died 4 January 1884 at Wonston. [Foster, *Alumni*; *Sherborne Mercury*, 23 August 1830; *Crockford* (1874); *Probate Calendar* 1884.]

William Josiah Irons DD

Instituted 12 May 1870 to rectory of Waddingham, on cession of Lewis Welsh Owen. Patron: Queen Victoria. [Reg. 41, p.307.]

Born 12 September 1812; son of Joseph I. of Hoddesdon (Hrt), gent. Educated: Queen's College, Oxford (matric. 1829; BA 1834; MA 1835; BD 1842; DD 1854). Deacon: 1835; priest: 1836 (Canterbury). Formerly: C. of St Mary, Newington, 1835–7; PC of St Peter, Walworth, 1837–8; V. of Barkway (Hrt), 1838–40; PC of Brompton, 1840–70; Bampton Lecturer, 1870. Resided at Waddingham Rectory. Also: Canon of St Paul's and Prebendary of Newington, 1860–83. Afterwards: R. of St Mary Woolnoth with St Mary Woolchurch, London, 1872–83; resided at 20 Gordon Square (Mx). Author: *Analysis of Human Responsibility* (1869); *Christianity as Taught by St Paul* (Bampton Lectures, 1870) and many other works. Died 18 June 1883 at 20 Gordon Square. ['Irons, William Josiah' in *ODNB*; Foster, *Alumni*; *Crockford* (1874); Census Returns 1871; *Probate Calendar* 1883.]

Edward Revell Eardley-Wilmot MA

Instituted 26 July 1872 to rectory of Waddingham, on cession of William Josiah Irons. Patron: Queen Victoria. [Reg. 41, p.360.]

Born 11 February 1814 at Leek Wootton (Wa), baptised there 22 July 1814; son of Sir John Eardley Eardley-Wilmot Bt. Served as officer in Bengal Artillery. Educated: Trinity Hall, Cambridge (matric. 1836; BA 1840; MA 1847). Deacon: 1840 (Winchester); priest: 1841 (Salisbury). Formerly: V. of Kenilworth, 1845–55; R. of All Souls Langham Place, 1855–72. Resided at Waddingham Rectory. Resigned 2 January 1882. Latterly of Clarina, Kenilworth Road, Leamington. Died there, 30 May 1899; buried at Kenilworth, 3 June 1899. [Burke, *Peerage* (1906), 1714; Warwicks RO, PR Leek Wootton; Venn, *Alumni*; *Crockford* (1898); White, *Lincolnshire* (1872); Census Returns 1881; RES A/27; *Probate Calendar* 1899; Warwicks RO, PR Kenilworth.]

Walter Lancelot Holland BA

Instituted 3 March 1882 to rectory of Waddingham, on resignation of Edward Revell Eardley-Wilmot. Patron: Queen Victoria. [Reg. 42, p.139.]

Born January 1852 at Shipley (Sx); son of Revd Charles H., Rector of Petworth. Educated: Haileybury and Corpus Christi College, Cambridge (matric. 1871; BA 1875; MA 1888). Deacon: 1875 (Winchester for Salisbury); priest: 1876 (Salisbury). Formerly: C. of Stalbridge (Do), 1875–7; R. of Puttenham (Sr), 1877–82. Married (27 September 1877) Edith Augusta, daughter of Revd Edward Revell Eardley-Wilmot (above). Father of Sir Eardley Lancelot Holland (1879–1967), obstetrician. Resided at Waddingham Rectory. Resigned 29 July (accepted 2 August) 1886. Afterwards: V. of All SS, Hatcham (Sr), 1886–91; Inc. of St Thomas, Edinburgh, 1891–5. Edited with a preface *Nunnery Life in the Church of England, or, Seventeen Years with Father Ignatius*, by Sister Mary Agnes (1891). Disclaimed his Orders. Latterly at 40 Lyndhurst Road, Hove. Died 11 April 1936; buried at Durrington (Wlt). [Venn, *Alumni*; *Crockford* (1885); Burke, *Peerage* (1906), 1715; 'Holland, Eardley Lancelot', in *ODNB*; RES 248/36; Bertie, *Scottish Episcopal Clergy*, 300; *Probate Calendar* 1936.]

Robert Gardner Smith

Instituted 24 August 1886 to rectory of Waddingham, on resignation of Walter Lancelot Holland. Patron: Queen Victoria. [Reg. 42, p.243.]

Born 28 November 1840; baptised 22 December 1840 at St Peter, Leeds; son of George S., thread manufacturer. Educated: Trinity College, Dublin (1867). Deacon: 1868; priest: 1869 (Ripon). Formerly: C. of St Andrew, Bradford, 1868–70; of St Philip, Ilfracombe, 1870–2; V. of St Mark, Manningham, Bradford, 1872–7; of All SS, Hatcham Park (Sr), 1877–86. Resided at Waddingham Rectory. Afterwards: R. of Castleford, 1892–1912. Retired to Aysgarth, Leamington. Latterly of 12 Lonsdale Road, Scarborough. Died there, 27 February 1930. [WYAS, PR Leeds St Peter; *Crockford* (1915, 1929); Census Returns 1891; *Probate Calendar* 1930.]

Joseph Simpson

Instituted 19 March 1892 to rectory of Waddingham, on cession of Robert Gardner Smith. Patron: Queen Victoria. [Reg. 42, p.342.]

Born *c*.1847 at Scorton (La). Congregational Minister at Erith (K), 1871. Educated: University College, Durham. Deacon: 1880; priest: 1881 (Ripon). Formerly: C. of Holmfirth, 1880–2; of Littleton (Mx), 1882–4; R. of Castleford, 1888–92. Resided at Waddingham Rectory. Resigned 31 March 1924. Latterly of Beeston St Andrew Hall (Nf). Died there, 19 March 1936. [*Crockford* (1935); Census Returns 1871 (Erith), 1901; RES A/106; *Probate Calendar* 1936.]

Robert Woods Wortley BA

Instituted 25 June 1924 to rectory of Waddingham, on resignation of Joseph Simpson. Patron: King George V. [Reg. 43, p.342.]

The Rectory of Snitterby was united to the Rectory of Waddingham by Order in Council dated 6 February 1928. [Reg. 43, p.428.]

Robert Woods Wortley BA

Instituted 12 March 1928 to the united benefice of the rectory of Waddingham with the rectory of Snitterby, as first incumbent thereof (the rectory of Snitterby being vacant by the resignation of Graeme Maurice Elliott). [Reg. 43, p.429.]

Born 1858; son of Robert W. of Suffield (Nf), gent. Educated: Fauconberge School, Beccles, and Caius College, Cambridge (matric. 1877; BA 1881). Deacon: 1882; priest: 1883 (Norwich). Formerly: C. of Dersingham (Nf), 1882–4; of Farnham Royal (Bk), 1884–6; V. of East with West Rudham (Nf), 1886–96; R. of Flempton with Hengrave (Sf), 1896–22; TCF 1914–19. Resided at Waddingham Rectory. Resigned 9 September (accepted 6 October) 1935. Died 5 November 1935 at Lindum Terrace, Lincoln. [Venn, *Alumni*; *Crockford* (1935); RES 1935/14; *Probate Calendar* 1937.]

George Hinchliffe BA
Instituted 23 March 1936 to united benefice of rectory of Waddingham with rectory of Snitterby, on resignation of Robert Woods Wortley. Patron: King George V. [Reg. 43, p.578.]

Educated: University of London (BA 1905; AKC 1910). Deacon: 1910; priest: 1911 (London). Formerly: C. of St Andrew, Alexandra Park, 1910–12; of St Peter, Plymouth, 1913–15; of Walton-on-the-Hill, Liverpool, 1916–19; V. of All SS, Newcastle-upon-Tyne, 1919–36. Resided at Waddingham Rectory. Resigned 14 June (accepted 30 June) 1954. Afterwards: C. of St Michael-on-the-Mount, Lincoln, 1955–6; Chaplain of St Wilfrid's Convent, Exeter, 1956–9. Latterly of 28 Bartholomew Street West, Exeter. Died 16 December 1959 after being knocked down by a bus while returning from a confirmation. [*Crockford* (1947, 1959–60); RES 1954/8; *LDM* (1960), 32; *Probate Calendar* 1960.]

Edmund Theodore Dickson BA
Instituted 23 September 1955 to united benefice of rectory of Waddingham with rectory of Snitterby, on resignation of George Hinchliffe. Patron: Queen Elizabeth II. [Reg. 44, p.215.]

Born 1898 at Sywell (Np); son of Thomas D. of Sywell Hall, resident estate agent. Educated: University of London (BA 1924); Ely Theological College (1924). Deacon: 1925; priest: 1926 (Southwark). Formerly: C. of Christ Church, Clapham, 1925–7; Missioner (UMCA) at Milo, 1927–36; P-in-C of Likoma (Nyasaland), 1936–8; Archdeacon of Nyasa and Canon of Likoma, 1938–52; Principal of St Paul's Training College, Liuli, 1947–54; Archdeacon of South West Tanganyika, 1952–4; Hon. Canon of Liuli, 1954. Resided at Waddingham Rectory. His 'dedicated missionary devotion … shone through his quiet unassuming shepherding of two small Lincolnshire villages'. Resigned 8 April (accepted 16 April) 1958. Died 31 December 1958 at St Matthew's Nursing Home, Northampton. [GRO, Birth Index; Census Returns 1901; *Crockford* (1957–8); *LDM* (1959), 31; RES 1958/7; *Probate Calendar* 1959.]

Eric John Wingfield BA ThL
Instituted 29 May1959 to united benefice of rectory of Waddingham with rectory of Snitterby, on resignation of Edmund Theodore Dickson. Patron: Queen Elizabeth II. [Reg. 44, p.273.]

Born 1916. Educated: University of Queensland (ThL 1943; BA 1951). Deacon and priest: 1944 (Brisbane). Formerly: in Australia, 1944–57; C. of St Matthew, Westminster, 1957–8. Afterwards: V. of Cowbit, 1977–81. Retired 1981. Served for many years as Treasurer of Confraternity of the Blessed Sacrament. Lived at 1A Fallowfield, Luton. Latterly at The College of St Barnabas, Blackberry Lane, Lingfield (Sx). Died there, 28 May 2006; buried at Waddingham. [*Crockford* (1989–90, 2006–7); *CBS Quarterly* (Sept–Oct 2006).]

WILLOUGHTON

The church of Willoughton was divided into two medieties, of which one was given by the Empress Matilda to the Abbey of St Nicholas at Angers, and the other by Simon de Canci to the Knights Templar. The Templars' mediety was closely linked with the preceptory of that Order in Willoughton. It was appropriated and a vicarage ordained; among the vicar's responsibilities was that of celebrating mass in the Templars' chapel. Although the two patrons may initially have presented to their separate medieties, by the end of the thirteenth century they appear to have agreed to present alternately to a vicarage of the whole church. This arrangement continued through the fourteenth century. After the suppression of the Knights Templar, their share passed to the Knights Hospitaller; when the possession of Angers were taken into the king's hands as those of an 'alien priory', the Crown presented in the Abbot's stead. By 1461 the Crown had granted this share of the advowson to King's College, Cambridge. The Hospitallers continued to present alternately until the Dissolution, after which their share passed eventually to the Sanderson family (later Earls of Castleton) from whom it passed (like Glentworth and Saxby) to the Lumleys (Earls of Scarbrough). In 1941 the Earl of Scarbrough and the College both transferred their shares of the advowson to the Bishop of Lincoln. The Bishop was patron in 1965. [*Records of the Templars*, clv–clvi, 78; *VCH Cambridge* iii. 381; *London Gazette* (35176), 30 May 1941; *LDC* (1965), 110–11.]

Lambert chaplain
Instituted in the eleventh pontifical year of Bishop Hugh of Wells (20 December 1219/19 December 1220) to vicarage of a mediety of church of Willoughton. Patron: Brethren of the Knights Templar. [*Rot. Welles* i. 213.]

John chaplain
Instituted in the eleventh pontifical year of Bishop Hugh of Wells (20 December 1219/19 December 1220) to vicarage of a mediety of church of Willoughton. Patron: Abbot and Convent of Angers. [*Rot. Welles* i. 214.]

Ralph de Hacwith chaplain
Instituted in the twenty-fourth pontifical year of Bishop Hugh of Wells (20 December 1232/19 December 1233) to vicarage of a mediety of church of Willoughton. Patron: br. Guy de Meles, Proctor General in England of Abbot and Convent of Angers. [*Rot. Welles* i. 234.]

James de Huntigdon chaplain
Instituted in the twenty-fifth pontifical year of Bishop Hugh of Wells (20 December 1233/19 December 1234) to vicarage of a mediety of church of Willoughton. Patron: br. Guy, as above. [*Rot. Welles* i. 236.]

Peter
Instituted before 18 June 1283. [*Reg. Sutton* viii. 4.]

William of Manningford chaplain
Instituted 18 June 1283 to vicarage of Willoughton, on death of Peter. Patron: Master of the Templars in England. [*Reg. Sutton* viii. 4.]

Simon de Wylmeleighton priest
Instituted 20 June 1323 to vicarage of Willoughton, on resignation of William de Manyngford. Patron: Br. William de Lesneill, monk of St Nicholas, Angers, proctor of Abbot and Convent of Angers. [*Reg. Burghersh* i. no.729.]

Ralph de Hale priest
Instituted 11 November 1333 to vicarage of Willoughton, on death of Simon. Patron: Br. Leonard de Tybertis, Prior of Hospitallers. [*Reg. Burghersh* i. no.780.]

John
Instituted before 8 February 1361/2. [Reg. 9, fo.173.]

William Marnham priest
Instituted 8 February 1361/2 to vicarage of Willoughton, on death of John. Patron: Br. John Pavely, Prior of Hospitallers in England. [Reg. 9, fo.173.]
Afterwards: V. of Risby, 1365.

William de Croxton priest
Instituted 28 January 1364/5 to vicarage of Willoughton, on resignation of William de Marnham (by exchange with vicarage of Risby). Patron: Br. John de Fessius, proctor in England of Abbot and Convent of St Nicholas, Angers. [Reg. 10, fo.127v.]
Formerly: V. of St Albin, Spridlington, 1358–9 (*q.v.*); V. of Risby, 1359–65. [Reg. 9, fo.169v.]

William de Herpeswell
Instituted before 23 April 1390. [Reg. 11, fo.104v.]
Afterwards: R. of Beesby, 1390–1; V. of Clarborough (Nt), 1391–2; R. of All Saints Peaseholme Green, York, 1392. [Reg. 11, fo.50; Train, *North Notts Clergy*, 36.]

John (Smyth) de Sutton (in Hoyland) priest
Instituted 23 April 1390 to vicarage of Willoughton, on resignation of William de Herpeswell (by exchange with church of Beesby). Patron: King Richard II (22 April 1390), by reason of the temporalities of the alien priory of Willoughton being in his hands on account of the war with France. [Reg. 11, fos 45, 104v; *CPR 1388–92*, 232–3.]

Priest: before 13 November 1375. Formerly: V. of Owersby, 1375–9; R. of Beesby, 1379–90. [Reg. 10, fos 77, 99v.]

Richard Sylby priest
Instituted 3 April 1394 to vicarage of Willoughton, on death of John. Patron: Br. John de Radyngton, Prior of Hospitallers in England. [Reg. 11, fo.111v.]

Richard Messengers
Instituted before 6 January 1407/8. [Reg. 14, fo.111v.]
Afterwards: V. of Upton (Nt), 1408.

Richard Chaterton
Instituted 6 January 1407/8 to vicarage of Willoughton, on resignation of Richard Messengers (by exchange with vicarage of Upton). Patron: King Henry IV, by reason of the temporalities of the alien Abbey of Angers being in his hands. [Reg. 14, fo.111v.]
Formerly: V. of Upton (Nt), to 1408.

Thomas Busk
Instituted before 14 March 1432/3. [Reg. 17, fo.16v.]

Thomas Chevalier priest
Instituted 14 March 1432/3 to vicarage of Willoughton, on resignation of Thomas Busk. Patron: Joan, Queen of England. [Reg. 17, fo.16v.]

William Dowcet
Instituted before 4 November 1451. [Reg. 19, fo.66v.]

William Spense
Instituted 4 November 1451 to vicarage of Willoughton, on resignation of William Dowcet. Patron: King Henry VI (13 October 1451). [Reg. 19, fos 66v, 80; *CPR 1446–52*, 494.]

Robert Jakson
Instituted before 20 August 1452. [Reg. 20, fo.157.]

Richard Pereson priest
Instituted 20 August 1452 to vicarage of Willoughton, on death of Robert Jakson. Patron: Br. Robert Bovyll, Prior of Hospitallers in England. [Reg. 20, fo.157.]

Thomas Barne chaplain
Instituted 4 July 1464 to vicarage of Willoughton, on death of Richard Persone. Patron: Provost (M. Robert Wodelarke) and Scholars of King's College of St Mary and St Nicholas, Cambridge. [Reg. 20, fo.161.]

John Hynkyrsell priest

Instituted 20 October 1472 to vicarage of Willoughton, on resignation of Thomas Baron. Patron: Br. William Tourney, Prior of Hospitallers in England. [Reg. 21, fo.31.]

John Sheffeld priest

Instituted 2 March 1479/80 to vicarage of Willoughton, on death of John Inkersale. Patron: Provost (M. Walter Feld) and Scholars of King's College of St Mary and St Nicholas, Cambridge. [Reg. 21, fo.35v.]

John Jakson chaplain

Instituted 25 May 1505 to vicarage of Willoughton, on resignation of John Sheffeld. Patron: Br. Thomas Newporte, Bailiff of Eagle and [lieutenant] of Br. Thomas Docwray, Prior of Hospitallers in England. [Reg. 23, fo.156.]

Assessed for subsidy (£3 6s 8d) in 1526. [*Subsidy*, 36.]

Roger Wardeley deacon

Instituted 29 March 1533 to vicarage of Willoughton, on death of last incumbent. Patron: Provost (Edward Foxe DD) and Scholars of King's College, Cambridge. [Reg. 27, fo.95.]

Priest: 12 April 1533 (Ascalon for Lincoln). [Reg. 26, fo.34.]

John Naler chaplain

Instituted 15 April 1536 to vicarage of Willoughton, on resignation of Roger Wardeley. Patron: Prior of Hospitallers in England. [Reg. 27, fo.96v.]

Witnessed Willoughton wills as curate, 1540–6. [Stow Wills 1530–52/73; 1530–52/207v; 1530–52/335v.]

Robert Otes

Instituted *c*.1537 (compounded for first-fruits, 28 January 1536/7). [FL.h.13.]

Nicholas Cusworthe

Instituted *c*.1548 (compounded for first-fruits, 24 August 1548). [FL.h.13.]

Priest: before 11 October 1534. Formerly: Chaplain of Burghersh Chantry in Lincoln Cathedral, 1534–48; allotted pension of £6 in 1548. Exhibited at Visitation in 1551. Witnessed Willoughton will, 20 March 1556. Died *c*.1558; will dated 22 January 1557/8. [*Chapter Acts* i. 184; *Ex-Religious*, 80; Vj 13, fo.58; Stow Wills 1553–67/179; LCC Wills 1557/ii/103v.]

Henry Grene

Instituted before 1565. [Stow Wills 1563–6/8v.]

Will dated 27 May 1565.

Nicholas Riley

Instituted before 25 February 1567/8. [Stow Wills 1568–75/11.]

Born *c*.1534. Education: 'ignorant of Latin; but little versed in sacred learning'. Priest: 27 February 1563/4 (Chester). Resident. Witnessed Willoughton will, 7 June 1568. Signed BTs at Willoughton 1600–4. Buried at Willoughton, 14 November 1604. Will (Stow). [*Bishop Cooper*, 167; *State of the Church*, 97, 330; Stow Wills 1568–70/45; BTs Willoughton; Stow Wills 1603–6/171.]

Garrett Holland MA

Instituted 22 November 1604 to vicarage of Willoughton, on death of last incumbent. Patron: Provost (Roger Coade DD) and Scholars of King's College of St Mary and St Nicholas, Cambridge (7 November 1604). [Reg. 30, fo.237v; PD 1604/26; IND/S/1.]

Born *c*.1577 at Newton (La). Educated: Emmanuel College (matric. 1594; BA 1597–9; MA 1601) and King's College, Cambridge. Priest: 22 November 1601 (Lincoln). Resident (1611): signed BTs at Willoughton 1605–12. Buried at Willoughton, 4 August 1612. [PD 1604/26; Venn, *Alumni*; LC 3, fo.100; BTs Willoughton.]

Nicholas Cartwright MA

Instituted 3 December 1612 to vicarage of Willoughton, on death of Gerard Holland. Patron: Sir Nicholas Saunderson Bt (10 August 1612), for this turn. [PD 1612/84.]

Born *c*.1586; of Worcestershire. Educated: Balliol College, Oxford (matric. 1602; BA 1605; MA 1608). Deacon and priest: 11 June 1609 (Lincoln). Signed BTs at Willoughton 1613–17. Afterwards: R. of Bourton-on-the-Hill (Gl), 1617–35. Will (PCC) dated 1 July 1634; proved 28 April 1635. [Foster, *Alumni*; PD 1612/84; LC 4, fo.10; PROB 11/167/447.]

Richard Raynsford

Instituted *c*.1617.

Signed BTs at Willoughton as Vicar, 1619–21. [BTs Willoughton.]

Henry Wilce

Instituted before 1624.

Signed BTs at Willoughton as Vicar, 1624. [BTs Willoughton.]

Between 1660 and 1718 the living of Willoughton was vacant and served by curates, including Samuel Holden (1662); William Branston (1666–71); John Hill (1677–81); Stephen Kaye (1690–4); Josiah Byard (1695–1706); Laurence Robinson (1710–17). [LC 5, fo.96; BTs Willoughton; LC 14, p.234.]

Thomas Reith BA

Instituted 23 December 1718 to vicarage of Willoughton, on death of last incumbent. Patron: King George I, by lapse. [Reg. 37, p.75.]

Signed BTs at Willoughton, 1719–42. Also: V. of Bishop Norton, 1704 (*q.v.*).

William Bassett
Instituted *c*.1742–3.
Signed BTs at Willoughton as Vicar, 1744–63. Also: V. of Glentworth, 1729–65 (*q.v.*).

George Bassett LLB
Instituted 27 February 1768 to vicarage of Willoughton, on death of last incumbent. Patron: King George III, by lapse. [Reg. 39, p.86.]
Also: V. of Glentworth (*q.v.*).

John Bassett
Instituted 17 April 1793 to vicarage of Willoughton, on resignation of George Bassett. Patron: George Augusta Lumley Sanderson, Earl of Scarbrough. [Reg. 39, p.574.]
Baptised 31 March 1748 at Glentworth; son of William B., Vicar of Glentworth (1729–65). Literate. Deacon: 18 December 1774; priest: 21 December 1774 (Lincoln). Also: R. of Broxholme, 1775–1805; V. of Saxby, 1779–1805; V. of Glentworth, 1788–93. Resided at Broxholme. Buried at Glentworth, 10 January 1805 (aged 56). [PR Glentworth; Reg. 39, p.246.]

Duke Yonge BA
Instituted 20 June 1805 to vicarage of Willoughton, on death of John Bassett. Patron: Provost and Scholars of King's College, Cambridge. [Reg. 40, p.96.]
Born 13 October 1779 at Yealmpton (Dev); son of Duke Y., C. of Yealmpton. Educated: Eton College and King's College, Cambridge (matric. 1800; BA 1803; MA 1808); Fellow of King's, 1802–6. Deacon: 10 June 1804; priest: 9 June 1805 (Lincoln). Non-resident at Willoughton, which was served by curates, including John Hartley (1792–1827) and Octavius Luard (1827–32). Also: V. of Anthony (Co), 1806–36; R. of Newton Ferrers (Dev), 1808–12. Died 29 July 1836 at the Plymouth residence of Dr Yonge his brother. [Venn, *Alumni*; Reg. 40, pp. 81, 96; BTs Willoughton; CR 1, pp. 42, 334; PR Willoughton; *GM* (September 1836), 331.]

Charles Gape
Instituted 25 October 1836 to vicarage of Willoughton, on death of Duke Yonge. Patron: Earl of Scarbrough (for this turn). [Reg. 40, p.443.]
Of Hertfordshire. Baptised 5 August 1799 at St Michael, St Albans; son of James Carpenter G., Vicar of Redbourn (Hrt). Educated: Peterhouse, Cambridge (matric. 1818; BA 1822; MA 1825). Deacon: 22 September 1822; priest: 21 September 1823 (Lincoln). Non-resident at Willoughton; resided at Sibsey (1841–2) and later at Hendon (Mx). Also: V. of Sibsey, 1826–71; V. of Hillington (Nf), 1837–40. Resigned 12 October (accepted 16 October) 1871. Lived at 12 Belsize Crescent (Mx). Died 24 February 1890 at 11 Exeter Road, Brondesbury (Mx). [IGI; Venn, *Alumni*; OR 1, pp. 9, 13; Census Returns 1841 (Sibsey), 1851 (Hendon); White, *Lincolnshire* (1842), 282; RES 246/45; *Probate Calendar* 1890.]

Edward Chapman Wilshere MA
Instituted 16 February 1872 to vicarage of Willoughton, on resignation of

Charles Gape. Patron: Provost (Revd Richard Okes DD) and Scholars of King's College, Cambridge, for this turn. [Reg. 41, p.344.]

Born *c*.1817 at Greenwich. Educated: St John's College, Cambridge (matric. 1838; BA 1842; MA 1850). Deacon: 1843 (Hereford for Exeter); priest: 1844 (Exeter). Formerly: C. of Chester-le-Street (Du), 1845; R. of St Andrew and St George, Scarborough, Tobago (West Indies), 1846–8; C. of Chester-le-Street (again), 1851; Chaplain at Gothenburg (Sweden), 1852–8; C. of Willoughton, 1859–72. Resided at Willoughton Vicarage. Died 14 April 1886, suddenly while visiting Willoughton National School. 'During his long ministry at Willoughton he had endeared himself to all classes.' [Venn, *Alumni*; *Crockford* (1886); Census Returns 1851 (Chester-le-Street), 1881; CR 4, fo.96; *Stamford Mercury*, 23 April 1886; *Probate Calendar* 1886.]

Henry Hacon

Instituted 19 November 1886 to vicarage of Willoughton, on death of Edward Chapman Wilshere. Patron: Aldred Frederick George Beresford Lumley, Earl of Scarbrough, of Sandbeck Park, Rotherham (for this turn). [Reg. 42, p.244.]

Born *c*.1835 at Swaffham (Nf). Educated: St Bees College (1860). Deacon: 1862; priest: 1863 (Rochester). Formerly: C. of Fairstead, 1862–3; of West Thurrock, 1864–7; Chaplain (Additional Clergy Society) at Indore, 1868–78; Assensole, 1879–80; Ajmere, Rajpootana, 1881–2; Arrah, 1883; Chinsurah, 1884–5; Midnapore, 1885–6. Resided at Willoughton Vicarage. Afterwards: V. of Searby with Owmby, 1895–1911. Died 11 April 1911 at Searby Vicarage. [Census Returns 1891; *Crockford* (1911); *Probate Calendar* 1911.]

Reginald Echalaz MA

Instituted 3 December 1895 to vicarage of Willoughton, on cession of Henry Hacon. Patron: Provost (Revd Augustus Austen Leigh MA) and Scholars of King's College of Our Lady and St Nicholas, Cambridge (for this turn). [Reg. 42, p.393.]

Born 1840; son of Theodore E. of Austrey (St), clerk in holy orders. Educated: Rossall School (to 1853); Exeter College (matric. 1858) and Queen's College, Oxford (BA 1862; MA 1865). Deacon: 1863; priest: 1864 (Lichfield). Formerly: C. of Bramshall (St), 1863–5; of Old Swinford, 1865. Lived with his mother at Ashby-de-la-Zouch (1871); an epileptic. Resided at Willoughton Vicarage. Resigned 30 January (accepted 31 January) 1901. Afterwards: Chaplain and Warden of St Anne's Bede Houses, 1909–15. Lived in Lincoln at 25 Bailgate (1901); St Anne's Lodge (1911); latterly of The Cottage, Queensway. Died 5 January 1926. [Foster, *Alumni*; *Rossall Register*, 37; *Crockford* (1923); Kelly, *Lincolnshire* (1900), 598; RES 248b/29; Census Returns (Ashby) 1871; (Lincoln) 1901, 1911; *Probate Calendar* 1926.]

Sidney Rupert Swalwell MA

Instituted 15 March 1901 to vicarage of Willoughton, on resignation of Reginald Echalaz. Patron: Aldred Frederick George Beresford Lumley, Earl of Scarbrough, of Sandbeck Park, Rotherham (for this turn). [Reg. 42, p.483.]

Born *c*.1868 at Scarborough; son of Revd John S. Brother of John S., Rector of Snitterby (*q.v.*). Educated: St Catharine's College, Cambridge (matric. 1888; BA 1891; MA 1899). Deacon: 1893; priest: 1895 (York). Formerly: C. of Coxwold (YNR), 1893–8; of Purston (YWR), 1898–1900; of Carleton, Pontefract, 1900–1. Resided at Willoughton Vicarage.

Died 7 April 1914 at Harrogate (aged 46). [Venn, *Alumni*; *Crockford* (1911); Census Returns 1911.]

William Burton Eastwood BA

Instituted 5 January 1915 by collation to vicarage of Willoughton, on death of Sidney Rupert Swalwell. Patron: Bishop of Lincoln (for this turn), by lapse. [Reg. 43, p.83.]

Born *c*.1867 at Stalybridge (Chs). Educated: Hatfield Hall, Durham (LTh 1892; BA 1896). Deacon: 1897 (York for Wakefield); priest: 1899 (Wakefield). Formerly: C. of Drighlington (YWR), 1897–1903; of St Andrew, Grimsby, 1903–7; of St Barnabas, Rotherhithe, 1907–10; of St Aidan, New Cleethorpes, 1910–15. Resided at Willoughton Vicarage. Bishop Hicks visited there (May 1918): 'By pony trap to Willoughton, where I read lessons & preached for Eastwood at 10. Saw his garden, & potato plot.' Died 26 September 1924 at Clinique St Joseph, 32 Rempart du Bassin, Bruges (Belgium), aged 58. [*Crockford* (1923); *Hicks Diaries*, no.1246; *LDC* (1925), 160; *Probate Calendar* 1925.]

George Argyll Ferguson

Instituted 26 June 1925 by collation to vicarage of Willoughton, on death of William Burton Eastwood. Patron: Bishop of Lincoln (for this turn), by lapse. [Reg. 43, p.366.]

Born *c*.1867. Educated: Manchester College, Oxford (1899) and Cuddesdon College (1918). Deacon: 1919 (Oxford for Lincoln); priest: 1920 (Lincoln). Formerly: C. of All Saints, Lincoln, 1919–21; of St John Spitalgate, Grantham, 1921–5. Resided at Willoughton Vicarage. Resignation accepted 1 April 1942. Lived at 34 Saxon Street, Lincoln. Latterly of Bentley Farm, Grasby. Author: *How a Modern Atheist Found God* (1912); *Why I Became a Christian Theosophist* (1918); *How a Unitarian Found the Saviour Christ* (1924); *Outlines of a Christian Philosophy* (1930). Died 26 May 1948. [GRO, Death Index; *Crockford* (1932, 1947); Reg. 43, p.673; *Probate Calendar* 1948.]

Hugh Frank Riches MA

Instituted 6 June 1942 by the Official *sede vacante* to vicarage of Willoughton, on resignation of George Argyll Ferguson. Patron: King George VI, for this turn by reason of the vacancy of the see of Lincoln. Note that on 14 May 1942, the Archbishop of Canterbury granted a dispensation enabling the said HFR to hold together the Rectory of Blyborough and the Vicarage of Willoughton. [Reg. 43, p.675.]

Born 2 November 1899; son of Frank Maplestone R. of Beaumont Fee, Lincoln, school-master. Educated: Hatfield College, Durham (LTh 1921; BA 1922; MA 1925; M.Litt. 1931) and St Paul's College, Burgh-le-Marsh (1919). Deacon: 21 December 1922; priest: 21 December 1923 (Lincoln). Formerly: C. of Bottesford, 1922–6; St John's School, Chepstow (Assistant Master), 1926–8; Hurstpierpoint College, 1928–9; St Paul's College, Burgh-le-Marsh: Tutor, 1929–30, Vice-Principal, 1930–1; R. of Stainton-le-Vale with Kirmond-le-Mire, 1931–6; V. of Torksey, 1936–42. Also: R. of Blyborough, 1942–52 (*q.v.*). Resided at Willoughton Vicarage. Also: Editor, *Lincoln Diocesan Leaflet*, 1936–62; Librarian of Lincoln Cathedral, 1950–67; RD of Aslacoe, 1951–2. Afterwards: R. of Lincoln St Mary Magdalene, 1952–67; PC of St Michael-on-the-Mount, Lincoln, 1959–67; Canon of Lincoln and Prebendary of Stow in Lindsey, 1961–7. Died 6 March 1967. [PR Lincoln St Martin; *Crockford* (1948, 1965–6); *LDC* (1968), 55.]

Jonathan Ernest Draper LTh

Instituted 5 December 1952 by collation to vicarage of Willoughton, on cession of Hugh Frank Riches. Patron: Bishop of Lincoln. Note that on 16 May 1952, the Archbishop of Canterbury granted a dispensation enabling the said JED to hold together the rectory of Blyborough and the vicarage of Willoughton. [Reg. 44, p.168.]

Born 5 August 1895; son of Jonathan D. of Derby, engine driver. Educated: St Paul's College, Burgh-le-Marsh (1915) and University of Durham (LTh. 1921). Deacon: 1921 (London for Colony); priest: 1922 (Waiapu). Formerly: C. of Dannevirke, 1921–3; of Hastings, 1923–5; V. of Opotiki, 1925–30; Holy Sepulchre, Auckland, 1930–6; R. of Halton Holegate, 1937–43; of Toynton St Peter with All SS, 1943–52. Also: R. of Blyborough, 1952–60 (*q.v.*); RD of Aslacoe, 1953–60; Canon of Lincoln and Prebendary of Heydour cum Walton, 1954–66. Resided at Willoughton Vicarage. Afterwards: R. of Caythorpe, 1960–6; RD of Loveden, 1960–4; Warden of St Anne's Bedehouses, Lincoln, 1966–72. Latterly at 17 Chellaston Lane, Aston-on-Trent (Db). Died 24 January 1984. [GRO, Death Index; Census Returns 1911; *Crockford* (1959–60, 1980–2).]

Benjamin Owen Whitfield BA

Instituted 23 September 1960 by collation to vicarage of Willoughton, on cession of Jonathan Ernest Draper. Patron: Bishop of Lincoln. Note that on 13 September 1960, the Archbishop of Canterbury granted a dispensation enabling the said BOW to hold together the rectory of Blyborough and the vicarage of Willoughton. [Reg. 44, p.302.]

Born 31 October 1917. Educated: University of Saskatchewan (BA 1943) and Emmanuel College, Saskatoon (LTh. 1943; BD 1953). Deacon 1943; priest 1944 (Brandon). Formerly: R. of Hamiota (MB), 1943–6; P-in-C of Shoal Lake, 1945–6; R. of Birtle, 1946–51; R. of St George, Brandon, 1951–4; R. of St Matthew, Brandon and Canon of Brandon, 1954–60; Dean of Brandon, 1957–60. Also: R. of Blyborough, 1960–2 (*q.v.*). Resided at Willoughton Vicarage. Afterwards: R. of Clee, 1962–70; V. of Gainsborough, 1970–81; Canon of Lincoln, 1970–89 and Prebendary of Corringham 1970–81, Prebendary of Kilsby, 1981–9; RD of Corringham, 1972–8; V. of St Paul, Morton, 1976–81; V. of Melton Ross with New Barnetby, 1981–6; V. of Wrawby, 1981–5. Latterly of 6 The Copse, Bigby High Road, Brigg. Died 17 March 1996. [GRO, Death Index; *Crockford* (1961–2, 1995–6); Lincoln Cathedral Obit Book.]

Edward Denzil Chetwood Wright MA

Instituted 20 December 1962 by collation to vicarage of Willoughton, on cession of Benjamin Owen Whitfield. Patron: Bishop of Lincoln. Note that on 22 November 1962, the Archbishop of Canterbury granted a dispensation enabling the said EDCW to hold together the rectory of Blyborough and the vicarage of Willoughton. [Reg. 44, p.340–1.]

Born 12 May 1907; son of Philip Chetwood Wright of Brattleby Hall. Educated: Marlborough College (1921–5); Magdalen College, Oxford (BA 1929; MA 1932) and Wells Theological College (1931). Deacon: 1931; priest: 1932 (Wakefield). Formerly: C. of Castleford, 1932–4; of Felkirk, 1934–8; V. of Penistone with Midhope, 1938–42; Chaplain RNVR, 1942–6; V. of Seamer with Cayton and East Ayton, 1946–62. Resided at Willoughton Vicarage to 1967, subsequently at Corringham Vicarage. Also: R. of Blyborough, 1962–72 (*q.v.*); R. of Heapham, 1967–72; V. of Corringham with Springthorpe,

1967–72; RD of Aslacoe, 1963–4; RD of Corringham, 1969–72. Married Diana Blanche, daughter of Major F. Strickland of Bridlington. Retired 1972. Latterly of The Yews, Brattleby. Died January 1990. [*Marlborough College Register*, 670; *Crockford* (1969–70, 1989–90); GRO, Death Index.]

DEANERY OF AVELAND

2. Deanery and Wapentake of Aveland.
Detail from A. Bryant, *Map of the County of Lincoln*
(London, 1828), (Lincoln Cathedral Library)

ASLACKBY

The church of Aslackby was given by Hubert de Ria to the Knights Templar in 1164. The Templars subsequently acquired further property in Aslackby and established a preceptory there towards the end of the twelfth century. Although the Gilbertines appeared to have made a claim to the advowson at this time, the Templars succeded in establishing their right to the church in 1202. A vicarage had been ordained by 1237–8. After the suppression of the Templars, the advowson passed to the Knights Hospitaller who continued to present to the vicarage until the Dissolution. In 1541 the advowson was granted by the Crown to Edward, Lord Clinton, whose descendants, the Earls of Lincoln, held it until the middle of the seventeenth century. The advowson subsequently came into the hands of the Barstow family of Yorkshire, who presented to the living from 1752 until 1959. In the 1960s the patronage was acquired by St John's Hall, Durham. [*Records of the Templars*, clxxxvi–clxxxvii; 3 ANC 1/3/2; *LDC* (1965), 66–7.]

William de Aldeberi chaplain
Instituted in the third pontifical year of Bishop Robert Grosseteste (17 June 1237/16 June 1238) to vicarage of Aslackby. Patron: The Templars in England. [Hoskin no.79.]

M. John de Melton
Instituted before 6 April 1280. [*Reg. Sutton* i. 2.]

William de Douseby chaplain
Instituted 6 April 1280 to vicarage of Aslackby, on resignation of M. John de Melton. Patron: Master of the Templars. [*Reg. Sutton* i. 2.]

Elias de Estwyk chaplain
Instituted 7 March 1301/2 to vicarage of Aslackby, on death of William. Patron: br. William de la More, Master of the Templars in England. [Reg. 2, fo.5v.]

Nicholas de Camelton priest
Instituted 25 March 1321 to vicarage of Aslackby, on death of Elias. Patron: br. Richard de Leicestre, proctor-general of Prior of Hospitallers in England. [*Reg. Burghersh* i. no 14.]
Formerly: V. of Chicksands (Bd), 1290–4; V. of Cople (Bd), 1294–1318; V. of St Peter, Kirkby Laythorpe, 1318–21. [*Reg. Sutton* viii. 106, 113; Reg. 2, fo.73v.]

John de Lidyngton priest
Instituted 6 May 1340 to vicarage of Aslackby, on death of Nicholas. Patron:

M. Henry de la Dale, clerk, by reason of a demise of the said church made to him by Prior of Hospitallers. [*Reg. Burghersh* i. no.635.]

Thomas de Peynton
Instituted 6 July 1349 to vicarage of Aslackby, on death of John. Patron: Prior of Hospitallers. [Reg. 9, fo.60v.]

William Calkewell
Instituted before 18 February 1371/2. [Reg. 10, fo.47.]

Afterwards: R. of Mavis Enderby, February–July 1372; R. of Newton-by-Folkingham, 1372 (*q.v.*).

John Petyt
Instituted 18 February 1371/2 to vicarage of Aslackby, on resignation of William Calkewell (by exchange with church of Mavis Enderby). Patron: br. Richard Overton, lieutenant of Prior of Hospitallers in England. [Reg. 10, fo.47.]

Priest: before 19 December 1361. Formerly: R. of Mavis Enderby, 1370–2. Also: R. of Reed (Hrt), 1361–84. Afterwards: R. of Tewing (Hrt), 1374–9; R. of Little Birch (Ess), 1379–82; V. of Tolleshunt d'Arcy (Ess), 1382; R. of Barkway (Hrt), 1384–5. [*Reg. Sudbury* i. 230; Reg. 10, fos 39v, 319v; Newcourt i. 803, 861; ii. 60, 605.]

John Prestwold
Instituted 9 November 1374 to vicarage of Aslackby, on resignation of John Petyt (by exchange with church of Tewing). [Reg. 10, fo.307v.]

Formerly: R. of Tewing (Hrt), 1361–74. Assessed for poll-tax, 1377, 1381. Afterwards: V. of Spaldwick (Hu), 1382–4. [Reg. 9, fo.412; *Clerical Poll-Taxes*, nos 700, 1329, 1918; Reg. 11, fo.247v.]

William Prestwold
Instituted 3 May 1382 to vicarage of Aslackby, on resignation of John Prestwold (by exchange with vicarage of prebendal church of Spaldwick). Patron: br. Hildebrand Inge, President of Hospitallers in England. [Reg. 10, fos 118v, 331v.]

Priest: before 16 August 1375. Formerly: V. of Spaldwick (Hu), 1375–82. [Reg. 10, fo.309v.]

Richard Malblank chaplain
Instituted 25 July 1424 to vicarage of Aslackby (cause of vacancy not stated). Patron: br. Henry Crounhale, preceptor of Eagle, lieutenant of br. William Hulles, Prior of Hospitallers in England. [*Reg. Chichele*, i. 322.]

Afterwards: V. of Deptford (K), 1457.

Thomas Hylton priest
Instituted 10 August 1457 to vicarage of Aslackby, on resignation of Richard

Malblank (by exchange with vicarage of Deptford, dioc. Rochester). Patron: br. Robert Botyller, Prior of Hospitallers in England. [Reg. 20, fo.128.]

Formerly: V. of Deptford (K), to 1457.

William Raven priest

Instituted 3 April 1484 to vicarage of Aslackby, on resignation of M. Thomas Hilton. Patron: br. William Weston, preceptor of Ansty and Trebigh, and lieu-tenant of br. John Weston, Prior of Hospitallers in England. Note that an annual pension of 4 marks was reserved to Thomas Hilton for life from the fruits of the vicarage. [Reg. 22, fo.134v.]

Henry Baxter

Instituted 19 January 1487/8 to vicarage of Aslackby, on resignation of William Ravyn. Patron: Prior of Hospitallers in England. [Reg. 22, fo.140.]

William Garstang chaplain

Instituted 18 March 1506/7 to vicarage of Aslackby, on death of Henry Baxter. Patron: br. Thomas Docwra, Prior of Hospitallers in England. [Reg. 23, fo.121.]

Edmund Thakwraa chaplain

Instituted 9 November 1518 to vicarage of Aslackby, on death of William Garstang. Patron: Prior of Hospitallers in England. [Reg. 25, fo.19v.]

Deacon: 18 April 1500; priest: 13 June 1500 (York). Assessed for subsidy (£7), 1526. Will dated 11 January 1533/4 ('to be buryed in the quere of Seyntt Jamys of Aslakbye'); proved 2 March 1533/4. [*York Ordinations 1500–1509*, 246; *Subsidy*, 58; *Lincoln Wills* iv. 265.]

Ralph Perse *alias* Smale priest

Instituted 4 March 1533/4 to vicarage of Aslackby, on death of Edmund Thakwra. Patron: br. William Weston, Prior of Hospitallers in England. [Reg. 27, fo.57v.]

Assessed for *Valor Eccesiasticus* in 1535. [*Valor*, iv. 104.]

M. John Williamson LLB

Instituted 24 March 1541/2 to vicarage of Aslackby, on death of Ralph Smalle. Patron: Nicholas Wilson (for this turn), by grant from Edward Clinton, Lord Clinton. [Reg. 27, fo.77.]

Thomas Ellis

Instituted 11 September 1544 to vicarage of Aslackby, on death of John Williamson. Patron: John Beche and Laurence Lawland of Rowston (14 July 1544), for this turn by grant from Edward Clinton, Lord Clinton of Sempringham. [Reg. 27, fo.83; PD 1544/18.]

Exhibited at Visitation in 1551. [Vj 13, fo.63.]

Thomas Stevinson

Instituted 16 July 1557 to vicarage of Aslackby, vacant both *de iure* and *de facto*. Patron: Miles Mordinge and Anthony Dickenson, for this turn by grant from Lord Clinton. [Reg. 28, fo.137v.]

Witnessed will of John Baley of Graby (August 1557). [LCC Wills 1558/i/34.]

Robert Maiborne

Instituted 29 January 1557/8 to vicarage of Aslackby. [*Bishop Cooper*, 220.]

Born *c*.1510. Education: 'but little skilled in Latin; but little versed in sacred learning'. Priest: 1534 (suffragan for Lincoln). Formerly: C. of Aslackby: witnessed wills of Agnes Wryghte (January 1555) and John Chamberlayne (August 1557). Resident: signed BTs 1562–88. Buried at Aslackby, 21 May 1589 [*Bishop Cooper*, 208; LCC Wills 1557/i/395; LCC Wills 1557/iii/162v; BTs Aslackby.]

Alexander Maiborne

Instituted 7 May 1590 to vicarage of Aslackby. [BC.]

Reader at Aslackby, 1585. Resident: signed BTs 1590–1605. Died 25 May 1605; buried at Aslackby, 26 May 1605. Probate inventory dated 30 May 1605. [*State of the Church*, 73; BTs Aslackby; INV 100/134.]

Ralph Palfreyman BA

Instituted 14 November 1605 to vicarage of Aslackby, on death of Alexander Maborne. Patron: Henry, Earl of Lincoln. [Reg. 30, fo.270v.]

Signed BTs at Aslackby 1606–10. Afterwards: R. of Folkingham, 1610–18 (*q.v.*).

George Wayte BA

Instituted 5 April 1611 to vicarage of Aslackby, on resignation of Ralph Palfreman. Patron: Henry, Earl of Lincoln (1 April 1611). [BC; PD 1611/2.]

Education: BA. Perhaps to be identified with GW of Trinity College, Cambridge (matric. 1576). Deacon: 17 July 1579 (Peterborough). Formerly: R. of Wittering (Np), 1586–1605. Resident at Aslackby: 'of good behaviour … no other benefice'. [Venn, *Alumni*; Longden xiv. 113; LC 3, fo.1.]

Samuel Asheton

Instituted 11 July 1614 to vicarage of Aslackby. [BC.]

Born *c*.1580. Educated: University College, Oxford (matric. 1601; BA). Deacon: 26 May 1605; priest: 20 December 1607 (Chester). Formerly V. of Threckingham, 1612–14 (*q.v.*). Signed BTs at Aslackby 1616–19, 1623–7. Buried at Aslackby, 26 June 1627. [PD 1612/74 (biographical details); Foster, *Alumni*; BTs Aslackby.]

Barjona Dove MA

Instituted 11 July 1627 to vicarage of Aslackby, on death of Samuel Asheton. Patron: Theophilus Fines, Earl of Lincoln (4 July 1627). Inducted 18 July 1627 by Tempest Wood, V. of Lavington. [PD1627/21; IND/L 1, fo.79.]

Educated: Emmanuel College, Cambridge (matric. 1609; BA 1612–13; MA 1616).

Deacon: 25 September 1614; priest: 26 September 1614 (Peterborough). Formerly: Master of Boston GS, 1613–16. Signed BTs at Aslackby 1628–41. Still Vicar in 1662. Died *c*.1667. [Venn, *Alumni*; Longden iv. 125; LC 4, fo.54; BTs Aslackby; LC 5, fo.22; LCC Wills 1667/ii/769.]

Robert Clipsham

Instituted 14 February 1662/3 to vicarage of Aslackby. Patron: Ann Hughes of Lammas (Nf), widow, administratrix of Lewis Hughes, clerk, decd. [AC; IND/L 1, fo.156.]

Also: V. of Billingborough, 1662–1702 (*q.v.*).

Thomas Raven MA

Instituted 18 July 1702 to vicarage of Aslackby, on death of Robert Clipsham. Patron: John Garland, gent. [Reg. 35, fo. 87.]

Born *c*.1668 at Louth, son of William R. Educated: Louth GS and Magdalene College, Cambridge (matric. 1684; BA 1687–8; MA 1702). Deacon: 10 June 1688; priest: 26 May 1689 (Lincoln). Formerly: C. of Wyham, 1688; C. of Wainfleet, 1689. Also: R. of South Ormsby, 1695. Resident at Aslackby but not in the Vicarage 'because it is too small, & unhealthy on account of the water under ground'; signed BTs 1703–20. Died 23 March 1720/1, aged 52; buried at Aslackby (MI). [Venn, *Alumni*; Reg. 34, fos 104v, 108v; *Speculum*, 6; BTs Aslackby; *Monson*, 8.]

Charles Bywater MA

Instituted 10 July 1721 to vicarage of Aslackby, on death of Thomas Raven. Patron: Daniel Douglas, gent. [Reg. 37, p.120.]

Born *c*.1697 at Chapeltown near Sheffield, son of Matthew B., currier. Educated: Leeds School and St John's College, Cambridge (matric. 1714; BA 1717–18). Deacon: 25 September 1720 (York); priest: 8 July 1721 (Lincoln). Signed BTs 1722–4, 1733–51. Died 9 November 1751, aged 55; buried at Aslackby (MI). [Venn, *Alumni*; *York Ordinations 1700–1749*, 11; Reg. 37, p.120; BTs Aslackby; *Monson*, 9; PR Aslackby.]

John Wheatley BA

Instituted 13 January 1752 to vicarage of Aslackby, on death of Charles Bywater. Patron: Michael Barstow of Wakefield, gent. [Reg. 38, p.506.]

Born *c*.1725 at Wakefield; son of Thomas W. Educated: Rotherham School and Christ's College, Cambridge (matric. 1744; BA 1748; MA 1753). Deacon: 25 September 1748; priest: 10 June 1750 (York). Formerly: C. of Rawmarsh (YWR), 1749. Non-resident at Aslackby: lived at Treeton nr Rotherham (YWR). Also: Chaplain to Duchess of Hamilton; R. of Claxby by Normanby, 1758–94. Died at Treeton, 10 April 1794, aged 68. [Venn, *Alumni*; Peile ii. 246; LC 31, p.75; *York Ordinations 1700–1749*, 70; *York Ordinations 1750–1799*, 109; *GM* 64 (1794), 387.]

Francis Barstow MA

Instituted 21 September 1794 to vicarage of Aslackby, on death of John Wheatley. Patron: Francis Barstow himself. [Reg. 39, p.597.]

Baptised 1 February 1749/50 at All Saints, Wakefield; son of Jeremiah Barstow. Educated: Emmanuel College, Cambridge (matric. 1768; BA 1772; MA 1775). Deacon: 29 September

1778 (Rochester); priest: 21 September 1794 (Lincoln). Resigned 2 November 1797. Latterly of Seale Bar Hall, near Otley. Died 1832 (aged 83). [WYAS, PR Wakefield All Saints; Venn, *Alumni*; CCED; Reg. 39, pp. 596, 644; *GM* 102 (1832), 651.]

Joseph Barwis

Instituted 6 June 1798 by collation to vicarage of Aslackby, on resignation of Francis Barstow. Patron: Bishop of Lincoln for this turn, by lapse. [Reg. 39, p.652.]

Deacon: 13 July 1786; priest: 22 July 1787 (Carlisle). Formerly: C. of Bolton, 1786–90; schoolmaster at Market Deeping, *c*.1792–8; C. of Market Deeping, 1797–8. Died 3 April 1828, aged 65 (MI); buried at Aslackby. [CCED; *Flinders* ii. 112–13; Reg. 39, p.636; *Monson*, 9; PR Aslackby.]

Richard Lee SCL

Instituted 15 March 1829 to vicarage of Aslackby, on death of Joseph Barwise. Patron: Francis Barstow of Scale Bar Park (Yorkshire), clerk. [Reg. 40, p.367.]

Born *c*.1802 at Leeds, son of Thomas L., gent. Educated: Lincoln College, Oxford (matric. 1820; BA 1830; MA 1840). Deacon: 21 December 1828; priest: 15 March 1829 (Lincoln). Married (23 January 1832) Charlotte Longton at St Saviour's, Southwark. Afterwards: R. of Darley (Db), 1838–47; R. of Stepney (Mx), 1847–69. Died 6 August 1869. [Foster, *Alumni*; OR 1, pp. 33, 35; LMA, PR Southwark St Saviour.]

William Job Charlton Staunton MA

Instituted 12 October 1838 to vicarage of Aslackby, on cession of Richard Lee. Patron: Richard Lee, himself. [Reg. 40, p.461.]

Born 16 July 1802; son of Revd John Aspinshaw of Calverton (Nt), who changed his name to Staunton in 1807 on inheriting the estate of Staunton (Nt). Educated: Eton College and Magdalen College, Oxford (matric. 1821; BA 1827; MA 1828). Deacon: 22 July 1827 (York); priest: 1 June 1828 (London for York). Married (3 March 1829) Isabella, daughter of George Gordon, Dean of Lincoln. Formerly: C. of Elton, 1827; R. of Matlock (Db), 1836–8 (Patron: George Gordon, Dean of Lincoln). Died 10 April 1840 at Aslackby; buried at Staunton (MI). [Burke, *Landed Gentry* (18th edn) ii. 585; *York Ordinations 1800–1849*, 174; *Eton School Lists*, 85; Foster, *Alumni*; PR Lincoln St Mary Magdalene.]

William Gurden Moore MA

Instituted 13 May 1840 to vicarage of Aslackby, on death of Job Charlton Staunton. Patron: John Barstow of Guiseley (Yorks.), esquire. [Reg. 40, p.470.]

Baptised at St Peter at Arches, Lincoln, 24 February 1794; son of George M. Educated: Corpus Christi College, Cambridge (matric. 1812; BA 1816; MA 1834). Deacon: 1817 (Exeter for York); priest: 1819 (Chester for York). Formerly: C. of North Muskham (Nt), 1817; R. of West Barkwith, 1832–40; V. of Stixwould, 1833–9. Resident at Aslackby Vicarage (1842); non-resident on account of ill-health, 1845–50. Author: *A Dream of Life, or, Augustine and Geraldine: a Poem* (1837). Died at Kensington, 30 March 1850 (aged 55). [PR Lincoln St Peter at Arches; Venn, *Alumni*; *York Ordinations 1800–1849*, 132; Census Returns 1841; White, *Lincolnshire* (1842), 729; NRL 9/57, 13/36; *GM* 187 (1850), 549.]

Edmund Alderson BA

Instituted 11 July 1850 to vicarage of Aslackby, on death of William Gurden Moore. Patron: John Barstow gent., Margaret Barstow widow and Joseph Whitehead farmer, Trustees under the will of John Barstow. [Reg. 40, p.527.]

Born *c*.1808; son of John Alderson, Curate of Blyton. Educated: St John's College, Cambridge (matric. 1827; BA 1831). Deacon: 1832; priest: 1833 (Chester). Formerly: C. of Luddington, 1834; C. of Epworth, 1839; C. of Aslackby, 1845; C. of West Halton, 1846. Resided at Aslackby Vicarage. Died 30 April 1873 at Aslackby. [Venn, *Alumni*; CCED; CR 2, pp. 94, 215; CR 3, pp. 69(2)v, 87; White, *Lincolnshire* (1856), 705; Census Returns 1861; *Probate Calendar* 1873.]

John Christopherson BA

Instituted 28 November 1873 to vicarage of Aslackby, on death of Edmund Alderson. Patron: John Barstow of Greengates near Otley (Yorkshire), esquire, surviving trustee under the will of John Barstow decd. [Reg. 41, p.423.]

Born 9 December 1816, baptised at Liverpool St Mark, 13 November 1817; son of John C. of Liverpool, merchant. Educated: Sedbergh School and Queens' College, Cambridge (matric. 1835; BA 1839). Deacon: 25 July 1841; priest: 10 July 1842 (Worcester). Formerly: C. of Knowle (Wa), 1847–9; C. of St Chad, Lichfield, 1851–65; Secretary of Society for the Evangelisation of the Jews, 1868–75. Resigned Aslackby 5 April 1876 (accepted 7 April 1876). Retired to Knowle. Died 9 January 1894; buried at Knowle, 11 January 1894. [Liverpool RO, PR Liverpool St Mark; *Sedbergh Register*, 190; Venn, *Alumni*; *Eccles. Gazette*, 10 August 1841, 12 July 1842; RES 247/59; *Probate Calendar*; Warwicks RO, PR Knowle.]

John Smithson Barstow MA

Instituted 7 July 1876 to vicarage of Aslackby, on resignation of John Christopherson. Patron: John Barstow, as above. [Reg. 41, p.532.]

Born *c*.1846 at Bramhope (Yorks); son of John B., gent. Educated: Leeds GS (1860); Queen's College, Oxford (matric. 1866; BA 1873; MA 1873); Scholae Cancellarii, Lincoln (Trinity 1874). Deacon: 20 December 1874 (Lincoln); priest: 7 November 1875 (Nottingham for Lincoln). Formerly C. of Freiston w. Butterwick, 1874–6. Married (1 February 1882) at All Souls, Hampstead, Elizabeth Charlotte, dau. of John George Coupland, gent. (and sister of R. S. Coupland, below). Died 12 March 1906 at Aslackby, aged 60. [*Leeds GS Admission Books*, 156; Foster, *Alumni*; LCL, LTC 1, no.10; OR 2, pp. 22, 25; *Crockford* (1878); LMA, PR Hampstead All Souls; *LDC* (1907), 136.]

Robert Stanley Coupland

Instituted 12 June 1906 to vicarage of Aslackby, on death of John Smithson Barstow. Patron: Elizabeth Charlotte Barstow of Aslackby, widow. [Reg. 42, p.548.]

Baptised 10 June 1855 at Freiston; son of John George C., gent. Educated: Scholae Cancellarii, Lincoln (1881). Deacon: 20 May 1883; priest: 8 June 1884 (Lincoln). Formerly: C. of Lincoln St Swithin, 1883–4 and 1890–1; UMCA Missionary at Misozwe, Usambara (East Africa), 1884–8 and 1896–9; C. of All Saints, Mile End New Town, 1891–4; C. of St John, Stamford Hill, 1895–6; C. of Willingale-Doe, 1901–2; C. of Sprowston, 1902–4;

C. of Caistor, 1904–6. Resided at Aslackby Vicarage. Resigned 29 January 1934. Died 15 April 1934, aged 79. [PR Freiston; LCL, LTC 1, no.145; OR 2, pp. 55, 60; *Crockford* (1909); Kelly, *Lincolnshire* (1913), 44; RES 1934/1; *LDC* (1935), 163.]

The Rectory of Kirkby Underwood was united to the Vicarage of Aslackby by Order in Council dated 22 March 1928. [Reg. 43, p.429.]

John Smithson Barstow MA BD

Instituted 29 March 1934 to united benefice of Aslackby with Kirkby Underwood, on resignation of Robert Stanley Coupland (Aslackby) and of Edward Michael Bland (Kirkby Underwood). Patron: John Smithson Barstow himself, for this turn. [Reg. 43, p.541.]

Born 1882 at Aslackby; son of Revd John Smithson Barstow (above). Educated: St John's Hall, Durham (BA 1913; MA 1917; BD 1926). Deacon: 1913 (Southwell); priest 1916 (York). Formerly: C. of Pleasley Hill, 1913–14; served in Royal Fleet Auxiliary, 1914–16; C. of St Andrew, Drypool, Hull, 1916–20; R. of Kirkby Underwood, 1920–2 (*q.v.*); R. of Somerby with Great Humby. 1922–34. Resided at Aslackby Vicarage. Afterwards: R. of Woolsthorpe, 1949–59. Latterly of West End, Harlaxton. Died 24 October 1961 at Grantham Hospital. [Census Returns 1901; *LDC* (1944), 44; *Crockford* (1961–2); *Probate Calendar* 1961.]

Arthur Mander Dutton

Instituted 8 July 1949 to united benefice of Aslackby with Kirkby Underwood, on cession of John Smithson Barstow. Patron: John Smithson Barstow of Woolsthorpe Rectory (Li), clerk in holy orders, for this turn. [Reg. 44, p.108.]

Born 17 August 1910 at Darlaston (St); son of Benjamin D. Educated: Burgh Missionary College (1932); St Aidan's College, Birkenhead (1937); University of Durham (1936). Deacon: 1939; priest: 1940 (Sheffield). Formerly: C. of Anston (YWR), 1939–41; of Blakenall Heath (St), 1941–2; of Cannock, 1942–4; V. of Buckminster with Sewstern (Le), 1944–8; V. of St John Divine, Leicester, 1948–9. Resided at Aslackby Vicarage. Afterwards: R. of Baxterley, 1952–5; V. of Merevale, 1952–5; R. of Newington Bagpath with Kingscote, 1955–8; R. of Nympsfield, 1955–8. At St Chad's School, Whitchurch Road, Wellington (Sa), 1961. V. of Ipstones, 1962–3. Retired 1963. Latterly of Greaves Bungalow, Draycott-in-the-Clay, Derby. Died April 1995. [GRO, Death Index; *Crockford* (1961–2, 1989–90); *LDC* (1950), 49.]

Denys Penkivil King MA

Instituted 29 July 1953 to united benefice of Aslackby with Kirkby Underwood, on cession of Arthur Mander Dutton. Patron: Gilbert James Heathcote Drummond Willoughby, Earl of Ancaster, of Swinstead Hall near Grantham, for this turn. [Reg. 44, p.180.]

Born 3 October 1899 at Pendleton (La); son of John Edward K., schoolmaster (later Head Master of Clifton College). Educated: Clifton College (1910–18) and Trinity College, Oxford (BA 1922; MA 1925); Wells Theological College (1922). Deacon: 1923; priest: 1924 (Wakefield). Formerly: C. of St John, Wakefield, 1923–6; Missioner, Trinity College

Mission, Stratford, 1926–34; PC of St Michael, Castleford, 1934–9; R. of Grasmere, 1939–45; V. of Holy Trinity, Millhouses, 1945–7; Asst to Education Secretary, SPCK, 1948–51; C. of St Nicholas, Lincoln, 1951–3. Resided at Aslackby Vicarage. Afterwards: R. of East Ilsley (Brk), 1958–70; RD of Newbury, 1966–70. Retired 1970; lived at 15 St George's Road, Twickenham. Died 15 March 1987. [GRO, Death Index; Census Returns 1901 (Pendleton), 1911 (Clifton); *Clifton College Register*, 451; *Crockford* (1980–2); *LDC* (1957), 51; *The Times*, 20 March 1987.]

Kenneth Thomas Street MA

Instituted 31 January 1959 to united benefice of Aslackby with Kirkby Underwood, on cession of Denys Penkivil King. Patron: Revd John Smithson Barstow of Woolsthorpe Rectory (Li), clerk in holy orders, for this turn. [Reg. 44, p.265.]

Born 18 April 1905 at Cookham (Brk); son of Thomas S., gardener. Educated: University of Durham (LTh 1930; BA 1940; MA 1955); St Augustine's College, Canterbury (1926). Deacon: 1930; priest: 1931 (Southwark). Formerly: C. of St Luke, Well Hall, Eltham, 1930–4; of St Mary, Wimbledon, 1934–7; P-in-C of Copper Belt (Northern Rhodesia), 1937–9; Acting C. of St Margaret, Durham, 1940–4; R. of Navenby, 1944–55; of Skinnand, 1950–5; Chaplain, Wellingore Open Prison, 1953–4; CF 1955–9. Retired 1983. Latterly at 4 Woodside East, Northorpe, Gainsborough. Died August 1985. [GRO, Death Index; Census Returns 1911 (Cookham); *Crockford* (1980–2, 1985–6).]

BILLINGBOROUGH

The church of Billingborough was granted by Roger Burnel to Sempringham Priory by *c*.1194 when it was confirmed to them by Bishop Hugh of Avalon. A vicarage, consisting of the whole altarage and the land of the church, was ordained before 1218. Sempringham presented to the vicarage until the Dissolution, after which the patronage passed to the Earls of Lincoln, who held it until the middle of the eighteenth century when they sold it to the Fortescue family. Successive Earls Fortescue continued to present until 1885. In 1890 Viscount Ebrington, son and heir of Earl Fortescue, transferred the patronage of Billingborough and Sempringham to the Crown, in exchange for the advowson of Exmoor. The living remained in the gift of the Crown in 1965. [*EEA* iv. no.177; *Acta of Hugh of Wells*, no.84; *London Gazette* (26023), 14 February 1890; *LDC* (1965), 66–7.]

Robert of Owmby chaplain

Instituted before 15 February 1217/18 to vicarage of Billingborough, newly ordained. Patron: Prior and Convent of Sempringham. [*Acta of Hugh of Wells*, no.84.]

Thomas de Horbeling chaplain

Instituted in the seventeenth pontifical year of Bishop Robert Grosseteste (17 June 1251/16 June 1252) to vicarage of Billingborough. Patron: Prior and Convent of Sempringham. [Hoskin no.512.]

William
Instituted before 1261/2. [*Rot. Gravesend*, 10.]

M. William de Greyby deacon
Instituted in the fourth pontifical year of Bishop Richard Gravesend (3 November 1261/2 November 1262) to vicarage of Billingborough, on death of William. Patron: Prior and Convent of Sempringham. [*Rot. Gravesend*, 10.]

M. Richard de Wylugby clerk in minor orders
Instituted 22 December 1296 to vicarage of Billingborough, on death of M. William de Greyby. Patron: Prior and Convent of Sempringham. [*Reg. Sutton* i. 216.]

Deacon: 22 December 1296 (Lincoln). Afterwards: R. of a mediety of Kirkby Underwood, 1304 (*q.v.*). [*Reg. Sutton* vii. 88.]

Henry de Carleby priest
Instituted 22 February 1304 to vicarage of Billingborough, on institution of M. Richard [de Wilugby] to mediety of church of Kirkby Underwood. Patron: Prior and Convent of Sempringham. [Reg. 2, fo.9v.]

John de Horblyng chaplain
Instituted 28 September 1317 to vicarage of Billingborough (having been granted the benefice *in commendam* 8 April 1317), on death of Henry de Carleby. Patron: Prior and Convent of Sempringham. [Reg. 2, fos 68, 337v; *Reg. Burghersh* iii. no.1652.]

Appointed a penitentiary for deanery of Aveland, 9 April 1321. Commissions to audit accounts of co-adjutor of Simon, R. of Hacconby, and of wardens of goods assigned to fabric of church of Silk Willoughby, 14 May 1321. Commissions to carry out testamentary business, May 1321. A commission by Bishop Dalderby to audit the churchwardens' accounts of Walcot was revoked, *c.*1326. [Reg. 5, fos 278v, 282; *Reg. Burghersh* iii. nos 1652, 1657, 1854.]

John Payn
Instituted before 5 August 1330. [*Reg. Burghersh* iii. no.1875.]

Commissions to carry out testamentary business, 5 August 1330, 13 March 1330/1. Afterwards: V. of Stow-by-Threckingham, 1346–9. [*Reg. Burghersh* iii. nos 1875, 1882.]

William son of Alan Wade de Horbelyng
Instituted 29 September 1346 to vicarage of Billingborough, on resignation of John Payn (by exchange with vicarage of Stow-by-Threckingham). Patron: Prior and Convent of Sempringham. [Reg. 6, fo.24.]

Formerly: V. of Stow-by-Threckingham 1337–46 (*q.v.*).

John de Stowe priest
Instituted 24 June 1366 to vicarage of Billingborough, on death of William Wade. Patron: Prior and Convent of Sempringham. [Reg. 10, fo.14.]

Simon de Rydesdale de Knaptoft

Instituted before 2 November 1373. [Reg. 10, fo.59v.]

Afterwards: V. of Laughton-by-Folkingham, 1373–4 (*q.v.*).

John de Loghton de Repynghale

Instituted 2 November 1373 to vicarage of Billingborough, on resignation of Simon de Rydesdale de Knaptoft (by exchange with vicarage of Laughton-by-Folkingham). Patron: Prior and Convent of Sempringham. [Reg. 10, fo.59v.]

Formerly: V. of Laughton-by-Folkingham, 1363–73 (*q.v.*). Assessed for poll-tax, 1377, 1381. Afterwards: R. of Harston (Le), 1389. [*Clerical Poll-Taxes*, nos 695, 1340, 1929; Hamilton Thompson, *Leicester Abbey*, 143.]

Geoffrey Canell priest

Instituted 8 August 1389 to vicarage of Billingborough, on resignation of John Loughton (by exchange with church of Harston). Patron: Prior and Convent of Sempringham. [Reg. 11, fo.40.]

Formerly: R. of Harston (Le), by 1377, until 1389. Died 1390. Will dated 13 April ('to be buried in the churchyard of St Andrew, Billingborough'), proved 28 June 1390. [Hamilton Thompson, *Leicester Abbey*, 143; *Clerical Poll-Taxes*, no.173; Reg. 12, fo.367; *Early Lincoln Wills*, 39.]

John son of Thomas de Thersway priest

Instituted 2 August 1390 to vicarage of Billingborough (cause of vacancy not stated). Patron: Prior and Convent of Sempringham. [Reg. 11, fo.46.]

John Bramcote chaplain

Instituted 13 April 1403 to vicarage of Billingborough (cause of vacancy not stated). Patron: Prior and Convent of Sempringham. [Reg. 13, fo.156v.]

Afterwards: R. of Nuthall (Nt), 1425; vacated before January 1434/5. [Train, *Central Notts Clergy*, 51.]

Richard Castelacre

Instituted 1 June 1425 to vicarage of Billingborough, on resignation of John Bramcote (by exchange with church of Nuthall). Patron: Prior and Convent of Sempringham. [*Reg. Fleming* i. no.253; *Reg. Fleming* ii. no.510.]

Priest: before 30 June 1416. Formerly: R. of Nuthall (Nt), 1416–25. [Train, *Central Notts Clergy*, 51.]

Robert Combe

Instituted before 23 May 1486. [Reg. 22, fo.139.]

William Poole

Instituted 23 May 1486 to vicarage of Billingborough, on death of Robert Combe. Patron: Prior and Convent of Sempringham. [Reg. 22, fo.139.]

Henry Hyne chaplain
Instituted 30 December 1506 to vicarage of Billingborough, on death of last incumbent. Patron: Prior and Convent of Sempringham. [Reg. 23, fo.117v.]

Richard White chaplain
Instituted 25 October 1508 to vicarage of church of St Andrew, Billingborough, on death of Henry Hynde. Patron: Prior and Convent of Sempringham. [Reg. 23, fo.133.]

Afterwards: R. of Stain, 1523–32. Died before 27 July 1532. [Reg. 27, fos 26, 54.]

Robert Lytherland priest
Instituted 30 June 1523 to vicarage of Billingborough, on resignation of Richard White. Patron: Prior and Convent of Sempringham. Note that an annual pension of 26s 8d was reserved to Richard White for life from the fruits of the vicarage. [Reg. 27, fo.26.]

Assessed for subsidy (£6) in 1526, when the pension to Richard White was still payable and had increased to 43s 4d. Assessed for *Valor Ecclesiasticus*, 1535. Died *c*.1538; probate inventory (n.d.) includes 'iij geese, j gander, xij hennys, iv capons, xij hyves of bees'. [*Subsidy*, 57; *Valor*, iv. 106; INV 7/4.]

William Tyngill
Instituted 3 April 1539 to vicarage of Billingborough, on death of last incumbent. Patron: King Henry VIII. [Reg. 27, fo.69.]

John Jackson
Instituted 26 November 1546 to vicarage of Billingborough, on death of last incumbent. Patron: King Henry VIII. [Reg. 27, fo.88.]

Born *c*.1495. Education: 'knows but little Latin; but little versed in sacred learning'. Priest: 1520 (Suffragan for York). Witnessed will as Vicar, 12 March 1552/3. Appears to have been deprived, *c*.1554; restored after 1558 (see below). Resident (1576): signed BTs 1562–6; witnessed wills as Vicar, 1562–7. Buried at Billingborough, 9 December 1576. [*Bishop Cooper*, 209; LCC Wills 1551–2/63; LCC Wills 1562/200; 1567/39, 274; BTs Billingborough; PR Billingborough; LCC Admons Aii, 230.]

Henry Wilson
Instituted *c*.1554 (compounded for first-fruits, 1 June 1554). [FL.h.12, 243.]

Anthony Langton
Occurs as Vicar, 1557.

Witnessed will as Vicar, 7 January 1556/7. [LCC Wills 1553–6/191.]

John Jackson
Restored after 1558 (see above).

John White
Instituted 20 May 1577 to vicarage of Billingborough, on death of John

Jackson. Patron: Robert Buckbere, by reason of a grant of next presentation made to him (13 February 1576/7) by Edward, Earl of Lincoln. [*Bishop
Cooper*, 19; PD 1577/3.]

Born *c*.1543. Education: 'knows Latin competently; and is to the same extent versed
in sacred learning'; 'bred in the schools'. Priest: 30 June 1568 or 1569 (Peterborough).
Formerly: V. of Hacconby, 1570–7 (*q.v.*). Signed BTs at Billingborough, 1577–91.
Assessed in Subsidy of Armour 1590. Buried at Billingborough, 24 June 1592. Probate
inventory dated 8 July 1592 ('his books, £3 6s 8d'). Will (LCC). [*Bishop Cooper*, 207,
220; *State of the Church*, 73, 148; BTs Billingborough; PR Billingborough; LCC Wills
1592/236; INV 82/353.]

Anthony Hill MA

Instituted 2 August 1592 to vicarage of Billingborough, on death of last
incumbent. Patron: Henry Fynes, Earl of Lincoln (13 July 1592). [BC; PD
1592/58.]

Educated: Christ's College, Cambridge (matric. 1576; BA 1579–80). Deacon and priest:
27 October 1580 (Lincoln). Formerly: R. of Blyborough, 1582–92 (*q.v.*). Resident at
Billingborough (1614): had no other benefice in England. Signed BTs at Billingborough
1592–1620. Buried at Billingborough, 22 March 1620/1. [Venn, *Alumni*; *Bishop Cooper*,
93; *State of the Church*, 96, 155; LC 4, fo.72; BTs Billingborough; PR Billingborough.]

William Carter

Instituted 11 April 1621 to vicarage of Billingborough. Patron: Thomas
Grene. [BC.]

Educated: Magdalene College, Cambridge (matric. 1614; BA 1617–18). Deacon: 1 March
1617; priest: 31 May 1618 (Peterborough). Signed BTs at Billingborough 1622–9. Afterwards: R. of Belton by Grantham, 1632–70; buried there, 5 November 1670. Will (LCC).
Probate inventory dated 9 November 1670 ('Bookes in the Studdie, £1 10s 0d'). [Venn,
Alumni; LC 5, fo.39; BTs Billingborough; PR Belton by Grantham; LCC Wills 1670/
ii/524.]

James Morton MA

Instituted 24 September 1632 to vicarage of Billingborough, on cession of
William Carter. Patron: Theophilus, Earl of Lincoln (17 September 1632).
[BC; PD 1632/18.]

Educated: Corpus Christi College, Cambridge (MA). Deacon: 21 September 1628; priest:
22 September 1628 (Peterborough). Signed BTs at Billingborough 1632–41. Also: V. of
Horbling, 1651–63. Perhaps ejected 1662. Buried at Billingborough, 9 November 1663
('late minester'). [Venn, *Alumni*; Longden ix. 271; *Calamy Revised*, 357; PR Billingborough.]

Robert Clipsham BA

Instituted 10 November 1662 to vicarage of Billingborough (cause of vacancy
not stated). Patron: Theophilus, Earl of Lincoln (4 November 1662). [Reg.
32, fo.22v; PD 1662/10.]

Born *c*.1640, son of Edward C., gent., of Braybrooke (Np). Educated: Bowden and Market
Harborough Schools and Caius College, Cambridge (matric. 1656–7; BA 1660–1; MA

1671). Priest: 30 March 1661/2 (Orkney). Also: V. of Horbling, 1662–3 (*q.v.*); V. of Aslackby, 1663–1702 (*q.v.*); Canon of Chichester and Prebendary of Somerley, 1681–1702. Buried at Billingborough, 7 February 1701/2. [Venn, *Alumni*; LC 14, p.1; *Le Neve Fasti: Chichester, 1541–1857*, 53; PR Billingborough.]

Robert Kelham BA

Instituted 1 June 1702 to vicarage of Billingborough, on death of Robert Clipsham. Patron: The Hon. Lady Vere Boothe, Samuel Rolle esquire and Hugh Fortescue esquire (7 May 1702). [Reg. 35, fo.86v; PD 1702/20.]

Born 23 January, baptised 6 February 1676/7 at Great Gonerby; son of Thomas K. Educated: Emmanuel College, Cambridge (matric. 1696; BA 1699–1700). Deacon: 26 May 1700; priest: 31 May 1702 (Lincoln). Formerly: C. of Evedon, 1700. Resided at Billingborough. Also: V. of Threckingham, 1703–52 (*q.v.*); Schoolmaster of Billingborough, 1704; Sequestrator of Walcot, 1721. Married (5 February 1709/10) at Sempringham, his cousin Mary, daughter and co-heir of John K. of Gonerby, esquire. Father of Robert K. (1717–1808), legal antiquary. Died 23 April 1752, aged 75 (MI); buried at Billingborough. Will (PCC) dated 23 February 1749, proved 9 May 1752. [PR Great Gonerby; Burke, *Landed Gentry* (1894), 1095; Venn, *Alumni*; Reg. 35, fos 65, 86; *Speculum*, 16; SUB V/6, fo.73; LC 18B, p.197; PR Sempringham; 'Kelham, Robert' in *ODNB*; *Monson*, 41; PR Billingborough; PRO, PROB 11/794/392.]

John Towers

Instituted 3 August 1752 to vicarage of Billingborough, on death of Robert Kelham. Patron: Matthew, Lord Fortescue. [Reg. 38, p.514.]

Born *c.*1719 in the Isle of Walney; son of James T., husbandman. Educated: Kendal and Urswick Schools and St John's College, Cambridge (matric. 1739; BA 1743–4). Deacon: 25 September 1743; priest: 9 June 1745 (Lincoln). Formerly: C. of Osbournby, 1743; of Swaton cum Spanby, 1745. Resident (1768, 1778). Also: V. of Threckingham, 1759–1802 (*q.v.*). Died 3 November 1802, aged 82; buried at Billingborough (MI). [Venn, *Alumni*; *St John's College Admissions* iii. 96; Reg. 38, pp. 434, 457; LC 18B, p.199; LC 32, p.75; *Monson*, 41; PR Billingborough.]

Thomas Latham MA

Instituted 20 January 1803 to vicarage of Billingborough, on death of John Towers. Patron: Hugh, Earl Fortescue (6 January 1803). [Reg. 40, p.48; PD 159/49.]

Baptised 13 January 1771 at Waltham-on-the-Wolds (Le); son of Charles L., gent. Educated: Brasenose College, Oxford (matric. 1788; BA 1793; MA 1794). Deacon: 1 December 1793; priest: 31 May 1795 (Lincoln). Formerly: C. of Coston (Le), 1793. Also: C. of Threckingham, 1814; V. of Sempringham, 1826–46 (*q.v.*). Licence for non-residence (1804), on account of house being unfit. Resided subsequently at Billingborough Vicarage. Died 11 May 1846, aged 76; buried at Billingborough (MI). [IGI; Foster, *Alumni*; Reg. 39, pp. 580–1, 605; CR 1, p.42; NRL 1804/53; Census Returns 1841; White, *Lincolnshire* (1842), 730; PR Billingborough.]

William Moxon Mann

Instituted 18 July 1846 to vicarage of Billingborough, on death of Thomas Latham. Patron: Hugh, Earl Fortescue. [Reg. 40, p.511.]

Baptised 14 June 1811 at St Mary, Lambeth; son of Charles M. Educated: Clare Hall, Cambridge (matric. 1830; BA 1834). Deacon: 1840; priest: 19 September 1841 (Carlisle). Formerly: PC of Thornthwaite (Cu), 1840–4; British Chaplain at Coblenz, 1844--6. Resided at Billingborough; built new Vicarage House in 1847–8 (architect, Thomas Pilkinton of Bourne). Resigned Billingborough 1 March 1855. Afterwards: V. of Tideswell (Db), 1855–8; C. of Bobbington (St), 1872–3. Married (23 April 1844) at Eccleston (Chs), Clara, daughter of Digby Thomas Carpenter of Hawke House, Sunbury (Mx) esquire (niece of Lord Stanley). Disappears from *Clergy List* 1877. His widow Clara died 13 August 1891. [LMA, PR Lambeth St Mary; Venn, *Alumni*; *Carlisle Journal*, 25 September 1841; Census Returns 1851; MGA 316; *Bonney's Church Notes*, 223; RES 244/1; *GM* (June 1844), 645; Census Returns 1871 (Bobbington); *Probate Calendar* 1891.]

John Kynaston MA

Instituted 17 May 1855 to vicarage of Billingborough, on resignation of William Moxon Mann. Patron: Hugh, Earl Fortescue. [Reg. 40, p.570.]

Born *c*.1803 at Wem (Sa); son of John Kynaston. Educated: Christ Church, Oxford (matric. 1822; BA 1826; MA 1829). Deacon: 21 May 1826; priest: 10 June 1827 (Lichfield). Formerly: C. of Broughton and Clive (Sa), 1827–9; Master of Market Drayton Free Grammar School, 1829; PC of Child's Ercall (Sa), 1829–37; V. of Tideswell (Db), 1837–55. Resided at Billingborough Vicarage. Died 4 August 1885 at Billingborough, aged 85; buried at Billingborough (MI). [Foster, *Alumni*; CCED; *Crockford* (1881); White, *Lincolnshire* (1856), 706; Census Returns 1861; PR Billingborough; *LDC* (1886), 97; *Probate Calendar* 1885.]

John Albert Greaves MA

Instituted 25 November 1885 to vicarage of Billingborough, on death of John Kynaston. Patron: Hugh, Earl Fortescue. [Reg. 42, p.231.]

Born *c*.1830; son of Thomas G. of Haversham (Bk), gent. Educated: Lincoln College, Oxford (matric. 1848; BA 1851; MA 1854). Deacon: 1852; priest: 1853 (Peterborough). Formerly: C. of Shearsby in Knaptoft (Le), 1852–5; of Bampton (Ox), 1855–7; in New South Wales, 1857–67; C. of Cosgrove, 1867–70; of Swinford (Le), 1870–1; V. of Towcester (Np), 1871–3; R. of Ivy Depôt, Virginia (USA), 1873–85; V. of Hellidon with Catesby (Np), 1885. Resided at Billingborough. Afterwards: R. of Great Leighs (Ess), 1891–3. Died 1 June 1893 at Hatfield Peverel (Ess). [Foster, *Alumni*; Longden vi. 33–5; *Crockford* (1885); Census Returns 1891; *Probate Calendar* 1893.]

William Mathew Thomas MA

Instituted 17 September 1891 to vicarage of Billingborough, on cession of John Albert Greaves. Patron: Queen Victoria. [Reg. 42, p.336.]

Baptised 13 March 1831 at Montgomery; son of Thomas T., Excise Officer. Educated: St John's College, Cambridge (matric. 1855; BA 1859; MA 1875). Deacon: 1859; priest: 1861 (Gloucester and Bristol). Formerly: C. of Alvington, 1859–63; of Tanfield, 1863–73; of St Andrew, Hove, 1873–4; of Esher, 1874–5; of Boscombe, 1875–91. Resided at Billingborough Vicarage. Author: *Practical Sermons* (1910). 'Old Mr Thomas, by his inefficiency, has emptied the Church, filled the chapels, & helped the Wesleyans to build a big new one!' (Bishop Hicks 1911). Died 6 July 1911 at Bencraig, King's Road, West Swanage (Do), aged 79. [Venn, *Alumni*; *Crockford* (1908); *Hicks Diaries*, no.74; *Probate Calendar* 1911; *LDC* (1912), 189.]

Charles Richard Thorold Winckley MA

Instituted 4 November 1911 to vicarage of Billingborough, on resignation [*sic*] of William Matthew Thomas. Patron: King George V. [Reg. 43, p.20.]

Baptised 11 April 1855; son of William W. of Harrow-on-the-Hill (FSA), bookseller. Educated: Aldenham School and St John's College, Cambridge (matric. 1873; BA 1877; MA 1880). Deacon: 1878; priest: 1879 (St Albans). Formerly: C. of Stansted Mount-fitchet (Ess), 1878–81; of St Matthias, Torquay, 1881–2; of Isleworth (Mx), 1882–5; Assistant Chaplain at Embassy Church, Paris, 1885–9; in Bengal, 1889–1909. Resided at Billingborough Vicarage. Married (16 January 1889) Amy, daughter of W. Underwood of St Cloud (France). Father of Charles Reginald W. (killed in action 20 July 1916). Resigned 11 October 1921. Latterly of Emsdale, 11 Vicarage Road, Lillington (Wa). Died 12 January 1941; buried at Lillington (MI). [Venn, *Alumni*; Kelly, *Lincolnshire* (1913), 69; RES A/98; Billingborough War Memorial; *Probate Calendar* 1942.]

Thomas Church

Instituted 8 March 1922 to vicarage of Billingborough, on resignation of Charles Richard Thorold Winckley. Patron: King George V. [Reg. 43, p.255.]

Born *c*.1868 at Northampton. Educated: King's College, London (AKC 1896). Deacon: 1896; priest: 1897 (London). Formerly: C. of St Andrew, Haverstock Hill, 1896–8; of St James the Great, Derby, 1898–1900; V. of Lowdham (Nt), 1900–2; in Winchester Diocese, 1902–6; V. of Tuddenham St Martin, 1906–11; in Southwark Diocese, 1911–15; R. of Halton Holegate, 1915–19; of St Cuthbert, Bedford, 1919–22. Married (2 May 1900) at St James the Great, Derby, Anne Elizabeth Swingler. Resigned 8 March (accepted 10 April) 1926. Lived at Friern Lodge, Ridgeway Road, Redhill (Sr). Died 11 December 1937. [Census Returns 1901 (Lowdham); Train, *Central Notts Clergy* i. 99; *Crockford* (1932); RES 1926/3; *Probate Calendar* 1938.]

Harold Mart Porter

Instituted 27 May 1926 to vicarage of Billingborough, on resignation of Thomas Church. Patron: King George V. [Reg. 43, p.396.]

Born 10 January, baptised 10 May 1879 at Holy Trinity, Kilburn (Mx); son of Caleb P. of Oakland House, West End Lane, Kilburn, fruiterer and wine merchant. Educated: London College of Divinity (1902). Deacon: 1904; priest: 1905 (London). Formerly: C. of St John Evangelist, Kilburn, 1904–6; of St Peter, Upper Holloway, 1906–7; of St Stephen, Old Ford (Mx), 1907–10; of St Mary, Woodbridge (Sf), 1910–12; of Walesby, 1912–13; of Ulceby with Croxton, 1913–14; of Ingatestone with Buttsbury (Ess), 1914–17; in St Edmundsbury and Ipswich Diocese, 1917–19; C. of St John Baptist, Felixstowe, 1919–22; of Diss, 1922–6. Resided at Billingborough Vicarage. Afterwards: V. of Langton-by-Wragby, 1932–5. Latterly of 44 Church Lane, Whitton (Sf). Died 14 September 1935 at East Suffolk and Ipswich Hospital, Ipswich. [LMA, PR Kilburn Holy Trinity; Census Returns 1911 (Woodbridge); *Crockford* (1932, 1934); *Probate Calendar* 1935.]

Samuel Skelhorn

Instituted 12 August 1932 to vicarage of Billingborough, on cession of Harold Mart Porter. Patron: King George V. [Reg. 43, p.510.]

Born *c*.1870 in Manchester. Congregational Minister: at Tideswell (Db), 1901. Financial journalist (1911). Educated: King's College, London (AKC 1915); University of Durham (LTh 1917). Deacon: 1915; priest: 1916 (Chichester). Formerly: C. of Seaford, 1915–19;

of St Augustine, Bristol, 1919–21; V. of Great Wollaston with Middleton, 1921–8; at Yate, 1928–9; at Christ Church, Weston-super-Mare, 1930–2. Resided at Billingborough Vicarage. Afterwards: R. of Fishtoft, 1934–6; V. of Holy Trinity, Warrington, 1936–9; R. of Hathern (Le), 1939–45; V. of St Saviour, Brockley Rise, 1945–7. Latterly of 233 Nelson Road, Whitton, Twickenham (Mx). Died 26 April 1947. [Census Returns 1901 (Tideswell), 1911 (Barnes); *Crockford* (1934, 1947); *Probate Calendar* 1947.]

Robert Spencer Gerald Sampey BA

Instituted 26 February 1935 to vicarage of Billingborough, on cession of Samuel Skelhorn. Patron: King George V. [Reg. 43, p.553.]

Born 11 November 1874 at Castlerea, Roscommon (Ireland); son of Alexander William S. Educated: Trinity College, Dublin (BA 1902; Div. Test. 1903). Deacon: 1903; priest: 1904 (Rochester). Formerly: C. of St John, Woolwich, 1903–5; of Church of Annunciation, Chislehurst, 1905–12; V. of Christ Church, Shooter's Hill, 1912–20; Chaplain of Brook Hospital, 1913–20; C. of All Saints, Clapton, 1921–3; of St John, Walham Green, 1923–4; of St Matthew, Hammersmith, 1924–34. Married (11 October 1920) at St Jude, Kensington, Adelaide Helen Gwendoline Saunders, widow. Resided at Billingborough Vicarage. Resigned 10 January (accepted 1 February) 1949. Latterly of Washingborough Hall. Died 6 November 1951; buried at Billingborough (MI). [*Crockford* (1951–2); LMA, PR South Kensington St Jude; *LDC* (1944), 54; RES 1949/1; *Probate Calendar* 1952.]

Leslie Ronald Swingler

Instituted 13 May 1949 to vicarage of Billingborough, on resignation of Robert Spencer Gerald Sampey. Patron: King George VI. Note that on 11 April 1949, the Archbishop of Canterbury granted a dispensation enabling the said LRS to hold together the vicarage of Billingborough and the vicarage of Sempringham. [Reg. 44, p.105.]

Born 25 November 1912. Educated: Lichfield Theological College (1935). Deacon: 1938 (Grantham for Lincoln); priest: 1939 (Lincoln). Formerly: C. of Flixborough with Burton-on-Stather, 1938–42; V. of Whaplode, 1944–9. Resided at Billingborough Vicarage. Also: V. of Sempringham with Pointon, 1949–58 (*q.v.*). Afterwards: V. of St Faith, Lincoln, 1958–62; R. of Finmere with Mixbury (Ox), 1962–74; Canon of Christ Church, 1973; Oxford Diocesan Youth and Community Officer, 1974–7. Retired 1977. Latterly at 54 Folly Road, Wymondham (Nf). Died August 1993. [GRO, Death Index; *Crockford* (1980–2, 1989–90); *LDC* (1957), 55.]

Charles Francis Ward

Instituted 28 August 1958 to vicarage of Billingborough, on cession of Leslie Ronald Swingler. Patron: Queen Elizabeth II. Note that on 11 July 1958, the Archbishop of Canterbury granted a dispensation enabling the said CFW to hold together the vicarage of Billingborough and the vicarage of Sempringham. [Reg. 44, p.259.]

Born *c*.1907. Educated: Lincoln Theological College (1943). Deacon and priest: 1945 (Grimsby for Lincoln). Formerly: C. of St James, Louth, with Welton-le-Wold and Withcall, 1945–8; R. of Swaby with South Thoresby, 1948–58; C-in-C of Burwell with Walmsgate, 1956–8. Resided at Billingborough Vicarage. Also: V. of Sempringham, 1958–62 (*q.v.*). Died 17 December 1962; buried at Sempringham (MI). [GRO, Death Index; *Crockford* (1961–2); *Probate Calendar* 1963.]

Peter Brian Hearn
Instituted 19 March 1964 to vicarage of Billingborough, on death of Charles
Francis Ward. Patron: Queen Elizabeth II. Note that on 16 January 1964,
the Archbishop of Canterbury granted a dispensation enabling the said
PBH to hold together the vicarage of Billingborough and the vicarage of
Sempringham. [Reg. 44, p.358.]

Born 1931. Educated: St John's College, Durham (1952). Deacon: 1955; priest:
1956 (Lincoln). Formerly: C. of Frodingham, 1955–9; R. of Belton, 1959–64; PC of
Manthorpe with Londonthorpe, 1959–64. Resided at Billingborough Vicarage. Also: V. of
Sempringham, 1964–73 (*q.v.*). Afterwards: V. of Flixborough with Burton Stather, 1973–
96; RD of Manlake, 1987–93; Canon of Lincoln and Prebendary of Welton Brinkhall,
1992–2001. Retired 1996. At 7 St Andrew's Drive, Burton-upon-Stather. [*Crockford*
(1965–6, 1980–2, 2010–11).]

BOURNE

The church of Bourne formed part of the foundation endowment of Bourne
Abbey, given by Baldwin Fitz Gilbert in 1138. The gift was made to 'establish an abbot and canons in that church', indicating that the parish church
became the abbey church itself. A parochial altar in the nave enabled the
parishioners to attend services and a vicar, fed at the canons' table, provided
pastoral care in the town on behalf of the Abbot. The Abbey continued to
present to the vicarage until the Dissolution, after which the advowson passed
to the Crown. In the seventeenth century it came to the Browne family of
Stamford. Between 1660 and 1712 the vicarage was under sequestration and
the parish was served by curates. The advowson subsequently passed into
the possession of a succession of different owners. An attempt to acquire it
by the Church Association in 1910 led to a case of simony. The patronage
was transferred subsequently to the Diocesan Board of Patronage. [Stenton,
Facsimiles of Early Charters, 18–20; Dickinson, *Austin Canons*, 150; *Rot.
Welles* iii. 87; *LDC* (1965), 66–7.]

Geoffrey de Brunne chaplain
Instituted between 1223 and 1226 to vicarage of Bourne. Patron: Abbot and
Convent of Bourne. [*Rot. Welles* iii. 87; 'Rolls of Hugh of Wells', 173–5.]

Hugh de Brunna chaplain
Instituted in the twentieth pontifical year of Bishop Hugh of Wells (20
December 1228/19 December 1229) to vicarage of Bourne. Patron: Abbot
and Convent of Bourne. [*Rot. Welles* iii. 168.]

Ralph chaplain
Instituted in the fourth pontifical year of Bishop Robert Grosseteste (17 June

9. Aslackby: village and church from the south
Engraving, from a drawing by J. B. Topham, published 1833 (Lincoln Cathedral Library).

10. Bourne: Church of St Peter and St Paul, from the east. The building on the right, known as Abbey House, served as the Vicarage House in the mid nineteenth century. Engraving, from a drawing by T. Phillips, published 1809 (Lincoln Cathedral Library).

11. Osbournby: Church of St Peter and St Paul, 1906.
(Lincoln Cathedral Library, Flintham Collection)

12. Folkingham: Church of St Andrew, west front.
Engraving, from a drawing by R. L. Wright, published 1825
(Lincoln Cathedral Library).

13. Dembleby: Rectory House, south elevation
(Stephen Dawson of Spalding for James Tillard Bonner, 1862–3).
(Detail from Lincolnshire Archives, MGA 437.
With the permission of Lincolnshire Archives.)

14. Newton-by-Folkingham, Church of St Botolph: fragments of inscription commemorating rebuilding of chancel by William de Helmeswell in 1308 (*Anno Domini millesimo tricentesimo octavo Willelmus [de] Helmswell Rector Ecclesiae de Newton…*).
(Gordon Plumb)

15. Scott Willoughby: seal of Thomas Wymbyssh attached to presentation deed of John Warde, 1492.
(Detail from Lincolnshire Archives, PD 1492/60. With the permission of Lincolnshire Archives.)

16. Horbling, Church of St Andrew: font (15th century). On 28 December 1904 Arthur Michael Ramsey, future Archbishop of Canterbury, was baptised here by his grandfather, Revd Plumpton Stravenson Wilson (Vicar of Horbling, 1876–1909). In 1977 Ramsey visited the church, exclaiming 'Oh font, font, font; this is where my Christian life began'.

In the name of God Amen &c.

I Thomas palfryman of Haceby in y County
of Lincoln Clerk being of p'fict mind and
memory doe make this my last will & testam't
in manner as followeth.

First I bequeath my soul into y hands of Almighty
God who gave it and I commit my Body to y
ground from whence it came to be decently
buried in the Churchyard of Haceby by my
father and mother who lye near the south wall
of the Chancell of y sd Church of Haceby in sure
and certain hope of a glorious resurrection unto
eternall life through y alone merits of my dearest
Lord & Saviour Jesus Christ, who dyed for me
and rose againe to make me righteous.

Item I give unto my dear & loving wife Ann
palfryman fiftie pounds of lawfull English
money to be put out for her use within six months
after my decease. And my farther will and testam't
is, yt shee continue with my dear & loving son &
daughter Francis, & Christian Hopps, at y Rector
of Haceby, and they to allow her Dyet, Lodging,
fire, washing, Candle, & five pounds p annu of
lawfull English money towards the maintaining her
with convenient apparell, and if it should so fall
out yt y sd Ann palfryman shall think good at
any time to removue from her aforesd son and
daughter, yt then they doe allow her furniture for
one Chamber and fifteen pounds p annu during
y term of her naturall life. &c.

Item I give unto y sd Ann palfryman my wife one

17. Will of Thomas Palfreman, Rector of Haceby (1670).
(Detail from Lincolnshire Archives, Stow Wills 1669–71/345.
With the permission of Lincolnshire Archives.

1238/16 June 1239) to vicarage of Bourne. Patron: Abbot and Convent of Bourne. [Hoskin no.101.]

Peter chaplain
Instituted in the eighth pontifical year of Bishop Robert Grosseteste (17 June 1242/16 June 1243) to vicarage of Bourne. Patron: Abbot and Convent of Bourne. [Hoskin no.262.]

William de [*blank*] chaplain
Instituted in the thirteenth pontifical year of Bishop Robert Grosseteste (17 June 1247/16 June 1248) to vicarage of Bourne. Patron: Abbot and Convent of Bourne. [Hoskin no.390.]

Robert
Instituted before 16 January 1272/3. [*Rot. Gravesend*, 53.]

Adam de Brunna chaplain
Instituted 16 January 1273 to vicarage of Bourne, on death of Robert. Patron: Abbot and Convent of Bourne. [*Rot. Gravesend*, 53.]

Sampson de Wynton
Instituted before 28 December 1274. [*Rot. Gravesend*, 61.]

William de Hacunby priest
Instituted 28 December 1274 to vicarage of Bourne, on resignation of Sampson de Wynton. Patron: Abbot and Convent of Bourne. [*Rot. Gravesend*, 61.]

William de Hacumby
Instituted 16 October 1275 to vicarage of Bourne, on death of William. Patron: Abbot and Convent of Bourne. [*Rot. Gravesend*, 67.]

John de Wermington chaplain
Instituted 22 September 1293 to vicarage of Bourne, on death of William de Hacumby. Patron: Abbot and Convent of Bourne. [*Reg. Sutton* i. 178.]
Afterwards: V. of Barholm, 1311–28. [*Reg. Burghersh* i. no.213.]

Simon Wolwyn chaplain
Instituted 23 September 1311 to vicarage of Bourne, on institution of John de Wermington to vicarage of Barholm. Patron: Abbot and Convent of Bourne. [Reg. 2, fo.37.]

William de Eston iuxta Graham chaplain
Instituted 7 April 1316 to vicarage of Bourne, on resignation of Simon de Burgo. Patron: Abbot and Convent of Bourne. [Reg. 2, fo.58v.]

Commission to carry out testamentary business, 25 March 1321. [*Reg. Burghersh* iii. no.1641.]

John
Instituted before 13 July 1349. [Reg. 9, fo.61.]

Simon de Rihale priest
Instituted 13 July 1349 to vicarage of Bourne, on death of John. Patron: Abbot and Convent of Bourne. [Reg. 9, fo.61.]

Occurs as Vicar, 13 July 1372. Assessed for poll-tax 1377. [*CPR 1370–74*, 184; *Clerical Poll-Taxes*, no.701.]

Reginald Penne
Instituted by 1381.

Assessed for poll-tax 1381. [*Clerical Poll-Taxes*, nos 1322, 1911.]

Geoffrey
Instituted before 10 May 1415. [Reg. 14, fo.73v.]

Robert Wynter de Gretteford priest
Instituted 10 May 1415 to vicarage of Bourne, on death of Geoffrey. Patron: Abbot and Convent of Bourne. [Reg. 14, fo.73v.]

John Notman
Instituted before 8 January 1440/1. [Reg. 18, fo.84v.]

Thomas Playndamore priest
Instituted 8 January 1440/1 to vicarage of Bourne on resignation of John Notman. Patron: Abbot and Convent of Bourne. [Reg. 18, fo.84v.]

Nicholas Melton
Instituted before 24 June 1476. [Reg. 21, fo.13.]

Thomas Lyndesey priest
Instituted 24 June 1476 to vicarage of Bourne, on resignation of Nicholas Melton. Patron: Abbot and Convent of Bourne. [Reg. 21, fo.13.]

Richard Wynthorp
Instituted 5 May 1486 to vicarage of Bourne, on death of Thomas Lynsey. Patron: Abbot and Convent of Bourne. [Reg. 22, fo.139.]

Christopher Massyngberd priest
Instituted 7 July 1505 to vicarage of Bourne, on death of Richard Wynthorp.

Patron: Abbot (Thomas) and Convent of Bourne. [Reg. 23, fo.97v; PD 1505/69.]

Of Holbeach. [PD 1505/69.]

M. Nicholas Holand priest
Instituted 20 July 1521 to vicarage of Bourne, on death of last incumbent. Patron: Abbot and Convent of Bourne. Note that the vicarage had been vacant since 11 February preceding. [Reg. 27, fo.21.]

Robert Harryson chaplain
Instituted 27 June 1522 to vicarage of Bourne, on death of Nicholas Holand. Patron: Abbot and Convent of Bourne. [Reg. 27, fo.23v.]

Assessed for subsidy (£8) in 1526 and for *Valor Ecclesiasticus* 1535. [*Subsidy*, 58; *Valor* iv. 106.]

Thomas Buddill clerk
Instituted 28 March 1542 to vicarage of Bourne, on death of last incumbent. Patron: King Henry VIII. [Reg. 27, fo.77.]

Witnessed Bourne wills, 1552–8. [LCC Wills 1551–3/194; 1557/i/138; 1557/iii/135v, 172, 196; 1558/i/34; 1558/ii/14v.]

Thomas Baxter
Instituted 7 May 1562 to vicarage of Bourne, on death of last incumbent. Patron: Queen Elizabeth I. Vacated by cession 1573. [Reg. 28, fo.210.]

Born *c*.1534. Education: 'has some little skill in Latin; well versed in sacred learning'. Priest: 1 February 1561/2 (London). Witnessed Bourne will, 13 June 1562; signed BTs, 1562–5. Also: R. of Draughton (Np), 1569–1606; resided there. Afterwards: V. of Thurlby by Bourne, 1573–86. Buried at Draughton, 24 October 1606. [*Bishop Cooper*, 212; LCC Wills 1562/261; Longden ii. 23.]

The vicarage of Bourne was vacant in 1576; it was served by Richard Fowler as curate (1577–8). [*Bishop Cooper*, 209; BTs Bourne.]

Richard Foster MA
Instituted 5 September 1581 to vicarage of Bourne (cause of vacancy not stated). Patron: Queen Elizabeth I (28 July 1581), by lapse. [*Bishop Cooper*, 29; PD 1581/41.]

Priest: 20 September 1561 (Peterborough). Afterwards: R. of Folkingham, 1585–91; R. of Scremby, 1591–1622; V. of Skendleby, 1593–1606. [*State of the Church*, 73.]

John Jackson
Instituted *c*.1585 to vicarage of Bourne, on resignation of last incumbent. Patron: Queen Elizabeth I (15 November 1585). [PD 1585/29.]

Deacon: 29 July 1578; priest: 8 April 1579 (Lincoln). C. of Folkingham, 1578–85. Resident (1611): signed BTs, 1586–1613. Assessed ('a Bowe') in Subsidy of Armour 1590. A Puritan preacher: cited (1603) for not wearing surplice and not conforming to the Prayer Book; JJ replied (1605) that 'he cannot yet be resolved to conform himself, and craves time'; a testimonial noted how he was 'well knowne to have taken greatt paines to feed his flock … and for a very smalle sallarie hitherto his christian care over them not sparinge mydnyght or cock crow to dyg and delve in season, and owt of season, hath he wrought in the lordes vinyard'. Presented again (1607–8) for not wearing surplice, not following the Book of Common Prayer, and not using the sign of the cross. At 1611 Visitation noted as of good behaviour, 'saveing that he nowe standes suspended being presented for unconformytie'. Died 30 January; buried at Bourne, 1 February 1612/13. [*Bishop Cooper*, 90–1, 220; BTs Folkingham; *State of the Church*, pp. cviii–cix, 73, 148; LC 3, fo.1; BTs Bourne; *PR Bourne*, pp. xi–xii, 170.]

Edmund Lolly MA

Instituted 30 March 1613 to vicarage of Bourne, on death of John Jackson. Patron: John Browne of Stamford, esquire (2 March 1612/13). [BC; PD 1613/38.]

Born *c*.1585. Educated: Magdalen College, Oxford (MA). Deacon and priest: 22 May 1608 (Peterborough). Resident (1614): signed BTs 1613–29. Died 11 July; buried at Bourne, 12 July 1632. Will (LCC), dated 11 July 1632; proved 23 May 1633. Desired to be buried 'in the Quire in Bourne'. To his son Edmund, 'all my books and my beste apparrell', entreating his gossips Thomas Browne and James Swifte 'to sell my Bookes and Apparrell for my said sonne and bring him up at the Schoole'. [PD 1613/38 (biographical details); Longden ix. 33; *PR Bourne*, 193, 217; LCC Wills 1633/378. Not in Foster, *Alumni*.]

Richard Titley MA

Instituted 23 November 1632 to vicarage of Bourne, on death of Edmund Lolly. Patron: Winifred Browne widow (6 August 1632). Inducted 18 December 1632 by Humphrey Boston, Vicar of Morton-by-Bourne. [BC; PD 1632/11; IND/L 1, fo.102.]

Baptised 9 December 1599 at Ufford (Np); son of Peter T., Rector of Ufford (1586–1641). Educated: Trinity College, Cambridge (matric. 1615; BA 1619–20; MA 1623). Deacon: 21 December 1623; priest: 22 December 1623 (Peterborough). Signed BTs at Bourne 1633–40. Afterwards: R. of Ufford, 1641. [Venn, *Alumni*; Longden xiii. 235; *PR Bourne*, pp. xii, 217.]

William Clarke BA

Instituted 7 April 1642 to vicarage of Bourne, on cession of Richard Titley. Patron: Winifred Browne widow (5 April 1642). [BC; Reg. 31, p.23; IND/L 1, fo.131.]

His daughter Ann was buried at Bourne, 22 July 1642; his wife Jane was also buried there, 23 November 1644; another daughter Ann was baptised at Bourne, 29 August 1647. In August 1646 an annual sum of £50 was sequestered to WC from the impropriate rectory of Heckington, as 'the vicarage in the best times was worth but thirty pounds a year'. [*PR Bourne*, pp. xii, 94, 207, 209.]

Richard Milward
Served as Minister from 19 August 1649. [*PR Bourne*, p.xii.]

His daughter Ann was baptised at Bourne in June 1651 and buried there in September 1655. [PR Bourne.]

Between 1660 and 1712 the living of Bourne was under sequestration and served by curates, including Thomas Ericke (1662), Nicholas Moysey (1671), Peter Stevens (1690–7). [LC 5, fo.22; LC 6, fo.1; LC 11, fo.27; LC 14, fo.2v.]

Edward Blithe MA
Instituted 24 July 1712 to vicarage of Bourne (cause of vacancy not stated). Patron: Queen Anne. [Reg. 36, p.183.]

Of Wansford (Np). Educated: Clare Hall, Cambridge (matric. 1699; BA 1701–2). Deacon: 31 May 1702; priest: 4 March 1704/5 (Peterborough). Formerly: C. of Wansford, 1702; C. of Bourne, 1706. Also: V. of Thurlby-by-Bourne, 1721–7. Buried at Bourne, 27 August 1727. [Venn, *Alumni*; Longden ii. 137; Reg. 36, p.21; PR Bourne.]

William Dodd BA
Instituted 23 October 1727 to vicarage of Bourne, on death of Edward Blithe. Patron: King George II. [Reg. 38, p.172.]

Of Cambridgeshire. Educated: Trinity Hall, Cambridge (matric. 1720; BA 1723–4). Deacon: 31 May 1724; priest: 24 September 1727 (Lincoln). Formerly: C. of Driby, 1724. Resident at Bourne. Also: C. of Kirkby Underwood. Father of William Dodd (1729–1777), the 'Macaroni Parson' executed for forgery in 1777. Died 7 August, buried 9 August 1756 at Bourne. [Venn, *Alumni*; Reg. 36, pp. 49, 51, 163; LC 18B, p.192; Philip Rawlings, 'Dodd, William' in *ODNB*; PR Bourne.]

Rowney Noel MA
Instituted 14 December 1756 to vicarage of Bourne, on death of William Dodd. Patron: Thomas Trollope Brown esquire. [Reg. 38, p.546.]

Born 26 July 1726; youngest son of Sir Clobery Noel Bt of Kirkby Mallory (Le) and Elizabeth his wife (daughter of Thomas Rowney of Oxford). Educated: St John's College, Oxford (matric. 1743) and All Souls College, Oxford (BA 1747; MA 1751; BD 1759); Fellow of All Souls. Deacon: 24 September 1752; priest: 23 September 1753 (Oxford). Non-resident at Bourne, which was served by Charles Grainger as curate. Afterwards: R. of Elmesthorpe (Le), 1763–86; R. of Kirkby Mallory (Le), 1763–86; Dean of Salisbury and Prebendary of Heytesbury in Salisbury Cathedral, 1780–6. Died 26 June 1786; buried in Salisbury Cathedral (MI). [*Complete Baronetage* iii. 76; Foster, *Alumni*; ORO, MS. Oxf. Dioc. Papers b.21, fos 38, 39v; PR Bourne; Reg. 39, p.17; *Le Neve Fasti: Salisbury 1541–1857*, 7; Harris, *Copies of the Epitaphs in Salisbury Cathedral* (1825), 46.]

Humphrey Hyde BA
Instituted 9 June 1763 to vicarage of Bourne, on resignation of Rowney Noel. Patron: Thomas Trollope Browne esquire. [Reg. 39, p.18.]

Also: R. of Dowsby, 1773–1807 (*q.v.*).

Thomas Denys MA
Instituted 8 July 1807 to vicarage of Bourne, on death of Humphrey Hyde.
Patron: George, Earl of Pomfret. [Reg. 40, p.121.]

Born *c*.1763; son of Peter D. of London, gent. Educated: Magdalen Hall, Oxford (matric.
1788; BA 1793; MA 1796). Deacon: 14 July 1793 (Peterborough). Formerly: V. of Easton
Neston (Np), 1795–1807. Resided at Bourne (1814). Also: C. of Thurlby-by-Bourne, 1814.
Latterly of St John's Wood (Mx); Joseph Dodsworth (below) officiated as curate. Died
22 January 1842 at Wellington Terrace, St John's Wood. [Foster, *Alumni*; Longden iv. 57;
CR 1, p.47; Bourne Par 5/1; White, *Lincolnshire* (1842), 732–3; *GM* (May 1842), 558.]

Joseph Dodsworth
Instituted 9 March 1842 to vicarage of Bourne, on death of Thomas Denys.
Patron: Henry Edmund Dodsworth of Billingborough Hall, esquire. [Reg.
40, p.483.]

Born 26 December 1797, baptised 5 February 1798 at Denton; son of John D., doctor,
and Charlotte his wife. Educated: Lincoln College, Oxford (matric. 1816). Deacon: 31
December 1820; priest: 13 January 1822 (Lincoln). Formerly: C. of Denton, 1820; of
Quarrington, 1821; of Sleaford, 1822; of Bourne, 1822; of Thurlby-by-Bourne, 1822.
Resided at The Abbey, Bourne, which was acquired in exchange for the old Vicarage
House in 1848. Died 9 May 1877 at Bourne. [PR Denton; Foster, *Alumni*; OR 1, pp. 2,
6; CR 1, pp. 125, 152, 161–2; White, *Lincolnshire* (1856), 710–11; Census Returns 1861,
1871; *Probate Calendar* 1877.]

George Eyre Massy BA
Instituted 27 July 1877 to vicarage of Bourne, on death of Joseph Dodsworth.
Patron: John Pritchard of Stanmore, near Bridgnorth (Shropshire), esquire,
on nomination of William Ostler of Arnold Field, Manthorpe cum Little
Gonerby, esquire. [Reg. 41, p.566.]

Born 25 May 1851 at Prendergast (Pemb); son of Edward Taylor Massy of Cottesmore,
esquire. Educated: Trinity College, Dublin (BA 1874; MA 1880); Gloucester College,
1875–6. Deacon: 1876; priest: 1877 (Gloucester and Bristol). Formerly: C. of Uley with
Owlpen (Gl), 1876–7. Afterwards: V. of Isle Brewers (So), 1881–4; R. of Gumfreston
(Pemb), 1884–1905. Died 20 September 1905 at Gumfreston Rectory. [Nicholas, *County
Families of Wales* (1872), 906; Lodge, *Peerage* (1867), 382; Census Returns 1861 (Prendergast); *Crockford* (1898); *Probate Calendar* 1905.]

Hugh McNeile Mansfield MA
Instituted 6 July 1881 to vicarage of Bourne, on resignation of George Eyre
Massy. Patron: Sir William Earle Welby Gregory of Denton Hall, Bt. [Reg.
42, p.122.]

Born at Trowbridge (Wlt), baptised 1 August 1845; son of Revd George M. Educated:
Felsted and St Paul's Schools; St John's College, Cambridge (matric. 1865; BA 1869;
MA 1872). Deacon: 1869; priest: 1871 (London). Formerly: C. of Bromley St Leonard,
1869–72; of St Saviour, Paddington, 1872–4; of St Thomas Portman Square, 1874–9; V.
of Isle Brewers (So), 1879–81. Resided at Bourne Vicarage. Died 10 September 1910 at
Bourne. [Venn, *Alumni*; *Crockford* (1908); *LDC* (1911), 145; *Probate Calendar* 1910.]

Thomas Cowpe Lawson MA

Instituted 13 June 1911 to vicarage of Bourne, on death of Hugh McNeile Mansfield. Patron: Hugh Mounteney Lely of Seaford (Sx), esquire. [Reg. 43, p.15.]

Educated: St Aidan's College, Birkenhead (1887); University of Oxford (BA and MA 1908). Deacon: 1890 (York); priest: 1891 (Beverley for York). Formerly: C. of Wadsley (YWR), 1890–1; of St James, Sheffield, 1891–1900; of St Philip, Sheffield, 1900–11. Deprived of Bourne 1913, his institution having been judged simoniacal since the patron had contracted to sell the advowson to the Church Association; Bishop Hicks wrote 'I feel convinced that [Lawson] is innocent of any malpractice, & knew nothing of any simony.' Afterwards: V. of Castle Bytham, 1913–28. Retired 1928. Lived at Copster, 38 Brittany Road, Hove. Died 14 June 1941. [*Crockford* (1932); *LRS News Review* 1, p.3; *Hicks Diaries*, no.313; *Probate Calendar* 1941.]

Harry Cotton Smith MA

Instituted 13 October 1913 to vicarage of Bourne, the benefice being legally void for simony under the provisions of 31 Elizabeth c.6. Patron: King George V (the presentation belonging to the Bishop of Lincoln for this turn only under the provisions of the said Act). [Reg. 43, p.57.]

Born *c*.1865 at Sheffield. Educated: Trinity College, Dublin (BA 1887; MA 1904). Deacon: 23 December 1888; priest: 22 December 1889 (Lincoln). Formerly: C. of Spilsby, 1888–91; of St Mary-le-Wigford, Lincoln, 1891–8; V. of Castle Bytham, 1898–1913. Resided at Bourne Vicarage. Afterwards: V. of St John, New Clee, 1919–27; V. of Nettleham, 1927–50; C. of Cherry Willingham with Greetwell, 1934–9. Latterly at 'Ericon', Washdyke Hill, Nettleham. Died 28 December 1952. [Census Returns 1911 (Castle Bytham); *LDM* (1888–9); *Crockford* (1951–2); *LDC* (1915), 91; *Probate Calendar* 1953.]

John Grinter

Instituted 14 October 1919 by the Official *sede vacante* to vicarage of Bourne, on cession of Harry Cotton Smith. Patron: Lady Laura Helen Pollock, wife of Sir Ernest Murray Pollock of 40 Thurloe Square (Mx) KC, MP. [Reg. 43, p.184.]

Baptised 23 October 1856 at Whitchurch Canonicorum (Do); son of John G., labourer. Married (26 July 1888) at St Stephen, Battersea, Mary Ann Gates Nixon, schoolmistress (daughter of John Potter Nixon, butler). Living in Battersea as Scripture Reader and Lay Preacher (1891). Deacon: 1894 (Honduras, in Christ Church, Lancaster Gate, London); priest: 1895 (Honduras). Formerly: C. of St Peter District, Orange Walk, Honduras, 1894–8; Head Master of St Peter's School, Orange Walk, 1895–8; R. of San José (Costa Rica), 1898–1908; Canon of St John's Cathedral, Belize, 1905–8; R. of Pettaugh (Sf), 1908–9; V. of Radford Semele (Wa), 1909–19. Resided at Bourne Vicarage. Also: RD of Aveland, 1924–34. Resigned 30 November 1935. Latterly at Cottin's Well House, Stonesfield (Ox). Died 5 May 1938, aged 82. [Dorset History Centre, PR Whitchurch Canonicorum; LMA, PR Battersea St Stephen; Census Returns 1891 (Battersea); *Crockford* (1932, 1938); Census Returns 1911 (Radford Semele); RES 1935/21; *LDC* (1939), 180.]

Charles Wynn Ellis Horne MA

Instituted 25 February 1936 to vicarage of Bourne, on resignation of John

Grinter. Patron: Lincoln Diocesan Trust and Board of Finance. [Reg. 43, p.576.]

Born 16 January 1876; son of Henry James Davidson H. of St Michael's, Hatfield (Hrt). Educated: Clifton College (1884–6) and Bedford Modern School; Selwyn College, Cambridge (matric. 1896; BA 1899; MA 1903); Ely Theological College (1899). Deacon: 1900; priest: 1901 (Lincoln). Formerly: C. of St John the Divine, Gainsborough, 1900–3; of St Nicholas, Skirbeck, 1903–7; in Canada: PC of Lobtstick, Alberta, 1907–10; C. of Pro-Cathedral of the Redeemer, Calgary, 1910–13; R. of Christ Church, Calgary, 1913–29; Chaplain, Canadian Forces, 1914–19; R. of St Mark, Calgary, 1915–17; Canon of St John in Calgary Cathedral, 1922–9; V. of Castle Hedingham (Ess), 1929–36. Resided at Bourne Vicarage. Resignation accepted 31 March 1951. Latterly of 99 North Road, Bourne. Died 4 April 1951 at The Butterfield Hospital, Bourne. [*Clifton College Register*, 196; Venn, *Alumni*; Census Returns 1881 (Hatfield); *Crockford* (1941); Reg. 44, p.138; *Probate Calendar* 1951.]

Daniel Stephen Rowlands BA

Instituted 29 May 1951 to vicarage of Bourne, on resignation of Charles Wynn Ellis Horne. Patron: Lincoln Diocesan Board of Patronage. [Reg. 44, p.141.]

Born 1901 at Stanley (Du); son of Revd William Handcock Rowlands (Rector of Allington 1917–29). Educated: St John's College, Durham (BA 1924). Deacon: 1925; priest: 1927 (Lincoln). Formerly: C. of Skegness, 1925–9; PC of Edenham, 1929–33; V. of Kilmersdon and R. of Babington (So), 1933–43; CF 1939–45; C. of Keighley (in charge of All Saints, Highfield), 1945–7; R. of Newton with Haceby, 1947–51 (*q.v.*); R. of Sapperton with Braceby, 1947–51. Resided at Bourne Vicarage. Also: Canon of Lincoln and Prebendary of St Mary Crackpole, 1954–8. Resignation accepted 31 October 1958. Afterwards: Chaplain at Moshi (Tanganyika), 1958–62; Canon of Central Tanganyika, 1958–62. Latterly at Thalatta, Aberporth (Card). Died 1968 (Carmarthen). [GRO, Birth Index; Census Returns 1911 (Hoyland Swaine); *LDC* (1957), 54; *Crockford* (1967–8); Reg. 44, p.261; GRO, Death Index.]

Hugh Peter Laurence

Instituted 9 January 1959 to vicarage of Bourne, on resignation of Daniel Stephen Rowlands. Patron: Lincoln Diocesan Board of Patronage. [Reg. 44, p.265.]

Born 7 April 1902. Educated: Emmanuel College, Saskatchewan (1924). Deacon: 1928; priest: 1929 (Saskatchewan). Formerly: C. of Maidstone, 1928–30; R. of Tisdale, 1930–2 (both Saskatchewan); R. of Thimbleby, 1932–46; CF 1939–45; C-in-C of Edlington with Wispington, 1945–6; V. of Horncastle, 1946–59; RD of Horncastle, 1946–57; R. of Martin with Thornton, 1951–9. Also: Canon of Lincoln and Prebendary of Liddington, 1950–77. Resided at Bourne Vicarage. Resignation of Bourne accepted 8 April 1970. Lived at Cresta, Thimbleby. Died 16 October 1987. [GRO, Death Index; *Crockford* (1961–2, 1980–2); Reg. 44, p.437; *The Times*, 20 October 1987.]

DEMBLEBY

The church of Dembleby originated as a chapel of Scott Willoughby. It was accorded this status in the two major tax assessments of the thirteenth century, and was described as such in the episcopal registers between 1335 and 1410. On the other hand, it was often referred to as a church in the thirteenth and fifteenth centuries and by 1603 it was regarded as a parsonage in its own right. Its parochial status was reflected in the regular series of institutions recorded in the registers. The advowson was held by the early thirteenth century by a branch of the knightly family of Lekeburn of Legbourne near Louth, who presented to the living between 1237–8 and 1331. By 1349 it had passed to William de Kelleseye, a clerk in the royal household, who presented on three occasions between 1349 and 1356. The manor and advowson subsequently came into the possession of John Bussy, Speaker of the Commons. On Bussy's forfeiture and execution in 1399, Dembleby was granted by King Henry IV to his loyal servant William Loveney for life. Loveney, who presented on several occasions between 1410 and 1433, died in 1435. It is possible that John, son of John Bussy, was able to regain his right to Dembleby at this time; the advowson shortly afterwards came into the possession of William Stanlowe of Silk Willoughby, who had married Joan, daughter of the younger John Bussy. The Stanlowe family continued to present until 1515; a century later the advowson had passed into the possession of the Pell family of Dembleby. On the death of Henry Pell in 1730, it descended to his daughter Jane, wife of Everard Buckworth of Spalding. The living remained in the gift of the Buckworth family, later of Cockley Cley (Nf), until the early twentieth century. By 1915 it had passed to Edmund Van Houtte Blyton of Spalding, solicitor. The Diocesan Board of Patronage held the advowson in 1965. [*Valuation of Norwich*, 246 (Scott Willoughby 'cum capella'); Taxatio, fo.10 ('Scotwyluby cum capella de Dembelby'); *Honors and Knights' Fees* ii. 106–9; *CPR 1399–1401*, 99; *History of Parliament: House of Commons 1386–1421* iii. 634–7; *Lincolnshire Pedigrees*, 216; PRO, CP 25/1/145/159, no.35; *Holles Church Notes*, 219; *Lincolnshire Pedigrees*, 769–71; *LDC* (1915), 134–5; *LDC* (1965), 94–5.]

William de Dembelb' chaplain
Instituted in the third pontifical year of Bishop Robert Grosseteste (17 June 1237–16 June 1238) to church of Dembleby. Patron: Henry de Lekeburn. [Hoskin, no.88.]

Richard de Wynepole
Instituted before 31 May 1287. [*Reg. Sutton* i. 96.]

Robert le Venur clerk in minor orders
Instituted 31 May 1287 to church of Dembleby (having received it *in*

commendam, 24 April 1287), on death of Richard de Wynepole. Patron: Robert de Lekeburn kt. Reinstituted 12 February 1289 (because he had not been ordained priest within a year of his first institution); patron: as above. [*Reg. Sutton* i. 96, 117.]

Deacon: 31 May 1287 (Lincoln for Canterbury). [*Reg. Sutton* i. 96.]

John de Hameslap acolyte
Instituted 8 April 1303 to church of Dembleby, on resignation of Robert le Venur. Patron: Henry de Lekeburn. [Reg. 2, fo.7v.]

Gilbert de Luda chaplain
Instituted 7 May 1309 to church of Dembleby, on death of John de Hampslap. Patron: Henry de Lekeburn kt. [Reg. 2, fo.28.]

Note that on 9 February 1322/3 the bishop issued a commission to inquire into presentation of Thomas de Luda acolyte to chapel of Dembleby by Matilda widow of Henry de Lekeburn kt, and if approved to institute him, at the same time proceeding ex officio against Gilbert, incumbent in possession of the chapel, and removing him from the same. Afterwards: V. of Ancaster, 1331–4. [Reg. 5, fo.333; *Reg. Burghersh* i. no.439.]

Geoffrey de Rouceby priest
Instituted 13 September 1331 to chapel of St Andrew, Dembleby, on resignation of Gilbert de Luda (by exchange with vicarage of Ancaster). Patron: Henry de Leukeburn kt. [*Reg. Burghersh* i. no.311.]

Priest: before 24 December 1321. Formerly: V. of Ancaster, 1321–31. [*Reg. Burghersh* i. no.36.]

Adam de Kelleseye
Instituted before 14 April 1349. [Reg. 9, fo.58.]

Peter de Kelleseye priest
Instituted 14 April 1349 to chapel of Dembleby, on resignation of Adam de Kelleseye. Patron: William de Kelleseye, Rector of Navenby. [Reg. 9, fo.58.]

William Mariot de Thornton priest
Instituted 12 December 1349 to chapel of Dembleby, on resignation of Peter de Kelleseye. Patron: William de Kelleseye, as above. [Reg. 9, fo.81.]

Afterwards: R. of Thornton-le-Moor, 1356–72. Died before 26 July 1372. [Reg. 9, fo.120; Reg. 10, fo.53v.]

Adam son of William Westren de Malbersthorp priest
Instituted 11 July 1356 to chapel of Dembleby, on institution of William Mariot to church of Thornton-le-Moor. Patron: William de Kelleseye, now Rector of Pulham (Nf). [Reg. 9, fo.120v.]

Assessed for poll-tax, 1377, 1381. His presentation (8 August 1370) by King Edward III to church of Newton-by-Folkingham, on an exchange with William Almer, was presumably ineffective. [*Clerical Poll-Taxes*, nos 686, 1335, 1924; *CPR 1367–70*, 455.]

Richard Brygge

Instituted 24 June 1410 to chapel of Dembleby, on resignation of Adam son of William Westrum de Malberthorp (by exchange with chantry of Walter de Ounesby in church of Aunsby and chapel of Crofton). Patron: William Loveney. [Reg. 14, fo.43.]

Afterwards: V. of Broxted (Ess), 1412.

Nicholas Adam

Instituted 1 February 1411/12 to church of Dembleby, on resignation of Richard Brygge (by exchange with vicarage of Broxted *(Chaureth)*, dioc. London). Patron: William Loveney esquire. [Reg. 14, fo.52v.]

Formerly: V. of Broxted (Ess), 1410–12. Afterwards: R. of Stockton (Nf), 1412. [Newcourt ii. 127.]

Thomas Yonge

Instituted 30 May 1412 to church of Dembleby, on resignation of Nicholas Adam (by exchange with church of Stockton, dioc. Norwich). Patron: William Loveney esquire. [Reg. 14, fo.56.]

Formerly: R. of Stockton (Nf), 1402–12. Afterwards: R. of Alfold (Sr), 1413. [Blomefield viii. 43.]

John Leman

Instituted 13 December 1413 to church of Dembleby, on resignation of Nicholas Adam (by exchange with church of Alfold, dioc. Winchester). Patron: William Loveney esquire. [Reg. 14, fo.91.]

Formerly: R. of Alfold (Sr), to 1413.

Richard Wryde priest

Instituted 2 December 1422 to church of Dembleby, on resignation of John Leman. Patron: William Loveney esquire. [*Reg. Fleming* i. no.173.]

Robert Sausmere priest

Instituted 3 December 1433 to church of Dembleby, on death of Richard Wryde. Patron: William Loveney esquire. [Reg. 17, fo.8v.]

Afterwards: R. of St Martin, Leicester, February–April 1439; R. of a mediety of Belchford, 1439. [Hamilton Thompson, *Leicester Abbey*, 164; Reg. 18, fo.81v.]

William Frawnces priest

Instituted 5 February 1438/9 to church of Dembleby, on resignation of Robert Sawsemer (by exchange with church of St Martin, Leicester). Patron: William Stanlaw of Silk Willoughby, squire. [Reg. 18, fo.80v.]

Priest: before 22 January 1435/6. Formerly: R. of St Martin, Leicester, 1436–9. [Hamilton Thompson, *Leicester Abbey*, 163.]

Richard Wynter
Instituted before 20 November 1476. [Reg. 21, fo.14.]

Thomas Hale priest
Instituted 20 November 1476 to chapel of Dembleby, on death of Richard Wynter. Patron: John Stanloo esquire. [Reg. 21, fo.14.]

Hugh Ingolsby priest
Instituted 17 March 1491/2 to church of Dembleby, on death of Thomas Hale. Patron: John Stanlowe esquire (14 March 1491/2). [Reg. 22, fo.149v; PD 1492/4.]

John Wilson chaplain
Instituted 20 December 1515 to church of Dembleby, on resignation of Hugh Ingoldesby. Patron: John Stanlowe. [Reg. 25, fo.13v.]

Assessed for subsidy (£6) in 1526 and *Valor Ecclesiasticus* 1535. Exhibited at Visitation, 1551. Witnessed Dembleby will, 1552; witnessed will of Thomas Thornbeke, R. of Scott Willoughby, 1557. Died in February 1561/2. Probate inventory (13 February 1561/2): 'all his books, 10s'. [*Subsidy*, 57; *Valor* iv. 105; Vj 13, fo.63; LCC Wills 1551–2/92; 1557/iii/186v; LCC Wills 1561/16; INV 40/433.]

Robert Tamworth
Instituted 14 July 1562 to church of Dembleby, on death of last incumbent. Patron: Edmund Bussey of Silk Willoughby, gent., and Elizabeth his wife. [Reg. 28, fos 5v, 213.]

Died 12 November 1569. [FL.h.11, 278.]

Thomas Buckeberye
Instituted *c.*1569–70, on death of Robert Tamworth.

Died 15 November 1570 at Scott Willoughby. [FL.h.11, 277.]

John Gamon
Instituted 29 June 1571 to rectory of Dembleby, on death of Thomas Buckeberye. Patron: Edmund Porter gent. (27 March 1571). [*Bishop Cooper*, 311.]

Born *c.*1540. Education: 'knows Latin moderately; moderately versed in sacred learning'. Priest: 7 December 1569 (Peterborough). Married. Resident (1576). Also: V. of Kirkby Green, 1577–96. Died before 12 February 1595/6 (probate inventory). [*Bishop Cooper*, 19, 208, 220; INV 86/234.]

Richard Tomlinson
Instituted 31 July 1589 to rectory of Dembleby, on resignation of John

Gamon. Patron: Edmund Porter gent. (31 July 1589), in right of Alice his wife. [PD 1589/14.]

Education: 'bred in the schools'; 'no graduate'. Deacon: 2 June 1577 (Chester); 11 February 1589 (Lincoln). Formerly: C. of Syston, 1585. Resident at Dembleby (1611, 1614). Assessed ('a Bowe') in Subsidy of Armour 1590. Died before 26 October 1614 (probate inventory: 'one bowe and one sheafe of arrows, 6d'; 'all his books, 13s 4d'). Will (LCC). [*State of the Church*, 70, 148; LC 3, fo.1v; LC 4, fo.72v; INV 116/100; LCC Wills 1614/ii/177.]

Richard Potter BA

Instituted 8 November 1614 to rectory of Dembleby, on death of Richard Tomlinson. Patron: Sir Anthony Pell kt. [BC; IND/L 1, fo.11.]

Signed BTs at Dembleby 1615–27. Buried 15 May 1627 at Dembleby. Administration (LCC) to Anne Potter of Dembleby, widow. Probate inventory: 'for the librare, 3s 6d'. [BTs Dembleby; LCC Admons 1627/150.]

Richard Pell MA

Instituted 1 September 1627 to rectory of Dembleby, on death of Richard Potter. Patron: Sir Anthony Pell of Dembleby kt (21 August 1627). [BC; PD 1627/31.]

Also: R. of Scott Willoughby, 1630–52 (*q.v.*).

Thomas Watson

Instituted *c*.1653. [Swaby, 112.]

George Campion MA

Instituted 24 November 1662 to rectory of Dembleby, on death of Thomas Watson. Patron: Elizabeth Pell widow (19 November 1662). [Reg. 32, fo.23; PD 1662/105.]

Educated: Clare Hall, Cambridge (matric. 1634; BA 1638–9). Deacon: 1 March 1639/40; priest: 19 September 1641 (Peterborough). Also: V. of Swarby, to 1670. Resided at Swarby but served Dembleby also: signed BTs there 1663–9. Buried at Swarby, 1 April 1670. Will (LCC). Probate inventory (30 April 1670): 'Minister of God's Word at Swarby'; 'in the Study, Bookes, £1'. [Venn, *Alumni*; Longden iii. 13; LC 5, fos 22v, 56v; BTs Dembleby; BTs Swarby; LCC Wills 1670/ii/472; INV 172/176.]

Richard Moore

Instituted 6 September 1670 to rectory of Dembleby, on death of last incumbent. Patron: Richard Pell esquire (2 September 1670). [Reg. 33, fo.133v; PD 1670/31.]

Born *c*.1641 at Hull; son of John M. Educated: Hull School and Christ's College, Cambridge (matric. 1659; BA 1662–3; MA 1668). Priest: 25 May 1665 (Lincoln). Formerly: C. of Grantham, 1664. Resident at Dembleby: signed BTs there 1671–1715. Also: R. of Scott Willoughby, 1668–1716 (*q.v.*). Died 8 January 1715/16, aged 77 (MI); buried at Dembleby. [Venn, *Alumni*; Reg. 33, fo.133v; *Speculum*, 40; *Monson*, 111.]

Benjamin Stokes

Appointed Sequestrator. Licensed curate, 26 June 1718. [*Speculum*, 40.]

Signed BTs at Dembleby 1718–20. Also: R. of Aunsby, 1711–21 (where he resided); buried there, 3 August 1721. [BTs Dembleby; *Speculum*, 8; PR Aunsby.]

John Jones MA

Instituted 12 September 1721 to rectory of Dembleby, on death of Benjamin Stokes. Patron: Henry Pell esquire (5 September 1721). [Reg. 37, p.124; PD 1721/28.]

Signed BTs at Dembleby 1721–31. Also: R. of Kirkby Underwood, 1722–52 (*q.v.*). [BTs Dembleby.]

Wyat Francis BA

Instituted 8 November 1731 to rectory of Dembleby, on cession of John Jones. Patron: Everard Buckworth esquire and Jane his wife; Elizabeth Pell and Katherine Pell. [Reg. 38, p.253.]

Baptised October 1707 at St Margaret, Lincoln; son of James F. (and grandson of Wyat F. (d.1715), Registrar of Dean and Chapter of Lincoln). Educated: Emmanuel College, Cambridge (matric. 1725; BA 1728–9). Deacon: 14 March 1730/1; priest: 7 November 1731 (Lincoln). Formerly: C. of Fillingham, 1731. Signed BTs at Dembleby 1732–54. Thereafter resided at Lincoln. Also: V. of Heckington, 1741–54; R. of Burton-by-Lincoln, 1754–80; V. of Gosberton, 1759–80; Canon of Lincoln and Prebendary of Crackpole St Mary, 1764–80. Died 1780; buried at St Margaret, Lincoln, 18 March 1780. [PR St Margaret, Lincoln; *Lincolnshire Pedigrees*, 371–2; Venn, *Alumni*; Reg. 38, pp. 240, 252; BTs Dembleby; LC 31, p.75; *Le Neve Fasti: Lincoln 1541–1857*, 59; Maddison, 'Lincoln Cathedral Choir 1750–1875'.]

Joseph Mills BA

Instituted 9 August 1780 to rectory of Dembleby, on death of Wyatt Francis. Patron: Everard Buckworth LLD. [Reg. 39, p.353.]

Baptised 25 January 1732/3 at Spalding; son of Thomas M., PC of Cowbit. Educated: Jesus College, Cambridge (matric. 1751; BA 1755). Deacon: 21 September 1755; priest: 6 March 1757 (Lincoln). Formerly: C. of Sutterton, 1755. Non-resident at Dembleby, which was served by John Nicholson as curate. Also: PC of Cowbit, 1760–1804; V. of Weston, 1787–1804. Died 19 December 1804; buried at Cowbit. [PR Spalding; Venn, *Alumni*; Reg. 38, pp. 538, 549, 580; PR Dembleby; PR Cowbit.]

Thomas Mills MA

Instituted 21 January 1805 to rectory of Dembleby, on death of Joseph Mills. Patron: Jane Buckworth and Anne Buckworth, both of St Martin, Stamford Baron, spinsters (19 January 1805). [Reg. 40, p.87; PD 161/30.]

Baptised 23 March 1774 at Cowbit; son of Joseph M., PC of Cowbit (1760–1804), above. Educated: Christ Church, Oxford (matric. 1792; BA 1796; MA 1800). Deacon: 18 September 1796; priest: 3 June 1798 (Lincoln). Formerly: C. of Weston, 1796; of Grantham, 1798. Non-resident at Dembleby (no Glebe house), which was served by curates, including John Nicholson, Bernard Cracroft, James David Glover and John Neville Calcraft. Also: Minor Canon of Peterborough Cathedral, 1806–45; V. of Helion Bumpstead (Ess), 1809–33; PC of Eye, 1816–32; V. of Bringhurst with Great Easton, 1824–33; R. of Northborough (Np), 1833–56; Canon of Peterborough, 1845–56. Died 21 July 1856. [PR Cowbit; Foster, *Alumni*; Reg. 39, pp. 622–3, 651–2; Longden ix. 229; CCED; NRL 10/30, 12/56, 16/25, 19/57; *Bonney's Church Notes*, 223; CR 1, pp. 10, 86, 171; CR 2, p.34; White, *Lincolnshire* (1856), 540.]

James Tillard Bonner SCL

Instituted 6 November 1856 to rectory of Dembleby, on death of Thomas Mills. Patron: Theophilus Russell Buckworth of Cockley Cley Hall (Nf), esquire. [Reg. 40, p.583.]

Born 18 October 1830 at Spalding; 6th son of Charles B., gent. Educated: Charterhouse School (1845–7); Lincoln College (matric. 1851) and New College, Oxford (SCL 1854; BA 1857). Deacon: 1854; priest: 1855 (Ely). Formerly: C. of Hadleigh (Sf), 1854–6; of Sapiston (Sf), 1856. Married (18 May 1858) at Richmond (Sr), Katherine Anne, daughter of Richard Godwin of Blandford (Do). Licensed for non-residence (1857–62), there being no house. Was living in 1861 with his mother-in-law at Sheen Villas, Richmond; Dembleby was served by John Neville Calcraft as curate. Resided thereafter at Dembleby in 'a commodious rectory house, built in 1864' (architect: Stephen Dawson of Spalding). Afterwards: V. of Great Hale, 1876–82; R. of Stanwick (Np), 1882–95. Retired 1895. Latterly of 'Kirkoswald', Chapel Park Road, St Leonards-on-Sea. Died there, 27 May 1904. [*Charterhouse Register 1769–1872*, 35; Foster, *Alumni*; Longden ii. 153; *Crockford* (1898); Bray, *Ely Lists*; NRL 21/35, 24/33, 26/25; Census Returns 1861 (Richmond); CR 4, fo.94v; Census Returns 1871; White, *Lincolnshire* (1872), 561; MGA 437; *Probate Calendar* 1904.]

William Sadler

Instituted 12 January 1877 to rectory of Dembleby, on cession of James Tillard Bonner. Patron: Everard Theophilus Buckworth of Lowestoft (Sf), a minor (with consent of his guardians, Pleasance Grace Buckworth of Lowestoft, widow; Thomas Edward Bagge of Islington Hall (Nf), esquire; and Chaloner William Chute of Old Square, Lincoln's Inn (Mx), esquire). [Reg. 41, p.546.]

Born *c*.1846 at Paddington (Mx). Deacon: 1868; priest: 1870 (Calcutta). Formerly: Classics Master at St Paul's School, Darjeeling, 1866–75; C. of Tilney (Nf), 1875–6. Married Charlotte Emelia, daughter of James Arden Crommelin of the Bengal Engineers. Also: R. of Aunsby, 1897–1930. Resided initially at Dembleby Rectory and at Aunsby from 1897. Bishop Hicks noted (1914) 'a rather sad, pessimistic old man … (Does he like his whisky nightcaps?).' Died 24 July 1930, aged 84. [*Crockford* (1898); Census Returns 1881; Census Returns 1901–1911 (Aunsby); Kelly, *Lincolnshire* (1913), 174; *Hicks Diaries*, no.571; *Probate Calendar* 1930; *LDC* (1931), 160.]

The Rectory of Dembleby was united to the Rectory of Aunsby by Order in Council dated 21 March 1924. [Reg. 43, pp. 337–40.]

DOWSBY

Matilda de Gynai held in 1212 as part of her dower the service of half a knight in Dowsby of the fee of the Archbishop of York; she presented to the church in 1229–30. Her holding had passed by 1242–3 to Hugh son of Ralph de Lavinton, who presented in 1249–50. The advowson passed in turn to Thomas son of William de Ros of Ingmanthorpe, who presented in 1298 and is recorded in 1303 as tenant of the fee formerly held by Hugh son of Ralph. The Ros family continued to present to the rectory until the early sixteenth century. Jane the daughter and heiress of Thomas Ros of Dowsby married first Edward Villers and secondly David Cecil; these two gentlemen or their representatives were involved in several presentations in the middle years of that century. The Dowsby estate passed to the Rigdon family, from whom it was purchased at the beginning of the reign of James I by Richard Burrell, citizen and grocer of London. The Burrell family presented to the living until the eighteenth century when the advowson passed to Thomas Foster through his grandmother Jane, daughter and co-heiress of Redmayne Burrell. In 1965 the rectory was in the gift of the Bishop of Lincoln. [*Book of Fees*, 181, 1027; *Feudal Aids* iii. 150; *Lincolnshire Pedigrees*, 830; Foster, *Burrell of Dowsby* (1885); *Lincolnshire Pedigrees*, 1227–8; *LDC* (1965), 66–7.]

Theobald de Reinevill subdeacon
Instituted in the twenty-first pontifical year of Bishop Hugh of Wells (20 December 1229/19 December 1230) to church of Dowsby. Patron: Matilda de Giney. [*Rot. Welles* iii. 182.]

Michael chaplain
Instituted in the fifteenth pontifical year of Bishop Robert Grosseteste (17 June 1249/16 June 1250) to church of Dowsby. Patron: Hugh son of Ralph. [Hoskin, no.457.]

Perhaps to be identified with Michael Passalewe, priest, who received papal dispensation (5 August 1255) to hold together the churches of Uggeshall (Sf) with *Duseby*, dioc. Lincoln. [*CPL* i. 321.]

Hugh Fucher
Instituted before 20 January 1298. [*Reg. Sutton* i. 221.]

Robert de Leyk chaplain
Instituted 20 January 1298 to church of Dowsby, on death of Hugh Fucher. Patron: Thomas son of Sir William de Ros of Ingmanthorpe. [*Reg. Sutton* i. 221.]

Robert de Tweng acolyte
Instituted 10 October 1307 to church of Dowsby, on death of Robert de Leek. Patron: Thomas de Ros kt. [Reg. 2, fo.21.]

Subdeacon by 25 September 1308. Dispensations for absence to study in England for 3 years, 25 September 1308; for 2 years, 20 September 1312. [Reg. 2, fos 315, 319v.]

John de Twenge acolyte
Instituted 19 December 1312 to church of Dowsby, on resignation of Robert. Patron: Thomas de Ros kt. [Reg. 2, fo.45.]

Dispensation for absence to study in England for 3 years, 19 December 1312. He is to proceed to the subdiaconate within a year. [Reg. 2, fo.320.]

Richard de Preston acolyte
Instituted 17 March 1314/15 to church of Dowsby, on resignation of John de Tweng. Patron: Thomas de Roos kt. [Reg. 2, fo.54v.]

Subdeacon by 18 May 1315. Dispensations for absence to study in England for 2 years, 18 May 1315; for a further 3 years, 23 February 1316/17. [Reg. 2, fos 322v, 324.]

William de Preston acolyte
Instituted 8 March 1318/19 to church of Dowsby, on death of Richard de Preston. Patron: Thomas de Ros kt. [Reg. 2, fo.77.]

Subdeacon: before 23 September 1319. Dispensations to study in England for 2 years, 23 September 1319; for 2 years, 26 September 1321; for 2 years (England or abroad), 30 January 1322/3. Licence to farm his church for 1 year, 13 January 1331/2. Mandate to archdeacon's official to issue monition to WP to reside on his benefice within 2 months, 14 May 1335. Licence to be in service of Robert, Bishop of Salisbury, for 1 year, 13 July 1335. Afterwards: Archdeacon of Salop, 1339–60. [*Reg. Burghersh* iii. nos 185, 365, 1295; Reg. 5, fos 190, 497v; *Le Neve Fasti: Coventry & Lichfield 1300–1541*, 17.]

William de Greyby priest
Instituted 19 March 1340 to church of Dowsby, on appointment of William de Preston as archdeacon of Salop. Patron: Thomas de Roos kt. [*Reg. Burghersh* i. no.625.]

Licensed to study in England (1 year), 18 September 1345; again (1 year), 23 September 1346. [Reg. 7, fos 127, 128v.]

John de Braydeston
Instituted before 26 March 1370. [Reg. 10, fo.39v.]

Peter de Scredyngton priest
Instituted 26 March 1370 to church of Dowsby, on resignation of John de Braydeston. Patron: John de Draycot, attorney-general of Thomas de Roos kt. [Reg. 10, fo.39v.]

Afterwards: R. of Fordington, 1395–1406; V. of Cherry Willingham, 1406–7. Died before 8 August 1407. [Reg. 14, fos 7, 110v.]

Elias Popley (Popolay)
Instituted 21 June 1395 to church of Dowsby, on resignation of Peter de

Skredyngton (by exchange with church of Fordington). Patron: Theobald de Swynford. [Reg. 11, fo.77.]

Formerly: R. of Fordington, 1392–5. Afterwards: V. of Shorne (K). [Reg. 11, fo.56v.]

Robert Fylle
Instituted 17 May 1398 to church of Dowsby, on resignation of Elias Popley (by exchange with vicarage of Shorne, dioc. Rochester). Patron: Helen de Swynford, widow of Thomas Roos. [Reg. 11, fo.92v.]

Formerly: V. of Shorne (K), to 1398. Afterwards: R. of Twinstead (Ess), September–November 1398. [Newcourt ii. 611.]

John Newman
Instituted 22 September 1398 to church of Dowsby, on resignation of Robert Fille (by exchange with church of Twinstead, dioc. London). Patron: Helen Swynford, widow of Theobald Swynford. [Reg. 13, fo.119.]

Formerly: R. of Twinstead (Ess), 1397–8. Afterwards: R. of Stoke Dry, 1411–19; R. of Hamerton (Hu), 1419–20. Died before 18 January 1419/20. [Newcourt ii. 611; Reg. 14, fos 369, 372.]

Robert Germthorp
Instituted 13 June 1411 to church of Dowsby, on resignation of John Newman (by exchange with church of Stoke Dry). Patron: not specified. [*Lambeth Institutions*, 5.]

Formerly: R. of Steppingley (Bd), to 1405; V. of Wolverton (Bk), 1405–6; R. of Stoke Dry (Ru), 1406–11. [Reg. 14, fos 219, 430.]

William de Wyllyngham priest
Instituted 14 October 1422 to church of Dowsby, on death of Robert Germethorp. Patron: William Roos of Dowsby, esquire. [*Reg. Fleming* i. no.161.]

William Dalaha priest
Instituted 15 March 1456/7 to church of Dowsby, on death of William Wyllyngham. Patron: Katherine Roos, widow of William Roos esquire. [Reg. 20, fo.126v.]

John Stumble priest
Instituted 27 April 1462 to church of Dowsby (cause of vacancy not stated). Patron: William Roos esquire. [Reg. 20, fo.136.]

Robert Castelford
Instituted before 19 November 1481. [Reg. 22, fo.128.]

William Malton
Instituted 19 November 1481 to church of St Andrew, Dowsby, on resignation of Robert Castelford. Patron: William Roos esquire. [Reg. 22, fo.128.]

John Estwood
Instituted 1 July 1487 to church of St Andrew, Dowsby, on resignation of William Malton. Patron: William Roos esquire. [Reg. 22, fo.137v.]

Robert Evedon priest
Instituted 11 May 1500 to church of Dowsby, on death of John Estwode. Patron: Thomas Roos esquire. [Reg. 23, fo.52v.]

John Fen chaplain
Instituted 12 January 1508/9 to church of Dowsby, on death of M. Robert Evyden. Patron: M. Henry Horneby DD for this turn, by grant of next presentation (dated 16 August 1508) made to him by Laurence Custe, true patron of Dowsby in right of his wife Margaret. [Reg. 23, fo.135v.]

Thomas Marmyon chaplain
Instituted 6 February 1518 to church of Dowsby, on death of M. John Fen. Patron: John Willughby esquire (Henry Willughby kt) and John Marmyon gent., for this turn by reason of a feoffment of the manor of Dowsby, made to them by Joan widow of John Tempest (then in her widowhood), now the wife of David Sacyll. [Reg. 25, fos 20, 20v.]

Assessed for subsidy (£10) in 1526 and *Valor Ecclesiasticus* 1535. [*Subsidy*, 56; *Valor* iv. 105.]

M. William Stafford
Instituted 20 April 1543 to church of Dowsby, on death of M. Thomas Marmyon. Patron: John Boocher de Maxhey, for this turn by reason of a grant of the advowson made to him by David Cycell late of Stamford and Joan his wife. [Reg. 27, fo.80.]

Exhibited at Visitation ('William Staforthe') in 1551. [Vj 13, fo.62.]

William Sherman
Instituted 9 June 1554 to church of Dowsby, on removal of last rector. Patron: Joan Boocher widow and executrix of the will of John Boocher of Stamford, by reason of a grant of the advowson made to the said John and others by Anthony Villers of Stamford. [Reg. 28, fo.110v.]

Christopher Villers
Instituted 1563 to church of Dowsby, on death of William Shereman. Patron: Edward Villers gent. [Reg. 28, fo.12.]

Signed BT at Dowsby 1566. Witnessed Dowsby wills, 1565–68. [BTs Dowsby; LCC Wills 1565/75v, 76v; LCC Wills 1568/102, 134v.]

William Stanehus
Instituted 8 July 1572 to church of Dowsby, on death of Christopher Villers.

Patron: William Stafford, by reason of a grant made to him by Edward Villers gent. [*Bishop Cooper*, 7, 243–4.]

Robert Buckberie

Instituted 24 December 1573 to church of Dowsby (cause of vacancy not stated). Patron: Rodolph Bowes esquire. [*Bishop Cooper*, 10.]

Born *c*.1549. Education: 'knows Latin moderately; moderately versed in sacred learning'. Priest: 22 December 1573 (Chichester). Resident (1576): signed BTs at Dowsby 1577–8, 1586–1611. Died before 16 September 1611 (probate inventory: 'his library, £3 6s 8d'). [*Bishop Cooper*, 208, 219; BTs Dowsby; INV 110/191.]

Edmund Assheton MA

Instituted 23 December 1611 to rectory of Dowsby, on death of Robert Buckberry. Patron: Robert Rigdon esquire (27 October 1611). [PD 1611/32.]

Son of Walter A. (d.1587) of Spalding and Etheldreda (who married 2ndly Sir William Rigdon kt of Dowsby). Educated: Corpus Christi College, Cambridge (matric. 1602; BA 1605–6; MA 1609). Deacon and priest: 22 December 1611 (Lincoln). Signed BTs at Dowsby 1612–41. Still Rector in 1655–6. Will (PCC) dated 21 December 1653: to be buried 'in my Chancell soe neare my Mothers Tombe as Conveniently may be'; to his son Edmund, 'the Deske in my Studdie which was his Grandfathers'; codicil dated 22 November 1654; proved 11 May 1657. [*Lincolnshire Pedigrees*, 1139–40; Venn, *Alumni*; LC 4, fo.72; BTs Dowsby; PRO, E134/1655–6/Hil3; PROB 11/264/143.]

Nathaniel Cony

Instituted *c*.1656. Patron: Abraham Burrell. [LPL, Comm. III/5, 212; Swaby, 111.]

Educated: St John's College, Cambridge (matric. 1629; BA 1632–3; MA 1636). Formerly: R. of Rempstone (Nt), 1642. Afterwards: R. of Broughton (Ox), 1657–62 (ejected 1662). Still alive in 1691, when it was reported that his 'condition is very Low, his very bed was Seized from under him, for his very bread that hee has to keep him alive, most of his helpers are dead, his Daughter as helpless as himselfe through poverty, hee is past preaching through age and other infirmities'. [Venn, *Alumni*; Swaby, 111; Godfrey, *Notts Churches: Rushcliffe*, 224; *Calamy Revised*, 131.]

John Rocket

Instituted 17 April 1658. [LPL, Comm. III/7, 11; Swaby, 112.]

Born *c*.1621; son of William R. of Nottingham. Educated: Lincoln College, Oxford (matric. 1636). Formerly: R. of Hickling (Nt), 1646; R. of Market Bosworth (Le), 1652; V. of Cheshunt (Hrt), 1654. Author: *Divisions Cut in Pieces by the Sword of the Lord* (1650). Died *c*.1669. Admon (LCC). [Foster, *Alumni*; ESTC; *Calamy Revised*, 414.]

Samuel Pancke

Instituted before 16 August 1660. [IND/L 1, fo.137v.]

Baptised 4 January 1628/9 at Thurlby-by-Bourne; son of William P. Educated: St John's College, Cambridge (matric. 1644; BA 1647–8; BD 1661). Also: R. of Fleet, 1657. Afterwards: R. of North Creake (Nf), 1662–86. [PR Thurlby-by-Bourne; Venn, *Alumni*; Swaby, 61, 112.]

George Burr MA

Instituted 16 August 1660 to rectory of Dowsby, on cession of Samuel Pancke. Patron: Redmayne Burrell esquire. [AC; IND/L 1, fo.137v.]

Of Bedfordshire. Educated: Emmanuel College (matric. 1635) and Trinity College, Cambridge; MA. Deacon: 19 December 1641 (Peterborough); priest: 18 May 1643 (Lincoln). Formerly: R. of Folksworth (Hu), 1645. Resident at Dowsby (1662): signed BTs there 1662–6. Also: V. of Thurlby-by-Bourne, 1663–7. Buried 2 February 1666/7 at Thurlby-by-Bourne. [Venn, *Alumni*; LC 5, fo.22v; BTs Dowsby; PR Thurlby-by-Bourne.]

Matthew Queningbrough MA

Instituted 6 February 1666/7 to rectory of Dowsby, on death of George Burr. Patron: Redmayne Burrell of Dowsby, esquire. [Reg. 33, fo.75.]

Of Lincolnshire. Educated: Emmanuel College, Cambridge (matric. 1656–7; BA 1660–1; MA 1664). Formerly: C. of Dunsby, 1663. Buried at Dowsby, 18 March 1669/70. [Venn, *Alumni*; CCED; BTs Dowsby.]

Nathaniel Bligh MA

Instituted 8 April 1670 to rectory of Dowsby, on death of Matthew Queningbrough. Patron: Redmayne Burrell esquire. [Reg. 33, fo.128v.]

Of Warwickshire. Educated: Emmanuel College, Cambridge (matric. 1659; BA 1662; MA 1666). Priest: 20 September 1667 (Ely). Buried at Dowsby, 1 October 1682. [Venn, *Alumni*; Reg. 33, fo.128v; BTs Dowsby.]

Ralph Thompson MA

Instituted 2 December 1682 to rectory of Dowsby, on death of Nathaniel Blyth. Patron: Redman Burrell esquire (21 November 1682). [Reg. 34, fo.71; PD 1682/58.]

Born *c*.1646; son of Christopher T. of Durham. Educated: Houghton-le-Spring School and Christ's College, Cambridge (matric. 1663; BA 1666; MA 1670). Deacon: 2 June 1667 (Peterborough); priest: 6 June 1669 (Durham). Formerly: C. of Dunsby, 1670; R. of Stubton, 1671–82. [Venn, *Alumni*; Reg. 34, fo.71; SUB V/5, fo.4v.]

Humphrey Hyde MA

Instituted 30 July 1690 to rectory of Dowsby, on death of Ralph Thompson. Patron: Matthew Trollope, William Trollope and William Hyde esquires (8 July 1690), trustees under will of Redmayne Burrell esquire. [Reg. 34, fo.117v; PD 1690/50.]

Born 2 January 1662/3 at Dowsby; son of William H. of Langtoft. Educated: Grantham School and Magdalene College, Cambridge (matric. 1678; BA 1681–2; MA 1685); Fellow 1684. Deacon: 20 December 1685; priest: 19 December 1686 (Lincoln). Resident: signed BTs at Dowsby 1692–1727. Also: V. of Long Sutton, 1687–1725; R. of Hayes with Norwood (Mx), 1689–1727. Father of Humphrey H., Rector of Dowsby (1727–54), below. Buried at Dowsby, 30 April 1727. Will (PCC) dated 23 April 1727, proved 21

June 1727; bequests to the poor of Dowsby (£5), of Long Sutton (£5), of Lutton (40s), of Sutton St Edmund (40s), of Sutton St James (40s), of Langtoft (40s) and of Hayes (£4). [*Lincolnshire Pedigrees*, 537–8; Venn, *Alumni*; Reg. 34, fos 89, 94v; LC 14, p.31; *Speculum*, 43, 121; BTs Dowsby; Newcourt i. 641; PRO, PROB 11/615/477.]

Humphrey Hyde

Instituted 25 September 1727 to rectory of Dowsby, on death of Humphrey Hyde. Patron: Thomas Burrell of Dowsby, esquire (3 May 1727). [Reg. 38, p.164; PD 1727/8.]

Baptised at West Deeping, 1 August 1701; son of Humphrey H., Rector of Dowsby (1690–1727), above. Educated: Lincoln College (matric. 1720) and Magdalen College, Oxford (BA 1724, MA 1727); Demy 1721–8. Deacon: 19 September 1725; priest: 24 September 1727 (Lincoln). Also: R. of Little Casterton (Ru), 1749–54. Resident until 1749: signed BTs at Dowsby 1728–48. Resided thereafter at Little Casterton, while Dowsby was served by John Vokes as curate. Married Philippa, daughter of John Wake. Died 17 March 1754 at Little Casterton; buried there (MI). [PR West Deeping; *Lincolnshire Pedigrees*, 538; Foster, *Alumni*; Bloxham vi. 200; Reg. 38, pp. 103, 163; BTs Dowsby; PR Stamford St Mary; Longden vii. 189.]

Brownlow Toller LLB

Instituted 24 August 1754 to rectory of Dowsby, on death of Humphrey Hyde. Patron: Thomas Burrell esquire. [Reg. 38, p.528.]

Born 17 July 1730 at Ryhall Hall (Ru); son of John T. of Billingborough, esquire. Educated: Oakham School and Clare Hall, Cambridge (matric. 1748; LLB 1754). Deacon: 9 June 1754; priest: 24 August 1754 (Lincoln). Inherited his father's estates at Ryhall and Billingborough. Married (26 December 1754) at St Mary, Stamford, Anne, daughter of Humphrey Hyde, Rector of Dowsby (1727–54) above, through whom he inherited the Dowsby estate. Resided at Barn Hill in Stamford. He 'displayed in the management of his property a scrupulous love of order and punctilious precision, which ran through all his conduct, and sometimes interfered with the peace and comfort of his household'. Died 4 September 1791 at the house of his daughter in Hart Street, Bloomsbury; buried at Billingborough (MI). [*Chester of Chicheley*, 669–70; *Lincolnshire Pedigrees*, 995; Venn, *Alumni*; Reg. 38, pp. 526, 528; *Monson*, 42.]

George Moore

Instituted 2 July 1761 to rectory of Dowsby, on cession of Brownlow Toller. Patron: William Pochin of Barkby, esquire (29 June 1761). [Reg. 38, p.584; PD 1761/33.]

Educated: Queens' College, Cambridge (matric. 1750; BA 1754; MA 1757). Priest: 21 September 1755 (Lincoln). Formerly: C. of Market Deeping, 1755; V. of Langtoft, 1755–61. Perhaps also: Minor Canon of Peterborough, 1756–64. Resigned Dowsby 3 June 1763. Died 1764. [Venn, *Alumni*; Reg. 38, pp. 538, 540; Longden ix. 249; RES 238/91.]

Thomas Foster LLB

Instituted 13 June 1763 to rectory of Dowsby, on resignation of George Moore. Patron: William Pochin of Barkby. Reinstituted 2 November 1763, on his own resignation; patron, William Pochin esquire. [Reg. 39, pp. 19, 25.]

Born 3 February, baptised at Bourne 22 March 1738/9; son of William F. of Bourne, attorney-at-law. Educated: Queens' College, Cambridge (matric. 1756; LLB 1763). Deacon: 20 December 1761 (Salisbury); priest: 12 June 1763 (Lincoln). Also: V. of Witham-on-the-Hill, 1763–72. Non-resident at Dowsby (1768), which was served by John Baskett as curate. Resided at Ryhall. Afterwards: V. of Ryhall with Essendine (Ru), 1773–98; R. of Careby, 1789–1825; R. of Tinwell (Ru), 1798–1825. Married (2 February 1769 by Humphrey Hyde, V. of Bourne) at Aslackby, Sarah, daughter of John Baskett, R. of Dunsby (1740–1802). Father of Thomas F., Rector of Tinwell (Ru), 1797–8; of John F., Rector of Wickersley (Y); and of Kingsman F., R. of Dowsby (1807–67), below. JP for Rutland and County Treasurer; promoter of schools of rural industry in Rutland. Sold the Dowsby and Ryhall estates in 1793; resided thereafter at Tinwell. Died 4 September 1825 at Tinwell, aged 87; buried at Tinwell. [*Notes on the Foster Family*, x–xi; Venn, *Alumni*; Longden v. 99; PR Aslackby.]

Humphrey Hyde MA
Instituted 6 December 1773 to rectory of Dowsby, on cession of Thomas Foster. Patron: Thomas Foster, as above. [Reg. 39, p.216.]

Baptised 14 February 1737/8 at Dowsby; son of Humphrey H. (1701–1754), Rector of Dowsby 1727–54, above. Educated: Queens' College, Cambridge (matric. 1756; BA 1760; MA 1774). Deacon: 21 September 1760 (Peterborough); priest: 7 March 1762 (Lincoln). Formerly: C. of Essendine (Ru), 1760. Also: V. of Langtoft, 1762–73; V. of Bourne, 1763–1807. Resided at Bourne 1763–73 ('lives at Bourne and serves his Church', 1768) and thereafter at Dowsby. Married (4 September 1766 by Thomas Foster, R. of Dowsby) at Bourne, Katharine, daughter and heir of John Hyde of Bourne, surgeon. Father of John H. (1767–1803), Minor Canon of Peterborough. Died 18 January 1807, aged 70; buried at Dowsby (MI). [PR Dowsby; *Lincolnshire Pedigrees*, 539; Venn, *Alumni*; Longden vii. 189; PR Bourne; LC 31, pp. 69, 75; PR Dowsby; *Monson*, 115.]

Kingsman Foster BA
Instituted 29 June 1807 to rectory of Dowsby, on death of Humphrey Hyde. Patron: Thomas Foster LLB of Tinwell (Ru), clerk (24 June 1807). [Reg. 40, p.121; PD 163/28.]

Baptised 27 June 1783 at Ryhall (Ru); son of Thomas Foster LLB, V. of Ryhall (and R. of Dowsby 1763–73), above. Educated: Oakham School and St John's College, Cambridge (matric. 1802; BA 1806; MA 1809). Deacon: 21 December 1806 (Lincoln for Peterborough); priest: 28 June 1807 (Peterborough). Also: C. of Kirkby Underwood, 1828; C. of Frampton (Do), 1851. Resided at Dowsby Rectory. Married (5 March 1812) at St Botolph, London, Mary, daughter of Kingsman Baskett St Barbe of London. Father of 13 children, including Kingsman Baskett F. (below). Licence for non-residence (1850–1), on account of daughter's ill-health; served curacy at Frampton. Died 18 April 1867 at Dowsby; buried at Dowsby. [*Lincolnshire Pedigrees*, 1228; Venn, *Alumni*; Longden v. 95; Reg. 40, p.112; CR 1, p.372; White, *Lincolnshire* (1842), 736; White, *Lincolnshire* (1856), 713–14; Census Returns 1841, 1861 (Dowsby), 1851 (Frampton); NRL 14/20; *Probate Calendar* 1867.]

Kingsman Baskett Foster BA
Instituted 4 October 1867 to rectory of Dowsby, on death of Kingsman Foster. Patron: Kingman Baskett Foster himself, for this turn. [Reg. 41, p.231.]

Born *c*.1813 at Dowsby; eldest son of Kingsman F., above. Educated: Lincoln College, Oxford (matric. 1831; BA 1836). Deacon: 25 September 1836; priest: 11 March 1838

(Lincoln). Formerly: C. of Dowsby, 1836. Resided at Dowsby Rectory. Licence for non-residence (1871–2), on account of ill-health (throat congested, loss of voice). Died 11 November 1896. [Foster, *Alumni*; OR 1, pp. 65, 71; CR 2, p.151; Census Returns 1891; NRL 35/57, 36/22; *Probate Calendar* 1897.]

Charles Edward Pochin Boyer BA

Instituted 27 March 1897 to rectory of Dowsby, on death of Kingsman Baskett Foster. Patron: Thomas Charge Boyer of Hazeldine, Farncomb Road, Worthing (Sx), esquire. [Reg. 42, p.411.]

Born *c.*1859 at Barton (YNR); son of Joseph B., surgeon. Educated: Emmanuel College, Cambridge (matric. 1878; BA 1883). Deacon: 1884; priest: 1888 (Worcester). Formerly: C. of King's Norton (Wa), 1884–6; of Harborough Magna (Wa), 1888–91. Resignation accepted 28 December 1898. Afterwards of 20 Cromwell Road, Hove. Died 24 August 1927 at Tregarthyn House Nursing Home, Hove. [Venn, *Alumni*; *Crockford* (1908, 1927); Census Returns 1861 (Barton), 1911 (Hove); Reg. 42, p.440; *Probate Calendar* 1927.]

Thomasin Albert Stoodley MA

Instituted 30 December 1898 to rectory of Dowsby, on resignation of Charles Edward Pochin Boyer. Patron: Mary Melesina Stoodley, wife of the said Thomasin Albert Stoodley of Folkingham. [Reg. 42, p.440.]

Born *c.*1846; son of Samuel S. of Ilminster (So), gent. Educated: Magdalen Hall (matric. 1863) and St Mary Hall, Oxford (BA 1869; BCL and MA 1870). Deacon: 1870; priest: 1871 (Ripon). Formerly: C. of Holy Trinity, Ripon, 1870–2; of St Cuthbert, Darlington, 1872–3; Assistant Chaplain, St Thomas Martyr, Newcastle-upon-Tyne, 1873–80; Second Master, Newcastle Royal GS, 1877–80; Head Master, Hereford County College, 1880–6; Head Master, Spalding GS, 1887–94; Chaplain, St Nicholas, Wykeham, 1889–94; R. of Folkingham with Laughton, 1894–8 (*q.v.*). Married (11 October 1894) Mary Melesina, daughter of Revd Francis Chenevix Trench, R. of Islip (Ox). Resided at Dowsby Rectory. In his 4½ h.p. De Dion motor car, took part in Lincolnshire Automobile Club rally at Grimsthorpe (July 1904). Licence for non-residence (1908–10), on account of ill-health; Dowsby served by William John Richards as curate. Bishop Hicks noted (1910): 'I gladly allowed him to be non-resident, for he has secured an excellent L[ocum] T[enens] & is so eccentric a Vicar that (I am told) his Parishioners had to request him sometimes to let them have the Apostles' Creed in Matins.' Resignation accepted 10 May 1912. Latterly of 73 Wimborne Road, Bournemouth. Died there, 27 February 1915. [Foster, *Alumni*; *Crockford* (1908); Burke, *Peerage* (1999), 124; NRL 70/12, 16, 20; Census Returns 1911; *Stamford Mercury*, 15 July 1904; *Hicks Diaries*, no.31; Reg. 43, p.26; *Probate Calendar* 1915.]

Thomas Gordon Murray Macmorran

Instituted 2 August 1912 to rectory of Dowsby, on resignation of Thomasin Albert Stoodley. Patron: Arthur Henry Brandt of Ivy House, Godstone (Sr), esquire. [Reg. 43, p.31.]

Born *c.*1865 Educated: King's College, London (AKC 1897). Deacon: 1898; priest: 1899 (St Albans). Formerly: C. of Great Wymondley with St Ippolyts (Hrt), 1898–1900; of Binfield (Brk), 1900–3; Southwark Diocese, 1903–5; C. of Coggeshall, 1905–8; of Godstone (Sr), 1908–9; Chaplain at Las Palmas, 1909–10; C. of Pulham St Mary Magdalene, 1910–12. Resided at Dowsby Rectory. Resignation accepted 25 June 1919. Afterwards: R. of Chiselborough with West Chinnock, 1919–29; V. of Nynehead (So),

1929–44. Retired to Westbere, Milverton (So). Died 1951. [*Crockford* (1949–50); *LDC* (1914), 88; Reg. 43, p.181; GRO, Death Index.]

Howard Smith Chesshire MA

Instituted 21 October 1919 by Official *sede vacante* to rectory of Dowsby, on resignation of Thomas Gordon Murray Macmorran. Patron: Arthur Henry Brandt, as above. [Reg. 43, p.185.]

Born 1857; son of Edwin C. of Birmingham, gent. Educated: Worcester College, Oxford (matric. 1877; BA 1881; MA 1884). Deacon: 1882; priest: 1883 (London). Formerly: C. of Stoke Newington, 1882–4; of St Andrew, Haverstock Hill, 1884–7; Chaplain at Havre, 1887–94; V. of St Catherine, Tranmere, 1894–1904; R. of Chiselborough with West Chinnock, 1904–19. Married (3 May 1887) at St Andrew, Haverstock Hill, Lucy Elizabeth Pridham. Resided at Dowsby. Resigned 27 December 1922 (accepted 1 January 1923). Latterly at Headlands, Foxhall, near Ipswich. Died 20 January 1929 at Ipswich Borough Royal Asylum. [Foster, *Alumni; Crockford* (1923); LMA, PR Haverstock Hill St Andrew; RES 248g/30; *Probate Calendar* 1929.]

Frederic Stanhope Worsley

Instituted 17 March 1923 to rectory of Dowsby, on resignation of Howard Smith Chesshire. Patron: Arthur Henry Brandt, as above. [Reg. 43, p.307.]

The Rectory of Dunsby was united to the Rectory of Dowsby by Order in Council dated 15 August 1929. [Reg. 43, p.452.]

Frederic Stanhope Worsley

Instituted 25 October 1929 to united benefice of Dunsby with Dowsby, as first Incumbent thereof, on resignation of Dunsby by Wordsworth Everard Jones. [Reg. 43, p.455.]

Born *c.*1864 at Bankipore (India); son of Charles Fortescue W., esquire. Educated: Magdalen College, Oxford (matric. 1882). Electrical engineer; living at Erdington (Wa), 1911. Deacon: 1920 (Coventry); priest: 1921 (Birmingham for Coventry). Formerly: C. of Stoke, Coventry, 1920–3. Resided at Dowsby Rectory. Resignation accepted 1 October 1945. Latterly at 4 Coleridge Walk, London NW11. Died 29 December 1950 at Caroline Nursing Home, Exeter Road, Exmouth. [Foster, *Alumni*; *Crockford* (1941); Reg. 44, p.40; *Probate Calendar* 1951.]

Harold Frederick David Stannard AKC

Instituted 21 May 1946 by the Official *sede vacante* to united benefice of Dunsby with Dowsby, on resignation of Frederic Stanhope Worsley. Patron: The Governors of Sutton's Hospital in Charterhouse, for this turn. [Reg. 44, p.53.]

Born 16 July 1912. Educated: King's College, London (AKC 1937). Deacon: 1937; priest: 1938 (Truro). Formerly: C. of St Columb Major, 1937–43; Chaplain, RAFVR, 1943–6. Resided at Dowsby Rectory. Afterwards: R. of West Quantoxhead (So), 1948–77. Retired 1977. Lived at Little Orchard, Bosinver Lane, Polgooth (Co). Died October 2003 in St Austell. [GRO, Death Index; *LDC* (1947), 56; *Crockford* (1971–2, 1989–90).]

Geoffrey Clarence Lewis
Instituted 26 August 1949 to united benefice of Dunsby with Dowsby, on cession of Harold Frederick David Stannard. Patron: Bishop of Lincoln for this turn, by lapse. [Reg. 44, p.110.]

Born 26 March 1909 at Vereeniging (Transvaal); son of Thomas Frederick L., Wesleyan Minister. Educated: University of Durham (1928); Queen's College, Birmingham (1928). Deacon: 1933; priest: 1934 (Manchester). Formerly: C. of St George, Hulme, 1933–5; at St Mary, Kingswinford (St), 1935–7; C. of Whitchurch Canonicorum, 1937–40; of Minehead, 1940–4; PC of St John, Holbeach Fen, 1944–9. Resided at Dowsby Rectory. Afterwards: R. of Bettiscombe with Pilsdon and Marshwood (Do), 1958–74. Latterly at 32 Denham Close, Maidenhead. Died 1975 (Slough). [Census Returns 1911 (Alford); *Crockford* (1973–4); *LDC* (1957), 51; GRO, Death Index.]

David Lamplough Scott MA
Instituted 3 October 1963 to united benefice of Dunsby with Dowsby, on cession of Geoffrey Clarence Lewis. Note that on 9 April 1963, an Order for Plurality was made under Section 5 of the Pastoral Reorganisation Measure 1949, authorising the said DLS to hold the benefices of Dunsby with Dowsby and Rippingale in plurality. [Reg. 44, p.352.]

Also: R. of Rippingale, 1955–74 (*q.v.*).

DUNSBY-BY-BOURNE

Although the church of Dunsby did not form part of the original endowment of Bourne Abbey, the advowson belonged to the Abbot and Convent by 1222–3. The Abbey, which never appropriated the church, continued to hold it until the Dissolution. In the early seventeenth century the manor and advowson were acquired by Thomas Sutton, who gave them as part of the original endowment of his Hospital of the Charterhouse. The first Master, John Hutton, was presented to the rectory in 1614. The Governors of the Hospital continued to present to the church thereafter; many of the rectors were educated at Charterhouse School. The advowson remained in the possession of the Governors in 1965. [Stenton, *Facsimiles of Early Charters*, 18; Porter, *The London Charterhouse*, 20; *LDC* (1965), 66–7.]

M. Elias de Lamburn clerk
Instituted in the fourteenth pontifical year of Bishop Hugh of Wells (20 December 1222/19 December 1223) to church of Dunsby-by-Bourne. Patron: Abbot and Convent of Bourne. [*Rot. Welles* iii. 122.]

M. Roger de Bedeford
Instituted 1 June 1237 to church of Dunsby-by-Bourne. Patron: Abbot and Convent of Bourne. Reinstituted in the twelfth pontifical year of Bishop

Robert Grosseteste (17 June 1246–16 June 1247); patron, as above. [Hoskin, nos 24, 369, 544.]

Also: R. of Thrapston (Np), 1246–7. [Hoskin, no.830.]

Ralph de Morton subdeacon
Instituted in the thirteenth pontifical year of Bishop Robert Grosseteste (17 June 1247/16 June 1248) to church of Dunsby-by-Bourne. Patron: Abbot and Convent of Bourne. [Hoskin, nos 416, 590.]

Had papal dispensation (2 January 1255/6) to hold another benefice with cure of souls. [*CPL* i. 325.]

Robert de Staumford
Instituted before 22 September 1291. [*Reg. Sutton* i. 158.]

M. Robert de Dunnesby clerk in minor orders
Instituted 22 September 1291 to church of Dunsby-by-Bourne, on death of Robert de Staumford. Patron: Abbot and Convent of Bourne. [*Reg. Sutton* i. 158.]

Subdeacon: 22 September 1291; deacon: 22 March 1292; priest: 20 September 1292 (Lincoln). Licence to choose a confessor, 20 January 1320/1. Licence to dwell in household of subdean of Lincoln, to help him and to study theology at Lincoln, by turns, 8 April 1321. Received royal letters of protection, dated 8 November 1327. [*Reg. Sutton* vii. 18, 26, 34; Reg. 5, fo.274; *Reg. Burghersh* iii. no.128; *CPR 1327–30*, 184.]

John de Wyveton subdeacon
Instituted 21 December 1328 to church of Dunsby-by-Bourne, on death of [blank]. Patron: Abbot and Convent of Bourne. [*Reg. Burghersh* i. no.212.]

Priest: before 30 November 1329. Licences for study for 1 year, 30 November 1329; in England or abroad for 3 years, 6 April 1331. [*Reg. Burghersh* iii. no.529; Reg. 5, fo.188.]

M. John de Staunford clerk
Instituted 4 August 1343 to church of Dunsby-by-Bourne, on death of John. Patron: Bishop of Lincoln, by lapse (the advowson having been disputed for over six months between br. Simon, Abbot of Bourne, and the Prior and Convent of the same). [Reg. 6, fo.6v.]

M. Wybert Campyon
Instituted before 19 March 1347/8.

Dispensation to study for 3 years, 19 March 1347/8. [Reg. 9C, fo.34v.]

M. Richard de Neuton priest
Instituted 30 January 1358/9 to church of Dunsby-by-Bourne, on death of Master Wybert. Patron: Abbot and Convent of Bourne. [Reg. 9, fo.136v.]

John de Huberd priest
Instituted 11 August 1363 to church of Dunsby-by-Bourne, on death of M. Richard de Neuton. Patron: Abbot and Convent of Bourne. [Reg. 10, fo.1v.]

Ralph de Hermethorp priest
Instituted 6 November 1366 to church of Dunsby-by-Bourne (cause of vacancy not stated). Patron: Abbot and Convent of Bourne. [Reg. 10, fo.16v.]
Formerly: R. of Folkingham, 1361 (*q.v.*). Afterwards: R. of Saundby (Nt), March–July 1376. Died before 4 July 1376. [Train, *North Notts Clergy*, 162.]

Henry Drury (de Helperthorp)
Instituted 17 March 1375/6 to church of Dunsby-by-Bourne, on resignation of Ralph de Hermesthorp (by exchange with church of Saundby, dioc. York). Patron: Abbot and Convent of Bourne. [Reg. 10, fo.76v.]
Priest: before 21 June 1361. Formerly: V. of Hemel Hempstead, 1361–3; R. of Teigh (Ru), 1363–8; R. of Owmby, 1368–74 (*q.v.*); R. of Saundby (Nt), 1374–6. Also: Canon of Lincoln and Prebendary of All Saints in Hungate, 1387 and again 1394–7; R. of Scotter, to 1394. Afterwards: R. of Dunsby (again), 1394–7. Assessed for poll-tax in 1381. Licences to be absent for 3 years and to farm his benefice, 28 April 1382; for a further 3 years and to farm his benefice, 10 February 1385/6. Will dated Saturday of Feast of St Agatha 1395; proved 5 February 1396/7. [Reg. 9, fo.410v; Train, *North Notts Clergy*, 162; *Le Neve Fasti: Lincoln 1300–1541*, 27; *Clerical Poll-Taxes*, nos 1325, 1914; Reg. 12, fos 238, 319, 442.]

M. John (Hode) de Bannebury
Instituted before 4 June 1394. [Reg. 11, fos 70v, 112v.]
Educated: University of Oxford (MA); Fellow of Merton *c.*1375–94. Acolyte: 19 September 1394 (London). Also: Canon of Lincoln and Prebendary of All Saints in Hungate, 1390–4. Afterwards: R. of Scotter, 1394–1400; R. of Hougham, 1400–20. Died before 25 September 1420. [Emden, *BRUO*, 102; Reg. 16, fo.209v.]

Henry Drury priest
Instituted 4 June 1394 to church of Dunsby-by-Bourne (and canonry of Lincoln and prebend of All Saints in Hungate), on resignation of M. John de Bannebury (by exchange with church of Scotter). Patron: Thomas, Archbishop of York; John, Bishop of Salisbury; John de Burton clerk; Philip Tilney kt and Philip Gernon *domicellus*, feoffees of Thomas de Pynchebek decd. [Reg. 11, fos 70v, 112v.]
See above.

Thomas Bawdewyn
Instituted 8 March 1396/7 to church of Dunsby-by-Bourne, on death of Henry Drury. Patron: Thomas, lately Archbishop of York and now of Canterbury, and Philip Gernon of Boston, feoffees of Thomas de Pynchebek, who had recovered the advowson in the king's court against John Mulsho. [Reg. 11, fo.86.]

TB's estate in the church ratified by the King, 22 January 1399. Afterwards: R. of Wilsford, 1407–9; V. of Stowmarket (Sf), 1409. [*CPR 1396–99*, 451; Reg. 14, fos 22, 33.]

Richard Butte

Instituted 22 November 1407 to church of Dunsby-by-Bourne, on resignation of Thomas Baudewyn (by exchange with church of Wilsford). Patron: Abbot and Convent of Bourne. [Reg. 14, fo.22.]

Formerly: V. of Grays Thurrock (Ess), 1395–8; R. of Denton (Hu), 1398–1404; R. of Wilsford, 1404–7. Afterwards: R. of Blisworth (Np), 1418–19; R. of Great Wigborough (Ess), 1419–42. Died before 26 January 1441/2. [Newcourt ii. 589, 663; Reg. 13, fo.172; Reg. 14, fo.277.]

William Gase priest

Instituted 28 August 1418 to church of Dunsby-by-Bourne, on resignation of Richard Butte (by exchange with church of Blisworth). Patron: Abbot and Convent of Bourne. [Reg. 14, fo.95v.]

Formerly: R. of Blisworth (Np), to 1418.

Roger Misterton

Instituted 8 August 1435 to church of Dunsby-by-Bourne (cause of vacancy not stated). Patron: Abbot and Convent of Bourne. [Reg. 17, fo.12v.]

William Bate priest

Instituted 24 November 1444 to church of Dunsby-by-Bourne (cause of vacancy not stated). Patron: Abbot and Convent of Bourne. [Reg. 18, fo.93.]

Thomas Caundelyn canon regular

Instituted 24 September 1473 to church of Dunsby-by-Bourne, on death of William Bate. Patron: Abbot and Convent of Bourne. [Reg. 21, fos 5v, 6.]

Richard Knoblowe priest

Instituted 27 March 1480 to church of Dunsby-by-Bourne, on death of Thomas Candelyn. Patron: Richard, Duke of Gloucester, for this turn, by grant of Abbot and Convent of Bourne. [Reg. 21, fo.26.]

Thomas Ridley priest

Instituted 7 February 1482/3 to church of Dunsby-by-Bourne, on death of Richard Knoblowe. Patron: Abbot and Convent of Bourne. Reinstituted 24 May 1483, on his own resignation; patron, as above. [Reg. 22, fos 131, 132v.]

Thomas Gan priest

Instituted 1 April 1491 to church of Dunsby-by-Bourne, on resignation of

Thomas Rydley. Patron: Abbot and Convent of Bourne (16 March 1490/1). [Reg. 22, fo.145; PD 1491/18.]

Resigned 17 August 1493. [RES 1493/9.]

Robert Wyhom chaplain
Instituted 24 April 1494 to church of Dunsby-by-Bourne, on resignation of Thomas Ganne. Patron: Abbot and Convent of Bourne (18 March 1493/4). [Reg. 22, fo.158; PD 1494/9.]

Dispensed for plurality, 1495. Assessed for subsidy (£9 9s 10d) in 1526. [*CPL* xvi no.496; *Subsidy*, 58.]

John Snowe priest
Instituted 30 March 1530 to church of Dunsby-by-Bourne, on resignation of last incumbent. Patron: Abbot and Convent of Bourne. Note that an annual pension of £6 was reserved to the resigning incumbent for life from the fruits of the church. [Reg. 27, fo.47.]

Assessed for *Valor Ecclesiasticus* 1535. Exhibited at Visitation in 1551. Appears to have been deprived, *c.*1554; restored after 1558 (see below). Died 1567. Will (LCC), dated 5 March 1565/6; proved 29 December 1567. Asked for 'my bodie to be buried in the parishe churche of Dunesbie'; bequests made to Christ's College, Cambridge (40s), to the poor of Dunsby, Rippingale, Hagnaby and Morton; residue to his wife, Alice. Probate inventory (30 December 1567): 'certaine bokes good and badd, both in latten and Englishe, xxvjs viijd'. [*Valor* iv. 106; Vj 13, fo.62; LCC Wills 1567/9v; INV 46/395A.]

Thomas Wood
Instituted *c.*1554 to rectory of Dunsby-by-Bourne (compounded for first-fruits, 28 August 1554). [FL.h.12, 375.]

Witnessed Dunsby wills 1557. [LCC Wills 1556–7/55, 81; 1557/i/111, 154v; 1557/iii/24.]

John Snowe
Restored after 1558 (see above).

William Bolton
Instituted *c.*1569 to rectory of Dunsby-by-Bourne (compounded for first-fruits, 26 January 1569). [FL.h.12, 375.]

Born *c.*1542. Education: 'Bred in the schools'; 'skilled in Latin; competently versed in sacred learning'. Priest: 30 November 1565 (Lincoln). Witnessed will as curate of Dunsby, 4 April 1567. Resident (1576). Died before 9 January 1614/15 (probate inventory: 'his books, 20s ... twelve swine, 4 turkies, £4 5s'). Will (LCC). [*Bishop Cooper*, 208; *State of the Church*, 73; LC 4, fo.72; LCC Wills 1567/278; INV 115/8; LCC Wills 1615/477.]

John Hutton MA
Instituted 9 November 1614 to rectory of Dunsby-by-Bourne. [BC; IND/L 1, fo.11.]

Educated: Trinity College (matric. 1584), King's College and St Catharine's Hall,

Cambridge (BA 1585–6; MA 1589). Deacon and priest: 24 August 1590 (Peterborough). Formerly: V. of Littlebury (Ess), 1595–1615; Master of the Charterhouse, 1613–14. Died *c*.1629. Will (PCC) dated 2 May 1626; administration granted to Mary Hutton widow, 12 January 1629/30. Bequeathed to Margaret Hutton (sister) the sum of £20 with remainder to children of Isabel Preston of Heversham (We), so that 'Roger Preston theire Father by no meanes, colour or perswasion shall finger any parte therof'; to the poor of Littlebury, £20; to the poor of Dunsby, £6 13s 4d; to the poor scholars of King's College, Cambridge, £10 (a 'widowes mite, the giver thereof sometimes beinge one of that same poore societie'); to the poor scholars of St Catharine's Hall, Cambridge, £6 13s 4d; to the Free School in Manchester, 'two school-bookes, viz. Doctore Cooper his Dictionary in folio, faire bound upp with a faire red cover clasped and bossed, and withal a faire and the best Calepine in folio, redd covered and clasped and garnished, with seaven kindes of words or languages, viz. Latin, Greeke, Hebrew, Galice, Italice, Germanice et Hispanice &c., to remaine there continually chayned upp for the use and helpe of the Schoollers …' [Venn, *Alumni*; Longden vii. 183; PRO, PROB 11/157, fo.54. The two books were the *Thesaurus* of Thomas Cooper (d.1594), sometime Bishop of Lincoln, first printed in 1565, and a polyglot edition of the Latin dictionary originally compiled by the late-medieval Italian lexicographer Ambrogio Calepino (d.1511).]

Percival Burrell MA

Instituted 13 December 1628 to rectory of Dunsby-by-Bourne, on death of last incumbent. Patron: Governors of the Charterhouse (31 October 1628). Inducted 2 February 1628/9 by Edmund Asheton, Rector of Dowsby. [PD 1628/34; IND/L 1, fo.82.]

Born *c*.1590; of London. Educated: Hart Hall (matric. 1607) and Christ Church, Oxford (BA 1609; MA 1612). Formerly: Preacher at Charterhouse, 1619–28. Buried at Dunsby, 16 September 1638. Will (PCC) dated 25 June 1638, proved 19 November 1638. To be 'decently layd in the grave against the time of the Archangells dead raisinge trumpett'; bequest to Ludgate Prison, £10 'for the redemption of twoe prisoners to be named by my brother Mr Robert Haslewood'. [Foster, *Alumni*; PR Dunsby-by-Bourne; PRO, PROB 11/178/562.]

Thomas Greaves

Instituted 10 October 1638 to rectory of Dunsby-by-Bourne. Patron: Hospital of Charterhouse. [AC.]

Born 1611; son of John G. (1579–1617), R. of Colmer (Ha). Educated: Charterhouse School (1619) and Corpus Christi College, Oxford (matric. 1628; BA 1630/1; MA 1633/4; BD 1641; DD 1661); Fellow 1636; Deputy Lecturer in Arabic, 1637–41. Deacon: 9 July 1639 (Peterborough); priest: 26 September 1642 (Lincoln). Also: R. of Minting, 1642–62; R. of Great Berkhamsted, 1660–70; R. of Gautby, 1665; R. of Benefield (Np), 1664–76. Resided in Oxford until 1648 when expelled by Parliamentary visitors. Resided at Dunsby (1649–60) where his children John (1649), Mary (1651), Elizabeth (1651), Thomas (1656), Frances (1658), Sarah (1659) were born. An oriental scholar, his published work was slight owing to his expulsion from Oxford in 1648 and his subsequent lack of access to books during the Interregnum. In a letter of 22 December 1657 he excused the meagre nature of his notes on the Persian Gospels on account of the remoteness of Dunsby from London and the universities. Died 22 May 1676; buried at Weldon (Np), in the chancel (MI). ['Greaves, Thomas' in *ODNB*; Foster, *Alumni*; Longden vi. 35; PR Dunsby; Todd, *Life of Walton* i. 228.]

Benjamin Johnson BD

Instituted 2 November 1676 to rectory of Dunsby-by-Bourne, on death of Thomas Greaves. Patron: Governors of Hospital of Charterhouse (24 June 1676). [Reg. 34, fo.13v; PD 1676/16.]

Baptised 26 August 1642 at Oundle; son of Thomas J., Master of Oundle School (1637–46). Educated: Oundle and Charterhouse Schools and Sidney Sussex College, Cambridge (matric. 1660; BA 1663–4; MA 1667; BD 1674); Fellow 1664. Priest: 3 March 1666/7 (Lincoln). Also: Canon of Salisbury and Prebendary of Bitton, 1685–6. Died before 10 January 1685/6. [Longden viii. 35; Venn, *Alumni*; Reg. 34, fo.13v; *Le Neve Fasti: Salisbury 1541–1857,* 31.]

William Bolton MA

Instituted 18 May 1686 to rectory of Dunsby-by-Bourne, on death of last incumbent. Patron: Governors of Hospital of Charterhouse. [LPL, Reg. Sancroft 2, fo.286v.]

Born *c*.1651; son of William B. of London. Educated: St John's College, Oxford (matric. 1667/8; BA 1672) and King's College, Cambridge (MA 1690). Formerly: Assistant Master at Charterhouse School. Also: Head Master of Harrow School, 1685–91. Non-resident at Dunsby, which was served by John Laney as curate. Resided at Harrow, the first Head Master to be provided with a separate house. A Tory, he published two sermons in support of the Stuart monarchy: *Joseph's Entertainment of his Brethren* (1684); *Core Redivivus* (1684). Also published: *A Poem Upon a Laurel Leaf* (1680), an account of the cure of his rheumatism. Buried at Harrow, 5 June 1691. [Foster, *Alumni*; Venn, *Alumni*; *Harrow Register 1571–1800*, 153; LC 11, fo.27; Tyerman, *Harrow School*, 69–71; ESTC.]

Charles Lidgould MA

Instituted 17 November 1691 to rectory of Dunsby-by-Bourne. Patron: Hospital of Charterhouse. [AC.]

Of St Martin-in-the-Fields (Mx). Educated: Charterhouse School and Clare Hall, Cambridge (matric. 1676; BA 1679–80; MA 1683); incorporated at Oxford 1683. Priest: 19 December 1687 (Lincoln). Children baptised at Dunsby, 1695–1700. Father of Charles (born 1695), R. of Holy Trinity, Colchester (1736–65) and John (born 1697), V. of Harmondsworth (1727–60). Buried at Dunsby, 27 August 1701. [Venn, *Alumni*; LC 14, fo.3; PR Dunsby-by-Bourne.]

John Stacy MA

Instituted 26 November 1701 to rectory of Dunsby-by-Bourne, on death of Charles Lidgould. Patron: Hospital of Charterhouse. [Reg. 35, fo.81.]

Born *c*.1653; son of John S. of London, gent. Educated: Charterhouse School and Magdalene College, Cambridge (matric. 1672; BA 1675–6; MA 1679); Fellow 1676. Deacon: 6 June 1680 (Lincoln). Formerly: C. of Wyville, 1680; C. of Sawston (Ca), 1680–1. Resident. Married (6 July 1703) at Dunsby, Anne Green. Died 1724. Will (PCC) dated 14 June 1723, proved 19 November 1724: to be buried 'under one of the Great Stones near the Vestry Door' in the chancel at Dunsby; to Richard Green clerk 'my dear wife's eldest son', £10 and 'all my books'. [Venn, *Alumni*; Reg. 34, p.49; *Speculum*, 43; PR Dunsby-by-Bourne; PRO, PROB 11/600/292.]

Robert Elliot

Instituted 23 February 1724/5 to rectory of Dunsby-by-Bourne, on death of John Stacy. Patron: Hospital of Charterhouse. [Reg. 38, p.84.]

Born *c*.1696; son of Robert E. of Southwark. Educated: Charterhouse School and Trinity College, Cambridge (matric. 1718); BA. Priest: 21 February 1724/5 (Lincoln). Buried at Dunsby, 9 August 1739. [Venn, *Alumni*; Reg. 38, p.82; SUB VII, p.85; PR Dunsby-by-Bourne.]

John Baskett MA

Instituted 26 January 1739/40 to rectory of Dunsby-by-Bourne, on death of Robert Elliot. Patron: Governors of Hospital of Charterhouse. [Reg. 38, p.375.]

Born 27 January 1714/15 at Blandford (Do); son of Samuel B. Educated: Charterhouse School and St John's College, Cambridge (matric. 1732; BA 1735–6; MA 1739). Priest: 28 May 1738 (London). Resident (1768): 'lives there and serves his church'. Non-resident (1778): 'Absent; lives at Blandford'; (1801): 'now and for many years past an Inhabitant of the Parish of Blandford St Mary'. Married 1stly (31 December 1737) at St Martin-in-the-Fields, Martha, daughter of Giles Eyre (buried at Dunsby, 13 December 1746); 2ndly (21 December 1748) at Blandford Forum, Lucy, daughter of Christopher Pitt MD (buried at Dunsby, 11 February 1764); 3rdly (22 January 1765) at Milborne St Andrew (Do), Rachael, daughter of John Cole (buried at Blandford St Mary, 22 December 1779); 4thly (12 October 1780) at Blandford Forum, Mary Fowle. Father of Sarah (born 1743), later wife of Thomas Foster, R. of Dowsby (1763–73). Died 8 August 1801 at Blandford. Will (Bristol CC) dated 3 July 1801, proved 26 August 1801. [Venn, *Alumni*; PR Dunsby; IGI; Dorset History Centre, PR Blandford Forum; PR Blandford St Mary; PR Milborne St Andrew; BC/W/B72.]

William Thomas Waters BA

Instituted 23 January 1802 to rectory of Dunsby-by-Bourne, on death of John Basket. Patron: Governors of Hospital of Charterhouse (19 January 1802). [Reg. 40, p.33; PD 158/51.]

Baptised 11 October 1771 at St George, Stamford; son of William W. of Stamford, surgeon and apothecary. Educated: Charterhouse School (1783–9) and St John's College, Cambridge (matric. 1789; BA 1793; MA 1815). Deacon: 29 June 1794 (Lincoln for Peterborough); priest: 11 June 1797 (Lincoln). Formerly: C. of Little Bytham with Castle Bytham, 1797–1802. Also: V. of Sempringham, 1813–26 (*q.v.*); R. of Rippingale, 1825–53 (*q.v.*); Chaplain to Lord Saltoun. Licence for non-residence (1804), on account of house being unfit. Resided subsequently at Dunsby; afterwards at Rippingale Rectory. Father of William Roe W. (baptised at Dunsby 1811), C. of Dunsby 1835–53; R. of West Bridgford (Nt), 1862–91. Buried at Rippingale, 11 February 1853. Will (PCC) dated 9 October 1849, proved 1 June 1853. [PR Stamford St George; *Charterhouse Register 1769–1872*, 352; Venn, *Alumni*; Reg. 39, pp. 594, 635; NRL 1804/64; PR Dunsby; White, *Lincolnshire* (1842), 736; Census Returns 1841, 1851 (Rippingale); PR Rippingale; PRO, PROB 11/2175/40.]

George Wilson Keightley MA

Instituted 26 May 1853 to rectory of Dunsby, on death of William Thomas Waters. Patron: Governors of Hospital of Charterhouse. [Reg. 40, p.540.]

Born 3 December 1825; son of John K. of Tralee, co. Kerry, esquire. Educated: Charterhouse School (1840–4) and Pembroke College, Oxford (matric. 1844; BA 1848; MA 1851). Deacon: 1850; priest: 1852 (London). Formerly: C. of Enfield (Mx), 1850–3. Married (27 September 1853) at Langton Long, Emily Elphinstone, daughter of William Donaldson of Lyttleton House, Blandford (Do) esquire. Resided at Dunsby Rectory. Afterwards: R. of Great Stambridge (Ess), 1879–99; of Little Stambridge, 1889–99. Latterly of Stone Cross, Lindfield (Sx). Died there 21 July 1911. [*Charterhouse Register 1769–1872*, 188; Foster, *Alumni*; *Crockford* (1908); *GM* (December 1853), 629; Census Returns 1871; White, *Lincolnshire* (1872), 582; *Probate Calendar* 1911.]

Perceval Hartley LLB

Instituted 27 February 1880 to rectory of Dunsby, on cession of George Wilson Keightley. Patron: Governors of Hospital of Charterhouse. [Reg. 42, p.102.]

Born 24 March, baptised 14 May 1814 at St Ann Blackfriars, London; son of James H. of New Bridge Street, London, gent. Educated: Charterhouse School (1826–31) and Trinity Hall, Cambridge (matric. 1833; LLB 1865). Rowed in University Boat Race, 1836. Admitted at Lincoln's Inn, 1836; called to the Bar, 1842. Deacon: 1849; priest: 1850 (Lichfield). Formerly: C. of Tamworth (St), 1849–54; PC of Wigginton (St), 1854–64; R. of Clonpriest, co. Cloyne (Ireland), 1864–72; R. of Staveley (YWR), 1872–78; R. of Creeton, 1878–80. Resided at Dunsby Rectory. Died 2 March 1891 at Boroughbridge; buried at Staveley. [LMA, PR St Ann Blackfriars; *Charterhouse Register 1769–1872*, 154; Venn, *Alumni*; *Crockford* (1885); *Probate Calendar* 1891.]

Wordsworth Everard Jones

Instituted 25 June 1891 to rectory of Dunsby, on death of Perceval Hartley. Patron: Governors of Hospital of Charterhouse. [Reg. 42, p.334.]

Born 23 May, baptised 3 July 1856 at St John Baptist, Hoxton; son of Revd Alfred J., Chaplain of Aske's Hospital. Educated: Charterhouse School (1867–71), St Paul's School and St Augustine's College, Canterbury (1875). Deacon: 1879; priest: 1881 (Rangoon). Formerly: SPG Missionary at Toungoo, Burma, 1877–90 (Principal of St Luke's Theological Institute Toungoo, 1882–90); C. of Potters Bar (Mx), 1890–1. Married (7 December 1886) at St John Baptist, Hoxton, Annie Christina, daughter of Revd George Purves Pownall (Vicar of Hoxton). Co-translator, *Book of Common Prayer into Sgau Karen* (1883); Editor and Translator, *Church Hymns into Sgau Karen* (1882). Applied for patent (1895) for 'improvements in paraffin lamps with side draught fittings'. Non-resident at Dunsby, which was served by curates, including Thomas Barker (1900–22). Experienced prolonged financial difficulties; appeared before Peterborough Bankruptcy Court (1900), 'stated that he had been in difficulties for years, but he had kept on in the hope that he would be able to improve his position little by little'. Lived in lodgings at Isleworth (1901) and Acton (1911). In June 1926 he was at 1 Royal Crescent, The Esplanade, Weymouth ('I need every penny through my wife's illness and as she [needed] rest and change, I have brought her here'). Resignation of Dunsby accepted 22 June 1926. Died 10 April 1938 at Newton Abbott. [LMA, PR Hoxton St John; *Charterhouse Register 1769–1872*, 186; *St Paul's School Admission Registers 1748–1876; Crockford* (1908); Muss-Arnolt, *BCP Among the Nations*, 223–7; *Hull Daily Mail*, 3 May 1895; Kelly, *Lincolnshire* (1913), 180; *Lincolnshire Chronicle*, 2 March 1900; Census Returns 1901 (Isleworth), 1911 (Acton); COR/B 7/I/D15; Reg. 43, p.397; GRO, Death Index.]

The Rectory of Dunsby was united to the Rectory of Dowsby by Order in Council dated 15 August 1929. [Reg. 43, p.451.]

FOLKINGHAM

The church of Folkingham was granted by Gilbert de Gant to Bardney Abbey; the grant was confirmed by Bishop Robert Chesney between 1148 and 1155. The church was not appropriated, but the Abbey retained a portion of the revenues, valued in 1291 at £6 13s 4d. In 1344, in consideration of her agreement to the appropriation by the Abbey of the valuable churches of Great Hale and Heckington, the Abbey obtained a royal licence to convey the advowson to Eleanor Beaumont, lady of Folkingham. The Beaumont family retained the patronage until the death of John, Viscount Beaumont, at the battle of Northampton, in 1460. In 1462 Folkingham was granted, with many other estates, to William Hastings, who presented in 1469. After Hastings's summary execution at the hands of King Richard III in 1483, the advowson passed to his feoffees (who presented in 1485) but, following the accession of King Henry VII after Bosworth, William Beaumont was restored to his father's estates. He is said to have lost his reason in 1487, custody being granted to John de Vere, Earl of Oxford (who presented in 1502). On Beaumont's death in 1507, Folkingham passed to the Crown. Henry VIII granted it to the Duke of Norfolk, on whose attainder in 1547 it was given to Lord Clinton; Queen Mary reversed the attainder, returning the estate to the Duke. An exchange made in 1561 secured the transfer of the property to Lord Clinton and he and his heirs (later the Earls of Lincoln) held it until the late seventeenth century. In 1691 the then Earl of Lincoln sold the estate to Richard Wynne of the Inner Temple, the son of a London merchant. Wynne, who presented to Folkingham in 1702, died in 1719. His son, another Richard, presented in 1720; after the death of his wife in 1734 he departed to live in Italy where, with Anna Gazzini (first his mistress and later his wife) he had five children. The eldest son, christened Riccardo Gulielmo Gasparo Melchior Baltazaro, succeeded to the estate in 1751 and presented to the rectory the following year. The heavy expenditure necessitated by paying the portions of his brother and sisters caused him to sell Folkingham in 1788 to Sir Gilbert Heathcote. The Heathcote family still held the advowson in 1965. [*EEA* i. no.74; Hamilton Thompson, 'Bardney Abbey', 44, 61–2, 65–6; 'Taxatio', fo.10; *GEC* ii. 59–64 (Beaumont); *CPR 1461–67*, 103; *Archivists' Report* 14 (1962–3), 16–17; *LDC* (1965), 66–7.]

Albric de Capellis subdeacon
Instituted 20 September 1238 to church of Folkingham. Patron: Abbot and Convent of Bardney. [Hoskin, nos 99, 554.]

Hugh de Scheltun
Instituted before 25 March 1273. [*Rot. Gravesend*, 54, 278.]

Robert de Hodum subdeacon
Instituted 25 March 1273 to church of Folkingham, on death of Hugh de Schelton. Patron: Abbot and Convent of Bardney. [*Rot. Gravesend*, 54, 278.]

Robert de Cava
Instituted before 1277/1278. [*Rot. Gravesend*, 79.]

William de Barton subdeacon
Instituted in the twentieth pontifical year of Bishop Richard Gravesend (3 November 1277/2 November 1278) to church of Folkingham, vacant because Robert de Cava entered the order of the Friars Minor at Oxford on the feast of St Andrew the Apostle. Patron: Abbot and Convent of Bardney. [*Rot. Gravesend*, 79.]

Afterwards: V. of Barton-upon-Humber, 1280–1304. [*Reg. Sutton* i. 1; Reg. 2, fo.10v.]

M. Henry de Beningworth subdeacon
Instituted 28 July 1284 to church of Folkingham, on institution of William de Barton to vicarage of Barton-upon-Humber. Patron: Abbot and Convent of Bardney. [*Reg. Sutton* i. 54.]

Educated: University of Oxford (DCnL). Also: Canon of Lincoln and Prebendary of Crackpole St Mary, 1292–4. Afterwards: Subdean of Lincoln, 1294–1318; Canon of Lincoln and Prebendary of Welton Westhall, 1294–1318. Died 1318; buried in Lincoln Cathedral where he founded a chantry. [Emden, *BRUO*, 171; *Le Neve Fasti: Lincoln 1066–1300*, 24, 63, 109; D&C A/1/8, no.77.]

M. Thomas de Benigworth clerk in minor orders
Instituted 26 February 1295 to church of Folkingham, on appointment of M. Henry de Benigworth to subdeanery of Lincoln. Patron: Abbot and Convent of Bardney. [*Reg. Sutton* i. 197.]

Brother of M. Henry de Beningworth (above). Subdeacon: 26 February 1295; deacon: 28 May 1295; priest: 18 February 1296 (Lincoln). Afterwards: R. of Ingoldmells, 1295–1303. Died before 25 November 1303. [*Reg. Sutton* i. 203; vii. 62, 66, 76; Reg. 2, fo.8v.]

William de Hale chaplain
Instituted 23 September 1296 to church of Folkingham, on institution of M. Thomas de Benigworth to church of Ingoldmells. Patron: Abbot and Convent of Bardney. [*Reg. Sutton* i. 212.]

Still Rector in 1300. [Reg. 3, fo.18.]

M. John de Beby
Instituted before 4 January 1321/2. [*Reg. Burghersh* iii. no.227.]

Licence for absence to study in England for 1 year, 4 January 1321/2. Commission to sequestrate revenues of churches of Aslackby and Donington while the right of the Hospitallers to them is pending, *c.*September 1321. Appointed coadjutor of M. William, R. of Newton by Folkingham, 9 October 1321; of the Prior of Newstead by Stamford, 23 May 1323. Commission to hear confessions of his parishioners and grant absolution, 12 March 1322/3. Commission to enquire into allegations made against Sr Joan de Donewyche, nun of Wothorpe, May 1323. Commissary to audit executors' accounts of will of Elias Druel, 13 September 1324. Licence for absence to be in service of Henry de Beaumont for 2 years, 1 March 1333/4. Commissaries appointed to act in cause of defamation pending between JB and John de Thorp of Lincoln, 13 January 1334/5. Licence to be absent from his church (1 year), 26 July 1346. [*Reg. Burghersh* iii. nos 227, 1190, 1831; Reg. 5, fos 293, 295v, 340r–v, 341v, 489v; Reg. 7, fo.138.]

Ralph de Hermethorp priest

Instituted 12 December 1361 to church of Folkingham, on death of M. John de Beby. Patron: Henry de Beaumont. [Reg. 9, fo.151v.]

Afterwards: R. of Dunsby-by-Bourne, 1366–76 (*q.v.*).

Thomas Boston

Instituted before 1381. [*CPR 1381–85*, 507.]

Assessed for poll-tax, 1377(?), 1381. Accused (1384) of coming armed, with others, to Fillingham, and ejecting John, Duke of Lancaster, from custody of land there of William, son and heir of William Fraunk kt. Commission (18 September 1386) to enquire into unauthorised devotion to statue known as *Jurden Cros* in the fields of Rippingale, where it was said that miracles were performed and consecrated bread left. [*Clerical Poll-Taxes*, nos 697, 1331, 1920; *CPR 1381–85*, 507; Reg. 12, fo.331v.]

John Pitte priest

Instituted 26 August 1399 to church of Folkingham, on death of Thomas de Boston. Patron: Katherine de Beaumont. [Reg. 13, fo.124.]

John Kyrmond chaplain

Instituted 23 August 1405 to church of Folkingham, on death of John Pytte. Patron: Katherine, Lady Beaumont. [Reg. 14, fo.4v.]

Afterwards: V. of Barton-upon-Humber, 1407–24. [Reg. 14, fo.20; *Reg. Chichele* i. 321.]

M. Hugh Harpeley clerk

Instituted 24 October 1407 to church of Folkingham, on institution of John Keremound to vicarage of Barton-upon-Humber. Patron: Katherine, Lady Beaumont. [Reg. 14, fo.21v.]

Educated: University of Cambridge (MA by 1393); Fellow of King's Hall, *c.*1382–1406. Afterwards: Warden of St Margaret's Chapel, Huntingdon, 1411; Master of Hospital of St Mary Magdalene, Sandown (Sr), 1413; RD of Clare (Sf), 1413. [Emden, *BRUC*, 289.]

William Thame priest

Instituted 13 December 1408 to church of Folkingham, on resignation of M. Hugh Harpeley. Patron: Henry de Beaumont, lord of Folkingham. [Reg. 14, fo.30v.]

Afterwards: R. of Edmondthorpe (Le), 1411–13. [Reg. 14, fo.174.]

Roger Estwell priest
Instituted 5 October 1411 to church of Folkingham, on resignation of William Thame, by exchange with church of Edmondthorpe (Le). Patron: lady Katherine de Beaumont. [Reg. 14, fo.51.]

Formerly: R. of Cossington (Le), 1408–9; R. of Edmondthorpe (Le), 1409–11. [Reg. 14, fos 149, 160.]

Thomas Newton priest
Instituted 18 October 1422 to church of Folkingham, on death of Roger Estwell. Patron: Katherine, lady Beaumont. [*Reg. Fleming* i. no.164.]

Robert Routh chaplain
Instituted 27 January 1424/5 to church of Folkingham, on resignation of Thomas Newton. Patron: Katherine, lady Beaumont. [*Reg. Chichele* i. 336.]

John Hardy priest
Instituted 25 January 1428/9 to church of Folkingham, on resignation of Thomas Newton [*sic*], by exchange with church of West Halton. Patron: King Henry VI. [*Reg. Fleming* i. no.303.]

William Surteys
Instituted before 28 September 1449. [Reg. 18, fo.104.]

George Tounlay priest
Instituted 28 September 1449 to church of Folkingham, on resignation of William Surteys. Patron: John, Viscount Beaumont. [Reg. 18, fo.104.]

Nicholas Rerysby Master of the Order of St Gilbert of Sempringham
Instituted 17 September 1455 to church of Folkingham, on resignation of George Tonlay. Patron: John, Viscount Beaumont. [Reg. 20, fo.125.]

Master of the Order by 2 November 1438. [*Heads* iii. 604.]

John Lincoln Canon of Sempringham, priest
Instituted 2 October 1469 to church of Folkingham, on resignation of the Master of the Order of Sempringham. Patron: William Hastynges, Lord Hastings. [Reg. 20, fo.150.]

Robert Goddysman priest
Instituted 10 June 1485 to church of Folkingham, on death of John Lincoln. Patron: M. William Chauntre and Thomas Kebull, feoffees of William

Hastynges, Lord Hastings, decd, of his castle or lordship of Folkingham *inter alia*. [Reg. 22, fo.135v.]

M. Gabriel Silvestre DD
Instituted 22 July 1502 to church of Folkingham, on death of Robert Godesman. Patron: John Veer, Earl of Oxford, Lord Great Chamberlain and High Admiral of England, by reason of his wardship of William, Viscount Beaumont, and his castles, manors and lands. [Reg. 23, fo.71v.]

Educated: Clare College, Cambridge (BD 1491–2; DD 1500; Fellow, 1489–96; Master, 1496–1506). Also: Canon of Stoke by Clare (Sf), to 1507; Canon of Lichfield and Prebendary of Weeford, 1507–12; R. of Wyberton, 1507–12; Canon of Chichester and Prebendary of Colworth, 1508–12. Member of Council of Lady Margaret Beaufort. Died 1512. Will (PCC) dated 29 September 1512, proved 20 October 1512: bequeathed to Folkingham Church, a vestment worth 26s 8d; to the poor of Folkingham, 10s. [Emden, *BRUC*, 573; PRO, PROB 11/17/216.]

Thomas Hall
Instituted 12 October 1512 to church of Folkingham, on death of M. Gabriel Silvester. Patron: King Henry VIII. [Reg. 23, fo.145.]

Assessed for subsidy (£8) in 1526. Assessed for *Valor Ecclesiasticus*, 1535. Still Rector in 1539. [*Subsidy*, 58; *Valor* iv. 106; Vj 11, fo.2.]

William Flatberye clerk
Instituted 4 October 1540 to church of Folkingham, on death of last incumbent. Patron: Thomas, Duke of Norfolk, Lord High Treasurer and Earl Marshal of England. [Reg. 27, fo.72v.]

John Harris
Instituted 25 May 1558 to church of Folkingham, on death of William Flatbury. Patron: Edward, Lord Clinton. [Reg. 28, fo.131v.]

Nicholas Clercke
Signed BTs as 'Pastor' 1563.

The rectory of Folkingham was vacant in 1576 and 1580. John Jackson was Curate in 1581 and 1585. [*Bishop Cooper*, 209, 220; *State of the Church*, 4, 73.]

Richard Foster MA
Instituted 11 November 1585 to rectory of Folkingham (cause of vacancy not stated). Patron: Queen Elizabeth I (11 November 1585), by lapse. [PD 1585/21.]

Priest: 20 September 1561 (Peterborough). Formerly: V. of Bourne, 1581–5. Signed BTs at Folkingham, 1586–91. Assessed at 'a Lighte horse' in Subsidy of Armour, 1590. Afterwards: R. of Scremby, 1591–1622; V. of Skendleby, 1593–1606. [*State of the Church*, 73, 148; BTs Folkingham.]

John Hoskin
Instituted 1 November 1592 to rectory of Folkingham (cause of vacancy not stated). Patron: Henry Fines, Earl of Lincoln (15 October 1592). [BC; PD 1592/20.]

Domestic chaplain of Earl of Lincoln. Signed BTs at Folkingham 1593–1602. [BTs Folkingham.]

Ralph Palfreman
Instituted 12 September 1610 to rectory of Folkingham, on death of John Hoskyns. Patron: Henry Fynes, Earl of Lincoln (8 July 1610). [BC; PD 1610/16.]

Born *c*.1550 at Sleaford. Educated: St John's College, Cambridge (matric. 1567). Deacon: 13 May 1569; priest: 20 September 1569 (Lincoln). Formerly: V. of Edlington, to 1577; V. of Billinghay, 1577–87; C. of Tattershall (by 1585); C. of Sempringham; V. of Threckingham, 1599–1607 (*q.v.*); V. of Aslackby, 1605–11 (*q.v.*). Resident (1611, 1614): signed BTs 1611–17. Buried at Folkingham, 23 November 1617. [PD 1598/15 for biographical details; Venn, *Alumni*; LC 3, fo.2; LC 4, fo. 72v; BTs Folkingham; LCC Admons 1618/164.]

Nicholas Price MA
Instituted 5 December 1617 to rectory of Folkingham, on death of Ralph Palfreman. Patron: John Smyth of Magdalene College, Cambridge, for this turn (by grant from Thomas, Earl of Lincoln). [IND/L 1, fos 36v–37; Additional Reg. 3, fo.68v.]

Educated: Magdalene College, Cambridge (BA 1604–5; MA 1608); Fellow. Deacon and priest: 12 March 1608/9 (Ely). Signed BTs at Folkingham 1618–19. Resigned 31 December 1624. [BTs Folkingham; RES 1624/7.]

Lot Maell MA
Instituted 12 January 1624/5 to rectory of Folkingham, on resignation of Nicholas Price. Patron: John White of the Middle Temple, London, for this turn only (7 January 1624/5). [BC; PD 1625/11.]

Of Cambridgeshire. Educated: Queens' College, Cambridge (matric. 1614; BA 1617–18; MA 1621). Deacon: 14 August 1620; priest: 15 August 1620 (Peterborough). Formerly: C. of Folkingham, 1623–5. Resident: signed parish register as Curate (1623–4) and as Rector (1625–53). Died 1656; buried at Folkingham, 15 December 1656 ('hee had preached the word of God to this parish above thyrtye and five yeares'). [Venn, *Alumni*; Longden ix. 87; PR Folkingham.]

Abraham Page
Instituted 1657 to rectory of Folkingham. Patron: Earl of Lincoln. Reinstituted 23 June 1662, on death of Lot Mael; patron: Theophilus, Earl of Lincoln. [Swaby, 112; Reg. 32, fo.17a.]

Born *c*.1622; son of Abraham P. of Northolt (Mx). Educated: Wadham College, Oxford (matric. 1640) and Magdalene College, Cambridge (matric. 1645; BA 1645–6; MA 1649). Deacon and priest: 10 August 1655 (Ardfert). Resident (1662): son Richard baptised at Folkingham (1665). Buried at Folkingham, 22 July 1673 ('who lived almost sixteen years in this parish and preached the word of God'). Will (LCC). Probate inventory ('In the Library: All the Bookes there, £16 … one Table, one Deske, and the shelves there, 5s'). [*Wadham Registers* i. 147; Venn, *Alumni*; LC 5, fo.22v; PR Folkingham; LCC Wills 1673/126; INV 174/17.]

Richard Brocklesby MA

Instituted 22 October 1673 to rectory of Folkingham, on death of Abraham Page. Patron: Edward, Earl of Lincoln. [SUB Va, fo.48v; IND/L 1, fo.211v.]

Born *c.*1635 at Tealby; son of George B., yeoman. Educated: Caistor School and Sidney Sussex College, Cambridge (matric. 1652; BA 1656–7; MA 1660). Deacon and priest: 2 June 1658 (Ardfert). Signed BTs at Folkingham 1675–1702. Also: R. of Kirkby-on-Bain, 1661. Deprived as a non-abjuror. Retired to Stamford where he immersed himself in theological study. Author: *An Explication of the Gospel-Theism and the Divinity of the Christian Religion* (1706), a work that influenced the Arianism of William Whiston. Buried at Folkingham, 15 February 1713/14. Will (PCC) dated 30 January 1713/14, proved 13 August 1714. Left legacies: for schoolmasters at Kirkby-on-Bain, Folkingham and Pidley (Hu) 'to teach the poor Children … their Chatichism and to read the holy Bible'; for 'the Propagation of the Gospel in the Eastern parts'; for French refugees 'that are poor and pious' and for Protestants of the Principality of Orange driven from their Country. [Venn, *Alumni*; LC 5, fo.52; LC 14, fo.3; BTs Folkingham; 'Brocklesby, Richard' in *ODNB*; PRO, PROB 11/541/213.]

Thomas Ixem BA

Instituted 10 November 1702 to rectory of Folkingham, on deprivation of Richard Brocklesby under the Act of Succession. Patron: Richard Wynne esquire. [Reg. 35, fo.90.]

Born *c.*1657 at Burton Lazars (Le); son of John I. Educated: Laughton-en-le-Morthen School and Christ's College, Cambridge (matric. 1674; BA 1677–8). Deacon: 15 June 1679; priest: 18 December 1681 (Lincoln). Formerly: C. of Clavering (Ess), 1679; C. of Great Munden (Hrt), 1681. Resided at Folkingham (but no Rectory House); signed BTs 1703–19. Buried at Folkingham, 3 March 1719/20. [Venn, *Alumni*; Reg. 34, fos 36, 64v; *Speculum*, 48; BTs Folkingham; PR Folkingham.]

Richard Toller MA

Instituted 29 July 1720 to rectory of Folkingham with vicarage of Laughton annexed, on death of Thomas Ixim. Patron: Richard Wynne esquire. [Reg. 37, p.104.]

Baptised 31 August 1688 at Billingborough; son of John T. of Billingborough Hall, esquire. Educated: Emmanuel College, Cambridge (matric. 1706; BA 1709–10; MA 1715); Fellow of Emmanuel 1715. Deacon: 21 February 1713/14 (Ely); priest: 19 September 1714 (Peterborough). Also: R. of South Ormsby, 1721–52; Chaplain to Earl of Northampton. Signed BTs at Folkingham 1722–50. Died 12 January 1752; buried at Folkingham, 15 January 1752 (MI). [*Chester of Chicheley*, 655; Venn, *Alumni*; LC 18B, p.198; BTs Folkingham; PR Folkingham; *Monson*, 126.]

William Murray

Instituted 14 February 1752 to rectory of Folkingham, on death of Richard Tollar. Patron: Riccardo Gulielmo Gasparo Melchior Baltazaro Wynne. [Reg. 38, p.507.]

Born *c*.1706; son of William M. of London. Educated: Pembroke College, Oxford (matric. 1722; BA 1727). Deacon: 20 September 1729 (Winchester); priest: 24 May 1730 (Ely). Formerly: C. of Mitcham (Sr), 1729; R. of Healing, 1732–52; V. of Stallingborough, 1737–52. Also: V. of Gainsborough, 1761–78; Canon of Lincoln and Prebendary of Corringham, 1761–78. Non-resident at Folkingham (1768, 1778), which was served by Isaac Cookson as curate. Was said to reside at Gainsborough. Died 18 December 1778; buried at Gainsborough, 24 December 1778 (MI). [Foster, *Alumni*; *Winchester Ordinations* ii. 22; *Le Neve Fasti: Lincoln 1541–1857*, 57; LC 31, p.76; PR Gainsborough.]

John Fountaine MA

Instituted 30 July 1779 to rectory of Folkingham with vicarage of Laughton annexed, on death of William Murray. Patron: Richard Wynne of Folkingham, esquire. [Reg. 39, p.336.]

Born *c*.1706; son of Robert F. of Easingwold (YNR). Educated: University College (matric. 1726) and Christ Church, Oxford (BA 1729–30) and King's College, Cambridge (MA 1738). Priest: 1 June 1740 (Lincoln). Formerly: C. of Berkhamsted St Mary (Hrt), 1740; R. of North Tidworth (Wlt), 1763–79. Non-resident at Folkingham, which was served by Isaac Cookson as curate. Died October 1787. Will (PCC) dated 10 July 1781, proved 23 October 1787; to be interred in the family vault in Marylebone churchyard. [Foster, *Alumni*; Venn, *Alumni*; Reg. 38, p.385; CCED; PR Folkingham; PRO, PROB 11/1158/2.]

John Moore Brooke MA

Instituted 24 November 1787, on death of John Fountain. Patron: Richard Arthur Knowles of Tinwell (Rutland), clerk. [Reg. 39, p.468.]

Born 10 June 1757; son of John B. of Westminster, Rector of Colney (Nf), and his wife Frances (1724–89), writer and playwright. Described (aged 14) by his mother as 'not a lively boy, but he will be a good scholar, has sense, & an excellent heart … he is in no danger but from women, on which score I tremble for him'. Educated: St Paul's School and Trinity College, Cambridge (matric. 1776; BA 1780; MA 1783); Fellow 1782–5. Deacon: 21 May 1780; priest: 4 June 1781 (Norwich). Also: V. of Helpringham, 1784–99. Resided with his mother in Sleaford; after her death at Folkingham Rectory and latterly at Leasingham. Married (6 January 1795) at St Mary Stamford, Robiana, daughter of Captain William Judd. Died 24 September 1798; buried at St Denys Sleaford (MI). Will (PCC) dated 27 July 1795, proved 21 March 1799. [Venn, *Alumni*; 'Brooke, Frances' in *ODNB*; Atkin, 'Frances Brooke', 16; PRO, PROB 11/1320/102.]

William Tait LLB

Instituted 13 February 1799 to rectory of Folkingham with vicarage of Laughton annexed, on death of John Moore Brooke. Patron: Sir Gilbert Heathcote of Normanton (Ru), Bt (23 October 1798). [Reg. 39, p.664; PD 155/54.]

Also: R. of Normanton (Ru), 1787–1814; V. of Fotheringhay (Np), 1790–1814; R. of Coningsby, 1792–1814. Non-resident at Folkingham, which was served by curates, including Richard Yerburgh, Edward Smith and Christopher Ellershaw. Died 30 August 1814 at Inverness. [Longden xiii. 141; PR Folkingham; *Scots Magazine*, 1 November 1814.]

Thomas Hardwicke Rawnsley MA
Instituted 22 December 1814 to rectory of Folkingham with vicarage of Laughton annexed, on death of William Tait. Patron: Sir Gilbert Heathcote of Normanton (Ru), Bt (6 December 1814). [Reg. 40, p.206; PD 170/3.]

Baptised 8 November 1789 at Bourne; son of Thomas R., gent. Educated: Eton College (1805) and Exeter College, Oxford (matric. 1807; BA 1811; MA 1814). Priest: 19 December 1813 (Lincoln). Also: PC of Spilsby, 1813–25; R. of Belleau with Aby, 1813–19; R. of Partney, 1819–25; R. of Halton Holegate, 1825–61. Married (16 November 1815) at Spilsby, Sophia, daughter of Revd Edward Walls of Boothby Hall. Non-resident at Folkingham, which was served by curates, including Christopher Ellershaw, Charles Day, Charles Hodgson, John Wilson, Joseph Hunt, Robert Burrell Drummond Rawnsley, William Charles Inman, William Hirst Simpson, John Thomas Brameld, John Shrapnel Warren and Henry Spurrier. Died 2 July 1861 at Halton Holegate Rectory. [PR Bourne; *Lincolnshire Pedigrees*, 1301; *Eton School Lists*; Foster, *Alumni*; *Registrum Collegii Exoniensis*, 214; Reg. 40, p.193; PR Spilsby; CR 1, pp. 62, 218, 361; CR 2, pp. 64, 237; CR 3, fos 6, 30v, 84v; CR 4, fos 30, 51v, 72; White, *Lincolnshire* (1842), 737–8; White, *Lincolnshire* (1856), 716; *Guardian* (1861), 643; *Probate Calendar* 1861.]

George Carter LLM
Instituted 15 November 1861 to rectory of Folkingham with vicarage of Laughton annexed, on death of Thomas Hardwicke Rawnsley. Patron: Arthur Heathcote of Durdans, Epsom (Sr), esquire. [Reg. 41, p.76.]

Born 25 October 1828. Educated: Oakham School and Emmanuel College, Cambridge (matric. 1847; LLB 1853; LLM 1859). Deacon: 1850 (Ely); priest: 19 December 1852 (Lincoln). Formerly: C. of Coningsby, 1852–61. Licences for non-residence (1864–73), on account of there being no house, but resided at Folkingham. Died 13 August 1894 at Laughton-by-Folkingham ('whilst engaged in conversation with a lady suddenly fell down and expired immediately'). Buried at Folkingham (MI). [MI Folkingham; Venn, *Alumni*; *Crockford* (1885); OR 1, p.129; NRL 28/7; NRL 29/23; NRL 31/21; NRL 33/15; NRL 35/9; NRL 37/33; Census Returns 1871, 1881; White, *Lincolnshire* (1872), 582; *Lincolnshire Echo*, 14 August 1894; *Probate Calendar* 1895.]

Thomasin Albert Stoodley MA BCL
Instituted 9 November 1894 to rectory of Folkingham with vicarage of Laughton annexed, on death of George Carter. Patron: Thomas Arthur Robert Heathcote of Folkingham, esquire. [Reg. 42, p.368.]

Afterwards: R. of Dowsby, 1898–1912 (*q.v.*).

John Herbert Heath MA
Instituted 2 June 1899 to rectory of Folkingham with vicarage of Laughton annexed, on cession of Thomasin Albert Stoodley. Patron: Thomas Arthur Robert Heathcote of Folkingham, esquire. [Reg. 42, p.448.]

Born *c*.1862 at Leamington; son of Revd Joseph Heath (PC of New Bolingbroke 1861–70). Brother of Francis Valentine H. (below). Educated: Ipswich GS and Pembroke College, Cambridge (matric. 1880; BA 1884; MA 1892). Deacon: 1885; priest: 1886 (Lichfield). Formerly: C. of St Mary, Tunstall (St), 1885–7; V. of Flintham (Nt), 1887–99. Resided at Folkingham Rectory. Afterwards: V. of Ledsham with Fairburn (YWR), 1906–10; V.

of Swinderby, 1910–9. Latterly at Cumnor House, Kenilworth. Died there 11 November 1938, aged 78. Buried at Swinderby. [Venn, *Alumni*; *Crockford* (1908); Census Returns 1901; *Probate Calendar* 1939.]

Francis Valentine Heath MA

Instituted 7 March 1906 to rectory of Folkingham with vicarage of Laughton annexed, on cession of John Herbert Heath. Patron: Thomas Arthur Robert Heathcote of Folkingham, esquire. [Reg. 42, p.545.]

Born 14 February 1869 at New Bolingbroke; son of Revd Joseph Heath (PC of New Bolingbroke 1861–70). Educated: Harlow College (Ess), Rossall School and Christ's College, Cambridge (matric. 1888; BA 1891; MA 1895). Deacon: 1893; priest: 1894 (Peterborough). Formerly: C. of St James, Northampton, 1893–5; of Lutterworth, 1895–1902; V. of Maxey with Deeping Gate (Np), 1902–6. Resided at Folkingham Rectory. Also: RD of Aveland 1934; Canon of Lincoln and Prebendary of Carlton-cum-Dalby, 1940–4. Latterly of West Cottage, Folkingham. Died 21 April 1944; buried at Folkingham. [Venn, *Alumni*; *Crockford* (1908); Census Returns 1911; Kelly, *Lincolnshire* (1913), 195; *Probate Calendar* 1944; PR Folkingham.]

William Thomas Henry Sampson

Instituted 15 November 1944 to rectory of Folkingham with vicarage of Laughton annexed, on death of Francis Valentine Heath. Patron: William Lionel Heathcote of 'Piper Holt', Billingborough, esquire. [Reg. 44, p.23.]

Born 7 June 1895 at Tonbridge (K); son of William John S., Temperance Hotel Proprietor. Living at Tonbridge (1911), working as clerk to a nurseryman. Educated: King's College, London (1930). Deacon: 1932; priest: 1933 (Rochester). Formerly: C. of Chelsfield, 1932–8; V. of St Mary, Green Street Green, 1938–41; R. of Pickworth with Walcot, 1941–4 (*q.v.*). Resided at Folkingham Rectory. Afterwards: R. of Bonnington with Bilsington, 1949–63; R. of Fawkenhurst, 1949–63; RD of North Lympne, 1960–3. Retired 1963. Afterwards lived at Hurstbourne, Aldington, Ashford. Died 1972. [Census Returns 1911 (Tonbridge); *Crockford* (1971–2); *LDC* (1947), 56; GRO, Death Index.]

Henry Evans BA

Instituted 24 January 1950 to rectory of Folkingham with vicarage of Laughton annexed, on cession of William Thomas Henry Sampson. Patron: William Lionel Heathcote, as above. [Reg. 44, p.121.]

Educated: University of Wales (BA 1912); St Michael's College, Llandaff (1912). Deacon: 1913; priest: 1914 (St David's). Formerly: C. of Llanstadwell, 1913–19; of Builth Wells with Llandeur'r Cwm, 1919–21; of Holy Trinity, Aberystwyth, 1921–3; R. of New Radnor (with Llanfihangel Nantmelan from 1927), 1924–31; V. of St James, Bolton, 1931–40; of Greengates, 1940–50. Resided at Folkingham Rectory. Also: V. of Threckingham, 1953–9 (*q.v.*). Afterwards lived at 51 Middleton Road, Felpham, Bognor Regis. Died there, 8 March 1979. [*Crockford* (1971–2); *LDC* (1957), 48; *London Gazette* (47811), 5 April 1979.]

Frank Reginald Money MA

Instituted 19 October 1960 to rectory of Folkingham with vicarage of Laughton annexed, on resignation of Henry Evans. Patron: Bishop of Lincoln for this turn, by lapse. Note that on 29 September 1960, the Archbishop of

Canterbury granted a dispensation enabling the said FRM to hold together the rectory of Folkingham with vicarage of Laughton annexed and the vicarage of Threckingham. [Reg. 44, p.303.]

Born 1905 at Nottingham. Educated: St Chad College, Durham (BA 1926; MA 1928). Deacon: 1928; priest: 1929 (Derby). Formerly: C. of St Werburgh, Derby, 1928–30; of St Luke with St George, Derby, 1930–4; V. of Holy Trinity, Ilkeston, 1934–49; V. of St Lawrence, Wootton (Ha), 1949–54; Chaplain of Park Prewett Mental Hospital, 1951–4; RD of Basingstoke, 1953–4; Canon Residentiary and Treasurer of Winchester, 1954–60. Resided at Folkingham Rectory. Also: V. of Threckingham, 1960–8; V. of Osbournby with Scott Willoughby, 1966–8; R. of Pickworth with Walcot, 1966–8 (*q.v.*); Canon of Lincoln and Prebendary of Leighton Beaudesert, 1966–8. Died 4 August 1968. [GRO, Birth Index; *Crockford* (1961–2, 1965–6); *LDC* (1969), 57.]

HACCONBY

The manor and advowson of Hacconby were granted by King John to Ralph de Hauvill, to hold by serjeanty of serving the king's falcons. By 1212 the land was held by Matilda de Hauvill, Ralph's widow. When the church became vacant in 1219, Matilda's right to present was challenged by William de Colville of Castle Bytham, whose father had presented at the last vacancy. An assize of darrein presentment was heard, at which it was proved that Colville has presented while Hacconby was in his custody during the reign of Henry II, but that the king had subsequently resumed the land into his own hand. The subsequent charter of King John granting the land to the Hauvills was produced. The hearing of this case no doubt explains the terms of the institution of John de Hoylande in 1218–19. The grant by King John must have been made before *c.*1204, when the king confirmed to the canons of Sempringham the gift made to them by Ralph de Hauvill of land in Upwell on the Norfolk/Cambridgeshire border, together with four churches (including Hacconby), to endow a small priory there. The evidence of the Lincoln episcopal registers indicates that nothing was in fact done to effect the gift of Hacconby to Sempringham until much later. The Hauvill family continued to present to the living until the middle of the fourteenth century. In 1340 the manor and advowson were settled on Robert Tiffour and Matilda his wife; Robert presented in 1347. Shortly after this, however, the church was finally given to Sempringham. On the eve of Trinity Sunday 1349 the priory church was hit by storm and flood, the water rising to the capitals of the pillars; many books were destroyed and eighteen sacks of wool damaged. The following November the king granted a licence to appropriate Hacconby church, although in the event this did not take place until Christmas 1392 when a vicarage was ordained. Sempringham Priory presented to the vicarage until the Dissolution, after which the advowson passed into the hands of the Bishop of Lincoln. It remained in the bishop's possession in 1965. [Stenton, *Rolls of the Justices in Eyre*, 358–9; Oggins, *The Kings and their Hawks*,

57; *Monasticon* vi. 2. 979; Golding, *Gilbertine Order*, 246–8; *CPR 1338–40*, 521; *VCH Lincoln* ii. 185; Reg. 12, fo.397; *LDC* (1965), 66–7.]

Church

M. John de Hoylande
Instituted by collation in the tenth pontifical year of Bishop Hugh of Wells (20 December 1218/19 December 1219) to church of Hacconby. Patron: Bishop of Lincoln, by authority of the Lateran Council. The right of anyone claiming the advowson in the future was reserved. [*Rot. Welles* i. 142.]

Hugh Luvel subdeacon
Instituted in the twenty-second pontifical year of Bishop Hugh of Wells (20 December 1230/19 December 1231) to church of Hacconby. Patron: Henry de Hauvill. [*Rot. Welles* iii. 193.]

Henry son of H[enry] de Hauvill
Instituted in the tenth pontifical year of Bishop Robert Grosseteste (17 June 1244/16 June 1245) to church of Hacconby. Patron: H[enry] de Hauvill, father of the said Henry. [Hoskin, no.287.]

Hugh de Alto Monte
Instituted before 26 June 1298. [*Reg. Sutton* i. 229.]

Simon de Stivekeya chaplain
Instituted 26 June 1298 to church of Hacconby, on death of Hugh de Alto Monte. Patron: Thomas de Hauvile kt. [*Reg. Sutton* i. 229.]

Vincent de Waterden appointed as his coadjutor; commission to audit coadjutor's accounts, 14 May 1321. Note that the bishop issued a commission relating to case of unjust suspension from entering church brought against Vincent de Waterden and John de Waterden, parochial chaplain of Hacconby, 9 April 1322. Appointment of M. Robert Bernard, R. of Great Carlton, as coadjutor of Simon who was weak, old and mentally ill, 31 December 1322. [Reg. 5, fos 282, 307v, 328.]

Robert de Folkingham priest
Instituted 22 March 1323 to church of Hacconby, on death of Simon de Stivekey. Patron: Matilda de Houill. [*Reg. Burghersh* i. no.70.]

Formerly: V. of St Peter, Kirkby Laythorpe, 1321–3. Charged (with others) with carrying away goods of John de Crumbewell at Hacconby and Morton, 16 September 1328. Ratification by Crown of RF as Rector of Hacconby, 24 July 1330. Feoffee (with others) of manor and advowson of Hacconby, 13 May 1340. [*CPR 1327–30*, 351, 543; *CPR 1338–40*, 521.]

John Wade priest
Instituted 10 November 1347 to church of Hacconby. Patron: Sir Robert de Tifford of Hacconby. [*LNQ* 1 (1888–9), 177.]

M. William Poutrell
Instituted before 28 February 1353/4. [Reg. 9, fo.109v.]
Formerly: V. of Horbling, 1349–51 (*q.v.*).

Augustine de Hagham priest
Instituted 28 February 1353/4 to church of Hacconby, on death of M. William
Poutrell. Patron: Prior and Convent of Sempringham. [Reg. 9, fo.109v.]

Thomas de Donyngton
Instituted *c.*1359 to church of Hacconby. Patron: King Edward III (3 February
1358/9). [*CPR 1358–61*, 172.]

Thomas de Brune priest
Instituted 21 October 1366 to church of Hacconby, on death of Thomas de
Donyngton. Patron: Prior and Convent of Sempringham. [Reg. 10, fo.15v.]
Still Rector in 1381. Buried *c.*1386 at Dunsby (MI). [*Clerical Poll-Taxes*, nos 1324, 1913;
Greenhill, *Incised Slabs*, 51.]

John Tylney
Instituted before 22 January 1386. [*CPR 1385–89*, 94.]
JT's estate in the church ratified by the King, 22 January 1386. Afterwards: V. of Whap-
lode, 1390.

John Ingram priest
Instituted 6 September 1390 to church of Hacconby, on resignation of John
Tylney (by exchange with vicarage of Whaplode). Patron: Prior and Convent
of Sempringham. [Reg. 11, fo.47.]
Formerly: R. of Covington (Hu), to 1377; V. of Whaplode, 1377–90. [Reg. 10, fo.84.]

Vicarage

John Moy de Hacumby priest
Instituted 13 February 1392/3 to vicarage of Hacconby, now first vacant.
Patron: Prior and Convent of Sempringham. Note that the ordination of the
vicarage is in the bishop's memoranda register. [Reg. 11, fo.63v.]
[For the ordination (25 December 1392), see Reg. 12, fo.397.]

Robert Terry de Repynghale chaplain
Instituted 24 January 1404/5 (in person of William Rasyn, vicar of Swaton,
his proctor) to vicarage of Hacconby, on death of John Moy. Patron: Prior
and Convent of Sempringham. [Reg. 13, fo.174.]

William Perotson priest
Instituted 5 June 1414 to vicarage of Hacconby, on resignation of Robert
Terry. Patron: Prior and Convent of Sempringham. [Reg. 14, fo.69v.]

Thomas Sharp priest
Instituted 29 January 1416/17 to vicarage of Hacconby, on resignation of William Perotson. Patron: Prior and Convent of Sempringham. [Reg. 14, fo.86.]

John Cobuldyke priest
Instituted 15 May 1430 to vicarage of Hacconby, on resignation of Thomas Shep. Patron: Prior and Convent of Sempringham. [*Reg. Fleming* i. no.351.]

Robert Drury
Instituted before 7 June 1443. [Reg. 18, fo.91.]

John Ledys priest
Instituted 7 June 1443 to vicarage of Hacconby, on resignation of Robert Drury. Patron: Prior and Convent of Sempringham. [Reg. 18, fo.91.]

William Browne
Instituted before 24 February 1461/2. [Reg. 20, fo.136.]

Br. John London, monk of Sempringham
Instituted 24 February 1461/2 to vicarage of church of St Andrew, Hacconby, with chapel of St Sythe, *Staynewhete*, on resignation of William Browne. Patron: Prior and Convent of Sempringham. [Reg. 20, fo.136.]

There was an image of St Sythe in the south aisle of Hacconby church in 1530. [*Lincoln Wills* iii. 77.]

John Warner priest
Instituted 7 August 1467 to vicarage of Hacconby, on death of John London. Patron: Prior and Convent of Sempringham. [Reg. 20, fo.146.]

Thomas Cliff priest
Instituted 12 March 1501/2 to vicarage of Hacconby, on death of John Warner. Patron: Prior and Convent of St Mary, Sempringham. Vacated by resignation by December 1533. [Reg. 23, fo.68v.]

Assessed for subsidy (£5 6s 8d) in 1526. Died 1534. Will (LCC) dated 7 February, proved 13 February 1533/4. [*Subsidy*, 58; *Lincoln Wills* iv. no.409.]

John Borowe priest
Instituted December 1533 to vicarage of Hacconby, on resignation of Thomas Cliff. Patron: Prior and Convent of Sempringham. Note that an annual pension was reserved to Thomas Cliff for life from the fruits of the vicarage. [Reg. 27, fo.36v.]

The day of the institution and the amount of the pension are left blank in the register. Assessed for *Valor Ecclesiasticus* 1535. [*Valor* iv. 105.]

John Batty
Instituted 16 March 1543/4 to vicarage of Hacconby, on death of last incumbent. Patron: King Henry VIII. [Reg. 27, fo.82v.]

Richard Nicholson
Instituted 1545 (compounded for first-fruits, 11 September 1545). [FL.h.13, 451.]

Exhibited at Visitation, 1551. Witnessed Hacconby wills, 1557–8. Signed BTs 1562–3. [Vj 13, fo.62; LCC Wills 1557/iii/2; 1558/i/183v; BTs Hacconby.]

Christopher Pratt
Instituted 3 November 1563. [SUB I, fo.18v.]

Witnessed Hacconby wills, 1564–7. Signed BTs 1566. Resigned 1 August 1570. [LCC Wills 1564/89; 1567/142, 277; BTs Hacconby; RES 1570/3.]

John White
Instituted 1 August 1570. [RES 1570/3.]

Afterwards: V. of Billingborough, 1577–92 (q.v.).

Thomas Gamon
Instituted 24 August 1577 by collation to vicarage of Hacconby, of which the last incumbent was John White. Patron: Bishop of Lincoln. [*Bishop Cooper*, 20.]

Education: 'bred in the schools'; 'no graduate'. Priest: 31 January 1577/8 (Lincoln). Signed BTs 1577, 1586–1614. Listed at Visitation in 1611, when 'he was monished by my Lord … to appear at Buckden before his Lordship touchinge his insufficiency in learninge'. Buried at Hacconby, 5 May 1614. [*Bishop Cooper*, 220; *State of the Church*, 73, 415; BTs Hacconby; LC 3, fo.2v.]

John Spencer
Instituted 15 July 1614 by collation to vicarage of Hacconby. Patron: Bishop of Lincoln. [BC; Borthwick, Sub. Bk. 2, fo.26v.]

Larkin (Lorkinus) Lively
Instituted 26 April 1615 to vicarage of Hacconby. [BC; Borthwick, Sub. Bk. 2, fo.34v.]

Baptised 8 September 1590 at Cambridge; son of Edward L., Regius Professor of Hebrew. Educated: Trinity College (matric. 1606) and King's College, Cambridge (BA 1613–14). Deacon: 18 December 1614; priest: 26 February 1614/15 (Peterborough). Signed BTs 1616, 1618–29. Afterwards: V. of Crondall (Ha), 1631–47 (ejected). Buried at Frimley (Sr), 30 December 1652. [Venn, *Alumni*; Longden ix. 9; BTs Hacconby; *Walker Revised*, 186.]

John Audley MA
Instituted 3 March 1630/1 to vicarage of Hacconby, on cession of Lorkinus

Lively. Patron: Samuel Custe of Hacconby, gent. (28 February 1630/1), by grant for this turn from Bishop of Lincoln. [BC; PD 1631/91.]

Educated: St Catharine's Hall, Cambridge (matric. 1622; BA 1627). Deacon: 27 September 1629; priest: 28 September 1629 (Peterborough). Signed BTs 1632–41. Buried at Hacconby (MI). [Venn, *Alumni*; Longden i. 117; BTs Hacconby; *Monson*, 156.]

Thomas Waters
Occurs between 1649 and 1655. [Swaby, 112.]

Humfrey Booth BA
Instituted 11 November 1661 by collation to vicarage of Hacconby (cause of vacancy not stated). Patron: Bishop of Lincoln. [Reg. 32, fo.13v.]

Born *c*.1635; son of Richard B. of Tottington, par. Bury (La). Educated: Bury School (La) and St John's College, Cambridge (matric. 1649; BA 1653–4). Deacon: 7 November 1661; priest: 9 November 1661 (Lincoln). Afterwards: V. of Langton-by-Wragby, 1663–79; buried there, 10 November 1679. [Venn, *Alumni*; Reg. 32, fo.13v; PR Langton-by-Wragby.]

Tristram Diamond
Licensed curate, 10 April 1662. [LC 5, fo.23.]

Signed BTs 1661–72. Also: V. of Morton-by-Bourne, 1662–73 (*q.v.*). [LC 5, fo.23; BTs Hacconby.]

James Brooke BA
Instituted 30 October 1673 by collation to vicarage of Hacconby, on death of Tristram Diamond. Patron: Bishop of Lincoln. [SUB Va, fo.49; IND/L 1, fo.212.]

Signed BTs 1674–7. Also: V. of Morton-by-Bourne, 1673–8 (*q.v.*).

William Hotchkin MA
Instituted 20 December 1678 by collation to vicarage of Hacconby (cause of vacancy not stated). Patron: Bishop of Lincoln. [Reg. 34, fo.32.]

Signed BTs 1678–98. Also: V. of Morton-by-Bourne, 1678–98 (*q.v.*).

Benjamin Place BA
Instituted 14 October 1698 by collation to vicarage of Hacconby, on death of William Hotchkins. Patron: Bishop of Lincoln. [Reg. 35, fo.52v; IND/L 2, fo.17.]

Born *c*.1659; son of Christopher P., Vicar of Clapham (Y). Educated: Lancaster School and Christ's College, Cambridge (adm. 1679). Priest: September 1696 (Ely). Signed BTs at Hacconby 1699–1708. Afterwards: V. of Ashby Puerorum, 1715–17; R. of Greetham, 1715–17. Buried at Greetham, 22 May 1717. [Venn, *Alumni*; PR Greetham.]

Richard Tonge BA
Instituted 27 May 1709 by collation to vicarage of Hacconby, on deprivation
of Benjamin Place. Patron: Bishop of Lincoln. [Reg. 36, p.112.]
Signed BTs 1710–37. Also: V. of Morton-by-Bourne, 1708–38 (*q.v.*).

**The vicarage of Hacconby was united to the vicarage of Morton by
Bourne on 7 July 1732. [Reg. 38, p.261.]**

HACEBY

The Domesday Survey lists a number of holdings in Haceby, of which that
of Guy of Craon included a priest and a church. Agnes de Walecot, who
presented to the church in 1241–2, was perhaps the daughter and co-heiress
of Robert de Haceby; she later married Simon de Nevill and presented to
Haceby again in 1246–7. The advowson subsequently came into the possession of Hugh Durevie; a member of the same family, William Durevie,
presented in 1286. The patronage then passed to the Kirketon family and
later to that of Walcot, members of whom presented to the living until the
sixteenth century. After the death of Humphrey Walcot in 1538, his second
wife Mary married John Booth of Killingholme, who presented in 1554 and
1560. The advowson was then acquired by Geoffrey Wace, who in 1587
conveyed it to Gabriel Savile of Newton. The Savile family exercised the
patronage into the seventeenth century; it was subsequently divided between
the daughters and co-heirs of William Savile (d.1682): Mary, who married in
1683 William Burnell of Winkburn (Nt), and her sister Alice, who married
in 1693 Sir Pury Cust. The Burnell share later passed to the Welby family.
Sir Oliver Welby held the patronage in 1965. [*Lincolnshire Domesday*, 181;
LNQ 20 (1928–9), 87–9; LAO, BNLW 1/1/25/1; *Lincolnshire Pedigrees*,
155, 1032; LAO, BNLW 1/1/36/6; *LDC* (1965), 66–7.]

Geoffrey de Folking' deacon
Instituted by collation in the eleventh pontifical year of Bishop Hugh of Wells
(20 December 1219/19 December 1220) to church of Haceby. Patron: Bishop
of Lincoln, by authority of the Lateran Council. The right of anyone claiming
the advowson in the future was reserved. [*Rot. Welles* iii. 104.]

Nigel de Breyteby subdeacon
Instituted in the seventh pontifical year of Bishop Robert Grosseteste (17 June
1241/16 June 1242) to church of Haceby. Patron: lady Agnes de Walecot.
[Hoskin, no.216.]

Robert de Lochton chaplain
Instituted in the twelfth pontifical year of Bishop Robert Grosseteste (17 June 1246/16 June 1247) to church of Haceby. Patron: lady Agnes de Nevill. [Hoskin, no.367.]

Richard de Draythorp
Instituted before 10 July 1286. [*Reg. Sutton* i. 85.]

Thomas de Trikingham chaplain
Instituted 10 July 1286 to church of Haceby (having first held it *in commendam* for six months), on death of Richard de Draythorp. Patron: William Durevie. [*Reg. Sutton* i. 85.]
Formerly: V. of Threckingham, 1262/3–86 (*q.v.*).

John de Kirketon clerk in minor orders
Instituted 22 December 1291 to church of Haceby, on death of Robert [*sic*] de Trikingham. Patron: Robert de Kirketon. [*Reg. Sutton* i. 161.]
Subdeacon: 22 December 1291; deacon: 20 September 1292; priest: 20 December 1292 (Lincoln). [*Reg. Sutton* vii. 22, 33, 36.]

Robert Malebise (de Enderby) priest
Instituted 3 May 1294 to church of Haceby, on death of M. John de Kirketon. Patron: Robert de Kirketon. Note that the patron had first presented Leonius, dean of Christianity in Lincoln. When Leonius became ill and was not expected to recover, RM was presented instead. Subsequently, however, the patron revoked his presentation of RM and represented Leonius who had regained his health. After some discussion, Leonius resigned his claim and RM was instituted. [*Reg. Sutton* i. 186–7.]
Afterwards: R. of Thorpe St Peter, 1295–7; R. of Mavis Enderby, 1297–1313. Died before 17 August 1313. [*Reg. Sutton* i. 198, 218–20; Reg. 2, fo.48.]

John de Blaykeston chaplain
Instituted 17 April 1295 to church of Haceby, on resignation of Robert de Enderby. Patron: Robert de Kirketon. [*Reg. Sutton* i. 198.]
Formerly: V. of Osbournby, 1276–95 (*q.v.*). Afterwards: R. of Aswarby, 1305–21. [Reg. 2, fo.16v; *Reg. Burghersh* i. no.21.]

M. Walter de Aswardeby acolyte
Instituted 23 December 1305 to church of Haceby, on resignation of John de Bleykeston. Patron: Cecilia widow of Robert de Kirketon. [Reg. 2, fo.16v.]

Richard Ristoft of Wisbech
Instituted before 30 September 1339. [*Reg. Burghersh* iii. no.762.]
Subdeacon: before 30 September 1339. Dispensation for absence to study in England

for 1 year, 30 September 1339. Assessed for poll-tax, 1377. [*Reg. Burghersh*. iii. no.762; *Clerical Poll-Taxes*, no.688.]

William (Maister) de Walcote priest
Instituted 13 June 1379 to church of Haceby, on death of Richard de Ristoft. Patron: John de Walcote. [Reg. 10, fo.94v.]
Assessed for poll-tax, 1381. [*Clerical Poll-Taxes*, nos 1334, 1923.]

William de Legburn chaplain
Instituted 23 March 1403/4 to church of Haceby, on death of William de Walcotes. Patron: Joan widow of John de Walcotes. [Reg. 13, fo.164v.]

Laurence Yorke
Instituted before 27 June 1418. [Reg. 14, fo.95.]

William son of Roger de Horkestowe priest
Instituted 27 June 1418 to church of Haceby, on death of Laurence Yorke. Patron: John Walcote of Walcot, esquire. [Reg. 14, fo.95.]

Thomas Cartwright
Instituted by 1473. [Vj 4, fo.58v.]

Richard Sleford priest
Instituted 6 November 1476 to church of Haceby, on death of Thomas Cartwright. Patron: Katherine Walkot widow, lady of Haceby. [Reg. 21, fo.14.]

John Tomson priest
Instituted 8 August 1481 to church of Haceby, on resignation of Richard Sleford. Patron: Katherine Walcot of Walcot, widow. [Reg. 22, fo.127.]

Christopher Mason
Instituted 27 September 1484 to church of Haceby, on resignation of John Tomson. Patron: John Walcote esquire. [Reg. 22, fo.135.]

William Dann priest
Instituted 1 August 1493 to church of Haceby, on death of Christopher Mason. Patron: John Walcott (31 July 1493). [Reg. 22, fo.155; PD 1493/58.]

Thomas Jercoke priest
Instituted 8 July 1497 to church of Haceby, on resignation of William Daname. Patron: John Walcote, lord of the manor of Haceby. [Reg. 23, fo.39v.]
Assessed for subsidy (£4 3s 2d) in 1526; assessed for *Valor Ecclesiasticus* 1535. [*Subsidy*, 57; *Valor* iv. 104.]

William Townroe

Instituted in the fourth year of King Edward VI (28 January 1550 x 27 January 1551) to church of Haceby, on death of Thomas Jercocke. Patron: Richard Mathewe LLB, for this turn, by reason of a grant of the advowson made by Humfrey Walcote esquire, decd, and Mary his widow, to Henry Williams, Dean of Lichfield, and others, and assigned to the said Richard Mathewe. [Reg. 28, fo.25.]

Exhibited at Visitation, 1551. Deprived 1554 (see below). Died before 11 February 1559/60 (probate inventory): 'in mony and goulde, £9 10s'. [Vj 13, fo.63; INV 36/712.]

Reginald Wadingtonne

Instituted 19 June 1554 to church of Haceby, on deprivation of William Towneroe. Patron: John Boothe and Mary his wife. [Reg. 28, fo.103v.]

Still Rector in 1558. [LCC Wills 1557/iv/123.]

Robert Mynnitt

Instituted 15 May 1560 to church of Haceby, on death of last incumbent. Patron: John Bothe of Killingholme, esquire, in right of Mary his wife. Vacated by death, before 5 February 1576/7. [Reg. 19, fo.96v; INV 59/330.]

Born c.1500. Education: 'skilled in Latin; moderately versed in sacred learning'. Priest: 24 September 1524 (Chalcedon for York). Resident (1576): signed BTs 1562. Witnessed Haceby will, 1566. Died before 5 February 1576/7 (probate inventory). [Bishop Cooper, 208; BTs Haceby; LCC Wills 1567/59; INV 59/330.]

Edward Bordman

Instituted 9 June 1577 to church of Haceby, on death of Robert Menytt. Patron: Geoffrey Wace gent. (8 June 1577). [Bishop Cooper, 19, 261.]

Education: BA. Priest: 1574 (Peterborough). Signed BTs 1577–99. Assessed ('a Bowe') in Subsidy of Armour 1590. Died before 5 March 1598/9 (probate inventory): 'his bookes and writinges, £6 13s 4d'. [Bishop Cooper, 220; State of the Church, 73, 148; BTs Haceby; INV 89/189.]

Robert Hawford

Instituted 5 May 1599 to rectory of Haceby, on death of Edward Boardman. Patron: Gabriel Savile esquire (3 May 1599). [Reg. 30, fo.108v; PD 1599/37.]

Born c.1571; of Graby, par. Aslackby. Educated: Christ's College, Cambridge (matric. 1587; BA ?1593–4; MA 1597). Deacon and priest: 17 September 1597 (Lincoln). Signed BTs 1600–4. Also: V. of Butterwick, 1599. Resigned Haceby 28 November 1604. Afterwards: R. of Brigsley, 1604–42. [PD 1599/37 (biographical detail); Venn, Alumni; BTs Haceby; RES 1604/21; LC 4, fo.33.]

Richard Norris BA

Instituted 5 December 1604 to rectory of Haceby, on resignation of Robert Hawford. Patron: Gabriel Savile of Newton, esquire. [Reg. 30, fo.238v; PD 1604/27.]

Baptised at Morton by Bourne, 10 February 1566/7. Educated: Jesus College, Cambridge (matric. 1584; BA 1587–8). Priest: 1 July 1590 (Lincoln). Formerly: C. of Ropsley; C. of Syston. Signed BTs at Haceby 1605–36. Died before 16 January 1637/8 (probate inventory): 'all his Bookes, £6 13s 4d'. Will 1637 (LCC). [PR Morton by Bourne; PD 1604/27; Venn, *Alumni*; BTs Haceby; INV 145/212; LCC Wills 1637/454.]

Thomas Palfreman MA

Instituted 21 May 1638 to rectory of Haceby, on death of Richard Norris. Patron: William Savile esquire. [LPL W3/32/1/3, no.50.]

Son of Richard P. of Haceby (and grandson of Thomas P. of Lusby, Merchant of the Staple). Educated: New Inn Hall, Oxford (BA 1633; MA 1635/6); incorporated at Cambridge (MA 1651). Deacon: 1635 (Oxford); priest (Bristol). Formerly: V. of Threckingham, 1637–8 (*q.v.*). Signed BTs at Haceby 1638–41 and 1662–70. Married (21 November 1639) at Bicker, Ann Harriman of Boston. Died 1670. Will dated 29 April, proved 6 July 1670: 'To be buried in Haceby churchyard by my father and mother who lye near the south wall of the chancel. ... To my wife Ann, £50 [and] my will is that she continue with my dear and loving son and daughter Francis and Christian Hopes at the Rectory of Haceby and they to allow her dyet, lodging, fire, washing, candle, and £5 per annum.' [*Lincolnshire Pedigrees*, 749; Foster, *Alumni*; Venn, *Alumni*; LC 5, fo.23; BTs Haceby; PR Bicker; Stow Wills 1669–71/345; A. R. Maddison, 'Hopes and Palfreyman families', *LNQ* 6 (1900–1), 118–20.]

Francis Hopes MA

Instituted 26 July 1670 to rectory of Haceby, on death of Thomas Palfreyman. Patron: Ann Palfryman widow. [Reg. 33, fo.132; IND/L 1, fo.198v.]

Born *c*.1642; son of Joseph H. of Richmond (YNR), draper. Educated: Durham School and St John's College, Cambridge (matric. 1660; BA 1663–4; MA 1667). Deacon and priest: 28 December 1664 (Lichfield). Also: R. of Aswarby, 1682–1704. Married (25 April 1670) at Haceby, Christian, daughter of Thomas Palfreman (above). Father of Christian (baptised at Haceby 1677), later wife of Sir Stephen Fox and grandmother of Charles James Fox. Buried at Aswarby, 15 March 1703/4. [Venn, *Alumni*; CCED; Reg. 33, fo.132; BTs Aswarby.]

Charles Baseley MA

Inducted 31 August 1704 to rectory of Haceby, on death of Francis Hopes. Patron: William Baseley of Churchover (Wa), gent., executor of Richard Baseley late of Churchover, decd. [IND/L 2, fo.29v.]

Baptised December 1666 at Churchover; son of Richard and Katherine B. Educated: Emmanuel College, Cambridge (matric. 1683–4; BA 1685–6; MA 1690). Deacon: 26 May 1689; priest: 22 September 1689 (Lincoln). Formerly: C. of Lutterworth, 1689; C. of Elton (Hu), 1689 (still there 1693); C. of Haceby, 1696–1704. Children: Charles (1696), Catherine (1698), Richard (1699), Rebecca (1702) baptised at Haceby. Also: C. of Swarby, 1724. Wife Susanna buried at Haceby, 8 May 1729. Died 1731; buried at Haceby, 6 October 1731. [Warwicks RO, PR Churchover; Venn, *Alumni*; Reg. 34, fos 108v, 110v; Reg. 35, fo.15; SUB V/6, fo.66; Reg. 38, p.52; SUB VII, p.62; PR Haceby.]

Richard Burrow MA

Instituted 15 October 1731 to rectory of Haceby, on death of Charles Beasley. Patron: William Burnell esquire. [Reg. 38, p.252.]

Perhaps to be identified with RB, baptised at Wakefield 5 June 1676, son of Rowland
B. of Wakefield; educated University College (matric. 1694; BA 1697) and St Edmund
Hall, Oxford (MA 1700); deacon: 5 March 1698/9; priest: 21 December 1701 (York).
Signed BTs at Haceby 1732–42. Buried at Haceby, 28 February 1742/3. [WYAS, PR
Wakefield All Saints; Foster, *Alumni*; *York Ordinations 1662–1699*, 12; *York Ordinations
1700–1749*, 10; PR Haceby.]

William Hasledine MA

Instituted 1 June 1743 to rectory of Haceby, on death of Richard Burrow.
Patron: Savile Cust esquire. [Reg. 38, p.430.]

Born 4 March, baptised 18 March 1713/14 at St Margaret-in-the-Close, Lincoln; son of
William H. of The Close of Lincoln, gent. Educated: Lincoln College (matric. 1730) and
Magdalen College, Oxford (BA 1734; MA 1736; BD 1747; DD 1748); Fellow of Magdalen
1733–64. Deacon: 28 May 1738; priest: 23 September 1738 (Oxford). Resided at Haceby;
signed BTs 1744–70. Resigned Haceby 6 October 1764 (accepted 17 December 1764) but
continued to serve Haceby thereafter as curate, until *c*.1769. Also: PC of Walcot, 1752–72
(*q.v.*). Afterwards: V. of Dinton (Wlt), 1762–73; R. of Wishford (Wlt), 1770–3. Died 3
December 1773. Buried at Dinton (MI): 'Undisturbed by violent passions and inordinate
desires, he enjoy'd a plentiful fortune, with moderation and decency.' Will (PCC) dated
24 March 1773, proved 29 December 1773. [PR Lincoln St Margaret; Foster, *Alumni*;
Bloxam vi. 225–7; ORO, MS. Oxf. Dioc. Papers b.21, fos 2, 3; LC 18B, p.198; BTs
Haceby; PR Haceby; LC 31, p.76; RES 238/96; Phillips, *Wiltoniae* ii. 80, 85, 87; PRO,
PROB 11/993/139.]

Charles Gery

Instituted 17 December 1764 to rectory of Haceby, on resignation of William
Hasledine. Patron: William Welby esquire, for this turn. [Reg. 39, p.37.]

Baptised 8 November 1740 at Welbourn; son of William G. of Welbourn esquire and
Eleanor (née Welby) his wife, one of 3 children 'born at one Birth'. Educated: Clare Hall,
Cambridge (matric. 1759; BA 1763; MA 1766). Deacon: 12 June 1763; priest: 1 November
1764 (Lincoln). Formerly: C. of Little Staughton (Bd), 1763. Also: R. of Sapperton,
1775–1813; R. of Toynton St Peter, 1784–1820. Non-resident at Haceby (house too
small). Resided at Bushmead (Bd), serving Little Staughton (1768). Subsequently lived
at Grantham. Married (16 October 1774) at Boston, Phyllis, daughter of Samuel Preston
esquire. Died 1820. Will (PCC) dated 14 October 1817, proved 12 September 1820. [PR
Welbourn; Venn, *Alumni*; Reg. 39, pp. 18, 36; NRL 1806/51b; 1808/51; 1810/34; PR
Boston; PRO, PROB 11/1634/168.]

John Earle Welby MA

Instituted 9 July 1813 to rectory of Haceby, on cession of Charles Gery.
Patron: William Earle Welby esquire. [Reg. 40, p.189.]

Born 11 September 1786 at Allington; son of Sir William Earle Welby Bt. Educated:
Eton College (1799) and Emmanuel College, Cambridge (matric. 1806; BA 1811; MA
1814). Deacon: 22 December 1811; priest: 27 September 1812 (Lincoln). Formerly: C. of
Harlaxton, 1811. Also: V. of Keddington, 1812–16; R. of Sapperton, 1813–16; R. of West
Allington, 1814–67. Afterwards: R. of Stroxton, 1816–67; R. of Harston (Le), 1816–67.
Died 9 July 1867 at Harston. [Venn, *Alumni*; *Eton College Lists*; Reg. 40, pp. 165, 174;
Probate Calendar 1867.]

James David Glover MA

Instituted 4 April 1816 to rectory of Haceby, on cession of John Earle Welby. Patron: John, Lord Brownlow, for this turn. [Reg. 40, p.239.]

Born 14 September, baptised 9 October 1771 at St Sepulchre Holborn, London; son of David G. and Ann his wife. Educated: Merchant Taylors' School (1781) and Magdalene College, Cambridge (matric. 1789; BA 1793; MA 1796). Deacon: 31 May 1795; priest: 3 June 1798 (Lincoln). Formerly: C. of Rearsby and Brooksby (Le), 1795; C. of Glen Magna (Le), 1814. Also: R. of Sapperton, 1816–32; C. of Dembleby, 1822. Licences for non-residence at Haceby (1816–27), on account of the house being unfit. Resided at Pickworth and served his parishes. Built new Rectory House at Haceby, 1828 (architect: J. S. Langwith of Grantham). Father of James David G., Rector of East Halton (1842–54). Died 9 March 1832, aged 61; buried at Pickworth (MI). [LMA, PR St Sepulchre Holborn; *Merchant Taylors' Register* ii. 149; Venn, *Alumni*; Reg. 39, pp. 605, 651; CR 1, pp. 11, 171; NRL 1816/60; 1821/5; 1823/25; 1825/22; 1827/9; MGA 144; *Monson*, 285.]

John Neville (Lucas) Calcraft MA

Instituted 1 May 1832 to rectory of Haceby, on death of James David Glover. Patron: Sir William Earle Welby Bt, for this turn. [Reg. 40, p.395.]

Baptised 9 July 1801 at Ancaster; son of John Charles Lucas-Calcraft of Ancaster Hall, esquire. Educated: Rugby School and Clare Hall, Cambridge (matric. 1820; BA 1824; MA 1828). Deacon: 27 February 1825; priest: 21 May 1826 (Lincoln). Formerly: C. of Normanton, 1825; C. of Barkston, 1828. Also: C. of Dembleby, 1832. Resided at Haceby Rectory. Died 11 July 1887 at Haceby. [PR Ancaster; Venn, *Alumni*; OR 1, pp. 19, 24; CR 1, pp. 261, 385, 479; CR 2, p.34; White, *Lincolnshire* (1842), 738–9; Census Returns 1851, 1871, 1881; *Probate Calendar* 1887.]

The rectory of Haceby was united to the rectory of Newton by Order in Council dated 24 October 1870. [Reg. 41, pp. 324–7.]

HORBLING

A mediety of the church of Horbling was given by Alexander Gudlein to Sempringham Priory *c.*1195, covenanting that he or his heirs would not give the other mediety to any other religious house. In 1222 Roger Joilein quit-claimed to the Priory his right in the advowson of a mediety of the church. The two medieties were united in the possession of the Priory by 1247 when papal permission was granted for the appropriation of the church, on the grounds that there were 200 women belonging to the Order who often lacked the necessities of life. A vicarage was ordained in 1265. The priory continued to present to the vicarage until the Dissolution. The advowson subsequently passed to the bishops of Lincoln, who still held it in 1965. [*Final Concords* i. 3, 163; Golding, *Gilbertine Order*, 378; *LDC* (1965), 66–7.]

Andrew son of Octavian Tecald a Roman citizen
Instituted by collation before 20 December 1218 to a mediety of church

of Horbling. Patron: Bishop of Lincoln. The right of anyone claiming the advowson in the future was reserved. [*Rot. Welles* i. 125.]

Joscius de Bilingburg clerk
Instituted in the thirteenth pontifical year of Bishop Hugh of Wells (20 December 1221/19 December 1222) to a mediety of church of Horbling. Patron: Prior of the Order of Sempringham and Prior and Convent of Sempringham. Note that Joscius was to proceed to the subdiaconate at the Michaelmas ordination in 1222 and to pursue his studies continually in the schools until he had learned to rule a parish. [*Rot. Welles* iii. 114.]

M. Reginald de Trigginham subdeacon
Instituted in the fifth pontifical year of Bishop Robert Grosseteste (17 June 1239/16 June 1240) to a mediety of church of Horbling. Patron: Master of the Order of Sempringham and Prior and Convent of Sempringham. [Hoskin, no.164.]

Vicarage

Robert de Flixton priest
Instituted 15 November 1265 to vicarage of Horbling, newly ordained. Patron: Prior and Convent of Sempringham. [*Rot. Gravesend*, 20.]

M. Hugh de Thurleby deacon
Instituted 2 April 1278 to vicarage of Horbling, on resignation of Robert (who had entered the order of Friars Minor). Patron: Master of the Order of Sempringham and Prior and Convent of Sempringham. [*Rot. Gravesend*, 80, 286.]

Died 1291; buried at Horbling. Grant of indulgence to all who pray for his soul, 20 October 1322; further indulgence, 4 November 1322. [Reg. 5, fos 322, 323v.]

William de Ringedon deacon
Instituted 28 October 1291 to vicarage of Horbling, on death of M. Hugh. Patron: Prior and Convent of Sempringham. [*Reg. Sutton* i. 160.]

Priest: 22 December 1291 (Lincoln). [*Reg. Sutton* vii. 24.]

John de Chikesand chaplain
Instituted 16 May 1300 to vicarage of Horbling, on death of William. Patron: Prior and Convent of Sempringham. [Reg. 2, fo.1v.]

John de Camylton
Instituted before 13 February 1330/1. [*Reg. Burghersh* i. no.289.]

John de Sempyngham priest
Instituted 13 February 1330/1 to vicarage of Horbling, on death of John de Camylton. Patron: Prior and Convent of Sempringham. [*Reg. Burghersh* i. no.289.]

William Poutrell de Prestwold priest
Instituted 30 July 1349 to vicarage of Horbling, on death of John. Patron: Prior and Convent of Sempringham. [Reg. 9, fo.67.]
Afterwards: R. of Hacconby, to 1354 (*q.v.*).

John de Irnham priest
Instituted 29 March 1351 to vicarage of Horbling, on resignation of M. William Poutrell. Patron: Prior and Convent of Sempringham. [Reg. 9, fo.89v.]
Assessed for poll-tax 1377. [*Clerical Poll-Taxes*, no.694.]

Thomas Howe de Leveryngton priest
Instituted 15 September 1380 to vicarage of Horbling, on death of John de Irnham. Patron: Prior and Convent of Sempringham. [Reg. 10, fo.105v.]
Assessed for poll-tax 1381. [*Clerical Poll-Taxes*, nos 1341, 1930.]

Robert Barette chaplain
Instituted 13 April 1403 to vicarage of Horbling (cause of vacancy not stated). Patron: Prior and Convent of Sempringham. [Reg. 13, fo.156.]

John Osburnby priest
Instituted 12 September 1458 to vicarage of Horbling (cause of vacancy not stated). Patron: Prior and Convent of Sempringham. [Reg. 20, fo.131.]

William Gamyll priest
Instituted 28 February 1458/9 to vicarage of Horbling (cause of vacancy not stated). Patron: Prior and Convent of Sempringham. [Reg. 20, fo.131v.]

Oswald Pyttes priest
Instituted 19 May 1505 to vicarage of Horbling (cause of vacancy not stated). Patron: Prior and Convent of Sempringham (16 May 1505). [Reg. 23, fo.96v; PD 1505/67.]

Thomas Wynter chaplain
Instituted 28 January 1505/6 to vicarage of Horbling, on death of Oswald Pyttes. Patron: Prior and Convent of Sempringham. [Reg. 23, fo.107.]

John Bullur alias Spyllesby BA priest
Instituted 22 September 1506 to vicarage of Horbling, on death of Thomas Wynter. Patron: Prior and Convent of Sempringham. [Reg. 23, fo.115v.]

Perhaps to be identified with JB of Sleaford; educated Magdalen College, Oxford (demy 1482); priest: 24 May 1483 (Lincoln). Resigned 5 November 1519. [Emden, *BRUO*, 303; RES 1519/2.]

Richard Baynton chaplain
Instituted 12 November 1519 to vicarage of Horbling, on resignation of John Buller. Patron: Prior and Convent of Sempringham. Note that an annual pension of 26s 8d was reserved to John Buller for life from the fruits of the vicarage. [Reg. 25, fo.22.]

Assessed for subsidy (£5 4s 0d) in 1526. [*Subsidy*, 57.]

Robert Haddesfrelde chaplain
Instituted 26 February 1532/3 to vicarage of Horbling, on death of Richard Baynton. Patron: Prior and Convent of Sempringham. [Reg. 27, fo.54v.]

Thomas Smyth chaplain
Instituted 29 April 1533 to vicarage of Horbling, on death of Robert Hatfeld. Patron: Prior and Convent of Sempringham. [Reg. 27, fo.56.]

Assessed for *Valor Ecclesiasticus* 1535. [*Valor* iv. 104.]

Anthony Langton
Instituted 25 October 1542 to vicarage of Horbling, on resignation of last incumbent. Patron: King Henry VIII. Reinstituted 5 June 1555 (compounded for first-fruits, 20 June 1555). Vacated by death before 25 March 1583. [Reg. 27, fo.78v; *Bishop Cooper*, 220; FL.h.13, 491; INV 69A/41.]

Born *c*.1513. Education: 'knows but little Latin; moderately versed in sacred learning'. Priest: 15 April 1536 (Philadelphia for Lincoln). Formerly: Canon of Sempringham Priory; allotted pension at the Dissolution, which he later sold. Compounded for first-fruits, 23 October 1542. Exhibited at Visitation in 1551. Signed BTs at Horbling 1562–78. Witnessed Horbling wills, 1557–73. Died before 25 March 1583 (probate inventory). Will (LCC). [*Bishop Cooper*, 207, 220; Reg. 26, fo.52; *Ex-Religious*, 68–9; FL.h.13, 491; Vj 13, fo.62v; BTs Horbling; LCC Wills 1556–7/7, 37; 1558/i/79v, 131, 204v; 1561/65v; 1562/131v, 132v; 1557–72/180v; LCC Wills 1583/ii/62; INV 69A/41.]

Richard Harrison BA
Instituted 24 March 1582/3 to vicarage of Horbling, on death of Anthony Langton. Patron: Bishop of Lincoln. [*Bishop Cooper*, 31.]

Educated: Trinity College, Cambridge (matric. 1569; BA 1572–3). Deacon and priest: 16 March 1573/4 (Peterborough). Formerly: V. of Quadring, 1578–83. Licensed preacher. Signed BTs at Horbling 1586–92. Died before 10 July 1593 (probate inventory). Inventory: described as 'Mynnister and Preacher of the Woorde of God within the foresaid Towne'; lists 'all his Bookes, £5'. [Venn, *Alumni*; Longden vi. 179; *Bishop Cooper*, 22, 31; *State of the Church*, 73; BTs Horbling; INV 84/151.]

Christopher Browne
Instituted 9 August 1593 to vicarage of Horbling, on death of Richard

Harryson. Patron: Henry Lambley, Francis Lambley and James Lambley, gents. (21 July 1593). [BC; PD 1593/25.]

Signed BT at Horbling 1593. Listed at Visitation in 1594. Died before 1 July 1595 (probate inventory). [BTs Horbling; *State of the Church*, 382; INV 86/313.]

Simon Bradstreet MA

Instituted 24 November 1596 to vicarage of Horbling, on death of Christopher Browne. Patron: Francis Lamley and James Lamley, gents (19 November 1596). [BC; PD 1596/30.]

Born at Gislingham (Sf). Educated: Christ's College, Cambridge (matric. 1570; BA 1575–6; MA 1579); Fellow of Emmanuel College. Deacon and priest: 22 November 1594 (Lincoln). Formerly: R. of Hinderclay (Sf), 1595–6. Resident at Horbling; signed BTs 1597–1621. Selected as preacher for Deanery of Aveland to give sermon at Folkingham on 25 April 1603 giving thanks for accession of King James I. A Puritan, who was treated with patience by the authorities: at 1604 Visitation the churchwardens noted that 'he hath not worne the surplis at eny tyme since his coming'. At 1607 Visitation was presented for not conforming to orders and ceremonies of the Prayer Book and Canons. At 1611 Visitation, entered as being of good behaviour, 'saving hee is not conformable'; 'geven till Michaelmas next come xij monthes to conforme himself'. Father of Simon B. (1604–97), later Governor of Massachusetts Bay Colony. Remained Vicar of Horbling until his death. Buried at Horbling, 9 February 1620/1. [Venn, *Alumni*; LC 3, fo.2; LC 4, fo.72v; BTs Horbling; *State of the Church*, pp. l, civ–cv; 'Bradstreet, Simon' in *ODNB*.]

Thomas Grainger

Instituted 12 March 1621 by collation to vicarage of Horbling. Patron: Bishop of Lincoln. [BC.]

Born *c*.1578 at Epworth. Educated: Peterhouse, Cambridge (matric. 1598; BA 1601–2; MA 1605). Deacon: 21 September 1606; priest: 20 September 1607 (Lincoln). Formerly: V. of Butterwick, 1606–21. Signed BTs at Horbling 1622–7. Died before 26 June 1627: probate inventory ('In his studdie … his librarie of Bookes, £11'). Will (LCC). [PD 1606/10 (biographical details); Venn, *Alumni*; BTs Horbling; INV 132/229; LCC Wills 1627/494.]

William Watson MA

Instituted 30 June 1627 by collation to vicarage of Horbling, on death of last incumbent. Patron: Bishop of Lincoln. [BC; IND/L 1, fo.78.]

Education: perhaps to be identified with WW of Christ's College, Cambridge (matric. *c*.1602; BA 1605–6; MA 1609). Formerly: Master of Boston GS, 1620–7. Afterwards: R. of Aswarby, 1641–61. [Venn, *Alumni*.]

John Howe MA

Instituted 4 June 1641 by collation to vicarage of Horbling, on cession of last incumbent. Patron: Bishop of Lincoln. Inducted 12 June 1641 by Edmund Ashton, R. of Dowsby. [Reg. 31, p.8; PD 1641/6; IND/L 1, fo.128.]

Education: perhaps to be identified with JH of Peterhouse, Cambridge (matric. 1618; BA 1618–19; MA 1622); incorporated at Oxford, 1623. Signed BT at Horbling 1641. Prosecuted before Committee of Plundered Ministers, 1646. [Venn, *Alumni*; Foster, *Alumni*; BTs Horbling; Foster, *Plundered Ministers*, 55–6.]

James Morton

Instituted 1650 to vicarage of Horbling, on cession of John Howes. [Swaby, 111.]

Listed at Visitation, 1662. Also: V. of Billingborough, 1632–62 (*q.v.*). [LC 5, fo.22v.]

Robert Clipsham BA

Instituted 24 December 1662 by collation to vicarage of Horbling (cause of vacancy not stated). Patron: Bishop of Lincoln. [Reg.32, fo.23v.]

Also: V. of Billingborough, 1662–1702 (*q.v.*).

Jonathan Cateline MA

Instituted 18 May 1663 by collation to vicarage of Horbling, on cession of last incumbent. Patron: Bishop of Lincoln. [Reg. 33, fo.6v.]

Son of Jeremiah C., Rector of Barham (Sf). Educated: Clare Hall, Cambridge (matric. 1650; BA 1654; MA 1658). Deacon: 12 July 1662; priest: 14 July 1662 (Lincoln). Formerly: V. of Baston, 1662–4. Signed BTs at Horbling 1664–1708. Buried at Horbling, 11 August 1708. [Venn, *Alumni*; Reg. 32, fos 17v, 23; LC 14, fo.4; BTs Horbling.]

Michael Taylor

Instituted 28 February 1708/9 by collation to vicarage of Horbling, on death of last incumbent. Patron: Bishop of Lincoln. [Reg. 36, p.99.]

Baptised 5 August 1658 at Ravenstonedale (We). Priest: 29 May 1687 (Chester). Formerly: C. of Kirkby-on-Bain, 1697. Also: C. of Tattershall, 1689–1730. Resided at Tattershall but signed BTs at Horbling 1709, 1713–18, 1730. Buried at Tattershall, 7 July 1730. [PR Tattershall (*sub* 1657); SUB V/6, fo.66; *Speculum*, 66, 125; PR Tattershall.]

John White MA

Instituted 25 September 1730 by collation to vicarage of Horbling, on death of last incumbent. Patron: Bishop of Lincoln. [Reg. 38, p.230.]

Also: C. of Totteridge (Hrt), 1724–46; Canon of Lincoln and Prebendary of Norton Episcopi, 1734–46. Buried at Totteridge, 16 May 1746. Will (PCC). [Reg. 38, p.47; SUB VII, p.52; *Le Neve Fasti: Lincoln 1541–1857*, 101; PRO, PROB 11/748/33.]

Miles Rowlandson

Instituted 29 May 1746, on death of John White. Patron: Bishop of Lincoln. [Reg. 38, p.466.]

Education: literate. Priest: 21 September 1707 (Lincoln). Formerly: C. of Horbling, 1711–46. Also: R. of Little Steeping, 1708–48. Non-resident at Little Steeping; resided at Horbling on account of his health. Signed BTs at Horbling: as curate 1711–12, 1719–45; as Vicar 1746–8. Buried at Horbling, 26 June 1748. [Reg. 36, p.54; Reg. 37, p.19; *Speculum*, 66, 117; BTs Horbling.]

Thomas Wilberfoss

Instituted 4 July 1748 by collation to vicarage of Horbling, on death of Miles Rowlandson. Patron: Bishop of Lincoln. [Reg. 38, p.482.]

Born *c.*1715; son of Robert W. of Sutton-on-Derwent (YER). Educated: Coxwold School; Sidney Sussex College (matric. 1732–3) and Peterhouse, Cambridge (BA 1735–6). Deacon: 21 December 1735; priest: 24 December 1738 (Lincoln). Formerly: C. of Holywell cum Needingworth (Hu), 1735; C. of Yelling (Hu), 1738. Also: R. of All Saints with St Peter, Stamford, 1756–85. Resided at Horbling to 1758 (signed BTs there 1752–8); afterwards at Stamford. Was too ill ('not able to stir') to attend Visitation in 1778. Died 24 January 1785; buried at All Saints Stamford (MI). Will (PCC) dated 22 November 1783, proved 21 February 1785. [Venn, *Alumni*; Reg. 38, pp. 310, 356; LC 31, pp. 71, 76; Peck, *Antiquities of Stamford* (1785), ii. 325; PRO, PROB 11/1127/34.]

John Smith MA

Instituted 7 April 1785 by collation to vicarage of Horbling, on death of Thomas Wilberfoss. Patron: Bishop of Lincoln. [Reg. 39, p.426.]

Joseph Lodington

Instituted 30 December 1785 by collation to vicarage of Horbling, on cession of John Smith. Patron: Bishop of Lincoln. [Reg. 39, p.441.]

Born 21 October 1754 at Carey Street, London: son of Thomas L., merchant. Educated: Soho Square and Oakham Schools; St John's College (matric. 1773) and Sidney Sussex College, Cambridge (BA 1777; MA 1780). Deacon: 28 September 1777; priest: 20 December 1778 (Peterborough). Formerly: C. of Oundle (Np), 1780–5. Also: Canon of Lincoln and Prebendary of Nassington, 1786–1806; V. of Oundle, 1796–1806. Resided at Southwick (Np). Married (5 June 1787) at St Mildred Poultry, London, Joanna Maria Smith. Died December 1806; buried 24 December 1806 at Benefield. Will (PCC) dated 28 December 1798, proved 26 March 1807. [Venn, *Alumni*; Longden ix. 27; Law, *Oundle's Story* (1922), 118; *Le Neve Fasti: Lincoln 1541–1857*, 98; Crisp, *Fragmenta Genealogica* xii. 49–50; LMA, PR St Mildred Poultry; PRO, PROB 11/1458/179.]

George Gordon BD

Instituted 14 January 1807 by collation to vicarage of Horbling, on death of Joseph Lodington. Patron: Bishop of Lincoln. [Reg. 40, p.115.]

Baptised 7 December 1763 at St Benedict, Cambridge; son of John G. (later Archdeacon of Lincoln). Educated: Rugby School and St John's College, Cambridge (matric. 1780; BA 1784; MA 1787; BD 1794; DD 1810); Fellow 1787. Deacon: 17 February 1788 (Ely); priest: 25 April 1788 (Lincoln). Formerly: R. of Gumley (Le), 1788–1807; Precentor of Exeter, 1789–1809. Non-resident at Horbling, which was served by curates, including John Shinglar, Joseph Irwin Eller, John Cross Morphew, Edmund Larken and Henry Harris. Also: R. of Sedgebrook with East Allington, 1792–1845; R. of West Deeping, 1807–10; Canon of Lincoln and Prebendary of Decem Librarum, 1808–45; Dean of Lincoln, 1810–45. 'Was distinguished all his life by a zealous and careful preservation of things as they were.' Died 2 August 1845 at Lincoln; buried in Lincoln Cathedral (MI). [IGI; Venn, *Alumni*; Reg. 39, pp. 475, 480; CR 1, pp. 12, 383; CR 2, pp. 48, 211; CR 3, fo.60v; White, *Lincolnshire* (1842), 740; *Le Neve Fasti: Lincoln 1541–1857*, 9, 63.]

Henry Harris

Instituted 29 August 1845 by collation to vicarage of Horbling, on death of George Gordon. Patron: Bishop of Lincoln. [Reg. 40, p.508.]

Born 28 June, baptised 29 June 1816 at Bicker; son of Revd Daniel H., Curate of Bicker.

Educated: St Catharine's Hall, Cambridge (matric. 1837; BA 1841). Deacon: 7 March 1841; priest: 20 February 1842 (Peterborough). Formerly: C. of All Saints, Northampton, 1842; of Bicker, 1842–4. Resident at Horbling where he built a new Vicarage House. 'Took an active part in all matters favorable to the temperance movement.' Died 15 March 1876 at Horbling. Buried at Horbling. [PR Bicker; Venn, *Alumni*; *Eccles. Gazette*, 13 April 1841, 8 March 1842; *Bonney's Church Notes*, 224; White, *Lincolnshire* (1856), 718; Census Returns 1851, 1861; *Grantham Journal*, 25 March 1876; *Probate Calendar* 1876; PR Horbling.]

Plumpton Stravenson Wilson MA

Instituted 18 April 1876 by collation to vicarage of Horbling, on death of Henry Harris. Patron: Bishop of Lincoln. [Reg. 41, p.528.]

Born *c*.1832 at Northover (So); eldest son of Plumpton W., Rector of Ilchester. Educated: Rugby School and Exeter College, Oxford (matric. 1849; BA 1853; MA 1856). Deacon: 1854; priest: 1855 (Peterborough). Formerly: C. of Hellidon (Np), 1854–6; of Roydon (Nf), 1856–60; of Ringstead (Nf), 1860–2; of Diss, 1863; V. of West Pinchbeck, 1863–76. Built new Vicarage House 1877 (Thomas Dickinson of Horbling, builder), where he resided. Father of Mary Agnes W. (1875–1927), mother of Archbishop Michael Ramsey. Resigned 25 November 1909. Latterly of 11 Devon Road, Fishponds, Bristol. Died there 19 January 1912. [Foster, *Alumni*; Longden xv. 137; *Crockford* (1885); MGA 628; Census Returns 1881, 1891, 1901; 'Ramsey, Arthur Michael' in *ODNB*; RES A/69; *London Gazette* (28316), 10 December 1909; *Probate Calendar* 1912.]

Cecil St John Wright BA

Instituted 17 January 1910 by collation to vicarage of Horbling, on resignation of Plumpton Stravenson Wilson. Patron: Bishop of Lincoln. [Reg. 42, p.630.]

Resided at Horbling Vicarage. Bishop Hicks noted (1911): 'Young wife, rather phthisical [*i.e.* consumptive]: ordered a fire in her bedroom, but too poor to have it. He looks hungry & gaunt. Old Cambridge man, & rowed in his college Eight. I sent him £5 …' Afterwards: R. of Pickworth with Walcot, 1919–33 (*q.v.*). [Census Returns 1911; Kelly, *Lincolnshire* (1913), 319; *Hicks Diaries*, no.74.]

Thomas Edward Meurig-Davies MA

Instituted 17 May 1919 by collation to vicarage of Horbling, on cession of Cecil St John Wright. Patron: Bishop of Lincoln. [Reg. 43, p.180.]

Born *c*.1885 at Gartheli (Card). Educated: St Catherine's Society, Oxford (BA 1908; MA 1914); St Michael's College, Llandaff (1908); Trinity College, Cambridge (1910). Deacon: 1909; priest: 1910 (St David's). Formerly: C. of Llandingat, 1909–10; of St Andrew, Cherry Hinton (Ca), 1910–11; of St Mary, Swansea, 1911–13; of Holy Trinity, Smethwick, 1913–14; Organising Secretary CETS for Lincoln Diocese, 1914–19. Afterwards: V. of Barnetby-le-Wold, 1922–9; V. of Great Carlton with Little Carlton, 1929–33; V. of Winchcombe with Gretton and Sudeley Manor (Gl), 1933–45; Chaplain of Boys' Home, Winchcombe, 1933–45; RD of Winchcombe, 1934–53; C-in-C of Didbrook with Stanway (Gl), 1943–5; Canon of Gloucester, 1945–61; R. of Bromsberrow (Gl), 1945–61. Died 10 November 1961. [Census Returns 1911 (Cherry Hinton); *Crockford* (1961–2); *Probate Calendar* 1962.]

George Edward Twamley

Instituted 21 June 1922 by collation to vicarage of Horbling, on cession of Thomas Edward Meurig-Davies. Patron: Bishop of Lincoln. [Reg. 43, p.261.]

Born c.1864 at Walcot, Bath; son of Martha T., laundress. Living in Wadhurst (Sx) as grocer's assistant (1891). Educated: Scholae Episcopi, Manchester (1898). Deacon: 1900; priest: 1901 (Manchester). Formerly: C. of St Mark, Bolton, 1900–3; of St Anne, Haughton (La), 1903–8; of St Michael, Northampton, 1908–16; of Waddingham, 1916–22. Resided at Horbling Vicarage. Died 22 January 1931. [Census Returns 1871 (Bath), 1891 (Wadhurst), 1911 (Northampton); *Crockford* (1923); Kelly, *Lincolnshire* (1930), 303; *Probate Calendar* 1931.]

Thomas Leonard Ivens

Instituted 18 March 1931 by collation to vicarage of Horbling, on death of George Edward Twamley. Patron: Bishop of Lincoln. [Reg. 43, p.479.]

Resided at Horbling Vicarage. Afterwards: R. of Pickworth with Walcot, 1933–41 (*q.v.*). [*Crockford* (1932).]

Joseph Westmoreland

Instituted 11 October 1933 by collation to vicarage of Horbling, on cession of Thomas Leonard Ivens. Patron: Bishop of Lincoln. [Reg. 43, p.532.]

Born 1902. Educated: Lincoln Theological College (1925). Deacon: 1928; priest: 1929 (Lincoln). Formerly: C. of St James, Grimsby, 1928–31; of Dunstable, 1931–3. Afterwards: PC of St Augustine, Grimsby, 1939–59; Chaplain of Holyrood House, South Leigh (Ox), 1959–62; V. of Sherborne with Windrush (Gl), 1962–70. Retired (1970) to Mead House, Sherborne. Latterly at The Glebe House, Northleach. Disappears from *Crockford* after 1987. [*Crockford* (1980–2, 1987–8).]

Charles Edwin Goshawk BD

Instituted 27 June 1939 by collation to vicarage of Horbling, on cession of Joseph Westmoreland. Patron: Bishop of Lincoln. [Reg. 43, p.637.]

Born 31 December 1896, baptised 14 February 1897 at St John Baptist, Greenhill, Harrow; son of George Edmund G. of Mavis Cottage, Oakley Road, Civil Servant. Educated: King's College, London (AKC 1920); University of London (BD 1921). Deacon: 1921; priest: 1922 (London). Formerly: C. of St James, Upper Edmonton, 1921–4; of Malvern Link, 1925–9; Chaplain, Queen Ethelburga's School, Harrogate, 1929; C. of St Bartholomew, Reading, 1929–32; PC of St Mary Magdalene, Millfield, Bishop Wearmouth, 1932–9. Resided at Horbling Vicarage. Also: V. of Threckingham, 1941–8. Afterwards: V. of St Faith, Lincoln, 1948–51; R. of Fifield with Idbury (Ox), 1951–62. Retired 1962; lived at Thorpe End, Abthorpe, Towcester (Np). Died September 1978. [LMA, PR Greenhill St John Baptist; *Crockford* (1971–2); *LDC* (1947), 50; GRO, Death Index.]

Frederick Guy Harrison

Instituted 11 August 1948 by collation to vicarage of Horbling, on cession of Charles Edwin Goshawk. Patron: Bishop of Lincoln. Note that on 8 July 1948, the Archbishop of Canterbury granted a dispensation enabling the said FGH to hold together the vicarage of Horbling and the vicarage of Threckingham. [Reg. 44, pp. 92–3.]

Born 3 June 1909 at Selly Park, Birmingham. Educated: Queen's College, Birmingham (1929). Deacon: 1932 (Manchester); priest: 1935 (Chester). Formerly: C. of St Matthew, Little Lever (La), 1932–3; of St John Evangelist, Weston, 1934–7; of St Helen, Tarporley, 1937–42; V. of Bicker, 1942–8. Also: V. of Threckingham, 1948–51 (*q.v.*). Afterwards: Dean of British Honduras and R. of St John's Cathedral, Belize, 1951–3; V. of Rillington, V. of Scampston and C-in-C of Yedingham (YER), 1953–6; R. of St Mary Bishopshill Senior with St Clement, York, 1956–64; V. of Oakworth (YWR), 1964–70; V. of Appleton Roebuck with Acaster Selby (YWR), 1970–4; C. of Bolton Percy, 1973–4. Retired 1974. Latterly at 14 Hunt Memorial Homes, Fulford, York. Died December 1981. [Census Returns 1911 (Northfield); *Crockford* (1970–1, 1977–9); GRO, Death Index.]

Leonard Benn Impson

Instituted 30 December 1952 to vicarage of Horbling, on resignation of Frederick Guy Harrison. Patron: Geoffrey Francis, Archbishop of Canterbury, for this turn only by lapse. Note that on 25 November 1952, the Archbishop of Canterbury granted a dispensation enabling the said LBI to hold together the vicarage of Swaton with rectory of Spanby annexed and the vicarage of Horbling. [Reg. 44, p.170.]

Also: V. of Swaton with Spanby, 1950–6 (*q.v.*).

Robert William Harris BSc

Instituted 5 July 1957 to vicarage of Horbling, on resignation of Leonard Benn Impson. Patron: Queen Elizabeth II for this turn only, by reason of the late avoidance of the see of Lincoln. Note that on 28 May 1957, the Archbishop of Canterbury granted a dispensation enabling the said RWH to hold together the vicarage of Horbling and the vicarage of Swaton with rectory of Spanby annexed. [Reg. 44, p.242.]

Born *c*.1895. Educated: University of Leeds (BSc 1923); Leeds Clergy School (1920); Westcott House, Cambridge (1924). Deacon: 1925; priest: 1926 (Wakefield). Formerly: C. of St Andrew, Huddersfield, 1925–7; of Warmfield (YWR), 1927–9; V. of Sharlston (YWR), 1929–45; CF 1940–5; V. of Armitage Bridge (YWR), 1945–50; R. of Well with Claxby and V. of Skendleby, 1950–7. Resided at Horbling Vicarage. Also: V. of Swaton with Spanby, 1957–64 (*q.v.*). Died 3 April 1964. [*Crockford* (1961–2); GRO, Death Index; *Probate Calendar* 1964.]

John Faber Scholfield Jones MA

Instituted 29 October 1964 to vicarage of Horbling, on death of Robert William Harris. Patron: Bishop of Lincoln. Note that on 20 October 1964, the Archbishop of Canterbury granted a dispensation enabling the said JFSJ to hold together the vicarage of Horbling and the vicarage of Swaton with rectory of Spanby annexed. [Reg. 44, p.365.]

Born 2 December 1903 at Oswestry; son of William Powell J., Music Teacher. Educated: University of Edinburgh (MA 1925); Scholae Cancellarii, Lincoln (1925). Deacon: 1926; priest: 1927 (Lincoln). Formerly: C. of Holy Trinity, Gainsborough, 1926–31; PC of St Paul, West Marsh, Grimsby, 1931–49; PC of St Botolph, Lincoln, 1949–64. Also: V. of Swaton with Spanby, 1964–9 (*q.v.*). Resignation accepted 31 March 1969. Died 3 November 1969. [Census Returns 1911 (Oswestry); *Crockford* (1961–2); Reg. 44, p.424; *LDC* (1970), 57.]

KIRKBY UNDERWOOD

One mediety of the church of Kirkby Underwood was given by William de Reinnes *c*.1160 to Sempringham Priory. The other mediety had been included by 1251 among the endowments of the prebend of Bedford Major in Lincoln Cathedral. This mediety was appropriated to the prebend but no vicarage was ever ordained and thus no institutions are recorded. The Priory last presented to their mediety in 1304 but by 1337 the advowson of this portion had passed to the Bishop of Lincoln. From 1511 the whole church was in the Bishop's gift. The advowson remained in the hands of the Bishop until 1918 when it was transferred to the Earl of Ancaster in exchange for that of Halton Holegate. The Earl remained the patron in 1965. [*Reg. Ant.* iii. 2–3; *Le Neve Fasti: Lincoln 1066–1300*, 52; *London Gazette* (30815), 26 July 1918; *LDC* (1965), 66–7.]

John de Brinklawe chaplain
Instituted in the third pontifical year of Bishop Robert Grosseteste (17 June 1237/16 June 1238) to a mediety of church of Kirkby Underwood. Patron: Prior and Convent of Sempringham. [Hoskin, no.57.]

Thomas
Instituted before 11 March 1276/7. [*Rot. Gravesend*, 75.]
Afterwards: V. of Threckingham (*q.v.*).

Nicholas de Bolingbroc subdeacon
Instituted 11 March 1276/7 to a mediety of church of Kirkby Underwood, on resignation of Thomas, Vicar of Threckingham. Patron: Prior and Convent of Sempringham. [*Rot. Gravesend*, 75.]

Alan de Wetwang subdeacon
Instituted 7 November 1277 to a mediety of church of Kirkby Underwood, on resignation of Nicholas. Patron: Master of the Order of Sempringham and Prior and Convent of Sempringham. [*Rot. Gravesend*, 78.]

Robert de Bilingburg chaplain
Instituted 13 April 1288 to [a mediety of] church of Kirkby Underwood, on deprivation of Alan de Wetehanger on account of misbehaviour. Patron: Prior and Convent of Sempringham. [*Reg. Sutton* i. 105 (benefice wrongly identified as Kirkby Green).]

M. Richard de Wilugby priest
Instituted 9 February 1303/4 to a mediety of church of Kirkby Underwood, on death of Robert. Patron: Prior and Convent of Sempringham. [Reg. 2, fo.9v.]

Had letters patent dated 5 May 1304 nominating John de Ounesby his attorney, as he was going to the court of Rome. [*CPR 1301–07*, 221.]

John Greneland de Islep clerk

Instituted 10 January 1336/7 to a mediety of church of Kirkby Underwood, on death of last rector. Patron: Bishop of Lincoln. [*Reg. Burghersh* i. no.522.]

William West of Buckingham clerk

Instituted 16 November 1337 to a mediety of church of Kirkby Underwood, on resignation of John Greyland de Islep. Patron: Bishop of Lincoln. [*Reg. Burghersh* i. no.558.]

Richard de Strensale clerk

Instituted 3 November 1364 to a mediety of church of Kirkby Underwood, on death of William West of Buckingham. Patron: Bishop of Lincoln. [Reg. 10, fo.9.]

Afterwards: R. of Wheathampstead (Hrt), 1366.

Henry Bernak priest

Instituted 11 January 1365/6 to a mediety of church of Kirkby Underwood, on resignation of Richard de Strensale (by exchange with church of Wheathampstead). Patron: Bishop of Lincoln. [Reg. 10, fo.13.]

Formerly: R. of Wheathampstead, 1361–6. [Cussans, *Hertfordshire* iii. 346.]

John Farburn

Instituted 8 June 1366 to a mediety of church of Kirkby Underwood (cause of vacancy not stated). Patron: Bishop of Lincoln. [Reg. 10, fo.14.]

Afterwards: Warden of Chantry of Wappenham (Np), 1367.

Thomas Prest (de Clyfton) priest

Instituted 21 January 1366/7 to a mediety of church of Kirkby Underwood, on resignation of John de Farburn (by exchange with chantry or wardenship of chantry of Wappenham). Patron: Bishop of Lincoln. [Reg. 10, fo.16v.]

Priest: before 5 August 1361. Formerly: Warden of Chantry of Wappenham (Np), 1361–7. Afterwards: R. of Glympton (Ox), 1374–81; V. of Harwell (Brk), 1381–93; Chaplain of Crane Chantry in Church of St Nicholas-in-the-Shambles, London, 1393. [Reg. 9, fo.235; Reg. 10, fos 360v, 376; *Reg. Waltham*, no.674.]

Philip Heron (Heyroun) priest

Instituted 18 January 1373/4 to a mediety of church of Kirkby Underwood, on resignation of Thomas Preest de Clyfton (by exchange with church of Glympton). Patron: Bishop of Lincoln. [Reg. 10, fo.61.]

Formerly: V. of West Hendred (Brk), to 1355; R. of Glympton (Ox), 1355–74. Assessed for poll-tax 1377, 1381. [Reg. 9, fo.266; *Clerical Poll-Taxes*, nos 696, 1328, 1917.]

Robert Attekyrk de Southscarle
Instituted 23 January 1392/3 to church of Kirkby Underwood (cause of vacancy not stated). Patron: Bishop of Lincoln. [Reg. 11, fo.63v.]
Afterwards: V. of South Scarle (Nt), 1393.

John Bayous
Instituted 30 March 1393 to church of Kirkby Underwood, on resignation of Robert Attekyrk de Southscarle (by exchange with vicarage of South Scarle, dioc. York). Patron: Bishop of Lincoln. [Reg. 11, fo.64v.]
Formerly: V. of South Scarle (Nt), to 1393.

[Name missing]
Instituted 13 April 1393 to church of Kirkby Underwood, on resignation of John Bayous. Patron: Bishop of Lincoln. [Reg. 11, fo.65.]

Thomas Raynard
Instituted before 29 January 1396/7.
Perhaps instituted 13 April 1393 (above). Pardoned (29 January 1396/7) for killing his servant Richard Jyme *alias* Jime at Kirkby Underwood on 14 September 1395 (or 1392). [*CPR 1396–99*, 61.]

Thomas Kyrkeham
Instituted before 26 November 1433. [Reg. 17, fo.8.]
Afterwards: R. of Wing (Ru), 1433.

Thomas Cook priest
Instituted 26 November 1433 to a mediety of church of Kirkby Underwood, on resignation of Thomas Kyrkeham (by exchange with church of Wing). Patron: Bishop of Lincoln. [Reg. 17, fo.8.]
Formerly: R. of Wing (Ru), to 1433.

Thomas Rayway
Instituted before 1 March 1441/2. [Reg. 18, fo.86v.]
Afterwards: R. of Collyweston (Np), 1442.

John Brantyngham
Instituted 1 March 1441/2 by collation to a mediety of church of Kirkby Underwood, on resignation of Thomas Rayway (by exchange with church of Collyweston). Patron: Bishop of Lincoln. [Reg. 18, fo.86v.]
Formerly: R. of Collyweston, to 1442. Afterwards: R. of Little Missenden (Bk), 1443.

[Name missing]
Instituted 3 August 1443 by collation to a mediety of church of Kirkby

Underwood, on resignation of John Brantyngham (by exchange with church of Little Missenden). Patron: Bishop of Lincoln. [Reg. 18, fo.91v.]

Formerly: R. of Little Missenden, to 1443.

William Flete
Instituted before 21 September 1493. [Reg. 22, fo.155v.]

Br. Robert Waterman alias Silston monk of St Mary Grace Dieu, dioc. Llandaff
Instituted 21 September 1493 (by papal dispensation enabling him to receive a benefice with or without cure of souls) to a mediety of church of Kirkby Underwood, on resignation of William Flete. Patron: Bishop of Lincoln. Note that an annual pension of 10 shillings was reserved to William Flete for life from the fruits of the church. [Reg. 22, fo.155v.]

M. Brian Higdon DCL
Instituted 3 July 1511 to church of Kirkby Underwood, on resignation of Robert Waterman. Patron: Bishop of Lincoln. [Reg. 23, fo.143.]

Educated: University of Oxford (BCL 1499; DCL 1506); Principal of Broadgates Hall, 1505–8. Acolyte: February 1504/5 (Hereford); subdeacon: 8 March 1504/5 (Lincoln); deacon: 21 March 1504/5 (Hereford); priest: 21 April 1508 (Lincoln). Formerly: R. of Bucknell (Ox), 1505. Licensed to hold another benefice in plurality, 1506. Also: Canon of Lincoln and Prebendary of Welton Ryval, 1503–13; of Clifton, 1513–23; of Aylesbury, 1523–39; Subdean of Lincoln, 1511–23; R. of Nettleton, 1513; Archdeacon of York, 1515–16; Canon of York and Prebendary of Ulleskelf, 1516–39; Dean of York, 1516–39; Canon of St Paul's and Prebendary of Nesden, 1536–9. Died 5 June 1539. Will (PCC) dated 3 June 1539, proved 5 May 1540. [Emden, *BRUO*, 930–1; 'Hygdon, Brian' in *ODNB*; *CPL* xviii. no.661; *Le Neve Fasti 1300–1541* i. 6, 26, 53, 128; vi. 8, 18, 86; xii. 14, 18; Cross, *York Clergy Wills* i. 35–7.]

Eugene Bold
Instituted before 13 July 1512. [Reg. 23, fo.144v.]

Robert Boston monk, late Prior of Bradwell
Instituted 13 July 1512 to church of Kirkby Underwood, on resignation of Eugene Bold. Patron: Bishop of Lincoln. [Reg. 23, fo.144v.]

Formerly: Monk of Tickford; Prior of Bradwell, 1504. Assessed for subsidy (£7) in 1526. [*Heads* iii. 21; *Subsidy*, 57.]

William Pigott chaplain
Instituted 3 July 1532 to church of Kirkby Underwood, on resignation of Robert Boston. Patron: Bishop of Lincoln. Note that an annual pension of 16s 8d was reserved to Robert Boston for life from the fruits of the church. [Reg. 27, fo.53v.]

Born *c*.1502. Education: 'understands but little Latin; but little versed in sacred learning'. Priest: 12 March 1523/4 (Mayo for Lincoln). Assessed for *Valor Ecclesiasticus* 1535. Exhibited at Visitation, 1551. Perhaps deprived 1554. Restored before 29 July 1568 (witnessed will). Resident: signed BTs 1562–3, 1566, 1577–8. Died 1580. Will (LCC), dated 27 April 1580; proved 11 November 1580. Made bequests for repair of churches of, and for the poor of, Mavis Enderby, West Keal, Rippingale and Dunsby; to William Greyge 'my reader', his best cloak or gown; to Guy Jekell, Rector of Irnham, 'my best gelding that he will chose'. [*Bishop Cooper*, 207; Reg. 26, fo.9; *Valor* iv. 104; Vj 13, fo.62v; LCC Wills 1568/72; BTs Kirkby Underwood; LCC Wills 1580/i/151; INV 65/68.]

Thomas Grawntham

Instituted *c*.1554 (compounded for first-fruits, 15 November 1554). [FL.h.13, 533.]

William Pigott

Restored after 1558 (see above).

Thomas Tipler

Instituted 11 October 1580 to church of Kirkby Underwood, on death of William Piggatte. Patron: Bishop of Lincoln. [*Bishop Cooper*, 27.]

Deacon and priest: 11 October 1580 (Lincoln). Afterwards: R. of Salmonby, 1588–91. Listed as a Puritan preacher in 1584. Buried at Salmonby, 9 February 1590/1. [*Bishop Cooper*, 93; *State of the Church*, pp. xxv–xxvi, 150.]

James Montcrief

Instituted 31 August 1584 to church of Kirkby Underwood. [*State of the Church*, 73.]

Education: 'bred in the schools'. Priest: 23 June 1584 (Peterborough). Assessed ('a Bowe') in Subsidy of Armour 1590. Signed BTs at Kirkby Underwood 1586–91. Buried at Kirkby Underwood, 8 April 1592. Admon (LCC). [*State of the Church*, 73, 148; BTs Kirkby Underwood; PR Kirkby Underwood; LCC Admons 1592/382.]

James Griffith

Instituted 23 May 1592 to rectory of Kirkby Underwood. [BC.]

Education: 'no graduate'; licensed preacher. Priest: 23 December 1568 (Gloucester). Also: R. of Little Ponton, where he resided (1611). Non-resident at Kirkby (1611), where his curate, Mr Llood, was inhibited by the bishop as being 'overmuch geven to drinke'. Griffiths as incumbent was suspended for not preaching every Sabbath at Little Ponton and 'for want of a preaching curate licensed to supply his absence here' at Kirkby. Buried at Kirkby Underwood, 16 October 1621. [LC 3, fo.2v; LC 4, fo.72v; *State of the Church*, 237; PR Kirkby Underwood.]

John Hacket MA

Instituted 2 November 1621 to rectory of Kirkby Underwood. Patron: King James I. [BC.]

Born 1 September 1592 in the Strand, par. St Martin-in-the-Fields (Mx); son of Andrew

H. Educated: Westminster School and Trinity College, Cambridge (matric. 1609; BA 1612–13; MA 1616; BD 1623; DD 1628); Fellow 1614. Deacon and priest: 20 December 1618 (London). Household Chaplain of Bishop John Williams, 1621. Non-resident at Kirkby Underwood, which was served by James Adamson as curate. Also: R. of Stoke Hammond (Bk), 1618–24; R. of Trumpington (Ca), 1621–2. Afterwards: R. of Barcombe (Sx), 1622–9; Canon of Lincoln and Prebendary of Aylesbury, 1623–61; R. of St Andrew, Holborn, 1624–61; R. of Cheam (Sr), 1624–61; Archdeacon of Bedford, 1631–61; Bishop of Coventry and Lichfield, 1661–70. Died 28 October 1670; buried in Lichfield Cathedral. ['Hacket, John' in *ODNB*; Venn, *Alumni*; BTs Kirkby Underwood; Bray, *Ely Lists*; *Le Neve Fasti: Lincoln 1541–1857*, 13, 34.]

Robert Haselwood MA

Instituted 8 December 1622 by collation to rectory of Kirkby Underwood, on resignation of John Hacket. Patron: Bishop of Lincoln. [BC; IND/L 1, fo.60.]

Born *c*.1596; of London. Educated: St John's College, Cambridge (matric. 1612); migrated to Christ Church, Oxford (matric. 1615; BA 1615; MA 1618); incorporated at Cambridge, 1623. Also: R. of Fleet, 1622–43. Resided initially at Fleet; Kirkby Underwood served by James Adamson as curate until 1631. Signed registers at Kirkby Underwood, 1632–52. Lent a horse to royal army, 1642; was said to be in arms against Parliament, 1643. Probably ejected 1656. Buried at Christ Church, Oxford, 20 April 1658. [Venn, *Alumni*; PR Kirkby Underwood; *Walker Revised*, 251; Swaby, 113.]

Edward Swift MA

Presented by the Lord Protector, 15 February 1656 (the living being void). [LPL, Comm II/401.]

Educated: Magdalene College, Cambridge (matric. 1641; BA 1644–5; MA 1655). Deacon: 22 February 1661/2; priest: 23 February 1661/2 (Lincoln). Resident (1662); signed register 1657–71. Buried at Kirkby Underwood, 26 March 1673. Will (LCC). [Venn, *Alumni*; Reg. 32, p.16; SUB IIa, fo.7; LC 5, fo.23; PR Kirkby Underwood; LCC Wills 1673/234b.]

Robert Haslewood BD

Instituted 31 July 1673 by collation to rectory of Kirkby Underwood, on death of Edward Swifte. Patron: Bishop of Lincoln. [Reg. 33, fo.163v; IND/L 1, fo.211.]

Educated: Corpus Christi College, Cambridge (matric. 1637; BA 1640; BD 1662). Also: R. of Fleet, 1662–84; Canon of Lincoln and Prebendary of Milton Manor, 1672–84. Signed BTs at Kirkby Underwood 1673–83. Buried at Kirkby Underwood, 6 December 1684. [Venn, *Alumni*; *Le Neve Fasti; Lincoln 1541–1857*, 96; BTs Kirkby Underwood; PR Kirkby Underwood.]

George Topham MA

Instituted 12 December 1684 by collation to rectory of Kirkby Underwood, on death of Robert Haslewood. Patron: Bishop of Lincoln. [Reg. 34, fo.82v.]

Also: V. of Baston, 1669–95; V. of Deeping St James, 1675–95; R. of Hallaton (Le), 1676-–7; Canon of Lincoln and Prebendary of Ketton, 1683–95; R. of Sawtry All Saints (Hu), 1687–95. Non-resident at Kirkby Underwood, which was served by Thomas Bland as curate. Resigned Kirkby Underwood, 4 June 1687. Resided at Deeping St James; buried there, 3 January 1694/5. [*Le Neve Fasti: Lincoln 1541–1857*, 73; BTs Kirkby Underwood; Reg. 34, fo.98v; RES 1687/3; PR Deeping St James.]

James Lightfoot MA

Instituted 6 June 1687 by collation to rectory of Kirkby Underwood, on resignation of George Topham. Patron: Bishop of Lincoln. [Reg. 34, fo.98v.]

Baptised 22 August 1647 at Bourne; son of James L., yeoman. Educated: Bourne School and St John's College, Cambridge (matric. 1663; BA 1665–6; MA 1669). Deacon: 29 May 1670 (Peterborough); priest: 5 June 1687 (Lincoln). Signed BTs at Kirkby Underwood 1687–1704. Buried at Kirkby Underwood, 4 June 1705. [*PR Bourne*, 94; *St John's Admissions* i. 157; Venn, *Alumni*; Longden viii. 261; Reg. 34, fo.98v; LC 14, fo.5; BTs Kirkby Underwood.]

Thomas Martin MA

Inducted 4 August 1705 to rectory of Kirkby Underwood, on death of last incumbent. Patron: Queen Anne (by reason of vacancy of see). [IND/L 2, fo.33v.]

Of Stamford. Educated: Clare Hall, Cambridge (matric. 1692; BA 1695–6; MA 1699). Deacon: 20 September 1696 (Lincoln); priest: 19 September 1697 (Peterborough). Also: Sequestrator of Swinstead, 1699–1719; R. of St John, Stamford, 1701–19. Chaplain to Duke of Ancaster; resided at Grimsthorpe. Signed BTs at Kirkby Underwood, 1706–19. Buried at Folkingham, 17 August 1719. [Venn, *Alumni*; *Speculum*, 75, 115, 124; BTs Kirkby Underwood; PR Folkingham.]

Henry Bransby

Instituted 5 August 1720 by collation to rectory of Kirkby Underwood, on death of Thomas Martin. Patron: Bishop of Lincoln. [Reg. 37, p.104.]

Baptised 31 December 1674 at North Somercotes; son of Robert B., farmer. Educated: Louth GS and Magdalene College, Cambridge (matric. 1695). Deacon: 20 March 1697/8; priest: 24 December 1699 (Lincoln). Formerly: C. of Bratoft, 1698. Also: V. of Cockerington St Leonard, 1699–1722; C. of Alvingham; C. of North Reston. Resided at Keddington. Died 1722. Will (LCC), dated 15 January 1721/2; proved 16 April 1722. Bequeathed to his son Charles 'the Silver Tankard, Cup and Eight Spoons which I bought of my Brother Bransby's Executors at Grimsby'. [PR North Somercotes; Venn, *Alumni*; Goulding, *Miscellany*, 197; Reg. 35, fos 47, 61; *Speculum*, 3, 34, 75, 99; LCC Wills 1722/i/8.]

John Jones LLB

Instituted 7 April 1722 by collation to rectory of Kirkby Underwood, on death of Henry Branceby. Patron: Bishop of Lincoln. [Reg. 37, p.152.]

Born 10 October 1694; son of William J. of St Mildred Poultry, London, apothecary. Educated: Merchant Taylors School (1703) and St John's College, Oxford (matric. 1712; BCL 1720); Fellow 1716. Deacon: 21 April 1717; priest: 21 December 1718 (Oxford). Formerly: Headmaster of Oundle School, 1718–22 (where he was known as 'a very Orbilius', a keen flogger). Also: R. of Dembleby, 1721–31 (*q.v.*); R. of Uppingham, 1743–52. Signed BTs at Kirkby Underwood 1722–4; thereafter non-resident, Kirkby Underwood being served by William Dodd as curate. Died at Uppingham; buried there, 20 July 1752. ['Jones, John' in *ODNB*; *Merchant Taylors' Register* ii. 11; Foster, *Alumni*; Longden viii. 47; ORO, MS. Oxf. Dioc. Papers c.266, fos 37, 39; BTs Kirkby Underwood.]

John Jones LLB (the younger)
Instituted 31 March 1752 by collation to rectory of Kirkby Underwood, on resignation of John Jones (the elder). Patron: Bishop of Lincoln. [Reg. 38, p.508.]

Born c.1723; son of John J. of Oundle, clerk (above). Educated: Lincoln College, Oxford (matric. 1741) and Emmanuel College, Cambridge (adm. 1742; matric. 1744; LLB 1748). Deacon: 9 June 1745; priest: 25 May 1746 (Lincoln). Formerly: C. of Wilshamstead (Bd), 1745; C. of Little Staughton (Bd), 1746. Signed BTs at Kirkby Underwood 1753–4. Non-resident (1768): 'Absent upon a cure in or near London'; the parish was served by John Vokes as curate. Died 1778. [Foster, *Alumni*; Venn, *Alumni*; Reg. 38, pp. 457, 466; BTs Kirkby Underwood; PR Kirkby Underwood; LC 31, p.72.]

John Searle BA
Instituted 13 October 1778 by collation to rectory of Kirkby Underwood, on death of John Jones. Patron: Bishop of Lincoln. [Reg. 39, p.323.]

Of Huntingdonshire. Educated: Jesus College, Cambridge (matric. 1744; BA 1747–8). Deacon: 12 March 1749/50; priest: 24 May 1752 (Ely). Formerly: C. of Chatteris (Ca), 1750. Also: V. of Buckden (Hu), 1773–9; Canon of Lincoln and Prebendary of Welton Brinkhall, 1773–9. Non-resident at Kirkby Underwood. Buried at Buckden, 23 September 1779. [Venn, *Alumni*; Bray, *Ely Lists*; *Le Neve Fasti: Lincoln 1541–1857*, 126.]

Edward Bowerbank BD
Instituted 30 September 1779 by collation to rectory of Kirkby Underwood, on death of John Searle. Patron: Bishop of Lincoln. [Reg. 39, p.341.]

Born c.1739; son of Edward B. of Lamonby (Cu). Educated: Queen's College, Oxford (matric. 1757; BA 1761; MA 1765; BD 1775). Priest: 2 March 1765 (Llandaff). Also: V. of Buckden, 1779–90; Canon of Lincoln and Prebendary of Welton Brinkhall, 1779–84, of Asgarby, 1784–6 and of Langford Manor, 1791–1805. Afterwards: V. of Holbeach, 1786–9; R. of Croft (YNR). Died 28 June 1805 at Ferrybridge 'on his road from Town, after a lingering illness'. [Foster, *Alumni*; CCED; *Le Neve Fasti: Lincoln 1541–1857*, 33, 80, 126; *Christian Observer* 4 (1805), 450.]

John Gutch MA
Instituted 15 November 1786 by collation to rectory of Kirkby Underwood, on cession of Edward Bowerbank. Patron: Bishop of Lincoln. [Reg. 39, p.454.]

Born 10 January 1746 at Wells; son of John G., Town Clerk of Wells. Educated: All Souls College, Oxford (matric. 1765; BA 1769; MA 1771); Chaplain of All Souls 1769–1831; Registrar of the University 1797–1824; Registrar of Chancellor's Court and Clerk of Oxford Market. Formerly: C. of Foxcote (So), 1768. Also: R. of Waterstock, 1777–89; R. of St Clement, Oxford, 1795–1831. Non-resident at Kirkby Underwood, which was served by curates, including Joseph Barwis (1814) and Kingsman Foster (1828). Resided at 8 Longwall Street, Oxford (which he rebuilt 1793–4). Married (1775) Elizabeth, daughter of Richard Weller, sometime butler of Magdalen College. Father of John Mathew G. (1776–1861), journalist and author, and of Robert G., Rector of Seagrave (Le) 1809–51. Author: *Collectanea Curiosa* (1781); editor of Anthony Wood's Histories of Oxford University. While devoted to antiquarian studies, 'as a parish priest his effort seems unremarkable'. Died 1 July 1831 at Oxford; buried in churchyard of St Peter-in-the-East. ['Gutch, John' in *ODNB*; Foster, *Alumni*; NRL 1804/24; 1805/7; 1808/17; 1814/1; CR 1, pp. 41, 372.]

George John Skeeles BA

Instituted 2 August 1831 by collation to rectory of Kirkby Underwood, on death of John Gutch. Patron: Bishop of Lincoln. [Reg. 40, p.387.]

Born 17 December 1790 at Peterborough; son of William Drury S., Librarian of Peterborough Cathedral and Rector of Polebrooke (Np). Educated: Rugby School (1805) and Christ's College, Cambridge (matric. 1809; BA 1813). Deacon: March 1813 (Ely); priest: 29 December 1813 (Norwich). Formerly: C. of Great Saxham (Sf), 1813–14 and 1829; C. of Denham (Sf), 1813–14; C. of Horringer; C. of Risby, 1829. Also: V. of Cranwell, 1833. Died December 1833; buried in Bury St Edmunds churchyard. [*Rugby School Register 1675–1842*, 138; Venn, *Alumni*; Peile ii. 360; Longden xii. 185.]

Charles Holmes

Instituted 25 December 1833 by collation to rectory of Kirkby Underwood, on death of John Skeeles. Patron: Bishop of Lincoln. [Reg. 40, p.410.]

Born 3 November 1788, baptised 4 January 1789; son of Revd John H., Curate of South Leverton (Nt). Education: literate. Deacon: 2 July 1820; priest: 16 December 1821 (York). Formerly: C. of Laughton-en-le-Morthen (YWR), 1820; of Quarrington, 1823–4; of Timberland, 1824–8; of Billinghay, 1825–33. His alleged neglect in failing to officiate at a funeral at Billinghay (1830) resulted in correspondence with Bishop Kaye; his subsequent appointment to Kirkby Underwood suggests that his explanation of the circumstances was accepted. Died 1 September 1838 ('suddenly, of apoplexy, whilst walking in a field'). [*York Ordinations 1800–1849*, 96; CR 1, pp. 246, 273; PR Quarrington; PR Timberland; PR Billinghay; *Kaye Parish Correspondence*, 94–100; *GM* (November 1838), 561; *Eccl. Gazette* (1838–9), 50; LCC Admons 1838/45.]

Frederick Septimus Emly MA

Instituted 12 September 1838 by collation to rectory of Kirkby Underwood, on death of Charles Holmes. Patron: Bishop of Lincoln. [Reg. 40, p.460.]

Born *c*.1803; 7th son of Samuel E. of St Martin's, Salisbury, esquire. Educated: Wadham College, Oxford (matric. 1818; BA 1822; MA 1826). Deacon: 29 May 1831; priest: 29 April 1832 (Peterborough). Formerly: C. of Deeping St James, 1834; V. of Deeping St James, 1834–8. Resided at Kirkby Underwood Rectory ('Good new Glebe house'). Died 4 March 1875 at Kirkby Underwood. [Foster, *Alumni*; Longden iv. 235; CR 2, p.87; White, *Lincolnshire* (1842), 740–1; *Bonney's Church Notes*, 226; Census Returns 1851, 1871; *Probate Calendar* 1875.]

Lemuel Saywell MA

Instituted 17 April 1875 by collation to rectory of Kirkby Underwood, on death of Frederick Septimus Emly. Patron: Bishop of Lincoln. [Reg. 41, p.494.]

Born *c*.1829 at Dorchester (Ox); son of Thomas S., carpenter. Sometime Assistant Master, King Edward VI GS, Bromsgrove (1854). Ordained as literate; deacon: 16 June 1861 (Exeter); priest: 1864 (Ely). Formerly: C. of Mariansleigh (Dev), 1861–2; of Sutton (Ca), 1862–4; V. of Napier (New Zealand), 1864–7; C. of South Witham, 1868–9; of Ingoldmells, 1869–71; of Fiskerton, 1871–5. Resided at Kirkby Underwood Rectory. Died 9 October 1888 at Kirkby Underwood. [*Oxford Journal*, 14 October 1854; *Royal Corn-*

wall Gazette, 21 June 1861; *Crockford* (1885); Bray, *Ely Lists*; Census Returns 1841 (Dorchester), 1881; *Probate Calendar* 1888.]

Robert Hurman

Instituted 2 January 1889 by collation to rectory of Kirkby Underwood, on death of Lemuel Saywell. Patron: Bishop of Lincoln. [Reg. 42, p.286.]

Born *c.*1828; son of Benjamin H. of Cossington (So), gent. Educated: St Mary Hall, Oxford (matric. 1874). Head Master, Wallingford GS, 1851–8; Principal of Oxford Diocesan School, Cowley, 1858–76. Deacon: 20 June 1886; priest: 27 May 1888 (Lincoln). Formerly: C. of Spilsby, 1886–8. Resided at Kirkby Underwood Rectory. Restored Kirkby Underwood Church (1893). Died 1 June 1907. [Foster, *Alumni*; *Crockford* (1898); *LDC* 1887, 1889; Census Returns 1891, 1901; *Stamford Mercury*, 5 May 1893; *Probate Calendar* 1907.]

Arthur Giles Madge MA LLD

Instituted 27 September 1907 by collation to rectory of Kirkby Underwood, on death of Robert Hurman. Patron: Bishop of Lincoln. [Reg. 42, p.585.]

Born *c.*1862 at Norwich. Educated: University of Cambridge, Non-Coll. (matric. 1883; BA 1886; MA 1890; LLM 1892; LLD 1898). Deacon: 1890; priest: 1891 (St Albans). Formerly: Second Master, Watford School, 1887–91; C. of Oxhey (Hrt), 1890; Head Master, Horncastle GS, 1891–1907. Resided at Kirkby Underwood Rectory. Afterwards: V. of North Willingham with Legsby, 1917–26. Died 5 September 1926 at Camberwell House, Peckham Road, London. [Venn, *Alumni*; *Crockford* (1908); Census Returns 1911; Kelly, *Lincolnshire* (1913), 345; *Probate Calendar* 1926.]

Wilfrid Henry Langworthy

Instituted 27 April 1917 by collation to rectory of Kirkby Underwood, on cession of Arthur Giles Madge. Patron: Bishop of Lincoln. [Reg. 43, p.148.]

Born at Islington, baptised privately 15 June 1875; son of Revd William Henry L. Living in Holbeach (1901), serving as Lay Reader. Deacon: 1904; priest: 1906 (Lincoln). Formerly: C. of Holy Trinity, Messingham, 1904–8; of Long Bennington with Foston, 1908–11; of Grantham, 1911–12; St Hugh's Missioner, Lincoln Diocese, 1912–17. Afterwards: R. of Claypole, 1919–33. Died 1 December 1933. [LMA, PR Stoke Newington St Matthias; Census Returns 1901 (Holbeach); *Crockford* (1932); *Probate Calendar* 1934.]

John Smithson Barstow MA

Instituted 7 May 1920 to rectory of Kirkby Underwood, on cession of Wilfrid Henry Langworthy. Patron: Gilbert Heathcote Drummond Willoughby, Earl of Ancaster, of Grimsthorpe Castle. [Reg. 43, p.195.]

Afterwards: V. of Aslackby with Kirkby Underwood, 1934–49 (*q.v.*).

Edward Grant Allison MA

Instituted 5 January 1923 to rectory of Kirkby Underwood, on cession of John Smithson Barstow. Patron: Gilbert Heathcote Drummond Willoughby, Earl of Ancaster, as above. [Reg. 43, p.301.]

Born 14 March, baptised 4 May 1860 at St James, Louth; 2nd son of William A. of Louth, solicitor. Educated: Lincoln College, Oxford (matric. 1879; BA 1883; MA 1885). Deacon: 1883; priest: 1884 (York). Formerly: C. of Doncaster, 1883–90; of St John Evangelist, Bradford, 1890–4; V. of Heckington, 1894–1919; R. of Howell, 1917–19; in Lincoln Diocese, 1919–23. Married (18 January 1901) at All Saints, St John's Wood, Ethel Annie, daughter of Revd John Gorton. Resignation of Kirkby Underwood accepted 9 November 1925. Afterwards lived at 77 Norton Road, Letchworth. Died 23 February 1932. [PR Louth St James; Foster, *Alumni*; *Crockford* (1932); LMA, PR St John's Wood All Saints; Reg. 43, p.382; *Probate Calendar* 1932.]

Percy Jules Hulbert

Instituted 13 April 1926 to rectory of Kirkby Underwood, on resignation of Edward Grant Allison. Patron: Gilbert Heathcote Drummond Willoughby, Earl of Ancaster, as above. [Reg. 43, p.393.]

Afterwards: V. of Sempringham, 1927–31 (*q.v.*).

Edward Michael Bland

Instituted 9 October 1928 to rectory of Kirkby Underwood, on cession of Percy Jules Hulbert. Patron: Gilbert Heathcote Drummond Willoughby, Earl of Ancaster, as above. [Reg. 43, p.437.]

Born 18 August 1851 at Wanstead (Ess). Educated: Haileybury and Corpus Christi College, Cambridge (matric. 1870). Deacon: 1875; priest: 1876 (Huron). Formerly: in Huron Diocese, Missioner at Dungannon, 1875–6; at Bervie, 1877–8; at Ingersoll, 1878–85; in Niagara Diocese, P-in-C (1885–8) then R. (1888–9) of St George, St Catherine's; P-in-C (1889–91) then R. (1891–1906) of Christ Church Cathedral, Hamilton; Canon of Niagara, 1891–1907; C. of Pembroke with Devonshire (Bermuda), 1906–10; returned to England 1910; C. of St Nicholas, Lincoln, 1911–13; R. of Langton-by-Horncastle and V. of Woodhall, 1913–16; R. of Keith, 1917–23; P-in-C of Tranent and Prestonpans, 1923–6; Chaplain of Etal (Nb), 1926–7; C-in-C of St Mary-le-Wigford, Lincoln, 1928. Resignation of Kirkby Underwood accepted 31 October 1933. Afterwards: Chaplain and Warden of St Anne's Bede Houses, Lincoln, 1933–6. Died 9 August 1936. [Venn, *Alumni*; *Crockford* (1935); Reg. 43, p.535; *Probate Calendar* 1936.]

The Rectory of Kirkby Underwood was united to the Vicarage of Aslackby by Order in Council dated 22 March 1928. [Reg. 43, p.429.]

LAUGHTON-BY-FOLKINGHAM

The church of Laughton-by-Folkingham was given by Hubert de Rye and Ralph Child to Sempringham Priory before 1189. It was appropriated *c*.1194. A dispute concerning a mediety of the church was settled in 1204 in favour of the Priory. A vicarage was ordained, consisting of the altarage and a house. The Priory continued to present to the vicarage until the Dissolution. In 1562 the vicarage was united with the rectory of Folkingham. [*EEA* iv. no.176; *Final Concords* i. 64; 'Rolls of Hugh of Wells', 173–5; Reg. 19, fo.153.]

Roger de Pikeworth chaplain
Instituted between 1223 and 1226 to vicarage of Laughton-by-Folkingham.
Patron: Prior and Convent of Sempringham. [*Rot. Welles* iii. 77; 'Rolls of
Hugh of Wells', 173–5.]

Robert priest
Instituted in the fourth pontifical year of Bishop Robert Grosseteste (17 June
1238/16 June 1239) to vicarage of Laughton-by-Folkingham. Patron: Prior
and Convent of Sempringham. [Hoskin, no.103.]

Stephen de Dereby chaplain
Instituted in the twelfth pontifical year of Bishop Robert Grosseteste (17 June
1246/16 June 1247) to vicarage of Laughton-by-Folkingham. Patron: Prior
and Convent of Sempringham. [Hoskin, no.358.]

Yvo
Instituted before 11 October 1267. [*Rot. Gravesend*, 24.]

Robert de Plesseley chaplain
Instituted 11 October 1267 to vicarage of Laughton-by-Folkingham, on death
of Yvo. Patron: Prior and Convent of Sempringham. [*Rot. Gravesend*, 24.]

Robert de Braiceby chaplain
Instituted 10 October 1302 to vicarage of Laughton-by-Folkingham, on death
of Robert. Patron: Prior and Convent of Sempringham. [Reg. 2, fo.6v.]
Formerly: V. of Sempringham, 1301–2 (*q.v.*). Appointed a penitentiary for deanery of
Aveland, 9 April 1321. [Reg. 5, fo.278v.]

John de Folkingham priest
Instituted 6 July 1331 to vicarage of Laughton-by-Folkingham, on death of
Robert de Braceby. Patron: Prior (John) and Convent of Sempringham. [*Reg.
Burghersh* i. no.302.]

Walter
Instituted before 1 March 1359/60. [Reg. 9, fo.142.]

William de Estlocton priest
Instituted 1 March 1359/60 to vicarage of Laughton-by-Folkingham, on
death of Walter. Patron: Prior and Convent of Sempringham. [Reg. 9, fo.142.]

William son of Thomas de Leyghton
Instituted before 21 December 1363. [Reg. 10, fo.5.]
Perhaps to be identified with William de Estlocton, above.

John son of John de Locton de Repynghale priest
Instituted 21 December 1363 to vicarage of Laughton-by-Folkingham,

on resignation of William son of Thomas de Leyghton. Patron: Prior and Convent of Sempringham. [Reg. 10, fo.5.]

Afterwards: V. of Billingborough, 1373 (*q.v.*).

Simon de Rydesdale de Knaptoft priest
Instituted 2 November 1373 to vicarage of Laughton-by-Folkingham, on resignation of John de Loghton de Repynghale (by exchange with vicarage of Billingborough). Patron: Prior and Convent of Sempringham. [Reg. 10, fo.59v.]

Formerly: V. of Billingborough, to 1373 (*q.v.*).

John Houdon de Somerby priest
Instituted 26 March 1373 [*recte* 1374] to vicarage of Laughton-by-Folkingham, on resignation of Simon de Redesdale. Patron: Prior and Convent of Sempringham. [Reg. 10, fo.62.]

Assessed for poll-tax, 1381. [*Clerical Poll-Taxes*, nos 1339, 1928.]

William Ywarn priest
Instituted 2 October 1391 to vicarage of Laughton-by-Folkingham (cause of vacancy not stated). Patron: Prior and Convent of Sempringham. [Reg. 11, fo.53.]

Ralph Smyth priest
Instituted 9 September 1416 to vicarage of Laughton-by-Folkingham, on resignation of William Ywerne. Patron: Prior and Convent of Sempringham. [Reg. 14, fo.82v.]

Nicholas Tarton
Instituted before 25 August 1429. [*Reg. Fleming* i. no.331.]

Robert Palmer priest
Instituted 25 August 1429 to vicarage of Laughton-by-Folkingham, on resignation of Nicholas Tarton. Patron: Prior and Convent of Sempringham. [*Reg. Fleming* i. no.331.]

--- Undyrwater
Instituted 24 September 1441 to vicarage of Laughton-by-Folkingham (cause of vacancy not stated). Patron: Bishop of Lincoln, for this turn, by lapse. [Reg. 18, fo.89v.]

Thomas Cartewright priest
Instituted 9 March 1458/9 to vicarage of Laughton-by-Folkingham (cause of vacancy not stated). Patron: Prior and Convent of Sempringham. [Reg. 20, fo.131v.]

Br. William Enderby monk of Sempringham
Instituted 24 February 1468/9 to vicarage of Laughton-by-Folkingham (cause of vacancy not stated). Patron: Bishop of Lincoln, for this turn, by lapse. [Reg. 20, fo.148v.]

Br. William Gryme monk of Sempringham
Instituted 13 March 1505/6 to vicarage of Laughton-by-Folkingham, on death of br. William Enderby. Patron: Prior and Convent of Sempringham. [Reg. 23, fo.108v.]

Thomas South priest
Instituted 18 November 1508 to vicarage of Laughton-by-Folkingham, on death of William Grym. Patron: Prior and Convent of Sempringham. [Reg. 23, fo.133v.]

William Cuthbart canon of Sempringham
Instituted 13 July 1512 to vicarage of Laughton-by-Folkingham, on resignation of Thomas South. Patron: Prior and Convent of Sempringham (1 July 1512). [Reg. 23, fo.144v; PD 1512/26.]
Assessed for subsidy (£4 6s 8d) in 1526; assessed for *Valor Ecclesiasticus* 1535. [*Subsidy*, 58; *Valor* iv. 104.]

Robert Baker clerk
Instituted 28 September 1536 to vicarage of Laughton-by-Folkingham, on death of William Cutbert. Patron: Prior and Convent of Sempringham. [Reg. 27, fo.63v.]

Thomas Harmeston chaplain
Instituted 17 September 1542 to vicarage of Laughton-by-Folkingham, on resignation of Robert Baker. Patron: King Henry VIII. [Reg. 27, fo.78v.]
Listed at Visitation in 1551. Witnessed will, 1553. [Vj 13, fo.63; LCC Wills 1553–6/11.]

The vicarage of Laughton was united to the rectory of Folkingham, 17 July 1562. [Reg. 19, fo.153.]

MORTON-BY-BOURNE

The church of Morton-by-Bourne formed part of the foundation endowment of Bourne Abbey, given by Baldwin Fitz Gilbert in 1138. The church was appropriated and a vicarage ordained before *c*.1224–5. The Abbey continued to present to the vicarage until the Dissolution, after which the advowson passed to the Bishop of Lincoln. The Bishop still held the patronage in 1965. [Stenton, *Facsimiles of Early Charters*, 18–20; 'Rolls of Hugh of Wells', 173–5; *LDC* (1965), 66–7.]

Robert de Morton chaplain
Instituted between 1223 and 1226 to vicarage of Morton-by-Bourne. Patron: Abbot and Convent of Bourne. [*Rot. Welles* iii. 88; 'Rolls of Hugh of Wells', 173–5.]

William de Banburg chaplain
Instituted in the twenty-first pontifical year of Bishop Hugh of Wells (20 December 1229/19 December 1230) to vicarage of Morton-by-Bourne. Patron: Abbot and Convent of Bourne. [*Rot. Welles* iii. 178.]

Peter
Instituted before 17 December 1272. [*Rot. Gravesend*, 53.]

William de Cottesmor deacon
Instituted 17 December 1272 to vicarage of Morton-by-Bourne, on death of Peter. Patron: Abbot and Convent of Bourne. [*Rot. Gravesend*, 53.]

Ralph de Glapthorn priest
Instituted 16 May 1277 to vicarage of Morton-by-Bourne, on death of William. Patron: Abbot and Convent of Bourne. [*Rot. Gravesend*, 76.]

Ralph de Clathorp
Instituted before 20 December 1297. [*Reg. Sutton* i. 221.]

Walter Erlin chaplain
Instituted 20 December 1297 to vicarage of Morton-by-Bourne, on death of Ralph de Clathorp. Patron: Abbot and Convent of Bourne. [*Reg. Sutton* i. 221.]

Roger Cissor
Instituted before 12 October 1369. [Reg. 10, fo.34.]
Afterwards: V. of Sleaford, 1369–76. [Reg. 10, fo.83.]

William Warde de Dunnesby priest
Instituted 12 October 1369 to vicarage of Morton-by-Bourne, on resignation of Roger Cissor (by exchange with vicarage of Sleaford). Patron: Abbot and Convent of Bourne. [Reg. 10, fo.34.]

Formerly: V. of Sleaford, to 1369. Afterwards: R. of Hardwick (Np), 1373–83; R. of Clipston Two Parts (Np), 1383–93; R. of Holcot (Np), 1393–5; R. of Ropsley, 1395. [Reg. 10, fo.193; Reg. 11, fos 123v, 165, 174.]

Nicholas Rose priest
Instituted 27 March 1372 [*recte* 1373] to vicarage of Morton-by-Bourne, on resignation of William Warde (by exchange with church of Hardwick). Patron: Abbot and Convent of Bourne. [Reg. 10, fos 55v, 193.]

Formerly: R. of Hardwick (Np), 1369–73. Afterwards: R. of Belton-by-Grantham, 1378–90; V. of Hinckley (Le), 1390. [Reg. 10, fo.178v; Reg. 11, fos 47v, 215v; *CPR 1388–92*, 302.]

John Hervy (Henry) de Depyng
Instituted 24 June 1378 to vicarage of Morton-by-Bourne, on resignation of Nicholas Rose (by exchange with church of Belton by Grantham). Patron: Abbot and Convent of Bourne. [Reg. 10, fo.89v.]

Formerly: V. of Castle Bytham, 1370–5; R. of Belton-by-Grantham, 1375–8. Assessed for poll-tax, 1381. Cited (as late vicar of Morton) for not appearing to answer touching a debt of 40 marks, 8 February 1389/90. [Reg. 10, fos 43v, 72v; *Clerical Poll-Taxes*, nos 1323, 1912; *CPR 1388–92*, 69.]

John de Halbertoft priest
Instituted 13 October 1385 to vicarage of Morton-by-Bourne (cause of vacancy not stated). Patron: Abbot and Convent of Bourne. [Reg. 11, fo.18v.]

Robert Halyday
Instituted before 1 September 1413. [Reg. 14, fo.65v.]

William Day priest
Instituted 1 September 1413 to vicarage of Morton-by-Bourne, on death of Robert Halyday. Patron: Abbot and Convent of Bourne. [Reg. 14, fo.65v.]

John Heyne alias Walden priest
Instituted 4 July 1430 to vicarage of Morton-by-Bourne, on death of William Deye. Patron: Abbot and Convent of Bourne. [*Reg. Fleming* i. no.362.]

Thomas Smythy priest
Instituted 24 October 1454 to vicarage of Morton-by-Bourne, on resignation of M. John Walden. Patron: Abbot and Convent of Bourne. [Reg. 20, fo.122.]

Richard Sponer priest
Instituted 29 April 1460 to vicarage of Morton-by-Bourne, on death of

Thomas Smythy. Patron: Abbot and Convent of Bourne. Note that an annual pension of 7 marks was reserved to M. John Walden, late Vicar, for life from the fruits of the vicarage. [Reg. 20, fo.133v.]

Richard Echerd priest
Instituted 4 April 1463 to vicarage of Morton-by-Bourne, on resignation of Richard Sponer. Patron: Abbot and Convent of Bourne. [Reg. 20, fo.138.]

Henry Echard
Instituted before 26 January 1496/7. [Reg. 23, fo.60.]

M. Robert Eveden clerk
Instituted 26 January 1496/7 to vicarage of Morton-by-Bourne, on death of Henry Echard. Patron: Abbot and Convent of Bourne. [Reg. 23, fo.60.]

John Feld chaplain
Instituted 1 February 1508/9 to vicarage of Morton-by-Bourne, on death of Robert Eviden. Patron: Abbot and Convent of Bourne. [Reg. 23, fo.135v.]

Richard Webster
Instituted by 1526.
Assessed for subsidy (£8) in 1526. [*Subsidy*, 58.]

William Dobson priest
Instituted 31 October 1530 to vicarage of Morton-by-Bourne, on resignation of Richard Webster. Patron: Abbot and Convent of Bourne. [Reg. 27, fo.48v.]

Henry Anderson chaplain
Instituted 16 October 1531 to vicarage of Morton-by-Bourne, on death of William Dobson. Patron: Abbot and Convent of Bourne. [Reg. 27, fo.51v.]
Assessed for *Valor Ecclesiasticus* 1535. Attainted. [*Valor* iv. 105.]

Thomas Rudocke clerk
Instituted 28 May 1544 to vicarage of Morton-by-Bourne, on attainder of Henry Andreson. Patron: King Henry VIII (19 May 1544). [Reg. 27, fo.82v; PD 1544/6.]

John Field
Occurs as Vicar, 1548.
Witnessed Morton will, 23 June 1548. [LCC Wills 1558/iii/9.]

Bartholomew Bowdocke
Instituted 1549 to vicarage of Morton-by-Bourne (compounded for first-fruits 9 May). [FL.h.13, 600.]

Exhibited at Visitation in 1551. [Vj 13, fo.62.]

Thomas Buddill

Instituted 13 December 1554 to vicarage of Morton-by-Bourne (cause of vacancy not stated). Patron: Bishop of Lincoln. [Reg. 28, fo.123v.]

Witnessed Morton wills, 1556–8. [LCC Wills 1553–6/189; 1557/i/270; 1558/i/30, 34, 35v, 177; 1558/iii/131.]

Robert Collingwood

Instituted 4 September 1560 to vicarage of Morton-by-Bourne, on cession of last incumbent. Patron: Bishop of Lincoln. [Reg. 19, fo.106.]

Witnessed Morton wills, 1560–2. Signed BTs at Morton 1562. Afterwards: R. of Rippingale Two Parts, 1562–1615; R. of Rippingale Third Part, 1565–1615 (*q.v.*). [LCC Wills 1561/19, 46, 87, 175; 1562/182v; BTs Morton-by-Bourne.]

Christopher Pratt

Instituted 3 November 1563 to vicarage of Morton-by-Bourne. [SUB I, fo.18v.]

Signed register 1565–8 ('Here endeth the regester written by Mr Pratt sometime Vicar of the Church of Morton'). Witnessed Morton wills, May 1565, April 1568. Afterwards: R. of a mediety of Leasingham, 1568–71. Died before 23 June 1571. [PR Morton-by-Bourne; LCC Wills 1565/139; 1568/139v; *Bishop Cooper*, 5.]

Thomas Francke

Instituted by 1 November 1568. [PR Morton-by-Bourne.]

Born *c.*1543. Education: 'is moderately skilled in Latin; and to the same extent versed in sacred learning'; 'no graduate'. Priest: 22 September 1565 (Lincoln). Signed register from 1 November 1568 'at which tyme Thomas Francke entred into the Church of Morton aforesaid as Vicar'. Signed BTs to 1617. Resident (1576, 1611). Witnessed Morton wills, 1569, 1573. Buried at Morton, 10 March 1617/18. Probate Inventory dated same day ('his books, xls'). [*Bishop Cooper*, 209; SUB I, fo.26; PR Morton-by-Bourne; LC 3, fo.2v; BTs Morton-by-Bourne; LCC Wills 1557–72/169; 1569/i/109; INV 121/58.]

Robert Pote MA

Inducted 27 June 1618 (by Edmund Ashton, Rector of Dowsby) to vicarage of Morton-by-Bourne, on death of Thomas Francke. Patron: Bishop of Lincoln. [IND/L 1, fo.43.]

Born *c.*1589; son of John P. of Ripon. Educated: Ripon School and Caius College, Cambridge (matric. 1606; BA 1610–11; MA 1614). Buried at Morton, 3 December 1618. [Venn, *Alumni*; PR Morton-by-Bourne.]

Humfrey Boston MA

Inducted 28 December 1618 (by Lorkin Liveley, Vicar of Hacconby) to vicarage of Morton-by-Bourne, on death of last incumbent. Patron: Bishop of Lincoln. [IND/L 1, fo.46.]

Educated: Christ's College, Cambridge (BA 1608–9; MA 1612). Priest: 1616 (Peterborough). Signed BTs 1619–41. Ejected 1646. Buried at Morton, 11 December 1650. [Venn, *Alumni*; BTs Morton-by-Bourne; Swaby, 113; PR Morton-by-Bourne.]

Henry Conington
Occurs 1648. [Swaby, 113; PR Morton-by-Bourne.]

Richard Quincey
Admitted 1653, on cession of last incumbent. [Swaby, 113.]

Samuel Dove
Admitted 1659. Patron: Lord Protector. [Swaby, 113.]

Baptised 22 January 1636/7; son of Barjonah D., V. of Aslackby. Educated: Emmanuel College, Cambridge (matric. 1651; BA 1654–5; MA 1658). Afterwards: C. of Tattershall, 1662; Chaplain to Earl of Lincoln at Tattershall, 1662; R. of Moorby, 1664–87; V. of Alford, 1669–79; R. of Martin, 1681–9. Buried at Horncastle, 1 August 1689. [Venn, *Alumni*; LC 5, fo.51; PR Horncastle.]

Tristram Dymond MA
Instituted 10 April 1662 by collation to vicarage of Morton-by-Bourne, on death of last incumbent. Patron: Bishop of Lincoln. [Reg. 32, fo.17; IND/L 1, fo.151v.]

Deacon: 30 July 1660; priest: 31 July 1660 (Chichester). Signed BTs 1663–70. Also: C. of Hacconby (*q.v.*). [LC 5, fo.23; BTs Morton-by-Bourne.]

James Brooke BA
Instituted 30 October 1673 by collation to vicarage of Morton-by-Bourne, on death of Tristram Diamond. Patron: Bishop of Lincoln. [SUB Va, fo.49; IND/L 1, fo.212.]

Priest: 25 May 1673 (Lincoln). Formerly: C. of Tealby, 1673. Signed BTs 1674–7. Also: V. of Hacconby, 1673–8. [Reg. 33, fo.161v; BTs Morton-by-Bourne.]

William Hotchkin
Instituted 20 December 1678 by collation to vicarage of Morton-by-Bourne, on death of James Brooke. Patron: Bishop of Lincoln. [Reg. 34, fo.32; IND/L 1, fo.229v.]

Baptised 19 August 1649 at Bourne; son of John H. Educated: Bourne School and St John's College, Cambridge (matric. 1667; BA). Deacon: 18 June 1671; priest: 24 September 1671 (Peterborough). Formerly: C. of Stickney, 1671; C. of Dunsby, 1671. Signed BTs at Morton 1678–97. Also: V. of Hacconby (*q.v.*). Buried 8 September 1698 at Morton-by-Bourne. Probate inventory (12 September 1698): 'His Library, £5'. [*PR Bourne*, 96; Longden vii. 113; Venn, *Alumni*; *St John's Admissions* ii. 1; LC 14, fo.4; SUB V/5, fos 5v, 8; BTs Morton-by-Bourne; PR Morton-by-Bourne; INV 193/330.]

Robert Baron MA
Instituted 27 December 1705 by collation to vicarage of Morton-by-Bourne (cause of vacancy not stated). Patron: Bishop of Lincoln. [Reg. 36, p.6.]

Son of Robert B. of Great Shelford (Ca), esquire. Educated: Jesus College, Cambridge (matric. 1683–4; BA 1687–8; MA 1691). Deacon: 8 July 1689; priest: 28 August 1689 (London). Afterwards: V.of Mumby, 1707–19. 'Gone beyond sea' (1711); perhaps as minister to Maryland. Died before 12 October 1719. [Venn, *Alumni*; *Speculum*, 90; Reg. 36, p.56; Reg. 37, p.87.]

Richard Tonge BA

Instituted 6 October 1708 by collation to vicarage of Morton-by-Bourne, on cession of Robert Baron. Patron: Bishop of Lincoln. [Reg. 36, p.93.]

Baptised 27 September 1683 at Gainsborough; son of John T., chandler. Educated: Kirton School and Magdalene College, Cambridge (matric. 1703; BA 1706–7; MA 1710). Deacon: 21 September 1707; priest: 30 May 1708 (Lincoln). Also: V. of Hacconby, 1709–32; Canon of Lincoln and Prebendary of Decem Librarum, 1728–38; R. of Belleau with Aby, 1732–8; Chaplain to Duke of Ancaster. Resident at Morton-by-Bourne; buried there, 27 February 1737/8. [PR Gainsborough; Venn, *Alumni*; Reg. 36, pp. 53, 82; *Le Neve Fasti: Lincoln, 1541–1857*, 62; *Speculum*, 57, 89; PR Morton-by-Bourne.]

The vicarage of Hacconby was united to the vicarage of Morton-by-Bourne on 7 July 1732. [Reg. 38, p.261.]

John Meyrick

Instituted 6 April 1738 by collation to vicarage of Morton with Hacconby, on death of Richard Tonge. Patron: Bishop of Lincoln. [Reg. 38, p.344.]

Deacon: 1734; priest: 1735 (Llandaff). Non-resident at Morton, which was served by Thomas Key as curate. [SPE 2, fo.82; PR Morton-by-Bourne.]

Thomas Key

Instituted 24 April 1758 by collation to vicarage of Morton with Hacconby, on death of --- Merick. Patron: Bishop of Lincoln. [Reg. 38, p.558.]

Deacon: 15 April 1734; priest: 17 June 1739 (Lincoln). Formerly: Chaplain to General Whetham's Regiment, 1739; C. of Morton-by-Bourne, 1741–58. Buried at Morton, 21 November 1766. [Reg. 38, pp. 286, 366; PR Morton-by-Bourne.]

John Hewthwaite MA

Instituted 31 December 1766 by collation to vicarage of Morton with Hacconby, on death of Thomas Key. Patron: Bishop of Lincoln. [Reg. 39, p.62.]

Born *c*.1729 at Pickering (YNR); son of Thomas H., attorney-at-law. Educated: Thresh-field School and St John's College, Cambridge (matric. 1747; BA 1750–1; MA 1757). Deacon: 2 June 1751; priest: 24 May 1752 (York). Formerly: C. of St Mary and St Nicholas, Beverley, 1751; V. of Cottingham (YER), 1757–66. Head Master of Lincoln School, 1758–92; resided at Lincoln on Waterside South. Non-resident at Morton, which was served by John Vokes as curate. Afterwards: V. of Messingham with Bottesford, 1768–73; V. of Great Carlton, 1773–6; V. of Bicker, 1776–1802. Died at Lincoln, 16 September 1802; buried at St Martin, Lincoln. [*St John's Admissions* iii. 121, 564; Venn, *Alumni*; *York Ordinations 1750–1799*, 52; Garton, 'Lincoln School,' pp. 1489, 1583; PR Morton-by-Bourne; PR Lincoln St Martin.]

Francis Tong MA

Instituted 8 September 1768 by collation to vicarage of Morton with Hacconby, on cession of John Hewthwaite. Patron: Bishop of Lincoln. Reinstituted 2 January 1783, on his own cession; patron: as above. [Reg. 39, pp. 97, 389.]

Born *c*.1735 at Beverley; son of John T., chapman. Educated: Beverley School and St John's College, Cambridge (matric. 1754; BA 1758; MA 1761). Deacon: 21 May 1758 (Lincoln for York); priest: 29 September 1759 (York). Formerly: C. of Hessle (YER), 1759. Resided at Morton from 1773 and served the church. Also: R. of Aisthorpe, 1783–95. Died 9 September 1795, at Burlington (Yorks) [*St John's Admissions* iii. 142, 628; Venn, *Alumni*; LC 31, p.72; PR Morton-by-Bourne.]

Samuel Edmund Hopkinson BD

Instituted 24 October 1795 by collation to vicarage of Morton with Hacconby, on death of Francis Tong. Patron: Bishop of Lincoln. [Reg. 39, p.609.]

Born 20 August 1754 at Sutton by Peterborough; son of William H., Minor Canon of Peterborough. Educated: Clare Hall, Cambridge (matric. 1773; BA 1777; MA 1780; BD 1793); Fellow of Clare 1776–82. Deacon: 17 March 1781 (Ely); priest: 23 December 1781 (Peterborough). Formerly: C. of Islip (Np), 1781–5; C. of Rotherhithe (Sr), 1786; C. of Christchurch (Sr), 1786–92. Also: R. of Etton (Np), 1786–1828; V. of Thorpe St Peter, 1834–8. Married (30 May 1782) at All Saints, Northampton, Elizabeth, daughter of John Portington of Northampton and formerly of Bourne. Resided at Morton; rebuilt Vicarage House (1796). 'An assiduous priest and devoted to his flock; every Sunday two poor men, in rotation through the parish, dined at Morton vicarage.' Died 17 July 1841 at Morton; buried at Hacconby. [Venn, *Alumni*; Longden vii. 99; Dioc/Misc/1/10; MGA 18; *GM* 171 (1841), 49–50.]

Thomas Colbeck Holdsworth MA

Instituted 25 October 1841 by collation to vicarage of Morton with Hacconby, on death of Samuel Edmund Hopkinson. Patron: Bishop of Lincoln. [Reg. 40, p.479.]

Baptised 23 November 1792; son of William H. of Otley, watchmaker. Educated: Clare Hall, Cambridge (admitted 6 December 1817). Deacon (as literate): 3 August 1817; priest: 14 July 1822 (York). Formerly: C. of Stainburn (YWR), 1817; C. of South Kelsey, 1828; V. of Saxilby, 1839–41. Resided at Morton Vicarage. Died 21 April 1862; buried at Morton (MI). His effects, offered for sale at Morton Vicarage on 2–4 June 1862, included a 'Cab Phaeton, with moveable front and glass doors' and paintings by Gainsborough, Rubens and others. [*York Ordinations 1800–1849*, 95; Venn, *Alumni*; CR 1, p.379; White, *Lincolnshire* (1842), 741; Census Returns 1851; *Probate Calendar* 1862; PR Morton-by-Bourne; *Lincolnshire Chronicle*, 23 May 1862.]

(Joseph) Walter Stockdale MA

Instituted 27 June 1862 to vicarage of Morton with Hacconby, on death of Thomas Colbeck Holdsworth. Patron: Bishop of Lincoln. [Reg. 41, p.90.]

Born 19 April, baptised 27 May 1810 at Kirton Lindsey; son of Revd Joseph S. (Vicar of Kingerby 1811–74). Educated: Charterhouse School (1823–8) and Trinity College, Cambridge (matric. 1829; BA 1833; MA 1845). Deacon: 22 September 1833; priest: 21 September 1834 (Lincoln). Formerly: C. of Linwood, 1835–61; V. of North Willingham, 1847–62. Resided at Morton Vicarage. Married (1838) Harriet, daughter of Revd

John Hale, Rector of Holton cum Beckering (1802–44). Died 30 June 1901; buried at Morton (MI). [PR Kirton Lindsey; *Charterhouse Register 1769–1872*, 316; Venn, *Alumni*; *Crockford* (1898); OR 1, pp. 53, 57; Census Returns 1871, 1881, 1891, 1901; White, *Lincolnshire* (1872), 586; *Probate Calendar* 1902; PR Morton-by-Bourne.]

Nisbet Colquhoun Marris MA
Instituted 11 October 1901 to vicarage of Morton with Hacconby, on death of Walter Stockdale. Patron: Bishop of Lincoln. [Reg. 42, p.491.]

Baptised 3 October 1858; son of Thomas M. of Ulceby, farmer. Educated: Clifton College (1875–7) and St John's College, Cambridge (matric. 1877; BA 1881; MA 1884). Deacon: 21 December 1884; priest: 20 December 1885 (Lincoln). Formerly: C. of Horncastle, 1884–92; of Crowle, 1892–1901. Resided at Morton Vicarage. Bishop Hicks noted (1912); '… to Morton & I preached at Marris' Church to a fine gathering of the Aveland Sunday School Association'. Afterwards: PC of Holy Trinity, Gainsborough, 1914–27; Canon of Lincoln and Prebendary of Sexaginta Solidorum, 1918–37; V. of Tathwell with Haugham, 1927–34. Latterly of 49 St Augustine's Avenue, Grimsby. Died 31 May 1937 at Grimsby. [*Clifton College Register*, 100; Venn, *Alumni*; *Crockford* (1932); OR 2, pp. 61, 63; Census Returns 1911; Kelly, *Lincolnshire* (1913), 467; *Hicks Diaries*, no.224; *Probate Calendar* 1937.]

John Herbert Boldero
Instituted 8 April 1914 (by Dean of Lincoln as Commissary) to vicarage of Morton with Hacconby, on cession of Nisbet Colquhoun Marris. Patron: Bishop of Lincoln. [Reg. 43, p.68.]

Born 1865 at Enville (St); son of Revd John Simon Boldero, Curate of Enville. By 1891 was Asst Master at Ellesmere College (Mathematics and Drawing). Educated: Scholae Cancellarii, Lincoln (1891). Deacon: 1893; priest: 1894 (Lincoln). Formerly: C. of Stow-in-Lindsey, 1893–5; V. of Martin-by-Timberland, 1895–1914. Resided at Morton Vicarage. Resignation accepted 31 May 1945. Retired to live at 22 North Street, Lostwithiel (Co). Died 20 August 1957 at Lostwithiel, aged 92; buried at Morton (MI). [GRO, Birth Index; Census Returns 1871 (Amblecote), 1891 (Ellesmere); *Crockford* (1874, 1941, 1951–2); *Probate Calendar* 1958.]

Justin Paul Taggart
Instituted 12 September 1945 to vicarage of Morton with Hacconby, on resignation of John Herbert Boldero. Patron: Bishop of Lincoln. [Reg. 44, p.39.]

Born 1911. Educated: Lincoln Theological College (1932). Deacon: 1934; priest: 1935 (Lincoln). Formerly: C. of St John Spitalgate, Grantham, 1934–40; of St Nicholas, Lincoln, 1940–5. Resided at Morton Vicarage. Afterwards: V. of St Peter, Woodhall Spa, R. of Langton-by-Horncastle with Woodhall, and C-in-C of Kirkstead, 1952–76; Canon of Lincoln and Prebendary of North Kelsey, 1968–77. Retired to live at Reedsbeck, Droghadfayle Road, Port Erin (IoM). [*Crockford* (1951–2, 1980–2).]

Edric George Close
Instituted 5 February 1953 to vicarage of Morton with Hacconby, on cession of Justin Paul Taggart. Patron: Bishop of Lincoln. [Reg. 44, p.173.]

Born 11 February 1910 at Dore (Db); son of John Battye C., anti-rust manufacturer. Educated: Chichester Theological College (1938). Deacon: 1941 (Lincoln); priest: 1942

(Grimsby for Lincoln). Formerly: C. of St John Spitalgate, Grantham, 1941–6; V. of St Matthew, Sutton Bridge, 1946–53. Resided at Morton Vicarage. Afterwards: R. of Thorpe-on-the-Hill, R. of North Scarle, and V. of Eagle, 1967–78. Retired to live at 4 Mill Moor Way, North Hykeham. Died July 1985 (Lincoln). [Census Returns 1911 (Dore); *Crockford* (1961–2, 1980–2); GRO, Death Index.]

Edward Cyril Blake MRST

Instituted 23 April 1968 to vicarage of Morton with Hacconby, on cession of Edric George Close. Patron: Bishop of Lincoln. [Reg. 44, p.411.]

Born 9 September 1912. Educated: MRST (1938); Lincoln Theological College (1945). Deacon: 1946; priest: 1947 (Chester). Formerly: C. of Christ Church, Latchford (Chs), 1946–9; V. of Gosberton Clough, 1949–52; V. of Cherry Willingham with Greetwell, 1952–4; V. of Welton, 1954–6; Director of Education, Lincoln Diocese, 1956–68. Also: Canon of Lincoln and Prebendary of Sanctae Crucis, 1960. Resided at Morton Vicarage. Afterwards: C. of Bourne, 1976–7. Retired to live at 3 Beech Avenue, Bourne. Died 12 September 1989. [*Crockford* (1971–2, 1980–2); Lincoln Cathedral Obit Book.]

NEWTON-BY-FOLKINGHAM

The church of Newton-by-Folkingham was surrendered by William the Clerk of Newton between 1160 and 1166 to Bishop Robert Chesney; the bishop then confirmed it as the possession of the monks of St Andrew, Northampton. The church was never appropriated. The Priory continued to present to the rectory, except during those times when its possessions, as those of an alien priory, were taken into the king's hands, until the Dissolution. After the Reformation the advowson passed into the hands of the Savile family of Newton, who presented to the living until the late seventeenth century. It was subsequently acquired by Richard Wynne, who sold it before 1784 to the Welby family of Denton. Sir Oliver Welby was patron in 1965. [*EEA* i. no.196; *LDC* (1965), 66–7.]

Amaury of Buckden

Instituted before 1247/8. [Hoskin, no.415.]

Also: Canon of Lincoln and Prebendary of North Kelsey, by October 1231; Archdeacon of Bedford, by 19 December 1231. [*Le Neve Fasti: Lincoln 1066–1300*, 42.]

James de Rebursa subdeacon

Instituted in the thirteenth pontifical year of Bishop Robert Grosseteste (17 June 1247/16 June 1248) to church of Newton-by-Folkingham, on death of A[maury of Buckden], Archdeacon of Bedford. Patron: Prior and Convent of St Andrew, Northampton. M. Hervey de Facham, formerly presented to the church, resigned his claim. Note that James held a papal dispensation. [Hoskin, no.415.]

Also: R. of Haltham on Bain. [Hoskin, no.254.]

John de Cantia subdeacon
Granted custody of the church of Newton-by-Folkingham, 24 December 1275.
Patron: Prior and Convent of St Andrew, Northampton. [*Rot. Gravesend*, 67,
283.]

Afterwards: R. of Potton (Bd), 1280–6. Died before 15 December 1286. [*Reg. Sutton*
viii. 93, 103.]

M. William de Helmeswell deacon
Instituted 20 November 1280 to church of Newton-by-Folkingham, on insti-
tution of John of Kent to church of Potton. Patron: Prior and Convent of St
Andrew, Northampton. [*Reg. Sutton* i. 9.]

Educated: University of Oxford (MA by 1270); Fellow of Merton in 1278–9. Gave books
to Merton College. Also: R. of Covenham St Mary, 1280–1. Granted temporary custody
of church of Ewerby 1286, until presentee came of age. Rebuilt chancel at Newton, 1308.
Licence to be absent from his church and farm his benefice, and appointment of M. John
de Beby, R. of Folkingham, as curator of him and his church during his absence, 17
September 1321. Appointment of the said M. John as coadjutor of M. William who was
old and had poor eyesight, 9 October 1321 (note that M. William had failed to nomi-
nate a coadjutor himself, despite being given additional time). M. John was subsequently
replaced as coadjutor by John, Vicar of Osbournby, 6 December 1321. [Emden, *BRUO*,
905; *Reg. Sutton* i. 4, 12, 91–2; Hebgin-Barnes, 196; Reg. 5, fos 294, 295v, 297, 300.]

John de Ditton chaplain
Instituted 14 September 1328 to church of Newton-by-Folkingham, on death
of M. William. Patron: Prior and Convent of St Andrew, Northampton. [*Reg.
Burghersh* i. no.203.]

Afterwards: R. of Authorpe, 1339–50. Died before 29 October 1350. [Reg. 9, fo.92.]

Ralph de Malberthorp priest
Instituted 29 January 1338/9 to church of Newton-by-Folkingham, on resig-
nation of John de Ditton (by exchange with church of Authorpe). Patron:
King Edward III (12 January 1338/9), by custody of priory of St Andrew,
Northampton. [*Reg. Burghersh* i. no.599; *CPR 1338–40*, 169.]

Formerly: R. of Authorpe, 1335–9. Licence to study in England for 1 year, 12 October
1339. [*Reg. Burghersh* i. no.452; Reg. 5, fo.200.]

Thomas son of Adam of Strubby
Presented 15 May 1342 to church of Newton-by-Folkingham (cause of
vacancy not stated). Patron: King Edward III. [*CPR 1340–43*, 429.]

William Almer de Saham clerk
Instituted 31 May 1366 to church of Newton-by-Folkingham (cause of
vacancy not stated). Patron: Prior and Convent of St Andrew, Northampton.
[Reg. 10, fo.13v.]

His presentation (8 August 1370) to chapel of Dembleby, on an exchange with Adam de

Malberthorp, was presumably ineffective. Afterwards: R. of Mavis Enderby, 1372. [*CPR 1367–70*, 455.]

William de Calkewell
Instituted 19 July 1372 to church of Newton-by-Folkingham, on resignation of William Almere (by exchange with church of Mavis Enderby). Patron: King Edward III. [Reg. 10, fo.57v.]

Formerly: V. of Aslackby, to 1372 (*q.v.*); R. of Mavis Enderby, February–July 1372. Assessed for poll-tax, 1377, 1381. Described as 'late parson of Newton', 1 November 1386. [*Clerical Poll-Taxes*, nos 687, 1332, 1921; *CPR 1385–89*, 252.]

John Bentley
Instituted 16 August 1386 to church of Newton-by-Folkingham (cause of vacancy not stated). Patron: King Richard II (25 July 1386). [Reg. 11, fo.24v; *CPR 1385–89*, 202.]

Godfrey Whytley de Braunston clerk
Instituted 17 September 1388 to church of Newton-by-Folkingham (cause of vacancy not stated). Patron: King Richard II (20 August 1388). [Reg. 11, fo.36v; *CPR 1385–89*, 502.]

John Thorpe priest
Instituted 26 July 1399 to church of Newton-by-Folkingham, on death of Godfrey de Brampston. Patron: King Richard II. [Reg. 13, fo.123v.]

Afterwards: Warden of College of Stanstead St Margaret, 1409.

John Wynter
Instituted 8 December 1409 to church of Newton-by-Folkingham, on resignation of John Thorpe (by exchange with office of master or warden of college of Stanstead St Margaret (*Thele*), dioc. London. Patron: King Henry IV (25 October 1409). [Reg. 14, fo.39v; *CPR 1408–13*, 141.]

Formerly: Warden of College of Stanstead St Margaret, to 1409. (For the history of the College, see Newcourt i. 891–3; *VCH Hertford* iv. 454–5. Neither John Thorpe nor John Wynter is included in the lists of wardens.) Afterwards: V. of Wragby, August–November 1414. [Reg. 14, fos 70v, 71.]

William Barton
Instituted 25 August 1414 to church of Newton-by-Folkingham, on resignation of John Wynter (by exchange with vicarage of Wragby). Patron: Prior and Convent of St Andrew, Northampton. [Reg. 14, fo.70v.]

Formerly: V. of Wragby, January–August 1414. [Reg. 14, fo.68.]

William Walcote priest
Instituted 26 March 1451 to church of Newton-by-Folkingham, on resignation of William Barton. Patron: Prior and Convent of St Andrew, Northampton. [Reg. 19, fos 60, 76.]

Thomas Maister priest
Instituted 1 June 1462 to church of St Botolph, Newton-by-Folkingham, on resignation of William Walcote. Patron: Prior and Convent of St Andrew, Northampton. [Reg. 20, fo.137.]

Thomas Swyfte priest
Instituted 17 June 1499 to church of Newton-by-Folkingham, on death of Thomas Mayster. Patron: Prior and Convent of St Andrew, Northampton. [Reg. 23, fo.64v.]

Michael Cottom
Instituted 29 November 1508 to church of Newton-by-Folkingham, on resignation of Thomas Swyft. Patron: Prior and Convent of St Andrew, Northampton. Note that an annual pension of £3 13s 4d was reserved to Thomas Swyft from the fruits of the church. [Reg. 23, fo.134.]

Assessed for subsidy (£10) in 1526; assessed for *Valor Ecclesiasticus* 1535. Exhibited at Visitation in 1551. Died before 28 November 1552 (probate inventory). [*Subsidy*, 57; *Valor* iv. 104; Vj 13, fo.63; LCC Wills 1551 & 1552/92; INV 20/289.]

Richard Turre
Instituted *c*.1553. Patron: Walter Wryght LLD, Archdeacon of Oxford (22 May 1553), by assignment of grant of advowson made by Prior and Convent of St Andrew, Northampton, to Henry Wyatt kt. [PD 1553/31, 39.]

Witnessed Newton will, September 1557. Died 15x24 January 1557/8. [LCC Wills 1557/i/339; 1557/iv/123.]

John Bryerley
Instituted 15 July 1558, on death of last incumbent. Patron: King Philip and Queen Mary I. [Reg. 28, fo.131.]

Robert Nelson (of Goxhill)
Instituted *c*.1559 (compounded for first-fruits, 8 June 1564). Patron: Queen Elizabeth I (22 April 1559). [FL.h.13, p.610; *CPR Elizabeth 1558–60*, 124.]

Born *c*.1494. Education: 'is moderately skilled in Latin; and to the same extent versed in sacred learning'. Priest: 23 February 1520/1 (Ariensis for Lincoln). Resident (1576); signed BTs 1562–6, 1577–8. Died 1579/80. [*Bishop Cooper*, 209; BTs Newton; INV 65/84.]

George Gamon
Instituted 30 December 1580 to rectory of Newton-by-Folkingham, on death of Henry [*sic*] Nelson. Patron: Thomas Gamon of Folkingham, gent. (25 November 1580). [*Bishop Cooper*, 27, 263.]

Education: 'bred in the schools'; 'no graduate'. Deacon: 26 July 1578; priest: 10 January 1578/9 (Lincoln). Also: V. of Burton Pedwardine, 1580. Assessed ('a Bowe') in Subsidy of Armour 1590. Resident (1611); signed BTs 1591–1622. Resigned 1622. Latterly of

Aslackby. Died before 14 June 1626 (probate inventory). [*State of the Church*, 66, 73, 148; *Bishop Cooper*, 90–1; LC 3, fo.3; BTs Newton-by-Folkingham; INV 131/193; LCC Wills 1626/653.]

Cordal Berrie BA

Instituted 6 April 1622 to rectory of Newton-by-Folkingham, on resignation of George Gamon. Patron: William Savile esquire (5 April 1622). [BC; PD 1622/3.]

Educated: Magdalene College, Cambridge (matric. 1614; BA 1617–8). Deacon: 19 September 1619; priest: 11 June 1620 (Peterborough). Formerly: at Pickworth (perhaps as curate) where his daughter Elizabeth was born, 19 November 1620. Other children, Susanna (1622), Frances (1624), William (1625), Margaret (1627), George (1628), John (1629), Thomas (1632), Samuel (1634), Katherine (1638) were baptised at Newton. Signed BTs at Newton, 1623–36. Buried at Newton, 28 April 1638. Probate inventory, 30 April 1638 ('his Libirary of Bookes, £10'). Will (LCC). [Venn, *Alumni*; Longden ii. 81; PR Pickworth; PR Newton-by-Folkingham; BTs Newton-by-Folkingham; INV 148/24; LCC Wills 1638/43.]

John Naylor

Instituted 2 June 1638 to rectory of Newton-by-Folkingham, on death of Cordal Berrie. Patron: William Savile gent. [AC; MCD 295/53.]

Signed BTs 1639–41. [BTs Newton-by-Folkingham.]

John Willowes

Instituted *c*.1650. [Swaby, 113]

Formerly: R. of Irnham, 1646–50. Died *c*.1654. Will (PCC) dated 8 October 1654. [PROB 11/248.]

Humphrey Lucas

Instituted 1655. Patron: William Savile, esquire. [LC 5, fo.23v; Swaby, 113.]

Of Northamptonshire. Educated: Queens' College, Cambridge (matric. 1645; BA 1648–9) and Magdalen Hall, Oxford (MA 1651). Deacon: 7 August 1662 (Lincoln). Also: V. of St Peter, Irthlingborough (Np), 1662. Signed BTs at Newton 1664–81. Married (27 October 1662) at Brockhall (Np), Martha, daughter of William Barlee, R. of Brockhall. Children: Katharine (1663), William (1664), Thomas (1666), John (1668), Barlee (1670), Richard (1676) were baptised at Newton. Buried 29 September 1682 in the chancel at Brockhall. [Venn, *Alumni*; Longden ix. 59; Reg. 32, p.19; LC 5, fo.23v; BTs Newton-by-Folkingham; PR Newton-by-Folkingham.]

Samuel Weed BA

Instituted 14 February 1682/3 to rectory of Newton-by-Folkingham, on death of Humphrey Lucas. Patron: Alice Savile widow and Mary Savile spinster. [Reg. 34, fo.72.]

Baptised at Doddington (Np), 4 March 1651/2; son of John W. Educated: Corpus Christi College, Cambridge (matric. 1670; BA 1673–4). Deacon: 19 September 1675 (Peterborough); priest: 25 June 1676 (Lincoln). Formerly: C. of Felmersham (Bd), 1675; V. of Felmersham, 1676; V. of Pavenham, 1682. Signed BTs at Newton 1684–6. Died 1687.

Will (LCC). Probate inventory (16 September 1687): 'Books in the Study, £10'. [Venn, *Alumni*; Longden xiv. 233; Reg. 34, fo.9; BTs Newton-by-Folkingham; LCC Wills 1688/i/179; INV 188/157.]

Isaac Laughton MA

Instituted 2 March 1687/8 to rectory of Newton-by-Folkingham, on death of Samuel Weed. Patron: Alice Savile, spinster (2 January 1687/8). [Reg. 34, fo.103; PD 1688/19–21.]

Born *c*.1657; son of William L. of Somerby. Educated: Knotting School (Bd) and Magdalene College, Cambridge (matric. 1674; BA 1675–6; MA 1679). Deacon: 24 September 1676 (Peterborough); priest: 21 December 1679 (Lincoln). Formerly: C. of Hougham cum Marston, 1677; C. of Somerby, 1679; C. of Brampton Ash (Np), 1680. Signed BTs at Newton 1688–9. Afterwards: R. of Ashby (Nf), 1691–1718; R. of Clippesby (Nf), to 1718. Died 1718. [Venn, *Alumni*; Longden viii. 181; SUB V/6, fo.24v; Reg. 34, fo.44r–v; BTs Newton-by-Folkingham.]

Thomas Milles

Instituted 2 May 1690 to rectory of Newton-by-Folkingham, on resignation of Isaac Laughton. Patron: Ann Middlemore of Winkburn (Nt), widow (18 March 1689/90), for this turn. [Reg. 34, fo.115; PD 1690/5.]

Perhaps to be identified with TM of Lincoln College, Oxford (matric. 1677; BA 1680). Deacon: 12 March 1681/2; priest: 25 May 1684 (Lincoln). Formerly: C. of Londonthorpe, 1682; C. of Ancaster, 1682; Usher of Grantham School, 1688. Resident: signed BTs at Newton 1690–1721. Buried at Newton, 4 September 1721. [Foster, *Alumni*; Reg. 34, fos 65v, 79; SUB V/6, fos 39, 55v; LC 14, fo.5; *Speculum*, 91; BTs Newton-by-Folkingham; PR Newton-by-Folkingham.]

James Stafford MA

Instituted 25 November 1721 to rectory of Newton-by-Folkingham, on death of Thomas Mills. Patron: Richard Wynne, esquire (23 November 1721). [Reg. 37, p.134; PD 1721/16.]

Born *c*.1690 at Little Ponton; son of John S., husbandman. Educated: Burton School and St John's College, Cambridge (matric. 1708; BA 1711–12; MA 1717). Deacon: 19 September 1713; priest: 24 September 1715 (Peterborough). Formerly: C. of Higham Ferrers (Np), 1713. Signed BTs at Newton 1721–34. Also: R. of Stonton Wyville (Le), 1727–36; Chaplain to Earl of Oxford. Died 1736. [*St John's Admissions* ii. 188; Venn, *Alumni*; Longden xiii. 29; BTs Newton-by-Folkingham.]

William Gower

Instituted 30 July 1736 to rectory of Newton-by-Folkingham, on death of James Stafford. Patron: Richard Winne of Bedwell Park, Essendon (Hrt), esquire (21 June 1736). [Reg. 38, p.319; PD 108/15.]

Born *c*.1702; son of Thomas G. of St Nicholas, Worcester, gent. Educated: Worcester College, Oxford (matric. 1715; BA 1719; MA 1722; BD and DD 1739); Provost of Worcester 1736–77. Deacon: 19 December 1725; priest: 5 June 1726 (Oxford). Non-resident at Newton; BTs signed by John Owen (1740–61) as curate. Died 19 July 1777. [Foster, *Alumni*; ORO, MS. Oxf. Dioc. Papers c.266, fos 57v, 58; BTs Newton-by-Folkingham; LC 18b, p.198.]

Arthur Cookson

Instituted 3 March 1749/50 to rectory of Newton-by-Folkingham, on resignation of William Gore DD. Patron: Richard Wynne, esquire (30 January 1749/50). [Reg. 38, p.493; PD 1750/6.]

Born 5 September baptised 19 September 1720 at Leeds; son of William C., Alderman. Educated: Leeds School and Magdalene College, Cambridge (matric. 1738; BA 1741–2; MA 1745). Deacon: 19 September 1742 (Lincoln). Formerly: C. of Eynesbury (Hu), 1742. Not always resident at Newton: 'Absent: said to be in the Country but is supposed not to have had notice – and yet is said to be at his Curate's' (1768); 'Lives at Bath or Ealing near London' (1778). Died 1781 at Bath. [WYAS, PR Leeds St Peter; Venn, *Alumni*; Reg. 38, p.420; LC 31, p.76.]

William Brown LLB

Instituted 15 March 1781 to rectory of Newton-by-Folkingham, on death of Arthur Cookson. Patron: William Brown DD and Daniel Douglas esquire, for this turn. [Reg. 39, p.361.]

Born *c*.1758; son of Edward B. of Walcot, esquire. Educated: Trinity College, Oxford (matric. 1775; LLB 1780). Deacon: 24 May 1780 (Oxford); priest: 11 March 1781 (Lincoln). [Foster, *Alumni*; ORO, MS. Oxf. Dioc. Papers b.21, fo.106; Reg. 39, p.360.]

John Rowland alias Litchford MA

Instituted 27 November 1784 to rectory of Newton-by-Folkingham, on death of William Brown. Patron: William Welby of Denton. [Reg. 39, p.420.]

Born 8 September, baptised 12 October 1748 at Boothby Pagnell; son of William R., attorney-at-law. Educated: Uppingham School and Emmanuel College, Cambridge (matric. 1767; BA 1771; MA 1785). Deacon: 26 May 1771; priest: 20 December 1772 (Lincoln). Formerly: C. of Boothby Pagnell, 1771. Also: R. of Boothby Pagnell, 1780–1818; R. of Westborough with Dry Doddington, 1802–9; V. of Bassingthorpe with Westby, 1805–19. Married (8 December 1778) at Grantham, Ann, daughter of Thomas Litchford esquire. Signed BTs at Newton 1785–1801. Died 25 November 1818, aged 70; buried at Boothby Pagnell (MI). [PR Boothby Pagnell; Venn, *Alumni*; Reg. 39, pp. 158–9, 191; PR Grantham St Wulfram; BTs Newton-by-Folkingham; *Monson*, 48.]

Montague Earle Welby BA

Instituted 19 December 1802 to rectory of Newton-by-Folkingham, on cession of John Rowland Litchford. Patron: Sir William Earle Welby of Denton House, Bt (1 December 1802). [Reg. 40, p.47; PD 158/5.]

Baptised 28 September 1778 at West Allington; 4th son of Sir William Earle Welby Bt. Educated: Emmanuel College, Cambridge (matric. 1797; BA 1801; MA 1804). Deacon: 31 May 1801; priest: 19 December 1802 (Lincoln). Formerly: C. of Muston and East Allington, 1801. Licence for non-residence at Newton (1804), on account of the house being unfit; Newton was served by curates, including Isaac Wilson, Robert Shepherd and John Pearson. Also: V. of Long Bennington, 1808–49. Afterwards resided at Allington House. Died 12 October 1871 at Allington, aged 93. [PR West Allington; Venn, *Alumni*; Reg. 40, pp. 24–5, 46; NRL 1804/62; CR 1, pp. 32, 55, 249, 344; White, *Lincolnshire* (1842), 742; Census Returns 1851, 1861, 1871 (Allington); *Probate Calendar* 1871.]

Thomas Earle Welby

Instituted 27 January 1847 to rectory of Newton-by-Folkingham, on resignation of Montague Earle Welby. Patron: Sir William Earle Welby, Bt. [Reg. 40, p.514.]

Born 11 July 1810; son of Sir William Earle Welby, 2nd Bt. Educated: Rugby School and Christ's College, Cambridge (admitted 1846; a 'ten year man'); MA (Lambeth) 1843; DD (Lambeth) 1862. Ensign in 26th Foot, 1826; Lieutenant, 1829; Lieutenant in 13th Light Dragoons, 1830; sold out 1837. Deacon and priest: 1840 (Toronto). Formerly: R. of Sandwich (Canada), 1842; C. of Burnham Westgate (Nf), 1846. Licence for non-residence at Newton (1848), on account of the house being unfit; the parish was served by Arthur Earle Welby as curate. Afterwards: Inc. of St Mark, George (Cape Town), 1851–61; Archdeacon of George Town, 1856–61; Bishop of St Helena, 1861–99. Killed 6 January 1899 in a carriage accident at James Town, St Helena. [Burke, *Peerage* (1938), 2539; Venn, *Alumni*; *Crockford* (1865); NRL 12/36; CR 3, fo.98v.]

Arthur Earle Welby BA

Instituted 5 December 1848 to rectory of Newton-by-Folkingham, on resignation of Thomas Earle Welby. Patron: Sir William Earle Welby, Bt. [Reg. 40, p.520.]

Born 22 August 1815 at Cowes (IoW); son of Sir William Earle Welby, 2nd Bt. Brother of Thomas Earle Welby, above. Educated: Balliol College, Oxford (matric. 1835); University of Durham (BA 1846). Married (13 May 1843) Julia Catherine, daughter of Captain George Macdonald. Deacon: 19 September 1847; priest: 24 September 1848 (Lincoln). Formerly: C. of Newton, 1847. Also: C. of Scott Willoughby, 1849. Resided at Newton, where a new Rectory House was built about 1851. Afterwards: R. of Holy Trinity Hulme, Manchester, 1858–84. Died 26 November 1884. [Burke, *Peerage* (1938), 2540; Foster, *Alumni*; *Crockford* (1874); OR 1, pp. 109, 113; CR 3, fos 98v, 122v; Census Returns 1851; White, *Lincolnshire* (1872), 587.]

Thomas Todd MA

Instituted 31 May 1858 to rectory of Newton-by-Folkingham, on resignation of Arthur Earle Welby. Patron: Sir Glynne Earle Welby of Denton Hall, Bt. [Reg. 40, p.595.]

Born *c.*1813; son of Joseph T. of West Newton (Cu), gent. Educated: Manchester GS and Queen's College, Oxford (matric. 1833; BA 1837; MA 1853). Deacon: 1840; priest: 1841 (Carlisle). Formerly: C. of Leeds Parish Church; R. of Holy Trinity Hulme, Manchester, 1843–58. Resided at Newton Rectory. Died 7 June 1892; buried at Newton (MI). [Foster, *Alumni*; *Crockford* (1885); White, *Lincolnshire* (1872), 587; Census Returns 1881, 1891; *Probate Calendar* 1892.]

The Rectory of Haceby was united with the Rectory of Newton-by-Folkingham by Order in Council dated 24 October 1870. [Reg. 41, pp. 324–7.]

Richard Lucas Calcraft BA

Instituted 30 September 1892 to rectory of Newton with Haceby, on death of Thomas Todd. Patron: Sir William Earle Welby Gregory of Denton Manor, Bt. [Reg. 42, p.347.]

Born 1 April 1846; son of John Neville C., Rector of Haceby 1832–87 (*q.v.*). Educated: Rossall School and Clare College, Cambridge (matric. 1865; BA 1869). Deacon: 1869; priest: 1870 (Ely). Formerly: C. of Swaffham Prior (Ca), 1869–70; of Polstead (Sf), 1870–1; of Freckenham (Sf), 1871–2; R. of Little Steeping, 1872–85; R. of Theddlethorpe St Helen with Mablethorpe St Peter, 1885–92. Afterwards: R. of Wilsford, 1897–1912. Married (31 July 1872) Emily Frances, daughter of Revd Thomas Preston, Vicar of Swaffham Prior. Died 20 December 1912. [Burke, *Landed Gentry* (1921), 263; Venn, *Alumni*; *Crockford* (1898); *Probate Calendar* 1913.]

John Dand Todd BA

Instituted 27 September 1897 to rectory of Newton with Haceby, on cession of Richard Lucas Calcraft. Patron: Sir William Earle Welby Gregory, Bt. [Reg. 42, p.421.]

Born 19 September 1852; son of Thomas T., Rector of Holy Trinity, Hulme (La), as above. Educated: Winchester College (1863; Cricket XI) and Lincoln College, Oxford (matric. 1871; BA 1875). Double Blue, football and sports. Deacon: 1876; priest: 1877 (Manchester). Formerly: C. of St Philip Hulme, Manchester, 1876–8; of St John, Broughton, Manchester, 1878–9; R. of Aunsby, 1883–97. Married (6 August 1878) Alice Gould, daughter of Henry Smith of Horbling. Resided at Newton Rectory. Died 12 August 1912 ('suddenly, after conducting evening service'), aged 59; buried at Newton (MI). [*Winchester College 1836–1906*, 194; Foster, *Alumni* (*sub* 'Todd, Thomas Dand'); *Crockford* (1908); Census Returns 1901; *Wisden* (1913); *Probate Calendar* 1912.]

Joseph Holden Stallard

Instituted 25 October 1912 to rectory of Newton with Haceby, on death of John Dand Todd. Patron: Sir Charles Glynne Earle Welby of Denton Manor (Li), Bt CB. [Reg. 43, p.39.]

Born 7 August 1864; son of Revd Joseph Orlando S., PC of Heath (Bd). Educated: Berkhamsted School and Pembroke College, Cambridge (matric. 1883; BA 1886; MA 1891). Deacon: 1887 (Ripon); priest: 1888 (Ripon for Wakefield). Formerly: C. of Horbury (YWR), 1887 94; V. of Allerton Bywater, 1894–1902; R. of Billington (Bd), 1902–12. Married (16 June 1897) Eva Catherine Beasley. Resided at Newton Rectory. Afterwards: R. of Hinton-on-the-Green (Gl), 1917–24; V. of Hallow (Wo), 1924–34. Retired to live at Worthing: 33 Belsize Road (1941); 145 Brighton Road (1951). Died 9 October 1952 at Worthing. [Venn, *Alumni*; Kelly, *Lincolnshire* (1913), 473; *Crockford* (1951–2).]

Frederick Hyde Adames

Instituted 3 August 1917 to rectory of Newton with Haceby, on cession of Joseph Holden Stallard. Patron: Sir Charles Glynne Earle Welby Bt, as above. [Reg. 43, p.151.]

Born *c.*1873 at Chichester. Educated: University of London (1904). Deacon: 1909 (Lincoln); priest: 1910 (Grantham for Lincoln). Formerly: C. of St Swithin, Lincoln, 1909–11; of St John Baptist, Atherton (La), 1911–17. Resided at Newton Rectory. Afterwards: V. of St John the Divine, Gainsborough, 1926–33; V. of Scothern, 1933–43. Died 4 July 1946. [Census Returns 1911 (Lincoln); *Crockford* (1923, 1941); *LDC* (1947), 179.]

David Jones

Instituted 28 July 1926 to rectory of Newton with Haceby, on cession of

Frederick Hyde Adames. Patron: Sir Charles Glynne Earle Welby Bt, as above. [Reg. 43, p.400.]

Educated: University of Wales (BA 1912); St Michael's College, Llandaff (1912). Deacon: 1913; priest: 1914 (St David's). Formerly: C. of St Paul, Llanelly, 1913–15; of Bolsover, 1915–16; of Elmton (Db), 1916–17; of Willoughby with Sloothby, 1917–24; V. of Killingholme, 1924–6. Resided at Newton Rectory. Also: R. of Sapperton with Braceby, 1933–46. Resigned 25 November (accepted 31 December) 1946. Retired to The Chestnuts, Welby, Grantham. Disappears from *Crockford* after 1965–6. [*Crockford* (1941, 1965–6); RES 1946/24.]

Daniel Stephen Rowlands BA

Instituted 20 March 1947 by the Official *sede vacante* to rectory of Newton with Haceby, on resignation of David Jones. Patron: Sir Oliver Charles Earle Welby Bt. Note that on 26 February 1947, the Archbishop of Canterbury granted a dispensation enabling the said DSR to hold together the rectory of Newton with vicarage of Haceby and the rectory of Sapperton with vicarage of Braceby. [Reg. 44, pp. 70–1.]

Afterwards: V. of Bourne, 1951–8 (*q.v.*).

John Frederick Theodore Martin

Instituted 8 October 1951 to rectory of Newton with vicarage of Haceby, on cession of Daniel Stephen Rowlands. Patron: Sir Oliver Charles Earle Welby of Denton Manor (Li), Bt. Note that on 28 September 1951, the Archbishop of Canterbury granted a dispensation enabling the said JFTM to hold together the rectory of Newton with vicarage of Haceby and the rectory of Sapperton with vicarage of Braceby. [Reg. 44, p.148.]

Born 6 May 1907. Educated: St Andrew's College, Whittlesford. Deacon: 1937; priest: 1938 (Southwell). Formerly: C. of Lowdham (Nt), 1937–47; R. of West Leake with Ratcliffe-on-Soar and Kingston-on-Soar, 1947–51. Resided at Newton Rectory. Also: R. of Sapperton with Braceby, 1951–4. Afterwards: V. of St Barnabas, Pleasley Hill, Mansfield, 1954–5; Chaplain of St Augustine's Hospital, Chartham (K), 1955–78. Latterly at Sherwood, Pilgrim's Lane, Chilham (K). Died 1982. [*Crockford* (1953–4, 1980–2); GRO, Death Index.]

Philip Hawker Hill MA

Instituted 5 November 1954 to rectory of Newton with vicarage of Haceby, on cession of John Frederick Theodore Martin. Patron: Lincoln Diocesan Board of Patronage and Sir Oliver Charles Earle Welby of Denton Manor, Bt, for this turn only. Note that on 9 April 1963, an Order for Plurality was made under Section 5 of the Pastoral Reorganisation Measure 1949, authorising the said PHH to hold the benefices of Aunsby with Dembleby and Newton with Haceby in plurality. [Reg. 44, p.202.]

Born 9 July 1894. Educated: St John's College, Oxford (BA 1921; DipTh 1922; MA 1926). Deacon: 11 June 1922; priest: 5 October 1924 (Durham). Formerly: C. of Houghton-le-Spring (Du), 1922–3; of Ryhope (Du), 1924–8; Vice-Principal, St Michael's UMCA Training College, Likwenu (Nyasaland), 1928–9; Principal, 1929–40; Missioner at Bolotwa (Grahamstown), 1940–54. Resided at Newton Rectory. Also: R. of Aunsby with Dembleby, 1954–72. Resigned 8 November 1972. Retired to live at 16 Ickworth Road, Sleaford. Died 3 April 1975. [*Crockford* (1961–2, 1973–4); Durham UL, DDR/EA/CL; Reg. 44, p.472; *St John's College Register*, 39.]

OSBOURNBY

The church of Osbournby was given to Kyme Priory; it was appropriated and a vicarage was ordained before 1219–20. The Priory continued to present to the vicarage until the Dissolution. The advowson subsequently came into the possession of the Bucke family of Hanby Hall; Sir John Bucke (d.1648) presented to the living in 1630. On the death of the last baronet, Sir Charles Bucke, in 1782, the property passed to his sister Anne, widow of Ambrose Isted of Ecton (Np); she presented in 1784. By 1797 the advowson, with the Hanby Hall estate, had been acquired by Sir William Manners. Through his mother he was the heir to the Earldom of Dysart, and on the death of his uncle in 1821 he took the surname of Talmash (for Tollemache) and was styled Lord Huntingtower. He presented to Osbournby in 1797 and 1826. In the event he died in 1833, seven years before his mother, and it was his son who eventually succeeded to the earldom. After his death the patronage was acquired by the Trustees of William Hulme's Estates, a charitable body that had been authorised by Act of Parliament in 1826 to acquire advowsons. In the first instance the right of presentation was to be exercised by Brasenose College, Oxford, in favour of one of the Hulme Exhibitioners attending that institution. By 1856, however, the Trustees had taken the advowson into their own hands and they made their first presentation in 1863. The Hulme Trustees still held the patronage in 1965. [*VCH Lincoln* ii. 173; *Lincolnshire Pedigrees*, 199–201; *GEC* iv. 565–6; White, *Lincolnshire* (1856), 548; *LDC* (1965), 96–7.]

David de Sancto Botulfo chaplain
Instituted in the eleventh pontifical year of Bishop Hugh of Wells (20 December 1219/19 December 1220) to vicarage of Osbournby. Patron: Prior and Convent of Kyme. [*Rot. Welles* iii. 71, 102.]

Roger de Lafford
Instituted in the twenty-fifth pontifical year of Bishop Hugh of Wells (20 December 1233/19 December 1234) to vicarage of Osbournby. Patron: Prior and Convent of Kyme. [*Rot. Welles* iii. 216.]

Anger de Thorp chaplain
Instituted in the second pontifical year of Bishop Robert Grosseteste (17 June 1236/16 June 1237) to vicarage of Osbournby. Patron: Prior and Convent of Kyme. [Hoskin, no.46.]

Robert de Horbling chaplain
Instituted 6 February 1266/7 to vicarage of Osbournby, on death of Anger.
Patron: Prior and Convent of Kyme. [*Rot. Gravesend*, 23.]

John de Blekiston deacon
Instituted 15 April 1276 to vicarage of Osbournby, on death of Robert. Patron:
Prior and Convent of Kyme. [*Rot. Gravesend*, 68.]
Afterwards: R. of Haceby, 1295–1305 (*q.v.*); R. of Aswarby, 1305.

John de Croketon chaplain
Instituted 17 February 1294/5 to vicarage of Osbournby, vacant because John
the last vicar had received other preferment. Patron: Prior and Convent of
Kyme. [*Reg. Sutton* i. 197.]
Appointed coadjutor of M. William, R. of Newton by Folkingham (*q.v.*), 6 December
1321. [Reg. 5, fo.300.]

Walter
Instituted before 1 August 1349. [Reg. 9, fo.67v.]

John Andrew de Grantham poor priest
Received collation 1 August 1349 from Bishop Gynwell (on the authority of
a papal provision of a benefice in the gift of Prior and Convent of Kyme) of
vicarage of Osbournby, on death of Walter. [Reg. 9, fo.67v.]
Afterwards: Chaplain of St Mary Chantry in Church of Digby, 1368.

Richard son of John son of James de Belton priest
Instituted 25 November 1368 to vicarage of Osbournby, on resignation of
John de Grentham (by exchange with chantry of St Mary, Digby). Patron:
Prior and Convent of Kyme. [Reg. 10, fo.26.]
Formerly: Chaplain of St Mary Chantry in Church of Digby, October–November 1368.
Assessed for poll-tax, 1377, 1381. [Reg. 10, fo.26; *Clerical Poll-Taxes*, nos 683, 1337,
1926.]

William Walmesford priest
Instituted 7 July 1384 to vicarage of Osbournby, on resignation of Richard
son of John son of James de Belton. Patron: Prior and Convent of Kyme.
[Reg. 11, fo.6.]

Henry Repham priest
Instituted 28 September 1392 to vicarage of Osbournby, on death of William.
Patron: Prior and Convent of Kyme. [Reg. 11, fo.60v.]
Afterwards: V. of Leake, 1393–4. [Reg. 11, fo.75.]

John de Foterby priest
Instituted 22 April 1393 to vicarage of Osbournby, on resignation of Henry

de Reffham (by exchange with vicarage of Leake). Patron: Prior and Convent of Kyme. [Reg. 11, fo.65.]

Priest: before 19 January 1385/6. Formerly: V. of Leake, 1386–93. [Reg. 11, fo.21.]

John son of William Lockyng de Waynflet chaplain
Instituted 8 May 1403 to vicarage of Osbournby, on death of John Foterby. Patron: Prior and Convent of Kyme. [Reg. 13, fo.157v.]

Thomas Saperton priest
Instituted 11 October 1410 to vicarage of Osbournby, on resignation of John Lokkyng. Patron: Prior and Convent of Kyme. [Reg. 14, fo.46v.]

Richard son of Geoffrey Colom priest
Instituted 16 August 1421 to vicarage of Osbournby, on death of Thomas Saperton. Patron: Prior and Convent of Kyme. [*Reg. Fleming* i. no.110.]

[Name missing] priest
Instituted 4 August 1427 to vicarage of Osbournby, on resignation of Richard Colne. Patron: Prior and Convent of Kyme. [*Reg. Fleming* i. no.286.]

[The name is left blank in the register. Richard Frodesham vacated the vicarage by resignation before 29 October 1431. See below.]

Richard Frodesham
Instituted before 29 October 1431.

Perhaps instituted 13 April 1393 (above).

William Grayfe priest
Instituted 29 October 1431 to vicarage of Osbournby, on resignation of Richard Frodesham. Patron: Prior and Convent of Kyme. [Reg. 17, fo.2.]

Thomas Trowdon priest
Instituted 9 April 1439 to vicarage of Osbournby, on death of William. Patron: Prior and Convent of Kyme. [Reg. 18, fo.81v.]

Robert Layke priest
Instituted 27 March 1483 to vicarage of Osbournby, on resignation of Thomas Denton *alias* Trowton. Patron: Prior and Convent of Kyme. [Reg. 22, fo.132.]

M. Thomas Gamull
Instituted by 1500. [Vj 5, fo.57.]

Thomas Maltby chaplain
Instituted 7 November 1505 to vicarage of Osbournby, on death of M. Thomas Gammut. Patron: Prior and Convent of Kyme. [Reg. 23, fo.103.]

Thomas Perch chaplain

Instituted 5 September 1508 to vicarage of Osbournby, on death of Thomas Maltby. Patron: Prior and Convent of Kyme. [Reg. 23, fo.132v.]

William Durham chaplain

Instituted *c*. January 1509/10 to vicarage of Osbournby, on death of Thomas Perch. Patron: Prior and Convent of Kyme. [Reg. 23, fo.139.]

(Date of institution omitted in register.) Assessed for subsidy (£5 13s 4d) in 1526. Will dated 20 March 1528/9, proved 27 September 1530. To be buried in church of SS Peter and Paul, Osbournby; legacies to churches of Scredington, Spanby, Stow-by-Threckingham, Walcot, Newton-by-Folkingham, Threckingham, Scott Willoughby, Aunsby and Aswarby; to the three gilds within Osbournby church; to the bells and the light of All Saints there. [*Subsidy*, 57; *Lincoln Wills* ii. 117–18.]

Thomas Jordan

Instituted 14 April 1529 to vicarage of Osbournby, on death of William Doram. Patron: Prior and Convent of Kyme. [Reg. 27, fo.44v.]

M. Thomas Jordan

Instituted 2 August 1529 to vicarage of Osbournby, on resignation of Thomas Jordan. Patron: Prior and Convent of Kyme. [Reg. 27, fo.45v.]

Edward Pratt chaplain

Instituted 26 February 1531/2. Patron: William Hall, Prior of Haverholme (by reason of a grant from Prior and Convent of Kyme). [Reg. 27, fo.52v.]

Assessed for *Valor Ecclesiasticus* 1535. RD of Aveland; exhibited at Visitation in 1551. [*Valor* iv. 106; Vj 13, fo.62v.]

Charles Welles

Instituted *c*.1555 (compounded for first-fruits, 21 June 1555). [FL.h.12, p.622.]

Died November 1569. Witnessed Osbournby wills, 1557–68. Will dated 5 November, proved 15 November 1569. Probate inventory dated 12 November 1569. [LCC Wills 1557/i/388; 1557/iii/15v; 1558/i/202v; 1558/iiii/15v; 1561/97, 113v, 218, 252; 1562/38, 273; 1563/69; 1564/47v; 1568/113, 250; 1569/i/62; INV 49/255.]

Clement Browne

Instituted *c*.1569. Patron: Queen Elizabeth I (24 November 1569). [FL.h.19, p.32.]

Born *c*.1538. Educated: Trinity College, Cambridge (matric. 1560; BA 1564–5) and Queens' College, Cambridge (MA 1568). Priest: 11 June 1564 (Lincoln). Resident (1576). Died *c*.1581. Will (LCC), dated 12 December 1581; proved 2 January 1581/2. Desired 'that Mr Cantrell shall have the chose of all my books to ellecte as he will and what he will'. [Venn, *Alumni*; *Bishop Cooper*, 207, 220; LCC Wills 1581/184; INV 66/262.]

Miles Whale BA

Instituted 2 February 1581/2 to vicarage of Osbournby, on death of Clement Browne. Patron: Queen Elizabeth I. [*Bishop Cooper*, 29.]

Educated: Christ's College, Cambridge (BA 1576–7). Deacon: 2 February 1581/2; priest: 6 July 1583 (Lincoln). Also: R. of Scott Willoughby, 1590–1630 (*q.v.*). Resident at Osbournby (1611, 1614); signed BTs 1586–1628. [Venn, *Alumni*; *Bishop Cooper*, 94, 97; LC 3, fos 3, 4; LC 4, fo.73.]

William Bardon BA

Instituted 22 July 1630 to vicarage of Osbournby, on death of Miles Whale. Patron: Sir John Bucke of Filey (Yorks), kt (15 July 1630). Inducted 25 July 1630 by Richard Pell, clerk. [PD 1630/38; IND/L 1, fo.88.]

Educated: St John's College, Cambridge (matric. 1619). Deacon: October 1627; priest: 23 December 1627 (Sodor and Man). Licensed preacher 1634. Resident (1662); signed BTs 1632–41, 1661–81. Prosecuted before Committee of Plundered Ministers, 1646; no evidence of sequestration. Buried at Osbournby, 26 April 1681. [Venn, *Alumni*; LC 5, fo.23v; BTs Osbournby; *Walker Revised*, 248; Foster, *Plundered Ministers*, 83–5.]

George Dickins

Appointed sequestrator 7 November 1681. Licensed curate same day. [LC 14, fo.6v.]

Priest: 21 December 1679 (Lincoln). Resident; signed BTs 1682–1720. Buried at Osbournby, 3 June 1720. [LC 14, fo.6v; *Speculum*, 93; PR Osbournby.]

John Burman MA

Instituted 8 September 1720 to vicarage of Osbournby, on death of George Dickins. Patron: Sir Charles Buck Bt. [Reg. 37, p.105.]

Born at Stamford. Educated: Clare Hall, Cambridge (matric. 1706; BA 1709–10; MA 1714). Deacon: 5 July 1713 (Lincoln). Formerly: C. of Burton Coggles, 1713; C. of Harston (Le), 1716; V. of Buckminster (Le), 1718–20. Also: V. of Scalford (Le), 1720–6; R. of Denton, 1726–30. Non-resident at Osbournby; BTs signed by Ralph Winterton as curate. Resided at Denton 'where he is Tutor to the sons of Mistress Welby'. Died 1730. Will (LCC), dated 12 January 1729/30. Bequeathed to Osbournby Church 'a Silver Salver for the Communion bread'. [Venn, *Alumni*; Reg. 36, p.197; Reg. 37, pp. 19, 50; BTs Osbournby; *Speculum*, 93; LCC Wills 1730/32.]

John Denison

Instituted 26 August 1730 to vicarage of Osbournby, on death of John Burman. Patron: Anne Buck of Hanby, widow. [Reg. 38, p.230.]

Born *c*.1687 at Furness (La); son of Samuel D., gent. Educated: Kendal School and St John's College, Cambridge (matric. 1705; BA 1708–9). Deacon: 23 September 1710 (Peterborough); priest: 15 August 1714 (Lincoln). Formerly: C. of Lavington, 1714; Master of Charity School at Folkingham (founded by Richard Brocklesby, Rector), 1718. Also: C. of Walcot. Signed BTs at Osbournby 1731–62. Resigned 11 April (accepted 8 June) 1763. [*St John's Admissions* ii. 174; Venn, *Alumni*; Longden iv. 59; *Speculum*, 78; Reg. 36, p.238; SUB V/6, fo.95; LC 18B, p.198; BTs Osbournby; RES 238/89.]

Isaac Cookson

Instituted 8 June 1763 to vicarage of Osbournby, on resignation of John
Denison. Patron: Sir Charles Buck Bt (25 April 1763). [Reg. 39, p.18; PD
1763/2.]

Priest: 10 June 1750 (Lincoln). Also: PC of Walcot, 1750–84 (*q.v.*); C. of Folkingham,
1751–84; Master of Folkingham GS, 1768–75; V. of Helpringham, 1769–84. Died 23
February 1784, aged 57; buried in Folkingham Church, by the altar (MI). 'He was a
learned, charitable & good man, and a true Christian.' [Reg. 38, p.496; LIC/PC&SCH/3/3;
LIC/SCH 2/19; PR Folkingham; *Monson*, 127.]

Robert Drury Rye MA

Instituted 7 May 1784 to vicarage of Osbournby, on death of Isaac Cookson.
Patron: Ann Isted of Walcot (Somerset), widow. [Reg. 39, p.411.]

Born *c*.1757; son of William Beauchamp R. of Northampton, doctor. Educated: Christ
Church (matric. 1776) and Magdalen College, Oxford (BA 1780; MA 1782); Demy
1776–80. Non-resident at Osbournby, which was served by John Nicholson as curate
(signed BTs 1784–1805). Died 1796 at Culworth (Np). [Foster, *Alumni*; Bloxam vii. 54;
BTs Osbournby]

John Corrie

Instituted 10 January 1797 to vicarage of Osbournby, on death of Drury Rye.
Patron: Sir William Manners of Hanby (9 December 1796). [Reg. 39, p.626;
PD 153/70.]

Also: C. of Colsterworth, 1787–1825; C. of Skillington, 1816. Non-resident at Osbournby
on account of unfitness of Vicarage House; resided at Colsterworth. Afterwards: R. of
Morcott (Ru), 1825–9. Died April 1829. Father of Daniel C. (1777–1837), First Bishop of
Madras. [PR Colsterworth; Reg. 39, p.479; CR 1, p.69; NRL 1804/6; NRL 1806/28; NRL
1808/33; NRL 1810/25; NRL 1814/23; Longden iii. 253; Venn, *Alumni*.]

John Pearson

Instituted 28 July 1826 to vicarage of Osbournby, on cession of John Corrie.
Patron: Lord Huntingtower. [Reg. 40, p.347.]

Baptised 26 October 1783 at Farndon (Nt). Education: literate. Deacon: 19 December
1813 (York); priest: 17 May 1818 (Lincoln). Formerly: C. of Ossett, 1813; of Stoke Rochford, 1815–24. Also: C. of Newton, 1827. Resided at Osbournby; built new Vicarage
House 1827 (John Johnson of Osbournby, surveyor and builder). Died 7 July 1863; buried
at Osbournby (MI). [*York Ordinations 1800–1849*, 144; Reg. 40, p.267; CR 1, pp. 89, 344;
MGA 138; White, *Lincolnshire* (1842), 659; *Bonney's Church Notes*, 228; Census Returns
1851, 1861; *Probate Calendar* 1863.]

Thomas Molineux Jackson MA

Instituted 6 November 1863 to vicarage of Osbournby, on death of John
Pearson. Patron: Trustees of William Hulme's estates. [Reg. 41, p.106.]

Born *c*.1822; son of Revd John J. of Bowdon (Chs). Educated: Brasenose College, Oxford
(matric. 1842; BA 1846; MA 1848). Deacon: 1848; priest: 1849 (Chester). Formerly: C.
of Over (Chs), 1848–52; PC of Little Marsden (La), 1852–63. Married (28 October 1858)
at Calderbridge (Cu), Mary, daughter of Revd John Hutchinson. Resided at Osbournby

Vicarage ('a handsome brick residence, with stone facings, rebuilt in 1864 by the present incumbent'). Osbournby Church was restored in 1873 during his incumbency. Resigned 6 April 1876. Afterwards lived at 4 Sussex Road, Southport. Latterly of Rosehill, Bowdon. Died 20 March 1894. [Foster, *Alumni*; *Brasenose Register*; *Crockford* (1885); *Carlisle Journal*, 5 November 1858; Census Returns 1871; White, *Lincolnshire* (1872), 567–8; *Grantham Journal*, 18 October 1873; RES A/12; *Probate Calendar* 1894.]

John Charles Bagshaw MA

Instituted 29 September 1876 to vicarage of Osbournby, on resignation of Thomas Molineux Jackson. Patron: Trustees of William Hulme's estates. [Reg. 41, p.537.]

Born *c*.1819; son of Thomas B. of Mossley near Ashton-under-Lyne (Chs), gent. Educated: Manchester GS and Brasenose College, Oxford (matric. 1840; BA 1844; MA 1846). Deacon: 1845; priest: 1846 (Chester). Formerly: C. of Deane (La), 1845–6; Mission Chaplain in South Australia, 1847–55; Mission Chaplain in New Zealand, 1855–69; Domestic Chaplain to Viscount Hill, 1871–5. Resided at Osbournby Vicarage. Died 17 May 1899. [Foster, *Alumni*; *Brasenose Register*; *Crockford* (1898); Census Returns 1881, 1891; *Probate Calendar* 1899.]

Alfred Bedson MA

Instituted 16 October 1899 to vicarage of Osbournby, on death of John Charles Bagshaw. Patron: Trustees of estates devised by William Hulme esquire. [Reg. 42, p.451.]

Born *c*.1855. Educated: Brasenose College, Oxford (matric. 1875; BA 1879; MA 1882). Deacon: 1882; priest: 1883 (Liverpool). Formerly: C. of Christ Church, Eccleston (La), 1882–5; of Burgh-le-Marsh with Winthorpe, 1885–6; of Braunston (Np), 1886–90; of Heydour, 1890–2; V. of Goodshaw (La), 1892–9. Resided at Osbournby Vicarage. Bishop Hicks noted (1917) 'an amusing, yet painful account' of a visit to Osbournby by C. G. Biddle (V. of Bardney) in connection with the National Mission: 'Found the altar v. untidy & the hangings thread-bare & cobwebbed … [After evening service], a *scene!* Fierce wrath of the Bedsons: Mrs B. whimpering, "Why, I took those hangings from my own dining room!" "Yes": said Biddle: "they had ceased to be good enough for your house, but you thought they would do for the House of God".' Also: R. of Scott Willoughby, 1906 (*q.v.*). Retired 1931. Latterly of Elm Cottage, Belton Lane, Grantham. Died there 25 November 1933; buried at Osbournby (MI). [Foster, *Alumni*; *Brasenose Register*, 640; *Crockford* (1932); Kelly, *Lincolnshire* (1913), 478; *Hicks Diaries*, no.1034; *Probate Calendar* 1934.]

The Rectory of Scott Willoughby was united to the Vicarage of Osbournby by Order in Council dated 26 May 1925. [Reg. 43, p.364.]

Jonathan Alfred Willmott Elwell BA

Instituted 24 November 1931 to united benefice of Osbournby with Scott Willoughby, on resignation of Alfred Bedson. Patron: Trustees of estates devised by William Hulme esquire, for this alternate turn. [Reg. 43, p.497.]

Born 1880 at Littlemore (Ox); son of Revd George Henry Elwell. Educated: St Catherine's Society, Oxford (BA 1910); Ridley Hall, Cambridge (1928). Schoolmaster, Incorporated

Thames Nautical Training College, HMS *Warspite* at Swanscombe (K), 1911. Married (7 June 1919) at St Stephen, Kirkstall, Ethel Mary Cook, widow. Deacon: 1929; priest: 1930 (Chelmsford). Formerly: C. of St Thomas, Becontree, 1929–31. Resided at Osbournby Vicarage. Also: R. of Aswarby with Swarby, 1945–62. Resignation accepted 31 December 1962. Retired; lived at 177 Brownhill Road, London SE6. Died 1967. [GRO, Birth Index; Census Returns 1891 (Brockley), 1911 (Swanscombe); WYAS, PR Kirkstall St Stephen; *Crockford* (1965–6); Reg. 44, p.341; GRO, Death Index.]

Frank Reginald Money MA

Instituted 8 March 1966 to united benefice of Osbournby with Scott Willoughby, on resignation of Jonathan Alfred Willmott Elwell. Note that on 1 November 1965, an Order for Plurality was made under Section 5 of the Pastoral Reorganisation Measure 1949, authorising the said FRM to hold the benefices of Folkingham with Laughton, Osbournby with Scott Willoughby, Pickworth with Walcot, and Threckingham in plurality. [Reg. 44, p.383.]

Also: R. of Folkingham, 1960–8 (*q.v.*).

PICKWORTH

The advowson of Pickworth belonged to the manor in the Longespee fee, held by Hugh de Pikeword in 1242–3 and by his son John in 1303. Adam de Pikworth presented in 1331 but by 1349 the patronage had passed to the Lovet family. During the fifteenth century a number of different patrons were involved in presentations, but in 1491 it was expressly stated that the advowson was attached to the manor held as feoffee by Margaret, widow of William Armine of Osgodby (d.1488) and then wife of John Stanlow. The Armine family continued to present through most of the sixteenth and seventeenth centuries. By 1722 the patronage had been acquired by the Carter family of Redbourne, whose heiress, Charlotte, daughter of Robert Carter Thelwall, married in 1791 Lord William Beauclerk, future Duke of St Albans. Lord William presented to the living in 1814. By the time of the next vacancy, the advowson had been sold to John Nicholas Andrews who presented himself in 1867. In 1918, under the terms of the wills of Mr Andrews and of his daughter, the advowson was transferred to the Dean and Chapter of Lincoln. The Chapter still held it in 1965. [*Book of Fees*, 1029; *Feudal Aids* iii. 135; Reg. 22, fo.147; *Lincolnshire Pedigrees*, 41–2; *GEC* xi. 291–2; *London Gazette* (30771), 28 June 1918; *LDC* (1965), 66–7.]

Roger de Pikewrd chaplain

Instituted in the eighteenth pontifical year of Bishop Hugh of Wells (20 December 1226/19 December 1227) to church of Pickworth. Patron: William de Newetun, by reason of his custody of the land and heir of Robert de Pikewrd. [*Rot. Welles* iii. 153.]

Richard de Stretton subdeacon
Instituted in the eighth pontifical year of Bishop Robert Grosseteste (17 June 1242/16 June 1243) to church of Pickworth. Patron: Hugh de Pikeword. [Hoskin, no.256.]

Alan de Stratton chaplain
Instituted 28 September 1273 to church of Pickworth, on death of Richard. Patron: John son of Hugh de Pykeword. [*Rot. Gravesend*, 279.]

Robert de Pykkewrth clerk
Instituted 22 December 1296 to church of Pickworth, on death of Alan de Stretton. Patron: John son of Hugh de Pikwrth. The advowson had been disputed by Robert Cosyn, who presented William de Roppele but subsequently withdrew his claim. [*Reg. Sutton* i. 215.]

Subdeacon: 22 December 1296; deacon: 8 June 1297; priest: 21 September 1297 (Lincoln). [*Reg. Sutton* vii. 87, 93, 98.]

Simon de Stowe chaplain
Instituted 12 March 1306/7 to church of Pickworth, on death of Robert. Patron: John de Picworth. [Reg. 2, fo.19.]

Formerly: V. of Dorrington, 1277–1307. [*Rot. Gravesend*, 78; Reg. 2, fo.19v.]

William son of Adam de Strubby clerk
Instituted 8 April 1331 to church of Pickworth, on death of Simon de Stowe. Patron: Adam de Pikworth. [*Reg. Burghersh* i. no.293.]

Acolyte: by 20 March 1331/2; deacon: by 26 January 1332/3. Dispensations to study for 1 year, 20 March 1331/2 (in England or abroad); for 1 year (in England), 26 January 1332/3. Licence to be in service of Ralph de Strubby, Rector of Gayton le Marsh, for 1 year, 24 February 1333/4. Licence to study in England for 1 year, 12 October 1339. [*Reg. Burghersh* iii. nos 594, 614, 1179; Reg. 5, fo.200.]

Walter
Instituted before 14 August 1349. [Reg. 9, fo.62v.]

Robert de Thirford priest
Instituted 14 August 1349 to church of Pickworth, on death of Walter. Patron: John Lovet de Neuton. [Reg. 9, fo.62v.]

John de Saperton clerk
Instituted 2 October 1369 to church of Pickworth, on death of Robert de Thirisford. Patron: Robert Mortimer de Ingoldesby and William Pylet de Skredyngton. [Reg. 10, fo.33v.]

Subdeacon: 8 June 1370 (London). JS's estate in the church ratified by the King, 20 June 1374. Assessed for poll-tax, 1377. [*Reg. Sudbury* ii. 84; *CPR 1370–74*, 443; *Clerical Poll-Taxes*, no. 699.]

Edmund de Fulbek priest
Instituted 23 December 1378 to church of Pickworth, on death of John de
Sap[er]ton. Patron: William de Boston and John Lovet. [Reg. 10, fo.92v.]

M. J[ohn] Thomas
Instituted 27 August 1379 to church of Pickworth (cause of vacancy not
stated). Patron: Bishop of Lincoln, by lapse. [Reg. 10, fo.97.]

Relative of Bishop Buckingham. Educated: Oxford University; LLB by October 1382.
Dispensations for study for 3 years, 6 May 1380; for 5 years, 26 November 1382. Assessed
for poll-tax in 1381. Commission from Bishop Buckingham, October 1382. Afterwards:
R. of Wheathampstead (Hrt), 1386–91. [Emden, *BRUO*, 1861; Reg. 12, fos 200, 248,
251v; *Clerical Poll-Taxes*, nos 1333, 1922; Reg. 11, fos 251, 265.]

John Atteloft de Stepynge clerk
Instituted 2 May 1386 to church of Pickworth, on resignation of M. John
Thomas (by exchange with church of Wheathampstead). Patron: William
Boston *domicellus*. [Reg. 11, fo.23.]

Formerly: R. of Wheathampstead (Hrt), to 1386.

John Mapulton the elder, priest
Instituted 29 June 1407 to church of Pickworth, on death of John Stepyng.
Patron: Bishop of Lincoln, by lapse. [Reg. 14, fo.19.]

John Smyth priest
Instituted 29 February 1424 to church of Pickworth, on resignation of John
Mapelton. Patron: John Walcote of Walcot, Thomas Repynghale of Rippin-
gale, Ralph Saperton of Pickworth and William Clerk of Thorpe. [*Reg.
Fleming* i. no.235.]

John Spaldyng
Instituted before 5 March 1433/4. [Reg. 17, fo.9.]

John Sherman priest
Instituted 5 March 1433/4 to church of Pickworth, on resignation of John
Spaldyng. Patron: Ralph Saperton of Pickworth, John Walcote of Walcot,
Thomas Repynghale of Rippingale and William Clerk of Thorpe. [Reg. 17,
fo.9.]

Thomas Wade priest
Instituted 4 June 1444 to church of Pickworth (cause of vacancy not stated).
Patron: Thomas Rypynghale and William Lascy. [Reg. 18, fo.94v.]

William Pety clerk
Instituted 26 May 1465 to church of Pickworth (cause of vacancy not stated).
Patron: Walter Blyssotte and John Williamson. [Reg. 20, fo.140v.]

Thomas Gannell MA priest

Instituted 19 September 1491 to church of St Andrew, Pickworth, on resignation of William Pety. Patron: John Stanlowe of the City of Lincoln, esquire, and Margaret his wife (formerly widow of William Ermyn late of Osgodby), in right of the said Margaret as feoffee of the manor of Pickworth to which the advowson of the church appertains. Note that an annual pension of 5 marks was reserved to William Pety for life from the fruits of the church. [Reg. 22, fo.147.]

Richard Jercoke priest

Instituted 18 April 1497 to church of Pickworth, on resignation of M. Thomas Gammull. Patron: John Doo de Pykworth for this turn, by reason of his mediety of the manor of Pickworth. [Reg. 23, fo.37v.]

Thomas Spenslay chaplain

Instituted 23 September 1508 to church of Pickworth, on death of Richard Jerkok. Patron: William Armyn esquire. [Reg. 23, fo.132v.]

Richard Ward chaplain

Instituted 18 December 1516 to church of Pickworth, on death of Thomas Spenceley. Patron: John Doo. [Reg. 25, fo.15.]

Assessed for subsidy (£11 6s 8d) in 1526; assessed for *Valor Ecclesiasticus* 1535. Was bequeathed a sarsnet tippet by Edmund Thakware of Aslackby in 1533/4. Buried at Pickworth ('Magister Ricardus Warde'), 4 December 1549. [*Subsidy*, 58; *Valor* iv. 104; *Lincoln Wills* iv. no.387; PR Pickworth.]

Robert Cooke clerk

Instituted 15 May 1550 to church of Pickworth, on death of Thomas [*recte* Richard] Warde. Patron: William Armyn of Osgodby, esquire. [Reg. 28, fo.24; *Bishop Cooper*, 220.]

Born *c*.1512. Education: 'bred in the schools'; 'is skilled in Latin; well versed in sacred learning'. Priest: 15 May 1550 (Lincoln). Resident; exhibited at Visitation in 1551. Deprived (perhaps for marriage) 1554 but subsequently restored. Witnessed Pickworth wills, 1564, 1569. Signed BTs 1562–97. Buried at Pickworth, 27 September 1597. [*Bishop Cooper*, 208, 220; *State of the Church*, 74; Vj 13, fo.63; LCC Wills 1564/60v; 1569/i/53v; BTs Pickworth; PR Pickworth.]

Robert Bacare clerk

Instituted 1554 to church of Pickworth, on deprivation of Robert Cooke. Patron: William Armyn esquire. [Reg. 28, fo.111v.]

Robert Cooke

Restored before 22 August 1563 when Joanna Cooke wife of Robert Cooke, Rector, was buried. [PR Pickworth.]

William Mapletoft BA
Instituted 2 November 1597 to rectory of Pickworth, on death of last incumbent. [Reg. 30, fo.77.]

Born at Barkston (Li). Educated: Trinity College, Cambridge (matric. 1583). Deacon: 24 February 1587/8 ; priest: 21 December 1588 (London). Resident (1611, 1614); signed BTs 1599–1625. Buried at Pickworth, 16 November 1624. Will (LCC). [Venn, *Alumni*; LC 3, fo.3; LC 4, fo.73; BTs Pickworth; PR Pickworth; LCC Wills 1624/366.]

John Weld
Instituted 25 November 1624 to rectory of Pickworth, on death of William Mapletofte. Patron: Sir William Armine Bt (15 November 1624). Inducted 3 December 1624 by Tempest Wood, V. of Lavington. [Lib. Inst., fo.113; PD 1624/64; IND/L 1, fo.67.]

Education: perhaps to be identified with JW of Christ's College, Cambridge (matric. 1607; BA 1611; MA 1614). Resident: signed BTs 1626–41. Married (1) Elinor, buried at Pickworth 19 October 1630; (2) Elizabeth, buried at Pickworth 11 September 1638 (both described as 'uxor charissima et dilectissima'). Sons John (1638) and Joseph (1642) baptised at Pickworth. Resigned 1646. Afterwards: R. of Bildeston (Sf), 1643–63; deprived. Died 1665; will (of Bildeston) dated 10 March 1664/5, proved 13 August 1665. [BTs Pickworth; PR Pickworth; *Calamy Revised*, 517.]

Michael Drake
Instituted 17 March 1646/7 to rectory of Pickworth. [Lib. Inst., fo.113.]

Born *c.*1622; son of John D. of Pikeley, Bradford. Educated: Halifax School; Magdalene College (matric. 1639) and St John's College, Cambridge (BA 1642–3; MA 1647). Member of Folkingham Classis and Tuesday Lecturer at Grantham. Ejected for nonconformity 1662. Afterwards lived at Fulbeck 'in a mean Habitation', preaching in Lincoln on Saturday evenings in John Disney's house. Licensed to preach at his house in Fulbeck, 16 May 1672. Latterly moved to Lincoln. Father of Joshua D., Vicar of Swinderby (1692–1728). Died 1696. [Venn, *Alumni*; *Calamy Revised*, 170; PR Pickworth.]

William Cooper MA
Instituted 11 April 1663 to rectory of Pickworth, on deprivation of Michael Drake. Patron: Lady Mary Armin of St Martin's (Mx), widow (9 April 1663). [Reg. 33, fo.2; PD 1663/61.]

Signed BTs at Pickworth 1663–75. Buried at Pickworth, 23 December 1675. [BTs Pickworth; PR Pickworth.]

Nathaniel Brown MA
Instituted 22 May 1676 to rectory of Pickworth, on death of William Cooper. Patron: Evers Armyne, esquire. [Reg. 34, fo.7v.]

Perhaps to be identified with NB son of Edward B. (Vicar of All Saints, Stamford), educated Oundle School and St Catharine's Hall, Cambridge (matric. 1665; BA 1668–9; MA 1672). Deacon and priest: 22 May 1676 (Lincoln). Signed BTs at Pickworth 1677. Buried at Pickworth, 17 February 1677/8. [Venn, *Alumni*; Reg. 34, fo.7v; PR Pickworth.]

Peter Clarke BA
Instituted 20 March 1677/8 to rectory of Pickworth, on death of Nathaniel Browne. Patron: Evers Armyne, esquire. [Reg. 34, fo.26.]

Priest: 20 March 1677/8 (London). Signed BTs at Pickworth 1679–1703. Married Phoebe: children Maria (1679), Anna (1680) and Edward (1682) baptised at Pickworth. Buried at Pickworth, 15 May 1703 (MI). Will (PCC) dated 9 May 1703, proved 11 August 1703. To be buried 'with smalle charge and noe pompe' in the chancel of Pickworth Church. [Reg. 34, fo.26; PR Pickworth; *Monson*, 285; PRO, PROB 11/471, fos 152v–154v.]

John Thompson MA
Inducted 13 November 1703 to rectory of Pickworth, on death of Peter Clerke. Patron: Faith Henneage, widow (28 September 1703). [IND/L 2, fo.25v; PD 1703/36.]

Born *c*.1674 at Wainfleet; son of Thomas T. Educated: Christ's College, Cambridge (matric. 1691; BA 1694–5; MA 1698). Deacon: 28 February 1696/7; priest: 19 June 1698 (Lincoln). Formerly: C. of Skegness, 1697; R. of Boothby Graffoe, 1702–3. Resident: signed BTs at Pickworth 1704–21. Buried at Pickworth, 18 February 1721/2. Will (LCC), dated 4 February 1721/2. [Venn, *Alumni*; Reg. 35, fos 39, 49; *Speculum*, 95; BTs Pickworth; PR Pickworth; LCC Wills 1721/i/165.]

Edward Tushingham
Instituted 17 March 1721/2 to rectory of Pickworth, on death of John Thompson. Patron: William Carter, esquire (for this turn). [Reg. 37, p.152.]

Born 1696; son of Thomas T. of London, gent. Educated: Jesus College, Cambridge (matric. 1715; BA 1718–19; MA 1722). Deacon: 18 February 1721/2; priest: 14 March 1721/2 (Ely). Resigned 25 March 1723. Afterwards: R. of Porlock (So), 1723–34. Buried at Porlock, 26 May 1734. [Venn, *Alumni*; PR Pickworth; Weaver, *Somerset Incumbents*, 421; PR Porlock.]

Roger Mostyn MA
Instituted 31 July 1723 to rectory of Pickworth, on cession of Edward Thusingham. Patron: William Carter, esquire (18 July 1723). [Reg. 38, p.7; PD 103/11.]

Born *c*.1696; son of John M. of Castle (Mont), clerk. Educated: Jesus College, Oxford (matric. 1713; BA 1717; MA 1720). Deacon: 21 December 1718; priest: 18 December 1720 (Oxford). Also: R. of Whitford (Flints), 1722; R. of Castle Caereinion (Mont), 1727–61. Non-resident at Pickworth. Resigned Pickworth, 25 March 1726. Died 13 July 1761. [Foster, *Alumni*; ORO, MS. Oxf. Dioc. Papers c.266, fos 39, 42; BTs Pickworth; PR Pickworth.]

John Owen
Instituted 5 May 1726 to rectory of Pickworth, on cession of Roger Mostyn. Patron: William Carter of Brigg, esquire (25 April 1726). [Reg. 38, p.126; PD 103/56.]

Born *c*.1698. Educated: All Souls College, Oxford (BA). Deacon: 22 September 1723 (Lincoln). Formerly: C. of Fenny Drayton (Le), 1723; C. of Saltfleetby St Peter, 1724. Signed BTs at Pickworth 1730–71. Also: C. of Newton-by-Folkingham, 1740–68 (*q.v.*).

Died 11 August 1771, aged 73; buried at Pickworth (MI). [Reg. 38, pp. 9, 52; SUB VII, pp. 26–7, 64, 127; BTs Pickworth; LC 31, pp. 76–7; PR Pickworth; *Monson*, 285.]

Jeoffry Snelson MA

Instituted 13 March 1772 by collation to rectory of Pickworth, on death of John Owen. Patron: Bishop of Lincoln (by lapse). Reinstituted 17 October 1772, on his own cession; patron, Robert Carter of Redbourne, clerk. Vacated by resignation, accepted 10 May 1775. [Reg. 39, pp. 172, 188, 254.]

Born *c*.1740; son of Thomas S. of Eccleshall (St), gent. Educated: Oriel College, Oxford (matric. 1757; BA 1761; MA 1764). Deacon: 25 September 1763; priest: 23 September 1764 (Coventry and Lichfield). Formerly: C. of Tamworth, 1763. Also: V. of Hanbury (St), 1772–90. Resigned Pickworth 5 April 1775. Afterwards: V. of Hendon (Mx), 1790; V. of Reigate (Sr), 1782–1812. Married (1779) at Lambeth, Mary Filewood. Father of Richard Filewood S. (Vicar of Reigate 1812–47). Catalogued parochial library at Reigate. Died 11 April 1812. [Foster, *Alumni*; CCED; PR Pickworth; *Canterbury Act Books* ii. 310; Brayley, *History of Surrey* (1841), 238; Perkins, 328–9.]

Thomas Hurst LLB

Instituted 27 May 1775 to rectory of Pickworth, on resignation of Jeoffry Snelson. Patron: Robert Carter Thelwall of Redbourne, clerk. [Reg. 39, p.254.]

Born *c*.1741; son of Rupert H. of Cheadle (St). Educated: St Mary Hall, Oxford (matric. 1761; BCL 1768). Deacon: 5 July 1767; priest: 28 February 1768. Formerly: C. of Cheadle, 1767. Also: R. of Stanford-on-Soar (Nt), 1775–1800. Non-resident at Pickworth: 'Absent: lives at Stanford near Loughborough' (1778); 'Illness and infirmity of body' (1803, 1808). Pickworth was served by Isaac Wilson as curate, 1772–1832. Resigned 31 March (accepted 2 April) 1814. [Foster, *Alumni*; CCED; LC 31, p.77; NRL 1803/50; NRL 1806/12; NRL 1808/2; NRL 1810/7; BTs Pickworth; CR 1, p.32; Godfrey, *Notts Churches: Ruschliffe*, 234; *Monson*, 285; RES 240/47.]

Thomas Skipworth

Instituted 21 May 1814 to rectory of Pickworth, on resignation of Thomas Hurst. Patron: Hon. William Beauclerk, commonly called Lord William Beauclerk (20 May 1814). [Reg. 40, p.199; PD 170/40.]

Baptised 15 October 1785 at Aylesby; son of Philip S. Education: literate. Deacon: 24 May 1812; priest: 20 June 1813 (Lincoln). Formerly: C. of North Kelsey, 1812. Also: PC of Belton-in-Axholme, 1814–67. Resided at Belton in the Rectory House ('a neat mansion, with tasteful pleasure-grounds') until 1855; Pickworth was served by curates, including William Handley Bland (1833–55). While at Belton he engaged in commercial activities, which resulted in a Fiat in Bankruptcy being declared (25 January 1847) against him as 'Thomas Skipworth of Belton … Clerk, Miller, Brick Maker, Dealer and Chapman'. Resident at Pickworth, 1855–62. Died 10 May 1867 at Folkingham; buried at Belton. [PR Aylesby; Reg. 40, pp. 170, 188; White, *Lincolnshire* (1842), 544; Census Returns 1841, 1851 (Belton), 1861 (Pickworth); CR 2, p.63; *London Gazette* (20763), 10 August 1847; PR Pickworth; PR Belton-in-Axholme.]

John Nicholas Andrews MA

Instituted 2 July 1867 to rectory of Pickworth, on death of Thomas Skipworth. Patron: John Nicholas Andrews, himself. [Reg. 41, p.226.]

Born 20 March, baptised 30 March 1820 at St Wulfram, Grantham; son of Robert Gordon A., Head Master of Grantham School, and Jane Elizabeth his wife, daughter of Revd John Wilson, V. of Leighton Buzzard (Bd). Brother of Christopher Robert A., Vicar of Hough-on-the-Hill (1855–1900). Educated: Clare Hall, Cambridge (matric. 1839; BA 1843; MA 1846). Deacon: 11 June 1843; priest: 2 June 1844 (Lincoln). Formerly: C. of Aswarby, 1843; of Baston, 1847–62. Resided at Pickworth where he built a new Rectory House (1867). Married (1 May 1849) at Bourne, Elizabeth, daughter of John Mawby (and sister of Mary Anne, wife of Christopher Robert Andrews above). Died 13 May 1905; buried at Pickworth, 13 May 1905 (MI). [PR Grantham St Wulfram; Venn, *Alumni*; OR 1, pp. 92, 96; CR 3, fos 39, 100; *Crockford* (1898); Census Returns 1851, 1861 (Baston); PR Baston; White, *Lincolnshire* (1872), 587; Census Returns 1871–1901 (Pickworth); PR Bourne; *Probate Calendar* 1905; PR Pickworth.]

William Christopher Houghton MA

Instituted 16 October 1905 to rectory of Pickworth, on death of John Nicholas Andrews. Patron: Elizabeth Charlotte Andrews of Pickworth, spinster, and Stephen Robert Andrews of Bourne, solicitor. [Reg. 42, p.537.]

Born 22 February 1849 at Matching (Ess); son of Revd John H., Vicar of Matching. Educated: Corpus Christi College, Cambridge (matric. 1868; BA 1875). Assistant Master at Stamford GS, 1872–5. Deacon: 1875; priest: 1877 (Peterborough). Formerly: C. of Tinwell (Ru), 1875–8; Chaplain of Stamford and Rutland Infirmary, 1877–9; C. of Ketton (Ru), 1878–9; C. of Haceby with Newton, 1888–92; V. of Threckingham, 1898–1900 (*q.v.*); R. of Scott Willoughby, 1900–5 (*q.v.*). Resided at Pickworth Rectory. Also: V. of Walcot, 1879–1918 (*q.v.*). Resigned 22 November 1918. Latterly at 'Passadena', King's Road, Paignton (Dev). Died there, 20 January 1923. [Venn, *Alumni*; Crockford (1908); Census Returns 1911; RES A/88; *Probate Calendar* 1923.]

The vicarage of Walcot was united to the rectory of Pickworth by Order in Council dated 22 March 1911. [Reg. 42, p.640.]

Cecil St John Wright BA

Instituted 8 February 1919 to rectory of Pickworth with vicarage of Walcot, on resignation of William Christopher Houghton. Patron: Dean (Thomas Charles Fry) and Chapter of Lincoln, for this turn. [Reg. 43, p.176.]

Born 23 April 1869 at Nottingham; 3rd son of Charles Edward W. of Daybrook. Educated: Nottingham High School and Queens' College, Cambridge (matric. 1887; BA 1890). Asst Master, Aske's School, Hatcham (K); Head Master of Corby GS (Li), 1903–9. Married (15 April 1903) at St Barnabas Kensington, Muriel Olive Mary Newcomb. Deacon: 1906; priest: 1907 (Lincoln). Formerly: C. of Little Bytham, 1906–8; V. of Stainfield with Apley, 1908–10; V. of Horbling, 1910–19 (*q.v.*); TCF 1917–19. Resided at Pickworth Rectory. Bishop Hicks noted at the institution: 'Mr St John Wright looks old, haggard & unhappy; lower teeth broken, & face without hope or brightness. I am afraid that all his life he has been repelling Poverty …' Also: V. of Threckingham, 1926–33. Afterwards: R. of Little Ponton with Stroxton, 1933–52. Latterly of 27 Grantham Road, Sleaford. Died 14 February 1958 at Manormead Nursing Home, Hindhead (Sr). [Venn, *Alumni*; LMA, PR Kensington St Barnabas; *Crockford* (1932, 1951–2); *Hicks Diaries*, no.1397; *Probate Calendar* 1958.]

Thomas Leonard Ivens

Instituted 31 July 1933 to rectory of Pickworth with vicarage of Walcot, on cession of Cecil St John Wright. Patron: Dean (Robert Andrew Mitchell) and Chapter of Lincoln, for this turn. Note that on 14 July 1933, the Archbishop of Canterbury granted a dispensation enabling the said TLI to hold together the said Rectory of Pickworth and Vicarage of Walcot with the Vicarage of Threckingham. [Reg. 43, p.526.]

Born 1879 at Whitton; son of Revd Coleman Ivens, Curate of Alkborough. Educated: Scholae Cancellarii, Lincoln. Deacon: 1904 (York); priest: 1905 (Beverley for York). Formerly: C. of St Margaret, Swinton (YWR), 1904–6; of St Nicholas, Lincoln, 1906–10; V. of Bilsby and Farlesthorpe, 1910–25; R. of Merredin (Western Australia), 1925–31; V. of Horbling, 1931–3 (*q.v.*). Resided at Pickworth Rectory. Also: V. of Threckingham, 1933–41 (*q.v.*). Afterwards: V. of Cranwell, 1941–4; V. of North Owersby with Thornton-le-Moor, 1944–64. Retired to The Bungalow, Wellingore. Died 20 February 1966. [Census Returns 1881 (Boynton); *Crockford* (1941, 1965–6); *LDC* (1967), 53.]

William Thomas Henry Sampson

Instituted 16 December 1941 to rectory of Pickworth with vicarage of Walcot, on resignation of Thomas Leonard Ivens. Patron: Gilbert Heathcote Drummond Willoughby, Earl of Ancaster, of Grimsthorpe Castle, for this turn. [Reg. 43, p.669.]

Afterwards: R. of Folkingham, 1944–9 (*q.v.*).

Roy Ellis MA

Instituted 3 February 1945 to rectory of Pickworth with vicarage of Walcot, on cession of William Thomas Henry Sampson. Patron: Dean (Robert Andrew Mitchell) and Chapter of Lincoln, for this turn. [Reg. 44, p.25.]

Born 24 August 1896. Educated: King Edward's School, Birmingham, and Keble College, Oxford (matric. 1915; BA 1918; MA 1922); Ridley Hall, Cambridge (1918). Deacon: 1919; priest: 1920 (London). Formerly: C. of Emmanuel, Paddington, 1919–21; of St Andrew, South Wimbledon, 1921–4; of Clapham, 1925–8; of St John Evangelist, Angell Town, Brixton, 1928–31; of Mortlake with Christ Church, East Sheen, 1931–2; V. of Baumber with Great Sturton, 1932–45. Married (1931) Elsie May Ridgewell. Resided at Walcot Vicarage. Afterwards: V. of Skillington, 1955–65. Latterly of 22 Grove Park, Tring (Hrt). Died 8 June 1966 at Tring. [*Keble Register*, 169; *Crockford* (1951–2, 1965–6); *Probate Calendar* 1966.]

Leslie George Barron LTh

Instituted 2 March 1956 to rectory of Pickworth with vicarage of Walcot, on cession of Roy Ellis. Patron: Dean (David Colin Dunlop) and Chapter of Lincoln, for this turn. [Reg. 44, p.222.]

Born 21 June 1887 at Bradford. Educated: London College of Divinity (1909; resident student 1911); University of Durham (LTh 1938). Deacon: 1912 (St Albans); priest: 1914 (Chelmsford). Formerly: C. of St Mark, Forest Gate (Ess), 1912–15; of Old Ford (Mx), 1916–19; of St Saviour, Westcliff-on-Sea, 1921–2; of Christ Church, Fenton (St), 1923–4; R. of South Witham, 1924–34; V. of St Luke, Bilston (St), 1934–52; R. of North Tamerton (Dev), 1952–4; R. of Ashwicken with Leziate (Nf), 1954–6. Married (26 December 1917) at Holy Trinity, Mile End Old Town, Stepney, Gladys Mary Atterbury. Resided at Walcot Vicarage. Resignation accepted 1 April 1963. Retired to 55 Blenheim Road, Clacton-on-Sea. Died 1969. [Census Returns 1911 (Highbury); *Crockford* (1961–2, 1965–6); LMA, PR Mile End Old Town Holy Trinity; Reg. 44, p.344; GRO, Death Index.]

Frank Reginald Money MA

Instituted 8 March 1966 to rectory of Pickworth with vicarage of Walcot, on resignation of Leslie George Barron. Note that on 1 November 1965, an Order for Plurality was made under Section 5 of the Pastoral Reorganisation Measure 1949, authorising the said FRM to hold the benefices of Folkingham with Laughton, Osbournby with Scott Willoughby, Pickworth with Walcot, and Threckingham in plurality. [Reg. 44, p.383.]

Also: R. of Folkingham, 1960–8 (*q.v.*).

RIPPINGALE

The church of Rippingale was divided early on into three parts, of which two parts came to be held as one benefice and the third part as another. The three parts appear to have been appurtenant to the several manors of Ringston, Downhall and Uphall. The patrons of the two parts held together (Ringston and Downhall) were, respectively, the Gobaud family and Shelford Priory. The two parties joined together to make the presentation of William de Burg in 1240–1 but at some stage the two patrons appear to have agreed to make alternate presentations, as was indicated by an inquiry of 1497. Shelford continued to present (at somewhat irregular intervals) to the 'Two Parts' until the Dissolution. The Gobaud share, held with a manor in Rippingale belonging to the Croun fee, was held by the Gobaud family in 1242–3 and in 1303 and by 1346 had passed to Robert de Colville. Subsequently this share of the 'Two Parts' advowson was exercised by Ralph Basset of Sapcote and later by his widow Alice, 'lady of Bytham', although their claim was successfully contested in 1394 and 1406 by the Swynburn family. The Basset share passed with the marriage of Elizabeth, daughter of Ralph and Alice, to Richard, Lord Grey of Codnor; his grandson Henry presented in 1494. By the early seventeenth century, the Shelford share in the 'Two Parts' had passed to Philip, Lord Stanhope, whose family had acquired the priory estates at the Dissolution, while the Grey share was in the possession of William Lister, whose father Thomas had purchased it from Edward Leigh of Rushall (St) in 1591. Stanhope presented in 1619, but in the same year he conveyed his share to Richard Brownlow, whose house at Ringston was in the parish of Rippingale. The advowson of the other benefice in Rippingale Church, known as the 'Third Part', was held in the thirteenth and early fourteenth centuries by the Repinghale family. Adam son of John de Repinghale presented in 1317. Adam's son John sold the property before 1327 to John de Stonor of Stonor in Oxfordshire. Thomas Stonor sold his Rippingale estate in 1425 and it passed into the hands of John, Viscount Beaumont, whose feoffees presented in 1443. It was later granted (like Folkingham) to William Hastings. By 1496 the advowson had been acquired by John Robinson of Boston; it was given to the Gild of St Mary in Boston by 1529. The patronage of this 'Third Part' was acquired by Richard Brownlow from William Hunston and Thomas Styles in 1618. The three parts of Rippingale were finally united on 18 August 1725. The patronage was also united in the Heathcote family, whence it passed to the Grimsthorpe estate. The Earl of Ancaster held the advowson in 1965. [Gibbons, *Visitation*, 23, 30; Reg. 14, fo.91v; Reg. 23, fo.36; *Book of Fees*, 1027; *Feudal Aids* iii. 163, 209; *GEC* vi. 127–9; LAO, 1ANC 2/A/6/4–5; *Stonor Letters and Papers*, 43; Reg. 38, p.97; *LDC* (1965), 68–9.]

Two Parts of the Church

Geoffrey de Deeping Precentor of Lincoln
Instituted in the twelfth pontifical year of Bishop Hugh of Wells (20 December 1220/19 December 1221) to a third part of church of Rippingale. Patron: Richard son of Ralph. [*Rot. Welles* iii. 111.]

Also: Precentor of Lincoln, *c*.1206–25. Resident at Lincoln; witnessed numerous charters as a member of Chapter. Died before 6 October 1225. [*Le Neve Fasti: Lincoln, 1066– 1300*, 13–14; *Acta of Hugh of Wells*, nos 150–1, 156, 177, 180, 186–90, 198–9, 208.]

M. Thomas de Collingham clerk
Instituted by collation in the seventeenth pontifical year of Bishop Hugh of Wells (20 December 1225/19 December 1226) to two third parts of church of Rippingale, on death of G[eoffrey de Deeping], late Precentor of Lincoln. Patron: Bishop of Lincoln. Note that the Prior of Shelford recovered his presentation to one third part against Hugh de Ringedun by assize of darrein presentment, that Richard de Repinghale kt as patron presented Alexander Picot clerk to the other third part, and that the Bishop, preferring (*satagens*) to institute one clerk to the two parts, collated them to M. Thomas with consent of all parties. M. Thomas promised to pay an annual pension of 20s to Alexander Picot until he should be provided with another benefice by the said Prior. [*Rot. Welles* iii. 142–3.]

William de Burg subdeacon
Instituted in the sixth pontifical year of Bishop Robert Grosseteste (17 June 1240/16 June 1241) to two third parts of church of Rippingale. Patron: Prior and Convent of Shelford for one third and John Gubaud for another third. A dispute between the guardians of Ralph son of Richard (a minor) and John Gubaud over the advowson of the second third had been settled by agree-

ment that Gubaud should present for this turn without prejudice to the right of Ralph when he came of age. [Hoskin, no.198.]

Richard de Trouwelle
Granted two parts of church of Rippingale *in commendam*, 22 April 1270. [*Rot. Gravesend*, 41.]

John Chaynel clerk
Instituted 12 June 1283 to two parts of church of Rippingale (following grant *in commendam* on 6 February 1282/3), on death of Richard de Trowell. Patron: Prior and Convent of Shelford (who recovered the advowson in the king's court after a dispute with John Gobaud). [*Reg. Sutton* i. 45–6.]

Subdeacon: 12 June 1283 (Lincoln). Issued with royal letters of protection (for 1 year), 20 May 1322; again (1 year) on 18 April 1327. Licensed for absence (2 years), August 1329. [*Reg. Sutton* i. 45; *CPR 1321–24*, 120; *CPR 1327–30*, 94; *Reg. Burghersh* iii. no.520.]

Richard Gobaud priest
Instituted 20 December 1329 to two parts of church of Rippingale, on death of John Schaynel. Patron: John Gobaud. [*Reg. Burghersh* i. no.247.]

Commission issued 20 January 1329/30 to Archdeacon of Lincoln to act in cause brought by RG against the executor of John Charneles, late Rector, concerning assessment of defects in the said two parts and in the rectory manse of the same. [Reg. 5, fo.400.]

William de Wylughby subdeacon
Instituted 21 July 1349 to two parts of church of Rippingale, on death of Richard. Patron: Prior and Convent of Shelford. [Reg. 9, fo.61v.]

Plaintiff (as co-executor of will of Richard de Wylughby kt) in plea against William Hutte of Lenton, October 1365. [*CPR 1364–67*, 170.]

Richard de Dornethorp
Instituted 10 August 1369 to two parts of church of Rippingale (cause of vacancy not stated). Patron: Ralph Basset of Sapcote kt. [Reg. 10, fo.31.]

Party to deed concerning chantry at Castle Bytham, 29 September 1371. Licensed to alienate in mortmain to Heynings Priory manor of *Braylond* in Leadenham, 25 June 1376. Assessed for poll-tax, 1377, 1381. [Reg. 12, fo.113; *CPR 1374–77*, 285; *Clerical Poll-Taxes*, nos 702, 1326, 1915.]

Robert de Morton
Instituted before 16 March 1393/4. [Reg. 11, fo.69.]

Afterwards: R. of Molesworth (Hu), 1394–6. [Reg. 11, fos 272v, 282v.]

Robert Caldecote priest
Instituted 16 March 1393/4 to two parts of church of Rippingale, on resignation of Robert de Morton (by exchange with church of Molesworth). Patron: Thomas Swynburn kt. [Reg. 11, fo.69.]

Formerly: R. of Molesworth (Hu), 1393–4. Afterwards: R. of Middleton Stoney (Ox), February–November 1396; R. of mediety of South Ferriby, 1396. [Reg. 11, fos 272v, 276v, 332, 334.]

John de Lidyngton clerk

Instituted 26 February 1395/6 to two parts of church of Rippingale, on resignation of Robert Caldecote (by exchange with church of Middleton Stoney). Patron: Prior and Convent of Shelford. [Reg. 11, fo.81v.]

Formerly: R. of Middleton Stoney (Ox), 1395–6. Afterwards: R. of Irnham, 1397–1407. [Reg. 11, fos 331v, 332; Reg. 14, fo.22v.]

John Brunne priest

Instituted 1 August 1397 to two parts of church of Rippingale, on resignation of John Lidyngton (by exchange with church of Irnham). Patron: Alice, lady of Bytham. [Reg. 11, fo.88.]

Formerly: R. of Irnham, 1393–7. Licensed for non-residence (1 year), 4 March 1398/9; similar licence (1 year), 9 April 1400. Afterwards: R. of Wadenhoe (Np), 1401–3; R. of Sudbrooke, 1403. [Reg. 11, fo.63; Reg. 13, fos 9, 24v; 224v, 239v.]

Robert Trays priest

Instituted 25 May 1401 to two parts of church of Rippingale, on resignation of John Browne (by exchange with church of Wadenhoe). Patron: M. John Kyngton and John Story of Sleaford. [Reg. 13, fo.136.]

Formerly: R. of Wadenhoe (Np). Afterwards: R. of All Saints, Hemswell, 1410 (*q.v.*).

John Charyte priest

Instituted 1 December 1406 to two parts of church of Rippingale, on resignation of Robert Trays. Patron: John Doreward, John Boys, Thomas Lampet, Clement Spyce and Ralph Chaumberleyn, feoffees of the lands and tenements of William Swynburn *domicellus*, who recovered the presentation in the king's court against Alice Basset, lady of Bytham, widow of Ralph Basset of Sapcote, who had presented Matthew Edenham priest. [Reg. 14, fo.14v.]

M. Thomas Hilton

Instituted before 12 June 1484. [Reg. 22, fo.134v.]

John Perte priest

Instituted 12 June 1484 to two parts of church of Rippingale, on resignation of M. Thomas Hilton. Patron: Henry, Lord Le Grey, kt. Note that an annual pension of £6 was reserved to M. Thomas Hilton for life from the fruits of the church. [Reg. 22, fo.134v.]

M. Robert Ednam priest

Instituted 18 August 1485 to two parts of church of Rippingale, on resignation of M. Thomas Hilton. Patron: Prior and Convent of Shelford, who recovered the advowson in the king's court against Henry Grey of Codnor kt. and John Perte clerk). [Reg. 22, fo.135v.]

Thomas Dikson priest

Instituted 13 February 1496/7 to two parts of church of Rippingale, on resignation of M. Robert Ednam. Patron: Henry Penyngton, for this turn by grant from Henry Grey kt. (An inquiry was held by which it was found that the said Henry Grey and the Prior and Convent of Shelford had the right to present on alternate turns.) Note that an annual pension of 40 shillings was reserved to M. Robert Ednam for life from the fruits of the church. [Reg. 23, fo.36.]

Assessed for subsidy (£20) in 1526. [*Subsidy*, 56.]

Edward Brereley chaplain

Instituted 22 December 1533 to two parts of church of Rippingale, on death of Thomas Dikson. Patron: James Foliambe esquire, by reason of a grant made to him by John Dunham of Kirklington (Nt), kt, and Benedicta his wife. [Reg. 27, fo.36v.]

Born *c*.1507. Formerly: Chaplain of St Mary Magdalene Chantry in Southwell Minster, 1530. Also: Vicar Choral of Southwell, 1531–47; allotted pension of £6 in 1548. Canon of Southwell and Prebendary of South Muskham, 1558–9. Exhibited (by Vicar of Morton-by-Bourne his proctor) at Visitation in 1551. Witnessed Rippingale will, 1551. Still Rector in 1554. [*Visitations of Southwell*, 174, 185–6; *Ex-Religious*, 116; Le Neve-Hardy iii. 433; Vj 13, fo.62; LCC Wills 1551–2/220.]

Robert Collingwood

Instituted 17 July 1562 to two parts of church of Rippingale, on death of last incumbent. Patron: Margaret Brerley (administratrix of the goods of John Brerley decd) by reason of a grant of advowson made by Prior (Henry) and Convent of Shelford to Brian Higden and others. Reinstituted 13 January 1580/1; patron, Queen Elizabeth I. [Reg. 28, fo.213v; *Bishop Cooper*, 27.]

Born *c*.1522. Education: 'bred in the schools'; 'knows Latin competently; well versed in sacred learning'. Priest: 27 or 28 July 1560 (Lincoln). Formerly: V. of Morton-by-Bourne, 1560–3 (*q.v.*). Also: R. of third part of Rippingale, 'twoe parsonages in one and the same churche'. Resident (1576, 1611, 1614). Witnessed Rippingale wills, 1563–69. Witnessed will of Ralph Cockerel, his predecessor as Rector of the third part (1564); witnessed will of John Snowe, R. of Dunsby (1566). Died 1615. [*Bishop Cooper*, 207, 219; *State of the Church*, 74, 237; LC 3, fo.3v; LC 4, fo.73v; LCC Wills 1563/61v; 1564/20v; 1567/9v; 1568/8; 1569/i/5; LCC Admons 1615/45–6.]

James Adamson

Instituted 12 January 1614/15 to two parts of church of Rippingale. Patron: William Williams BD, by grant for this turn from William Lister esquire. Note that the presentation was unsuccessfully disputed by Sir Philip Stanhope kt. Adamson was inducted on 24 July by John Hutton, Rector of Dunsby. [BC; Borthwick, Sub.Bk. 2, fos 31v, 32; IND/L 1, fo.13.]

Formerly: Schoolmaster at Rippingale, admitted 6 May 1606. The advowson of the two parts was subsequently contested in Chancery and was recovered by Sir Philip Stanhope; on 10 May 1619 the Bishop was directed to remove James Adamson and institute a suitable person on Stanhope's presentation. Afterwards: C. of Kirkby Underwood, 1622–31 (*q.v.*). [LC 4, fo.73v; 1 ANC/2/A/6/8.]

Adam Cranwell MA
Instituted 1 June 1619 to two parts of church of Rippingale (cause of vacancy not stated). Patron: Philip, Lord Stanhope. Inducted 8 June 1619 by Edmund Ashton, Rector of Dowsby. [IND/L 1, fo.48.]

Educated: Trinity College (matric. 1606) and St Catharine's Hall, Cambridge (BA 1609). Deacon: 17 September 1609; priest: 17 December 1609 (Peterborough). Formerly: C. of Woolsthorpe, 1613. Also: R. of Rippingale Third Part, 1615–46 (*q.v.*). Lent a horse to royal army, 1642. Petitioned (5 June 1646) to compound on Newark Articles, being there at its surrender; left his dwelling and went into the garrison but was never in arms. Sequestered for deliquency, 1646. [Venn, *Alumni*; Longden iii. 285; LC 4, fo.68; *Walker Revised*, 249; *CCC* Pt II, 1311; Swaby, 114.]

George Beck
Admitted 14 August 1646, on sequestration of Adam Cranwell. [*Walker Revised*, 249.].

Son of Robert B. of Lincoln. Educated: Magdalene College, Cambridge (matric. 1625; BA 1628–9; MA 1632). Priest: 21 September 1634 (Lincoln). Formerly: R. of Stanhoe (Nf), 1638; R. of Mareham-le-Fen, 1645–6. Chaplain to Earl of Manchester during Civil War, attending him during battle of Winceby. Member of Folkingham Classis; Tuesday Lecturer at Grantham. Also: R. of Rippingale Third Part, 1646–56 (*q.v.*). Afterwards: R. of West Allington, 1656; ejected 1662. Resided afterwards in London, whence he was driven by the plague, which 'follow'd him to Tottenham … and there put an end to his Persecution and Mortality'. Will (PCC) dated 24 June 1665; proved 6 January 1665/6. [Venn, *Alumni*; LC 5, fo.39; *Calamy Revised*, 43; Swaby, 66, 98, 114; PRO, PROB 11/319/102.]

John Bucke
Instituted 6 March 1656/7. Patron: Thomas Lister, esquire. [Swaby, 114.]

Son of Peregrine B. of Syston. Educated: Stamford School and Magdalene College, Cambridge (matric. 1649; BA 1652–3; MA 1656); Fellow. Formerly: V. of East Dereham (Nf), 1654–6. Also: R. of Rippingale Third Part, 1657–8 (*q.v.*). Buried at Rippingale, 16 January 1657/8. [*Lincolnshire Pedigrees*, 199; Venn, *Alumni*; *Walker Revised*, 264; PR Rippingale.]

Timothy Dove
Instituted *c.*1658 (compounded for first-fruits, 27 April). Reinstituted 14 November 1660, on death of John Buck. Patron: Sir John Brownlow, Bt. (26 October 1660). [FL.h.13, 665; Reg. 32, fo.2; PD 1660/75.]

Baptised 11 September 1631 at Aslackby; son of Barjonah D., Vicar of Aslackby (*q.v.*). Educated: Emmanuel College (matric. 1653) and St John's College, Cambridge (BA 1654–5; MA 1670). Deacon and priest: 7 or 17 July 1660 (Ardfert). Also: R. of Rippingale Third Part, 1669–91 (*q.v.*). Married (1663) Elinor, daughter of Ephraim Garthwaite, Rector of Barkston (1641). Father of Barjonah D., Rector of Croxton Kerrial (Le), 1701.

Buried at Rippingale, 3 September 1691. Will (LCC). [PR Aslackby; Venn, *Alumni*; LC 5, fo.24; Reg. 33, fo.124v; *Lincolnshire Pedigrees*, 390; PR Rippingale; LCC Wills 1691/ ii/99.]

Daniel Nicholls (the younger) MA

Instituted 9 January 1691/2, on death of Timothy Dove. Patron: John Lister, gent. [IND/L 1, fo.270v; LC 14, fo.6.]

Son of Daniel N., Rector of Scotton (1673–1711). Educated: St Paul's School and Jesus College, Cambridge (matric. 1677; BA 1680–1; MA 1684). Deacon: March 1682/3 (York); priest: 30 May 1686 (Lincoln). Formerly: C. of Scotton, 1686. Also: R. of Rippingale Third Part, 1698–1725 (*q.v.*). Signed BTs at Rippingale 1692–1720, 1724. Latterly 'resides mostly with his brother, John Nevile of Thorney, on account of his health'. Buried at Rippingale, 6 March 1724/5. [Venn, *Alumni*; *York Ordinations 1662–1699*, 49; Reg. 34, fo.92; LC 14, fo.6; BTs Rippingale; *Speculum*, 100.]

Third Part of the Church

Alan de Repingal subdeacon

Instituted in the twenty-second pontifical year of Bishop Hugh of Wells (20 December 1230/19 December 1231) to a third part of church of Rippingale. Patron: John son of Hugh de Repingal. [*Rot. Welles* iii. 188.]

M. Hugh de Houcton deacon

Instituted in the thirteenth pontifical year of Bishop Robert Grosseteste (17 June 1247/16 June 1248) to a third part of church of Rippingale, on resignation of Alan. Patron: John, son of Hugh de Repinghal, kt. [Hoskin, no.413.]

Educated: University of Cambridge (MA); Chancellor of the University, 1246. Also: Subdean of Lincoln, *c.*1250–64; Canon of Lincoln and Prebendary of Welton Westhall, *c.*1250–64. [Emden, *BRUC*, 316; *Le Neve Fasti: Lincoln 1066–1300*, 23, 109.]

Alan de Repingale

Instituted before 15 December 1277. [*Rot. Gravesend*, 78.]

John de Helmeden subdeacon

Instituted 15 December 1277 to third part of church of Rippingale, on resignation of Alan de Repingale. Patron: John de Repingehal. [*Rot. Gravesend*, 78.]

William de Chele

Instituted before 1 July 1281. [*Reg. Sutton* i. 14–15.]

Afterwards: R. of Helpston (Np), 1281–97. [*Reg. Sutton* ii. 9, 138.]

John de Helmeden subdeacon

Instituted 1 July 1281 to third part of church of Rippingale, on institution of William de Chele to church of Helpston. Patron: John son of John de

Repinghale, kt. Note that the presentation was unsuccessfully disputed by Amabel, mother of the said John. [*Reg. Sutton* i. 14–15.]

Thomas de Fenneditton chaplain
Instituted 17 November 1317 to third part of church of Rippingale, on death of John de Helmeden. Patron: Adam son of John de Repynghale kt. [Reg. 2, fo.68v.]

John
Occurs 1335.

Commission issued 11 November 1335 to act in cause pending between Prior and Convent of Shelford and John, Rector of a third part of Rippingale, concerning the retention by the latter of an annual pension of 5 shillings due to the Priory. [Reg. 5, fo.516v.]

Thomas Segyn
Instituted before 9 June 1352. [Reg. 9, fo.101v.]

Thomas de Luyton priest
Instituted 9 June 1352 to third part of church of Rippingale, on death of Thomas Segyn. Patron: John de Stonore kt. [Reg. 9, fo.101v.]

Educated: Oxford University (MA). Formerly: R. of Sulhamstead Abbots (Brk), 1350–2. Died 10 January 1368/9 in rectory house at Rippingale. [*BRUO*, 1183; Reg. 10, fo.28.]

John de Belyngburgh priest
Instituted 23 February 1368/9 to third part of church of Rippingale, on death of M. Thomas de Luton. Patron: William [of Wykeham], Bishop of Winchester, by reason of a grant of the manor of *Uphale* in Rippingale together with the advowson of the said third part, made to him by Edmund, son and heir of John de Stanore kt, decd. [Reg. 10, fo.28.]

Assessed for poll-tax, 1377, 1381. [*Clerical Poll-Taxes*, nos 702, 1326, 1915.]

Robert Davy priest
Instituted 19 May 1381 to third part of church of Rippingale, on death of John de Billingburgh. Patron: Edmund Stonore. [Reg. 10, fo.113v.]

John Bray clerk
Instituted 29 January 1417/18 to third part of church of Rippingale, on death of Robert Davy. Patron: John Thorp, Archdeacon of Suffolk, by reason of a grant made to him by Thomas Stonore, lord of the manor of *Ly Uphall* in Rippingale, to which the advowson of the said third part appertains, of the right to present to the said third part at any vacancy during a term of nine years dating from Monday after the Feast of the Assumption, 3 Henry V (19 August 1415). [Reg. 14, fo.91v.]

Robert Robynson
Instituted before 24 June 1443. [Reg. 18, fo.91.]

John Rokke priest
Instituted 24 June 1443 to third part of church of Rippingale, on resignation of Robert Robynson. Patron: Richard Byngham, Thomas Lughburgh clerk, and Robert Wytham, feoffees of John Viscount Beaumont. [Reg. 18, fo.91.]

Henry Lewys
Instituted before 22 February 1465/6. [Reg. 20, fo.143.]

Henry Thornton (or Brabaner) priest
Instituted 22 February 1465/6 to third part of church of Rippingale, on resignation of Henry Lewys. Patron: William Hastynes kt, lord of Hastings. [Reg. 20, fo.143.]

William Whatton chaplain
Instituted 6 October 1491 to third part of church of Rippingale, on death of Henry Thornton. Patron: Katherine Hastingys widow, lady of Hastings. [Reg. 22, fo.147v.]

Richard Caade priest
Instituted 8 November 1496 to third part of church of Rippingale, on resignation of William Walton. Patron: John Robynson. [Reg. 23, fo.34v.]

Richard Compton priest
Instituted 7 November 1498 to third part of church of Rippingale, on resignation of Richard Cade. Patron: John Robynson the younger of Boston, gent. [Reg. 23, fo.46.]

William Turre priest
Instituted 31 December 1499 to third part of church of Rippingale, on resignation of Richard Compton. Patron: John Robynson the elder, of Boston. [Reg. 23, fo.51.]

Thomas Dikson
Instituted 20 August 1509 to third part of church of Rippingale, on resignation of William Turr. Patron: John Robynson of Boston. [Reg. 23, fo.137v.]

Walter Mawdes priest
Instituted 4 November 1529 to third part of church of Rippingale, on resignation of Thomas Dixson. Patron: Thomas Dixson esquire, Alderman of the Gild of Boston, and Laurence Belman and William Wadnay, Chamberlains of the said Gild. [Reg. 27, fo.34v.]

Assessed for *Valor Ecclesiasticus* 1535. [*Valor* iv. 105.]

Thomas Hogekynson

Instituted 23 September 1542 to third part of church of Rippingale, on death of Walter Mawdes. Patron: William Kyde, Alderman, and John Wendon and Robert Dobb, Chamberlains, of the Gild of St Mary of Boston. [Reg. 27, fo.78v.]

Exhibited at Visitation in 1551. Witnessed Rippingale will, 1551. [Vj 13, fo.62; LCC Wills 1551–2/220.]

Ralph Cockrell

Instituted 25 June 1552 (in the [blank] year of King Edward VI; compounded for first-fruits, 8 July 1552) to third part of church of Rippingale, on death of last incumbent. Patron: John Bell of Boston, by grant of the advowson for this turn from the Chamberlains of the Gild of St Mary of Boston. [Reg. 28, fo.111v; FL.h.13, 662.]

Witnessed Kirkby Underwood will, February 1559; witnessed Rippingale will, 1561. Died before 17 January 1564/5 (probate inventory). Will (LCC). [LCC Wills 1558/i/140v; 1561/82; LCC Wills 1564/20v; INV 43/253.]

Robert Collingwood

Instituted 27 June 1565 to third part of church of Rippingale, on death of last incumbent. Patron: William Hunston of Boston, esquire. [Reg. 28, fo.6.]

Also: R. of Rippingale Two Parts, 1562–1615 (*q.v.*).

Adam Cranwell MA

Instituted 13 January 1614/15 to third part of church of Rippingale, on death of Robert Collingwood. Patron: Thomas Stiles gent. Inducted 17 January 1614/15 by Edmund Lolley, Vicar of Bourne. [BC; IND/L 1, fo.11.]

Also: R. of Rippingale Two Parts, 1619–46 (*q.v.*). Ejected 1646. [Swaby, 114.]

George Beck

Instituted 1646. [Swaby, 114.]

Also: R. of Rippingale Two Parts, 1646–56 (*q.v.*).

John Bucke

Instituted 23 July 1656. Patron: Oliver Cromwell. [Swaby, 114.]

Also: R. of Rippingale Two Parts, 1656–8 (*q.v.*).

Robert Sharp

Instituted 24 May 1658 (compounded for first-fruits, May 1658). Patron: Sir John Brownlow Bt. [LC 5, fo.24; Swaby, 114; FL.h.13, 663.]

Educated: Magdalene College, Cambridge; BD (by 1662). Priest: 20 December 1629 (Peterborough). Resident (1662). Also: V. of Heckington, 1635–62; Chaplain to Frances, widow of John Cobham, 1661; V. of Alford, 1665–9. Buried at Alford, 10 November 1669. Will. [Longden xii. 123; LC 5, fos 24, 54v; BTs Alford; LCC Wills 1670/i/136; INV 172/251.]

Timothy Dove MA

Instituted 7 December 1669, on death of Robert Sharpe. Patron: Sir John Brownlow, Bt. [Reg. 33, fo.124v.]

Also: R. of Rippingale Two Parts, 1658–91 (q.v.).

Richard Knight MA

Instituted 11 December 1691 to third part of church of Rippingale, on death of Timothy Dove. Patron: Sir John Brownlowe, Bt. [AC; IND/L 1, fo.270v.]

Of Lincolnshire. Educated: Emmanuel College, Cambridge (matric. 1674; BA 1677–8; MA 1681). Deacon: 3 January 1678/9; priest: 21 December 1679 (Lincoln). Formerly: V. of St Gabriel, Binbrook, 1679–91; C. of Sapperton, 1680; R. of Sapperton, 1688–92. Also: R. of Carlby, 1690–8. Buried at Carlby, 25 April 1698. Will (LCC). [Venn, *Alumni*; Reg. 34, fos 32v, 44; LC 14, fos 6, 79; SUB V/6, fo.35; PR Carlby; LCC Wills 1697&8/ii/428.]

Daniel Nicols MA

Instituted 17 May 1698 (cause of vacancy not stated). Patron: Alice Brownlow widow (mother and guardian of the daughters of Sir John Brownlow Bt, decd) (5 May 1698). [Reg. 35, fo.48v; PD 1698/36.]

Also: R. of Rippingale Two Parts, 1691–1725 (q.v.).

The three parts of the church of Rippingale were united on 18 August 1725. [Reg. 38, p.97.]

Francis Inman

Instituted 7 July 1725 and 23 August 1725 to rectory of Rippingale, on death of Daniel Nicoals. Patron: Sir Gilbert Heathcote, Alderman of London, kt. [Reg. 38, pp. 94, 98.]

Education: literate. Deacon: 9 March 1717/18; priest: 21 December 1718 (Lincoln). Formerly: C. of Datchworth (Hrt), 1718. Signed BTs at Rippingale, 1726–37. [Reg. 37, pp. 48, 74; BTs Rippingale.]

Daniel Debat MA

Instituted 13 December 1738 to rectory of Rippingale, on death of Francis Inman. Patron: Sir John Heathcote, Bt. [Reg. 38, p.355.]

Born c.1688; son of James D. of London. Educated: Gloucester Hall, Oxford (matric. 1703; BA 1706; MA 1710). Deacon: 27 May 1711 (Oxford). Formerly: R. of Holdenby (Np), 1730–8. Also: Prebendary of Heredum Marney in Collegiate Church of St Endellion (Co), 1738. Signed BTs at Rippingale, 1739–65. Died 'of a Fever', aged 65; buried at Rippingale, 18 August 1765. [Foster, *Alumni*; Longden iv. 49; BTs Rippingale.]

Wade Gascoigne LLB

Instituted 30 December 1765 to rectory of Rippingale, on death of Daniel Debat. Patron: Sir Gilbert Heathcote of Normanton, Bt. [Reg. 39, p.51.]

Born *c.*1733; son of John G. Educated: Westminster School (1743–50) and Trinity College, Cambridge (matric. 1750; LLB 1757). Deacon: 6 March 1757; priest: 11 March 1759 (Lincoln). Formerly: C. of South Witham, 1757; C. of Castle Bytham with Little Bytham, 1759–65. Also: R. of Terrington St John (Nf), 1767–1801. Resided at Rippingale: 'Absent – No excuse – but is said to live at Rippingale & to be regular' (1768); 'Resides and does the duty' (1778). Signed register at Rippingale 1766–1800. Died 19 May 1801; buried at Rippingale (MI). [*Record of Old Westminsters* i. 365; Venn, *Alumni*; Reg. 38, pp. 548, 565; PR Castle Bytham; LC 31, p.72; *Norfolk Benefices*, 18; PR Rippingale; *Monson*, 303.]

Bernard Cracroft

Instituted 17 November 1801 to rectory of Rippingale, on death of Wade Gascoigne. Patron: Sir Gilbert Heathcote of Normanton, Bt. [Reg. 40, p.28.]

Born 28 December 1752, baptised 1 February 1753 at Louth; son of Robert C., esquire. Educated: Queen's College, Oxford (matric. 1770). Deacon: 24 September 1775; priest: 24 February 1777 (Lincoln). Formerly: R. of Cold Hanworth, 1777–1801 (*q.v.*); V. of Bardney, 1778–85; V. of Stixwould, 1778–1801. Also: V. of South Elkington, 1781–1821; R. of West Keal, 1785–1821; C. of Dembleby, 1817. Resided at Folkingham. Died 6 May 1821 'suddenly in Horbling Church'. [*Lincolnshire Pedigrees*, 282; PR Louth St James; Foster, *Alumni*; Reg. 39, pp. 260, 286; CR 1, p.86.]

Charles Douglas BA

Instituted 6 November 1816 to rectory of Rippingale, on resignation of Bernard Cracroft. Patron: Sir Gilbert Heathcote of Normanton Park (Ru), Bt (27 October 1816). [Reg. 40, p.244; PD 172/4.]

Born 10 March, baptised 18 April 1791 at St Marylebone; son of Hon. John D. (son of James 14th Earl of Morton and his 2nd wife Bridget, daughter of Sir John Heathcote of Normanton, Bt) and Frances his wife. Educated: Trinity College, Cambridge (matric. 1810; BA 1815; MA 1818). Deacon: March 1816 (Winchester); priest: 9 June 1816 (Salisbury). Formerly: C. of Kilmeston (Ha), 1816. Also: V. of Laxton (Nt), 1818–26. Signed registers at Rippingale 1820–5. Afterwards: R. of Donagheady, co. Tyrone, 1825. Lived at Earl's Gift, co. Tyrone. Married (2 March 1816) Lady Isabella Gore, daughter of 2nd Earl of Arran. Children Julia Mary (1822), William Grant (1824) and Charles Edward (1825), baptised at Rippingale. Died 28 January 1857. [Burke, *Peerage* (2003), 2788; *Winchester Ordinations* i. 137–8; CCED; Venn, *Alumni*; PR Rippingale; *Ecclesiastical Register of Ireland* (1827), 308.]

William Thomas Waters MA

Instituted 18 November 1825 to rectory of Rippingale, on resignation of Charles Douglas. Patron: Sir Gilbert Heathcote, Bt. [Reg. 40, p.344.]

Also: R. of Dunsby, 1802–53 (*q.v.*).

William Cooper BA

Instituted 11 May 1853 to rectory of Rippingale, on death of William Thomas

Waters. Patron: Trustees of the will of Sir Gilbert Heathcote of Normanton Park, Bt (decd). [Reg. 40, p.540.]

Born *c*.1813 at Lambeth; son of William C. of Islington (Mx), mercer. Educated: King's College School, London; Trinity College (matric. 1832) and Pembroke Hall, Cambridge (BA 1838; MA 1872). Deacon: 1840; priest: 1842 (Winchester). Formerly: C. of Epsom, 1841; of Banstead (Sr), 1843–5. Living at Chalk Lane, Epsom (1851). Resided at Rippingale Rectory. Licences for temporary non-residence (1858–60), on account of his ill-health; Rippingale served by Joseph Heath as curate. Died 9 June 1885 at Rippingale. [Venn, *Alumni*; Census Returns 1851 (Epsom); White, *Lincolnshire* (1856), 721; NRL 22/26; NRL 24/21; CR 4, fo.69v; Census Returns 1871, 1881; White, *Lincolnshire* (1872), 588; *Probate Calendar* 1885.]

William Wright Layng MA
Instituted 18 September 1885 to rectory of Rippingale, on death of William Cooper. Patron: Gilbert Henry Heathcote Drummond Willoughby, Lord Aveland. [Reg. 42, p.229.]

Born 15 July 1845 at Overstone (Np); son of Revd William L., later R. of Creeton (1850–77). Educated: St Mary Hall, Oxford (matric. 1866; BA and MA 1873). Deacon: 1869; priest: 1870 (Worcester). Formerly: C. of St John, Dudley, 1869–71; of Langtoft, 1871–3; V. of Spilsby, 1873–85; of Hundleby, 1883–5; RD of Hill, 1880–5. Also: RD of Aveland, 1907–23; Canon of Lincoln and Prebendary of Stow-in-Lindsey, 1907. Resided at Rippingale Rectory. Married (1871) at St John, Dudley, Caroline Mary Terry. Father of Herbert William L., Rector of Creeton (1902–11). Bishop Hicks noted (July 1913): 'By the 12.57 to Rippingale, to take part in the Village Revels, & speak in Canon Layng's Rectory garden for the CETS. Lovely weather & scene: children's morris dancing.' Retired 1923. Afterwards lived at Arcroft, Rosemary Hill, Kenilworth. Died 9 February 1936. [*Who Was Who 1929–1940*, 789; Foster, *Alumni*; *Crockford* (1932); Census Returns 1891–1911; Kelly, *Lincolnshire* (1913); *Hicks Diaries*, no.347; *Probate Calendar* 1936.]

Joseph Ernest Williams MA
Instituted 2 April 1924 to rectory of Rippingale, on resignation of William Wright Layng. Patron: Gilbert Heathcote Drummond Willoughby, Earl of Ancaster, of Grimsthorpe Castle. [Reg. 43, p.341.]

Born *c*.1882 at Liverpool; son of Thomas Henry Williams, later Rector of Bradfield St Clare (Sf). Educated: Christ's College, Cambridge (BA 1911; MA 1915). Deacon: 1912; priest: 1913 (London). Formerly: C. of Emmanuel, Paddington, 1912–14; of St Luke, Hampstead, 1914–15; TCF 1915–19; Residential Chaplain, St Dunstan's Hospital for Blinded Soldiers, 1919–24. Married (5 March 1917) at St Mary, Balham, Elsie May Trampleasure. Resided at Rippingale Rectory. Also: RD of Aveland, 1944–9; Canon of Lincoln and Prebendary of Ketton, 1946–9. Afterwards: R. of Walton-on-the-Hill (Sr), 1949–62. Retired 1962. Latterly at 9 Victoria Road South, Bognor Regis. Died 9 February 1964. [Census Returns 1901 (Liverpool); LMA, PR Balham St Mary; *Crockford* (1961–2); *Probate Calendar* 1964.]

William Williams MA
Instituted 21 July 1949 to rectory of Rippingale, on resignation of Joseph Ernest Williams. Patron: Gilbert Heathcote Drummond Willoughby, Earl of Ancaster, of Grimsthorpe Castle. [Reg. 44, p.109.]

Born 14 October 1876 at Pontyclûn, Cardiff. Educated: Queens' College, Cambridge (matric. 1900; BA 1902; MA 1907). Deacon: 1902; priest: 1903 (Llandaff). Formerly: C. of Caerphilly, 1902–6; of St Paul, Newport (Monm), 1906–9; of Temple Church, Bristol, 1909–14; V. of St Lawrence, Bristol, 1914–18; V. of All Saints, Newport (Monm), 1918–24; C. of Wilton with Netherhampton (Wlt), 1924–31; R. and V. of Bishopstone with Stratford Tony (Wlt), 1931–6; R. of Walton-on-the-Hill (Sr), 1936–49. Resided at Rippingale Rectory. Resignation accepted 30 April 1955. Retired. Disappears from *Crockford* after 1955–6. [Venn, *Alumni*; *Crockford* (1951–2, 1955–6); Reg. 44, p.210.]

David Lamplough Scott MA

Instituted 24 October 1955 to rectory of Rippingale, on resignation of William Williams. Patron: Gilbert James Heathcote Drummond Willoughby, Earl of Ancaster, of Swinstead Hall. [Reg. 44, p.215.]

Born 14 May 1921. Educated: Selwyn College, Cambridge (BA 1942; MA 1948); Ripon Hall, Oxford (1942). Deacon: 1944; priest: 1945 (York). Formerly: C. of St James, Sutton-in-Holderness, 1944–7; of Christ Church, Chelsea, 1947–9; R. of Creeton with Counthorpe and Swinstead, 1949–55. Resided at Rippingale Rectory. Also: C-in-C of Dowsby with Dunsby, 1960–3; R. of Dowsby with Dunsby, 1963–74 (*q.v.*). Afterwards: V. of Hale, Liverpool, 1974–86. Retired 1986. Lived afterwards at 8 Langwith Drive, Holbeach. Died December 1992. [*Crockford* (1980–2, 1989–90); GRO, Death Index.]

SEMPRINGHAM

The church at Sempringham formed part of the endowment of the Gilbertine Order from its inception. It had been given to Gilbert of Sempringham by his father on his return from studying in France – perhaps in the late 1110s – and when he left the household of Bishop Alexander and went back to Sempringham, his income from the church helped to fund his first community of anchoresses. The nuns inhabited an enclosure on the north side of the church. When after 1147 the Order was established, a new priory church was constructed and the parish church became once more solely for parochial use. Its endowments remained appropriated to the use of Sempringham Priory and a vicarage was ordained. The vicar was to receive eleven quarters of marketable wheat and for his servant boy two loaves every day, no doubt from the priory kitchen. He was also to receive 1d on All Saints Day, 3d at Christmas, 2d at Easter and 1d on the patronal festival of the church. He would receive the 'second legacy' or mortuary and 1d at every funeral and wedding, besides fifteen shillings of silver annually, and a competent house. The Prior was to provide him with a horse whenever he needed to travel on the church's business. The Prior and Convent presented regularly to the vicarage up to the Dissolution. Afterwards the advowson passed with the site of the priory to Lord Clinton and his descendants, the Earls of Lincoln. There were several periods after the Reformation (1576–1638, 1678–1702 and 1723–1812) when the vicarage was under sequestration and the parish served by curates. In the nineteenth century the patronage was in the possession of Earl Fortescue.

In 1890 Viscount Ebrington, son and heir of Earl Fortescue, transferred the patronage of Billingborough and Sempringham to the Crown, in exchange for the advowson of Exmoor. The living remained in the gift of the Crown in 1965. [Golding, *Gilbertine Order*, 13, 15, 353, 363; *Rot. Welles* iii. 77; *London Gazette* (26023), 14 February 1890; *LDC* (1965), 68–9.]

Gilbert de Sempingham
Instituted (no date) to vicarage of Sempringham. Patron: Master and Convent of Sempringham. [*Rot. Welles* iii. 77.]

Gilbert Wade chaplain
Instituted 16 February 1268/9 to vicarage of church of St Andrew, Sempringham, on resignation of Gilbert. Patron: Prior and Convent of Sempringham. [*Rot. Gravesend*, 35.]

William de Gayton priest
Instituted 26 October 1274 to vicarage of Sempringham, on resignation of Gilbert. Patron: Prior and Convent of St Mary, Sempringham. [*Rot. Gravesend*, 60.]

Gerinus priest
Instituted 25 February 1278/9 to vicarage of Sempringham, on resignation of William de Gayton. Patron: Prior and Convent of Sempringham. [*Rot. Gravesend*, 83.]

Benedict de Ringesdon chaplain
Instituted 24 February 1281/2 to vicarage of Sempringham, on resignation of Gerinus of Stow. Patron: Prior and Convent of Sempringham. [*Reg. Sutton* i. 21.]

John de Herlauston priest
Instituted 6 April 1283 to vicarage of Sempringham, on resignation of Benedict de Ringesdon. Patron: Prior and Convent of Sempringham. [*Reg. Sutton* i. 40.]

Robert de Bilingburg (Dilingburg) chaplain
Instituted 4 March 1283/4 to vicarage of Sempringham, on institution of John de Herlauxton to vicarage of Ketton. Patron: Prior and Convent of Sempringham. [*Reg. Sutton* i. 51.]
Afterwards: R. of mediety of Kirkby Underwood, 1288–1304 (*q.v.*).

Peter de Birthorp chaplain
Instituted 30 August 1288 to vicarage of Sempringham, on resignation of Robert de Bilingburg. Patron: Prior and Convent of Sempringham. [*Reg. Sutton* i. 111.]
Afterwards: V. of Stow-by-Threckingham, 1290–1 (*q.v.*).

Henry de Carleby chaplain
Instituted 9 May 1291 to vicarage of Sempringham, on institution of Peter de Birthorp to vicarage of Stow. Patron: Prior and Convent of Sempringham. [*Reg. Sutton* i. 154.]

Afterwards: V. of Stow-by-Threckingham, 1292–1304 (*q.v.*); V. of Billingborough, 1304–17 (*q.v.*).

John de Folkyngham chaplain
Instituted 29 April 1292 to vicarage of Sempringham, on institution of Henry to vicarage of Stow. Patron: Prior and Convent of Sempringham. [*Reg. Sutton* i. 166.]

Afterwards: V. of Buxton (Nf), 1301.

Robert de Braiceby chaplain
Instituted 11 June 1301 to vicarage of Sempringham, on institution of John de Folkingham to vicarage of Buxton (*Buckeston*), dioc. Norwich. Patron: Prior and Convent of Sempringham. [Reg. 2, fo.4.]

Afterwards: V. of Laughton-by-Folkingham, 1302.

Adam de Lavington chaplain
Instituted 10 October 1302 to vicarage of Sempringham, on resignation of Robert de Braiceby. Patron: Prior and Convent of Sempringham. [Reg. 2, fo.6v.]

John Barn priest
Instituted 12 June 1330 to vicarage of Sempringham, on death of Adam. Patron: Prior and Convent of Sempringham. [*Reg. Burghersh* i. no.265.]

John de Irnham priest
Instituted 8 October 1349 to vicarage of Sempringham, on death of John. Patron: Prior and Convent of Sempringham. [Reg. 9, fo.76v.]

John de Stowe iuxta Trikyngham priest
Instituted 26 May 1351 to vicarage of Sempringham, on resignation of John de Irnham. Patron: Prior and Convent of Sempringham. [Reg. 9, fo.92.]

Thomas Caworth de Irnham priest
Instituted 7 March 1361/2 to vicarage of Sempringham, on resignation of John. Patron: Prior and Convent of Sempringham. [Reg. 9, fo.152v.]

Roger de Camelton de Sempyngham priest
Instituted 5 May 1372 to vicarage of Sempringham, on resignation of Thomas Chaworth de Irnham. Patron: Prior and Convent of Sempringham. [Reg. 10, fo.47v.]

Assessed for poll-tax, 1377, 1381. [*Clerical Poll-Taxes*, nos 698, 1330, 1919.]

John Crees priest
Instituted 4 March 1388/9 to vicarage of Sempringham, on resignation of Roger de Camulton. Patron: Prior and Convent of Sempringham. [Reg. 11, fo.38v.]

William son of William Perotson de Coryngham priest
Instituted 3 August 1393 to vicarage of Sempringham, on resignation of John Crece. Patron: Prior and Convent of Sempringham. [Reg. 11, fo.66.]
Afterwards: R. of Flowton (Sf), 1409.

John Cham
Instituted 19 July 1409 to vicarage of Sempringham, on resignation of William Perotson (by exchange with church of Flowton, dioc. Norwich). Patron: Prior and Convent of Sempringham. [Reg. 14, fo.36.]
Formerly: R. of Flowton (Sf), to 1409. Afterwards: V. of Anwick, January–March 1413. [Reg. 14, fos 60v, 62.]

Nicholas Horne
Instituted 3 January 1412/13 to vicarage of Sempringham, on resignation of John Cham (by exchange with vicarage of Anwick). Patron: Prior and Convent of Sempringham. [Reg. 14, fo.60v.]
Formerly: V. of Ardeley (Hrt), to 1412; V. of Anwick, 1412–13. [Reg. 14, fos 55v, 303v.]

William Perotson priest
Instituted 12 January 1416/17 to vicarage of Sempringham, on death of Nicholas Horne. Patron: Prior and Convent of Sempringham. [Reg. 14, fo.85.]

Richard Seman priest
Instituted 28 September 1431 to vicarage of Sempringham, on death of William Perotson. Patron: Prior and Convent of Sempringham. [Reg. 17, fo.1v.]

Thomas Browne priest
Instituted 8 August 1469 to vicarage of Sempringham, on resignation of Richard Seyman. Patron: Prior and Convent of Sempringham. [Reg. 20, fo.149v.]

Thomas Clyff priest
Instituted 2 April 1494 to vicarage of Sempringham, on death of Thomas Browne. Patron: Prior and Convent of Sempringham (2 April 1494). [Reg. 22, fo.157v; PD 1494/51.]

Richard Hansby priest
Instituted 27 April 1503 to vicarage of Sempringham, on resignation of Thomas Clife. Patron: Prior and Convent of Sempringham. [Reg. 23, fo.75v.]

John Durhaunt priest, canon of Sempringham
Instituted 22 October 1509 to vicarage of Sempringham, on resignation
of Richard Hensby. Patron: Prior and Convent of Sempringham. [Reg. 23,
fo.138.]

John Raggit chaplain
Instituted 10 June 1525 to vicarage of Sempringham, on death of John
Durrant. Patron: Prior and Convent of Sempringham. [Reg. 27, fo.38v.]

Assessed for subsidy (£4 13s 4d) in 1526; assessed for *Valor Ecclesiasticus* 1535. [*Subsidy*,
58; *Valor* iv. 104.]

Hugh Gryssington chaplain
Instituted 14 May 1539 to vicarage of Sempringham, on death of last incumbent. Patron: Thomas, Duke of Norfolk, Lord High Treasurer and Earl
Marshal of England, by reason of a grant of the advowson made to him by
the lately dissolved Prior and Convent of Sempringham. [Reg. 27, fo.69.]

Robert Baker chaplain
Instituted 17 October 1541 to vicarage of Sempringham, on death of Hugh
Gressington. Patron: Edward Clynton, Lord Clinton and Saye (20 July 1541).
[Reg. 27, fo.76; PD 1541/22.]

Exhibited at Visitation in 1551. Witnessed Sempringham will 1552. [Vj 13, fo.62v; LCC
Wills 1551–3/176.]

The vicarage of Sempringham was vacant in 1576. The living was served
by curates: Roger Rodiate (between 1576 and 1589), James Lloyd (or
Floyd) (occurs 1594 and 1597), Henry Holywell (occurs 1604 and 1607),
Samuel Skelton (occurs 1619–21) and Thomas White (occurs 1624–35).
[*Bishop Cooper*, 209; *State of the Church*, 6, 10, 74, 175, 383, 397, 415;
BTs Sempringham.]

Samuel Stoneham MA
Instituted 18 December 1638 to vicarage of Sempringham (cause of vacancy
not stated). Patron: King Charles I, by lapse. [AC; IND/L 1, fo.119.]

Of Lincolnshire. Educated: St Catharine's Hall, Cambridge (matric. 1629–30; BA 1633;
MA 1638). Deacon: 21 September 1634 (Peterborough). Signed BT 1638. Afterwards: R.
of Brockdish (Nf), 1648. [Venn, *Alumni*; BTs Sempringham.]

John Marshall
Instituted by 1662. [LC 5, fo.24.]

Signed BTs 1660–75. Also: V. of Threckingham 1662–76 (*q.v.*). [BTs Sempringham.]

Thomas Morton BA
Instituted 12 February 1676/7 to vicarage of Sempringham, on death of last
incumbent. Patron: Charles Bates, esquire. [Reg. 34, fo.17.]

Baptised at Withern, 13 June 1647; son of Robert M., Rector of Withern (1644) and grandson of Adam M., Rector of Hinton-in-the-Hedges (1608–53). Educated: Lincoln College (matric. 1666) and New Inn Hall, Oxford (BA 1670). Deacon: 25 September 1670; priest: 18 June 1671 (Peterborough). Signed BTs at Sempringham 1677. Afterwards: R. of Beesby, 1678–1709. [PR Withern; Longden ix. 277; Foster, *Alumni*; Reg. 34, fo.17; BTs Sempringham.]

From 1678 until 1702 Sempringham was served by Henry Brerewood as curate. [LC 14, fo.7; BTs Sempringham.]

Samuel Galley

Instituted 22 November 1704 to vicarage of Sempringham. [SUB VI, 165.]

Born *c.*1661 in Cheshire; son of Richard G., husbandman. Educated: Wrexham School and St John's College, Cambridge (matric. 1681; BA 1683–4). Also C. of Helpringham. Resided at Sempringham 'but not in the Vicarage, because it is unsuited'; later, 'in the Vicarage'. Signed BTs at Sempringham 1704–22. Buried at Sempringham, 23 June 1723. [*St John's Admissions* ii. 78; Venn, *Alumni*; Speculum, 63, 106; BTs Sempringham; PR Sempringham.]

From 1723 until 1812 Sempringham was served by curates, including Miles Rowlandson (1723–46), Edward Edwards (1758–69), Irton Murthwaite (1771–84) and John Shinglar (1785–1812). [BTs Sempringham; LC 31, p.77]

William Thomas Walters (Waters) MA

Instituted 13 April 1813 to vicarage of Sempringham, on death of last incumbent. Patron: King George III, by lapse. Vacated by resignation, 9 November 1825. [Reg. 40, p.180; RES 240/78.]

Also: R. of Dunsby, 1802–53 (*q.v.*).

Thomas Latham MA

Instituted 18 February 1826 to vicarage of Sempringham, on resignation of William Waters. Patron: Earl Fortescue. [Reg. 40, p.345.]

Also: V. of Billingborough, 1803–46 (*q.v.*).

Samuel John Hillyerd

Instituted 12 August 1846 to vicarage of Sempringham, on death of Thomas Latham. Patron: Hugh, Earl Fortescue. [Reg. 40, p.512.]

Baptised 14 March 1784 at St Mary, Rotherhithe; son of Nicholas H. and Mary his wife. Education: literate. Deacon: March 1819 (Exeter for York); priest: 3 August 1823 (York). Formerly: C. of Denby (YWR), 1819; PC of Tattershall, 1824–46. Resided at West Street, Pointon. Died 29 June 1861 at Pointon; buried at Sempringham (MI). [*York Ordinations 1800–1849*, 93; PR Tattershall; Census Returns 1851, 1861 (Pointon); White, *Lincolnshire* (1856), 723; *Probate Calendar* 1861; PR Sempringham.]

John Charles Kitching Saunders MA

Instituted 13 September 1861 to vicarage of Sempringham, on death of Samuel John Hillyerd. Patron: Hugh, Earl Fortescue, of Castle Hill, South Molton (Dev). [Reg. 41, p.75.]

Born *c*.1824; son of John S. of St Andrew's, Plymouth, gent. Educated: St Edmund Hall, Oxford (matric. 1846; BA 1850; MA 1854). Deacon and priest: 1851 (York). Formerly: C. of Withernwick (YER), 1851–2; of South Molton (Dev), 1853–61. Resided at Pointon where a new Vicarage House was built (1865). During his incumbency he also secured the building of the school at Pointon and the restoration of the church. Signed registers at Sempringham 1861–9. Afterwards: R. of Thornton-le-Moor, 1869–75; R. of Friesthorpe with Snarford, 1875–90. Retired 1890; lived at 3 Salisbury Road, St Jude's, Plymouth. Died 19 March 1910 at Plymouth. [Foster, *Alumni*; *Crockford* (1898); Kelly, *Lincolnshire* (1889), 387; PR Sempringham; *Probate Calendar* 1910.]

Robert Keith Arbuthnot MA

Instituted 17 December 1869 to vicarage of Sempringham, on cession of John Charles Kitching Saunders. Patron: Hugh, Earl Fortescue. [Reg. 41, p.302.]

Born 10 August 1838 at Nassek (East Indies); son of Sir Robert Keith Arbuthnot, 2nd Bt. Educated: Trinity College, Dublin (BA 1861; MA 1864). Deacon: 1861; priest: 1862 (London). Formerly: C. of St Martin-in-the-Fields (Mx), 1861–3; of Kimpton (Hrt), 1864–9. Married (17 June 1868) Mary Agnes, daughter of Edward Vaughan, Rector of Harpenden and Canon of St Albans. Resided at Sempringham Vicarage House in Pointon ('a commodious residence'). Afterwards: V. of St Luke, Holbeach Hurn, 1874–80; V. of St James, Ratcliffe, London, 1880–94. Died 5 December 1894. [Burke, *Peerage* (1959), 82; *Crockford* (1885); Census Returns 1871; White, *Lincolnshire* (1872), 588–9; *Probate Calendar* 1895.]

John James Hodgson MA

Instituted 18 June 1874 to vicarage of Sempringham, on cession of Robert Keith Arbuthnot. Patron: Hugh, Earl Fortescue, as above. [Reg. 41, p.463.]

Born *c*.1835; son of Alfred H. of Snaith (YWR), doctor. Educated: Magdalene College, Cambridge (matric. 1854; BA 1858; MA 1861). Deacon: 1858; priest: 1859 (Ely). Formerly: C. of Holy Trinity, Ely, 1859–60; of St Lawrence, York, 1860–2; of Holbeach, 1862–74. Resided at Pointon Vicarage. Died 25 August 1877, following a fall sustained while demonstrating gymnastic exercises to his children. Buried at Sempringham (MI). [Venn, *Alumni*; *Crockford* (1874); Bray, *Ely Lists*; *Probate Calendar* 1877; *Grantham Journal*, 1 September 1877; PR Sempringham.]

Thomas Charles Litchfield Layton MA

Instituted 23 November 1877 to vicarage of Sempringham, on death of John James Hodgson. Patron: Hugh, Earl Fortescue. [Reg. 42, p.4.]

Born *c*.1823 at Windsor; son of Charles L., gent. Educated: Pembroke College, Oxford (matric. 1839; BA 1845; MA 1846); Scholar 1839–54; Fellow 1854–6. Deacon: 1846; priest: 1847 (Oxford). Formerly: C. of St Andrew, Plymouth, 1852–5; R. of St Aldate, Oxford, 1856–9; C. of Calne (Wlt), 1859–62; of Marston Magna (So), 1866–7; of St Thomas, Exeter, 1867–70; of Wellington (So), 1870–2; of Emmanuel Chapel, Weston-super-Mare, 1872–5; of Charles, Plymouth, 1875–7. Signed registers at Sempringham

1877–83, intermittently thereafter. Licences for non-residence (1884–6), on account of the ill-health of his wife and daughters. Resigned 19 November (accepted 26 November) 1887. Afterwards: V. of Newnham (Hrt), 1887–9. Latterly of Ivy Cottage, 4 Bedford Street, Hitchin. Died 30 April 1893. [Foster, *Alumni*; *Crockford* (1891); PR Sempringham; NRL 48/16; NRL 49/12; NRL 50/13; RES 248/43; *Probate Calendar* 1893.]

Edwin Wrenford

Instituted 10 December 1887 to vicarage of Sempringham, on resignation of Thomas Charles Litchfield Layton. Patron: Hugh, Earl Fortescue, of Castle Hill, par. Filleigh (Dev). [Reg. 42, p.264.]

Born *c*.1829 at Liverpool; son of William W., Collector of Inland Revenue. Educated: St Bees College (1851); University of Röstock (PhD 1867). Deacon: 26 June 1853; priest: 2 July 1854 (Durham). Formerly: C. of St Hilda, South Shields, 1853–5; of Christ Church, Carlisle, 1855–8; of Blackburn, 1858–60; of Guilden Morden (Ca), 1860–5; of St Paul, Newport (Monm), 1879–81; V. of Newnham (Hrt), 1881–7. Married (11 August 1853) at Otley (YWR), Sarah, daughter of Benjamin Stinson, wine merchant. Author: *First-fruits of Sacred Song* (1876); *Carmina Regia and other Songs of the Heart* (1878); *'The Kiss of Death' and 'In Memoriam': Alice Maud Mary, Princess of England* (1878). Resided at Sempringham Vicarage in Pointon. Built mission church of St John Evangelist at Pointon (1892); added south porch at Sempringham Church to commemorate Queen Victoria's Diamond Jubilee. Died 18 January 1901 at Kesteven County Asylum, Grantham, aged 71. Buried at Sempringham (MI). [Census Returns Wales 1851 (Newport); *St Bees College Calendar* (1859), 75; Durham UL, DDR/EA/CL; *Crockford* (1898); WYAS, PR Otley All Saints; Census Returns 1891; *Probate Calendar* 1901; *Stamford Mercury*, 25 January 1901.]

Edward Ernest Harrisson MA

Instituted 6 May 1901 to vicarage of Sempringham, on death of Edwin Wrenford. Patron: Hon Hugh Fortescue, commonly called Viscount Ebrington of Exmoor, for this alternate turn. [Reg. 42, p.484.]

Born 20 June 1863 at 64 Great Portland Street, London; son of Henry H., surgeon. Baptised 4 August 1863 at All Souls, Marylebone. Educated: King's School, Ely, and Corpus Christi College, Cambridge (matric. 1882; BA 1888; MA 1892). Deacon: 16 June 1889; priest: 12 June 1892 (Durham). Formerly: C. of Marley Hill, Durham, 1889–92; of St Cuthbert, Gateshead, 1892–4; of Bedale (YNR), 1894–9; of Sedbergh with Howgill (YWR), 1899–1901. Resided at Sempringham Vicarage. Bishop Hicks noted (March 1914): 'through his own (and his wife's) blindness [he] is to resign'. Resigned 1914. Latterly of St Gilbert's, North Road, Bourne. Died 9 January 1917. [LMA, PR St Marylebone; Venn, *Alumni*; Durham UL, DDR/EA/CL; *Crockford*; Census Returns 1911; *Hicks Diaries*, no.454; *Probate Calendar* 1917.]

Thomas Edward Pritchett

Instituted 5 February 1915 to vicarage of Sempringham with Pointon and Birthorpe, on resignation of Edward Ernest Harrisson. Patron: King George V. [Reg. 43, p.84.]

Baptised 18 May 1853 at St Michael, Stockwell; son of Edward P. of 3 Lorn Road, hosier. Educated: University of Oxford, Non-Coll. (matric. 1877); St Alban Hall (BA 1880); Merton College (MA 1895); Wycliffe Hall (1881). Deacon: 1881 (Oxford); priest: 1884 (Perth). Formerly: C. of Middle Claydon (Bk), 1881–2; of Faringdon, 1882–4; Assistant Chaplain and Precentor of Perth Cathedral, 1884–5; R. of Gingin with Chittering Lake (Western Australia), 1885–98; C. of Holy Trinity, Wakefield, 1895–6; Chaplain at Turin, 1898–9; in Canterbury Diocese, 1903–10; R. of Stratford St Andrew (Sf), 1910–15. Resided at Sempringham Vicarage. Afterwards: V. of Elmbridge (Wo), 1924–9. Retired to live at The Rodd, Glenair Road, Parkstone (Do). Died 28 April 1932 at Cornelia Hospital, Poole. [LMA, PR Stockwell St Michael; Foster, *Alumni*; *Crockford* (1923, 1932); *Probate Calendar* 1932.]

William Thomas Henley Bradley

Instituted 23 December 1924 to vicarage of Sempringham with Pointon and Birthorpe, on cession of Thomas Edward Pritchett. Patron: King George V. [Reg. 43, p.354.]

Educated: Scholae Cancellarii, Lincoln. Deacon: 1914; priest: 1915 (Southwark). Formerly: C. of Tooting Graveney, 1914–16; of All Saints, Wandsworth, 1917–18; of St Mark, Battersea, 1918–19; of St John Evangelist, Redhill (Sr), 1919–21; of St John, Peterborough, 1921–4. Afterwards: V. of Ashby-de-la-Launde, 1927. Died 23 November 1930. [*Crockford* (1923); *LDC* (1931), 160.]

Percy Jules Hulbert

Instituted 24 March 1927 to vicarage of Sempringham with Pointon and Birthorpe, on cession of William Thomas Henley Bradley. Patron: King George V. [Reg. 43, p.413.]

Born 14 May, baptised 14 June 1871 at St Peter, De Beauvoir Town, Hackney; son of John Attwood H., merchant. Educated: Scholae Cancellarii, Lincoln (1904). Deacon: 10 June 1906; priest: 26 May 1907 (Lincoln). Formerly: C. of Alford with Rigsby, 1906–8; of Frampton, 1908–10; V. of Frampton, 1910–15; V. of Spaldwick with Barham (Hu), 1915–19; R. of Gate Burton with Knaith, 1919–20; P-in-C of St Ninian, Invergordon, 1921–2; R. of St Olaf, Kirkwall, 1922–4; C. of Wishaw, 1924–5; in Lincoln Diocese, 1925–6; R. of Kirkby Underwood, 1926–7 (*q.v.*). Resided at Sempringham Vicarage. Afterwards: R. of Belleau and Claythorpe with Aby and Greenfield, 1931–3; in Chichester Diocese, 1933–40; P-in-C of St Ninian, Invergordon, 1940. Latterly of St Ninian's, Lancing (Sx). Died 15 September 1945. [LMA, PR Hackney St Peter; *Crockford* (1929, 1941); *LDM* (1906–7); *Probate Calendar* 1945.]

Albert Edward Parsons

Instituted 13 November 1931 to vicarage of Sempringham with Pointon and Birthorpe, on cession of Percy Jules Hulbert. Patron: King George V. [Reg. 43, p.495.]

Educated: St Michael's College, Llandaff (1925). Deacon: 1926; priest: 1928 (Llandaff). Formerly: C. of St Andrew, Cardiff, 1926–30; of Branksome Park with St Aldhelm (Do), 1930–1. Resided at Sempringham Vicarage. Afterwards: V. of Ringland with Morton-on-the-Hill (Nf), 1936–9. Died 31 May 1939 at Ringland Vicarage. [*Crockford* (1932); *Probate Calendar* 1939.]

Leonard Garnier Pilkington

Instituted 22 February 1937 (by Bishop of Grimsby as Commissary) to vicarage of Sempringham with Pointon and Birthorpe, on cession of Albert Edward Parsons. Patron: King Edward VIII. [Reg. 43, p.593.]

Born 1877 at Worcester; son of Revd Charles H. Pilkington, Vicar of The Tything, Worcester; also great-nephew of Thomas Garnier, Dean of Lincoln. Living at Bristol (1911); working as Warden of Boys' Club for J. S. Fry and Sons, Cocoa Manufacturers. Deacon: 1929; priest: 1930 (London). Formerly: C. of Christ Church, Crouch End, 1929; of St George, Hornsey (Mx), 1929–37. Resided at Sempringham Vicarage in Pointon. Died there 14 December 1945; buried at Sempringham (MI). [GRO, Birth Index; Census Returns 1911 (Bristol); *Crockford* (1941); *Probate Calendar* 1946.]

Gerald Wilfred Fardell Howard

Instituted 10 December 1946 to vicarage of Sempringham with Pointon and Birthorpe, on death of Leonard Garnier Pilkington. Patron: King George VI. [Reg. 44, p.66.]

Born 1884 at Littleport (Ca); son of Wilfred H., medical practitioner. Educated: Scholae Cancellarii, Lincoln (1908). Deacon: 1910; priest: 1911 (York). Formerly: C. of St Lawrence, York, 1910–12; of Stansted, 1912–15; of Pulham St Mary (Nf), 1915–17; TCRN 1917–19; C. of North Walsham (Nf), 1919–20; of Great Yarmouth, 1920–2; V. of St James with Pockthorpe, Norwich, 1922–9; R. of Mutford with Rushmere (Sf), 1929–32; R. of Winterton with East Somerton (Nf), 1932–45; Chaplain, RAFVR, 1941–6. Resided at Sempringham Vicarage. Afterwards: R. of Tivetshall St Mary with St Margaret, 1947–55. Retired to Tower Cottage, Winterton-on-Sea. Died 1960. [GRO, Birth Index; Census Returns 1891 (New Buckenham), 1911 (York); *Crockford* (1959–60); *LDC* (1947), 51; GRO, Death Index.]

Leslie Ronald Swingler

Instituted 13 May 1949 to vicarage of Sempringham, on cession of Gerard Wilfred Fardell Howard. Patron: King George VI. Note that on 11 April 1949, the Archbishop of Canterbury granted a dispensation enabling the said LRS to hold together the vicarage of Billingborough and the vicarage of Sempringham. [Reg. 44, pp. 105–6.]

Also: V. of Billingborough (*q.v.*).

Charles Francis Ward

Instituted 28 August 1958 to vicarage of Sempringham, on cession of Leslie Ronald Swingler. Patron: Queen Elizabeth II. Note that on 11 July 1958, the Archbishop of Canterbury granted a dispensation enabling the said CFW to hold together the vicarage of Billingborough and the vicarage of Sempringham. [Reg. 44, p.259.]

Also: V. of Billingborough (*q.v.*).

Peter Brian Hearn

Instituted 19 March 1964 to vicarage of Sempringham, on death of Charles Francis Ward. Patron: Queen Elizabeth II. Note that on 16 January 1964, the Archbishop of Canterbury granted a dispensation enabling the said PBH to hold together the vicarage of Billingborough and the vicarage of Sempringham. [Reg. 44, p.358.]

Also: V. of Billingborough (*q.v.*).

STOW-BY-THRECKINGHAM

The church of St Aethelthryth, Stow-by-Threckingham, with its chapel at Birthorpe was given by William Pikenot to Sempringham Priory; it was confirmed to them by Bishop Robert Chesney before 1166. It was appropriated and a vicarage ordained, which consisted of the altarage, a house and one quarter of marketable wheat annually. A dispute in 1222 over the advowson of Birthorpe chapel appears to have been settled in the Priory's favour. The Priory continued to present to the vicarage until the early fifteenth century. The grant by King Henry III in 1268 of an annual fair at Stow Green helped the village to flourish for a time but by 1428 it was reported that there were only eight inhabitants in Stow and Birthorpe. The last institution was made in 1423. [*EEA* i. App. 1 (no.23); *EEA* iv. nos 174–5; *VCH Lincoln* ii. 181; *Rot. Welles* iii. 77; *Feudal Aids* iii. 338.]

Warin chaplain
Instituted between 1223 and 1226 to vicarage of Stow-by-Threckingham. Patron: Prior and Convent of Sempringham. [*Rot. Welles* iii. 77; 'Rolls of Hugh of Wells', 173–5.]

Gilbert
Instituted before 31 August 1264. [*Rot. Gravesend*, 17.]

John de Saueton priest
Instituted 31 August 1264 to vicarage of Stow-by-Threckingham, on death of Gilbert. Patron: Prior and Convent of Sempringham. [*Rot. Gravesend*, 17.]

Ralph de Bolyngbroc chaplain
Instituted 27 March 1273 to vicarage of Stow-by-Threckingham, on death of John. Patron: Prior and Convent of Sempringham. [*Rot. Gravesend*, 54.]

Ralph de Lyndeseye
Instituted before 15 March 1281/2. [*Reg. Sutton* i. 22.]

Geoffrey de Gumcestre chaplain
Instituted 15 March 1281/2 to vicarage of Stow-by-Threckingham, on death of Ralph de Lyndeseye. Patron: Prior and Convent of Sempringham. [*Reg. Sutton* i. 22.]

Peter de Birthorp chaplain
Instituted 18 November 1290 to vicarage of Stow-by-Threckingham, on resignation of Geoffrey de Gurmecestre. Patron: Prior and Convent of Sempringham. [*Reg. Sutton* i. 146.]
Formerly: V. of Sempringham, 1288–90 (*q.v.*).

William de Ringedon chaplain
Instituted 1 October 1291 to vicarage of Stow-by-Threckingham, on death of Peter. Patron: Prior and Convent of Sempringham. [*Reg. Sutton* i. 159.]
Afterwards: V. of Horbling, 1291–1300 (*q.v.*).

Henry de Carleby chaplain
Instituted 18 January 1291/2 to vicarage of Stow-by-Threckingham, on institution of William de Ringesdon to vicarage of Horbling. Patron: Prior and Convent of Sempringham. [*Reg. Sutton* i. 162.]
Formerly: V. of Sempringham, 1291–2 (*q.v.*). Afterwards: V. of Billingborough, 1304–17 (*q.v.*).

John de Sempingham chaplain
Instituted 22 February 1303/4 to vicarage of Stow-by-Threckingham, on institution of Henry de Carleby to vicarage of Billingborough. Patron: Prior and Convent of Sempringham. [Reg. 2, fo.9v.]

William de Barton
Instituted before 29 June 1327. [*Reg. Burghersh* i. no.167.]

John de Camelton priest
Instituted 29 June 1327 to vicarage of Stow-by-Threckingham, on resignation of William de Barton. Patron: Prior and Convent of Sempringham. [*Reg. Burghersh* i. no.167.]

Simon de Walcote chaplain
Instituted in accordance with bishop's commission dated 15 September 1335 to vicarage of Stow-by-Threckingham. Patron: Prior and Convent of Sempringham. [Reg. 5, fo.225v.]

William son of Alan Wade de Horbelyng priest
Instituted in accordance with bishop's commission dated 24 September 1337 to vicarage of Stow-by-Threckingham. Patron: Prior and Convent of Sempringham. [Reg. 5, fo.239.]
Afterwards: V. of Billingborough, 1346–66 (*q.v.*).

John Payn priest
Instituted 29 September 1346 to vicarage of Stow-by-Threckingham, on resignation of William son of Alan Wade de Horbelyng (by exchange with vicarage of Billingborough). Patron: Prior and Convent of Sempringham. [Reg. 6, fo.24.]
Formerly: V. of Billingborough, to 1346 (*q.v.*).

Richard son of Robert son of Henry de Wilughby super Wald priest
Instituted 22 August 1349 to vicarage of Stow-by-Threckingham, on death of
John. Patron: Prior and Convent of Sempringham. [Reg. 9, fo.64.]

William de Wylughby
Instituted before 30 October 1350. [Reg. 9, fo.88.]

John de Salteby priest
Instituted 30 October 1350 to vicarage of Stow-by-Threckingham, on resig-
nation of William de Wylughby. Patron: Prior and Convent of Sempringham.
[Reg. 9, fo.88.]
Afterwards: V. of Saltby (Le), 1357.

Thomas (son of Hugh) de Sproxton (alias Salteby) priest
Instituted 24 October 1357 to vicarage of Stow-by-Threckingham, on resig-
nation of John de Salteby (by exchange with vicarage of Saltby). Patron:
Prior and Convent of Sempringham. [Reg. 9, fos 130, 368v.]
Priest: before 5 December 1351. Formerly: V. of Saltby (Le), 1351–7. Afterwards: V. of
Ingham, 1370–95 (q.v.). [Reg. 9, fo.352v.]

John de Luda priest
Instituted 9 December 1370 to vicarage of Stow-by-Threckingham, on resig-
nation of Thomas de Salteby (by exchange with vicarage of Ingham). Patron:
Prior and Convent of Sempringham. [Reg. 10, fos 43v, 136v.]
Formerly: V. of Ingham, March–December 1370.

Robert de Basingham
Instituted before 21 July 1382. [Reg. 10, fo.120.]

Robert Vescy de Conyngesburgh priest
Instituted 21 July 1382 to vicarage of Stow-by-Threckingham, on resignation
of Robert de Basingham. Patron: Prior and Convent of Sempringham. [Reg.
10, fo.120.]

Richard (Makeblith de) Rolleston
Instituted before 1 September 1390. [Reg. 11, fo.47.]
Afterwards: V. of Cosby (Le), 1390–1403; V. of Alrewas (St), 1403. [Reg. 13, fo.199.]

Matthew de Upton priest
Instituted 1 September 1390 to vicarage of Stow-by-Threckingham, on resig-
nation of Richard Rolleston (by exchange with vicarage of Cosby). Patron:
Prior and Convent of Sempringham. [Reg. 11, fo.47.]

Formerly: V. of Selston (Nt), to 1388; V. of Cosby (Le), 1388–90. [Train, *Central Notts Clergy* iii. 11; Reg. 11, fos 210v, 215v.]

Henry Berbe priest
Instituted 26 [September] 1391 to vicarage of Stow-by-Threckingham, on resignation of Matthew Upton. Patron: Prior and Convent of Sempringham. [Reg. 11, fo.52v.]

Thomas de Demelby priest
Instituted 28 September 1392 to vicarage of Stow-by-Threckingham, on resignation of Henry Barbe. Patron: Prior and Convent of Sempringham. [Reg. 11, fo.60v.]

William Wyberd priest
Instituted 13 February 1421/2 to vicarage of Stow-by-Threckingham (cause of vacancy not stated). Patron: Prior and Convent of Sempringham. [*Reg. Fleming* i. no.130.]

M. William Paynell priest
Instituted 10 December 1423 to vicarage of Stow-by-Threckingham (cause of vacancy not stated). Patron: Prior and Convent of Sempringham. [*Reg. Fleming* i. no.226.]

SWATON

The church of Swaton formed part of the manor there held at the time of the Domesday Survey by Colswein. This passed to his daughter Muriel, who married Robert de Haia. During the reign of Henry I, Robert gave Swaton Church to Lessay Abbey in Normandy but it reverted later to the tenure of the Haia family. Robert's granddaughter, the redoubtable Nichola de Haia, presented to the rectory in 1221–2; she died at Swaton in 1230. The manor and advowson then passed to Idonea, daughter of Nichola and Gerard de Camville, who married William II de Longespee; he presented in 1231–2. William died in 1250, while on crusade, at Mansura on the Nile; his son, William III, died in 1257 from injuries sustained at a tournament at Blyth (Nt). The estate then passed to Margaret, daughter of William III, who married Henry de Lacy, Earl of Lincoln. Their daughter Alice married Thomas, Earl of Lancaster, who was beheaded at Pontefract in 1322 after the defeat of his rebellion against King Edward II at the battle of Boroughbridge. Three months after his execution, Alice granted the manor and advowson of Swaton to Barlings Abbey of which she, through her descent from Colswein and the Haia family, was the hereditary patron. The church was appropriated on 23 June 1332 by John Stratford, Bishop of Winchester, in accordance with a papal bull dated 16 October 1331. A vicarage was ordained by Bishop Burgh-ersh on 9 March 1332/3. It was to consist of part of the rectory manse, with arable land (7 acres), meadow (3 acres), common of pasture, all oblations, mortuaries and small tithes. The vicar was to find a chaplain to celebrate in the chapel at Spanby; he was to pay procurations, synodals and laetere, to keep the books, vestments and ornaments in repair, and to undertake minor repairs of the chancel. Barlings continued to present to the vicarage until the Dissolution, after which the patronage passed to the Earls of Lincoln. Towards the end of the seventeenth century the advowson was acquired by Samuel Heyrick, citizen and stationer of London. It then passed to William Ducros, Rector of Swaton from 1729 to 1745, whose widow Mary presented in 1745. It descended from her to Jerome Knapp, her stepson, and continued in the Knapp family until the nineteenth century. In 1965 the living was in the gift of the Diocesan Board of Patronage. [*Lincolnshire Domesday*, 122–3; Sanders, *English Baronies*, 109, 112; *Honors and Knights Fees* ii. 220–2; *GEC* xi. 382–5; *Custodians of Continuity*, 360–9; Colvin, *White Canons*, 75; *Reg. Burghersh* i. nos 375, 397; *LDC* (1965), 68–9.]

Church

Bartholomew clerk
Instituted in the thirteenth pontifical year of Bishop Hugh of Wells (20 December 1221/19 December 1222) to church of Swaton. Patron: lady Nichola de Haya. [*Rot. Welles* iii. 115.]

Augustine de Wycumb subdeacon
Instituted in the twenty-third pontifical year of Bishop Hugh of Wells (20 December 1231/19 December 1232) to church of Swaton. Patron: William Lungespee, in right of his wife. [*Rot. Welles* iii. 197–8.]

H. of Penn
Instituted before 17 June 1295. [*Reg. Sutton* i. 199.]

M. Robert de la Vanne chaplain
Instituted 17 June 1295 to church of Swaton, on death of H … of Penn. Patron: Henry de Lacy, Earl of Lincoln. [*Reg. Sutton* i. 199.]

Also: Chaplain of Bishop of Albano; Canon of Wimborne Minster (Do); R. of Kirkby Thore (We): had papal dispensation (12 May 1300) to retain Kirkby and Swaton, notwithstanding he had held them for five years without dispensation. [*CPL* i. 588.]

William Nunny chaplain
Instituted 1 September 1309 to church of Swaton (having been granted the benefice *in commendam* 13 February 1308/9), on death of M. Robert de la Vanne. Patron: Henry, Earl of Lincoln. [Reg. 2, fos 31, 333.]

Elias de Stapilton deacon
Instituted 13 October 1316 to church of Swaton, on death of William Nunny.
Patron: Thomas, Earl of Lancaster. [Reg. 2, fo.62v.]

Geoffrey de Edenham priest
Instituted 16 December 1328 to church of Swaton, on death of Elias. Patron:
Abbot and Convent of Barlings. [*Reg. Burghersh* i. no.209.]

Commission to act as co-adjutor to Philip, R. of Braceborough, 5 December 1330. [Reg.
5, fo.441.]

Vicarage

William de Scredyngton priest
Instituted 18 March 1332/3 to vicarage of Swaton, newly ordained. Patron:
Abbot (Thomas) and Convent of Barlings. [*Reg. Burghersh* i. no.376.]

Appointed a commissary to audit accounts of administrators of goods of John Yoman, 23
January 1335/6. [*Reg. Burghersh* iii. no.1956.]

William de Oxeton
Instituted before 4 October 1357. [Reg. 9, fo.129.]

Afterwards: V. of Kensington (Mx), 1357.

John de Tichemerssh
Instituted 4 October 1357 to vicarage of Swaton, on resignation of William
de Oxeton (by exchange with vicarage of Kensington, dioc. London). Patron:
Abbot and Convent of Barlings. [Reg. 9, fo.129.]

Formerly: V. of Kensington (Mx), to 1357. [Neither Oxeton nor Tichemerssh is listed
among the vicars of Kensington in Hennessy, 256.]

John de Hille
Instituted before 4 August 1363. [Reg. 10, fo.1v.]

Afterwards: V. of Ashbourne (Db), 1363.

William de Exton
Instituted 4 August 1363 to vicarage of Swaton, on resignation of John de
Hille (by exchange with vicarage of Ashbourne, dioc. Coventry and Lich-
field). Patron: Abbot and Convent of Barlings. [Reg. 10, fo.1v.]

Formerly: R. of Shelley (Ess), to 1363; V. of Ashbourne (Db), January–August 1363.
[*Reg. Sudbury* i. 22.]

Adam de Lubynham priest
Instituted 15 June 1369 to vicarage of Swaton, on death of William de Exton.
Patron: Abbot and Convent of Barlings. [Reg. 10, fo.28v.]

Afterwards: V. of Riseley (Bd), 1372.

William Gaunt priest
Instituted 10 August 1372 to vicarage of Swaton, on resignation of Adam de Lobenham (by exchange with vicarage of Riseley). Patron: Abbot and Convent of Barlings. [Reg. 10, fo.50.]

Priest: before 19 July 1349. Formerly: V. of Riseley (Bd), 1349–72. [Reg. 9, fo.419.]

William de Northiby de Glentham priest
Instituted 21 December 1373 to vicarage of Swaton, on death of William. Patron: Abbot and Convent of Barlings. [Reg. 10, fo.60v.]

Robert Tollare de Threkyngham
Instituted by 1381. [*Clerical Poll-Taxes*, nos 1342, 1931.]

Afterwards: R. of St Mary *ad pontem*, Stamford, 1382–3; Master of Hospital of St John Baptist, Sevenoaks (K), 1383. [Reg. 10, fo.122; Reg. 11, fo.1.]

Henry de Barneby priest
Instituted 13 December 1382 to vicarage of Swaton, on resignation of Robert Tollare de Threkyngham (by exchange with church of St Mary *ad pontem*, Stamford). Patron: Abbot and Convent of Barlings. [Reg. 10, fo.122.]

Formerly: R. of St Mary *ad pontem*, Stamford, to 1382. Afterwards: R. of Somerby-by-Grantham, 1386–90; R. of St Andrew, Hertford, 1390. [Reg. 11, fo.44v.]

John son of Alan de Wigtoft priest
Instituted 4 May 1386 to vicarage of Swaton, on resignation of Henry Barneby (by exchange with church of Somerby-by-Grantham). Patron: Abbot and Convent of Barlings. [Reg. 11, fo.23.]

Priest: by 31 May 1385. Formerly: R. of Somerby-by-Grantham, 1385–6. Afterwards: R. of Allexton (Le), 1388–9; V. of Frieston, 1389. [Reg. 11, fos 14v, 210, 212v.]

Thomas Everarde priest
Instituted 24 August 1388 to vicarage of Swaton, on resignation of John Wictoft (by exchange with church of Allexton). Patron: Abbot and Convent of Barlings. [Reg. 11, fo.36.]

Formerly: R. of Ufton Richard (*Ofton Rycher*) (Brk), to 1382; R. of North Scarle, 1382–4; R. of Allexton (Le), 1384–8. Afterwards: R. of Sudborough (Np), 1388–90; R. of Syston, June–July 1390; R. of Broughton (Np), 1390–5; R. of Northborough (Np), 1395–6; R. of mediety of East Keal, 1396. [Reg. 11, fos 45v, 46, 147v, 155, 174v, 183v, 195v, 210.]

Thomas Bitterley priest
Instituted 21 September 1388 to vicarage of Swaton, on resignation of Thomas Everard (by exchange with church of Sudborough). Patron: Abbot and Convent of Barlings. [Reg. 11, fo.36.]

Formerly: R. of Thrapston (Np), to 1379; V. of Enderby (Le), 1379–83; R. of Sudborough (Np), 1383–8. While at Thrapston he was outlawed for not appearing before the justices of the Bench to answer concerning a debt of £10 to John Reve citizen of London, taylor;

his outlawry was pardoned (18 May 1379) on his surrender to the Fleet prison. [Reg. 10, fos 270v, 280; *CPR 1377–81*, 330.]

William Long de Rasen priest

Instituted 9 October 1394 to vicarage of Swaton, on resignation of Thomas Bitterley. Patron: Abbot and Convent of Barlings. [Reg. 11, fo.72v.]

Henry Fouler priest

Instituted 8 April 1415 to vicarage of Swaton, on resignation of William Rasen (by exchange with church of Broxholme). Patron: Abbot and Convent of Barlings. [Reg. 14, fos 73v, 126.]

Priest: by 23 October 1408. Formerly: R. of Broxholme, 1408–15. [Reg. 14, fo.113.]

John Metham

Instituted before 10 June 1429. [*Reg. Fleming* i. no.318.]

Afterwards: R. of a mediety of Stoke, 1429–32; R. of Boothby Pagnell, 1432. [Reg. 17, fo.4v.]

Robert Grene de Querndon

Instituted 10 June 1429 to vicarage of Swaton, on resignation of John Metham (by exchange with a mediety of church of Stoke). Patron: Abbot and Convent of Barlings. [*Reg. Fleming* i. no.318.]

Formerly: V. of Plungar (Le), to 1414; V. of Castle Bytham, 1414–15; R. of Stenigot, 1415–16; V. of Sixhills, 1416–19; V. of Market Rasen, 1419–22; R. of Owmby, 1422–4 (*q.v.*); R. of Coppingford (Hu), 1424; V. of Lowesby (Le), to 1428; R. of a mediety of Stoke, 1428–9. Afterwards: R. of Screveton (Nt), 1431–3. [Reg. 14, fos 69v, 74, 78v, 99v; *Reg. Fleming* i. nos 292, 318, 420; Godfrey, *Notts Churches: Bingham*, 385.]

John Sargeaunt

Instituted 2 October 1431 to vicarage of Swaton, on resignation of Robert Grene (by exchange with church of Screveton alias *Kyrketon*, dioc. York). Patron: Abbot and Convent of Barlings. [Reg. 17, fo.2.]

Formerly: R. of Screveton (Nt), 1430–1. Afterwards: V. of Calceby, 1432–3; V. of Stickford, 1433. [Godfrey, *Notts Churches: Bingham*, 385; Reg. 17, fo.6v.]

Robert Heryng

Instituted 17 April 1432 to vicarage of Swaton, on resignation of John Sargeaunt (by exchange with vicarage of Calceby). Patron: Abbot and Convent of Barlings. [Reg. 17, fo.3.]

Formerly: V. of Calceby, to 1432.

John Grype priest

Instituted 9 August 1432 to vicarage of Swaton, on resignation of Robert Heryng. Patron: Abbot and Convent of Barlings. [Reg. 17, fo.3.]

Robert Marston priest
Instituted 14 October 1461 to vicarage of Swaton (cause of vacancy not stated). Patron: Abbot and Convent of Barlings. [Reg. 20, fo.135.]

William Grigge priest
Instituted 7 March 1477/8 to vicarage of Swaton, on death of Robert Marston. Patron: Abbot and Convent of Barlings. [Reg. 21, fo.19.]

Robert Malteby priest
Instituted 25 February 1498/9 to vicarage of church of St Andrew, Swaton, on death of William Gregg. Patron: Abbot and Convent of Barlings. [Reg. 23, fo.48.]

Br. John Waltham canon of Barlings, priest
Instituted 29 March 1501 to vicarage of Swaton, on death of Robert Malteby. Patron: Abbot and Convent of Barlings. [Reg. 23, fo.61v.]

Br. John Thomas canon of Barlings
Instituted 8 May 1506 to vicarage of Swaton, on death of br. John Waltham. Patron: Abbot and Convent of Barlings. [Reg. 23, fo.109v.]

William Sawnderson chaplain
Instituted 2 June 1522 to vicarage of church of St Andrew, Swaton, on death of John Thomas. Patron: Abbot and Convent of St Mary, Barlings. [Reg. 27, fo.24v.]

Assessed for subsidy (£6) in 1526. [*Subsidy*, 57.]

Thomas Smale chaplain
Instituted 6 April 1531 to vicarage of Swaton, on resignation of William Saunderson. Patron: John Monson esquire, by reason of a grant made to him for this turn by Abbot and Convent of Barlings. [Reg. 27, fo.49v.]

Assessed for *Valor Ecclesiasticus* 1535. Exhibited at Visitation in 1551. Witnessed Swaton wills, 1552–3. Perhaps deprived 1554. Restored by 6 July 1560 when witnessed a Dunsby will as Vicar of Swaton. Witnessed Swaton wills, 1562–5. Died before 8 July 1566 (probate inventory). Will (LCC). [*Valor* iv. 104; Vj 13, fo.62v; LCC Wills 1553–6/10v, 12v; 1561/219; 1562/184v; 1563/109v; 1564/185v, 186v; INV 45/142; LCC Wills 1563, 66 & 69/134v.]

Robert Gibson
Instituted in the first year of Queen Mary I (19 July 1553 x 5 July 1554) to vicarage of Swaton (cause of vacancy not stated). Patron: Queen Mary I. Compounded for first-fruits, 12 June 1554. [Reg. 28, fo.112v; FL.h.13, 778.]

Robert Raynes
Instituted 13 February 1557/8 to vicarage of Swaton (cause of vacancy not stated). Patron: King Philip and Queen Mary I. [Reg. 28, fo.132v.]

Thomas Smale (again)
Restored after 1558 (see above).

Richard Carrington
Instituted 25 November 1566 to vicarage of Swaton (cause of vacancy not stated). Patron: Queen Elizabeth I. [Reg. 28, fo.4v.]

Born *c*.1540. Education: 'is competently skilled in Latin; and to the same extent versed in sacred learning'; 'bred in the schools'. Priest: 21 September 1564 (Peterborough). Resident (1576). Witnessed Swaton wills, 1568–73. Died before 25 August 1611 (probate inventory: 'his bookes, 25s'). [*Bishop Cooper*, 207; *State of the Church*, 74; LCC Wills 1557–72/157; 1568/73; 1570/66v, 180v, 188v; INV 110/104.]

Edward Hassell MA
Instituted 2 September 1611 to vicarage of Swaton with Spanby, on death of Richard Carrington. Patron: Henry Fiennes, Earl of Lincoln (21 August 1611). [BC; PD 1611/23.]

Educated: St John's College, Cambridge (matric. 1595; BA 1599–1600; MA 1603). Deacon and priest: 20 November 1603 (Peterborough). Died 1633. Will (LCC), dated 10 February 1632/3: to be buried in the churchyard of Swaton; bequeathed 'unto the poorest people of Swaton, five shillinges'. [Venn, *Alumni*; LCC Wills 1633/14.]

Thomas Wallace MA
Instituted 25 April 1633 to vicarage of Swaton cum Spanby, on death of Edward Hasel. Patron: Theophilus, Earl of Lincoln (20 April 1633). [BC; PD 1633/22.]

Born *c*.1607; son of Robert W. of Huntingdon, chandler. Educated: Huntingdon School and Sidney Sussex College, Cambridge (matric. 1623–4; BA 1627; MA 1631). Priest: 25 April 1633 (Lincoln). Afterwards: R. of Hadstock (Ess), 1645; of Stansted Mountfichet, 1664–7. Died 1667. [Venn, *Alumni*.]

Peter Saunders MA
Instituted 22 January 1662/3 to vicarage of Swaton cum Spanby, on resignation of Thomas Wallis. Patron: Theophilus Clynton alias Fynes, Earl of Lincoln (15 January 1662/3). [Reg. 32, fo.25; PD 1663/104.]

Of Cambridgeshire. Educated: St Catharine's Hall, Cambridge (matric. 1635; BA 1638–9; MA 1642). Deacon and priest: 7 August 1645 (Lincoln). Resident (1662); signed BTs at Swaton 1663–73. [Venn, *Alumni*; LC 5, fo.24v; BTs Swaton.]

John Spademan BA
Instituted 12 December 1673 to vicarage of Swaton, on death of Peter Sanders. Patron: Edward, Earl of Lincoln. Inducted same day. [SUB Va, fo.50; IND/L 1, fo.213.]

Born *c*.1649; son of Thomas S., Vicar of Althorpe (1648–62). Educated: Sheffield School and Magdalene College, Cambridge (matric. 1665; BA 1668–9; MA 1674). Deacon and priest: 4 November 1673 (Bristol). Also: R. of a mediety of Llandinam (Mont), 1674. Signed BTs at Swaton 1674–80. Resigned 1681. Afterwards: Co-pastor (with Joseph Hill his uncle) of English Church at Rotterdam, 1681–98; later settled in London. Died 14 February 1707/8. [Venn, *Alumni*; Swaby, 1; SUB Va, fo.50; BTs Swaton; *Calamy Revised*, 453.]

Joseph Oulton BA

Instituted 30 May 1681 to vicarage of Swaton, on resignation of John Spademan. Patron: Edward Fiennes Clinton, Earl of Lincoln (25 April 1681). [Reg. 34, fo.60v; PD 1681/63.]

Born *c*.1658; son of Isaac O. of Crewe, yeoman. Educated: Barthomley School and St John's College, Cambridge (matric. 1674–5; BA 1678–9). Priest: 28 May 1681 (Lincoln). Signed BTs at Swaton 1681–97. Buried at Swaton, 3 October 1697. Will (LCC). Probate inventory ('his Library, £10'). [*St John's Admissions* ii. 53; Venn, *Alumni*; Reg. 34, fo.60v; LC 14, p.7; BTs Swaton; LCC Wills 1697&8/ii/479; INV 193/256.]

Jonathan Whaley MA

Instituted 15 October 1697 to vicarage of Swaton cum Spanby, on death of Joseph Oulton. Patron: Samuel Heyrick, citizen and stationer of London. [Reg. 35, fo.45v.]

Born *c*.1661 at Laughton (YWR); son of John W., wheelwright. Educated: Laughton School and St John's College, Cambridge (matric. 1680; BA 1683–4; MA 1694). Deacon: 15 March 1684/5 (York); priest: 31 July 1687 (Lincoln). Formerly: C. of Dinnington (YWR), 1685; C. of Sawtry St Andrew (Hu), 1687. Also: C. of All Hallows, London, 1697; Chaplain to Colonel Sanderson's Regiment of Marines, 1702. Non-resident at Swaton, which was served by John Spriggs as curate (signed BTs 1699–1702). [*St John's Admissions* ii. 76; Venn, *Alumni*; *York Ordinations 1662–1699*, 72; Reg. 34, fo.99v; LMA, Marriage Bonds and Allegations (1696/7); BTs Swaton.]

John Spriggs BA

Instituted 21 September 1702 to vicarage of Swaton cum Spanby, on death of Jonathan Whaley. Patron: Samuel Heyrick, citizen and stationer of London. [Reg. 35, fo.89.]

Born *c*.1675; perhaps son of John S. of Cottingham (Np). Educated: All Souls College, Oxford (matric. 1692; BA 1696). Deacon: 20 September 1696 (Peterborough); priest: 20 September 1702 (Lincoln). Formerly: C. of Corby (Np), 1696; C. of Swaton, 1699–1702. Signed BTs as Vicar 1703. Non-resident thereafter: resided 'on account of his health' at Braunston near Oakham, where he served as curate for Dean and Chapter of Lincoln. Swaton meanwhile was served by Robert Smith as curate (signed BTs 1704–39). [Foster, *Alumni*; Longden xiii. 23; Reg. 35, fo.88v; BTs Swaton; *Speculum*, 123.]

William Ducros

Instituted 8 May 1729 to vicarage of Swaton cum Spanby, on death of John Spriggs. Patron: John Masson, Rector of Aswarby (3 May 1729). [Reg. 38, p.203; PD 103/88.]

Deacon: 1701; priest: 1707 (London). Non-resident at Swaton, which was served by Robert Smith and William Holgate as curates.. A French Huguenot. He acquired the advowson of Swaton, which passed on his death to his widow Mary and thence via their daughter Isabel to her husband Jerome Knapp. [SPE 2, p.113; BTs Swaton; *GM* (February 1843), 211.]

John Stephen Masson

Instituted 18 March 1744/5 to vicarage of Swaton with Spanby, on death of William Ducross. Patron: Mary Ducros of St George, Westminster, widow (16 March 1744/5). [Reg. 38, p.455; PD 109/23.]

Deacon: 21 September 1735; priest: 19 December 1736 (Lincoln). Formerly: C. of Aswarby, 1735. Also: V. of Scredington, 1744–76. Lived at Spanby; signed registers at Swaton 1752–64. Died 1777. Will (LCC), dated 22 April 1777. Bequeathed to his son Samuel, 'all my Books, except a small number which I have before given to my daughter Louisa'; to his son John (to whom he had advanced some £1200), 'I hereby forgive and discharge him of all that is due to me, considering his distresful situation, earnestly intreating the Almighty to bless his honest endeavours for his future well doing in life'. [Reg. 38, pp. 306, 323; LC 31, p.77; Trollope, *Sleaford*, 448; PR Swaton; LCC Wills 1777/108.]

Samuel Masson BA

Instituted 1 October 1777 to vicarage of Swaton St Michael with Spanby, on death of Stephen Masson. Patron: Jerome Knapp of Haberdashers Hall, London, esquire. [Reg. 39, p.297.]

Born *c*.1750; son of John M. of Aswarby, clerk. Educated: Lincoln College, Oxford (matric. 1768; BA 1772). Deacon: 20 September 1772; priest: 25 September 1774 (Lincoln). Formerly: C. of Swaton, 1772. Also: V. of Scredington, 1776–86. Resident at Swaton (1778). Buried at Spanby, 11 July 1786. [Foster, *Alumni*; Reg. 39, pp. 181, 233; LC 31, p.77; PR Spanby.]

James Pigott MA

Instituted 10 August 1786 to vicarage of Swaton with Spanby, on death of Samuel Mason. Patron: Jerome Knapp of Haberdashers Hall, London, esquire. [Reg. 39, p.451.]

Born *c*.1738 at Wimbledon (Sr); son of Charles Newsham P. Educated: Christ's Hospital School and Pembroke Hall, Cambridge (matric. 1754; BA 1758; MA 1761). Deacon: 21 September 1760 (London); priest: 20 December 1761 (Salisbury). Formerly: V. of St Nicholas, Leicester, 1769–78. Also: V. of Wigston Magna (Le), 1762–1812; Head Master of Leicester GS, 1769–99. Died 28 December 1812 at Wigston Magna, aged 74. [Venn, *Alumni*; CCED; Reg. 39, pp.1, 113; *GM* 82 (1812), 674.]

John Shinglar

Instituted 2 February 1813 to vicarage of Swaton cum Spanby, on death of James Pigott. Patron: Jerome William Knapp of Bedford Row (Mx), esquire (30 January 1813). [Reg. 40, p.178; PD 169/43.]

Also: PC of Walcot, 1798–1828 (*q.v.*).

Thomas Darby BA

Instituted 21 September 1828 to vicarage of Swaton with Spanby, on death of John Shinglar. Patron: Edmund Darby of Aston (Hrt), esquire (for this turn). [Reg. 40, p.362.]

Born *c*.1801 at Aston (Hrt); son of Edmund D. Educated: Hertford School; Trinity College (matric. 1822) and Downing College, Cambridge (BA 1828). Deacon: 23 December 1827; priest: 21 September 1828 (Lincoln). Formerly: C. of Walkern (Hrt), 1827. Resided at Swaton. Submitted return of places of worship for Swaton and Spanby, 1829. Died 9 October 1840. Will (PCC). [Venn, *Alumni*; OR 1, pp. 30, 34; CR 1, p.346; Ambler, 'Return', 63; *Spectator*, 17 October 1840; PRO, PROB 11/1937/206.]

Henry Knapp MA

Instituted 13 February 1841 to vicarage of Swaton with rectory of Spanby annexed, on death of Thomas Darby. Patron: Eleanor Knapp of Cheltenham (Gl), widow. [Reg. 40, p.475.]

Born 2 January, baptised 1 February 1811 at St Michael, Wood Street, London; son of Thomas George K. of Haberdasher's Hall, London, gent. (and nephew of Eleanor Knapp, the patroness). Educated: St John's College, Oxford (matric. 1829; BA 1833; MA 1836). Formerly: C. of Norwood, 1834; of Chedworth (Gl); of Bangor Monachorum (Flints), 1836. Married (3 October 1836) at Overton (Flints), Anna Maria, daughter of George Kenyon of Cefn Park, Wrexham. Father of Thomas Lloyd K., V. of Threckingham 1902–26 (*q.v.*). Resided at Swaton where he built a new Vicarage House (1844). Also: RD of Aveland; Canon of Lincoln and Prebendary of Stoke, 1873–9. Died 20 December 1879 at Swaton Vicarage. [Foster, *Alumni*; Grimaldi, *Miscellaneous Writings*, 323–4; *GM* (February 1843), 211; Census Returns 1841–61; White, *Lincolnshire* (1856), 551; White, *Lincolnshire* (1872), 570; *Crockford* (1874); *Probate Calendar* 1880.]

Richard Henry Mann BA

Instituted 17 March 1880 to vicarage of Swaton with rectory of Spanby annexed, on death of Henry Knapp. Patron: Archibald James Campbell of No 3 Wilton Terrace, Belgrave Square (Mx), esquire. [Reg. 42, p.103.]

Born *c*.1850 at Saxmundham (Sf); son of Revd Robert Mann. Educated: Harrow School (1864–8) and Emmanuel College, Cambridge (matric. 1869; BA 1873). Deacon: 1873; priest: 1874 (Lincoln). Formerly: C. of Great Hale, 1873–5; of Swaton, 1875–80. Married (5 April 1877) at Swaton Church, Mary Emma, daughter of Revd Henry Knapp (above). Resided at Swaton Vicarage. Retired 1930. Latterly of The Old Place, Horbling. Died 16 February 1932. [*Harrow Register 1800–1911*, 378; Venn, *Alumni*; *Crockford* (1932); *The Guardian*, 11 April 1877; Census Returns 1881–1911; *Probate Calendar* 1932.]

Percival Frederick Foottit

Instituted 27 June 1930 to vicarage of Swaton with rectory of Spanby annexed, on resignation of Richard Henry Mann. Patron: Evelyn Jack Needham of 5 Westbourne Terrace, Hyde Park, London, late a Captain in HM Army; Robert Philip Needham of Wentworth Dormy House Club, Virginia Water (Sr), esquire; Archibald George Seymour of Chapel Brampton (Np), a Brigadier General in HM Army, DSO; and Charles Evelyn Seymour of Kilbees Farm, Winkfield (Brk), esquire. [Reg. 43, p.468.]

Born 1889 at Threckingham; son of Revd Charles Edward Walker F., Vicar of Threckingham 1884–90 (*q.v.*). Educated: University of Durham (LTh 1911); Lincoln Theological College (resident student 1911). Deacon: 1912; priest: 1913 (Bristol). Formerly: C. of Wroughton, 1912–21; TCF 1917–20; V. of Burton Pedwardine, 1921–30; C. of Heckington with Howell, 1923–33. Afterwards: V. of Scredington, 1936–61. Died 17 July 1961 at St George's Hospital, Lincoln. [GRO, Birth Index; Census Returns 1891 (Burton Pedwardine), 1911 (Lincoln); *Crockford* (1961–2); *Probate Calendar* 1961.]

George Kendall Wrigley MA

Instituted 28 September 1936 to vicarage of Swaton with rectory of Spanby annexed, on cession of Percival Frederick Foottit. Patron: Evelyn Jack Needham of 6 Bryanston Court, London, late a Captain in HM Army; Robert Philip Needham of Wentworth Dormy House Club, Virginia Water (Sr), esquire; and Charles Evelyn Seymour of Kilbees Farm, Winkfield (Brk), esquire. [Reg. 43, p.587.]

Baptised 20 June 1895 at All Hallows, Leeds; son of John James W. of 12 Woodsley Street, gas engineer. Living at home (12 Woodside Avenue, Leeds) in 1911; working as commercial clerk at ironworks. Educated: University of Leeds (BA 1922; MA 1934). Deacon: 1924; priest: 1925 (Lincoln). Formerly: Chaplain, St Paul's Missionary College, Burghle-Marsh, 1924–6; Lecturer, St Botolph, Boston, 1926–9 and 1935–6; V. of Sutton-le-Marsh, 1929–33. Afterwards: P-in-C of Almirante and Bocas del Toro (Panama), 1937–41 and 1945–7; of San José, Costa Rica, 1941–3; of Stann Creek (Honduras), 1943–5; of Holy Trinity, La Ceiba (Honduras), 1948–9; V. of Hackness with Harwood Dale (YNR), 1950–4; in Barbados Diocese, 1954–5; V. of Weaverthorpe with Helperthorpe (YER), 1955–8; R. of Falmouth (Jamaica), 1959–63. Latterly at Muschett Home, Duncans, Trelawny, Jamaica. [WYAS, PR Leeds All Hallows; Census Returns 1911 (Leeds); *Crockford* (1961–2, 1971–2).]

Henry Blacker Fairclough BA

Instituted 6 April 1938 to vicarage of Swaton with rectory of Spanby annexed, on resignation of George Kendall Wrigley. Patron: Evelyn Jack Needham, Robert Philip Needham and Charles Evelyn Seymour, as above. [Reg. 43, p.614.]

Baptised 28 December 1879 at Mirfield (YWR); son of Thomas Butter F. of Knowle, surgeon. Educated: St David's College, Lampeter (BA 1901). Deacon: 1902; priest: 1903 (Manchester). Formerly: C. of Holy Trinity, Coldhurst, 1902–5; of St Paul, Grangetown, 1905–6; of Netherbury with Solway Ash, 1907–8; of All Saints, Hereford, 1908–9; of Stoulton, 1909–10; of Leigh with Bransford (Wo), 1910–11; of St Luke, Dudley, 1911–14; of Beaufort, 1914–16; of Avan Vale, 1916–18; of Maindee, 1918–19; of St Luke, Beeston Hill, Leeds, 1919–20; of Oulton, Leeds, 1920–2; of Glenfield with Braunstone and Kirby Muxloe, 1922–3; of Ledsham with Fairburn, 1923–5; R. of Maltby-in-the-Marsh, 1925–38. Afterwards: V. of Latton, 1942–50. Died 1961 (Spilsby). [WYAS, PR Mirfield St Mary; Census Returns 1881 (Mirfield); *Crockford* (1961–2); GRO, Death Index.]

Aubrey Wyld Steedman BA

Instituted 2 December 1942 to vicarage of Swaton with rectory of Spanby annexed, on cession of Henry Blacker Fairclough. Patron: Evelyn Jack Needham of Forest House Cottage, Hatchet Lane, Winkfield (Brk), late a Captain in HM Army; Robert Philip Needham of Sunningdale Hotel, Sunningdale (Sr), esquire; and Charles Evelyn Seymour of Kilbees Farm, Winkfield (Brk), esquire. [Reg. 43, p.681.]

Born 16 April 1911 at Nottingham. Educated: University of Durham (BA 1940; MA 1943); St Aidan's College, Birkenhead (1934). Deacon and priest: 1938 (Southwell). Formerly: C. of St Mary Magdalene, Sutton-in-Ashfield, 1938; of Bulwell, 1938–9; of Blyth, 1941–2. Also: Chaplain RAFVR 1943–7. Afterwards: R. of Beckingham with Fenton, 1949–89. Latterly at 38 Bullpit Road, Balderton (Nt). Died December 1993 (Newark). [GRO, Birth Index; *Crockford* (1961–2, 1989–90); GRO, Death Index.]

Leonard Benn Impson

Instituted 22 November 1950 to vicarage of Swaton with rectory of Spanby annexed, on cession of Aubrey Wyld Steedman. Patron: Lincoln Diocesan Board of Patronage. [Reg. 44, p.131.]

Born 7 January 1905 at Grange-over-Sands (La); son of Robert Philip I., draper. Educated: Edinburgh Theological College (1937). Deacon: 1939; priest: 1940 (Edinburgh). Formerly: C. of St Peter, Edinburgh, 1939–41; CF 1941–7; C. of St Peter, Hersham (Sr), 1947–50. Also: V. of Horbling, 1952–6 (*q.v.*). Resided at Swaton Vicarage. Afterwards: R. of Kondinin-Corrigin (Western Australia), 1956–8; Domestic Chaplain to Bishop of Bunbury, 1958–9; R. of Welby and V. of Heydour with Culverthorpe, 1959–62; V. of Wilden with Colmworth and Ravensden (Bd), 1962. Died 1974 (Bedford). [Census Returns 1911 (Cark in Cartmel); *Crockford* (1951–2, 1971–2); GRO, Death Index.]

Robert William Harris BSc

Instituted 5 July 1957 to vicarage of Swaton with rectory of Spanby annexed, on resignation of Leonard Benn Impson. Patron: Bishop of Lincoln, for this turn (by lapse). Note that on 28 May 1957, the Archbishop of Canterbury granted a dispensation enabling the said RWH to hold together the vicarage of Horbling and the vicarage of Swaton with rectory of Spanby annexed. [Reg. 44, p.242.]

Also: V. of Horbling, 1957–64 (*q.v.*).

John Faber Scholfield Jones MA

Instituted 29 October 1964 to vicarage of Swaton with rectory of Spanby annexed, on death of Robert William Harris. Patron: Lincoln Diocesan Board of Patronage. Note that on 20 October 1964, the Archbishop of Canterbury granted a dispensation enabling the said JFSJ to hold together the vicarage of Horbling and the vicarage of Swaton with rectory of Spanby annexed. [Reg. 44, p.365.]

Also: V. of Horbling, 1964–9 (*q.v.*).

THRECKINGHAM

Gilbert de Gant was recorded as holding land in Threckingham at the time of the Domesday Survey. His barony of Folkingham descended to his son Walter (d.1139), then to Gilbert II, son of Walter (d.1156), and then to Gilbert II's daughter Alice. Alice married Simon de St Liz, Earl of Northampton and Huntingdon. During the reign of Henry II, Alice and Simon gave the church of Threckingham to the Hospital of Burton Lazars (Le). In 1204 the Hospital reached a settlement with Gilbert III de Gant whereby Gilbert released all claim to Threckingham to Burton Lazars. The church was appropriated and a vicarage was ordained, consisting of the whole altarage and a toft where the vicar resided. The Master and Brethren of the Hospital continued to present to the vicarage until the Dissolution. Afterwards the patronage was acquired by the Earls of Lincoln, then passed (as with Folkingham) to the Wynne family and subsequently to Sir Gilbert Heathcote. The fourth baronet presented in 1803 and 1829. After his death in 1851 the advowson passed to his nephew Francis, whose daughter Ida Grosvenor Wilson (née Heathcote) presented between 1884 and 1902. The advowson continued in the Wilson-Heathcote family during the twentieth century. [*Lincolnshire Domesday*, 114; Sanders, *Baronies*, 46; Marcombe, *Leper Knights*, 197; *Lincolnshire Feet of Fines*, 92; *Rot. Welles* iii. 91; Burke, *Peerage* (1999), 1369–70.]

Reginald de Trikingeham chaplain
Instituted between 1223 and 1226 to vicarage of Threckingham. Patron: Brethren of Hospital of Burton Lazars. [*Rot. Welles* iii. 91; 'Rolls of Hugh of Wells', 173–5.]

Reginald de Wistowe chaplain
Instituted in the fifth pontifical year of Bishop Robert Grosseteste (17 June 1239/16 June 1240) to vicarage of Threckingham. Patron: Master and Brethren of Hospital of Burton Lazars. [Hoskin, no.143.]

Richard de Makwrthe priest
Instituted in the fourth pontifical year of Bishop Richard Gravesend (3 November 1261/2 November 1262) to vicarage of Threckingham, on death of Reginald. Patron: Hospital of Burton Lazars. [*Rot. Gravesend*, 10.]

Thomas de Trikingham deacon
Instituted in the fifth pontifical year of Bishop Richard Gravesend (3 November 1262/2 November 1263) to vicarage of Threckingham, on death of Richard. Patron: Master and Brethren of House of St Lazarus at Burton Lazars. [*Rot. Gravesend*, 12.]

Also: R. of a mediety of Kirkby Underwood, to 1277. Afterwards: R. of Haceby, 1286–91 (*q.v.*).

Geoffrey de Screytfeld chaplain
Instituted 24 August 1286 to vicarage of Threckingham, on resignation of
Thomas. Patron: Master and Brethren of House of St Lazarus at Burton
Lazars. [*Reg. Sutton* i. 87.]

Thomas de Henney chaplain
Instituted 21 October 1293 to vicarage of Threckingham, vacant because
Geoffrey had joined the Dominicans. Patron: Master and Brethren of Hospital
of St Lazarus at Burton Lazars. [*Reg. Sutton* i. 180.]

Hugh le Toller de Trikyngham
Instituted *c.*1321 by collation to vicarage of Threckingham, on death of
Thomas. Patron: Bishop of Lincoln, by lapse (Hugh's earlier presentation by
Master and Brethren of Hospital of Burton Lazars having been ineffective
because the Master was excommunicate). [*Reg. Burghersh* i. no.15.]

Commission to act as co-adjutor to Philip, R. of Braceborough, 5 December 1330.
Appointed commissary to audit executors' accounts of wills of Nicholas Squier of Rippin-
gale and of Margaret wife of John de Billingburgh, 13 March 1330/1. [Reg. 5, fo.441;
Reg. Burghersh iii. no.1882.]

Robert Templer de Babbegrave priest
Instituted 15 February 1349/50 to vicarage of Threckingham, on death of
Hugh. Patron: Master and Brethren of Hospital of St Lazarus at Burton
Lazars. [Reg. 9, fo.83.]

Thomas de Brampton priest
Instituted 26 February 1352/3 to vicarage of Threckingham, on death of
Robert de Belgrave. Patron: Master and Brethren of the Knights of St Lazarus
at Burton Lazars. [Reg. 9, fo.104.]

Afterwards: V. of Westfield (Sx), 1367.

Richard Gamul
Instituted 28 July 1367 to vicarage of Threckingham, on resignation of
Thomas de Brampton (by exchange with vicarage of Westfield, dioc. Chichester). Patron: Master and Brethren of Hospital of Burton Lazars. [Reg. 10,
fo.18v.]

Formerly: V. of Westfield (Sx), to 1367. Afterwards: V. of Stretton (Ru), 1369–71; V. of
Barholm, 1371. [Reg. 10, fos 44, 178v, 184v.]

Henry Busshe (de Gretham) priest
Instituted 4 October 1369 to vicarage of Threckingham, on resignation of
Richard Gamul de Worthyngton (by exchange with vicarage of Stretton,
Rutland). Patron: Master and Brethren of the Knights of St Lazarus at Burton.
[Reg. 10, fo.33v.]

Priest: before 23 February 1356/7. Formerly: V. of Stretton (Ru), 1357–69. [Reg. 9, fo.216.]

Thomas Cronke de Demilby priest
Instituted 3 June 1374 to vicarage of Threckingham, on death of Henry. Patron: Master and Brethren of the Knights of Burton Lazars. [Reg. 10, fo.33v.]

Afterwards: Chaplain of St Nicholas Chantry in Church of Newark (Nt), 1385.

Richard de Kelme
Instituted 20 October 1385 to vicarage of Threckingham, on resignation of Thomas Croke (by exchange with chantry at altar of St Nicholas in church of Newark, dioc. York). Patron: Master (br. Nicholas) and Brethren of Hospital of Burton Lazars. [Reg. 11, fo.18v.]

Formerly: Chaplain of St Nicholas Chantry in Church of Newark (Nt), to 1385. Afterwards: V. of Slipton (Np), 1389–92. [Reg. 11, fos 149v, 162v.]

Thomas Northampton priest
Instituted 12 January 1388/9 to vicarage of Threckingham, on resignation of Richard Kelm (by exchange with vicarage of Slipton, Northants). Patron: Master and Brethren of Burton Lazars. [Reg. 11, fo.38.]

Deacon: before 23 March 1376/7. Formerly: V. of Evington (Le), 1377–84; V. of Slipton (Np), 1384–9. Afterwards: R. of Wyfordby (Le), 1397–1402; Chaplain of St Mary Chantry in Manor of Weston in Arden, par. Bulkington (Wa), 1402. [Reg. 10, fo.267; Reg. 11, fos 129, 149v; Reg. 13, fo.197.]

Raymond Barker priest
Instituted 2 April 1397 to vicarage of Threckingham, on resignation of Thomas Northampton (by exchange with church of Wyfordby, Leics). Patron: Master (Walter Lynton) and Brethren of Hospital of Burton Lazars. [Reg. 11, fo.86v.]

Formerly: V. of Rothley (Le), to 1392; R. of Wanlip (Le), 1392–4; R. of Wyfordby (Le), 1394–7. [Reg. 11, fos 221v, 227.]

Nicholas Fort priest
Instituted 12 May 1400 to vicarage of Threckingham, on death of last incumbent. Patron: Master (br. Walter Lynton) and Brethren of Hospital of Burton Lazars. [Reg. 13, fo.128.]

Afterwards: V. of Aldworth (Brk), 1401.

Walter Clent
Instituted 25 October 1401 to vicarage of Threckingham, on resignation of Nicholas Fort (by exchange with vicarage of Aldworth, dioc. Salisbury). Patron: Master and Brethren of Burton Lazars. [Reg. 13, fo.141v.]

Formerly: V. of Aldworth (Brk), to 1401. Afterwards: R. of Potsgrove (Bd), 1406.

William Smyth priest

Instituted 13 August 1406 to vicarage of Threckingham, on resignation of Walter Clent (by exchange with church of Potsgrove). Patron: Master (br. Walter Lynton) of Hospital of Burton Lazars. [Reg. 14, fo.11v.]

Priest: before 26 October 1402. Formerly: R. of Potsgrove (Bd), 1402–6. Afterwards: V. of Hagnaby, 1418. [Reg. 13, fo.256.]

John Gryme

Instituted 28 January 1417/18 to vicarage of Threckingham, on resignation of William Smyth (by exchange with vicarage of Hagnaby). Patron: Master and Brethren of Hospital of Burton Lazars. [Reg. 14, fo.91v.]

Formerly: V. of Hagnaby, to 1418.

John Tyas priest

Instituted 11 March 1420/1 to vicarage of Threckingham (cause of vacancy not stated). Patron: Master and Brethren of Burton Lazars. [*Reg. Fleming* i. no.87.]

Afterwards: Chaplain of Chantry in Harrington Church, 1423.

Thomas Soper

Instituted 5 April 1423 to vicarage of Threckingham, on resignation of John Tyas (by exchange with chantry in church of Harrington). Patron: Master and Brethren of Burton Lazars. [*Reg. Fleming* i. no.185.]

Formerly: Chaplain of Chantry in Harrington Church, 1423.

Richard Sleford priest

Instituted 5 August 1440 to vicarage of Threckingham, on resignation of Thomas Sopere. Patron: Master of Burton Lazars. [Reg. 18, fo.84.]

William Tundur priest

Instituted 18 July 1452 to vicarage of Threckingham, on resignation of Richard Sleford. Patron: Master (br. William Sutton) and Brethren of Burton Lazars. [Reg. 20, fo.117.]

Robert Lord priest

Instituted 22 September 1452 to vicarage of Threckingham, on resignation of William Tundur. Patron: Master and Brethren of Burton Lazars. [Reg. 20, fo.118.]

Robert Baxster priest

Instituted 9 April 1457 to vicarage of Threckingham, on deprivation of Robert Lorde. Patron: Master (William Sutton) and Brethren of Burton Lazars. [Reg. 20, fo.127v.]

William Doram priest
Instituted 17 March 1491/2 to vicarage of Threckingham, on death of Robert Baxtar. Patron: Master and Brethren of Hospital of Burton Lazars. [Reg. 22, fo.149v.]

John Lancaster priest
Instituted 26 February 1506/7 to vicarage of Threckingham, on resignation of William Dorram. Patron: Master (Thomas Norton) of Burton Lazars. [Reg. 23, fo.120.]

Thomas Lambart chaplain
Instituted 4 February 1521/2 to vicarage of Threckingham, on resignation of John Lancaster. Patron: Master (Thomas Norton) of Burton Lazars. [Reg. 27, fo.23.]
Assessed for subsidy (£5 6s 8d) in 1526; pension of 20s payable to John Lancaster. Assessed for *Valor Ecclesiasticus* 1535. Exhibited at Visitation in 1551. Witnessed Threckingham will, 1551. [*Subsidy*, 57; *Valor* iv, 106; Vj 13, fo.62v; LCC Wills 1551–2/224.]

Ambrose Baynes
Presented 2 November 1556 to vicarage of Threckingham. Patron: King Philip and Queen Mary I. [*CPR 1555–57*, 367.]
Witnessed Threckingham will as Vicar, 24 February 1556/7. [LCC Wills 1557/iii/4.]

Robert Nelsonne
Instituted 4 June 1557 to vicarage of Threckingham, on death of last incumbent. Patron: King Philip and Queen Mary I. [Reg. 28, fo.138.]
Witnessed Threckingham wills as Vicar, 1558–9. [LCC Wills 1558/i/192, 203; 1558/iiii/104.]

John Graye
Instituted 20 February 1561/2 to vicarage of Threckingham, on death of last incumbent. Patron: Queen Elizabeth I (10 November 1561). [Reg. 19, fo.129; *CPR Elizabeth I: 1560–1563*, 130.]

Richard Carrington
Instituted before 4 April 1564.
Witnessed Threckingham will as Vicar, 4 April 1564. Aftewards: V. of Swaton, 1566–1611 (*q.v.*) [LCC Wills 1564/187v.]

Roger Price
Presented 17 November 1565 to vicarage of Threckingham. Patron: Queen Elizabeth I. [FL.h.19, 24.]

John Mitchell
Instituted by 1566. [BTs Threckingham.]

At Bishop Cooper's visitation on 21 August 1576 it was noted that the vicarage of Threckingham was vacant. Nicholas Antonie occurs as curate on 20 December 1575 and again in 1580, 1585 and 1592. [*Bishop Cooper*, 209, 220; *State of the Church*, 74; LCC Wills 1592/401.]

William Browne

Instituted 30 June 1593 to vicarage of Threckingham, on death of last incumbent. Patron: Henry Fynes, Earl of Lincoln (3 February 1592/3). [BC; PD 1593/8.]

Buried at Threckingham, 25 June 1597. [PR Threckingham.]

Henry Tompson MA

Instituted 4 February 1596/7 to vicarage of Threckingham (cause of vacancy not stated). Patron: Queen Elizabeth I, by lapse (31 January 1596/7). [BC; PD 1597/1.]

Educated: Pembroke College, Cambridge (matric. 1579; MA). Deacon: 31 October 1583 (Lincoln); priest (Peterborough). Listed as Vicar for election of proctors, September 1597. [Venn, *Alumni*; PD 1597/1; *State of the Church*, 175.]

Richard Carrington

Instituted 20 September 1597 to vicarage of Threckingham, on death of William Browne. Patron: Henry Fynes, Earl of Lincoln (18 September 1597). [Reg. 30, fo.75; PD 1597/53.]

Resident: signed BT in 1597. [BTs Threckingham.]

Ralph Palfreman

Instituted 22 January 1598/9 to vicarage of Threckingham (cause of vacancy not stated). Patron: Henry Fines, Earl of Lincoln (8 July 1598). [Reg. 30, fo.103v; PD 1598/15.]

Also: V. of Aslackby, 1605–11 (*q.v.*).

Henry Halliwell MA

Instituted 15 May 1607 to vicarage of Threckingham (cause of vacancy not stated). Patron: Henry Fines, Earl of Lincoln (28 April 1607). [Reg. 30, fo.305; PD 1607/2.]

Born *c*.1559 at Tong (YWR). Education: 'no graduate'. Priest: 18 October 1603 (Lincoln). Formerly: C. of Sempringham (occurs 1604, 1607). Buried at Threckingham, 25 May 1612. [PD 1607/2; *State of the Church*, 397, 415; LC 3, fo.4; PR Threckingham.]

Samuel Ashton BA

Instituted 24 November 1612 to vicarage of Threckingham, on death of Henry Holliwell. Patron: Henry Fines, Earl of Lincoln (30 September 1612). [BC; PD 1612/74.]

Afterwards: V. of Aslackby, 1614–27 (*q.v.*).

Henry Hough
Instituted 22 December 1614 to vicarage of Threckingham. [BC.]

Deacon: 20 September 1607; priest: 20 December 1607 (Chester). [CCED.]

Richard Greaves BA
Inducted 4 August 1616 to vicarage of Threckingham, on cession of Henry Houghe. Patron: Thomas Greene esquire. [IND/L 1, fo.20.]

Perhaps to be identified with RG of Nottinghamshire, educated at Corpus Christi College, Cambridge (admitted 1610; BA 1613–14). Buried at Threckingham, 9 July 1625. [Venn, *Alumni*; PR Threckingham.]

John Peachie
Instituted 28 December 1625 to vicarage of Threckingham, on death of Richard Graves. Patron: William Boyer *alias* Gamble, citizen and vintner of London, and Christopher Gustard gent. (19 December 1625). Inducted 2 January 1625/6 by Thomas White, Curate of Sempringham. [BC; PD 1625/60; IND/L 1, fo.71.]

Baptised 6 November 1603 at Oakham; son of William P., Vicar of Oakham (1596–1643). Educated: St John's College, Cambridge (matric. 1620; BA 1623–4; MA 1627); incorporated at Oxford (1628). Deacon: 26 April 1625; priest: 5 March 1625/6 (Peterborough). Afterwards: at Bourne (1633) where John son of John Peachey, minister, was baptised; R. of Morborne (Hu) in 1640–52; Chaplain to East India Company at Poplar, 1665. Died 1669. [Venn, *Alumni*; Longden x. 213; *PR Bourne*, 76.]

Thomas Lambe
Instituted 31 October 1629 to vicarage of Threckingham, on resignation of John Peachie. Patron: William Bowyer *alias* Gamble esquire and Christopher Gustard gent. (29 October 1629). [BC; PD 1629/37.]

Thomas Palfreyman MA
Instituted 4 April 1637 to vicarage of Threckingham, on resignation of Thomas Lambe. Patron: Theophilus, Earl of Lincoln (20 March 1637). [BC; PD 1637/1.]

Also: R. of Haceby, 1638–70 (*q.v.*).

Ephraim Garthwaite MA
Instituted 29 October 1638 to vicarage of Threckingham, on cession of Thomas Palframan. Patron: Theophilus, Earl of Lincoln. [AC; IND/L 1, fo.118v.]

Baptised 18 May 1600 at Fulbeck; son of Miles G., Rector of Fulbeck. Educated: Brasenose College, Oxford (matric. 1619/20; BA 1620/1; MA 1623). Deacon: 18 September 1625; priest: 19 September 1625 (Peterborough). Afterwards: R. of Barkston, 1641–52; R. of King's Cliffe (Np) by sequestration, 1645. Father of Ephraim, baptised at Barkston 22 August 1647 (later R. of Ropsley 1692–1719). Died 1652. Admon (PCC). [PR Fulbeck; *Lincolnshire Pedigrees*, 390; Foster, *Alumni*; Longden v. 183; PR Barkston; Swaby, 99.]

William Douglas

Instituted 14 July 1642 to vicarage of Threckingham, on resignation of Ephraim Garthwaite. Patron: Theophilus, Earl of Lincoln (2 May 1642). [Reg. 31, fo.29; PD 1642/33.]

Baptised 2 February 1614/15 at St Peter, Leeds; son of William D., clothier. Educated: Leeds School and Caius College, Cambridge (matric. 1631; BA 1633–4; MA 1637). Afterwards: perhaps at Yoxford (Sf). [Venn, *Alumni*; Swaby, 114.]

Thomas White

Instituted before 10 July 1662. [PD 1662/84.]

John Marshall

Instituted 30 August 1662 to vicarage of Threckingham, on death of Thomas White. Patron: Theophilus, Earl of Lincoln (10 July 1662). [Reg. 32, fo.19v; SUB IIa, fo.26v; PD 1662/84.]

Also: V. of Sempringham, 1662–76 (*q.v.*). Signed BTs at Threckingham 1667–76. Died 1676. Will (LCC). Probate inventory (6 October 1676): 'the Study for his Libery, £15'. [BTs Threckingham; LCC Wills 1676/143; INV 179/217.]

Henry Brerewood

Instituted 29 May 1677 by collation to vicarage of Threckingham, on death of John Marshall. Patron: Bishop of Lincoln. [Reg. 34, fo.21; IND/L 1, p.224.]

Priest: 28 May 1677 (Gloucester). Resided at Sempringham. Died 1703. Will (LCC), dated 25 May 1700; proved 13 October 1703. [Reg. 34, fo.21; LCC Wills 1703/19.]

Robert Kelham BA

Inducted 15 November 1703 to vicarage of Threckingham, on death of Henry Brerewood. Patron: Richard Wynne, esquire (19 October 1703). [IND/L 2, fo.26; PD1703/43].

Also: V. of Billingborough, 1702–52 (*q.v.*).

Charles Potter

Instituted 9 June 1752 to vicarage of Threckingham, on death of Robert Kelham. Patron: Riccardo Gulielmo Gasparo Melchior Baltazaro Wynne. [Reg. 38, p.513.]

Baptised 11 October 1727 at St Peter, Dorchester; son of Charles P., clerk. Educated: Bury St Edmunds and Oakham Schools; St John's College, Cambridge (matric. 1745; BA 1748–9). Deacon: 11 March 1749/50 (Bath and Wells); priest: 22 December 1751 (Lincoln). Non-resident at Threckingham which was served by John Towers as curate. Also: C. of Little Bytham, 1751–8. Buried at Little Bytham, 13 November 1758. Will dated 24 October, proved 2 December 1758. [Dorset History Centre, PR Dorchester St Peter; Venn, *Alumni*; Reg. 38, p.506; SPE 2, fo.119v; BTs Threckingham; PR Little Bytham; PRO, PROB 11/842/163.]

John Towers

Instituted 18 September 1759 by collation to vicarage of Threckingham, on death of Charles Potter. Patron: Bishop of Lincoln, by lapse. [Reg. 38, p.569.]

Also: V. of Billingborough, 1752–1802 (*q.v.*).

David Henry Urquhart MA

Instituted 30 March 1803 to vicarage of Threckingham, on death of John Towers. Patron: Sir Gilbert Heathcote of Normanton (Ru), Bt. [Reg. 40, p.67.]

Born 23 November, baptised 27 December 1754 at Great Yarmouth; son of David U. of Hobland Hall (Sf), esquire. Educated: Magdalen College, Oxford (matric. 1771; BA 1775; MA 1778). Deacon: 30 May 1779; priest: 6 June 1784 (Norwich). Formerly: C. of Gorleston, 1784; V. of Wigtoft, 1791; V. of Gainsborough, 1791–1805; Canon of Lincoln and Prebendary of Corringham, 1791–1805. Also: R. of West Knighton with Broadmayne (Do), 1805–29. Non-resident (on account of his wife's illness) at Threckingham, which was served by curates, including Thomas Latham (1814). Died 22 May 1829 at Broad-mayne. [CCED; Foster, *Alumni*; *Le Neve Fasti: Lincoln 1541–1857*, 57; NRL 1803/9; CR 1, p.42; *GM* (June 1829), 571.]

Charles Spencer Ellicott

Instituted 20 July 1829 to vicarage of Threckingham, on death of David Henry Urquhart. Patron: Sir Gilbert Heathcote, Bt. [Reg. 40, p.370.]

Born 6 February 1793 at Little Hallingbury (Ess); son of John E., Vicar of Exton (Ru). Educated: Trinity Hall, Cambridge (matric. 1815; LLB 1821). Deacon: 14 December 1817; priest: 17 May 1818 (Lincoln). Formerly: C. of Lavendon (Bk), 1817. Also: R. of Whitwell (Ru), 1818–77; RD of Oakham, 1848–64. Married Ellen, daughter of John Jones. Father of Charles John E., Bishop of Gloucester (1863–1905). Resided at Whitwell; non-resident at Threckingham, which was served by curates, including John Cross Morphew, Edmund Roberts Larken, Henry Harris, Julian John Webb Probyn and Octavius Pyke Halsted. Subsequently lived at Cheltenham (1861). Resigned Threckingham, 9 October 1877. Latterly at 8 Royal York Crescent, Clifton, Bristol, where he died, 5 June 1880. [Venn, *Alumni*; Reg. 40, pp. 261, 267; CR 1, p.87; 'Ellicott, Charles John' in *ODNB*; Census Returns 1841–1851 (Whitwell), 1861 (Cheltenham), 1871 (Clifton); CR 2, pp. 47, 210; CR 3, fos 60v, 113v, 135v; White, *Lincolnshire* (1856), 724; Reg. 42, p.2; *Probate Calendar* 1880.]

Frederick Hammond

Instituted 4 October 1878 to vicarage of Threckingham, on resignation of Charles Spencer Ellicott. Patron: David Lloyd Morgan MD CB, late of 9 Spring Gardens, Charing Cross (Mx), Deputy Inspector General in the Royal Navy (for this turn). [Reg. 42, p.49.]

Born *c.*1831 at Cirencester. Deacon: 1871; priest: 1873 (Exeter). Formerly: C. of Porthleven (Co), 1871–3; of Brixham with Churston Ferrers (Dev), 1873–4; V. of Talland (Co), 1876–8. Resided at Threckingham (in a 'private house now used by Vicar'). Resigned 1883. [*Crockford* (1885); Census Returns (1881).]

Charles Edward Walker Foottit BA

Instituted 2 May 1884 to vicarage of Threckingham, on resignation of

Frederick Hammond. Patron: Ida Grosvenor Wilson of The Grove, Market Drayton (Sa). [Reg. 42, p.201.]

Born *c*.1858 at Beckingham; son of Revd James F., Curate of Fenton with Stragglethorpe. Educated: University College, Durham (BA 1881). Deacon: 17 December 1882 (Lincoln); priest: 6 April 1884 (Nottingham for Lincoln). Formerly: C. of Threckingham, 1882–4. Resided at Threckingham. Afterwards: V. of Burton Pedwardine, 1889–1921. Father of Percival Frederick F., Vicar of Swaton 1930–6 (*q.v.*). Died 28 July 1927 at Burton Pedwardine. [*Crockford* (1908); OR 2, pp. 53, 59; Census Returns 1891 (Burton Pedwardine); *Probate Calendar* 1927.]

Alfred Hodge

Instituted 22 March 1890 to vicarage of Threckingham, on cession of Charles Edward Walker Foottit. Pat: John Wilson Wilson of The Grove, Market Drayton (Sa), esquire, in his own name and that of his wife Ida Grosvenor Wilson. Note that on 3 March 1890, the Archbishop of Canterbury granted a dispensation enabling the said AH to hold together the vicarage of Threckingham and the vicarage of Scredington. [Reg. 42, p.309.]

Born *c*.1832 at Keynsham (So). Educated: Scholae Cancellarii, Lincoln (1872). Deacon: 20 December 1874; priest: 19 December 1875 (Lincoln). Formerly: C. of Heckington, 1874–83. Also: V. of Scredington, 1883–97. Resided at Scredington Vicarage. Father of Walter Fallows Hodge, Rector of Benington (1913–38). Died 4 August 1897, aged 65; buried at Scredington (MI). [*Crockford* (1885); OR 2, pp. 22, 25; Census Returns 1891 (Scredington); *Probate Calendar* 1897; PR Scredington.]

William Christopher Houghton BA

Instituted 3 January 1898 to vicarage of Threckingham, on death of Alfred Hodge. Pat: John Wilson Wilson as above, in his own name and that of his wife Ida Grosvenor Wilson. Note that on 15 December 1897, the Archbishop of Canterbury granted a dispensation enabling the said WCH to hold together the vicarage of Threckingham and the vicarage of Walcot. [Reg. 42, p.425.]

Afterwards: R. of Pickworth, 1905–18 (*q.v.*).

John Frederick Tanfield (formerly Punch) BA

Instituted 26 January 1901 to vicarage of Threckingham, on cession of William Christopher Houghton. Patron: Ida Grosvenor Wilson of The Grove, Market Drayton (Salop), widow. [Reg. 42, p.482.]

Born 28 April 1875 at Middlesbrough; son of John Punch. Educated: Middlesbrough GS; Ealing GS; Christ's College, Cambridge (matric. 1896; BA 1899; MA 1903). Deacon: 1899; priest: 1900 (Ripon). Formerly: C. of Low Moor (YWR), 1899–1901. Lived at Folkingham (1901), boarding at the Greyhound Hotel. Afterwards: C. of Spalding, 1902–8; V. of St Jude, Liverpool, 1908–9; R. of Holywell with Needingworth (Hu), 1909–13; V. of Burnham-on-Crouch (Ess), 1913–15; of Earby (YWR), 1915–24; R. of Thornton-in-Craven, 1915–31. Married (1 July 1907) Dorothy Ermytrude, daughter of Stanley Maples of Spalding. Retired 1931. Latterly of Ravensdale, Ben Rhydding, Ilkley. Died 24 June 1940 at Crichton Royal, Dumfries. [Venn, *Alumni*; *Crockford* (1932); Census Returns 1901 (Folkingham); *Probate Calendar* 1940.]

Thomas Lloyd Knapp MA

Instituted 27 September 1902 to vicarage of Threckingham, on resignation of John Frederick Tanfield. Patron: Ida Grosvenor Wilson of The Grove, Market Drayton (Sa), widow. [Reg. 42, p.501.]

Born 30 December 1841 at Swaton; son of Henry K., Rector of Swaton (*q.v.*). Educated: Lancing College (1857–60) and St John's College, Oxford (matric. 1860; BA 1864; MA 1867). Deacon: 1865; priest: 1866 (Lincoln). Formerly: C. of Morton-by-Bourne, 1865–9; of St Mary, Hulme, Manchester, 1869–78; V. of St James, Oldham, 1878–1902. Married (9 January 1879) Sarah Anne, daughter of Robert Smith of Papcastle, Cockermouth. Resided at Threckingham Vicarage. Resignation accepted 22 February 1926. Died 2 October 1926; buried at Threckingham (MI). [*Lancing Register*, 28–9; Foster, *Alumni*; *Crockford* (1898); Census Returns 1911; Kelly, *Lincolnshire* (1913), 607; Reg. 43, p.390; *Probate Calendar* 1926.]

Cecil St John Wright BA

Instituted 19 October 1926 to vicarage of Threckingham, on resignation of Thomas Lloyd Knapp. Patron: Cecil Grosvenor Wilson-Heathcote of Ashurst House, Pulborough (Sx), esquire. Note that on 22 September 1926, the Archbishop of Canterbury granted a dispensation enabling the said CSW to hold together the rectory of Pickworth with vicarage of Walcot and the vicarage of Threckingham. [Reg. 43, p.405.]

Also: R. of Pickworth with Walcot, 1919–33 (*q.v.*).

Thomas Leonard Ivens

Instituted 31 July 1933 to vicarage of Threckingham, on cession of Cecil St John Wright. Patron: Cecil Grosvenor Wilson-Heathcote, as above. Note that on 14 July 1933, the Archbishop of Canterbury granted a dispensation enabling the said TLI to hold together the rectory of Pickworth with vicarage of Walcot and the vicarage of Threckingham. [Reg. 43, p.526.]

Also: R. of Pickworth with Walcot, 1933–41 (*q.v.*).

Charles Edwin Goshawk BD

Instituted 21 October 1941 to vicarage of Threckingham, on resignation of Thomas Leonard Ivens. Patron: Cecil Grosvenor Wilson-Heathcote of Woodlands Vale, Ryde (IoW), esquire. Note that on 8 September 1941, the Archbishop of Canterbury granted a dispensation enabling the said CEG to hold together the vicarage of Horbling and the vicarage of Threckingham. [Reg. 43, p.666.]

Also: V. of Horbling, 1939–48 (*q.v.*).

Frederick Guy Harrison

Instituted 11 August 1948 to vicarage of Threckingham, on cession of Charles Edwin Goshawk. Patron: Cecil Grosvenor Wilson-Heathcote of Woodlands Vale, Ryde (IoW), esquire. Note that on 8 July 1948, the Archbishop of

Canterbury granted a dispensation enabling the said FGH to hold together the vicarage of Horbling and the vicarage of Threckingham. [Reg. 44, pp. 92–3.]

Also: V. of Horbling, 1948–51 (*q.v.*).

Henry Evans BA
Instituted 24 April 1953 to vicarage of Threckingham, on resignation of Frederick Guy Harrison. Patron: Bishop of Lincoln, for this turn (by lapse). Note that on 20 March 1953, the Archbishop of Canterbury granted a dispensation enabling the said HE to hold together the rectory of Folkingham with vicarage of Laughton annexed and the vicarage of Threckingham. [Reg. 44, pp. 176–7.]

Also: R. of Folkingham, 1950–9 (*q.v.*).

Frank Reginald Money MA
Instituted 19 October 1960 to vicarage of Threckingham, on resignation of Henry Evans. Patron: Bishop of Lincoln, for this turn (by lapse). Note that on 29 September 1960, the Archbishop of Canterbury granted a dispensation enabling the said FRM to hold together the rectory of Folkingham with vicarage of Laughton annexed and the vicarage of Threckingham. [Reg. 44, p.303.]

Also: R. of Folkingham, 1960–8 (*q.v.*).

WALCOT

The Domesday Survey records half a church at Walcot as part of the Gant fee. Some time before 1230 the church was given to Sempringham Priory. It seems that a member of the Nevill family was involved in this gift. Simon de Nevill was holding land in Walcot of Gilbert de Gant in 1242–3 and when a dispute arose between the Prior of Sempringham and Agnes de Walecot in 1234 over the advowson of Walcot, the Prior produced as evidence a charter of Hugh de Nevill. The Master of the Order joined with the Prior and Convent in presenting to Walcot in 1230–1. In 1248 Pope Innocent IV licensed the Priory to appropriate Walcot. No vicarage was ordained, however, and no institutions are recorded in the medieval registers. In 1526 the parish was being served by a curate and a stipendiary chaplain. The registering of licences and institutions began again in the eighteenth century, the patronage being in the possession of the Grimsthorpe estate. [*Lincolnshire Domesday*, 114; *Book of Fees*, 1030; *Curia Regis Rolls* xiii. 415; *CPL* i. 259; Golding, *Gilbertine Order*, 378; *Subsidy*, 57.]

Geoffrey de Wuleward subdeacon
Instituted in the twenty-second pontifical year of Bishop Hugh of Wells (20

December 1230/19 December 1231) to church of Walcot. Patron: Master of Order of Sempringham and Prior and Convent of Sempringham (after a dispute over the advowson). [*Rot. Welles* iii. 186.]

The rectory of Walcot was appropriated but not endowed with a vicarage. It was served by a curate. [*State of the Church*, 301; *Speculum*, 136; LC 18B, p.200.]

William Hasledine DD
Licensed 26 June 1752 to curacy of Walcot. [Reg. 38, p.513.]
Also: R. of Haceby, 1743–64 (*q.v.*).

Isaac Cookson
Licensed 26 March 1772 to free chapel or curacy of Walcot, on cession of William Hasledine. Nominated by Sir Gilbert Heathcote, Bt. [Reg. 39, p.174.]
Also: V. of Osbournby, 1763–84 (*q.v.*).

Isaac Cookson
Licensed 18 March 1784 to free chapel or curacy of Walcot, on death of Isaac Cookson. Nominated by Sir Gilbert Heathcote of Normanton (Ru), Bt. [Reg. 39, p.408.]
Baptised 31 July 1759 at Folkingham; son of Revd Isaac C. (above). Educated: Christ's College, Cambridge (matric. 1780). Deacon: 22 December 1782; priest: 21 December 1783 (Lincoln). Formerly: C. of Osbournby, 1782. Died 16 November 1797; buried at Folkingham (MI). [PR Folkingham; Venn, *Alumni*; Reg. 39, pp. 388, 404.]

John Shinglar
Licensed 10 May 1798 to perpetual curacy of Walcot, on death of John [*sic*] Cookson. Nominated by Sir Gilbert Heathcote of Normanton (Ru), Bt (1 May 1798). [Reg. 39, p.651; PD 154/45.]
Education: literate. Deacon: 26 May 1782; priest: 6 June 1784 (Lincoln). Formerly: C. of Leighton Bromswold (Hu), 1782. Also: C. of Horbling, 1785–1828; C. of Sempringham, 1785–1812; C. of Billingborough, 1797; V. of Swaton cum Spanby, 1813–28 (*q.v.*). Kept a private school at Horbling, which was attended by Matthew Flinders, 1786. Licence for non-residence (1804, 1808), on account of there being no house. Gave two silver chalices and a paten to Walcot Church (1813). Died 25 June 1828 at Horbling, aged 72; buried at Walcot (MI). [Reg. 39, pp. 378, 412; *Flinders* ii. 30; NRL 1804/77; NRL 1808/60; *Bonney's Church Notes*, 231; *GM* 98 (1828), 473; *Monson*, 396.]

Charles Tomblin MA
Instituted 22 October 1828 to vicarage of Walcot, on death of John Shinglar. Patron: Sir Gilbert Heathcote, Bt. [Reg. 40, p.363.]
Born *c*.1800; son of Robert T. of Edith Weston (Ru), esquire. Educated: Uppingham School and Emmanuel College, Cambridge (matric. 1821; BA 1825; MA 1828). Non-

resident at Walcot, which was served by curates, including William Holland, William Theed, Francis Hopkinson and William Roe Waters. Also: V. of Langoft, 1834–58, where he resided. Died 20 December 1857 at Langtoft Vicarage. [Venn, *Alumni*; CR 2, p.233; CR 3, fos 40, 68v, 111; Census Returns 1841, 1851 (Langtoft); *Probate Calendar* 1859.]

John Bennett MA

Instituted 23 April 1858 to vicarage of Walcot, on death of Charles Tomblin. Patron: Gilbert John, Lord Aveland of Normanton Park (Ru). [Reg. 40, p.594.]

Born *c*.1827; son of Thomas B. of Market Overton (Ru), gent. Educated: Lincoln College, Oxford (matric. 1846; BA 1849; MA 1852). Deacon: 1850; priest: 1851 (Lincoln). Formerly: C. of Long Bennington, 1850–1; of Harston (Le). Resided at Folkingham (in house of John Rose, schoolmaster). Died 22 May 1866 at Folkingham. [Foster, *Alumni*; Census Returns 1841 (Market Overton), 1851 (Foston), 1861 (Folkingham); *Crockford* (1865); CR 3, fo.127; *Probate Calendar* 1867; *GM* (1866), 115.]

Robert Gerard Anderson BA

Instituted 26 October 1866 to vicarage of Walcot, on death of John Bennett. Patron: Gilbert John, Lord Aveland, of Normanton Park (Ru). [Reg. 41, p.161.]

Born 9 June, baptised 11 August 1830 at Holy Trinity, Clapham; son of Thomas A. of Old Broad Street, London, merchant. Educated: King's College School, London, and Trinity College, Cambridge (matric. 1854; BA 1858; MA 1886). Deacon: 1858; priest: 1859 (York). Formerly: C. of Lythe with Ugthorpe (YNR), 1858–9; V. of Manton (Ru), 1859–66. Resided at Market Place, Folkingham (1872). Afterwards of Maison Louis Masson, Veytaux, Switzerland (1885). Latterly of Craven House, Prestbury (Gl). Died 20 April 1889 at Bath. [LMA, PR Clapham Holy Trinity; Venn, *Alumni*; *Crockford* (1885); White, *Lincolnshire* (1872), 582; *Probate Calendar* 1889.]

William Christopher Houghton BA

Instituted 18 April 1879 to vicarage of Walcot, on resignation of Robert Gerard Anderson. Patron: Gilbert Henry Heathcote Drummond Willoughby, Lord Aveland. [Reg. 42, p.83.]

Also: R. of Pickworth, 1905–18 (*q.v.*).

The vicarage of Walcot was united to the rectory of Pickworth by Order in Council dated 22 March 1911. [Reg. 42, p.640.]

SCOTT WILLOUGHBY

During the thirteenth and fourteenth centuries, the advowson of Scott Willoughby was held by the Wavere family. By the early fifteenth century it had passed to the Sothill family of Redbourne and later to the Stanlow family who also held the advowson of Dembleby. Towards the end of the fifteenth century the patronage came into the hands of the Wymbish family of Nocton from whom it descended to the Townleys. By 1668 it had been acquired by the Brownlow family with whom it remained into the twentieth century. In 1950 Lord Brownlow transferred his right in the patronage to the Bishop of Lincoln, who held it in 1965. [*Lincolnshire Pedigrees*, 921; 'Notes for a History of Nocton', 356–9; Reg. 44, p.125; *LDC* (1965), 96–7.]

Richard de Apeltre subdeacon
Instituted by collation in the seventeenth pontifical year of Bishop Hugh of Wells (20 December 1225/19 December 1226). Patron: Bishop of Lincoln, saving to M. Michael Belet the right of presentation at a future vacancy (after the advowson had been disputed between the said M. Michael on the one hand and br. Geoffrey, Master of Stixwould, and Simon de Nevill on the other). [*Rot. Welles* iii. 148.]

[Blank] subdeacon
Instituted in the fourth pontifical year of Bishop Robert Grosseteste (17 June 1238/16 June 1239) to church of Scott Willoughby. Patron: M. Michael Beleth (after the advowson had been disputed unsuccessfully by Simon de Neovill). [Hoskin, no.102.]

Elyas de Hertford
Instituted by collation in the thirteenth pontifical year of Bishop Robert Grosseteste (17 June 1247/16 June 1248) to church of Scott Willoughby. Patron: Bishop of Lincoln. Note that with the agreement of the Rector the Bishop granted a vicarage in the church for life to Richard de Thornton chaplain, who was to have the entire income of the church, paying to the Rector 100s per annum. [Hoskin, no.408.]

John Pykard
Instituted by collation before 30 January 1278/9 to church of Scott Willoughby. Patron: Bishop of Lincoln, by lapse. [*Rot. Gravesend*, 83, 287.]

M. Hugh Hamelin subdeacon
Instituted 30 January 1278/9 to church of Scott Willoughby, on resignation of John Pykard. Patron: Robert de Wauer, who had recovered the presenta-

tion against Geoffrey de Nevill by an assize of darrein presentment. [*Rot. Gravesend*, 83, 287.]

Educated: University of Oxford (MA). Formerly: R. of Clent (Wo), 1276. Afterwards: R. of Wymondham (Le), 1287–1317. [Emden, *BRUO*, 862; *Reg. Sutton* viii. 38.]

Thomas de Prestwold subdeacon
Instituted 23 September 1279 to church of Scott Willoughby, on resignation of M. Hugh Hamelin. Patron: Robert de Wauuce. Re–instituted 2 February 1280/1, because he had not been ordained priest within a year of his institution; patron, Robert de Wavere kt. [*Rot. Gravesend*, 85, 289; *Reg. Sutton* i. 10.]

Eustace de Cotesbech clerk
Instituted 21 December 1286 to church of Scott Willoughby (having been granted the benefice *in commendam* 18 August 1286), on institution of Thomas de Prestwold to church of Barrow. Patron: Robert de Wavere kt. [*Reg. Sutton* i. 89–90.]

Subdeacon: 21 December 1286 (Lincoln). [*Reg. Sutton* i. 203.]

Henry de Cottesbech clerk
Instituted 17 December 1295 to church of Scott Willoughby, on resignation of Eustace. Patron: Robert de Waure kt. [*Reg. Sutton* i. 203.]

Subdeacon: 17 December 1295; deacon: 19 May 1296; priest: 22 December 1296 (Lincoln). [*Reg. Sutton* vii. 72, 79, 89.]

John de Wauer clerk
Instituted 24 September 1300 to church of Scott Willoughby, on death of Henry de Cotesbech. Patron: Robert de Wauer kt. [Reg. 2, fo.2.]

Subdeacon: 24 September 1300 (Lincoln). Afterwards: R. of mediety of Leasingham, 1315–37. Died before 20 January 1336/7. [Reg. 2, fos 2, 55; *Reg. Burghersh* i. no.523.]

James de Wauere acolyte
Instituted 3 August 1315 to church of Scott Willoughby, on institution of John de Wauere to a mediety of Leasingham. Patron: William de Wauere (after a dispute over advowson with William de Spanneby, who withdrew his claim). [Reg. 2, fo.56v.]

Licences to be absent for study for 1 year, 22 July 1321 (England); for 1 year, 25 August 1330. [*Reg. Burghersh* iii. no.158; Reg. 5, fo.185v.]

John de Folkyngham de Sleford priest
Instituted 11 July 1349 to church of Scott Willoughby, on death of James. Patron: Robert de Waur. [Reg. 9, fo.60.]

William de Horseth priest
Instituted 10 September 1349 to church of Scott Willoughby, on death of John. Patron: Robert de Waure. [Reg. 9, fo.69.]

William de Northfolk
Instituted before 2 November 1380. [Reg. 10, fo.108.]

John Westryn de Malbirthorp priest
Instituted 2 November 1380 to church of Scott Willoughby, on death of William de Northfolk. Patron: John de Wauere *domicellus*. [Reg. 10, fo.108.]
Assessed for poll-tax, 1381. [*Clerical Poll-Taxes*, no.1336.]

John Elsham
Instituted before 8 February 1428/9. [*Reg. Fleming* i. no.305.]

William Thorold priest
Instituted 8 February 1428/9 to church of Scott Willoughby, on death of John Elsham. Patron: Gerard, son and heir of Gerard Sothill kt. [*Reg. Fleming* i. no.305.]

John Thorp de Wyloghby priest
Instituted 23 June 1432 to church of Scott Willoughby, on death of William Tarald. Patron: Gerard Sotehyll esquire. [Reg. 17, fo.3.]

Robert Kepyk chaplain
Instituted 11 July 1435 to church of Scott Willoughby, on resignation of John Thorp. Patron: Gerard Suttell esquire. [Reg. 17, fo.12.]

John Helpringham priest
Instituted 22 May 1446 to church of Scott Willoughby (cause of vacancy not stated). Patron: William Stanlow. [Reg. 18, fo.98v.]

Robert Sparowe
Instituted before 2 May 1457. [Reg. 20, fo.127v.]

Thomas Skyrlowe chaplain
Instituted 2 May 1457 to church of Scott Willoughby, on death of Robert Sparowe. Patron: William Stanlowe esquire. [Reg. 20, fo.127v.]

John Pynchebek priest
Instituted 24 January 1461/2 to church of Scott Willoughby, on death of Thomas Skyrlowe. Patron: William Stanlowe esquire. [Reg. 20, fo.136.]

John Warde priest
Instituted 26 May 1492 to church of Scott Willoughby, on death of John Pynchebeke. Patron: Thomas Wymbyssh of Nocton, esquire (15 May 1492). [Reg. 22, fo.150v; PD 1492/60.]

Robert Rede chaplain
Instituted 13 January 1512/13 to church of Scott Willoughby, on death of John Warde. Patron: John Wymbiche esquire (14 October 1512). [Reg. 23, fo.145v; PD 1512/19.]
Resigned 19 August 1522. [RES 1522/11.]

Thomas Gybbe priest
Instituted 4 September 1522 to church of Scott Willoughby, on resignation of Robert Red. Patron: John Wynbyshe of Nocton, esquire. [Reg. 27, fo.25.]
Assessed for subsidy (£6) in 1526; assessed for *Valor Ecclesiasticus* 1535. [*Subsidy*, 57; *Valor* iv. 105.]

Christopher Calvart
Instituted 1549 (compounded for first-fruits, 13 December) to church of Scott Willoughby, on death of Thomas Gybbe. Patron: Thomas Wymbishe esquire. [Reg. 28, fo.24v; FL.h.13, 896.]
Exhibited at Visitation in 1551. [Vj 13, fo.62v.]

Thomas Thirnebeck
Instituted 1554 (compounded for first-fruits, 29 August) to church of Scott Willoughby. [FL.h.13, 896.]
Died 8 x 13 October 1557. [LCC Wills 1557/iii/186v; INV 29/446.]

Cuthbert Bailie
Instituted 19 October 1557 to church of Scott Willoughby, on death of last incumbent. Patron: Francis Norton and Alexander Ratclif, esquires. [Reg. 28, fo.136.]

Robert Tamworth
Instituted 2 September 1558 to church of Scott Willoughby, on death of Cuthbert Bailiffe. Patron: Alexander Ratclif and Francis Norton, esquires. [Reg. 28, fo.130v.]
Died 12 November 1569. [FL.h.11, 278.]

Thomas Buckbery
Instituted *c*.1570 (compounded for first-fruits, 26 January 1569/70) to church of Scott Willoughby. [FL.h.13, 896.]
Died 15 November 1570. [FL.h.11, 277.]

Nicholas Long
Instituted 5 May 1571 to church of Scott Willoughby, on death of last incumbent. Patron: Hugh Bawdes gent. (1 May 1571), by reason of a grant of advowson made to him. [*Bishop Cooper*, 5; PD 1571/6.]
Born *c*.1526. Education: 'unskilled in Latin; and but little versed in sacred learning'. Priest:

2 November 1567 (Oxford). Resident. Buried at Scott Willoughby, February 1583/4. Will (LCC), dated 11 November 1583 (witness, Michael Beane, Rector of Aunsby); proved 6 April 1584. Asked to be buried in Scott Willoughby Church, 'near unto the upper ende thereof'. [*Bishop Cooper*, 208; PR Scott Willoughby; LCC Wills 1584/208.]

William Glen

Instituted 19 May 1584 to church of Scott Willoughby, on death of Nicholas Longe. Patron: John Towneley and Mary Towneley. [Reg. 19, fo.143.]

Humphrey Walwine

Instituted 18 June 1584 to church of Scott Willoughby. [*State of the Church*, 74.]

Education: 'bred in the schools'. Priest: 24 February 1560/1 (London). Buried at Scott Willoughby, 11 October 1589. [*State of the Church*, 74; BTs Scott Willoughby.]

Miles Whale BA

Instituted 23 September 1590 to church of Scott Willoughby, on death of Humphrey Walwine. Patron: John Bussey of Heydour, esquire (18 September 1590). [BC; PD 1590/15.]

Also: V. of Osbournby, 1582–1630 (*q.v.*).

Richard Pell MA

Instituted 5 July 1630 to rectory of Scott Willoughby, on death of Miles Whale. Patron: Sir Anthony Pell of Dembleby kt (30 June 1630). Inducted 9 July 1630 by Cordal Berrie, clerk. [BC; PD 1630/49; IND/L 1, fo.88.]

Son of Robert P. of Dembleby. Educated: Peterhouse, Cambridge (matric. 1620; BA 1623–4; MA 1627). Deacon: 7 July 1627; priest: 2 September 1627 (Peterborough). Still Rector in 1641. Also: R. of Dembleby, 1627–52 (*q.v.*). Buried at Scott Willoughby, 20 September 1652. [*Lincolnshire Pedigrees*, 769–70; Venn, *Alumni*; BTs Dembleby; PR Scott Willoughby.]

John Armstrong

Instituted *c*.1653. [Swaby, 115.]

Born *c*.1627; son of Thomas A. of Belton. Educated: Christ Church, Oxford (matric. 1644) and St John's College, Cambridge (matric. 1645); BA. Deacon and priest: 23 January 1652/3 (Ardfert). His children were baptised at Scott Willoughby, 1653–8. Signed BTs at Scott Willoughby 1663–7. Also: C. of Aunsby, by 1662. [Venn, *Alumni*; LC 5, fos 24v, 53; PR Scott Willoughby.]

Richard Moore BA

Instituted 2 December 1668 to rectory of Scott Willoughby, on death of John Armstrong. Patron: Sir John Brownlow, Bt. [Reg. 33, fo.113.]

Also: R. of Dembleby, 1670–1716 (*q.v.*).

George Dickins BA

Instituted 20 June 1716 to rectory of Scott Willoughby, on death of Richard

Moore. Patron: John Cecil, Earl of Exeter; Francis North, Lord Guilford; Peregrine Bertie, Marquis of Lindsey, and Sir John Brownlow Bt (2 May 1716). [Reg. 37, p.17; PD 1716/6.]

Also: C. of Osbournby, 1681–1720 (*q.v.*).

William Cawthorne BA

Instituted 20 October 1720 to rectory of Scott Willoughby, on death of John [*sic*] Dickins. Patron: John, Viscount Tyrconnel (12 October 1720). [Reg. 37, p.107; PD 1720/41.]

Born 4 September, baptised 15 September 1694 at Careby; son of William C., Rector of Careby (1689–1732). Educated: Magdalene College, Cambridge (matric. 1712; BA 1715–16; MA 1723). Deacon: 22 September 1716 (Peterborough); priest: 21 September 1718 (Lincoln). Formerly: C. of Greatford, 1718. Signed BTs at Scott Willoughby 1721–41. Also: R. of Partney, 1728; R. of Willoughby-in-the-Marsh, 1728–53. Resigned Scott Willoughby 7 September 1739. Buried at Willoughby-in-the-Marsh, 21 November 1753. [PR Careby; Venn, *Alumni*; Longden iii. 69; Reg. 37, p.68; RES 1739/5; PR Willoughby cum Sloothby.]

Richard Palmer BA

Instituted 2 June 1740 to rectory of Scott Willoughby, on resignation of [William] Cawthorn. Patron: Lord Tyrconnel. [Reg. 38, p.385.]

Educated: Jesus College, Cambridge. Deacon: 25 September 1737; priest: 1 June 1740 (Lincoln). Fomerly: C. of Canwick, 1737. Also: R. of Snelland, 1747–78. Non-resident (1768): 'no House there: lives at Grantham – has no Parish, the Houses being all dilapidated'. Died 7 May 1805. [Venn, *Alumni*; Reg. 38, pp. 337, 385; LC 31, p.72.]

Hon. Henry (Cockayne) Cust

Instituted 6 July 1805 to rectory of Scott Willoughby, on death of Richard Palmer. Patron: Brownlow, Lord Brownlow, of Belton. [Reg. 40, p.97.]

Born 28 September 1780; son of Sir Brownlow Cust, 1st Lord Brownlow. Educated: Eton College (1791) and Trinity College, Cambridge (matric. 1800; MA 1803). Deacon: 10 June 1804; priest: 23 June 1805 (Peterborough). Formerly: C. of Sywell (Np), 1804. Also: V. of Middle Rasen Drax, 1806–32; R. of Sywell, 1806–61; R. of Cockayne Hatley (Bd), 1806–61; Canon of Windsor, 1813–61. Married (20 June 1816) Anna Maria, daughter of Francis, 1st Earl of Kilmorey. Licensed for non-residence at Scott Willoughby on account of the house being unfit ('a mere cottage'); the parish was served by curates including William Holland, William Theed, Francis Hopkinson, George Edwin Pattenden, Arthur Earle Welby and Octavius Pyke Halsted. Resided at Cockayne Hatley in 'a Mansion of his own in the Parish'; restored the church there, introducing historic furnishings from the continent including a pulpit (1559) from St Andrew, Antwerp (now in Carlisle Cathedral). Died 19 May 1861 at Windsor. [Burke, *Peerage* (1938), 408; *Eton School Lists*; Venn, *Alumni*; Longden iii. 329; Reg. 40, pp. 103, 109; *Fasti Wyndesorienses*, 64; NRL 1815/58; NRL 1816/18; NRL 1/99; CR 3, fos 6v, 43v, 69, 110, 122v; CR 4, fo.10v; Bedfordshire Archives, P104/0/1–2; Pickford, *Bedfordshire Churches* ii. 331–8; *Probate Calendar* 1861.]

Octavius Pyke Halsted BA

Instituted 8 November 1861 to rectory of Scott Willoughby, on death of

Henry Cockayne Cust. Patron: John William Spencer Brownlow Egerton, Earl Brownlow (with consent of Lady Marianne Margaret Alford and Peregrine Francis Cust, his guardians). [Reg. 41, p.75.]

Baptised 1 July 1818 at Great Thurlow (Sf); son of Revd Samuel H. and Decima his wife. Educated: St John's College, Cambridge (matric. 1842; BA 1847). Formerly: C. of All Saints, Worcester, 1849–51; C. of Threckingham, 1851 (residing at Osbournby with his mother); C. of Scott Willoughby, 1852–61. Resided at Scott Willoughby from 1863 when a new Rectory House was built (architect: Edward Browning of Stamford). Died 31 December 1899; buried at Scott Willoughby (MI). [Venn, *Alumni*; CR 3, fo.135v; CR 4, fo.10v; Census Returns 1851, 1861 (Osbournby); MGA 440; Census Returns 1871 (Scott Willoughby); *Probate Calendar* 1900.]

William Christopher Houghton BA

Instituted 5 May 1900 to rectory of Scott Willoughby, on death of Octavius Pyke Halsted. Patron: Adelbert Wellington Brownlow, Earl Brownlow. Note that on 23 March 1900, the Archbishop of Canterbury granted a dispensation enabling the said WCH to hold together the rectory of Scott Willoughby and the vicarage of Walcot. [Reg. 42, p.475.]

Afterwards: R. of Pickworth, 1905–18 (*q.v.*).

Alfred Bedson MA

Instituted 7 April 1906 to rectory of Scott Willoughby, on cession of William Christopher Houghton. Patron: Adelbert Wellington Brownlow, Earl Brownlow. Note that on 16 February 1906, the Archbishop of Canterbury granted a dispensation enabling the said AB to hold together the rectory of Scott Willoughby and the vicarage of Osbournby. [Reg. 42, p.546.]

Also: V. of Osbournby, 1899–1931 (*q.v.*).

The Rectory of Scott Willoughby was united to the Vicarage of Osbournby by Order in Council dated 26 May 1925. [Reg. 43, p.364.]

INDEX OF PERSONS AND PLACES

(Places where no county or country is given are usually in Lincolnshire. The main sequence of incumbents for parishes included in this volume is shown in bold.)

Aswardeby, M. Walter de, R. of Haceby, 250
Atherby, Adtherby, M. Walter de, R. of Firsby, 50–1
Atherton (La), vicar, 295
Atkinson
   Francis (father of George), cotton manufacturer, 35
   George, V. of Coates by Stow, 35
   Robert, V. of Glentworth, xxxviii, 63
Attekyrk, *see* Southscarle
Atteloft, *see* Stepyng
Atterbury, Gladys Mary, *see* Barron
Auckland (New Zealand), church of Holy Sepulchre, vicar, 176
Audley (St), curate, 132
Audley, Audeley, Daudele
   Elizabeth, wife of Nicholas, 26
   Hugh, the younger, 92
   John, V. of Hacconby, xxxviii, 247–8
   Nicholas kt, 26
     Elizabeth, wife of, 26
Audoyin, Cardinal, Prebendary of Norton Episcopi in Lincoln Cathedral, 117
Aunsby
   burial, 212
   church, 300
     chantry of Walter de Ounesby in, 209
   curate, 369
   rectors, 212–13, 295–7, 369
   union of benefice, 213
Austin, John, V. of Glentham; V. of Normanby-by-Spital, 58, 116
   William, father of, 58
Austrey (St), 174
Authorpe, rectors, 288
Avan Vale (Glam), curate, 349
Aveland (Li), deanery, xxxiii
   penitentiaries, 190, 276
   preacher, 259
   rural deans, 205, 242, 325, 348
   Sunday School Association, 286
   value of benefices in, xxxiv
Aveland, Lord, *see* Willoughby
Axeby, *see* Haxeby
Aylesby, baptism, 310
Aylington, M. John de, R. of Normanby by Spital, 111
Aynho (Np)
   hospital of St James and St John, master, 41
   rector, 41
Ayton, East (YNR), 176

Babbegrave, Belgrave, Robert Templer de, V. of Threckingham, 352
Babington (So), rector, 206
Bacare, Robert, R. of Pickworth, 307
Bacheler, John, V. of Ingham, 105–6

Badshot Lea (Sr), church of St George, Minister, 22
Bagge, Thomas Edward, 213
Baggenderby, William de, V. of Cammeringham, 24
Bagshaw, Bagshawe
   Christopher, V. of Normanby by Spital, 115
     George, father of, 115
   George, V. of Haselbech; father of Christopher, 115
   John Charles, V. of Osbournby, 303
     Thomas, father of, 303
   Thomas, of Mossley; father of John Charles, 303
Bailie, Bailiffe, Cuthbert, R. of Scott Willoughby, 368
Baker
   John, *see* Elton
   Robert
     V. of Laughton by Folkingham, 278
     V. of Sempringham, 330
Balderton (Nt), 350
Baley, John, 184
Balguy, Balgay, Thomas, Prebendary of Norton Episcopi in Lincoln Cathedral, 120–1
Balham (Sr), church of St Mary, marriage, 325
Ballarat, diocese, ordinations in, 133
Ballarat, Victoria (Australia), St Aidan's Theological College, 133
   acting subwarden, 134
Balsall Heath (Wo), vicar, 109
Bamburg, Simon de, V. of St Albin, Spridlington, 144
Bampton (Ox), curate, 195
Banburg, William de, V. of Morton by Bourne, 279
Bancks, Banckes, *see* Banks
Bangor, bishop of, 156
Bangor Monachorum (Flints), curate, 348
Bankipore, Bihar (India), 223
Banks, Bancks, Banckes, Bankes
   John, Headmaster of Boston School; V. of Cammeringham, xxxvii, 30
     John, father of, 30
   Thomas, R. of Owmby by Spital, 128
   William, 10
Bannebury, M. John Hode de, R. of Dunsby by Bourne, 226
Banstead (Sr), 153
   curates, 133, 325
Banyster, Christopher, R. of St Peter, Waddingham, 161
Barbados (West Indies), 12
   diocese, 349
Barbe, Berbe, Henry, V. of Stow by Threckingham, 339
Barber
   John, V. of Coates by Stow, 36–7

Cayton (YNR), 176
Cecil, Cycell, Sacyll
    David, 214, 217
        Jane (Ros), wife of, 214, 217
    John (d.1721), Earl of Exeter, 370
    William Thomas Brownlow, Marquess of
        Exeter, domestic chaplain of, 38
Central Tanganyika, cathedral, *see* Dodoma
Cervington, Elizabeth, *see* Bunting
Cestrefeld, *see* Chestrefeld
Chaderton, William, Bishop of Lincoln, xxx
Chafford, Robert of, V. of St Albin,
    Spridlington, 144
Chalcedon, suffragan bishop of, 252
Chalton (Ha), rector, 4
Chalvey (Bk), 36
Cham, John, V. of Sempringham, 329
Chamberlain, Chamberlayne
    Clifford Coleridge, R. of Snitterby, 142
        Henry Edwin, father of, 142
    Edward Eustace, 142
    Henry Edwin, C. of Chelwood; father of
        Clifford Coleridge, 142
    John, 184
Chandos, Chaundos, John, kt, 91
Chapeltown (YWR), 185
Chapman, Robert, V. of Glentworth, 63
Charles I, King, 44, 128, 162
Charles II, King, 9, 17, 162
Charles, King of France, 93
Charlotte, Princess, sub-preceptor and chaplain
    to, 130
Charlton (K), 116
Charminster (Do), curate, 78
Charneles, *see* Chaynel
Chartham (K), St Augustine's Hospital,
    chaplain, 296
Charwelton (Np), curate, 19
Charyte, John, R. of two parts of Rippingale,
    316
Chaterton, Richard, V. of Willoughton, 170
Chatham (K), church of St John, curate, 67
Chatteris (Ca), curate, 272
Chaumberlayn, Chaumberleyn
    Ralph, 316
    Robert, *see* Aslokby
Chaundos, *see* Chandos
Chauntre, M. William, 236
Chaworth, *see* Irnham
Chaynel, Charneles, Schaynel, John, R. of two
    parts of Rippingale, 315
Cheadle (St), 310
    curate, 310
Cheam (Sr), rector, 270
Chedworth (Gl), curate, 348
Chele, William de, R. of third part of
    Rippingale, 319
Chelmorton (Db), vicar, 22

Chelmsford, diocese, ordinations in, 110, 304,
    312
Chelmsford (Ess), cathedral, canon of, 79
Chelsea (Mx), 12
    churches
        Christ Church, curate, 326
        Holy Trinity, baptism, 155
    water works, 98
Chelsfield (K), curate, 242
Cheltenham (Gl), 348, 359
    college, 154
    marriage, 165
Chelwood (So), curate, *see* Chamberlain
Chepstow (Monm), St John's School, assistant
    master, 175
Cheshire, county, 331
Cheshunt (Hrt)
    Bishops' College, 109, 123
    vicar, 218
Chesney, Robert, Bishop of Lincoln, 134, 146,
    233, 287, 336
Chesshire
    Edwin, of Birmingham; father of Howard
        Smith, 223
    Howard Smith, R. of Dowsby, 223
        Lucy Elizabeth, wife of, 223
    Lucy Elizabeth (Pridham), wife of Howard
        Smith, 223
Chester, diocese, ordinations in, 18, 20, 95,
    152, 172, 184, 186–7, 210, 260, 264, 287,
    302–3, 357
    bishop, *see* Cotes
Chester
    cathedral
        canon, 42
        dean, 43
        church of St Bridget with St Martin, curate,
            21
Chester le Street (Du), curates, 154–5, 174
Chester, Chestre
    John de, R. of Owmby by Spital, 125
    William, R. of Firsby, 51–2
Chestrefeld, Cestrefeld
    Richard de, Prebendary of Norton Episcopi
        in Lincoln Cathedral
    Br. William de, canon of Welbeck; V. of
        Coates by Stow, 32
Chetour, Cheytoure, John
    R. of Cold Hanworth, 81
    V. of St Albin, Spridlington, 145–6
Chevalier, Thomas, V. of Willoughton, 170
Cheytoure, *see* Chetour
Chichester, diocese, 334
    ordinations in, 17–18, 122, 141, 154, 196,
        218, 283
Chichester, 295
    cathedral
        canon, 40

Field
John, V. of Morton by Bourne, 281
see also Feld
Fiennes, *see* Fines
Fifield (Ox), rector, 263
Filewood, Mary, *see* Snelson
Fille, Fylle, Robert, R. of Dowsby, 216
Filleigh (Dev), Castle Hill, 332
Fillingham, 27, 44–9, 137, 235
advowson, xxxiii, xxxvi, 39
burials, 44, 47–9
church, xxxv
value of, xxxiv
curates, 29, 48, 58, 85, 107, 138
pension, 39
'rantanning' in, 48
rectors, xxxv–xxxvi, xxxviii, 30, **39–49**, 109–10
rectory house, 48–9, 109
Filyngham, Thomas son of Simon de Houton de, R. of mediety of Hackthorn; V. of Glentworth, 61, 70, 72
Finedon (Np), curate, 142
Fines, Fiennes, Fynes
Edward (d.1692), Earl of Lincoln, 239, 345–6
Henry, Earl of Lincoln, 193, 238, 345, 356
domestic chaplain of, 238
Theophilus, Earl of Lincoln, 184, 193, 238, 345, 357–8
Thomas, Earl of Lincoln, 238
Finmere (Ox), rector, 197
Firsby
advowson, 50
church, 50
grant *in commendam*, 50
rectors, **50–2**, 125
Fishborne, Fishburne, Fissheburn, Fisseburn, Fycheborn
Brian, V. of Ingham, 106
Gervase, V. of Bishop Norton, 119
M. Peter de, R. of Blyborough, 4
Fishlake (YWR), rector, 4
Fishtoft
curate, 20
rector, 197
Fiskerton, 109
curate, 273
rector, 130
Fisseburn, Fissheburn, *see* Fishborne
Brian, V. of Ingham, 106
M. Peter de, R. of Blyborough, 4
Fitzwilliam, Thomas, 82
Flatberye, Flatbury, William, R. of Folkingham, 237
Fledborough (Nt), rector, 36
Fleet, rectors, 218–19, 270

Fleming
M. John le, proctor-general in England of Lessay Abbey, 39–40
Richard, Bishop of Lincoln, xxix, 93
M. Thomas le, R. of Fillingham, 39
Flempton with Hengrave (Sf), rector, 167
Flete, William, R. of mediety of Kirkby Underwood, 268
Fligher, Flygher, William son of John, V. of Ingham, 105
Flinders, Matthew, 363
Flint
Charles Ramsay, V. of Glentworth, xxxvii, 66
Charles William, father of, 66
Frances, wife of, 66
Frances (Fowler), wife of Charles Ramsay, 66
Flintham (Nt)
curate, 98
vicar, 241
Flixborough
curate, 197
vicar, 198
Flixton, Robert de, Franciscan; V. of Horbling, 256
Flowers, William Henry
C. of Cammeringham, 30
C. of Hackthorn, 76
Flowton (Sf), rectors, 329
Floyd, *see* Lloyd
Flygher, *see* Fligher
Foam Lake, Saskatchewan (Canada), incumbent, 68
Fochabers (Moray), rector, 157
Fogheler, John, V. of Coates by Stow, 33
Foliambe, James, 317
Foliot, Folyot
Jordan, 50, 134
Richard kt, 50
Robert, 50–1
William, 134
Folkingham, 310, 324, 364
advowson, 233
baptism, 363
barony, 351
burials, 238–9, 241–2, 271, 302, 363
castle, 237
church
altar, 302
vestment, 237
Classis, 308, 318
curates, 202, 237–8, 240–1, 302
Greyhound Hotel, 360
Market Place, 364
poor, 237
rectors, xxxiv–xxxvi, xxxviii, 184, 201, 222, 226, **233–43**, 288, 301, 304, 312–13, 362

Innocent IV, Pope, 362
Invergordon (Ross), church of St Ninian, priest
   in charge, 334
Inverness, 240
Ipstones (St), vicar, 188
Ipswich, suffragan bishop of, 155
Ipswich (Sf)
   church of St Matthew
      curate, 100
      rector, 79
   Grammar School, 241
   hospitals
      Borough Royal Asylum, 223
      East Suffolk and Ipswich, 196
Irby in the Marsh, vicar, 123
Irby on Humber, 83
   rector, 83
Ireland, 108
   Royal University, 100
Irnham, rectors, 291, 316
   see also Jekell
Irnham
   John de
      V. of Horbling, 257
      V. of Sempringham, 328
   Thomas Chaworth (Caworth) de, V. of
      Sempringham, 328
Irons
   Joseph, of Hoddesdon; father of William
      Josiah, 165
   William Josiah, R. of St Mary with St Peter,
      Waddingham, 165
      Joseph, father of, 165
Irthlingborough (Np), church of St Peter, vicar,
   291
Isle Brewers (So), vicars, 204
Islep, John Greneland (Greyland) de, R. of
   mediety of Kirkby Underwood, 266
Isleworth (Mx), 232
   curate, 196
Islington (Mx), 8, 274, 325
   churches
      St Mary, baptism, 132
      St Peter, curate, 99
Islington (Nf), Hall, 213
Islip (Np), curate, 285
Isted
   Ambrose, 297
      Anne, wife of, 297
   Anne (Bucke), widow of Ambrose, 297, 302
Itchenor (Sx), 143
Ivens
   Coleman, C. of Alkborough; father of
      Thomas Leonard, 312
   Thomas Leonard, R. of Pickworth
      with Walcot; V. of Horbling; V. of
      Threckingham, 263, 312, 361
      Coleman, father of, 312

Ivy Depôt, Virginia (USA), rector, 195
Ixem, Ixim
   John, of Burton Lazars; father of Thomas, 239
   Thomas, R. of Folkingham, 239
      John, father of, 239
Izmir (Turkey), chaplain, 79

Jackes, *see* Norton
Jackson, Jakson, Jakeson
   John (Revd), of Bowdon; father of Thomas
      Molineux, 302
   John
      C. of Folkingham, 237
      V. of Bourne, xxxviii, 201–2
   John, V. of Billingborough, xxxv, 192–3
   John, V. of Willoughton, 171
   Mary (Hutchinson), wife of Thomas
      Molineux, 302
   Robert, V. of Willoughton, 170
   M. Thomas, R. of Fillingham, 41
   Thomas Molineux, V. of Osbournby, 302–3
      John, father of, 302
      Mary, wife of, 302
   William, PC of All Saints, Hemswell; V. of
      Ingham, 97, 107
Jacobstow (Co)
   rectors, 67
   rectory house, 67
Jamaica (West Indies), House of Assembly,
   speaker of, 130
James I, King, 8–9, 74–5, 162, 269
   chaplain to, 44
James II, King, 129, 162
Jamestown (Saint Helena), 294
Janney, Janny
   Robert father of Robert, V. of Bowden, 64
   Robert
      C. of Harpswell, 89
      V. of Glentworth, 64
      Robert, father of, 64
Jarrow (Du)
   perpetual curate, 19
   rector, 80
Jarvis
   Edwin George
      C. of Hackthorn, 76
      V. of Hackthorn with Cold Hanworth,
         xxxvi, 77
         father, *see* George Ralph Payne
         son, *see* Francis Amcotts
         wife, *see* Frances Amcotts
   Frances Amcotts (Cracroft), wife of Edwin
      George, 77
   Francis Amcotts, Rector of Burton Stather;
      Rector of Kettlethorpe, 77
   George Ralph Payne, of Doddington, 77
Jeffrason, Jeffrayson, John, R. of St Peter,
   Waddingham, 159–60

Richard, R. of Dembleby; R. of Scott
Willoughby, 211, 369–70
John, father of, 211
Richard Greaves, C. of Hackthorn, 76
William Gurden, V. of Aslackby, xxxvii,
186–7
George, father of, 186
Morborne (Hu), rector, 357
Morcott (Ru), rector, 302
Mordinge, Miles, 184
More, Br. William de la, Master of Templars,
181
Morepath, Morpath, William, R. of Owmby by
Spital, 126
Morey, Richard, PC of Snitterby, 141
Richard Marden, father of, 141
Morgan, David Lloyd, 359
Morphew, John Cross
C. of Horbling, 261
C. of Threckingham, 359
Mortimer, see Ingoldesby
Mortlake (Sr), curate, 312
Morton by Bourne, 244
advowson, xxxii-xxxiii, 279
baptism, 253
burials, 282–6
church, appropriation, 279
curates, 284, 361
poor, 228
union of benefice, 249, 284
vicarage house, 285–7
vicars, xxxvii–xxxviii, 202, 248, **279–87**,
317
Morton by Gainsborough, church of St Paul,
vicar, 176
Morton on the Hill (Nf), 334
Morton
Adam, R. of Hinton in the Hedges; father of
Robert, 331
James, V. of Billingborough; V. of Horbling,
193, 260
Ralph de, R. of Dunsby by Bourne, 225
Robert de, 92
Robert de, R. of two parts of Rippingale,
315
Robert, R. of Withern; father of Thomas,
331
Adam, father of, 331
Robert de, V. of Morton by Bourne, 279
Thomas, V. of Sempringham, 330–1
Robert, father of, 331
Morwode, Roger de, 69
Moseley (Wo), curate, 22
Moseley, Edmund, V. of Glentworth, 62
Moshi, Kilimanjaro (Tanzania), chaplain, 206
Mossley (Chs/La), 303
Mostyn
John, of Castle; father of Roger, 309

Roger, R. of Pickworth, 309
John, father of, 309
Mounson, see Monson
Mount Dandenong, Victoria (Australia),
minister, 134
Mount Forest, Ontario (Canada), incumbent,
668
Moy, see Hacunby
Moysey, Nicholas, C. of Bourne, 203
Mulsho, John, 226
Mumby, vicar, 284
Munden, Great (Hrt), curate, 239
Munden, Little (Hrt), curate, 132
Mundesley (Nf), rector, 130
Mundon (Ess), vicar, 150
Munk, see Monck
Murray
William, of London; father of William, 240
William, R. of Folkingham, 239–40
William, father of, 240
Murthwaite, Irton, C. of Sempringham, 331
Murtoa, Victoria (Australia), curate in charge,
133
Muskham, North (Nt), curate, 186
Muston (Le), curate, 293
Muswell Hill (Mx), 48
Mutford with Rushmere (Sf), rector, 335
Myddle (Sa), curate, 47
Mynnitt, Menytt, Robert, R. of Haceby, 252
Mynting, John, V. of Hackthorn, 73

Naler, see Naylor
Nanney
Hugh, R. of Caenby; V. of Saxby with
Firsby, xxxvi, 19, 140
Hugh, V. of Haltwhistle, 19
Lewis, 19
Barbara (Middleton), mother of, 19
Thomas Middleton, R. of Caenby; V. of
Saxby with Firsby, 19–20, 140
Napier, Hawke's Bay (New Zealand), vicar,
273
Nashik (Nassek), Maharashtra (India), 332
Navenby, rector, 189
see also Kelsay
Navenby alias Severesby, John de, R. of
Harpswell, 87–8
Naylor, Nayler, Naler
James, R. of Owmby by Spital, 128
John, R. of Newton by Folkingham, 291
John, V. of Willoughton, 171
Richard, 17
Neatishead (Nf), vicars, 33
Nebraska (USA), 79
Needham, Nedham
Evelyn Jack, 348–9
Francis, Earl of Kilmorey, 370
Ann Maria, daughter of, see Cust

St Martin in the Fields, 230, 270, 308
  curate, 332
  marriage, 231
St Matthew, curate, 167
St Thomas, Regent Street, curate, 108
schools
  Soho Square, 261
  Westminster School, 8, 10, 48, 66, 130, 270, 324
streets and places
  Belgrave Square, 348
  Carey Street, 261
  Charing Cross, 359
  Great Portland Street, 333
  Hanover Square, 130
  Westbourne Terrace, 348
  Wimpole Street, 131
Whitehall, 130
Westmoreland, Joseph, V. of Horbling, 263
Weston (Chs), *see* Runcorn
Weston (Li)
  curate, 212
  vicar, 212
Weston, Colly (Np), rectors, 267
Weston, Edith (Ru), 363
Weston super Mare (So), Emmanuel Chapel, curate, 332
Weston under Lizard (St), curate, 96
Weston
  Br. John, Prior of Hospitallers, 183
  Br. William, Prior of Hospitallers, 183
Westrasen, *see* Herford
Westren, Westrum, Westryn, *see* Malberthorp
Wetehanger, *see* Wetwang
Wetherall, Waterall, John, R. of St Hilary, Spridlington, xxxv, 152
  Anne (Bogg), wife of, 152
Wethern, *see* Wythern
Wetwang, Wetehanger, Alan de, R. of mediety of Kirkby Underwood, 265
Weybread (Sf), vicar, 99
Weybridge (Sr), curate, 156
Weymouth (Do), 232
Whale, Miles, R. of Scott Willoughby; V. of Osbournby, 301, 369
Whaley
  John, of Laughton, wheelwright; father of Jonathan, 346
  Jonathan, V. of Swaton, 346
  John, father of, 346
Whalley (La), curate, 133
Whaplode, vicar, 197
Whatton (Nt), vicars, 122, 245
Whatton, Walton, William, R. of third part of Rippingale, 321
Wheatfield (Ox)
  baptism, 153
  rector, *see* Taylor

Wheathampstead (Hrt), rectors, 6, 266, 306
Wheatley, John, V. of Aslackby, 185
  Thomas, father of, 185
Whelpdale
  Richard, R. of Caenby, 17
  Robert, V. of Glentham, 55
Wheteley
  Elias de, R. of Caenby, 15
  Hugh de, R. of Stainton-by-Langworth, 15
Whetham, Thomas, General in HM Army, 284
Whetstone (Le), 44
Whichcote, Whichcot
  Elizabeth daughter of George, *see* Bassett
  George, of Harpswell, 65, 139
    Elizabeth, daughter of, 65
    John, son of, 139
  Sir George Bt, 87, 90–1
  John, V. of Saxby, 139
    George, father of, 139
Whistler
  Edward Webster, father of Rose Fuller, 121
  Rose Fuller, V. of Bishop Norton, 121–2
    Edward Webster, father of, 121
Whiston, William, 239
Whitchurch (He), rectors, 98, 154
Whitchurch (Ox), rector, *see* Hammond
Whitchurch Canonicorum (Do), 205
  curate, 224
White
  John, of Middle Temple, 238
  John, V. of Billingborough; V. of Hacconby, 192–3, 247
  John, V. of Horbling, 260
  Richard, V. of Billingborough, 192
  Thomas, C. of Sempringham, 330, 357
  Thomas, V. of Threckingham, 358
  William, C. of All Saints, Hemswell, xxxvii, 97
Whitehaven (Cu), 99
Whitehead
  John, C. of All Saints, Hemswell, 96
  Joseph, 187
Whitelwode, Stephen de, R. of Owmby by Spital, 125
Whitewell, Whittewell, Stephen de, R. of Harpswell, 88
Whitfield, Benjamin Owen, R. of Blyborough; V. of Willoughton, 13, 176
Whitford (Flints), rector, 309
Whithead, Hugh, Prior of Durham, 7–8
Whitlam, William, C. of Coates by Stow, 35
Whitley (Nb), curate, 19
Whitstable (K), 133
Whittewell, *see* Whitewell
Whittington (Sa), curate, 131
Whittlesford (Ca), St Andrew's Theological College, 296